LEGAL FOUNDATIONS

LEGAL FOUNDATIONS

Keir Bamford

Kevin Browne

Jacqueline Kempton

Lesley King

Valerie Vickery

CLP

Published by

The University of Law,
2 Bunhill Row, London EC1Y 8HQ

British Library Cataloguing-in-Publication Data
A catalogue record for this book is available from the British Library.

ISBN: 978 1 80502 170 4

Typeset by Style Photosetting Ltd, Mayfield, East Sussex
Tables and index by Moira Greenhalgh, Arnside, Cumbria

Preface

This book is divided into five Parts, the first four each dealing with one of the topics which pervade the syllabus of the Legal Practice Course. These topics are: Revenue Law, Professional Conduct, EU Law and Human Rights. Part V deals with the core subject, Probate and Administration. The material contained in this book is intended to be an introduction to the pervasive and core topics, and is designed for those with little or no previous knowledge of the subjects. It has been written primarily to support and complement the Legal Practice Course undertaken by trainee solicitors. The approach taken to the subjects is essentially practical and is enhanced by worked examples showing the application of the topics in a practical context.

The law is generally stated as at May 2025.

KEIR BAMFORD
KEVIN BROWNE
JACQUELINE KEMPTON
LESLEY KING
VALERIE VICKERY
The University of Law

Contents

Table of Cases

M

N

O

P

Q

R

Table of Primary Legislation

Page numbers in **bold** refer to full text of material

Bill

EU primary legislation

International legislation

Table of Secondary Legislation

Page numbers in **bold** refer to full text of material

Guidance and Warning Notices

Table of Abbreviations

ABS	alternative business structure
AEA 1925	Administration of Estates Act 1925
AEA 1971	Administration of Estates Act 1971
APR	annual percentage rate
ATP	authorised third person
CGT	capital gains tax
CJEU	Court of Justice of the European Union
COB Rules	SRA Financial Services (Conduct of Business) Rules
COFA	Compliance Officer for Finance and Administration
COLP	Compliance Officer for Legal Practice
COREPER	Committee of Permanent Representatives
CPR	Civil Procedure Rules 1998
CTM	Community trade mark
DPB	designated professional body
EAT	Employment Appeal Tribunal
ECA 1972	European Communities Act 1972
ECHR	European Convention for the Protection of Human Rights and Fundamental Freedoms 1950
ECJ	European Court of Justice
ECSC	European Coal and Steel Community
ECtHR	European Court of Human Rights
EEA	European Economic Area
EFTA	European Free Trade Agreement
EIS	Enterprise Investment Scheme
ESC	Economic and Social Committee
EurAtom	European Atomic Energy Community
FCA	Financial Conduct Authority
FPO 2005	Financial Services and Markets Act 2000 (Financial Promotion) Order 2005
FSA	Financial Services Authority
FSMA 2000	Financial Services and Markets Act 2000
GDPR	General Data Protection Regulation
HMCTS	HM Courts and Tribunals Service
HMRC	HM Revenue & Customs
HRA 1998	Human Rights Act 1998
ICTA 1988	Income and Corporation Taxes Act 1988
IHT	inheritance tax
IHTA 1984	Inheritance Tax Act 1984
IP	intellectual property
I(PFD)A 1975	Inheritance (Provision for Family and Dependants) Act 1975
IPDI	immediate post-death interest
ISA	Individual Savings Account
ITA 2007	Income Tax Act 2007
ITEPA 2003	Income Tax (Earnings and Pensions) Act 2003
ITTOIA 2005	Income Tax (Trading and Other Income) Act 2005
LASPO 2012	Legal Aid, Sentencing and Punishment of Offenders Act 2012
LCS	Legal Complaints Service
LCT	lifetime chargeable transfer
LeO	Legal Ombudsman for England and Wales

LPA 1925	Law of Property Act 1925
MCA 2005	Mental Capacity Act 2005
MEP	member of the European Parliament
MEQR	measure having equivalent effect to a quantitative restriction
MLRO	money laundering reporting officer
NCA	National Crime Agency
NCPR 1987	Non-Contentious Probate Rules 1987
NSNDI	non-savings, non-dividend income
OEICs	open-ended investment companies
PAYE	Pay As You Earn
PEP	Politically Exposed Person
PET	potentially exempt transfer
PR	personal representative
RAO 2001	Financial Services and Markets Act 2000 (Regulated Activities) Order 2001
RPI	Retail Prices Index
Scope Rules	SRA Financial Services (Scope) Rules
SRA	Solicitors Regulation Authority
TA 1925	Trustee Act 1925
TA 2000	Trustee Act 2000
TEU	Treaty on European Union
TFEU	Treaty on the Functioning of the European Union
TLATA 1996	Trusts of Land and Appointment of Trustees Act 1996
VATA 1994	Value Added Tax Act 1994
VCT	Venture Capital Trust

PART I

REVENUE LAW

CHAPTER 1

VALUE ADDED TAX

LEARNING OUTCOMES

After reading this chapter you will be able to understand:

- the circumstances that give rise to a VAT charge
- the current rates at which VAT is charged and supplies that are exempt from VAT
- the penalties for failing to comply with the VAT legislation.

1.1 INTRODUCTION

1.1.1 Sources of VAT law

The main charging statute relating to value added tax (VAT) is the Value Added Tax Act 1994 (VATA 1994), as amended by later Finance Acts and certain statutory instruments. Detailed provisions implementing the Act are to be found in the VAT Regulations 1995 (SI 1995/2518) and other statutory instruments. In addition, His Majesty's Revenue & Customs (HMRC) issues VAT Notices which, although lacking legal force, express its views on the law.

1.1.2 Charge to tax

In the current tax year, the standard rate of VAT is 20%.

Generally, VAT is charged whenever a business supplies goods or services. The business charges the customer VAT at 20% on the value of the goods or services. This is known as 'output tax'. The business deducts from the output tax which it collects any VAT it has paid ('input tax') on goods or services received and pays the difference to HMRC.

	Value of goods (£)	*VAT charged to buyer (£)*	*VAT paid to HMRC (£)*
(a) A manufacturer buys raw material costing £200 plus VAT from a producer	200	40	
Producer pays to HMRC			40
(b) The manufacturer sells finished article to a retailer for £1,000 plus VAT	1,000	200	
Manufacturer pays to HMRC			160 (200 – 40)

	Value of goods (£)	*VAT charged to buyer (£)*	*VAT paid to HMRC (£)*
(c) The retailer sells the finished article to a consumer for £2,000 plus VAT	2,000	400	
Retailer pays to HMRC			200 (400 – 200)
Total paid to HMRC			400

Note: (i) VAT does not cost the business anything as any VAT paid is recouped from VAT charged.

(ii) Each business accounts for VAT on the 'value added' to the goods whilst in the possession of the business. The value added by the manufacturer is £800 (£1,000 – £200). Twenty per cent of £800 is £160, the sum paid to HMRC.

(iii) The ultimate burden falls on the consumer, who pays £2,000 plus £400 VAT for the product. The £400 VAT has been paid to HMRC in three stages.

1.2 CHARGE TO VAT

1.2.1 Definition

Value added tax is 'charged on any supply of goods or services made in the United Kingdom where it is a taxable supply made by a taxable person in the course or furtherance of any business carried on by him' (VATA 1994, s 4(1)). Tax will be charged on the 'value of the supply' (VATA 1994, s 2(1)). The elements of this charge are defined widely to prevent avoidance.

1.2.2 Supply of goods or services

1.2.2.1 Supply of goods

Any transfer of the whole property in goods is a supply of goods (VATA 1994, Sch 4). As well as more obvious transactions like the sale of consumer goods, this includes a supply of power or heat, the grant of an interest in land, and even a gift of goods.

1.2.2.2 Supply of services

Anything that is not a supply of goods but which is done for a consideration is a supply of services (VATA 1994, s 5(2)). This includes the provision of a solicitor's services for a fee, but not a gratuitous supply of services.

1.2.3 Taxable supply

Any supply of goods or services (other than an exempt supply) is taxable (VATA 1994, s 4(2)). Exempt supplies are listed in VATA 1994, Sch 9 and include supplies of residential land, insurance, postal services, education and health services.

1.2.4 Taxable person

A taxable person is a person who makes or intends to make taxable supplies and who is or is required to be registered under the Act (VATA 1994, s 3(1)). A person is required to register if they make taxable supplies in a defined period which have exceeded a limit, which is set each year, or will exceed that limit. Currently, a person must register if the value of their taxable supplies in the preceding 12 months exceeded £90,000.

Any person who makes taxable supplies is entitled to be registered if they so request (see 1.3.4). A person who makes only exempt supplies cannot register.

Once registered, a taxable person (individual, partnership or company) receives a VAT number which is issued for all businesses operated by that person.

1.2.5 Course of business

'Business' includes any trade, profession or vocation (VATA 1994, s 94). A supply in the course of business includes the disposal of a business or any of its assets.

1.2.6 Value of supply

Value added tax is charged on the value of the supply of goods or services. This is what the goods or services would cost were VAT not charged and is often shown as part of the price. For example, a television may be advertised as costing '£400 plus VAT'; £400 is the value of the supply.

If the supply is shown as being for a VAT inclusive amount (eg, a television costs '£240'), the value of supply is 'such amount as, with the addition of the tax chargeable, is equal to the consideration' (VATA 1994, s 19(2)). In the case of the television, the value of supply would be £200 and the VAT £40. A price is deemed to include VAT unless the contrary is stated.

If the supply is not for a consideration in money, the value of supply is taken to be its market value (VATA 1994, s 19(3)).

1.2.7 Rate of tax

The standard rate of VAT is 20%. However, there is a large category of supplies which are taxed at 0%. 'Zero-rated' supplies are listed in VATA 1994, Sch 8 and include most types of food (but subject to a number of exceptions including food supplied in the course of catering), books and newspapers, transport and construction of dwellings. A reduced rate of 5% is applied to certain supplies, including domestic fuel, installation of energy-saving materials and child car seats (VATA 1994, Sch 7A). Some supplies are exempt from VAT and include the supply of education and training and many types of land-related supplies (VATA 1994, Sch 9)

1.2.8 Time of supply

A taxable person must account for VAT one month after the end of each quarter (see **1.3.1**). The time of supply (tax point) determines the accounting period within which a supply of goods or services falls.

In the case of goods, the basic tax point is the time goods are removed, or the time they are made available to the person to whom they are supplied. In the case of services, the basic tax point is the time the services are performed (VATA 1994, s 6).

The basic tax point can be varied in a number of cases. For example, it can be brought forward, if the supplier issues a tax invoice (see **1.3.5**) or receives a payment, to the time when the invoice is issued or payment received. It can be delayed, if the supplier issues a tax invoice within 14 days after the basic tax point, to the time when the invoice is issued. Thus the time for accounting for VAT may be brought forward or delayed.

1.3 TAX PAYABLE TO HM REVENUE & CUSTOMS

1.3.1 Introduction

A person who is registered for VAT must send a return to HMRC showing the VAT payable by them, together with a cheque for this amount, generally within one month after the end of each quarter.

The amount payable is the VAT the person has charged on all supplies of goods and services in the course of their business ('output tax'), less any VAT they have paid in the course of their business ('input tax'). If input tax exceeds output tax, the person will receive a rebate.

1.3.2 Zero-rated and exempt supplies

Zero-rated and exempt supplies are similar to each other, in that the customer does not pay any VAT. However, a person who makes zero-rated supplies will be able to reclaim the VAT they have paid from HMRC. A person who makes only exempt supplies cannot register (see 1.2.4) and so cannot reclaim VAT.

> **EXAMPLE**
>
> A baker and a doctor in private practice are converting premises into a shop and a surgery respectively. They will both pay VAT on the cost of their conversions. The baker, who makes zero-rated supplies of food, will be able to reclaim the VAT; the doctor, who makes exempt supplies of health services, will not be able to do so.

1.3.3 Taxable and exempt supplies

Where a person makes both exempt and taxable supplies, for example a doctor in private practice who also acts as an expert witness in personal injury claims, only part of their input tax will be deductible from the output tax charged on the fees for acting as an expert witness (see the VAT Regulations 1995, SI 1995/2518).

1.3.4 Voluntary registration

A person who makes taxable supplies of £90,000 or less per annum is not required to register and charge VAT. This can be an advantage as such a supplier may be able to undercut larger rivals who are obliged to charge VAT.

However, only those people who are registered can reclaim any input tax they have paid. For example, a builder with a small business who bought a van could not reclaim VAT payable on the purchase of the van if they were not registered.

When deciding whether to register voluntarily, people in business must weigh up the advantage of being able to reclaim VAT against the disadvantage that customers might be put off by higher prices.

1.3.5 Tax invoices

A person making a taxable supply to a taxable person must provide them with a tax invoice. A tax invoice is an ordinary invoice or bill which contains specified information about the transaction, such as the VAT number, the tax point, the value of supply and the rate of tax charged.

The tax invoice is important because a person who is claiming to deduct input tax must have tax invoices in respect of all the tax claimed.

1.4 PENALTIES

1.4.1 Introduction

A person who fails to comply with the VAT legislation is liable to a range of criminal and civil penalties in addition to being required to pay any unpaid tax with interest. There are very few defences to these provisions, although the civil penalties may be mitigated. A number of these penalties are dealt with in outline below.

1.4.2 Fraudulent evasion of tax

A person knowingly concerned in the fraudulent evasion of tax is liable, on conviction on indictment, to an unlimited fine and imprisonment for a term not exceeding 14 years (VATA 1994, s 72).

1.4.3 Breaches of regulations

Regulations impose many obligations on taxable persons. Breach of a regulation will lead to a civil penalty. There is a penalty of £500 for failure to keep certain records. Other breaches attract a penalty calculated at a daily rate over the period of the breach (VATA 1994, s 69).

1.4.4 Penalties for late payments and late submission of VAT returns

Interest is charged on late payments of VAT. There are fixed penalties for the late filing of returns imposed via a points system based on the frequency of submissions.

CHAPTER 2

INCOME TAX

LEARNING OUTCOMES

After reading this chapter you will be able to:

- identify chargeable income
- identify allowable reliefs
- identify the appropriate personal allowance for a taxpayer
- understand the difference between income (except savings and dividend income) and savings and dividend income
- identify the tax rates applicable to taxable income
- complete a full income tax calculation.

2.1 INTRODUCTION

2.1.1 The importance of income tax

Income tax is the tax which produces the greatest revenue for the UK Government. For example, in the most recent year for which figures are available (2024/25), total tax revenues collected by HMRC reached £857 billion, of which some £300 billion was generated by income tax (source: ONS: HMRC Tax & NIC Receipts, April 2025). Income tax is, therefore, a vital source of revenue from which public services such as health, education, welfare, transport and defence can be funded. Income tax is collected by HMRC (see **2.9**).

2.1.2 Sources of income tax law

2.1.2.1 Statute

The charging statute for income tax is the Income Tax Act 2007 (ITA 2007) as amended by later Finance Acts. Also of importance are the Income Tax (Trading and Other Income) Act 2005 (ITTOIA 2005) and the Income Tax (Earnings and Pensions) Act 2003 (ITEPA 2003).

Income tax is an annual tax renewed each year by Act of Parliament.

2.1.2.2 Case law

The meaning and extent of the statutory provisions are decided by the judiciary.

An appeal by a taxpayer against an assessment to tax is heard by the First-tier Tribunal. Appeals from the decision of the First-tier Tribunal are made to the Upper Tribunal (Tax and

Chancery Chamber). There is a right of appeal from the Upper Tribunal on a point of law to the Court of Appeal and, with leave, to the Supreme Court.

2.1.2.3 Official Statements

There would be an impossible workload if all questions as to the meaning and extent of tax legislation were taken to court. Official Statements made by HMRC are therefore an important source of information. The two most important types of statement are Extra-Statutory Concessions and Statements of Practice.

Extra-Statutory Concessions

These are published by HMRC. If a taxpayer satisfies the terms of an Extra-Statutory Concession, HMRC waives its right to collect tax which would otherwise be due.

Statements of Practice

These are announced by press release and published in the professional journals. They indicate what view HMRC will take of particular tax provisions.

Note that these Official Statements do not bind the courts.

2.1.3 What is income?

There is no statutory definition of 'income' and the courts have failed to impose a judicial definition. A distinction must be made between income and capital profits: the former is subject to income tax; the latter are subject to capital gains tax. Generally, money received will be income if there is an element of recurrence, for example, a salary or partnership profit share received every month, or interest paid on a bank or building society account every quarter.

2.1.4 Who pays income tax?

The following are liable to pay income tax:

(a) individuals;

(b) partnerships (partners are individually responsible for the tax due on their share of partnership profits);

(c) personal representatives (who pay the deceased's outstanding income tax and income tax chargeable during the administration of the estate); and

(d) trustees (who pay income tax on the income produced by the trust fund).

Companies pay corporation tax (see ***Business Law and Practice***).

Charities are generally exempt from paying tax. There are tax-efficient ways of giving money to charities, for example, Gift Aid.

2.1.5 The tax year

Income tax is paid with reference to the 'tax year' or 'year of assessment', which runs from 6 April until 5 April the following year. It is referred to by the calendar years which it straddles: for example, the tax year beginning on 6 April 2025 is referred to as the tax year 2025/26. So, in the simple tax calculation below at **2.1.8**, Amy's salary received between 6 April 2025 and 5 April 2026 will be charged to tax in the tax year 2025/26.

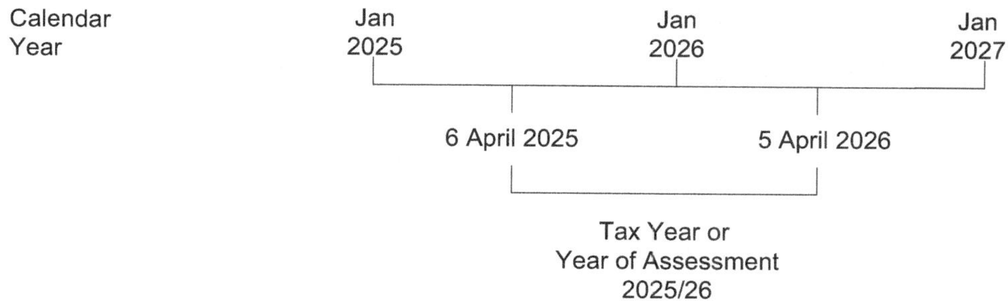

2.1.6 Anti-avoidance legislation

Income tax is one of the taxes subject to the 'general anti-abuse rule' (GAAR) introduced by the Finance Act 2013. The GAAR is an addition to the existing anti-avoidance legislation in this area and is designed to allow HMRC to counteract 'abusive' tax avoidance schemes intended to exploit loopholes in the legislation covering the rules for calculating tax.

2.1.7 How much income tax is payable?

Income tax is a 'progressive' tax, ie a tax where the rate of tax increases as the income of the taxpayer increases, with the result that taxpayers with higher incomes pay a higher average rate of tax than those on lower incomes.

Tax is payable on taxable income, which is calculated by deducting any available reliefs and allowances taxed at the appropriate rate or rates. The allowances and rates are different for the various types of income. Therefore, before a final calculation is made, the different types of income must be separated from one another into three categories. The categories are:

(a) non-savings, non-dividend income ('NSNDI'), comprising all sources of income except income derived from savings and dividends;

(b) savings income, which is interest from various sources, for example building society accounts, most National Savings accounts, unit or investment trusts and corporate or government bonds and gilts; and

(c) dividend income.

The steps to work through to calculate the amount of tax payable are as follows:

Step 1: Calculate the total income

↓

Step 2: Deduct any allowable reliefs

↓

The resulting sum is net income

↓

Step 3: Deduct any personal allowances

↓

The resulting sum is taxable income

↓

Step 4: Separate NSNDI, savings income and dividend income, and calculate the tax on each type of income at the applicable rate(s) (starting rate, basic rate, higher rate and additional rate)

↓

Step 5: Add together the amounts of tax from Step 4 (to give the overall income tax liability)

Note: As explained below, income tax is charged on an individual's taxable income for 2025/26 in bands at a variety of rates ranging from 0% to 45% depending on the amount and type of income (see **2.5**).

2.1.8 Simple income tax calculation

The five steps may be used to carry out a simple tax calculation. For example, Amy has the following income for 2025/26: £62,270 share of partnership profits, and £10,000, after deduction of expenses, from writing learned articles. She is liable to make interest payments of £2,000 per annum on a qualifying loan. Amy's income tax may be calculated as follows:

		£
STEP 1	Calculate the total income	
	Partnership profits	62,270
	Learned articles	10,000
	TOTAL INCOME	72,270
STEP 2	Deduct any allowable reliefs (interest)	(2,000)
	NET INCOME	70,270
STEP 3	Deduct any personal allowance	(12,570)
	TAXABLE INCOME	57,700
STEP 4	Calculate the tax at the applicable rate(s)	
	£37,700 at 20%	7,540
	£20,000 at 40%	8,000
	£57,700	
	Note: Income from partnership profits and from writing learned articles are both NSNDI so are taxed at the same rates.	
STEP 5	Add together the amounts of tax from Step 4	
	OVERALL INCOME TAX LIABILITY	15,540

The calculation above indicates the principles used to establish an individual's liability to income tax. The remainder of this chapter will consider each step of the calculation in more detail.

2.2 TOTAL INCOME

Total income is the aggregate of the taxpayer's income from all sources which is charged to income tax.

2.2.1 What income is charged to income tax?

2.2.1.1 The chargeable sources of income

Income is charged to income tax if it comes from a source specified by the ITTOIA 2005 and the ITEPA 2003. The most important sources are listed below.

Location	*Source*
ITTOIA 2005	
Part 2	Trading income (Profits of a trade, profession or vocation. Part 2 therefore charges the self-employed and applies to sole traders, trading partnerships, sole practitioners and professional partnerships)
Part 3	Property income (Rents and other receipts from land in the UK)
Part 4	Savings and investment income (Interest, annuities and dividends)
Part 5	Certain miscellaneous income (Annual income not otherwise charged)

Location	*Source*
ITEPA 2003	Employment and pensions income (Income arising out of employment and including social security payments such as sick pay and maternity payments)

2.2.1.2 How do the chargeable sources of income work?

If income is shown to be derived from one of the sources, it will be charged to income tax. For example, if an individual receives rent from land, they will pay income tax under Part 3 of the ITTOIA 2005. Income not having a chargeable source cannot be charged to income tax at all.

2.2.1.3 Why is it divided into chargeable sources?

Each Part of the ITTOIA 2005 and the ITEPA 2003 has its own rules for calculating the amount of income. For example, under Part 3 of the ITTOIA 2005 (which taxes income from land) the charge is on rents and other receipts, but the landlord may deduct expenses such as repairs on the property, ie expenses of an income nature. This means that income tax is charged on the profit element rather than the gross income.

Further details of how the ITTOIA 2005 and the ITEPA 2003 operate can be found in ***Business Law and Practice***.

2.2.2 Exempt income

Certain items are free of income tax. They include:

(a) certain State benefits;
(b) interest on National Savings and Investments (NS&I) Savings Certificates;
(c) scholarships;
(d) interest on damages for personal injuries or death;
(e) income from investments in an individual savings account (ISA) (see **5.3**);
(f) gross income up to £7,500 a year from letting a furnished room in the taxpayer's home;
(g) annual payments under certain insurance policies, for example, where insurance benefits are provided in times of sickness; and
(h) premium bond winnings.

Most of the above items are set out in the ITTOIA 2005, Part 6 (Exempt Income). In addition, a number of items are exempted from tax because of Extra-Statutory Concessions (see **2.1.2.3**).

2.2.3 Calculating the total income

It should now be possible to calculate the total income.

The total income is the aggregate of chargeable income computed according to the rules of the various chargeable sources. To work out the total income of a taxpayer it is necessary to find out what sources of income they have, calculate the income arising under each source and then add all the *'gross'* income together. For example:

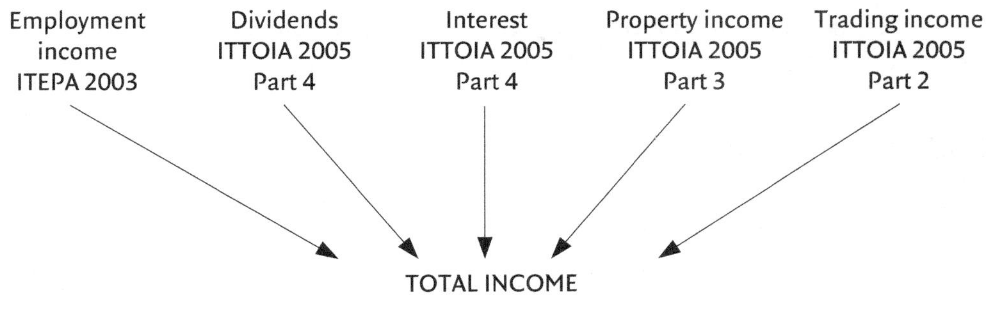

Most types of income are received by the taxpayer without any tax having been deducted prior to receipt. These types of income are said to be received 'gross'. Trading, property, interest and dividend income are received gross.

2.2.3.1 Tax deducted at source

For most taxpayers, their main source of income will be employment income, from which tax will have been deducted at source. The payee receives the net amount, not the gross amount. This is to ensure a steady flow of tax to HMRC and then on to central government to fund public services throughout the year.

Any sum received after deduction of tax at source must be grossed up to find the original sum from which the tax was deducted. This gross figure must be entered into the payee's calculation of total income. This is because the tax calculation is a way of checking that, overall, the taxpayer pays the right amount of tax.

At the end of the tax calculation, the tax that has already been paid will be credited to the taxpayer so that they will owe HMRC only the outstanding amount.

Salaries and other employment income are assessable under ITEPA 2003 using the Pay As You Earn system (PAYE). Under the PAYE system, the employer deducts from the employee's salary and then pays to HMRC income tax at the appropriate rate at the time the salary is paid. The PAYE system also takes account of personal allowances.

Employment income cannot be grossed up using a simple formula because deduction at source may not be just at one single rate. Under the PAYE scheme, income tax at various rates and National Insurance contributions will be deducted from salaries by the employer using tables and information supplied by HMRC and taking into account the employee's personal reliefs. A certificate of tax paid (P60), showing the gross figure, is given by the employer to the employee on a yearly basis and the employee can put this figure into their tax return. A taxpayer must complete a tax return if they have other sources of income.

2.2.3.2 Savings and dividend income

Interest and dividends are paid gross, and both savings and dividend income have the benefit of annual tax-free allowances (see **2.5.4.2** and **2.5.5.1**). Both savings and dividend income still form part of Total Income, and must be aggregated with other income at this stage

2.3 ALLOWABLE RELIEFS

Total Income
Less
Allowable Reliefs
=
Net Income

2.3.1 Net income

Net income is total income less certain specified commitments known as allowable reliefs, for example interest on qualifying loans. Allowable reliefs remove sums of money from the income tax calculation.

2.3.2 Interest payments on qualifying loans

Most interest payments receive no tax relief at all, for example ordinary bank overdrafts, credit card interest and hire purchase interest payments. The borrower pays the interest out of taxed income.

However, in certain cases, tax relief may be available for interest paid on money borrowed. A taxpayer obtains income tax relief for certain interest payments by deducting them from their total income as an allowable relief. To obtain tax relief, interest must be payable on a 'qualifying loan'.

Qualifying loans include the following.

2.3.2.1 A loan to buy a share in a partnership or to contribute capital or make a loan to a partnership

EXAMPLE

Dawn, a partner, has total income of £25,000. She borrows £10,000 to make a loan to the partnership to be used wholly and exclusively for partnership business. The interest rate on the loan is 4% per annum. Dawn's net income is:

	£
Total income	25,000
Deduct any allowable reliefs	
(interest on qualifying loan)	400
Net income	24,600

There is a cap of £50,000 or 25% of 'adjusted total income' on the amount of relief that can be claimed under this provision. 'Adjusted total income' is taxable income less allowable pension contributions. See **Business Law and Practice** for further details.

2.3.2.2 A loan to invest in a close trading company

See ***Business Law and Practice.***

2.3.2.3 A loan to personal representatives to pay inheritance tax

See **30.6.3.5.**

2.4 PERSONAL ALLOWANCES

Personal allowances are deducted from net income to obtain the taxpayer's taxable income. This means that a certain amount of income is free each year.

The availability of allowances depends not on the type of income involved, but on the taxpayer's personal circumstances, for example disability or the amount of income received each tax year.

The taxpayer must claim their allowances each year in their tax return. The principal allowances available and deducted at this stage are as follows.

2.4.1 Personal Allowance

Net Income
Less
Personal Allowance
=
Taxable Income

The Personal Allowance available for 2025/26 is £12,570. It is set to remain at this level until 2028. This is, however, subject to an income limit of £100,000 (see below). It may be set against income of any kind. It is applied in this order: first against NSNDI; then, if there is a surplus, against savings income; and finally any remaining surplus is applied against dividend income. For most employees, their Personal Allowance will be used up by their employment income, unless such income is below £12,570.

If the Personal Allowance exceeds the net income of the taxpayer, the surplus is unused and cannot be carried forward for use in future years (subject to the Marriage Allowance – see **2.4.2**).

This allowance may be claimed by taxpayers resident in the UK. Those who are married or in a civil partnership are treated as separate individuals for income tax purposes, independently liable for tax on their own income, and each benefits from their own Personal Allowance (but see **2.4.2**).

The Personal Allowance is reduced where the taxpayer's income exceeds the income limit of £100,000. This reduction applies irrespective of age. The Personal Allowance is reduced by £1 for every £2 of income above the £100,000 limit. The effect of the reduction is that for a taxpayer with income of £125,140 or more, no Personal Allowance will be available. In order to calculate the adjusted Personal Allowance for a taxpayer with a net income in excess of £100,000 but under £125,140, a formula may be used:

$$\text{£}12{,}570 - \frac{(\text{net income} - \text{£}100{,}000)}{2} = \text{adjusted Personal Allowance}$$

The adjusted Personal Allowance should be rounded up to nearest £1.

EXAMPLE 1

Jo has a net income of £50,570. Jo is entitled to deduct the full Personal Allowance of £12,570 from her net income of £50,570 to obtain a taxable income figure of £38,000.

EXAMPLE 2

Miriam has a net income of £110,000. Miriam is not entitled to deduct the full Personal Allowance as her net income exceeds the £100,000 income limit. Using the above formula, Miriam's adjusted Personal Allowance can be calculated.

$$\text{£}12{,}570 - \frac{(\text{£}110{,}000 - \text{£}100{,}000)}{2}$$

$$\text{£}12{,}570 - \frac{\text{£}10{,}000}{2}$$

£12,570 – £5,000 = £7,570

Miriam is entitled to deduct £7,570 from her net income of £110,000 to obtain a taxable income figure of £102,430.

2.4.2 Marriage Allowance

A transferable 'marriage allowance' is available to married couples and civil partners. Where one spouse or partner does not have enough income to use their Personal Allowance fully for that tax year, they may transfer £1,260 of their Personal Allowance to their spouse or civil partner. The recipient must not be a higher or additional rate taxpayer.

2.4.3 Blind Person's Allowance

A taxpayer who is a registered blind person receives an allowance of £3,130. If a husband and wife are both registered blind, they can each claim the Blind Person's Allowance.

2.4.4 Property and trading allowances

Allowances for small amounts of property income and trading income are, generally, available to all UK taxpayers. Where individuals are in receipt of gross property income or gross trading income below £1,000, the income will not be subject to income tax and taxpayers are not required to submit a tax return or, where they have other income, declare it in their tax return. Where gross property or trading income is in excess of £1,000, the taxpayer can choose to take the £1,000 allowance as a deduction against gross income instead of deducting actual expenses to arrive at their taxable income figure.

2.5 RATES OF TAX

2.5.1 Types of income

The taxable income is taxed at the appropriate rate or rates. As stated above, income tax is a progressive tax. The rates of tax increase as the taxpayer's income increases. In addition, the rates are different for the various types of income. Therefore, before the rates can be applied, the different types of income must be separated from one another (see **2.1.7**).

To find out how much taxable income is comprised of NSNDI and how much of savings and dividend income, the savings and dividend income are deducted from the Taxable Income figure arrived at in Step 3.

Taxable Income
Less
Savings and Dividend Income
=
Taxable NSNDI
This is the amount of NSNDI which will be subject to tax at the relevant rate(s)

(In most cases, use of this calculation results in the taxpayer receiving the maximum benefit from any allowable reliefs and the personal allowance (because NSNDI is taxed at higher rates). In practice, the taxpayer may choose to allocate the personal allowance between their various types of income in the way that is most beneficial to them, but as a different allocation will only be relevant to a minority of taxpayers, for ease, this will not be considered further.)

2.5.2 Order of taxation

Once the different types of income have been separated out, they must be taxed in order: NSNDI first, then savings income, then dividends. The rates of tax are different for each type of income. These tax rates are applied in 'bands' according to the level of the taxpayer's income: the higher the amount of income, the higher the tax rate. These rates and bands are fixed annually. A summary of the main rates is as follows:

Taxable income	**Tax rates**
£0–£33,700	Basic rate: NSNDI 20% Savings 20% Dividends 8.75%
£33,701–£125,140	Higher/Upper rate: NSNDI 40% Savings 40% Dividends 33.75%

Taxable income	Tax rates
Above £125,140	Additional rate: NSNDI 45% Savings 45% Dividends 39.35%

Note: There is also a 'starting rate' for savings income (see **2.5.4.1**)

Under its devolved powers, the Welsh Parliament sets the rates of income tax on NSNDI for Welsh taxpayers (ie those who either live in Wales or have their main residence in Wales). The rate of tax is calculated by reducing the above rates of tax by 10% and then adding the rate set annually by the Welsh Parliament. The rate set by the Welsh Parliament is currently 10%. This means that for 2025/26 the rates of tax paid by Welsh taxpayers are the same as those for English taxpayers, although there is clearly potential for the rates to differ. The amounts of allowances and the rates on savings and dividend income are set by the UK Parliament.

2.5.3 NSNDI

NSNDI is taxed first. Once the NSNDI has been calculated, it is taxed at the basic rate, followed by the higher rate and the additional rate, if the amount of NSNDI is large enough. The rates for the tax year 2025/26 are set out above.

EXAMPLE

Timothy has a taxable income of £180,000, of which £20,000 is savings and dividend income. Timothy's NSNDI amounts to:

Taxable income	£180,000
Less savings and dividend income	£20,000
NSNDI	£160,000

Timothy's NSNDI will be liable to tax:

(a) at the basic rate of 20% on the first £37,700;

(b) at the higher rate of 40% to the extent that it is above the basic rate limit of £37,700 but falls below the higher rate limit of £125,140. Therefore, £87,440 (£125,140 – £37,700) will be taxed at 40%; and

(c) at the additional rate of 45% on the income in excess of the £125,140 limit (£34,860).

The tax liability in respect of his NSNDI will be:

£37,700	@ 20%	£7,540
£87,440	@ 40%	£34,976
£34,860	@ 45%	£15,687
£160,000		£58,203

The savings and dividend income is calculated separately (not shown here).

2.5.4 Savings income

Any savings income is taxed next.

2.5.4.1 Starting rate

In addition to the tax rates set out above, savings income benefits from a starting rate. The starting rate is 0% on the first £5,000 of savings income. The starting rate works in a different way to the other rates in that its availability is gradually reduced as the taxpayer's income increases. In effect, every £1 of NSNDI that the taxpayer has above the personal allowance

(£12,570) reduces the starting rate by £1. Applying that formula, the starting rate ceases to be available at all once the taxpayer's NSNDI is above £17,570.

> **Example**
>
> Winston has a salary of £14,000 and receives interest of £750 a year. As Winston's non-savings income is below £17,570, he benefits from the starting rate. However, the amount available is reduced by the amount by which his NSNDI exceeds his personal allowance (ie £1,430). The starting rate available is reduced from £5,000 to £3,570. This is sufficient to cover all of Winston's savings income which is therefore taxed at 0%.

2.5.4.2 Personal Savings Allowance (PSA)

The PSA (which must be distinguished from the Personal Allowance (see **2.4**)) can be set against savings income, so that up to the first £1,000 of savings income will, in effect, be tax free.

The amount of PSA to which a taxpayer is entitled depends on whether they are a basic, higher or additional rate taxpayer. This is calculated by reference to the taxpayer's taxable income, as calculated at Step 3. Basic rate taxpayers are entitled to a PSA of £1,000; higher rate taxpayers are entitled to a PSA of £500; additional rate taxpayers do not receive a PSA.

> **Example 1**
>
> Asaad has a salary of £22,000 and receives interest of £750 a year. (He has no relevant allowable reliefs.) For the purposes of calculating how much PSA Asaad is entitled to, Asaad is a basic rate taxpayer, as his total taxable income is below the basic rate threshold. He therefore has a PSA of £1,000.

> **Example 2**
>
> Janine has a salary of £61,000 and receives interest of £550 a year from her bank and building society savings accounts. For the purposes of calculating how much PSA Janine is entitled to, Janine is a higher rate taxpayer, as her taxable income is above the basic rate threshold (and below the additional rate threshold). She therefore has a PSA of £500.

Although termed an 'allowance', in reality the PSA applies a nil rate (ie 0% tax rate) to the first part of savings income. Note in particular that the PSA (unlike the Personal Allowance) does not reduce the amount of the taxpayer's taxable income.

The PSA is applied once the Personal Allowance and the starting rate (if any) have been exhausted. Any PSA unused in the tax year is lost – it cannot, for example, be carried forward to set against savings income in future years.

2.5.4.3 Taxing savings income

Having established the amount of the taxable savings income, this must be taxed at the appropriate rates.

The starting rate (if any) will be applied first.

Any savings income remaining to be taxed will be subject to the taxpayer's PSA (if any). The effect of the PSA is to tax the first 'slice' of savings income at 0% regardless of the tax band into which that income falls.

Any remaining savings income will be taxed at the basic, higher or additional rate for savings according to the taxpayer's level of income.

Example 1

Eric has taxable income of £6,500 (after deduction of his personal allowance), of which £4,500 is NSNDI and £2,000 is interest. As Eric's NSNDI income is below £17,570, he benefits from the starting rate for savings. However, the amount available is reduced by the amount by which his NSNDI exceeds his personal allowance (ie £4,500). The starting rate available is therefore reduced from £5,000 to £500. Eric is a basic rate taxpayer and so will be entitled to a PSA of £1,000. He will be liable to tax:

(a) at the basic rate of 20% on the £4,500 of NSNDI (£90);

(b) at the starting rate for savings of 0% on the first £500 of savings income (£0);

(c) at 0% under his PSA on the next £1,000 of savings income (£0); and

(d) at the basic rate of 20% on the remaining £3,500 of savings income (£700).

Example 2

Deka has taxable income (after deduction of her personal allowance) of £43,700, of which £41,700 is NSNDI and £2,000 is interest. As Deka's NSNDI income is above £17,570, she is not entitled to the starting rate for savings income. Deka is a higher rate taxpayer. She will be entitled to a PSA of £500. All of her remaining savings income falls within the savings higher rate band. She will be liable to tax:

(a) on the NSNDI:

  (i) at the basic rate of 20% on the first £37,700 (£7,540); and

  (ii) at the higher rate of 40% on the remaining £4,000 (£1,600);

(b) at 0% under her PSA on the first £500 of savings income (£0); and

(c) at the savings higher rate of 40% on the remaining £1,500 of savings income (£600).

Example 3

Josh has taxable income (after allowances and reliefs) of £135,140, of which £115,140 is NSNDI and £20,000 is interest. Josh is an additional rate taxpayer. He is not entitled to a PSA. He will be liable to tax:

(a) on the NSNDI:

  (i) at the basic rate of 20% on the first £37,700 (£7,540); and

  (ii) at the higher rate of 40% on the remaining £77,440 (£30,976); and

(b) on the interest:

  (i) at the savings higher rate of 40% to the extent that it falls below the higher rate limit of £125,140, so £10,000 (£125,140 – £115,140) will be taxed at 40% (£4,000); and

  (ii) at the savings additional rate of 45% on the remaining £10,000 (£4,500).

2.5.5 Dividend income

Dividend income is treated as the 'top slice' of taxable income, above both NSNDI and savings income.

2.5.5.1 Dividend Allowance

The Dividend Allowance can be set against dividend income, so that the first £500 of a taxpayer's dividend income is in effect tax free. All taxpayers (whether basic, higher or additional rate taxpayers) are entitled to the £500.

As with the PSA (see **2.5.4.2**), although termed an 'allowance', in reality the Dividend Allowance applies a nil rate (ie 0% tax rate) to the first part of dividend income. The Dividend Allowance (unlike the Personal Allowance) does not reduce the amount of the taxpayer's taxable income.

2.5.5.2 Taxing dividend income

Having established the amount of the taxable dividend income, this must be taxed at the appropriate rates.

The Dividend Allowance is applied first. The effect of the Dividend Allowance is to tax the first 'slice' of dividend income at 0% regardless of the tax band into which that income falls.

EXAMPLE 1

Arthur has taxable income (after allowances and reliefs) of £6,000, of which £4,500 is NSNDI and £1,500 is dividend income. (He has no savings income.) Arthur is a basic rate taxpayer. He is entitled to a Dividend Allowance of £500, which is taxed at 0%. All of his remaining dividend income falls within the basic rate. He will be liable to tax:

(a) at the basic rate of 20% on the £4,500 of NSNDI (£900);

(b) at 0% under his Dividend Allowance on the first £500 of dividend income (£0); and

(c) at the dividend ordinary rate of 8.75% on the remaining £1,000 of dividend income (£87.50).

EXAMPLE 2

Sanjay has taxable income (after allowances and reliefs) of £50,700, of which £41,700 is NSNDI and £9,000 is dividend income. (He has no savings income.) Sanjay is a higher rate taxpayer. He is entitled to a Dividend Allowance of £500, which is taxed at 0%. All of his remaining dividend income falls within the upper rate. He will be liable to tax:

(a) on the NSNDI:

 (i) at the basic rate of 20% on the first £37,700, (£7,540); and

 (ii) at the higher rate of 40% on the remaining £4,000 (£1,600); and

(b) at 0% under his dividend allowance on the first £500 of dividend income (£0); and

(c) on the remaining dividend income (£8,500), at the dividend upper rate of 33.75% (£2,868.75).

2.5.6 Taxing both savings and dividend income

The examples above illustrate the position where the taxpayer has either savings or dividend income in addition to taxable NSNDI. The example below shows a simple calculation where the taxpayer has both savings and dividend income, as well as taxable NSNDI (and see **2.7**).

EXAMPLE

Ben has taxable NSNDI of £17,700, savings income of £1,250 and dividend income of £9,000. As his NSNDI exceeds £17,570, he is not entitled to the starting rate for savings income. Ben is a basic rate taxpayer and is entitled to a PSA of £1,000 and a Dividend Allowance of £500.

(a) Ben will be liable to tax on the NSNDI at the basic rate: £17,700 at 20% (£3,540).

His NSNDI will use up only £17,700 of the basic rate band, leaving £20,000.

The savings income is taxed next. The PSA is applied first. The remaining taxable savings income all falls within the £37,700 threshold and is taxed at the savings basic rate.

(b) Ben will be liable to tax at 0% under his PSA on the first £1,000 of savings income (£0); and on the remaining savings income at the savings basic rate: £250 at 20% (£50).

This has used up a further £1,250 of the basic rate band, leaving £18,750.

The dividend income is taxed last. The £500 Dividend Allowance is applied first. His remaining taxable dividend income all falls below the £37,700 threshold.

(c) Ben will be liable to tax at 0% under his Dividend Allowance on the first £500 of dividend income (£0); and on the remaining dividend income at the dividend ordinary rate: £8,500 at 8.75% (£743.75).

2.6 CALCULATING THE TAX DUE

The five steps described above will enable a taxpayer to calculate their overall tax liability for a tax year. However, deductions can be made for any tax deducted at source.

Salaries and other employment income

Tax is deducted at source using the PAYE system (see **2.2.3.1**). The amount of tax paid (shown in a taxpayer's P60) is deducted from the taxpayer's overall tax liability. If the tax paid exceeds that liability, a refund will be due.

2.7 A FULL INCOME TAX CALCULATION

Frederick carries on a business in partnership and his share of [trading] profit from the partnership for 2025/26 is £40,435. However, to buy his share of this partnership he took out a loan from the Blankshire Bank, and the interest on that loan is £1,165 per annum.

Frederick also has an account at the Guildfleet Building Society on which he receives interest of £4,500 in 2025/26. He also owns shares in a company and receives dividends of £10,000 net in 2025/26.

To calculate Frederick's tax bill for 2025/26:

	£
Step 1: Calculate total income	
Trade profits (ITTOIA 2005, Part 2)	40,435
Interest (ITTOIA 2005, Part 4)	4,500
Dividends (ITTOIA 2005, Part 4)	10,000
Total Income	54,935
Step 2: Deduct allowable reliefs	
Loan interest to Blankshire Bank	(1,165)
Net Income	53,770

Step 3: Deduct personal allowances

Personal Allowance	(12,570)
Taxable Income	41,200

Step 4: Separate NSNDI and savings and dividend income and calculate tax at the applicable rate(s)

(a) NSNDI

Taxable income	41,200
Less savings income	(4,500)
Less dividend income	(10,000)
= NSNDI	26,700

This element of Frederick's taxable income falls £11,000 short of the £37,700 basic rate threshold and so is taxed at the basic rate of 20%:

£26,700 @ 20% = £5,340

(b) *Savings income*

The total of his NSNDI and savings income (£31,200) falls £6,500 short of the £37,700 basic rate threshold.

As Frederick is a higher rate taxpayer (his taxable income exceeds £37,700), he is entitled to a PSA of £500, which is taxed first at 0%.

The remaining savings income (£4,000) all falls within the basic rate band, and so is taxed at 20%.

£500 @ 0% = £0
£4,000 @ 20% = £800
£800

(c) *Dividend income*

The total of his NSNDI, savings and dividend income (£41,200) exceeds the £37,700 basic rate threshold by £3,500.

Frederick is entitled to a Dividend Allowance of £500, regardless of whether he is a basic or higher rate taxpayer. This is taxed first at 0%.

To the extent that the remaining dividend income (£9,500) falls within the remaining basic rate band (£6,000), it is taxed at the dividend ordinary rate of 8.75%; the excess over the basic rate threshold (£3,500) is taxed at the dividend upper rate of 33.75%.

£500 @ 0% = £0
£6,000 @ 8.75% = £525.00
£3,500 @ 33.75% = £1,181.25
£1,706.25

Step 5: Add together the amounts of tax from Step 4

OVERALL INCOME TAX LIABILITY (£5,340 + £800 + £1,706.25)	£7,846.25

There are no relevant deductions, as none of Frederick's income was deducted at source.

Income tax to pay	£7,846.25

2.8 COLLECTION OF INCOME TAX AND DATES FOR PAYMENT

2.8.1 HM Revenue & Customs

Before considering the collection of income tax (see **2.8.2**), it is worth noting that HMRC is also responsible for:

(a) administering corporation tax, capital gains tax, petroleum revenue tax, inheritance tax, stamp duties, VAT, customs duties and excise duties;
(b) collecting National Insurance contributions;
(c) advising on tax policy;
(d) advising on valuation policy and providing valuation services;
(e) enforcing the National Minimum Wage; and
(f) recovering student loan repayments.

2.8.2 Collection of income tax: deduction at source

There are two methods of collection of tax: deduction at source and the self-assessment regime.

As explained above (see **2.2.3**), for certain types of income, tax is deducted at source. The payer of the income acts as a tax collector by deducting from the payment the appropriate amount of income tax and handing it to HMRC. The taxpayer therefore receives the payment net of income tax.

2.8.3 Collection of income tax: self-assessment

The self-assessment regime covers all income tax due. There is a set of payment dates for all sources of income and a single tax bill for the year. However, where income tax has been deducted at source, the taxpayer will declare this income on their tax return and their overall tax liability will be reduced by the amount of income tax already paid.

Examples of when income will be declared on a tax return and the appropriate amount of income tax collected under the self-assessment regime are:

(a) Trading profit (ITTOIA 2005, Part 2). Any income profits of a trade which a taxpayer has made will be assessed under ITTOIA 2005, Part 2 and collected under the self-assessment regime.
(b) Rent (ITTOIA 2005, Part 3). A landlord (taxpayer) receiving gross rent from the tenant will be assessed to tax under ITTOIA 2005, Part 3 and any income tax payable will be collected under the self-assessment regime.

The self-assessment method assumes that the taxpayer has actually received the sum on which they are to pay tax and can send part of it to HMRC to satisfy their income tax liability. There is a risk that the taxpayer will spend the income received before HMRC can claim its share.

2.8.3.1 The tax return

Under the self-assessment regime, the taxpayer completes an annual tax return, which includes computation pages to enable the taxpayer to calculate their own income tax. Tax returns are issued soon after 5 April. There are different returns for different types of income. HMRC now encourages taxpayers to use an online tax return.

Even if a taxpayer does not normally receive a tax return, there is a statutory obligation to notify HMRC that they have income that is liable to tax. This must be done within six months of the end of the relevant tax year. There is a penalty for default.

2.8.3.2 Dates for payment

The online tax return and any payment must be filed by 31 January following the tax year to which the return relates. If the taxpayer would rather send a paper return, this must be submitted no later than 31 October.

The taxpayer is automatically required to make two payments on account towards the income tax due for any year, and then a third and final balancing payment to meet any tax still outstanding. The first payment on account is due on 31 January in the tax year in question.

The second payment on account is due on 31 July after the end of the tax year. Any balancing payment is due on the next 31 January.

Each payment on account should be approximately one half of the income tax liability for the year. They are calculated by reference to the previous year's income tax liability, and are reduced to give credit for tax deducted at source. No payments on account are required if this 'relevant amount' is below a certain limit. This limit is set at a level that ensures most employees and pensioners (and others who receive the bulk of their income after deduction of income tax at source or who have relatively small outstanding tax liabilities) do not have to make payments on account.

EXAMPLE

Josie's income tax liability for 2025/26 came to £15,000, of which £7,000 was deducted at source. Her return for 2025/26 will be issued in April 2026 and a paper return must be submitted to HMRC by 31 October 2026, or an online return by 31 January 2027 at the latest. For 2025/26 she will make interim payments on account of ½ × (£15,000 – £7,000) = £4,000 on 31 January 2026 and 31 July 2026. Her final adjustment for 2025/26 is due on 31 January 2027.

Taxpayers have the right to claim a reduction or cancellation of payments on account where they have grounds for believing that payments based on the tax liability for the previous year will lead to an overpayment of tax in the current year.

2.8.3.3 Penalties for default

Interest is charged on any amount of tax unpaid at the due date for payment whether that tax is due as a payment on account or as a balancing payment. There are also fixed penalties for late or non-payment.

Throughout the self-assessment regime the onus is on the taxpayer, and there is a statutory requirement to maintain adequate records to support the return, backed up by a penalty for default. HMRC has extensive powers, for example random audits and specific enquiries, to check the accuracy of any return. Appeals against assessments and determinations are made to the First-tier Tribunal.

SUMMARY

There is no statutory definition of income but income payments and receipts have an element of recurrence.

Income tax is payable by individuals, partners, PRs and trustees.

Income tax is payable on income only if it derives from a source specified in either ITTOIA 2005 or ITEPA 2003. Income, which does not derive from one of these sources, is not taxable and some income is specifically exempted from tax.

Income tax is paid on income received during a tax year. The tax year runs from 6 April to 5 April.

There are five steps to be used to calculate a taxpayer's income tax liability.

Step 1: Calculate total income

This is achieved by adding together all the taxpayer's *gross* income arising under each source. Some income (eg employment income) is received net and will have to be grossed up before being added to the gross income from other sources.

Step 2: Deduct any allowable reliefs to give net income

Interest on a qualifying loan is an example of a payment which may be deducted at this stage.

Step 3: Deduct any personal allowance to give taxable income

Generally, the only allowance which may be deducted at this stage is the personal allowance of £12,570. This allowance is subject to an income limit of £100,000.

Step 4: Calculate the tax at the applicable rate(s)

Before applying the tax rates, separate the income (except savings and dividend income) from the savings and dividend income. This is achieved as follows:

	Taxable income
LESS	Savings and dividend income
	Non-savings, non-dividend income

First, tax the income (except savings and dividend income) as follows:

Basic rate	£0–£37,700 @ 20%
Higher rate	over £37,700–£125,140 @ 40%
Additional rate	over £125,140 @ 45%

Next, having made adjustment for the Personal Savings and Dividend Allowances, tax the savings and dividend income, starting with any interest received.

To the extent that the starting rate for savings, basic rate and higher rate bands remain available after taxing the income (except savings and dividend income), interest received is taxed as follows:

Starting rate for savings	£0–£5,000 @ 0%
Savings basic rate	over £5,000–£37,700 @ 20%
Savings higher rate	over £37,700–£125,140 @ 40%
Savings additional rate	over £125,140 @ 45%

Finally, tax any dividend income element of the savings and dividend income.

To the extent that the dividend ordinary rate and upper rate bands remain available after taxing the non-savings, non-dividend income, dividends are taxed as follows:

Dividend ordinary rate	£0–£37,700 @ 8.75%
Dividend upper rate	over £37,700–£125,140 @ 33.75%
Dividend additional rate	over £125,140 @ 39.35%

Step 5: Add together the amounts of tax from Step 4 to give the taxpayer's overall tax liability

Having calculated the taxpayer's overall liability, reduce that liability by any income tax deducted at source (and therefore paid direct to HMRC). The resulting figure is the income tax which the taxpayer is obliged to pay to HMRC.

The taxpayer will submit a tax return to HMRC by 31 January following the tax year to which the return relates. The taxpayer will make payments on account on 31 January in the tax year in question and on 31 July after the end of tax year in respect of their income tax liability. Any balancing payment must be made by 31 January after the end of the tax year.

CHAPTER 3

CAPITAL GAINS TAX

LEARNING OUTCOMES

After reading this chapter you will be able to understand:

- the circumstances that give rise to a capital gains tax charge
- the method for calculating a taxpayer's chargeable gain(s) for the tax year
- the means by which the taxpayer can claim tax relief on their capital losses.

3.1 INTRODUCTION

3.1.1 Sources of capital gains tax law

The principal charging statute is the Taxation of Chargeable Gains Act 1992.

3.1.2 The charge to tax

Capital gains tax (CGT) is charged on the chargeable gains made by a chargeable person on the disposal of chargeable assets in a tax year (6 April to following 5 April).

3.1.3 Chargeable assets

All forms of property are treated as assets for CGT purposes (including debts, options, incorporeal property and property created by the person disposing of it). Sterling is excluded from the definition so disposals of cash do not attract CGT liability. The legislation does provide for a limited category of non-chargeable assets, the main example being private motor vehicles. The legislation also provides that certain assets which are not non-chargeable shall be wholly or partly exempt from CGT – see **3.4**.

Who pays CGT?

Chargeable persons are:

(a) individuals;

(b) business partners (each partner is charged separately for their share of the partnership gains when there is a disposal of a chargeable partnership asset);

(c) personal representatives (who pay CGT when there is a disposal of the deceased's chargeable assets);

(d) trustees (who pay CGT when there is a disposal of a chargeable asset from the trust fund).

Companies pay corporation tax on income and capital gains (see **Business Law and Practice**). Charities are generally exempt from paying tax.

3.1.4 How much CGT will an individual pay?

The steps required to calculate the amount of CGT payable are as follows:

3.1.4.1 Step 1: Disposal of a chargeable asset

It is first necessary to identify the disposal of a chargeable asset, for example the sale of land.

3.1.4.2 Step 2: Calculation of the gain

This, in basic terms, will be the consideration received when the asset is sold less cost.

3.1.4.3 Step 3: Consider reliefs

Various reliefs may be available (see **3.4**). Early examples assume that none of these apply for the sake of simplicity.

3.1.4.4 Step 4: Aggregate gains/losses; deduct annual exemption

An individual does not pay tax on all the gains they make. There is an exemption for the first £3,000 of total net gains made by an individual in the current tax year (2025/26).

The annual exemption for most types of trust is £1,500 in the current tax year.

3.1.4.5 Step 5: Apply the appropriate rates of tax

When calculating the appropriate rate(s) of tax, gains are treated as if they were the top slice of the taxpayer's income for the tax year. There are four possible rates:

(a) Subject to para (c) below, if an individual's gains and taxable income added together do not exceed the threshold for basic rate income tax (£37,700), the rate of tax on the gains is 18%.

(b) Subject to para (c) below, if an individual's gains and taxable income added together exceed the basic rate income tax threshold, any part of the gains up to the basic rate threshold is taxed at 18%, but the rate of tax on the gains that exceed the threshold is 24%.

(c) Any gains that qualify for business asset disposal relief (see **3.4.8**) are taxed at a flat rate of 14%.

Where an individual has gains that qualify for business asset disposal relief and other gains that do not, the business asset disposal relief gains (taxed at a flat rate of 14%) will be added to the individual's income first with the result that their other gains will be treated (for the purpose of calculating the appropriate rate) as the very top slice of their income and so be more likely to be taxed at 24%.

Note: All examples in this chapter assume that business asset disposal relief is not available. Please refer to **Chapter 28** of **Business Law and Practice** for a detailed explanation of how business asset disposal relief is applied in practice.

Gains realised by trustees and personal representatives are taxed at a flat rate of 24%.

EXAMPLE

In August, Sarah sells shares for £92,000. The shares cost her £70,000. It is her only disposal during the tax year. Sarah has a taxable income for the tax year of £50,000, which means that all of her gain is taxed at 24%.

Step 1: Identify the disposal
Sale of shares

Step 2:	Calculate the gain	
	Proceeds of disposal	£92,000
	Less: Cost	(£70,000)
		£22,000
Step 3:	Consider exemptions and reliefs	Nil
Step 4:	Gain	£22,000
	Deduct annual exemption	(£3,000)
	Chargeable gain	£19,000
Step 5:	What is the rate of tax?	
	CGT at 24% on £19,000 is £4,560.	

3.1.5 Assessment and payment of CGT

Capital gains tax is assessed on the aggregate net gain of the current tax year and so it is necessary to consider all the disposals made during the tax year. Generally, tax for individuals is payable on or before 31 January following the end of the tax year (or 30 days from the making of an assessment if later). However, a taxpayer disposing of a property not exempted by principal private residence relief (see **3.4.2**) must submit a return and pay an estimate of tax due within 60 days of completion of the sale.

The above example shows the principles used to establish an individual's liability for CGT. The remainder of this chapter will consider each step of the calculation in more detail.

3.2 DISPOSALS

3.2.1 The sale or gift of a chargeable asset

There must be a disposal of a chargeable asset. Disposal is widely defined and includes a sale or a gift. If a gift is made then HMRC taxes the gain the taxpayer is deemed to have made on the disposal. This is done by using the market value of the asset at the time of the gift instead of consideration received.

EXAMPLE

In September, Barbara makes a gift of a Ming vase worth £271,000. She had bought the vase for £180,000. It is her only disposal during the tax year. Barbara's taxable income for the tax year is £60,000.

Step 1:	Identify the disposal	
	Gift of vase	
Step 2:	Calculate the gain	
	Market value of vase	£271,000
	Less: Cost	(£180,000)
		£91,000
Step 3:	Consider exemptions and reliefs	Nil
Step 4:	Gain	£91,000
	Deduct annual exemption	(£3,000)
	Chargeable gain	£88,000
Step 5:	What is the rate of tax?	
	CGT at 24% on £88,000 is £21,120.	

3.2.2 The disposal of part of an asset

A sale of part of an asset or a gift of part of an asset is a disposal, for example the sale of part of a field. This is considered in detail in **3.8**.

3.2.3 The death of the taxpayer

On death there is no disposal by the deceased, so there is no charge to CGT. The personal representatives acquire the deceased's assets at the market value at the date of death (the probate value). This has the effect of wiping out gains which accrued during the deceased's lifetime so that these gains are not charged to tax.

> **EXAMPLE**
>
> Christopher dies owning shares worth £150,000. He had bought the shares for £60,000. Since death is not a disposal, there is no charge to CGT when Christopher dies. His personal representatives will acquire the shares at the market value at his death, ie at £150,000. The gain of £90,000 is wiped out and is not charged to tax. The £90,000 is the difference between the cost of the shares and the market value of the shares at the date of Christopher's death.

3.3 CALCULATION OF GAINS

The basic aim is to tax the gain in value that the asset has realised from the date of acquisition to the date of disposal. Consequently, the gain is generally the consideration for the disposal (or market value if the taxpayer gives away the asset) less any of the following expenditure incurred by the taxpayer:

Initial expenditure

(a) The cost price of the asset (or its market value at the date of acquisition if the asset was given to the taxpayer; or the probate value if the taxpayer acquired the asset by will or intestacy) plus incidental costs of acquisition. Examples of incidental costs of acquisition are legal fees, valuation fees, stamp duty.

(b) Expenditure wholly and exclusively incurred in providing the asset. An example is the cost of building a weekend cottage.

Subsequent expenditure

(a) Expenditure wholly and exclusively incurred to enhance the value of the asset, which is reflected in the value of the asset at the time of disposal. An example is the cost of building an extension to a house. The cost of routine maintenance, repairs and insurance, on the other hand, is not deductible.

(b) Expenditure wholly and exclusively incurred in establishing, preserving or defending title to the asset. An example is the cost of legal fees incurred to resolve a boundary dispute.

Incidental costs of disposal

Examples are legal fees and estate agent's fees.

Note that expenditure which is deductible for income tax purposes cannot be deducted when calculating a capital gain.

> **EXAMPLE**
>
> Paul sells his holiday cottage for £184,800. He bought the cottage for £50,000 and spent £700 on a survey and £1,300 on legal fees when he purchased it. He spent £7,600 improving the cottage. Legal fees when he sells the cottage are £800 and the estate agent's commission is £3,400. For the current tax year Paul has a taxable income of £27,700.

Step 1:	Identify the disposal			
	Sale of holiday cottage			
Step 2:	Calculate the gain			
	Proceeds of disposal			£184,800
Less:				
Incidental costs of disposal				
Legal fees			£800	
Estate agent's commission			£3,400	
				(£4,200)
Net proceeds of disposal				£180,600
Less:				
Initial expenditure				
Acquisition cost		£50,000		
Survey fee		£700		
Legal fees		£1,300		
			£52,000	
Subsequent expenditure				
Cost of improvements			£7,600	
				(£59,600)
GAIN				£121,000
Step 3:	Consider exemptions and reliefs			Nil
Step 4:	Gain			£121,000
	Deduct annual exemption			(£3,000)
	Chargeable gain			£118,000
Step 5:	What is the rate of tax?			
	CGT at 18% on the first £10,000			
	(ie amount of gain below the basic rate threshold) =			£1,800
	CGT at 24% on remaining £108,000			
	(ie amount of gain above the basic rate threshold) =			£25,290
	Total CGT			£27,720

Note: As the cottage is not Paul's main home, the gain is not exempted by principal private residence relief (see **3.4.2**).

3.3.1 The indexation allowance

For gains realised before 6 April 2008, an indexation allowance was used when calculating the gain on an asset which had been owned for any period between 31 March 1982 and 5 April 1998. The purpose of the indexation allowance is to remove inflationary gains from the CGT calculation so that a smaller gain is charged to tax. Inflation is measured by reference to the Retail Prices Index (the RPI). The indexation allowance is calculated by applying to the initial and subsequent expenditure the percentage increase in the RPI from the date the expenditure was incurred to the date of disposal (or April 1998 if earlier). Tables published by HMRC express this information as an indexation factor for ease of calculation.

The allowance still has some relevance to gains, the charge to which has been deferred before 6 April 2008 by the use of various roll-over or hold-over reliefs – see **3.4**. This is because, on a subsequent disposal after 6 April 2008, the rolled-over or held-over gain will be reduced by the appropriate amount of indexation allowance, provided the relevant assets were owned for some time between 31 March 1982 and 5 April 1998.

The same point applies to inter-spouse disposals made before 6 April 2008 – see **3.9**.

3.3.2 Assets owned on 31 March 1982

Where a taxpayer disposes of an asset which they owned on 31 March 1982, special rules are applied. The aim of these rules is to exclude from the tax calculation the part of the gain that accrued before 31 March 1982, so that no CGT is paid on that part of the gain.

As a result, the gain on such assets is calculated by using the market value of the assets on 31 March 1982, rather than actual expenditure.

3.3.3 Losses

The formula 'consideration received (or market value) less cost' can produce a capital loss.

EXAMPLE

Christine bought shares for £10,000 three years ago. She sells them for £10,300 but her incidental costs of acquisition were £250 and her incidental costs of disposal were £200.

Step 1:	Identify the disposal		
	Sale of shares		
Step 2:	Calculate the gain/loss		
	Proceeds of disposal		£10,300
Less:			
Incidental costs of disposal			
	Broker's commission		(£200)
Net proceeds of disposal			£10,100
Less:			
Initial expenditure			
	Acquisition cost	£10,000	
	Broker's commission	£200	
	Stamp duty	£50	
			(£10,250)
LOSS			£150

The treatment of losses will be considered at **3.6** and **3.7**.

3.4 RELIEFS

After calculating the gain, the next step is to consider whether any reliefs apply. Generally, reliefs may be available due to the nature of the asset being disposed of. The majority of reliefs are aimed at smaller businesses, to encourage investment in this sector of the economy.

The following is a non-exhaustive list of CGT reliefs.

3.4.1 Tangible moveable property

Wasting assets (ie assets with a predictable life of less than 50 years) are generally exempt. Most consumer goods will fall into this category, for example televisions and washing machines.

Not all items of tangible moveable property are wasting assets. Some will go up in value, for example antiques. However, they will be exempt from CGT if the disposal consideration is £6,000 or less.

3.4.2 Private dwelling house

Principal private residence relief operates to make a gain on the disposal by an individual of a dwelling house, including grounds of up to half a hectare, completely exempt, provided it has been occupied as their only or main residence through their period of ownership (ignoring the last 9 months of ownership).

For most people, their home is their most valuable asset. The effect of this relief is that the house can be sold (or given away) without CGT liability being incurred.

3.4.3 Damages for personal injury

The recovery of damages or compensation may amount to the disposal of a chargeable asset; however, the receipt of damages for personal injury is exempt.

3.4.4 Hold-over relief

Hold-over relief enables an individual to make a gift of certain types of business assets without paying CGT. However, if the donee disposes of the asset, the donee will be charged to tax not only on their own gain but on the donor's gain as well. Because hold-over relief defers the charge to tax until a disposal by the donee, there must be an election by donor and donee to claim hold-over relief.

3.4.5 Relief for replacement of business assets ('roll-over' relief)

This relief encourages expansion and investment in qualifying business assets by enabling the sale of those assets to take place without an immediate charge to CGT, provided the proceeds of sale are invested in other qualifying business assets. The charge to CGT is postponed until the disposal of the new asset.

3.4.6 Roll-over relief on incorporation of a business

This relief again defers a CGT charge. It is applied (subject to conditions) when an individual sells their interest in an unincorporated business (sole trader, partnership) to a company. The gain is rolled over into the shares received as consideration for the interest being sold to the company. The CGT charge is postponed until the disposal of the shares.

3.4.7 Relief for re-investment in certain unquoted shares

To encourage investment in small company shares, it is possible for an individual to defer payment of CGT on any chargeable gain provided the proceeds of sale are re-invested in certain shares in an unquoted trading company. This is dealt with in **5.4**.

3.4.8 Business asset disposal relief

This relief (in the form of a reduced rate of tax) is available on gains made by individuals on the disposal (ie on a sale or a gift) of certain assets, including:

(a) all or part of a trading business the individual carries on as a sole trader or in partnership;

(b) shares in a trading company, subject to certain conditions, including (but not limited to) that the individual's holding is at least 5% of the ordinary voting shares of the company (ie, it is their 'personal' trading company);

(c) assets owned and used by the individual's personal trading company or trading partnership.

The detailed workings of the business reliefs are set out in ***Business Law and Practice***.

3.5 THE ANNUAL EXEMPTION

The annual exemption is applied to make exempt the first slice of the taxpayer's net capital gains for the tax year. Unlike the reliefs referred to in **3.4**, it is not applied to any particular disposal but is rather a general deduction from the total net gain. However, where someone makes gains on several disposals in a tax year and those gains are liable to CGT at different rates, the taxpayer is permitted to apply the exemption first to the gains that would otherwise attract the higher rates (see **3.6**).

As explained in **3.1.4.4**, the amount of the exemption for tax year 2025/26 is £3,000. If a taxpayer's net gain is smaller than the annual exemption the unused part of the exemption cannot be carried forward to the following tax year.

Personal representatives and trustees of settlements are also entitled to an annual exemption; see **Part V: Probate and Administration**.

3.6 CGT CALCULATION WHERE THERE IS MORE THAN ONE DISPOSAL IN A TAX YEAR

As explained in **3.1.4.5**, different rates of tax apply to disposals, not only depending on the taxpayer's income tax position but also due to the type of assets disposed of. In this respect, chargeable assets essentially fall into two categories – those assets which qualify for business asset disposal relief and those which do not. Because of the different rates that apply, gains made on assets within each category must be aggregated in separate compartments.

Where the taxpayer realises gains in both categories, any losses and the annual exemption can be deducted from gains in the best way possible for the taxpayer (ie to the gains that would otherwise attract the higher rates), so from non-business asset disposal relief gains first and then business asset disposal relief gains.

EXAMPLE 1

Gordon made the following disposals during 2025/26. Gordon has a taxable income in the tax year of £40,000.

On 17 July 2025, he sold his shareholding in Pibroch Ltd for £11,600. He bought it for £4,000 on 16 April 1999. This shareholding satisfies the requirements to be Gordon's personal trading company for the purposes of business asset disposal relief.

On 12 August 2025, he sold his holiday cottage, 'Landseer Lodge', for £190,000. He acquired it on his mother's death on 11 January 2002, when its market value was £30,000.

On 8 January 2026, he sold his units in TVT Unit Trust for £5,000. He had purchased them on 16 May 2003 for £9,000.

Note: For the sake of simplicity, the example ignores incidental costs of acquisition and disposal on all of the transactions, and it is assumed that the only relief available is business asset disposal relief on the shares (as Landseer Lodge is not Gordon's home, it does not qualify for principal private residence relief).

	Pibroch Ltd	Landseer Lodge	TVT
Step 1: Identify the disposal	Sale of shares	Sale of holiday cottage	Sale of unit trust units
Step 2: Calculate the gain. Proceeds of disposal	£11,600	£190,000	£5,000
Less: Acquisition expenditure	(£4,000)	(£30,000)	(£9,000)
Gain/(Loss)	£7,600	£160,000	(£4,000)
Step 3: Consider exemptions and reliefs	None	None	None
Step 4: Aggregate net gains/ losses	Business asset disposal relief gain	Non-business asset disposal relief gain	
	7,600	160,000	
Deduct current year loss		(4,000)	
		156,000	
Deduct annual exemption		(3,000)	
Chargeable gains	7,600	153,000	
Step 5: What are the rates of tax?			
CGT at 14% on £7,600 gain on Pibroch shares is		£1,064	
CGT at 24% on £153,000 gain on Landseer Lodge is		£36,720	
Total CGT		£37,784	

3.7 UNABSORBED LOSSES

It is, of course, possible that a taxpayer's CGT losses in a tax year may exceed their overall CGT gains. If so, setting the losses against the gains will wipe them out completely and the taxpayer will have no CGT to pay. In such a situation, the setting-off of current year losses to wipe out the gains entirely means that the taxpayer loses the use of their annual exemption. The exemption cannot be carried forward to use against gains of future tax years.

If, after setting losses against gains, there are still unabsorbed losses, these may be carried forward to future years and then used to the extent necessary to reduce gains to the limit of the annual exemptions available in those future years. Unabsorbed losses can be carried forward indefinitely. The approach should be:

(a) work out the gain or loss on each disposal made during the tax year;

(b) deduct any losses of the current year from gains;

(c) deduct any losses brought forward from previous years to reduce any remaining gains to the limit of the annual exemption;

(d) deduct the annual exemption from any remaining gains.

Note: As previously stated, the losses and annual exemption should be applied in the most advantageous way for the taxpayer.

EXAMPLE 2 (CONTINUED FROM 3.6)

Year of loss

In 2024/25, the year before the **3.6** scenario, Gordon made gains of £30,000, and losses of £70,000. He had no unused losses from previous years.

Gains for the year	£30,000
Less: losses for the year	£70,000
Net loss for the year	£40,000

The £30,000 gain is wiped out, and the unused loss of £40,000 is carried forward to the next year.

As there is no net gain for 2024/25, the annual exemption cannot be used in this year and it cannot be carried forward to later years.

Year following year of loss

In 2025/26, Gordon's loss of £40,000 carried forward from 2024/25 would be set against the gain on Landseer Lodge (as this is taxed at the higher rate of 24%) after the deduction of the current year loss of £4,000. The annual exemption would also be applied against the remaining gain on Landseer Lodge for the same reason.

Step 4: Aggregate net gains/losses	Business asset disposal relief gain	Non-business asset disposal relief gain	
	7,600	160,000	
Less current year loss		(4,000)	
Less previous year loss		(40,000)	
		116,000	
Deduct annual exemption		(3,000)	
Chargeable gains	7,600	113,000	

Step 5: What are the rates of tax?

CGT at 14% on £7,600 gain on Pibroch shares is	£1,064
CGT at 24% on £113,000 gain on Landseer Lodge is	£27,120
Total CGT	£28,184

FURTHER EXAMPLE

If Gordon's unabsorbed loss in 2024/25 had been greater, eg £180,000, it would be carried forward and used in 2025/26 as follows:

As the available losses are greater than the aggregate gains for 2025/26, these will be wiped out altogether and so there is no need to consider the order in which the taxpayer might like to apply the losses. In this situation the losses would simply be deducted from the total gains of £167,600. First, the deduction of the current year loss of £4,000 would mean that the aggregate net gains for the current tax year are £163,600. The brought-forward loss of £180,000 would then be set against this figure until the gains are reduced to the limit of the annual exemption of £3,000. The balance of the loss (£19,400) remains unused and can be carried forward to set against gains of future years.

	Loss carried forward	*2025/26 gains*
	£	£
2024/25 loss	180,000	
2025/26 aggregate net gains/losses		7,600
		160,000
		(4,000)
Use part loss	(160,600)	(160,600)
		3,000
Deduct annual exemption		(3,000)
2025/26 taxable gains		nil
Balance of loss to be carried forward	19,400	

3.8 PART DISPOSALS

Where the disposal is of only part of the asset the initial and subsequent expenditure are apportioned when calculating the gain.

EXAMPLE

Anna bought a large plot of commercial property for £100,000 in 2002. She sells part of it for £90,000 in October 2025. The remaining property is worth £360,000. This is her only disposal in the tax year.

Anna's taxable income for the year is £32,700.

Identify the disposal: sale of part of commercial property.

Calculation of the gain on the land sold:

The consideration received is £90,000.

What is the cost of the part sold?

The total value of the two pieces of land is £450,000, ie £90,000 plus £360,000.

The part sold is worth $\frac{1}{5}$ of the total value, ie £90,000 is $\frac{1}{5}$ of £450,000.

Therefore, take $\frac{1}{5}$ of the cost as the relevant figure for the calculation, ie $\frac{1}{5}$ of £100,000, that is £20,000.

	£
Proceeds of disposal	90,000
Less:	
Apportioned cost	(20,000)
Gain	70,000
Deduct annual exemption	(3,000)
Chargeable gain	67,000
What is the rate of tax?	
CGT at 18% on the first £5,000	
(ie amount of gain below the basic rate threshold) =	£900
CGT at 24% on remaining £62,000	
(ie amount of gain above the basic rate threshold) =	£14,880
Total CGT	£15,780

3.9 HUSBAND AND WIFE

3.9.1 Disposals between spouses

Where spouses or civil partners are living together, a disposal by one to the other is treated as being made for such a consideration as to provide neither a gain nor a loss. This means that a spouse (or civil partner) can dispose of property to the other without paying CGT on the disposal. The donor's gain is not wiped out but merely deferred. If the donee disposes of the asset, the donee will be charged to tax not only on the donee's gain but on the donor's gain as well.

EXAMPLE

David gives a portrait to his wife Jane. David will not pay CGT on this disposal.

The portrait was worth £100,000 at the time of the gift. It cost David £80,000 three years ago.

Usually, when a gift is made the acquisition cost of the donee is the market value at the time of the gift (£100,000) but because the portrait was a gift from her husband, Jane will acquire it with a value of £80,000, ie the amount David paid for the painting.

If Jane disposes of the asset, she will have a lower acquisition cost to set against her gain and she will be charged to tax on both her own gain and her husband's gain.

Assume Jane sells the painting for £150,000, five years later.

The calculation will be:

Consideration received	£150,000
Less: Cost	£80,000
	£70,000

If Jane had not acquired the painting from her husband, so that the ordinary rules applied, the calculation would have been:

Consideration received	£150,000
Less: Cost	£100,000
	£50,000

A comparison of the above calculations shows that a larger gain is produced on Jane's disposal where she acquired the portrait from her husband; but, of course, David avoided any CGT charge at the time of the gift to Jane.

3.9.2 Tax planning point: making full use of annual exemptions and lower rate of tax

The fact that both spouses are entitled to a separate annual exemption in each tax year can lead to tax-planning opportunities. By way of example, assume that the wife wishes to dispose of a number of assets in the tax year and that these disposals would realise gains that use up all of her annual exemption and leave some of the gains chargeable. On the other hand, the husband would not be making any disposals and so would not use his annual exemption at all. In this situation, it may be beneficial for the wife to transfer some of the assets to the husband (remember that this is a disposal that would not create a gain or a loss – see **3.9.1**), so that they both make gains and both can use their own annual exemption to make exempt gains up to £6,000, rather than £3,000.

Also, if the asset-holding spouse would be taxed on gains at the higher rate of 24% but the other would be taxed at the basic rate of 18%, it would again be sensible to make an inter-spouse transfer so that the disposal is made by the spouse who is subject to the basic rate.

CHAPTER 4

INHERITANCE TAX

LEARNING OUTCOMES

After reading this chapter you will be able to:

- understand the overall structure of inheritance tax
- explain how a person's death estate is taxed
- explain how certain lifetime transfers are taxed
- appreciate the rules on liability, burden and timing of payments of inheritance tax.

4.1 INTRODUCTION

This chapter explains the basic principles of inheritance tax (IHT). Some form of death duty has existed in the UK since the 19th century and has varied in name and approach over that period, beginning with estate duty then capital transfer tax and now IHT. Inheritance tax is governed principally by the Inheritance Tax Act 1984 (IHTA 1984). Despite its name, the tax does not apply only to death estates but can also catch transfers made during life.

There are three main occasions when IHT may be charged:

(a) on death;

(b) on lifetime gifts made to individuals within seven years prior to death;

(c) on lifetime gifts to a company or into a trust.

4.1.1 Death

Inheritance tax is intended primarily to take effect on death. When an individual dies, IHT is charged on the value of their estate (broadly, their assets less their liabilities) subject to various exemptions and reliefs.

4.1.2 Lifetime gifts made to individuals within seven years prior to death

If IHT were limited to a charge on death, one way to avoid tax would be to reduce the size of one's estate by making lifetime gifts; IHT is therefore also charged on certain lifetime gifts or 'transfers' if the donor dies within seven years after making them. Such gifts to individuals are called 'potentially exempt transfers', because at the time when the transfer is made no IHT is chargeable; the transfer is 'potentially exempt'. If the transferor survives for seven years, the transfer becomes exempt. If the transferor dies within that period, the transfer becomes chargeable.

4.1.3 Lifetime gifts to a company or into a trust

Inheritance tax might also be avoided by the use of a trust or corporate entity. At present a lifetime gift to a company or into a trust is immediately chargeable to IHT at the time when it is made, unless the trust is for a disabled person.

4.1.4 Anti-avoidance legislation

As with income tax and capital gains tax, IHT is one of the taxes subject to the 'general anti-abuse rule' (GAAR) introduced by the Finance Act 2013, which is designed to allow HMRC to counteract 'abusive' tax avoidance schemes intended to exploit loopholes in the legislation covering the rules for calculating IHT.

4.2 THE MAIN CHARGING PROVISIONS

Inheritance tax is charged on 'the value transferred by a chargeable transfer'. The term 'chargeable transfer' is defined as 'a transfer of value which is made by an individual but is not an exempt transfer' (IHTA 1984, ss 1, 2).

This charge may apply in any of the three situations outlined above, because the term 'chargeable transfer' may refer to:

(a) the transfer on death; or
(b) a lifetime transfer which is potentially exempt when it is made but becomes chargeable because the transferor dies within seven years; or
(c) a lifetime transfer which is immediately chargeable at the time when it is made.

In each case, the method by which tax is calculated is broadly similar, and may be approached by applying a sequence of logical steps.

4.2.1 Step 1: Identify the transfer of value

A lifetime transfer of value is any disposition which reduces the value of the transferor's estate. On death, tax is charged as if the deceased had made a transfer of value of their estate.

4.2.2 Step 2: Find the value transferred

For a lifetime transfer, this is the amount of the reduction in the transferor's estate.

On death, it is the value of the estate.

4.2.3 Step 3: Apply any relevant exemptions and reliefs

Various exemptions and reliefs exist for public policy reasons which can reduce or eliminate the IHT charge on any given transfer.

Some exemptions apply both to lifetime transfers and to the transfer on death (eg transfers to spouse or civil partner). Others are more restricted, and many apply only to lifetime transfers (eg annual exemption).

The main reliefs are business and agricultural property relief, which may apply both to lifetime transfers of such property and to the transfer on death.

4.2.4 Step 4: Calculate tax at the appropriate rate

Rates of tax

A range of tax rates apply to IHT, the lowest being zero per cent. There are two bands for which this is relevant:

(a) the nil rate band (currently £325,000) – available for all transfers of value;
(b) the residence nil rate band (currently £175,000) – available only on a transfer on death where there is a 'qualifying residential interest'.

The rate of tax that applies in excess of the nil rate band and the residence nil rate band (where applicable) varies according to the type of transfer (details are given in context below).

Cumulation

The nil rate band will not necessarily be available in full (or at all) for any given transfer. In order to calculate the available nil rate band on any transfer, whether during lifetime or on death, one must first look back over the seven years immediately preceding the transfer. Any chargeable transfers made by the transferor during that period must be taken into account in order to determine how much of the nil rate band remains available. This process is known as 'cumulation' and is used solely to calculate whether the nil rate band is available for any chargeable transfer.

As the residence nil rate band is not available for lifetime transfers, it will be available in full on death, subject to any adjustments in relation to estates over £2 million (see **4.3.6**). Cumulation is not relevant.

This chapter will consider the detailed application of the steps outlined above to each of the three types of transfer in turn. Note that, for ease of reference in the examples provided, any mention of the nil rate band assumes that the band has always been £325,000. In fact, it has increased over the years to its current level. In real calculations one may have to identify the previous bands.

4.3 TRANSFERS ON DEATH

The steps outlined at **4.2** above apply as follows.

4.3.1 Step 1: Identify the transfer of value

When a person dies, they are treated for IHT purposes as having made a transfer of value immediately before their death, ie there is a deemed transfer of value. The value transferred is the value of the deceased's 'estate' immediately before their death.

4.3.1.1 Definition of 'estate'

A person's estate is defined by IHTA 1984, s 5(1) to mean all the property to which they were beneficially entitled immediately before their death, with the exception of 'excluded property'.

Property included within this definition falls into three categories, as set out below.

(a) *Property which passes under the deceased's will or on intestacy.*

The deceased was 'beneficially entitled' to all such property immediately before they died.

(b) *Property to which the deceased was 'beneficially entitled' immediately before their death but which does not pass under their will or on intestacy.*

This applies to the deceased's interest in any joint property passing on their death by survivorship to the surviving joint tenant(s). In most cases, the deceased will be taken to have owned an equal share in the property with the other joint tenant(s).

(c) *Property included because of special statutory provisions.*

By statute, the deceased is treated as having been 'beneficially entitled' to certain types of property which would otherwise fall outside the definition. These rules apply to

(i) certain trust property; and

(ii) property given away by the deceased in their lifetime but which is 'subject to a reservation' at the time of death.

Each of these categories is explained further below.

4.3.1.2 Trust property included in the estate for IHT purposes

In certain circumstances, a person who is entitled to the income from a trust is treated for IHT purposes as 'beneficially entitled' to the capital which produces that income. This means that where a beneficiary who is entitled to all the income from such a trust dies, the trust fund is taxed as if it were part of the beneficiary's estate.

The type of beneficial interest covered by these provisions is known as a 'qualifying interest in possession'. To be an interest in possession, it must be an interest under which the beneficiary is entitled to claim the income from the trust property (or enjoy trust property in some equivalent way, such as living in it) with no power on the part of the trustees to decide whether or not the beneficiary should receive it. An interest in possession arising before 22 March 2006 will be a qualifying interest in possession. The rules changed on that date and where an interest in possession arises on or after 22 March 2006, it will only be a qualifying interest in possession in limited circumstances. The main example is where the interest is an 'immediate post-death interest' (IPDI). An IPDI is, broadly, an interest in possession arising on the death of the settlor under their will or intestacy.

EXAMPLE 1

Gina died in January 2018. In her will, she left all her estate to her executors/trustees, Tom and Tessa, on trust to pay the income to Gina's son, Simon, for life with remainder to Rose absolutely. Both Simon and Rose are over 18 years old.

Tom and Tessa must invest the property to produce income. Simon is entitled to the income during his life. Tom and Tessa must pay it to him. Thus Simon, the life tenant, has an interest in possession.

When Simon dies, his rights under the trust cease. Under the terms of the trust instrument (Gina's will), Rose is now entitled to the trust fund, and Tom and Tessa must transfer all the trust property to her.

For IHT purposes, Simon had a qualifying interest in possession by virtue of it being an IPDI. Although he was entitled only to the income from the trust property and had no control over the disposition of the fund on his death, he is treated for tax purposes as 'beneficially entitled' to the whole trust fund. The fund is taxed on his death as part of his estate. The tax on the trust property will be paid from the trust fund.

EXAMPLE 2

The facts are as in Example 1, except that Gina did not die in January 2018. Instead, she created the trust on that date by transferring the funds to Tessa and Tom and signing a declaration that they were to hold on trust for Simon for life with remainder to Rose. While the beneficiaries' rights under the trust will be exactly the same as in Example 1, the trust will not be an IPDI. Instead it will be taxed under the 'relevant property' regime. Details of this regime are outside the scope of this chapter.

4.3.1.3 Property subject to a reservation

The Finance Act 1986 contains provisions designed to prevent people from avoiding tax by giving property away more than seven years before death but continuing to enjoy the benefit of the property. The rule applies where the deceased gave away property during their lifetime but did not transfer 'possession and enjoyment' of the property to the donee, or was not entirely excluded from enjoying the property. If property is subject to a reservation at the time of the donor's death, the donor is treated as being 'beneficially entitled' to the property.

> **EXAMPLE**
>
> In 2018, Diana gave her jewellery, worth £100,000, to her daughter Emma, but retained possession of it. Diana dies in 2025, when the jewellery (still in her possession) is worth £120,000. Although the jewellery belongs to Emma, tax is charged on Diana's death as if she were still beneficially entitled to it. The jewellery, valued at £120,000, is taxed as part of Diana's estate. The tax on the jewellery will be borne by Emma.

4.3.1.4 Property outside the estate for IHT purposes

From the above, it can be seen that the definition of 'estate' turns on whether the deceased was (or was deemed to be) beneficially interested in property immediately before their death. Property in which the deceased did not have such an interest falls outside the definition. Two common examples of property outside the definition are a life assurance policy once it is written in trust for a named beneficiary (because the proceeds are no longer payable to the deceased's estate) and a discretionary lump sum payment made from a pension fund to the deceased's family (because the pension trustees are not obliged to pay it to the deceased's estate).

4.3.1.5 Excluded property

Certain property which would otherwise be included in the estate for IHT purposes is defined in IHTA 1984 as 'excluded property'. Excluded property is not part of the estate for IHT purposes. One example of excluded property is a 'reversionary interest'. For IHT purposes this means a future interest under a settlement, for example an interest in remainder under a trust, created before 22 March 2006.

> **EXAMPLE**
>
> In 2005, Faith created a settlement placing £500,000 on trust for Guy for life, remainder to Hazel absolutely. Whilst both Guy and Hazel are alive, Guy has a qualifying interest in possession and Hazel has a reversionary interest (that is excluded property).

4.3.2 Step 2: Find the value transferred

4.3.2.1 Basic valuation principle

Assets in the estate are valued for IHT purposes at 'the price which the property might reasonably be expected to fetch if sold in the open market' immediately before the death (IHTA 1984, s 160).

This means that the value immediately before death of every asset forming part of the estate for IHT purposes must be assessed and reported to HMRC. Some assets, such as bank and building society accounts and quoted shares, are easy to value. Others, such as land, may be more difficult, especially where it was jointly owned (in some cases it may be possible to reduce the value of the share of the deceased to reflect the difficulty in selling a share in a jointly-owned property). Negotiations may be required (in the case of land, with the district valuer) in order to reach an agreed valuation.

The value of an asset agreed for IHT purposes is known as the 'probate value'.

4.3.2.2 Modification of the basic valuation principle: s 171

The IHTA 1984, s 171 provides that, where the death causes the value of an asset in the estate to increase or decrease, that change in value should be taken into account.

> **EXAMPLE**
>
> Brian has insured his life for £50,000. The benefit of the policy belongs to him (ie the policy is not written in trust). Immediately before Brian's death, the value of the policy to him is its 'surrender value' (ie the value if he surrendered his rights back to the insurance company in return for a payment). This will be considerably less than its maturity value of £50,000. Under s 171, the effect of Brian's death on the value of the policy is taken into account: its value for IHT purposes is £50,000.

4.3.2.3 Valuing quoted shares

The value of quoted shares is taken from the Stock Exchange Daily Official List for the date of death (or the nearest trading day). The list quotes two prices. To value the shares for IHT, take one-quarter of the difference between the lower and higher price and add it to the lower price.

> **EXAMPLE**
>
> John died owning 200 shares in ABC plc. On the date of John's death the quoted price per share is 102p/106p. The value of each share for IHT is 103p, and so the value of John's holding is £206.

4.3.2.4 Debts and expenses

Liabilities owed by the deceased at the time of death are deductible for IHT purposes provided that they were incurred for money or money's worth (IHTA 1984, s 5(3) and 5(5)). Thus debts such as gas and telephone bills may be deducted. In addition, the deceased may not have paid enough income tax on the income they received before they died; this amount may also be deducted.

Reasonable funeral expenses are also deductible (IHTA 1984, s 162).

4.3.3 Step 3: Apply any relevant exemptions and reliefs

The main exemptions applicable on death depend on the identity of the beneficiary. Reliefs depend on the nature of the property in the estate. Thus it is important to see who is entitled to the property on death and whether the property qualifies for a relief.

4.3.3.1 Spouse or civil partner exemption

Section 18 of the IHTA 1984 provides as follows:

> A transfer of value is an exempt transfer to the extent that the value transferred is attributable to property which becomes comprised in the estate of the transferor's spouse or civil partner.

Any property included in the estate for IHT purposes is exempt if it passes to the deceased's spouse or civil partner under the deceased's will or intestacy or, in the case of joint property, by survivorship. (But note that under s 18(2), if the transferor is a long-term UK resident but the transferee is not, the level of the exemption is limited to £325,000. Alternatively, the transferee can elect to be treated as a long-term UK resident for IHT purposes and so receive the full exemption.)

The rule applicable to qualifying interest in possession trusts is that IHT is charged as if the person with the right to income owned the capital (see **4.3.1.2**). This rule applies for the purpose of spouse exemption, both on creation of the trust (whether by will or on intestacy) and on the death of a life tenant.

> **EXAMPLE**
>
> In his will, Dan leaves his estate worth £300,000 to trustees on trust for his wife, Jane, for life with remainder to their children. Although Jane only has the right to the income from Dan's estate for her lifetime, the trust is treated for IHT purposes as if Jane owned the capital. On Dan's death, his whole estate will, therefore, be spouse exempt.

Note that this exemption does not apply to cohabitees.

4.3.3.2 Charity exemption

The IHTA 1984, s 23(1) provides as follows:

> Transfers of value are exempt to the extent that the values transferred by them are attributable to property which is given to charities.

Any property forming part of the deceased's estate for IHT purposes which passes on death to charity is exempt. The exemption most commonly applies to property which passes to charity under the deceased's will. However, if the deceased had a life interest in trust property which passes under the terms of the trust to charity, the charity exemption applies.

A similar exemption applies to gifts to certain bodies such as museums and art galleries, and to political parties.

When large charity gifts are made by the deceased, not only is the transfer itself exempt, but it may affect the tax rate on the rest of the death estate (see **4.3.4**).

4.3.3.3 Business and agricultural property relief

Business property relief applies to reduce the value transferred by a transfer of 'relevant business property' by a certain percentage, provided that the transferor owned the property for the two years immediately before the transfer.

The reduction is 100% for:

(a) a business, or an interest in a business (such as a share in a partnership); and

(b) unquoted shares.

The reduction is 50% for:

(a) quoted shares which gave the transferor control of the company; and

(b) certain land, buildings and machinery owned by the transferor but used in their company or partnership.

Agricultural property relief applies in a similar manner to reduce the agricultural value of agricultural property.

Further details of these reliefs are given in ***Business Law and Practice***.

4.3.4 Step 4: Calculate tax at the appropriate rate

4.3.4.1 Nil rate band

Generally, the position is that, if the deceased has made no chargeable transfers in the seven years before death, the rate of tax on the first £325,000 of their estate (the 'nil rate band') is 0%. If their estate exceeds the nil rate band, IHT is normally charged on the excess at 40%. In a small number of cases, provisions introduced in the Finance Act 2012 may apply. These provisions are aimed at increasing charitable giving and will apply a 36% tax rate in place of the normal 40% rate when at least 10% of a defined 'component' of a person's net estate (after deduction of other exemptions, reliefs and the available nil rate band) passes to charity. The provisions will rarely apply as most people will not want to give anything close to 10% of their net estate to charity, whereas those that do want a charity as their main beneficiary (often because they have no close family) tend to leave the vast majority of their estate to that charity with any other gifts falling within the nil rate band. For further details, see **Private Client: Wills, Trusts and Estate Planning**.

If the deceased died on or after 9 October 2007 having survived a spouse or civil partner, the nil rate band in force at the date of death of the survivor is increased by whatever percentage of the nil rate band of the first to die was unused by them (subject to a maximum increase of 100%).

> **EXAMPLE**
>
> Emily, a widow, dies on 21 August 2025. Her husband Guy died 10 years earlier leaving all his estate to Emily. There was no tax to pay on Guy's death as his whole estate was spouse exempt, and his nil rate band was not used. Emily's estate benefits from a 100% uplift in her nil rate band, so that the rate of tax on the first £650,000 of her estate is 0%.

Cumulation

If the deceased did make any chargeable transfers in the seven years before death the cumulation principle outlined at **4.2.4** will apply. The effect is that the lifetime transfers use up the deceased's nil rate band first, reducing the amount available for the estate. Most lifetime gifts are potentially exempt from IHT and become chargeable only if the transferor dies within seven years. Less commonly, the deceased may also have made gifts in the seven years before death which were immediately chargeable to IHT at the time they were made, eg a gift into a trust. The cumulation principle applies to both types of transfer.

The 'values transferred' by such transfers must be aggregated. This means that any lifetime exemptions or reliefs which operate to reduce the value transferred are taken into account.

> **EXAMPLE 1**
>
> In 2021, David made a gift to his daughter. The value transferred (after exemptions and reliefs) was £175,000.
>
> In August 2025, David dies, leaving his estate, valued at £200,000, to his son. The estate did not include a qualifying residential interest.
>
> (It may help you, when calculating cumulative totals, to draw a timeline showing the relevant transfers. An example is given below.)

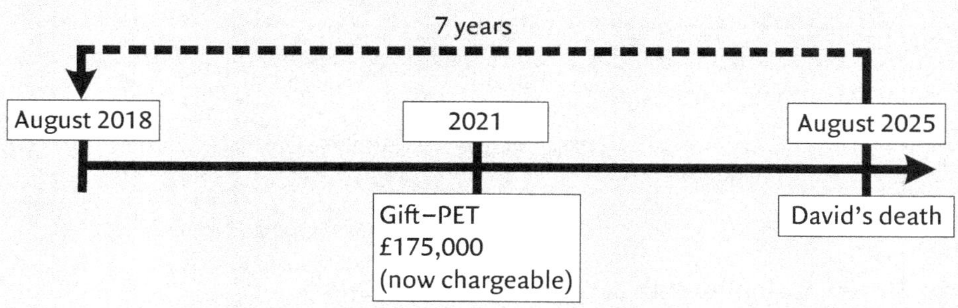

> The 2021 transfer was potentially exempt from IHT but has now become chargeable. David's cumulative total is £175,000.

The nil rate band applicable to David's estate on death is	£325,000
less cumulative total	£175,000
= remaining nil rate band	£150,000
Tax on David's estate:	
£150,000 @ 0% =	nil
£50,000 @ 40% =	£20,000

For further details of the effect of the cumulation principle, see **4.6**.

4.3.4.2 Example of the application of IHT to an estate on death

Facts

Veronica dies intestate on 3 August 2025 survived by her partner William (they were not married or in a civil partnership) and their children Brian (19) and Carla (22). She holds the following property:

	£
Bank accounts (in joint names with William): value of shares:	
(1) savings account	90,000
(2) current account	5,000
Life assurance policies:	
(1) payable to estate: maturity value	195,000
(2) written in trust for William: maturity value	30,000
Unquoted shares: 15% holding in a trading company (held for 10 years)	15,000
Building society account	19,000
Car and chattels	15,000

There are various debts, including funeral expenses, which total £4,000.
Two years before her death, Veronica made a gift of £211,000 in cash to William.
She made no other substantial lifetime gifts.

Step 1: identify the estate

Property to which Veronica was beneficially entitled immediately before death:

Passing on intestacy (to children):	life assurance policy (1) unquoted shares building society account car and chattels
Passing by survivorship (to William):	interest in bank accounts

(Life assurance policy (2) is not included in the estate for IHT purposes because Veronica was not beneficially entitled to it immediately before her death.)

Step 2: value the estate

	£	£
Passing on intestacy:		
life assurance policy (1) (full maturity value)	195,000	
unquoted shares (market value)	15,000	
building society account	19,000	
car and chattels	15,000	
		244,000
Joint property:		
interest in the bank accounts		95,000
		339,000
Less debts (including funeral expenses)		4,000
Value of estate (before reliefs)		335,000

Step 3: apply exemptions and reliefs

No exemptions apply to Veronica's estate as she had no spouse and left no property to charity.

The unquoted shares qualify for business property relief at 100%:

100% of £15,000	15,000
Value of estate for IHT	320,000

Step 4: calculate tax at the appropriate rate

Cumulate the value transferred by chargeable transfers made in the seven years before death. The gift to William was a potentially exempt transfer which has now become chargeable.

	£
Value of gift	211,000
Less two annual exemptions (see **4.4.3**)	6,000
Value transferred	205,000

Only £120,000 of Veronica's nil rate band remains available on her death.

Calculate tax on the estate of £320,000:

on £120,000 @ 0%	nil
on £200,000 @ 40%	£80,000

4.3.4.3 Residence nil rate band

The nil rate band is set to remain at £325,000 until April 2028. For deaths occurring after 6 April 2017, the residence nil rate band (RNRB) has been available in addition to the nil rate band. The RNRB has increased in the years following its introduction and is now at £175,000. It is set to remain at that level until 2028.

For the RNRB to apply, the deceased must die owning a 'qualifying residential interest' which is 'closely inherited':

(a) A qualifying residential interest is an interest in a dwelling house which has at any time been the deceased's residence and which forms part of the deceased's estate.

(b) For a property to be 'closely inherited', it must pass to:

   (i) a child, grandchild or other lineal descendant of the deceased outright or on certain types of trust. Lineal descendants are defined as children, step-children, adopted children, foster children, or children where the deceased had been appointed as a guardian;

   (ii) the current spouse or civil partner of the deceased's lineal descendants; or

   (iii) the widow, widower or surviving civil partner of a lineal descendant who predeceased the deceased, unless such persons have remarried or formed a new civil partnership before the deceased's death.

The RNRB will apply only up to the value of the deceased's residence. You cannot claim for more than the property is worth. When calculating the tax, the RNRB is taxed first at 0%, reducing the amount of the total chargeable estate, then, subject to cumulation, the nil rate band is taxed next at 0% and finally the remaining death estate at 40%.

Where the estate is valued at £2 million or more, the RNRB is reduced by £1 for every £2 over the £2 million threshold. To calculate the adjusted RNRB for an estate over £2 million, the following formula may be used:

$$£175{,}000 - \frac{(\text{value of estate} - £2\text{ million})}{2} = \text{adjusted RNRB}$$

If the deceased has not used all of their RNRB, like the nil rate band, any unused RNRB may be claimed by a surviving spouse, even if the first spouse died before 6 April 2017.

EXAMPLE

Angela dies on 4 September 2025, leaving her entire estate to her two children in equal shares. The value of her estate, after payment of debts and funeral expenses, is £1,750,000 and includes a house worth £1,250,000. Her husband, Richard, died four years earlier, leaving all his estate (worth less than £2 million) to Angela.

On Richard's death, the whole estate was spouse exempt, and the RNRB was not available to Richard's executors. As Richard has not used any of his RNRB, the amount transferred to Angela is an additional 100% of the RNRB, but at the current rate.

Therefore, when Angela dies, her executors can claim her own personal RNRB of £175,000 and Richard's unused RNRB of £175,000 (£350,000). This is the amount of RNRB current at the time of the death of the second spouse. This is in addition to the £650,000 nil rate band (2 x £325,000) from which Angela's estate will also benefit (see **4.3.4**).

The Finance Bill 2016 introduced a downsizing allowance to prevent (particularly older) people from hanging on to unsuitable properties in order to claim the full benefit of the allowance. If, after 8 July 2015, the deceased has downsized prior to death to a less valuable property, or sold their property in order, for example, to move to a care home, the personal representatives can still claim the RNRB to which the deceased would have been entitled, provided the property would have qualified for the RNRB had it been retained, and the replacement property or other assets of an equivalent value (where the property had been sold) is left to lineal descendants.

4.3.4.4 Example of the application of IHT to an estate on death which includes a closely inherited qualifying residential interest

Facts

If we take the facts from the example above, Angela, who died on 4 September 2025, left her entire estate to her two children in equal shares. Her husband, Richard, died four years earlier, leaving all his estate (worth less than £2 million) to Angela.

Angela's estate includes the following assets:

	£
House	1,250,000
Bank and Building Society Accounts	25,000
Quoted shares	455,000
Chattels, including a car	25,000

There are various debts, including funeral expenses, amounting to £5,000. Angela has not made any lifetime gifts.

Step 1: Identify the transfer of value

Property to which Angela was entitled immediately before death

Step 2: Identify the value transferred

House	1,250,000
Bank and Building Society Accounts	25,000
Quoted shares	455,000
Chattels, including a car	25,000
	1,755,000
Less debts (including funeral expenses)	(5,000)
Value of estate (before reliefs)	1,750,000

Step 3: Apply exemptions and reliefs

No exemptions or reliefs apply on the facts

Step 4: Calculate the tax at the appropriate rates

Cumulation is not relevant as Angela did not make any lifetime gifts.

Calculate tax on estate of £1,750,000, remembering that Angela benefits from both the nil rate band (NRB) and the RNRB transferred from Richard:

(1)	Tax Total RNRB @ 0%:	£350,000 @ 0% nil
(2)	Tax Total NRB @ 0%:	£650,000 @ 0% nil
		£1,000,000 (leaving £750,000)
(3)	Tax remaining £750,000 @ 40%	£300,000

Note that both the RNRB and the NRB operate to reduce the amount of the *total* chargeable estate.

4.4 LIFETIME TRANSFERS: POTENTIALLY EXEMPT TRANSFERS

The definition of a potentially exempt transfer (PET) includes any gift made by an individual to another individual or into a disabled trust (IHTA 1984, s 3A(1A)), to the extent in either case that the gift would otherwise be chargeable.

This means that all lifetime gifts to an individual are 'potentially exempt' to the extent that no immediate exemption applies.

4.4.1 Step 1: Identify the 'transfer of value'

The term 'transfer of value' is defined to mean any lifetime disposition made by a person ('the transferor') which reduces the value of their estate (IHTA 1984, s 3(1)). In principle, therefore, any lifetime gift falls within the definition.

Certain dispositions are excluded from the definition, such as a transfer for the maintenance, education or training of the transferor's child under 18, or over that age if still undergoing full-time education or training, or for the maintenance of a dependent relative (IHTA 1984, s 11). Such dispositions have no significance for IHT.

4.4.2 Step 2: Find the value transferred

The second step is to find the value transferred by the transfer of value. In the case of a lifetime transfer, this is the amount by which the value of the transferor's estate is 'less than it would be but for' the transfer (IHTA 1984, s 3(1)). In other words, the value transferred is the loss in value to the estate of the transferor brought about by the transfer. The transferor's 'estate' is the aggregate of all the property to which they are beneficially entitled (IHTA 1984, s 5).

In practice, the loss to the estate will usually be the market value of the property transferred, although this does not follow in every case.

EXAMPLE

Vanessa owns a pair of matching bronze statuettes. The market value of the pair together is £80,000, but individually each one is worth £25,000. If Vanessa were to give away one statuette to her son, the loss to her estate would be calculated as follows:

	£
Value of pair	80,000
Less value of remaining statuette	25,000
Loss to estate	55,000

Related property

The related property rules are designed to prevent tax avoidance in relation to a group or set of assets. The rules apply most often to property transferred between husband and wife.

> **EXAMPLE (CONTINUED)**
>
> Suppose Vanessa gives one of the statuettes to her husband Boris (an exempt transfer to spouse). Without the related property rules Vanessa and Boris would each then own one statuette worth £25,000.
>
> However, the two statuettes owned by Vanessa and Boris are related property. Under the related property valuation rule, the value of each statuette is the appropriate portion of the value of the pair, ie half of £80,000 which is £40,000. If Vanessa was then to give away her statuette, the value transferred would be £40,000.

4.4.3 Step 3: Apply any relevant exemptions and reliefs

As seen at **4.4**, a gift is potentially exempt only to the extent that it would otherwise be chargeable. At the time when a lifetime gift is made it may be clear that an exemption applies. Some lifetime exemptions, however, may apply to only part of a lifetime transfer, so that the excess is potentially exempt.

The main exemptions and reliefs applicable on death apply also to lifetime transfers. In addition, there are some further exemptions which apply only to lifetime transfers.

4.4.3.1 Spouse or civil partner and charity exemptions

These exemptions, outlined at **4.3.3**, apply to lifetime transfers as well as to the transfer on death. So any lifetime gift to the transferor's spouse or civil partner or to charity is exempt, even if the transferor dies within seven years.

4.4.3.2 Business and agricultural property relief

The reliefs set out at **4.3.3** apply to reduce the value transferred by transfers of business or agricultural property made during lifetime as well as on death. However, if the transferor dies within seven years after the transfer, the relief will generally be available only if the transferee still owns the property or qualifying replacement when the transferor dies (see **4.6.2**).

4.4.3.3 Order of application of exemptions and reliefs

Spouse or civil partner and charity exemptions are applied before reliefs, since their effect is to make the transfer wholly exempt. If, for example, a transferor gives relevant business property to her husband, business property relief is academic – the transfer is exempt.

The 'lifetime only' exemptions, however, may apply to only part of a transfer. Since the reliefs apply to reduce the value transferred, they should be applied before such exemptions are considered.

4.4.3.4 Lifetime only exemptions

The annual exemption (IHTA 1984, s 19)

The annual exemption applies to the first £3,000 transferred by lifetime transfers in each tax year. Any unused annual exemption may be carried forward for one year only, so that a maximum exemption of £6,000 may be available. The current year's exemption must be used before the previous year's exemption can be carried forward.

> **EXAMPLE**
>
> On 1 May 2022, Annie gives £3,000 to her son Ben. The transfer falls within Annie's annual exemption for 2022/23 and is exempt. Annie does not make any further gifts until 1 May 2025.
>
> On 1 May 2025, Annie gives £7,000 to her daughter Claire. Annie may apply her annual exemption for 2025/26 and may carry forward her unused annual exemption for 2024/25. Thus £6,000 of the transfer is exempt at the time of the gift. (The remaining £1,000 will be 'potentially exempt', as explained below.)

If a transferor makes more than one transfer of value in any one tax year, then the exemption is used to reduce the first transfer. Any unused exemption is set against the second and any further transfers until it is used up.

> **EXAMPLE**
>
> Sarah gives £10,000 to Jessica on 30 April 2025 and £10,000 to Kirsty on 1 May 2025. She has made no previous transfers. The annual exemptions for 2025/26 and 2024/25 will be set against the transfer to Jessica and reduce it to £4,000. (The remaining part of Jessica's gift and the whole of Kirsty's gift will be 'potentially exempt', as explained below at **4.4.3.5**.)

Small gifts (IHTA 1984, s 20)

Lifetime gifts in any one tax year of £250 or less to any one person are exempt. This exemption cannot be set against a gift which exceeds £250.

Normal expenditure out of income (IHTA 1984, s 21)

A lifetime transfer is exempt if it can be shown that:

(a) it was made as part of the transferor's normal expenditure; and

(b) it was made out of the transferor's income; and

(c) after allowing for all such payments, the transferor was left with sufficient income to maintain their usual standard of living.

> **EXAMPLE**
>
> Andrew, who is a highly-paid company director, has a niece at drama college. He sends his niece £100 each month (paid from his income) to assist her with her living expenses. These transfers are exempt as normal expenditure out of Andrew's income (provided Andrew's remaining income is sufficient to support his normal standard of living).

Gifts in consideration of marriage (IHTA 1984, s 22)

Lifetime gifts on marriage are exempt up to:

(a) £5,000 by a parent of a party to the marriage;

(b) £2,500 by a remoter ancestor of a party to the marriage (eg, a grandparent); and

(c) £1,000 in any other case.

4.4.3.5 Potentially exempt status

As long as the lifetime transfer is not immediately chargeable (see **4.5**), any value remaining after exemptions and reliefs have been applied at step 3 is potentially exempt. The transfer will become chargeable *only* if the transferor dies within seven years. The transferor does not need to take any action at the time when such a lifetime transfer is made, and if the transferor survives for seven years it will automatically become exempt. However, if the transferor dies within the seven-year period, the transfer becomes chargeable and must be assessed as such. (For further explanation of the effect of death within seven years, see **4.6**.)

> **EXAMPLE**
>
> On 1 July 2025, Jane gives £130,000 to her brother, Brian. She has made no previous lifetime gifts. The disposition is a transfer of value because the value of Jane's estate is reduced. The value transferred is £130,000, the loss to Jane's estate.
>
> | | £ |
> |---|---|
> | Value transferred | 130,000 |
> | Less: annual exemptions for 2025/26 and 2024/25 | 6,000 |
> | Potentially exempt transfer | 124,000 |
>
> No tax is payable at the time of the gift. Jane has made a PET. If Jane survives until 1 July 2032, the PET will become completely exempt. If Jane dies before that date, the PET will become a chargeable transfer.

4.5 OTHER LIFETIME TRANSFERS: LIFETIME CHARGEABLE TRANSFERS

Any lifetime transfer which does not fall within the definition of a PET (see **4.4**) is immediately chargeable as a 'lifetime chargeable transfer' (LCT). The main example is a lifetime transfer made on or after 22 March 2006 into any trust (other than a disabled trust) or to a discretionary trust or company (whether made before, on or after 22 March 2006). The charge to IHT on lifetime creation of trusts is part of a wider regime under which further charges to tax arise during the existence of the trust and on its ending. The details of these further charges are beyond the scope of this book. The examples below refer to transfers into trusts: in each case it is assumed that the trusts are not disabled trusts.

4.5.1 Calculating tax on a lifetime chargeable transfer

Where an individual makes an LCT, the IHT calculation begins with application of the first three steps as described at **4.4.1**, **4.4.2** and **4.4.3**. Once relevant exemptions and reliefs have been applied (except the small gifts exemption which is not available to LCTs), the balance is chargeable to IHT and tax must be calculated by applying step 4.

The rates of tax applicable to LCTs are:

(a) 0% on the first £325,000 (the nil rate band); and

(b) 20% on the balance of the chargeable transfer (this rate being half the rate for transfers which are chargeable on death).

4.5.1.1 The effect of cumulation

Chargeable transfers made in the seven years before the current chargeable transfer reduce the nil rate band available to that current transfer. In other words, the value transferred by chargeable transfers made in the seven years before the current chargeable transfer must be 'cumulated' with that transfer (whilst the transferor is alive, any PETs made by the transferor are ignored for cumulation purposes because they may never become chargeable).

EXAMPLE 1

In this example, it is assumed that Venetia has used up her annual exemptions in each relevant tax year.

On 1 May 2024, Venetia transfers £50,000 to the trustees of a trust.

She has previously made the following lifetime chargeable transfers (after applying relevant annual exemptions):

1 May 2016 £100,000
1 May 2019 £280,000

She has made no other lifetime transfers (and makes no more in the current tax year).

To calculate the IHT due on the chargeable transfer of £50,000, the values transferred by any chargeable transfers made in the seven years prior to 1 May 2024 must be 'cumulated'.

(Remember that it may help you when calculating cumulative totals to draw a time line, showing the relevant transfers. An example is given below.)

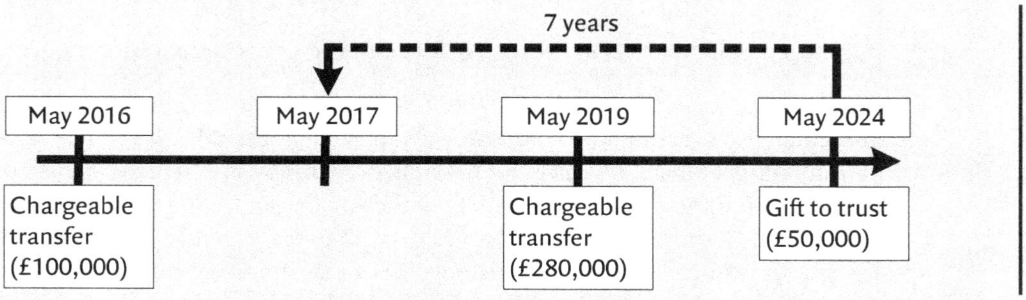

Venetia's cumulative total consists of the £280,000 transferred on 1 May 2019 (less than seven years before the present transfer).

The transfer of £100,000 was made more than seven years ago and can be ignored.

	£
Nil rate band	325,000
less cumulative total	280,000
= remaining nil rate band	45,000

Tax on current chargeable transfer of £50,000:
£45,000 at 0% = nil
£5,000 at 20% = £1,000

Note that only chargeable transfers are relevant for cumulation. If the May 2019 transfer had been an outright gift of cash, it would have been a PET and not chargeable (as Venetia is still alive). It would not have been relevant for cumulation purposes, and the whole nil rate band would be available in relation to the 2024 gift to the trust.

Remember that each transfer has its own cumulation period. If a new transfer is made, it is necessary to re-calculate the cumulative total.

EXAMPLE 2

On 1 May 2025, Venetia makes a further transfer of £100,000 to the trustees of the trust. The rates of IHT remain the same as for 2024/25, so her position for IHT would be as follows:

Nil rate band exhausted by transfers of 1 May 2019 and 1 May 2024.

Tax on current chargeable transfer of £100,000:

£100,000 at 20% = £20,000

EXAMPLE 3

Venetia makes the following further transfer to the trustees of the trust:

1 July 2026 £200,000

Assuming the rates of IHT remain the same as for 2025/26, Venetia's position for IHT would be as follows:

The transfer on 1 May 2019 was made more than seven years ago and can be ignored.

Venetia's cumulative total consists of the £50,000 transferred on 1 May 2024 and the £100,000 transferred on 1 May 2025.

	£	£
Nil rate band		325,000
less cumulative total		
1 May 2024	50,000	
1 May 2025	100,000	150,000
= remaining nil rate band		175,000

Tax on current chargeable transfer of £200,000:
£175,000 at 0% = nil
£25,000 at 20% = £5,000

Note that the effect of death on lifetime chargeable transfers is considered at **4.6.3**.

4.6 EFFECT OF DEATH ON LIFETIME TRANSFERS

4.6.1 Introduction

The death of a transferor may result in a charge (or additional charge) to IHT on any transfers of value which they have made in the seven years immediately preceding their death, whether those transfers were PETs or LCTs when they were made. First, PETs made in that period become chargeable and the transferee will be liable for any IHT payable. Secondly, the IHT liability on LCTs made in that period is recalculated and the trustees will be liable for any extra tax payable. In either case, as the liability arises on death, the rate of tax, once the nil rate band and, if relevant, the RNRB are exceeded, is 40%.

Once the transfers that must be (re)assessed have been identified by checking the seven-year period before the transferor's death, each of those transfers must be analysed chronologically, starting with the transfer furthest back in time and working through the transfers (ending with the calculation of death on the death estate). If a transfer was originally a PET, the rules are those set out at **4.6.2**; if it was a LCT, the rules at **4.6.3** are used.

4.6.2 Effect of death on PETs

Potentially exempt transfers are defined and explained in **4.4**. There is no liability on a PET at the time of the transfer, and it will become wholly exempt if the transferor survives for seven years after the transfer. Many gifts will thus escape a charge to IHT.

A PET will become chargeable *only* if the transferor dies within seven years of making the transfer.

4.6.2.1 Steps 1–3

As seen at **4.4**, the first three steps are applied to determine the size of the PET. Business property relief and/or agricultural property relief may apply to reduce the value transferred, provided that the transferee still owns the business or agricultural property (see ***Business Law and Practice***).

4.6.2.2 Step 4: Calculate tax at the appropriate rate

The final step is to identify the rate or rates of tax applicable to the transfer in question. In order to do this, one must first establish the transferor's cumulative total of transfers at the time of the PET, as this will reduce the available nil rate band. The cumulative total will be made up of:

(a) any LCTs made in the seven years *before the PET being assessed* (even if the LCT was made more than seven years before the transferor's death – therefore a taxpayer who makes an LCT may have to survive for 14 years before it ceases to have any impact); and

(b) any other PETs made during the seven years *before the PET being assessed* which have become chargeable as a result of the transferor's death.

The rates of tax applicable to chargeable transfers made within seven years of death of the transferor are:

(a) 0% on the available nil rate band; and

(b) 40% on the balance (the lower 36% charity rate is not applicable).

EXAMPLE 1

On 5 May 2022, Adam gives quoted shares worth £356,000 to his daughter, Emma.

On 21 April 2025, Adam dies, leaving his estate (consisting of quoted shares and bank deposits worth £200,000) to his son, Matthew. He made no other significant lifetime gifts.

The transfer on 5 May 2022 was a PET which has now become chargeable as the transferor has died within seven years.

(1) Tax on the PET	£
Loss to estate	356,000
Less annual exemptions 2022/23; 2021/22	6,000
	350,000

Adam had made no chargeable transfers in the seven years preceding 5 May 2022, so his nil rate band was intact.

Tax on £325,000 @ 0%	Nil
Tax on £25,000 @ 40%	£10,000 (payable by Emma).

(2) Tax on the estate

The cumulation principle means that Adam's nil rate band has been used up by the chargeable transfer made within the preceding seven years.

Tax on £200,000 @ 40%	£80,000 (payable by Adam's PRs from the estate passing to Matthew)

EXAMPLE 2

Gina gave the following gifts of cash to her children:

1 September 2020	£200,000 to Claire
25 June 2022	£200,000 to James

Gina died on 30 May 2025 leaving her estate of £400,000 (consisting of a house worth £350,000 and bank accounts worth £50,000) to the two children equally. She had made no other significant gifts.

Both gifts were PETs which have now become chargeable as Gina has died within seven years.

(1) Tax on the 2020 PET	£
Loss to estate	200,000
Annual exemptions 2020/21; 2019/20	6,000
	194,000

Gina had made no chargeable transfers in the seven years before 1 September 2020 so her nil rate band was intact.

Tax on £194,000 @ 0%	Nil

(2) Tax on the 2022 PET	£
Loss to estate	200,000
Annual exemptions 2022/23; 2021/22	6,000
	194,000

Gina's cumulative total of chargeable transfers made in the seven years up to 25 June 2022 was £194,000 (the 2020 transfer to Claire). Only £131,000 of Gina's nil rate band remains.

Tax on £194,000	
£131,000 @ 0%	Nil
£63,000 @ 40%	£25,200 (payable by James)

(3) Tax on Gina's estate: The house is a qualifying residential interest which has been closely inherited, so Gina is entitled to the RNRB of £175,000. Gina's nil rate band has been used up by the two chargeable transfers in the last seven years.

Tax on £175,000 @ 0%	
Tax on £225,000 @ 40%	£90,000 (payable by Gina's PRs from the property passing to the children)

4.6.2.3 Tapering relief

Where a PET has become chargeable, tapering relief is available if the transferor survives for more than three years after the transfer. The relief works by reducing any *tax payable* on the PET.

Tax is reduced to the following percentages:

(a) transfers within three to four years before death: 80% of death charge
(b) transfers within four to five years before death: 60% of death charge
(c) transfers within five to six years before death: 40% of death charge
(d) transfers within six to seven years before death: 20% of death charge

EXAMPLE

1 January 2019	Leonora makes a gift of £96,000 to Isadora Leonora's cumulative total before the gift is made is £325,000
1 July 2025	Leonora dies

Effect of death:	£
Transfer of value	96,000
Less: Annual exemptions 2018/19; 2017/18	6,000
PET (which is now chargeable)	90,000
Rate of tax: Cumulative total £325,000 so all £90,000 is in the 40% band	
£90,000 @ 40%	36,000
Tapering relief applies. Leonora died within six to seven years of the PET so 20% of this figure is payable	
Tax payable by Isadora 20% of £36,000	7,200

4.6.3 Effect of death on LCTs

If a transferor dies within seven years of making an LCT, the IHT payable must be recalculated and more IHT may be payable by the trustees. The tax bill may be increased not only because the full death rate of IHT will now apply, but also because PETs made *before* the LCT may have become chargeable. They will increase the cumulative total and so reduce the nil rate band applicable to the LCT.

4.6.3.1 Steps 1–3

As described at **4.5.1**, the first three steps apply to find the value transferred by the LCT that is chargeable to tax. It will be necessary to check whether any reliefs claimed at step 3 when the LCT was made (such as BPR or APR) are still available.

4.6.3.2 Step 4: calculate tax at the appropriate rate(s)

Inheritance tax is recalculated in accordance with the rates of tax in force at the transferor's death if these are less than the rates in force at the time of the transfer; if not, the death rates at the time of the transfer are applied (the lower 36% charity rate is not applicable).

The cumulative total relevant to the LCT will determine how much (if any) of the nil rate band is available. The cumulative total is made up of:

(a) any other LCTs made in the seven years *before the LCT being assessed* (even if such earlier LCTs were made more than seven years before the transferor's death); and

(b) any PETs made during the seven years *before the LCT being assessed* which have become chargeable as a result of the transferor's death.

Remember that each transfer that becomes chargeable or rechargeable has its own cumulation period, which means that a taxpayer who makes an LCT may have to survive for 14 years before it ceases to have an impact. This is sometimes known as the '14 year rule.'

EXAMPLE 1

Jasmin dies in November 2025. During her lifetime, she made the following gifts. In December 2018, she gave her son £100,000 in cash and, in January 2012, she transferred £300,000 to a discretionary trust for the benefit of her grandchildren. (Assume that Jasmin used her annual exemption each year.)

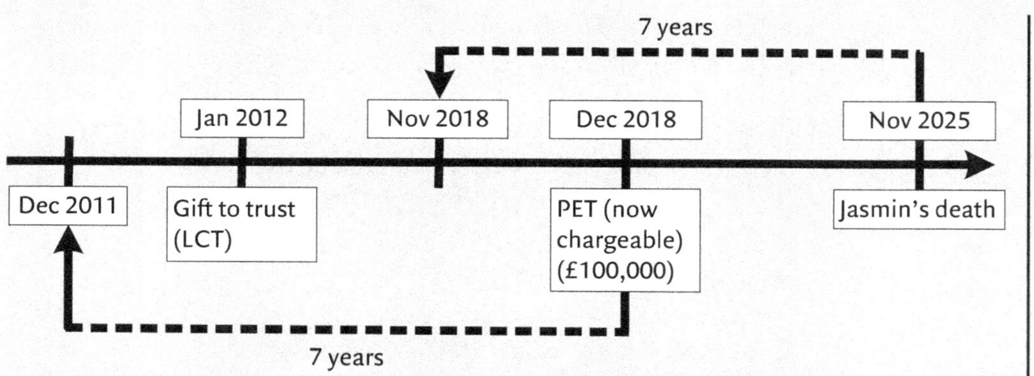

The December 2018 PET is just within 7 years of Jasmin's death, and has now become chargeable. As a result, it now has its own cumulation period, so you must look back 7 years from December 2018, when the PET was made, to see if any *chargeable* transfers were made during that period. If there is either a chargeable PET, as here (or a rechargeable LCT) in the 7 years before the death, you need to go back another 7 years to see how much of the nil rate band is left. The January 2012 LCT is just within the 7 years from December 2018 and must be cumulated. As a result, there is only £25,000 nil rate band left for the December 2018 PET.

Notes:

(a) As Jasmin survived for more than 7 years from the January 2012 LCT, it is not rechargeable. It is only relevant for cumulation purposes.

(b) Had the January 2012 transfer been a PET, as Jasmin survived for more than 7 years, it would never have become chargeable, and so would not be taken into account when calculating the cumulative total.

(c) The cumulative total for the death estate, looking back 7 years from November 2025, is £100,000, ie the amount taken by the PET which has become chargeable. The January 2012 LCT has no effect on the death estate as it is outside the 7 years before Jasmin's death.

4.6.3.3 Tapering relief and credit for IHT already paid

Once the IHT on the LCT has been recalculated, and if more than three years have elapsed between the transfer and the subsequent death, tapering relief applies to reduce the recalculated tax (using the rules set out at **4.6.2.3**). Credit is then given for any IHT paid on the LCT at the time it was made but if the recalculated bill is lower than the original amount paid (which may occur if tapering relief is available) no tax is refunded.

EXAMPLE 1

On 1 May 2021, George transferred £381,000 into a trust on condition that the trustees must pay the IHT. He had made no other lifetime gifts.

(a) On 1 May 2021, George made an LCT.

	£
Value transferred	381,000
Less: Annual exemptions 2021/22; 2020/21	6,000
	375,000
Calculate tax.	
£325,000 @ 0%	0
£50,000 @ 20%	10,000
Tax payable by trustees	10,000

(b) George dies on 1 September 2025, within seven years of the LCT.
Recalculate tax at death rates.

	£
£325,000 @ 0%	0
£50,000 @ 40%	20,000
	20,000

George died between four and five years after the transfer, so apply tapering relief

	£
60% of £20,000	12,000
Less: tax already paid (see part (a))	10,000
Further tax payable by trustees	2,000

EXAMPLE 2

Drusilla dies on 1 August 2025. During her lifetime she made only the following transfers of value:

1 July 2019 Gift of £150,000 to Rukhsana
1 July 2022 Gift of £332,000 on discretionary trusts

The consequences are as follows:

(a) On 1 July 2019, Drusilla made a PET:

	£
Value transferred	150,000
Less: Annual exemptions 2019/20; 2018/19	6,000
Potentially exempt transfer	144,000

(b) On 1 July 2022, Drusilla made an LCT:
Charge to tax on 1 July 2022:

		£
Value transferred		332,000
Less: Annual exemptions 2022/23; 2021/22		6,000
		326,000
Rate of tax	Cumulative total zero	
	£325,000 @ 0%	0
	£1,000 @ 20%	200
Tax payable by trustees		200

(c) Recalculation of tax on PET following death: Drusilla has died within seven years after 1 July 2019, so the PET of £144,000 to Rukhsana has become chargeable. There is no IHT on the transfer as it falls within Drusilla's nil rate band, but her cumulative total is now £144,000.

(d) The tax on the LCT of 1 July 2022 must be recalculated.

Rate of tax: Cumulative total £144,000 so £181,000 of nil rate band left

	£
£181,000 @ 0%	0
£145,000 @ 40%	58,000
£326,000	58,000

Tapering relief applies. Drusilla died between three and four years after the LCT so the recalculated tax is reduced to 80%.

	£
80% of £58,000	46,400
Less: IHT already paid	200
Tax payable by trustees	46,200

(e) Effect on Drusilla's death estate. In the seven years before her death, Drusilla made two chargeable transfers. Her cumulative total at the time of her death is:

	£
1 July 2019 PET (now chargeable)	144,000
1 July 2022 LCT	326,000
	470,000

This means that, when calculating tax on Drusilla's estate on death, her nil rate band has been used up. Assuming that her estate did not include a qualifying residential interest, tax on her estate will be charged at a flat rate of 40%.

4.7 LIABILITY AND BURDEN OF PAYMENT

4.7.1 Meaning of 'liability' and 'burden'

The rules that follow concern the question of who is liable to account to HMRC for the payment of IHT and who bears the burden of the tax. HMRC is concerned with obtaining payment of the tax (ie liability). Payment will usually be obtained from people who are not beneficially entitled to the property but who hold property in a representative capacity (ie PRs and trustees). Those who ultimately receive the property are concurrently liable with such representatives, but in most cases tax will have been paid before the beneficiaries receive the property. The concept of 'burden' concerns who ultimately bears the burden of the tax.

4.7.2 The estate rate

The term 'estate rate' means the average rate of tax applicable to each item of property in the estate for IHT. When tax on the estate has been calculated, it may be necessary for various reasons to work out how much of the tax is attributable to a particular item of property in the estate. For example:

(a) since tax on certain types of property, such as land, may be paid in instalments, the personal representatives (PRs) must calculate how much of the tax relates to that property;

(b) the PRs may not be liable to pay all the tax on the estate. If the estate for IHT purposes includes trust property, the trustees are liable to pay the tax attributable to that property;

(c) the will may give a legacy 'subject to tax' so that the recipient has the burden of tax relating to that legacy.

The principle is that tax is divided between the various assets in the estate proportionately, according to their value. This may be applied by calculating the average rate of tax on the estate as a percentage, ie the 'estate rate'. For example, if the deceased's nil rate band was completely used up by lifetime transfers, the 'estate rate' would normally be 40%. However, it is not always necessary to calculate the estate rate as a percentage; instead, the amount of tax on a particular item of property in the estate may be calculated by applying to the value of that property the proportion which the total tax bill bears to the total chargeable estate.

EXAMPLE

Graham, who has made no lifetime transfers, leaves a house, valued at £210,000, to his brother, Henry, subject to payment of IHT, and the rest of his estate, valued at £190,000 net, to his nephew, Ian.

Tax on Graham's estate:	£325,000 @ 0%			nil
	£75,000 @ 40%			£30,000

The 'estate rate' is: $\frac{\text{£30,000 (total tax bill)}}{\text{£400,000 (total chargeable estate)}} \times 100 = 7.5\%$

Henry pays tax on the house: $\text{£210,000} \times \frac{\text{£30,000}}{\text{£400,000}} = \text{£15,750}$

Ian pays tax on the residue: $\text{£190,000} \times \frac{\text{£30,000}}{\text{£400,000}} = \text{£14,250}$

The same result would be achieved if the estate rate of 7.5% was applied to the value of the house and residue respectively.

4.7.3 Liability for IHT on death

4.7.3.1 The PRs: tax on the non-settled estate

The PRs are liable to pay the IHT attributable to any property which 'was not immediately before the death comprised in a settlement' (IHTA 1984, s 200). This includes:

(a) the property which vests in the PRs (ie the property which passes under the deceased's will or intestacy); and

(b) property (other than trust property) which does not pass to the PRs but is included in the estate for IHT because the deceased was beneficially entitled to it immediately before death (eg, joint property which passes by survivorship).

Thus the PRs are liable to pay the IHT on joint property even though that property does not vest in them. Their liability is, however, limited to the value of the assets they received, or would have received but for their own neglect or default.

Concurrently liable with the PRs is 'any person in whom property is vested ... at any time after the death or who at any such time is beneficially entitled to an interest in possession in the property' (IHTA 1984, s 200(1)(c)). This means that tax on property passing by will or intestacy may in principle be claimed by HMRC from a beneficiary who has received that property. Similarly, HMRC may claim tax on joint property from the surviving joint tenant. Such tax is normally paid by the PRs and it is relatively unusual for HMRC to claim tax from the recipient of the property.

4.7.3.2 The trustees: tax on settled property

If the estate for IHT purposes includes any property which was 'comprised in a settlement' immediately before the death, the trustees of the settlement are liable for IHT attributable to that property. This principle is relevant where the deceased had a qualifying interest in possession under a trust (see **4.3.1.2**). Again, any person in whom the trust property subsequently vests or for whose benefit the trust property is subsequently applied is concurrently liable with the trustees.

EXAMPLE

In 1999, Ruth's father died leaving shares now worth £300,000 on trust for Ruth for life with remainder to Arthur. Ruth dies leaving property worth £200,000 which passes under her will to her niece, Tessa. The trust fund is taxed as part of Ruth's estate as she had a qualifying interest in possession for IHT purposes. She had made no lifetime transfers.

Tax on Ruth's death:

on	£325,000 @ 0%	nil
on	£175,000 @ 40%	£70,000

The trustees are liable to pay the tax on the trust fund (calculated according to the estate rate):

$$£300,000 \times \frac{£70,000}{£500,000} = £42,000$$

Arthur, the remainderman, is concurrently liable if any of the trust property is transferred to him before the tax has been paid.

Ruth's PRs are liable to pay the tax on Ruth's free estate (the remaining £28,000).

4.7.3.3 Additional liability of PRs

Property which the deceased gave away during their lifetime is treated as part of their estate on death if the donor reserved a benefit in the property which they continued to enjoy immediately before death (see **4.3.1**). The donee of the gift is primarily liable to pay tax attributable to the property. However, if the tax remains unpaid 12 months after the end of the month of death, the PRs become liable for the tax.

4.7.4 Liability for IHT on PETs

Where a person dies within seven years of making a PET, the transfer becomes chargeable and IHT may be payable. The transferee is primarily liable but, again, the PRs become liable if the tax remains unpaid 12 months after the end of the month of death.

The liability of the PRs is limited to the extent of the assets they actually received, or would have received but for their neglect or default. However, PRs cannot escape liability on the grounds that they have distributed the estate and so they should ideally delay distribution until IHT on any such lifetime gifts has been paid.

4.7.5 Liability for IHT on LCTs

4.7.5.1 Trustees pay

The transferor is primarily liable for IHT, although HMRC may also claim the tax from the trustees. In practice, the trustees often pay IHT out of the property they have been given.

EXAMPLE

Ahmed transfers £146,000 cash into a trust. His cumulative total is £285,000 and he is entitled to two annual exemptions. Ahmed stipulates that the trustees must pay any IHT.

		£
Value transferred		146,000
Less:	Two annual exemptions	6,000
		140,000
Rate of tax:	Cumulative total £285,000, so £40,000 of the nil rate band is left	
	£40,000 @ 0%	0
	£100,000 @ 20%	20,000
Tax payable by trustees:		20,000

4.7.5.2 Transferor pays: grossing up

If the transferor pays, the amount of tax will be more than it would be if the trustees paid.

This is because IHT is charged on the value transferred, ie the loss to the transferor's estate brought about by the gift (see **4.4.2**). If the transferor pays, the loss is increased by the amount of tax the transferor pays.

EXAMPLE

Henrietta transfers £80,000 in cash to trustees of a trust. Earlier in the tax year, she gave them £331,000 in cash. She has made no previous chargeable transfers.

The annual exemptions for this tax year and last have already been used by the gift of £331,000 and her cumulative total stands at £325,000. All the current transfer will be taxed at 20%.

If trustees pay IHT:

The loss to her estate is £80,000. Tax payable is 20% of £80,000, which is £16,000.

If Henrietta pays IHT:

The total loss to her estate (ie the value transferred) is £80,000 plus the IHT payable on that transfer.

> Therefore, in order to ascertain the value transferred, it is necessary to calculate what sum would, after deduction of tax at the appropriate rate (ie 20%), leave £80,000 (ie the transfer must be grossed up).
>
> Gross up £80,000 at 20%
>
> $£80{,}000 \times \frac{100}{80} = £100{,}000$
>
> The gross value transferred is £100,000.
>
> Calculate tax on £100,000:
>
> £100,000 @ 20% = £20,000
>
> The tax payable by Henrietta is more than the tax payable by the trustees.
>
> However, if she pays, the trustees are left with the full amount of the property transferred, £80,000, as opposed to £64,000 if they pay.

4.7.5.3 Additional liability following the transferor's death

If additional IHT becomes due on a LCT following the transferor's death, the rules for those liable for the additional tax are set out in IHTA 1984, s199 (as summarised at **4.7.4** above).

4.7.6 Burden of IHT

Unlike liability, the question of where the burden of tax should fall is one for the transferor to decide. For example, the burden of tax could fall on the transferees of any gifts (including PETs and LCTs) or the transferor could choose to relieve them of that burden by paying any IHT on lifetime gifts and directing that any IHT arising following their death be paid from the residue of their estate. Further details of the default rules that apply when administering the deceased's estate are contained in **31.8**.

4.8 TIME FOR PAYMENT

4.8.1 Death estates

4.8.1.1 The basic rule

The basic rule is that IHT is due for payment six months after the end of the month of death (although PRs will normally pay earlier in order to speed up the administration of the estate as any IHT due must be paid before the grant of representation can be obtained; see **30.6**).

If the tax due is not paid on time, interest runs on the outstanding amount.

4.8.1.2 The instalment option

Some property, such as land and certain types of business property, attracts the instalment option. Any tax attributable to instalment option property may be paid in 10 equal yearly instalments, the first falling due six months after the end of the month of death. The tax on the estate is apportioned using the estate rate to find how much tax is attributable to the instalment option property.

The instalment option applies to:

(a) land of any description;

(b) a business or an interest in a business;

(c) shares (quoted or unquoted) which immediately before death gave control of the company to the deceased;

(d) unquoted shares which do not give control if either:

  (i) the holding is sufficiently large (a holding of at least 10% of the nominal value of the company's shares and worth more than £20,000); or

(ii) HMRC is satisfied that the tax cannot be paid in one sum without undue hardship; or

(iii) the IHT attributable to the shares and any other instalment option property in the estate amounts to at least 20% of the IHT payable on the estate.

4.8.1.3 Interest

Where the instalment option is exercised in relation to tax on shares or any other business property or agricultural land, instalments carry interest only from the date when each instalment is payable. Thus, no interest is due on the outstanding tax provided that each instalment is paid on the due date.

In the case of other land, however, interest is payable with each instalment (apart from the first) on the amount of IHT which was outstanding for the previous year.

4.8.1.4 Sale

If the instalment option property is sold, all outstanding tax and interest becomes payable.

4.8.2 PETs

Any IHT on a PET that has become chargeable is due six months after the end of the month of death. The instalment option outlined above may be available depending on the circumstances (IHTA 1984, s 227).

4.8.3 LCTs

4.8.3.1 At the time of the transfer

Any IHT on LCTs made after 5 April and before 1 October in any year is due on the 30 April in the following year. Inheritance tax on LCTs which are not made between those dates is due six months after the end of the month in which the LCT is made.

4.8.3.2 Following subsequent death within seven years

Any additional IHT on the reassessment of a LCT following the transferor's death is due six months after the end of the month of death.

Again, the instalment option may be available (IHTA 1964, s 227).

4.8.4 Example of the rules on liability, burden and timing

EXAMPLE

Xander, who was divorced, dies on 4 May 2025, leaving an estate on which the total IHT due is £150,000. His taxable estate (of £800,000) comprises instalment property (a house) worth £240,000 and non-instalment property worth £560,000 (of which £200,000 is Xander's share of a joint bank account held with this brother, Zak). Xander left a valid will, leaving the residue of his estate to his nephew, but which makes no mention of the burden of IHT.

Liability

The executors of Xander's estate are liable for the entire IHT due of £150,000.

Burden

As the will makes no contrary provision, the default rule is that the IHT on the share of the joint bank account is borne by Zak as the surviving joint tenant:

$$£200,000 \times \frac{£150,000}{£800,000} = £37,500$$

IHT on the property passing via the will is paid from the residuary estate as a testamentary expense:

$$£600{,}000 \times \frac{£150{,}000}{£800{,}000} = £112{,}500$$

Timing

The house qualifies as instalment option property:

$$£240{,}000 \times \frac{£150{,}000}{£800{,}000} = £45{,}000$$

This tax can be paid in 10 equal annual instalments, with the first instalment of £4,500 payable on 30 November 2025 (six months after the end of the month of death).

The remaining IHT of £105,000 is all due no later than 30 November 2025, but if the executors submit the IHT account before that date, they will have to pay the tax at that time. They will have a right of recovery from Zak for the £37,500 in respect of the joint bank account for which they have liability to HMRC but for which he bears the burden.

SUMMARY

The main occasions of charge to IHT are:

(a) on death on the value of an individual's estate;

(b) on lifetime gifts made by one individual to another made within seven years prior to death;

(c) on lifetime gifts to a company or into a trust.

Lifetime gifts to an individual are only chargeable to IHT if the donor dies within the seven years after making the gift. At the time such a gift is made it is a 'potentially exempt transfer' (PET). It becomes exempt if the donor survives for seven years or chargeable if they die during that period.

Lifetime gifts into a trust or to a company are immediately chargeable to IHT at the time they are made. They are known as 'lifetime chargeable transfers' (LCTs).

There are four steps to be used to calculate liability to IHT.

Step 1: Identify the transfer of value

On death this means the value of the estate, ie all the property to which the deceased was beneficially entitled.

For lifetime transfers this means any transaction which reduces the value of the transferor's estate. This includes any gift or a sale at an undervalue.

Step 2: Find the value transferred

On death this means the value of the property in the estate, valued at open market value.

For lifetime transfers this means the amount by which the transferor's estate has been reduced as a result of the transfer.

Step 3: Apply exemptions and reliefs

Transfers to spouse or charity are exempt whether in lifetime or on death.

Some exemptions apply only to lifetime transfers. These include annual exemption (£3,000 pa), small gifts, marriage gifts and gifts made as normal expenditure out of income.

Business property relief applies to reduce the value transferred by a transfer of certain types of business property by 100% or 50%. This may apply to transfers made in lifetime or on death.

Step 4: Calculate tax at the appropriate rate

If the estate includes a qualifying residential interest which is closely inherited, tax is charged at 0% on the first £175,000 (the residence nil rate band).

Tax is then charged at 0% on the first £325,000 of other transfers (the nil rate band).

In order to calculate IHT on any transfer, chargeable transfers made during the preceding seven years must be taken into account. Such transfers will reduce the nil rate band available for the current transfer.

The balance of the transfer in excess of the nil rate band is taxed at 40% (or, rarely, 36%) if the transfer is on death or 20% for LCTs.

Potentially exempt transfers (PETs) made within seven years of the transferor's death become chargeable as a result of their death. The rate of tax is 40%, but the amount of tax is tapered if the transferor survived for more than three years after the transfer.

If a transferor dies within seven years of making a LCT, tax must be recalculated at death rates, applying taper if the death was more than three years after the transfer.

CHAPTER 5

Tax-efficient Investments

LEARNING OUTCOMES

After reading this chapter you will have a basic understanding of the different forms of tax relief available on a range of investments.

5.1 INTRODUCTION

An individual with high levels of income or capital gains can reduce their exposure to tax by making tax-efficient investments. Depending on which investment vehicle is chosen, it may be possible to:

(a) obtain income tax relief on the investment (and so pay less income tax in the current year);

(b) ensure that future income or capital gains escape tax;

(c) avoid paying CGT on a capital gain by re-investing it.

The rest of this chapter introduces the main features of some investments which meet these objectives. However, no investor should allow a tax advantage to cloud their judgement as to the merits or risk of any particular investment. The list is not comprehensive, but gives examples of the opportunities available. Fuller treatment of these complex matters can be found in *Simon's Direct Taxes* (LexisNexis Butterworths).

5.2 INVESTMENTS ELIGIBLE FOR INCOME TAX RELIEF

5.2.1 Enterprise Investment Scheme (EIS)

This relief is designed to encourage investment in smaller (and riskier) companies. An individual is allowed to subscribe up to £2 million (note that any amount over £1 million must be invested in one or more qualifying knowledge-intensive companies) each tax year in the ordinary shares of qualifying unquoted companies. Broadly, this means trading companies that are not listed on The Stock Exchange, so there is no ready market for their shares. Certain asset-based activities, for example share dealing, property development, farming, shipbuilding and coal and steel production are excluded. During the two years before and three years after the subscription, the individual must not be 'connected with' the company. Thus, the combined shareholdings of the investor and their 'associates' (which includes spouse and close family) must not exceed 30%; neither the investor nor their associates are normally permitted to be paid employees or directors, although there are exceptions to this rule.

The relief is given by deducting a sum equal to 30% of the amount invested from the shareholder's income tax liability for the tax year of the investment, provided they continue to satisfy the personal qualifying conditions throughout the next three years. A further attraction is that gains on disposal will be exempt from CGT; conversely, if the enterprise fails, the investor's loss on their shares may be set against their income or capital gains.

5.2.2 Seed Enterprise Investment Scheme (SEIS)

This relief is similar to the EIS, in that the qualifying conditions are broadly similar, but it is aimed at small start-up companies with less than 25 full-time employees and assets of up to £200,000. The maximum qualifying investment is £200,000 and the rate of income tax relief is 50%. Subject to certain restrictions and provided the SEIS shares are held for more than three years, a gain on the sale of SEIS shares is also free from capital gains tax.

If the SEIS investment makes a loss, an individual will also be able to offset the capital loss against income.

5.2.3 Venture Capital Trust (VCT)

A VCT is a quoted company run by professional fund managers as a vehicle to hold shares in a range of unquoted trading companies which match the EIS criteria. Smaller enterprises are thus given access to funds and the investor buying shares in the VCT can invest indirectly in smaller businesses, at the same time reducing the risk attendant on investment in a single unquoted company.

Such VCTs carry tax advantages similar to EISs, but to qualify the shares must be held for five years and the maximum investment each tax year is £200,000. A sum equal to 30% of the amount invested can be deducted from the investor's income tax liability (so the maximum tax deduction in any one tax year is £60,000). Gains on disposal are also CGT exempt. The added feature is that dividend income from a VCT is exempt from income tax.

5.3 INVESTMENTS PRODUCING TAX-FREE INCOME OR CAPITAL GAINS

5.3.1 Individual Savings Account (ISA)

Two types of ISA have existed since they were introduced in 1999: the Cash ISA and the Stocks and Shares ISA. Other specialised ISAs have been introduced over the years including the Innovative Finance ISA (aimed at facilitating peer to peer loans), Lifetime ISAs (to help people save for their first home, or for retirement) and Junior ISAs (for children). This section describes the Cash ISA and Stocks and Shares ISA only.

In each tax year, an individual aged 18 or above (or 16 for a Cash ISA) and resident in the UK can put money into either or both types of ISA. If both types are used, they can be held with different providers.

A Cash ISA resembles an ordinary savings account and deposits are generally held in bank or building society accounts.

A Stocks and Shares ISA is a wrapper that can be put around a wide range of investment products, including unit trusts and investment trusts.

The ISA investment allowance for the current tax year is £20,000. This can be held in any mix of cash or stocks and shares and the funds can be freely moved between these categories, so giving the taxpayer the option of investing the whole ISA allowance in cash, stocks and shares or any combination of the two.

The tax benefits of ISAs are as follows.

(a) No income tax liability on income produced by the ISA.
(b) No CGT liability on gains arising from ISA investments.
(c) Tax relief is not forfeited when money is taken out of the scheme.

Money can be withdrawn from either type of ISA at any time without losing the tax benefits. Additionally, provided investors have what is called a 'flexible ISA', they will be allowed to dip into their current year investments, then replenish the balance in the same tax year without the transaction affecting any unused portion of their annual allowance. For example, if an investor puts £10,000 into a flexible ISA and then withdraws £3,000, they can still pay in a further £13,000 in the tax year (the remaining allowance of £10,000 plus the £3,000 withdrawn), in contrast to £10,000 if the ISA is not flexible.

5.3.2 Enterprise Investment Scheme (EIS) and Seed Enterprise Investment Scheme (SEIS)

Capital gains are CGT exempt (see **5.2.1** and **5.2.2**).

5.3.3 Venture Capital Trust (VCT)

Both income and capital gains are exempt (see **5.2.3**).

5.4 INVESTMENT TO ESCAPE A CGT LIABILITY

5.4.1 Deferral relief on re-investment in EIS shares

Unlimited deferral of capital gains arising on the disposal of any asset is available where an individual subscribes wholly for cash for shares in a company which qualifies under the EIS. (As the shares must be acquired for cash, this relief will not usually be available to a partner or sole trader who transfers their business to a company, as the shares acquired following such a transfer are usually in return for the non-cash assets of the business.)

(a) This deferral relief is available where the shares acquired meet the requirements of the EIS (see **5.2.1**).

(b) The relief is complex but, in general terms, the individual's chargeable gain on the disposal of the asset (up to the subscription cost of the shares) is deferred until they dispose of the shares. The deferred gain is taxed at the rate applicable to the taxpayer in the tax year of the disposal of the EIS shares.

(c) The relief is available where the EIS shares are acquired within one year before or three years after the disposal.

(d) As regards the 'true gain' on the disposal of the EIS shares themselves, a slightly different relief applies. Such gains will be exempt from CGT if held for three years, but only if the investor is not 'connected' with the company (see **5.2.1**).

EXAMPLE

Shares in X Co Ltd (not EIS) have been held by Andrew for two years. He sells them and realises a gain of £60,000. This gain is deferred when he subscribes for shares in Y Co Ltd (an EIS company) for £100,000. Andrew holds the shares in Y Co Ltd for four years and then sells them for £120,000. His deferred gain of £60,000 is now chargeable to CGT. The 'true' gain of £20,000 on the disposal of the shares in Y Co Ltd will be exempt if all the qualifying conditions are met.

5.4.2 Partial relief on re-investment in SEIS shares

There is a CGT exemption on 50% of gains reinvested in SEIS qualifying investments.

Tax Rates Summary

SUMMARY OF RATES AND ALLOWANCES FOR 2025/26 FOR INDIVIDUALS

Value Added Tax

Rates:	Standard rate:	20%
	Lower	5%
	Zero	0%
Registration threshold:		£90,000

Income Tax

Rates for non-savings, non-dividend income

Rates:	Basic rate	£0–£37,700	20%
	Higher rate	over £37,700–£125,140	40%
	Additional rate	over £125,140	45%

Rates for savings and dividend income			Interest	Dividends
Rates:	Starting rate	£0–£5,000	0%	8.75%

Note: the starting rate for savings income of 0% does not apply where the taxpayer's non-savings income exceeds the starting rate limit of £5,000.

	Basic rate	over £5,000–£37,700	20%	8.75%
	Higher rate	over £37,700–£125,140	40%	33.75%
	Additional rate	over £125,140	45%	39.35%

Income tax allowances:

	Personal Allowance	£12,570
	Income limit for full Personal Allowance	£100,000

Personal Savings Allowance:

	Basic rate:	£1,000 (taxed @ 0%)
	Higher rate:	£500 (taxed @ 0%)
	Additional rate:	£0

Dividend Allowance: £500 (taxed @ 0%)

Capital Gains Tax

Rates on gains:

	Gains below the basic rate income tax threshold	18%
	Gains above the basic rate income tax threshold	24%
	Gains qualifying for business asset disposal relief	14%

Annual exempt amount:

	Individuals	£3,000
	Most forms of trust	£1,500

Inheritance Tax

Rates:

£0 to £325,000	nil %
over £325,000	40%

Note 1: For estates, where 10% or more of a person's net estate is left to charity, transfers exceeding the nil rate band of £325,000 are taxed at 36%.

Note 2: A surviving spouse or civil partner may claim the unused proportion (or percentage) of the nil rate band of an earlier deceased spouse or civil partner. The unused proportion is based on the amount of the nil rate band available at the time of the death of the second spouse or civil partner.

Note 3: From April 2017 an additional nil rate band applies when a main residence is passed on death to a direct descendant. This is currently £175,000. Any unused nil rate band will be able to be transferred to a surviving spouse or civil partner. For estates valued at more than £2 million, the additional threshold (and any transferred additional threshold) will be gradually tapered away.

Transfer on death

Full rates apply.

Lifetime transfers

(a) Potentially exempt transfers

Gifts to individuals, and gifts into trusts for the disabled.

(i) On or within seven years of death

On death, the full rates apply with a tapered reduction in the tax payable on transfers as follows:

Years between gift and death	Percentage of full charge
0–3	100
3–4	80
4–5	60
5–6	40
6–7	20

Note: the scale in force at date of death applies

(ii) More than seven years before death – gift is exempt therefore NIL tax payable

(b) Chargeable transfers

Gifts into and out of most types of trusts and gifts involving companies.

At the time of gift, half the full rates apply.

If the gift falls within seven years of death:

- the transfer is reassessed at the full death rate;
- any tax paid at the time of the transfer will be credited against tax due on death;
- (a)(i) above applies, so that the full death rate is tapered in the same way as for PETs.

PART I SUMMARIES

REVENUE LAW

Chapter 2: Income Tax

Topic	*Summary*	*References*
Occasions of charge	Individuals, partners, personal representatives and trustees could all incur IT liability on the receipt of taxable income.	
Income or capital?	Income receipts must be distinguished from capital receipts. Only income can be subject to IT; capital gains may be subject to capital gains tax.	2.1.3
Chargeable income	To be chargeable, the income must come from a specified source and not be exempt.	2.2.1 and 2.2.2
	In practice, most income receipts are chargeable. In each tax year, all chargeable income from the different sources are added together to find the taxpayer's total income.	2.2.3
Deduction at source	Employers are obliged to deduct the recipient's basic rate IT liability, before payment, and send this direct to HMRC under the PAYE system. In such cases, it is necessary to gross-up the payment received by the taxpayer, in order to find their true income from that source. The grossed-up (as opposed to the net) income will be added to their total income.	2.2.3.1 to 2.2.3.2
Reliefs	The taxpayer may deduct allowable reliefs (eg interest on loans to invest in their business) from their total income. The resulting figure is their net income.	2.3
Allowances	The taxpayer may deduct relevant personal allowances (eg the personal allowance and/or the blind person's allowance) from their net income. The resulting figure is their taxable income.	2.4
	Taxpayers are also entitled to a Personal Savings Allowance on interest of £1,000 for basic rate taxpayers and £500 for higher rate taxpayers and a Dividend Allowance of £500 for any taxpayer. These allowances operate as nil rate bands for the relevant type of income, and are taxed at 0%.	2.2.3.2, 2.5.4.2 and 2.5.5.1
Savings and dividend income and non-savings, non-dividend income (NSNDI)	Interest and dividends are savings and dividend income. All other income is non-savings, non-dividend income (NSNDI).	2.1.7 and 2.5.1

Topic	Summary	References
Rates of tax	Generally, taxable income falls into three bands – the basic rate band, the higher rate band and the additional rate band. Within these three bands, however, different rates apply, depending on whether the income is classed as NSNDI or savings and dividend income. NSNDI is taxed first, followed by interest and then dividends.	2.5.2
Tax credits	Once the taxpayer's total IT liability is worked out, credit is given for any tax deducted at source (eg by their employer). The remaining balance is then sent to HMRC, to meet the taxpayer's outstanding liability.	2.6
IT – liability and time for payment	In general terms, the recipient of taxable income must pay the balance of their tax liability to HMRC by 31 January following the tax year in which the income was earned. Special rules apply to the self-employed.	2.8

Chapter 3: Capital Gains Tax

Topic	Summary	References
Occasions of charge	Individuals, partners, personal representatives and trustees could all incur CGT liability when they dispose of chargeable assets.	
Disposals	For CGT to arise there must be a disposal of a chargeable asset. Disposals include gifts, as well as sales, but do not include property passing on death.	
Chargeable assets	Most forms of property are chargeable. The main exemption is sterling. In general terms, depreciating assets are also non-chargeable. This prevents the taxpayer from setting losses on these types of assets against their other chargeable gains.	3.1.3
Calculation of the gain	In basic terms, this is the sale price less allowable expenditure. The main element of allowable expenditure will usually be the acquisition cost of the asset but other expenditure is also deductible.	3.3
	To work out the notional gain made on a gift, the asset is deemed to be disposed of at its market value on the date of the gift.	3.2.1
Reliefs	Various reliefs are available, depending on the circumstances. Most of the reliefs available are aimed at encouraging business investment. Otherwise, a major relief for the ordinary taxpayer is the principal private residence exemption.	3.4.1
Disposals between spouses (and civil partners)	These are treated as being for such consideration as to provide neither a gain nor a loss. On a subsequent disposal by the donee spouse, the gain will be assessed by using the donor spouse's acquisition cost.	3.9.1

Topic	*Summary*	*References*
Losses	Losses can be set against gains of the same tax year to reduce the net chargeable gain. Unabsorbed losses can be taken forward to set against gains of future tax years, but in such a way that the taxpayer does not lose the use of their annual exemption in future years.	3.7
Rates of tax	(a) On normal gains, after deducting an annual exemption from an individual's net aggregate gains, the balance is added onto their taxable income. After doing this, if any part of the gains is below the basic rate income tax threshold it is taxed at 18%, while any part of the gains above the threshold is taxed at 24%. (b) Gains qualifying for business asset disposal relief are calculated separately from other gains and are taxed at a flat rate of 14%. (c) Gains realised by trustees and PRs are taxed at a flat rate of 24%.	3.1.4.5
Liability and time for payment	Any taxpayer still having net aggregate gains after applying their annual exemption, is (in most cases) liable to pay CGT on them by 31 January following the tax year in which the gains were made.	3.1.6

Chapter 4: Inheritance Tax

Topic	*Summary*	*References*
Occasions of charge	A charge to IHT can arise on transfers into most types of trust or to companies, on other lifetime transfers made within seven years of the transferor's death and on property passing on death.	4.3 and 4.4
Transfer of value	IHT is charged on the value transferred by a chargeable transfer. A chargeable transfer is a transfer of value made by an individual but which is not an exempt transfer. A transfer of value is any disposition which reduces the value of the transferor's estate.	4.3 and 4.4
Value transferred	This is the amount of the reduction in the transferor's estate. On death, it is the value of the estate.	4.3.2.1 and 4.4.1
Exemptions applying to all types of lifetime transfer	Any property passing to a spouse (or civil partner) and to a charity is exempt. Business property relief (and agricultural property relief) may be available on relevant business (and agricultural) property, to reduce the value transferred by either 50% or 100%.	4.3.3
	In addition, lifetime transfers may be exempted by a number of other exemptions, including the small gifts exemption, gifts in consideration of marriage and the annual exemption.	4.4.3.4
Transfers into most types of trust	To the extent that exemptions are not available, these are immediately chargeable to IHT and are referred to as lifetime chargeable transfers (LCTs).	4.5

Topic	Summary	References
Rate of tax on LCTs at time of transfer	All amounts above the available nil rate are charged at a flat rate of 20%.	
Other lifetime transfers	The main example of these is a transfer to an individual. To the extent that other exemptions are not available, the transfer is a potentially exempt transfer (PET). As PETs, they are exempt from any IHT charge at the time of the transfer and will become unconditionally exempt if the transferor survives for seven years after the transfer.	4.4
IHT – effect of death of transferor within seven years of any type of lifetime transfer	To the extent that they do not fall within the nil rate band, LCTs made within seven years of the transferor's death must be re-assessed at the death rate of 40%.	4.6.3
	Any PETs made within seven years of transferor's death become chargeable transfers (failed PETs) and, to the extent that they do not fall within the nil rate band, are then chargeable at the death rate of 40%.	4.6.2, 4.6.2.1 and 4.6.2.2
IHT – cumulation	To assess the rate of tax on any individual transfer, it is necessary to take into account the value of any other chargeable transfers made within the seven years before the transfer being assessed. The nil rate band is applied to transfers in chronological order, so chargeable transfers within the previous seven years will have taken up some or all of the nil rate band, leaving only the balance for the transfer being assessed.	4.2.4, 4.3.4, 4.5.1 and 4.6.2
IHT – tapering relief	If any lifetime transfer (LCT or failed PET) was made between three and seven years before the death of the transferor, any IHT charge to which it is subject is progressively reduced by between 80% and 20% of the full liability.	4.6.2.3
IHT – transfers on death	The deceased is deemed to have made a transfer of value immediately before death. The value transferred is the value of their 'estate' immediately before death. The estate includes all property to which the deceased was beneficially entitled. Property held by the deceased on trust for others does not form part of the estate.	4.3
	Although property held by the deceased as a beneficial joint tenant passes automatically by survivorship to the remaining joint tenant(s), the value of the deceased's share in the property will form part of their estate for IHT purposes. Also included in the estate is property, which the deceased transferred in their lifetime but which they continued to have the use of until their death (gifts with a reservation of benefit).	4.3.1
	Liabilities of the deceased at the time of death and reasonable funeral expenses are deductible from the value of the estate.	4.3.2.4

Topic	Summary	References
IHT – exemptions applicable to death transfers	Any property passing to a spouse (or civil partner) and to a charity is exempt. Business property relief (and agricultural property relief) is available on relevant business (and agricultural) property, to reduce the value transferred by either 50% or 100%.	4.3.3
IHT – rate of tax on death transfers	Amounts falling within the residence nil rate band or nil rate band (subject to cumulation) are charged at 0%. The excess is taxed at 40% (except where a large enough amount passes to charity to trigger the lower 36% rate).	
IHT – liability and time for payment	Primary liability for IHT falls on the donee of a failed PET, the transferor of a LCT and the personal representatives of the deceased's estate. In the case of lifetime transfers, if the transfer was made between 1 October and 5 April, the date for payment is six months from the end of the month in which the transfer was made. Otherwise, the payment date is on 30 April following the date of the transfer. On death, the general rule is that IHT is payable six months after the end of the month in which the death occurred. However, in the case of certain assets, such as land and shares, the tax may be paid in 10 yearly instalments.	

PART II

PROFESSIONAL CONDUCT

Author's notes

- This Part has been compiled from the versions of the SRA Codes of Conduct and Regulations current at the time of writing.
- This book is not intended as a definitive guide to the subject.
- This book is not intended to constitute legal advice. The publisher and author are not responsible or liable for the results of any person acting (or omitting to act) on the basis of information contained within this publication.
- The examples given in this Part are intended to illustrate a point only, and not as model examination answers.

CHAPTER 6

THE LEGAL PROFESSION

LEARNING OUTCOMES

After reading this chapter you will be able to understand:

- what is meant by 'professional conduct'
- the role of The Law Society and Solicitors Regulation Authority
- different aspects of practice.

6.1 PROFESSIONAL CONDUCT

'Professional conduct' is the term that is often used to describe the rules and regulations with which a solicitor must comply. Solicitors, like every other person, must comply with the laws of the country. However, additional requirements are placed upon solicitors due to the nature of their job.

A solicitor is said to be a member of a profession. Other examples of members of professions include doctors and accountants. The public must be able to place a great deal of trust in such professionals due to the work that they carry out. For example, on a simplistic level, both solicitors and accountants often handle large amounts of clients' money. A client must be able to trust that this money will be safe in the hands of those professionals.

In addition to holding client monies, solicitors must be able to be trusted to act in the best interests of clients. Clients often seek advice from solicitors concerning transactions worth millions of pounds. With that amount of money at stake, the client must be certain that the solicitor will provide honest advice and take every step to protect that client's interests. Equally, clients often seek a solicitor's advice on sensitive matters. The client must be reassured that whatever the matter, the solicitor can be trusted to keep the information confidential and not, for example, sell it to third parties like the press.

Law firms, like any other commercial organisation, must comply with general regulatory requirements such as the Bribery Act 2010, which came into force on 1 July 2011. The Act creates a new offence under s 7, which can be committed by commercial organisations that fail to prevent persons associated with them (including employees) committing bribery on their behalf. It is, however, a full defence for an organisation to prove that, despite bribery having occurred, it nevertheless had in place adequate procedures to prevent bribery by persons associated with it. Guidance about such procedures has been published by the Ministry of Justice, and firms will need to ensure that they comply with this.

In addition to the general law, the Solicitors Regulation Authority (SRA) publishes a number of rules and regulations (such as the Codes of Conduct) with which the solicitor and bodies authorised by the SRA (and those who work with solicitors) must comply at all times. These rules and requirements apply to the entire profession, including trainee solicitors. The aim of these rules is to ensure the protection of the public and to uphold the integrity of the profession itself.

Breach of these rules and requirements can have severe consequences. For example, where a solicitor breaches certain requirements relating to the service provided to clients, they may be ordered to pay the client compensation of up to £50,000. The ultimate sanction for breach of the requirements of professional conduct is to be 'struck off'. This effectively ends the solicitor's career and prevents them from acting as a solicitor.

6.2 THE LEGAL SERVICES BOARD

The Legal Services Board was created by the Legal Services Act 2007. It supervises the 'approved regulators' of the legal profession. These regulators include the SRA (for solicitors), the Bar Council (for barristers), the Chartered Institute of Legal Executives (for legal executives), the Council of Licensed Conveyancers (for licensed conveyancers), the Chartered Institute for Patent Attorneys (for patent attorneys), the Chartered Institute of Trade Mark Attorneys (for trade mark attorneys), the Association of Law Costs Draftsmen (for law costs draftsmen), and the Master of the Faculties (for notaries public).

6.3 THE SOLICITORS REGULATION AUTHORITY

The SRA was established by The Law Society in January 2007 to take over the regulation of solicitors from The Law Society itself. The SRA also controls matters such as training and admission to the profession.

In its own words, the purpose of the SRA is 'to protect the public by ensuring that solicitors meet high standards, and by acting when risks are identified'. The SRA is governed by a board of 10 members. This board comprises four solicitors and six lay members. Details of the members of the SRA's board can be found at www.sra.org.uk.

The headquarters of the SRA are at The Cube, Birmingham, and there is an office in central London. Its budget is funded from the practising certificate fee (see **18.2**).

The regulation of the profession is considered in detail in **Chapter 7**.

6.4 THE LAW SOCIETY

6.4.1 Introduction

The Law Society is the representative body for solicitors in England and Wales. It was founded in 1825 to raise the reputation of the profession. Today it fulfils a number of roles.

The Law Society represents solicitors within England and Wales. For example, The Law Society lobbies the Government in respect of changes in the law, and campaigns for better working conditions for solicitors, particularly on behalf of solicitors undertaking publicly funded work. The Law Society also seeks to improve the reputation of the profession as a whole, and to promote the benefits of using a solicitor to the general public.

6.4.2 Membership

After admission, membership of The Law Society is voluntary. However, all members of the profession are bound by the requirements of professional conduct whether they are members of The Law Society or not.

6.4.3 Governance

The Law Society is governed by the Council of The Law Society. The Council delegates many of its powers and decision-making responsibilities to various Boards, such as the Management Board and the Regulatory Affairs Board.

6.4.4 Local law societies

There are approximately 54 local law societies throughout England and Wales. These often provide representation, training and facilities (such as law libraries) to local firms within their area. They also help to provide a link between The Law Society and local solicitors. Local law societies do not have any disciplinary powers.

6.5 DIFFERENT ASPECTS OF PRACTICE

The legal profession is made up of a number of different types of organisations. Within these organisations there are a number of roles that a solicitor may fill.

The SRA Authorisation of Firms Rules set out the ways in which legal services authorised by it may be provided to the public, and these are detailed below.

6.5.1 As a recognised sole practice or the employee of a recognised sole practice

A sole practitioner is a solicitor who chooses to practise on their own. They almost certainly will employ administration staff, such as secretaries, etc and may also employ other solicitors or paralegals. However, they will own, and therefore be responsible for, the firm in its entirety.

Whilst sole practitioners used to be fairly common, there is a general trend for solicitors to practise in larger organisations. There are a number of reasons for this. One prominent reason is cost. In recent times, a solicitor's practice has become more reliant on information technology. Solicitors' firms use such equipment for researching legal issues, for running sophisticated accounts programs, and for the day-to-day management of clients' files. Both the hardware and software required to perform these operations are expensive. Accordingly, it is easier to share this cost out amongst a number of partners, rather than for one person (ie the sole practitioner) to cover the entire cost.

Another reason is practicality. When a partner, or other fee earner, in a law firm goes on holiday, their clients' matters may temporarily be taken over by another solicitor within the firm. The sole practitioner may not have this option. Accordingly, the sole practitioner may have to arrange for a locum solicitor to supervise their absence from the office.

There is also a growing trend for solicitors to specialise in one particular area of law, for example family law or insolvency. Unless the sole practitioner is running a niche practice, this option is not open to them.

Since 1 November 2015, sole practitioners have been authorised under the same authorisation rules as other types of firm. Accordingly, their organisation is authorised by the SRA as a 'recognised sole practice' rather than recognising the individual as a sole practitioner. Recognised sole practices are entitled to carry out the activities set out at **6.5.2.3**. Individual solicitors are permitted to work freelance without being authorised as a recognised sole practice under certain conditions (see **6.5.3**).

6.5.2 As a recognised body

6.5.2.1 Eligibility criteria

A 'legal services body' in which all of the managers and interest holders are legally qualified is eligible to apply for authorisation by the SRA as a recognised body. The term 'legal services body' is defined in the Administration of Justice Act 1985 and, in general terms, means where at least 75% of the body's managers are legally qualified, the proportion of shares and voting rights held by legally qualified persons is at least 75% and managers who are not legally qualified are approved by the SRA. In addition, at least one manager must be a solicitor (or registered European lawyer).

6.5.2.2 Form of a recognised body

A recognised body may take the following forms:

Partnerships

Most solicitors' firms operate as partnerships. The firm is owned and run by the partners, who then employ other solicitors and administration staff to work for them. As the partners own the firm, they are entitled to share the profits generated by the firm between them.

Some large firms have two types of partners – 'equity' partners and 'salaried' partners. A salaried partner is the first step on the partnership ladder. A salaried partner may not be entitled to share in the profits of the firm, but they will receive a salary from the firm in excess of that paid to other non-partner fee earners. After a number of years, a salaried partner may be promoted to an equity partner, whereupon they will be entitled to share in the profits of the firm.

Limited liability partnerships

An LLP is an incorporated partnership. Instead of partners, LLPs have members. The members will share in the profits of the LLP.

Companies

A solicitors' practice may be incorporated as a company registered under the Companies Act 2006. The company will have directors and shareholders like any other company.

6.5.2.3 Effect of authorisation

Once authorised (and unless the SRA specifies otherwise) the body is entitled to carry on all 'reserved legal activities' (except notarial activities). This term is defined in s 12 of the Legal Services Act 2007 and includes conducting court proceedings, the preparation/lodging of documents relating to the transfer or charging of land and the preparation of probate documents. It can also carry out immigration work (as defined in the SRA Glossary).

The business of a recognised body is limited to:

(a) professional services of the sort provided by individuals practising as solicitors and/or lawyers of other jurisdictions; and

(b) other professional services set out in annex 2 of the Rules, for example, alternative dispute resolution, estate agency and financial services.

It must at all times have an individual who is designated as its Compliance Officer for Legal Practice (COLP), and one who is designated as its Compliance Officer for Finance and Administration (COFA) and whom the SRA has approved.

6.5.2.4 Licensed bodies

The provision of legal services in England and Wales has changed radically with the introduction of alternative business structures (ABSs), a concept introduced by the Legal Services Act 2007. These structures allow non-lawyers to offer legal services alongside non-legal services. They also, for the first time, allow non-lawyers to own and invest in firms that provide legal services.

The first ABSs were licensed in early 2012 and so became 'licensed bodies' for the purposes of the SRA Authorisation and Practising Requirements. The SRA is a licensing authority for this purpose and licensed its first three ABSs in March 2012, including Co-operative Legal Services. An example of an ABS is BMA Law Ltd, which was licensed in 2015. It offers legal advice and other services to members of the British Medical Association and is run as a not-for-profit organisation. A register of ABSs can be found on the SRA website.

Eligibility criteria

For a body to be eligible to apply for authorisation as a licensed body, there must be at least one manager who is authorised by the SRA (eg, a solicitor) or another approved regulator (eg, the Council of Licensed Conveyancers (see **6.2**)) to carry on a legal activity as defined in s 12 of the Legal Services Act 2007. It also has to be a 'licensable body'. A body ('B') will be a 'licensable body' if a non-authorised person (ie, someone not authorised by the SRA or another approved regulator):

(a) is a manager of B; or

(b) is an interest holder of B (eg, a person who holds shares in it or is entitled to exercise any voting rights).

Alternatively (or in addition to the above), a body ('B') will be a licensable body if:

(a) another body ('A') is a manager of B, or is an interest holder of B; and

(b) non-authorised persons are entitled to exercise, or control the exercise of, at least 10% of the voting rights in A.

Effect of authorisation

Once authorised, a licensed body is entitled to carry out the same range of activities as a recognised body (see **6.5.2.3**) in accordance with the terms of the licence granted by the SRA. As with recognised bodies, it must at all times have individuals designated as compliance officers, but for licensed bodies these are termed a Head of Finance and Administration (HOFA) and a Head of Legal Practice (HOLP).

6.5.3 Solicitors working in unregulated entities and freelance solicitors

One of the outcomes of the SRA's 'Looking to the Future' programmes has been to liberalise the restrictions on how a solicitor can practise. With the introduction of the new SRA Standards and Regulations on 25 November 2019, solicitors are allowed to deliver 'non-reserved legal activities' to the public from within a business not regulated by a legal services regulator (see **6.2**), for example, family, employment or personal injury work and general legal advice. However, such solicitors are not permitted to hold client money (for example, damages received by a client as settlement of a case) in their own name. An example given by the Law Society of this new model is an accountancy firm expanding its business to offer legal services to its client without having to apply for licensed body authorisation as an ABS (see **6.5.2.4**).

A further change under the new SRA Standards and Regulations is that, for the first time, individual solicitors will be able to work and offer legal services to the public on a freelance basis. Such solicitors must notify the SRA of their intention to practise in that way but are not required to maintain the same level of client protection (for example, as to professional indemnity insurance) as is normally required, depending on the type of work carried out. Under the SRA Authorisation of Individuals Regulations, an individual solicitor does not have to be authorised by the SRA as a recognised sole practice if either:

(a) their practice consists entirely of carrying on activities which are 'non-reserved legal activities' (see above); or

(b) any 'reserved legal activities' are provided through an authorised body or an authorised non-SRA firm, ie a firm authorised to carry on legal services by one of the other approved legal regulators (see **6.2**), or if certain requirements are met. For example, the solicitor must have practised as a solicitor for a minimum of three years since admission, they are self-employed and practise in their own name, they must take out 'adequate and appropriate' indemnity insurance in respect of the services they provide, they do not employ anyone in connection with those services and they can only hold limited categories of client money. Solicitors whose only reserved legal activity is to administer oaths or statutory declarations outside of their normal practice are able do so without being regarded as a freelance solicitor so long as they do not charge other than the statutory fee for this service and they do not provide this service by way of business. Solicitors who provide pro bono services outside of a firm can do so without being required to notify the SRA of their intention to practise as a freelancer.

6.5.4 Employed solicitors

An 'employed solicitor' is a solicitor who is employed by a non-legal services employer. They may also be referred to as 'in-house counsel'. A number of large companies have in-house legal departments to advise on issues that arise from their business activities. Law firms often second their solicitors to work for their larger clients on a temporary basis. It is not uncommon for these solicitors to leave their law firm and go on to work for these clients on a full-time basis as employed solicitors.

Employed solicitors are subject to the same rules and regulations as solicitors in private practice, including the Code of Conduct for Solicitors.

6.5.5 Registered European Lawyers (RELs) and Registered Foreign Lawyers (RFLs)

Foreign lawyers who wish to become managers or owners of law firms authorised by the SRA must register as RFLs. This also enables them to practise in the law of their home state and advise on English and Welsh law, and to provide unreserved legal services and a limited range of reserved legal services (but they cannot practise as a sole practitioner). RFLs are subject to the Code of Conduct for Solicitors. European lawyers who wished to practise in England and Wales were able do so under an EU directive upon registering with the SRA as RELs. However, following the UK's exit from the EU, the REL regime has ended and RELs have lost their associated practice rights in the UK. This is with the exception of Swiss lawyers who, under a separate arrangement with the government, may continue to be RELs and continue to apply to become RELs. They too are subject to the Code of Conduct for Solicitors. The options for other former RELs are to provide unreserved legal activities only, to qualify as a solicitor or to register as a RFL.

6.6 LAW CENTRES

Law centres are run by solicitors, other legal advisers and community workers, to provide free legal advice and case work to disadvantaged individuals within local communities. There are 42 of these centres in England, Wales and Northern Ireland. The Law Centres Federation acts as a co-ordinating body for law centres nationally.

A solicitor who works for a law centre must still comply with all of the requirements of professional conduct, including the Code of Conduct for Solicitors. Where they are carrying out reserved legal activities and those services are being provided to the public, they must ensure that the organisation takes out and maintains adequate and appropriate indemnity insurance (see **18.5**).

6.7 LEGAL ADVICE CENTRES

A legal advice centre is a place where the public may attend for legal advice but where no case work is undertaken. In many parts of the country legal advice centres are operated by the Citizens' Advice Bureaux and solicitors will attend to give free legal advice either as honorary legal advisers, or on a rota scheme. The University of Law itself runs legal advice centres, staffed by its students under the supervision of a qualified solicitor.

6.8 DUTY SOLICITOR SCHEMES

The police station duty solicitor scheme aims to provide advice and assistance to people at police stations who otherwise would not be legally represented.

The court duty solicitor scheme aims to provide emergency legal representation at magistrates' courts on a rota basis to those who are not otherwise represented.

In both cases, the scheme is staffed by contracted solicitors on a rota basis, with fees being paid by the Legal Aid Agency.

There is also a Housing Possession Court Duty Scheme, which provides emergency on-the-day legal advice and advocacy for those facing possession proceedings in the civil courts.

SUMMARY

(1) A solicitor is said to be part of a profession. Accordingly, a higher standard of behaviour is expected of them than of a member of the public.

(2) The Solicitors Regulation Authority regulates the legal profession. It publishes rules and regulations with which a solicitor must comply in addition to the general law.

(3) These rules and regulations must be obeyed by all solicitors, whether they are members of The Law Society or not.

(4) The Law Society represents the legal profession.

(5) The legal profession is made up of a number of different types of practices.

CHAPTER 7

REGULATING THE PROFESSION

LEARNING OUTCOMES

After reading this chapter you will be able to understand:

- how the profession is regulated
- how complaints against solicitors and those who work with/for them are dealt with
- the sanctions for breaches of professional conduct
- the role of the Solicitors Disciplinary Tribunal.

7.1 INTRODUCTION

The previous chapter looked at the legal profession and the fact that a higher standard of behaviour is expected from the profession than from an ordinary citizen. This is because solicitors are often trusted with large amounts of client money and/or a client's confidential information.

This chapter will consider who is responsible for specifying the rules and requirements which ensure that this higher standard of behaviour is met, and also how these rules are enforced.

7.2 HOW THE PROFESSION REGULATES ITSELF

7.2.1 The Solicitors Regulation Authority

As was noted in **Chapter 6**, the Solicitors Regulation Authority (SRA) was created by The Law Society in January 2007 to deal with the regulation of solicitors in England and Wales. Following the introduction of reforms brought about by the Legal Services Act 2007, the SRA now regulates solicitors, the bodies in which they operate and all those working within those bodies. However, a separate organisation, the Legal Ombudsman, is often the first point of contact for the public when complaining about solicitors (see **7.5**).

The SRA was created in anticipation of the Legal Services Act 2007. As we have already seen, the Legal Services Board supervises the SRA's regulation of the profession.

The SRA can publish and enforce rules governing how solicitors behave and conduct their business. As mentioned in **Chapter 6**, since early 2012, alternative business structures (ABSs) have enabled lawyers and non-lawyers to share the management and control of businesses providing legal services. In anticipation of this, the SRA decided to undertake a complete review of the regulation framework.

The result was the SRA Code of Conduct 2011 and accompanying sets of rules and regulations which underpinned the regulation of both traditional law firms and ABSs. The 2011 Code replaced the Solicitors' Code of Conduct 2007 which was a detailed set of prescriptive rules. The 2011 Code consisted of 10 Principles and mandatory 'Outcomes' organised into sections dealing with different aspects of practice. The 'Outcomes' were supplemented by non-mandatory 'Indicative Behaviours'. These provided examples of the kinds of behaviour which tended to show whether the Outcomes had or had not been achieved and therefore whether the Principles had been complied with. Although still comparatively detailed, the 2011 Code was considerably more streamlined and reflected the SRA's stated aim to focus more on the quality of what a solicitor was delivering to the client, rather than prescribing how the solicitor reached that stage.

In 2014 the SRA began a programme of reform, 'Looking to the Future', to further review its regulatory approach. It was felt by the SRA that this was necessary in order to better reflect the realities of a rapidly changing market in legal services and to keep pace with those changes. Solicitors, firms and other organisations were looking to provide legal services to the public and businesses in new ways and using different business models, and there was a perception that the regulatory regime was still unnecessarily restrictive and bureaucratic.

After a long period of consultation, in 2018 the SRA announced its intention to introduce a shorter, simplified set of Standards and Regulations, with the stated aim of helping to 'drive high professional standards, remove unnecessary bureaucracy and free up solicitors to work in new markets'. There are currently two separate Codes of Conduct: one for solicitors and one for firms. The new Codes are considerably shorter than the 2011 Code, with a combined length of 14 pages (a reduction of more than half) and comprise sets of 'Standards' which solicitors and firms are required to uphold. New sets of rules and regulations governing the profession have also been introduced, along with a revised Enforcement Strategy and transitional arrangements for the introduction of the Solicitors Qualifying Examination. All of the defined terms contained in the Codes, rules and regulations (which appear in italics in the text) are contained in the SRA Glossary. The SRA also intends to issue guidance from time to time to supplement the Codes. The new Codes, rules and regulations came into force on 25 November 2019.

7.2.2 The SRA Standards and Regulations and approach to regulation

The SRA Standards and Regulations apply to everyone regulated by the SRA. They consist of the SRA Principles, the two Codes, the SRA Accounts Rules and a number of other rules and regulations. The SRA indicated that the 'Looking to the Future' programme had been:

> focused on delivering a regulatory regime that:
>
> - sets clear, high, professional standards for those we regulate;
> - offers flexibility, both for providers in how they structure their businesses and for consumers in how they choose to access legal services;
> - can keep up with rapid developments in the market while also maintaining appropriate protections for consumers and the public; and
> - is user friendly, so our rules can be understood by the people and businesses we regulate and their customers.

7.2.2.1 SRA Principles

There are seven Principles that are mandatory and apply to all those regulated by the SRA and to all aspects of practice. They underpin all of the Standards and Regulations.

7.2.2.2 SRA Codes of Conduct

The Code of Conduct for Solicitors, Registered European Lawyers (RELs) and Registered Foreign Lawyers (RFLs) applies to individuals authorised by the SRA to provide legal services. The introduction to the Code indicates that such individuals must exercise their judgement in applying the standards to the situations they are in and deciding on a course of action, taking into account factors such as their roles and responsibilities, areas of practice and nature of their clients.

The Code of Conduct for Firms applies to all bodies authorised by the SRA to provide legal services (see **6.5**). The introduction to the Code indicates that a serious failure to meet its standards may lead to the SRA taking regulatory action against the body itself as an entity, or its managers or compliance officers. It may also take action against employees working within the body for any breaches for which they are responsible.

Both the Principles and the Codes are underpinned by the SRA's Enforcement Strategy (see **7.6**). The provisions of the Codes are considered in detail in the following chapters. The SRA issues guidance from time to time to supplement the Standards and Regulations.

7.2.2.3 Overseas and cross-border practice

The SRA Overseas and Cross-border Practice Rules, Part A (Overseas Rules) apply to regulated individuals who are practising overseas (outside England and Wales) and to authorised bodies with an overseas practice as defined in the SRA Glossary. It contains the Overseas Principles that are a modified version of the SRA Principles (see **Chapter 8**) to take into account the different legal, regulatory and cultural context of practice in other jurisdictions. Part B (Cross-border Practice Rules) applies to European cross-border practice as defined in the SRA Glossary.

7.3 THE PERVASIVE NATURE OF CONDUCT

Conduct is said to be a pervasive subject – it cannot be viewed in isolation. It pervades all aspects of a solicitor's life and work, regardless of the area of work in which the solicitor chooses to practise. The topics covered in this book are of general application.

7.4 COMPLAINTS AGAINST SOLICITORS, AUTHORISED BODIES AND THOSE WHO WORK FOR THEM

A solicitor must ensure that they either establish and maintain, or participate in, a procedure for handling complaints in relation to the legal services they provide (Code of Conduct for Solicitors, para 8.2). A solicitor must ensure that clients are informed in writing at the time of engagement about:

(a) their right to complain about the solicitor's services and charges;
(b) how complaints may be made and to whom; and
(c) any right they have to make a complaint to the Legal Ombudsman and when they can make such complaint (Code of Conduct for Solicitors, para 8.3).

Under the SRA Transparency Rules, certain information about complaints procedures is required to be published on a firm's website, or made available upon request if the firm has no website (see **9.3.2.4**).

When a client has made a complaint, if this has not been resolved to the client's satisfaction within eight weeks following the making of a complaint, the solicitor must ensure that the client is informed in writing:

(a) of any right they have to complain to the Legal Ombudsman, the timeframe for doing so and full details of how to contact the Legal Ombudsman (see **7.5**); and

(b) if a complaint has been brought and the complaints procedure has been exhausted:
   (i) that the solicitor cannot settle the complaint;
   (ii) the name and website address of an alternative dispute resolution (ADR) approved body which would be competent to deal with the complaint; and
   (iii) whether you agree to use the scheme operated by that body. (Code of Conduct for Solicitors, para 8.4)

The Chartered Trading Standards Institute (CTSI) has approved a number of ADR entities that will be able to provide ADR services. The obligation is to provide information about an ADR approved body and to indicate whether the solicitor is agreeable to using it, and so they are not required to submit complaints to the body unless they wish to. Clients' complaints must be dealt with promptly, fairly and free of charge (Code of Conduct for Solicitors, para 8.5).

The same requirements concerning complaints apply to firms by virtue of para 7.1(c) of the Code of Conducts for Firms.

7.5 THE LEGAL OMBUDSMAN

The Legal Ombudsman for England and Wales ('LeO') became operational on 6 October 2010. It was set up by the Office for Legal Complaints under the Legal Services Act 2007 and is based in Birmingham. It deals with complaints made not only against solicitors, but also against barristers, legal executives, licensed conveyancers, notaries and patent attorneys, ABSs (amongst others), and it replaced the Legal Complaints Service (LCS) so far as complaints against solicitors are concerned. It therefore brings all legal service complaint handling under one roof for the first time.

The Scheme Rules provide that only certain types of client can complain to the LeO, including individuals, 'micro-enterprises' (broadly speaking, an enterprise with fewer than 10 staff and a turnover or balance sheet value not exceeding €2 million), charities, clubs and associations with an annual income net of tax of less than £1 million, and personal representatives or beneficiaries of a person's estate. The complaint must relate to an act/omission by the solicitor and must relate to the services which the solicitor provided. The LeO also accepts complaints in relation to services which the solicitor offered, provided or refused to provide to the complainant.

Ordinarily, the complainant cannot use the LeO unless the solicitor's complaints procedure has been used (see **7.4**), but can do so if:

(a) the complaint has not been resolved to the complainant's satisfaction within eight weeks of being made to the solicitor; or
(b) the LeO considers that there are exceptional reasons to consider the complaint sooner, or without it having been made first to the solicitor; or
(c) the LeO considers that in-house resolution is not possible due to irretrievable breakdown in the relationship between the solicitor and the complainant.

With effect from April 2023, the complaint should be brought no later than:

- one year from the act/omission; or
- one year from when the complainant should reasonably have known there was cause for complaint.

However, the LeO has a discretion to extend the time limits to the extent it considers fair. When the LeO accepts a complaint for investigation, it aims to resolve it by whatever means it considers appropriate, including informal resolution. If the LeO considers that an investigation is necessary, both parties will be given an opportunity to make representations. A hearing will be held only where the LeO considers that the complaint cannot be determined fairly without one. A 'determination' will then be made and sent to the parties and the SRA (as the approved regulator), with a time limit for response by the complainant. Once the complainant accepts or rejects the determination (or fails to respond), the solicitor and the SRA will be notified of the outcome. The details of the procedure are set out in the Scheme Rules.

The LeO's determination may direct the lawyer to:

(a) apologise;

(b) pay compensation (together with interest) for any loss suffered and/or inconvenience/ distress caused;

(c) ensure (and pay for) the putting right of any error or omission;

(d) take (and pay for) any specified action in the interests of the complainant;

(e) pay a specified amount for the costs of the complainant in pursuing the complaint;

(f) limit the solicitor's fees (including that all or part of any amount paid is refunded, with or without interest, or that all or part of the fees are remitted).

The determination may contain one or more of the above directions. There is a limit of £50,000 on the total value that may be awarded in respect of compensation and the costs in respect of (c) and (d) above. The limit does not apply to (a), (e) or (f) above, or to interest on compensation for loss suffered.

If the complainant accepts the determination, it is binding on the parties and final, and neither party may start or continue any legal proceedings in respect of the subject matter of the complaint. It may be enforced through the High Court or county court by the complainant, and the report may also be published. If the complainant rejects the determination, both parties remain free to pursue other legal remedies (such as suing for negligence).

Although the LeO has the power to adjudicate on acts/omissions as a result of which the complainant has suffered loss, in the event that the LeO considers that the resolution of a particular legal question is necessary in order to resolve a dispute, it may refer that question to the court.

Lastly, where the LeO receives a complaint which discloses any alleged professional misconduct on the part of the solicitor, it will inform the SRA.

The LeO has published an online list of lawyers or law firms involved in complaints which have led to a formal decision by the LeO since April 2012. The list is updated quarterly.

More information about the LeO may be found at <www.legalombudsman.org.uk>.

7.6 BREACH OF PROFESSIONAL CONDUCT

7.6.1 Professional misconduct

'Professional misconduct' primarily concerns breaches of the SRA's Codes of Conduct. For example, if a solicitor gave an undertaking (see **Chapter 14**) to post their client's witness statement to another solicitor on 1 May and then failed to do so, they would not have complied with para 1.3 of the Code of Conduct for Solicitors and so would be said to breach the requirements of professional conduct.

7.6.2 The Solicitors Regulation Authority

Although all complaints from the general public are received through the Legal Ombudsman, complaints primarily concerning a breach of professional conduct will be dealt with by the SRA.

The role of the SRA is to protect the public. Accordingly, having received an allegation that a solicitor or authorised body has committed professional misconduct or committed, or is responsible for, a serious breach of any of the SRA's regulatory obligations, the SRA will carry out an investigation and inform the individual or firm about whom the allegation has been made and their employer (where relevant). Notice will be given to that individual or firm setting out the allegation and facts in support and other relevant information, and inviting them to respond with written recommendations within a specified time period. The details of the process are contained in the SRA Regulatory and Disciplinary Procedure Rules.

In addition to the powers set out below, the SRA has the statutory power to carry out an intervention into a practice (see **7.8.1**).

7.6.3 SRA Enforcement Strategy

The SRA Standards and Regulations are underpinned by the SRA Enforcement Strategy, which sets out how the SRA will use its enforcement powers and what is expected of those it regulates. The Codes of Conduct place obligations on firms and individuals regulated by it to report any facts or matters which are reasonably believed to be capable of amounting to a serious breach of its standards and requirements (see **18.9.2.1**). The SRA explains that its approach to enforcement will:

(a) focus on the most serious breaches. The concept of a 'serious breach' is described in the Enforcement Strategy by reference to a number of factors, such as the nature of the allegation, intent and motivation, harm and impact and the role, experience and seniority of the individual. However, the SRA makes it clear that other factors may be taken into account and that not all of them have to be present. For example, harm to others may have less impact in relation to conduct which raises serious questions about a solicitor's integrity, and evidence of intent or harm may not be required in cases involving the use of a firm's client account as a banking facility;

(b) take account of aggravating or mitigating factors, focused on any concerns about the protection of the public interest; and

(c) place an emphasis upon the importance of constructive engagement to support firms and individuals to achieve compliance. This will in turn require an open and cooperative approach by the firms and individuals involved.

In carrying out its investigations, the SRA will consider the position of both the firm and the individuals within the firm in deciding against whom enforcement action should be taken. Action will be taken against individuals where they are personally responsible for the misconduct. However, it is likely that the SRA will take action against the firm alone (or in addition to an individual) where there is a breach of the Code of Conduct for Firms, for example, when the matter demonstrates a failure of the firm's internal systems or supervision arrangements.

7.6.4 Outcomes – professional misconduct

The enforcement action of the SRA following a finding of professional misconduct depends upon the subject of the complaint and various factors surrounding it. Its approach is set out in the SRA Enforcement Strategy in the form of an explanation of the purpose of each of its powers and the factors which may be taken into account either in favour or against its use. Some of these powers are detailed below.

The SRA may do the following:

(a) *Take no further action with or without issuing advice or a warning about future conduct*

The SRA may then decide at any stage that no further action is necessary and, in doing so, may decide to issue advice to the individual or firm against whom the allegation was made or issue a warning to them about their future conduct or behaviour. This may be appropriate to respond to a minor regulatory breach which does not require action to protect the public/public interest and is not sufficiently serious to require action to restrict their ability to practise or to rebuke or impose a financial penalty.

(b) *Impose a financial penalty or written rebuke*

The Legal Services Act 2007 gave the SRA new powers to rebuke and/or direct a solicitor or firm to pay a penalty. The maximum penalty is £25,000 (increased from £2,000 as from July 2022) for solicitors and their employees, recognised bodies and their managers or employees, £250 million for licensed bodies and £50 million for managers and employees of licensed bodies. The SRA introduced a fixed penalties scheme in May 2023 for specified breaches by firms, eg, failure to provide information or documentation to the SRA in response to requests or requirements, and certain breaches of the SRA Transparency Rules (see **9.3.2.2**). Under this scheme the penalty is £750 for a first breach and £1,500 for a subsequent breach of the same category within three years of the first penalty, or for a continuation of the first breach after the SRA issued the penalty. As from 1 January 2008, the SRA has made its regulatory decisions public. This allows the general public to search under the name of the solicitor they propose to use, to establish whether they have been subject to any regulatory sanction.

(c) *Control how the firm/regulated person practises*

The SRA may impose conditions on, or suspend, a solicitor's practising certificate, or make an order to control the person's activities in connection with legal practice. It may also impose conditions on, revoke or suspend the terms and conditions of authorisation of a firm.

(d) *Refer the matter to the Solicitors Disciplinary Tribunal*

In some cases, the SRA does not make a final decision but refers alleged misconduct to the Tribunal, where it is responsible for prosecuting the matter. The Tribunal is independent from the SRA (see **7.7** below).

(e) *Disqualify an individual from acting as a HOLP, HOFA, manager or employee of a licenced body (see* **6.5.2.1**).

Any of the decisions set out in (b) to (e) above may be made by agreement between the SRA and the individual or firm in question.

7.6.5 Distinction between complaints about professional services and negligence

A solicitor owes a duty of care to their client in the law of tort. Where the solicitor breaches this duty and the client suffers loss as a result, the solicitor may be sued by the client for negligence (see further **7.10** below).

The client does not have to suffer any loss for the Legal Ombudsman to make a determination against the solicitor arising from a complaint about the services provided by them. The mere fact that the solicitor has provided services which are not of the quality reasonably to be expected of a solicitor is enough. For example, a solicitor may miss a deadline in respect of issuing proceedings, which would then deprive their client of the opportunity to pursue the matter in court. The service provided would clearly be below what it is reasonable to expect from a solicitor. However, it would also constitute negligence, as the solicitor has breached their duty of care to their client and as a result the client has suffered a foreseeable loss (ie, the client will not be able to pursue their matter in court and recover damages).

The Legal Ombudsman and the SRA have no power to adjudicate upon issues of negligence in a legal sense, ie they are not courts and so do not have the power to adjudicate on legal issues. However, where there is an overlap between negligence and complaints about professional services, the Legal Ombudsman may adjudicate on those services where its powers of redress would be adequate to compensate the client.

7.7 THE SOLICITORS DISCIPLINARY TRIBUNAL

7.7.1 Introduction

The Solicitors Disciplinary Tribunal hears and determines applications relating to allegations of unbefitting conduct and/or breaches of the requirements of professional conduct by solicitors, RELs, RFLs, recognised bodies, managers of recognised bodies and employees of recognised bodies/sole practices (see **6.5**). Since 23 December 2011, the Disciplinary Tribunal has also dealt with appeals made in relation to ABSs and the application of the SRA Authorisation of Firms Rules. Most applications to the Disciplinary Tribunal are made on behalf of the SRA. The SRA may make an application to the Tribunal where it is satisfied that there is a realistic prospect of the Disciplinary Tribunal making an order in respect of the allegation and it is in the public interest to make the application. However, except where the Solicitors Act 1974 expressly provides otherwise, any person may make an application directly to the Tribunal without first making a complaint to the SRA.

The Disciplinary Tribunal was established by s 46 of the Solicitors Act 1974 and is independent of The Law Society and the SRA. The members of the Disciplinary Tribunal are appointed by the Master of the Rolls. There is no statutory maximum on the number of members, and at the time of writing it comprised 46 members, of whom approximately two-thirds are solicitor members and one-third lay members. The solicitor members must have been admitted for at least 10 years, and the lay members must be neither solicitors nor barristers. The Disciplinary Tribunal sits in divisions of three members, each made up of two solicitors and one lay person. The decisions of the Disciplinary Tribunal may be delivered by a single member. The standard of proof is that applicable in civil proceedings.

7.7.2 Tribunal procedure

The Disciplinary Tribunal has power, exercisable by statutory instrument, to make rules governing its procedure and practice. These rules are made with the concurrence of the Master of the Rolls. The SRA maintains a panel of solicitors in private practice who prosecute applications before the Disciplinary Tribunal on its behalf. In most cases, either the SRA's own advocates or the panel solicitor will present the case before the Disciplinary Tribunal. In complex cases, counsel may be instructed to present the case. The Disciplinary Tribunal does not have powers of investigation nor will it collect evidence itself.

7.7.3 Application to the Tribunal

An application to the Disciplinary Tribunal must be made in the prescribed form, supported by evidence (this will be prepared by the panel solicitor, or the SRA's advocate where the applicant is the SRA). The Disciplinary Tribunal will consider the application and, if satisfied that there is a case to answer, will fix a hearing date. Either party may be represented at the hearing by a solicitor or counsel. Evidence is given on oath and witnesses may be called.

The decisions of the Disciplinary Tribunal are called 'Judgments' and 'Orders'. The Order itself, together with brief reasons for the decision, is made available at the end of the hearing. The Order takes effect once it is filed with The Law Society. A detailed written Judgment containing reasons, findings and repeating the Order is made available to the parties, The Law Society and The Law Society's *Gazette* after the hearing (usually within seven weeks of the hearing).

Where (unusually) an application is made directly to the Disciplinary Tribunal, the Tribunal may refer the matter to the SRA for investigation before proceeding with the application. Where in such a case the SRA investigates the complaint and finds it to be substantiated, it may take over the application on the applicant's behalf (or deal with the matter by using the powers of the SRA discussed at **7.6** above).

7.7.4 Powers of the Tribunal

The Solicitors Act 1974, s 47 gives the Disciplinary Tribunal power to make such order against a solicitor as in its discretion it thinks fit, including the following:

(a) striking a solicitor off the roll;
(b) suspending a solicitor from practice or imposing restrictions upon the way in which a solicitor can practise;
(c) imposing an unlimited fine payable to HM Treasury;
(d) reprimanding the solicitor;
(e) requiring the payment by any party of costs or a contribution towards costs.

7.7.5 Restoration to the roll

Once struck off the roll of solicitors, the Tribunal may also restore a solicitor to the roll.

7.7.6 Appeals

Appeal from a substantive decision of the Disciplinary Tribunal is made to the Administrative Court.

7.8 OTHER POWERS OF THE SOLICITORS REGULATION AUTHORITY

7.8.1 Intervention

The aim of an intervention is to protect clients' interests and money. The practical effect of an intervention is that the practice is closed. The practice monies vest in the SRA, and the SRA takes possession of the practice documents, including client papers. An agent appointed by the SRA carries out the intervention and the practice is liable for the costs of this. An intervention may also occur where a sole practitioner is unable to continue their practice through ill health, an accident or death. The SRA Statutory Trust Rules set out what the SRA does with the monies it takes possession of following an intervention.

7.8.2 Delivery of files

In order to investigate complaints of misconduct, the SRA has the power, under s 44B of the Solicitors Act 1974, to serve a notice on a solicitor or recognised body requiring the delivery of a file or documents in the possession of the solicitor to the SRA in certain circumstances, eg, to investigate whether there has been professional misconduct. The Codes of Conduct impose an obligation to respond promptly to the SRA and provide information and documents in response to any such request (Code of Conduct for Solicitors, para 7.4 and Code of Conduct for Firms, para 3.3).

7.9 POWERS OF THE COURT

A solicitor is an officer of the court. Accordingly, the court has jurisdiction to discipline the solicitor in respect of costs within any matter before the court. The court may order the solicitor to pay costs to their own client, or to a third party (see CPR, rr 44 and 45).

7.10 NEGLIGENCE

7.10.1 Introduction

In addition to or instead of the actions that the SRA or Legal Ombudsman may take, a solicitor may be sued by their client in the tort of negligence. A solicitor owes their clients a duty of care. Where a solicitor breaches this duty, and the client suffers loss as a result of that breach, the solicitor may be sued in negligence. A solicitor may also be sued for breach of contract in these circumstances. Firms must carry compulsory indemnity insurance against such actions (see 18.4).

7.10.2 Steps to be taken on discovery of a claim

The Codes of Conduct provide that solicitors and firms must be 'honest and open' with clients if things go wrong, and if a client suffers loss or harm as a result, matters are to be put right (if possible) and a full and prompt explanation given as to what has happened and the likely impact. If requested to do so by the SRA, a solicitor or firm must investigate whether anyone may have a claim against them, provide the SRA with a report on the outcome of the investigation and notify relevant persons that they may have such a claim accordingly (Code of Conduct for Solicitors, para 7.9 and Code of Conduct for Firms, para 3.5).

In circumstances where the client notifies the solicitor of their intention to make a claim, or where the solicitor discovers an act or omission which might give rise to a claim, consideration must be given as to whether a conflict has arisen (see **Chapter 13**) and/or whether the client should be advised to obtain independent advice. It will be very rare that a conflict of interest does not arise in such a situation.

However, The Law Society's guidance states that solicitors should respond to complaints even if they believe the allegations concern negligence and a referral to the firm's insurance provider will be necessary.

Where the solicitor does cease to act for the client, and is asked to hand over the papers to another solicitor who is giving independent advice on the merits of a claim, the solicitor should keep copies of the original documents for their own reference.

7.11 THE SRA COMPENSATION FUND

The SRA Compensation Fund is maintained by the SRA under ss 36 and 36A of the Solicitors Act 1974. The Fund is governed by the SRA Compensation Fund Rules and exists as a discretionary fund of last resort to make grants to persons whose money has been stolen or otherwise not accounted for as the result of an act or omission of those regulated by the SRA, and to relieve losses for which SRA authorised bodies should have had insurance but did not (see **18.5.1**). It is funded by mandatory contributions by all solicitors and SRA authorised bodies. Applications to this Fund may be made where an individual/organisation has suffered loss due to a defaulting practitioner's dishonesty, or where the individual/organisation is suffering loss and hardship due to a defaulting practitioner's failure to account for monies they have received. The term 'defaulting practitioner' includes a solicitor, a recognised body and a licensed body (or managers, employees or owners of such bodies).

Eligibility criteria setting out those applicants that may be able to apply for a grant are set out in the SRA Compensation Fund Rules.

Individuals/organisations are not automatically entitled to a grant from the Fund (they have to apply and their claims will be assessed). The Fund does not pay out sums of more than £2 million per claim (unless the SRA is satisfied that there are exceptional circumstances in the public interest that justify a higher sum). Where there are multiple related or connected claims, the SRA may impose a cap of £5 million on the total amount paid.

Where payment is made from the Fund, the SRA will seek to be subrogated to the rights of the applicant and can therefore take proceedings against the defaulting solicitor to recover the amount paid out of the Fund. The client may be asked to exhaust any legal remedy before applying to the Fund.

The Codes of Conduct impose an obligation on solicitors and firms to ensure that clients understand the regulatory protections available to them, and this will include eligibility to claim under the Fund (Code of Conduct for Solicitors, para 8.11, which also applies to firms by virtue of para 7.1(c) of the Code of Conduct for Firms).

SUMMARY

(1) The SRA is empowered by the Solicitors Act 1974 to publish rules and requirements for the regulation of conduct of solicitors, recognised/licensed bodies, members of recognised/licensed bodies, and employees of recognised/licensed bodies/sole practices.

(2) These rules and requirements are enforced by the SRA and the Legal Ombudsman.

(3) The SRA deals with breaches of the requirements of professional conduct, whereas the Legal Ombudsman primarily deals with complaints about services provided by legal practitioners, including solicitors.

(4) The Legal Ombudsman deals with complaints relating to an act/omission by a legal practitioner and which relates to services provided by the practitioner. The client does not need to suffer any loss as a result of the service provided in order to raise the issue.

(5) The SRA may impose disciplinary sanctions for a breach of the requirements of professional conduct, or in serious cases may refer the matter to the Solicitors Disciplinary Tribunal.

(6) The Legal Ombudsman has numerous sanctions at its disposal. These include directing the solicitor to limit their fees, or directing the solicitor to compensate the client up to £50,000. The SRA/Legal Ombudsman has no power to pay compensation to the client itself.

(7) The Solicitors Disciplinary Tribunal may fine a solicitor, suspend the solicitor or, as an ultimate sanction, strike the solicitor off the roll.

(8) A solicitor will be negligent if they breach a duty of care to their client and foreseeable loss results as a consequence of that breach. Where the solicitor has been negligent, they may be sued by the client for damages.

(9) The SRA Compensation Fund is maintained by the SRA. Payment may be made from the Fund when a client has suffered loss as a result of a defaulting practitioner's act or omission or to cover claims against uninsured firms.

CHAPTER 8

THE PRINCIPLES

LEARNING OUTCOMES

After reading this chapter you will be able to understand the essentials of professional conduct.

8.1 INTRODUCTION

The profession is regulated by the Government (eg, the Proceeds of Crime Act 2002), in some instances by the Financial Conduct Authority, as well as by the Solicitors Regulation Authority (SRA) itself. As was noted in **Chapter 7,** the SRA's regulatory arrangements are contained in the Code of Conduct for Solicitors (including registered European lawyers and registered foreign lawyers), the Code of Conduct for Firms and accompanying sets of rules and regulations.

The starting point for the consideration of the regime is the SRA Principles ('the Principles'). The Principles are all-pervasive and underpin all of the SRA's regulatory arrangements.

8.2 THE PRINCIPLES

The introduction to the Principles states that:

> The SRA Principles comprise the fundamental tenets of ethical behaviour that we expect all those we regulate to uphold ...
>
> Should the Principles come into conflict, those which safeguard the wider public interest (such as the rule of law, and public confidence in a trustworthy solicitors' profession and a safe and effective market for regulated legal services) take precedence over an individual client's interests ...

The Principles are mandatory and apply to all individuals and bodies regulated by the SRA, whether traditional firms of solicitors, ABSs or in-house. They apply outside of a solicitor's practice as well as within it and, if not met, are likely to give rise to action being taken by the SRA in accordance with its Enforcement Strategy (see **Chapter 7**). Where an individual or authorised body is practising overseas, the Overseas Principles (almost identical in form) will apply instead (see **7.2.2.3**).

8.3 PRINCIPLE 1: JUSTICE AND THE RULE OF LAW

Principle 1 provides that a solicitor must act in a way that upholds the constitutional rule of law and the proper administration of justice. This applies not only in relation to clients but also to the court and to third parties with whom the solicitor may deal. A solicitor's obligations to the court and third parties are discussed in **Chapter 16**.

8.4 PRINCIPLE 2: PUBLIC TRUST

Both the SRA and The Law Society are keen to improve the reputation of the profession in the eyes of the general public. Accordingly, this Principle provides that a solicitor must act in a way that upholds public trust and confidence in the solicitors' profession and in legal services provided by those who are authorised by the SRA or another approved regulator to carry out legal activities.

For example, if a solicitor were to use money from their client account to fund the purchase of a new car then they would not only breach the SRA Accounts Rules, but they would almost certainly harm the public's trust in the profession and breach Principle 2. Cases in which solicitors have been found by the SRA or Solicitors Disciplinary Tribunal to have breached this Principle include involvement in high risk or fraudulent investment schemes, the sending of offensive and derogatory emails to the opponent's solicitor during litigation, and unintentionally sending out a large volume of misleading leaflets to the public.

A solicitor may harm the public's trust in the profession by behaviour outside of their solicitors' practice. For example, conviction of a criminal offence would lead the solicitor to breach Principle 2.

8.5 PRINCIPLE 3: INDEPENDENCE

A solicitor must act with independence. 'Independence' in this context means a solicitor's own and their firm's independence, and not merely their ability to give independent advice to a client. A solicitor should, therefore, avoid situations which might put their independence at risk, eg giving control of their practice to a third party which is beyond the regulatory reach of the SRA or other approved regulator. Independence includes independence from the client:

> A solicitor is independent of [their] client and having regard to [their] wider responsibilities and the need to maintain the profession's reputation, [they] must and should on occasion be prepared to say to [their] client 'What you seek to do may be legal but I am not prepared to help you to do it.' (*In the matter of Paul Francis Simms*, Solicitors Disciplinary Tribunal, 2002)

8.6 PRINCIPLE 4: HONESTY

A solicitor must act with honesty, and this is arguably one of the most fundamental principles underpinning the solicitors' profession. This Principle applies not only to a solicitor's professional practice but also to their life outside practice. Where a solicitor is convicted of an offence involving dishonesty, or a finding of dishonesty is made against them in disciplinary proceedings, it is likely that they will be struck off the roll of solicitors.

In *Bolton v Law Society* [1993] EWCA Civ 32 the Court made it clear that the standard of honesty required for solicitors is that they may be 'trusted to the ends of the earth'. The reason for this is because, for example, solicitors advise on and deal with substantial amounts of money or other valuable assets on behalf of their clients, they are officers of the court and they often act for clients in difficult, complex and sensitive matters.

8.7 PRINCIPLE 5: INTEGRITY

This Principle provides that a solicitor must act with integrity. This will include all professional dealings with clients, the court, other lawyers and the public. A solicitor is in a position of trust, and so must behave in an appropriate manner to reflect that position.

Whilst it may be the case that there is some overlap in the concepts of integrity and honesty (Principle 4), the SRA has split these into separate Principles to make it clear that the two requirements are not interchangeable and that it would not be necessary to show that both have been proven in the context of a breach. The concept of integrity is wider than just acting dishonestly. The court has indicated that, in the context of professional codes of conduct, the term 'integrity' refers to the higher standards which society expects from those professionals and which the professions expect from their members. Accordingly, if a solicitor were to mislead, or take unfair advantage of, clients or third parties, this could amount to a lack of integrity for the purpose of a finding by the SRA. This Principle also applies to a solicitor's private life and could be breached in circumstances in which the conduct touches realistically upon their practice of the profession (*Ryan Beckwith v SRA* [2020] EWHC 3231 (Admin)) or where the conduct is sufficiently serious enough that it calls into question whether they meet the high standards required of a member of the profession (SRA Guidance on Acting with Integrity).

8.8 PRINCIPLE 6: EQUALITY, DIVERSITY AND INCLUSION

A solicitor and a firm must act in a way that encourages equality, diversity and inclusion. This would include, for example, making reasonable adjustments to ensure that disabled clients, employees or managers are not placed at a disadvantage compared to those who are not disabled. It would also include firms treating their employees fairly, creating an inclusive workplace environment and having systems and procedures in place to address issues such as bullying, harassment, discrimination or victimisation.

In addition to complying with all anti-discrimination legislation, including the Equality Act 2010, a solicitor is under a much wider duty not to discriminate in their professional dealings. Paragraph 1.1 of the Code of Conduct for Solicitors provides that a solicitor must not unfairly discriminate by allowing their personal views to affect their professional relationships and the way in which they provide their services. The identical obligation appears at para 1.1 of the Code of Conduct for Firms. A finding of unlawful discrimination outside practice could also amount to a breach of Principles 1 and 2.

Paragraph 1.5 of the Code of Conduct for Firms requires that firms monitor, report and publish workforce diversity data as prescribed by the SRA from time to time.

8.9 PRINCIPLE 7: BEST INTERESTS OF THE CLIENT

This Principle provides that a solicitor must act in the best interests of each client. This derives from the common law, as a solicitor is said to be in a fiduciary position in relation to their client. This fiduciary relationship is considered further in **Chapter 10.**

Ensuring that clients are provided with a proper standard of service in terms of client care, competence and standard of work is also encompassed by this Principle.

For example, imagine that a client is seeking to instruct a solicitor in respect of a complex dispute regarding a contract of insurance. If the solicitor in question knows very little about insurance law then they will be unable to act in the best interests of the client. The best interests of the client in this case would be for the solicitor to refer the client to an expert (ideally this would be a colleague, or alternatively someone in another firm) in the relevant field of law.

Equally, a solicitor must consider whether they have the capacity (in terms of work volume) to take on a particular matter. If a solicitor was to take on work when they did not have the capacity to deal with it effectively, they would be unlikely to be able to provide a proper service to that client and so would not be acting in the client's best interests.

8.10 EXAMPLES

EXAMPLE 1

Question You are asked to act for Mr Monks, who wishes to sue X Co Ltd for a substantial amount of money. The case, if successful, would also generate a substantial amount of bad publicity for X Co Ltd, which would result in fewer sales for that company. You hold a significant number of shares in X Co Ltd. Should you act for Mr Monks?

Answer You need to act in the best interests of your client (Principle 7), and you must also ensure that your independence is not compromised (Principle 3). If the case is successful, this may well lead to a substantial reduction in the share price of X Co Ltd, and you would stand to lose out financially in respect of your shares.

In these circumstances, could you act in the best interests of your client (when these interests conflict with your own) and provide unbiased and objective advice?

For these reasons you must decline to act.

EXAMPLE 2

Question You are a sole practitioner who specialises in patent disputes. You are considered an expert in your field. However, you are already overworked and are struggling to keep up with your existing caseload.

You are approached by a large American company, which wishes to bring an action for a breach of one of its patents. You consider that this work would be very lucrative for your firm. Should you take on this work?

Answer You must act in the best interests of your client (Principle 7), which includes providing a proper standard of service. Your expertise is not in question. However, it would appear that you do not have the capacity to take on the work. Therefore you should decline to act, even if you would lose out on this lucrative work.

SUMMARY

(1) The SRA sets out standards and requirements concerning professional conduct.

(2) The starting point for consideration of the Codes of Conduct and the other regulatory requirements is the seven Principles.

(3) The Principles set out the fundamental requirements which all individuals and firms regulated by the SRA must satisfy in practice.

(4) Breach of the Principles may constitute professional misconduct.

CHAPTER 9

Obtaining Instructions

LEARNING OUTCOMES

After reading this chapter you will have learned about:

- the general principles of obtaining instructions
- advertising
- arrangements with third parties.

9.1 INTRODUCTION

A solicitors' firm is a business, and has much in common with any high street store. Obviously a firm of solicitors sells services rather than goods, but just like a high street store it needs a regular supply of customers to survive. Without clients, a solicitors' firm cannot generate income to pay staff salaries, the rent on premises, or for the upkeep of the office equipment. Accordingly, just like a high street store, a firm of solicitors must take steps to try to maintain and increase its market share. The two most common ways of trying to achieve this are through advertising and referrals.

9.2 GENERAL PRINCIPLES

As noted above, a solicitors' firm must take steps to try to maintain and increase its market share in order to prosper as a business. However, no matter how urgent these financial pressures may be, a solicitor must at all times comply with the requirements of professional conduct, and in particular with the Principles (see **Chapter 8**). A solicitor's primary duty is to their client. Accordingly, a solicitor must not do anything that would compromise their independence. Therefore a solicitor must not do anything, or enter into any arrangement, that would restrict them from acting in the best interests of their client.

For example, a firm of solicitors may be offered a large financial incentive to refer all clients requiring advice on financial services to a particular firm of brokers. However, the firm must not accept this offer if it would prevent the solicitors acting in the best interests of their clients.

9.3 ADVERTISING

9.3.1 Introduction

In the past, it was common for solicitors to rely on their personal reputation to obtain work. For example, a solicitor would earn a reputation for a certain type of work (eg, family law) by word of mouth in a town or city. This method of obtaining work is still valuable today. One of the best ways of attracting clients is by personal recommendation of a friend or colleague who has experienced similar problems. There are also publications, such as the Legal 500, which list the names of the 'top' solicitors in a particular legal field and geographical location.

However, in recent times firms have invested a lot of money with a view to attracting new clients through different means. For example, firms will advertise their services in local newspapers, on their websites or through promotional literature. The use of radio and television advertisements has become more frequent in recent years (particularly in the area of personal injury). The use of social media is also increasingly being embraced by the profession in order to engage with current and potential clients and to market its services.

The aim of these advertisements is to increase the general public's awareness of the firm in question, and of the services that the firm offers (ie, how the firm could help the potential client). Therefore, when a potential client needs the services of a solicitor, they will know which firm to contact.

Solicitors are generally free to publicise their practice, provided that they comply with:

(a) the general laws on advertising and data protection in force at the time. These include:
    (i) the UK Code of Non-broadcast Advertising and Direct and Promotional Marketing (CAP Code),
    (ii) the UK GDPR and the Data Protection Act 2018, and
    (iii) the Privacy and Electronic Communications (EC Directive) Regulations 2003 (SI 2003/2426);
(b) paras 8.6 to 8.11 of the Code of Conduct for Solicitors (which also apply to firms).

9.3.2 Client information and publicity under the Codes of Conduct

9.3.2.1 General

The SRA considers that there is an imbalance of knowledge between the general public on the one hand and the solicitor providing the service on the other. Accordingly, publicity in relation to the firm must be accurate and not misleading, including that relating to charges and the circumstances in which interest is payable by or to clients (Code of Conduct for Solicitors, para 8.8, and applied to firms by para 7.1(c) of the Code of Conduct for Firms). The term 'publicity' is very widely defined and includes all promotional material and activity, including the name and description of the firm, stationery, advertisements, brochures, websites, directory entries, media appearances, promotional press releases, and direct approaches to potential clients and other persons, whether conducted in person, in writing or electronic form (SRA Glossary). It does not, however, include press releases prepared on behalf of a client.

9.3.2.2 The SRA Transparency Rules

The Transparency Rules came into effect in December 2018 with the stated aim of making sure that consumers of legal services have the information they need to make an informed choice of legal services provider, including understanding what the costs may be. The Rules require all firms regulated by the SRA (and individual freelance solicitors and solicitors providing services to the public from outside SRA authorised firms – see **6.5.3**), who publish as part of their usual business the availability of any of the services specified in the Rules, to publish certain information about the costs of those services. This does not apply to publicly funded work.

The specified services in relation to individuals are:

- residential conveyancing;
- uncontested probate (where all assets are within the UK);
- motoring offences (summary only offences);
- employment tribunals (claims for unfair or wrongful dismissal);

- immigration (excluding asylum applications).

The specified services in relation to businesses are:

- debt recovery (up to £100 000);
- employment tribunals (defending claims for unfair or wrongful dismissal);
- licensing applications for business premises.

The information on the costs must include the following:

(a) the total cost of the service or, where this is not practicable, the average cost or range of costs, and details of any disbursements;
(b) the basis for the charges (including any hourly rate or fixed fees);
(c) what services are included within the displayed price and details of any services which might reasonably be expected to be included in the price but are not;
(d) the experience and qualifications of anyone carrying out the work (and their supervisors);
(e) whether VAT is payable on the fees or disbursements and, if so, if this is included in the price;
(f) typical timescales and the key stages of the matter.
(g) if conditional fee or damages-based agreements are used, the circumstances in which clients may have to make any payments themselves for the services received (including from any damages) (see **11.7.3**).

It is a requirement that the costs information outlined above must be published in a clear and accessible way and in a prominent place on the website. Where the firm or solicitor does not have a website, the Rules require that the information must be made available on request.

9.3.2.3 Unsolicited approaches

A solicitor may wish to 'cold call' individuals in order to promote their business. As mentioned above at **9.3.1**, a solicitor must comply with the general law applicable to such marketing. This means that the solicitor must have all consents required by the relevant data protection legislation for the type of marketing they intend to carry out.

In December 2024, the SRA issued a warning notice to law firms about prohibited marketing practices, such as cold calling, door knocking and directly targeted online messaging.

Data protection legislation permits all individuals to request that their details are not used for direct marketing purposes, and therefore if a solicitor receives such a request, it should be taken seriously and complied with.

In addition, the Codes of Conduct prohibit a solicitor or firm from making unsolicited approaches to individual members of the public (Code of Conduct for Solicitors, para 8.9, which applies to firms by virtue of para 7.1(c) of the Code of Conduct for Firms) which, even if permitted by law, may feel unwelcome or intrusive. The exception is in respect of current or former clients in order to advertise legal services provided by the firm or solicitor. Even in circumstances when such approaches are permitted, solicitors should still be mindful of complying with the provisions of the relevant legislation mentioned at **9.3.1**. Approaches made to current or potential business connections would not count as approaches to 'members of the public' for these purposes and so would be permitted provided that they complied with the general law.

Solicitors are permitted to advertise their services to the public in general, as long it is done in a non-targeted way. For example, adverts placed in local newspapers, radio, TV, online or billboards are allowed. So too is sending out leaflets to people's homes (but not if distributed only to selective homes or individuals based on information known about them, for example). However, in its December 2024 warning notice, the SRA warned firms to make sure that marketing and recruitment materials used to attract clients do not have the potential to mislead consumers.

9.3.2.4 Letterheads, websites and emails

The Code of Conduct for Solicitors provides that a solicitor must not be a manager, employee, member or interest holder of a business that has a name which includes the word 'solicitors' or describes its work in a way that suggests that it is a solicitors' firm unless it is a body authorised by the SRA (para 5.4).

Likewise, there is an obligation to ensure that clients understand whether and how the services provided are regulated, including explaining which activities will be carried out as a person authorised by the SRA, any services which may be regulated by another approved regulator (see **6.2**) and ensuring that no business or employer is represented as being regulated by the SRA when it is not (Code of Conduct for Solicitors, para 8.10 and Code of Conduct for Firms, para 7.1(c)).

The Transparency Rules (see **9.3.2.2**) require that a body authorised by the SRA must display in a prominent place on its website its SRA number and the SRA's 'digital badge' (a clickable logo which confirms that it is regulated and links to information on the protections this offers its clients). The website must also publish the firm's complaints handling process, details about how to complain to the SRA and how to complain to the Legal Ombudsman (see **7.5**). In addition, its letterhead and emails must show its SRA authorisation number and the words 'authorised and regulated by the Solicitors Regulations Authority'.

9.3.2.5 Social media

Whilst there are no specific provisions in the Codes that apply to the use of social media by solicitors and firms, regard must still be had to the Principles and the relevant standards in the Codes when using social media as a marketing tool. For example, if a relationship with a client is established and continued via social media, the solicitor must still comply with the standards in the Code of Conduct for Solicitors on service and competence (see **Chapter 10**) and with regard to confidentiality and disclosure (see **Chapter 12**). A Law Society practice note on social media gives as an example a solicitor commenting on X (formerly Twitter) that he is in a certain location at a certain time which may result in him unintentionally disclosing that he is working with a client, so breaching the duty to keep the affairs of clients confidential (para 6.3 of both Codes).

Where a solicitor is using social media for personal use, they must still be mindful that they could be associated with views expressed, comments and activities that are available to view by a wider audience online, and so should consider compliance with, for example, Principle 2, ie behaving in a way that maintains the trust the public places in the profession (see **Chapter 8** and **16.5.4**).

9.3.2.6 Inducements

Under the Criminal Justice and Courts Act 2015, solicitors and firms are banned from offering a benefit to a potential client where the benefit amounts to an inducement relating to a personal injury claim and is not related to the provision of legal services in connection with the claim. Firms considering whether to offer inducements or incentives to potential clients in other types of matters will need to ensure that the Principles and Standards under the Codes of Conduct are adhered to and that the services provided by the firm are not linked to the inducements offered. In particular, it would be necessary to ensure that an own interest conflict, or a significant risk of one, is avoided by such an offer (see **13.5**).

9.4 ARRANGEMENTS WITH THIRD PARTIES

9.4.1 Introduction

In addition to targeting the general public, a solicitor may also wish to enter into an agreement with a third party to introduce clients to the solicitor. For example, a solicitor could enter into an agreement with a local estate agent, so that the agent will 'introduce' to the solicitor's firm any potential house buyers looking for a solicitor to complete their conveyancing, or with a claims management company to 'introduce' clients who wish to claim for losses arising from a motor vehicle accident. Likewise, the solicitor may want to enter into an agreement to refer clients to a third party, such as another lawyer or a financial services provider. Any such arrangement must comply with the Principles (the most relevant being Principles 2, 3, 6 and 7) and the relevant paragraphs of the Codes of Conduct.

9.4.2 Referrals, introductions and fee-sharing

As the relationship between a solicitor and their client should be built on trust, it follows that any arrangement with a third party should not jeopardise that trust and that a solicitor must not abuse their position by taking unfair advantage of clients or others (para 1.2 of both Codes of Conduct).

In respect of any referral of a client by a solicitor to a third party or of any third party introducing business to the solicitor, clients must be informed of any financial or other interest which a solicitor, their business or employer has in referring the client to another person/body, or which an introducer has in referring the client to the solicitor (Code of Conduct for Solicitors, para 5.1(a)). The term 'introducer' in the Code is defined in the SRA Glossary as 'any person, business or organisation who or that introduces or refers clients to your business, or recommends your business to clients or otherwise puts you and clients in touch with one another'. A solicitor must not receive payments relating to a referral or make payment to an introducer in respect of clients who are the subject of criminal proceedings (Code of Conduct for Solicitors, para 5.1(d)). Any client referred to the solicitor by an introducer must not have been acquired in a way which would breach the SRA's regulatory arrangements if the person acquiring the client were regulated by the SRA (Code of Conduct for Solicitors, para 5.1(e)). So, for example, the client must not have been acquired as a result of 'cold calling' (see **9.3.2.3**). The SRA Warning Notice, 'Marketing your services to members of the public', says that the solicitor must be able to demonstrate that the third party did not acquire the client through prohibited means and must make sure that the third party is aware of the solicitor's regulatory duties and how these impact on the way that the third party works.

Fee-sharing would occur if a solicitor made a payment to a third party in respect of a percentage of the solicitor's gross or net fees for a particular period. Clients must be informed of any fee-sharing arrangement that is relevant to their matter, and the fee-sharing agreement must be in writing (Code of Conduct for Solicitors, para 5.1(b) and (c)).

The provisions in the Code of Conduct for Solicitors on introductions, referrals and fee-sharing apply equally to firms by virtue of para 7.1(b) of the Code of Conduct for Firms.

9.4.3 Referral fees

In March 2004 the ban on solicitors paying referral fees to third parties introducing clients to solicitors was lifted. These arrangements were used mainly in areas such as personal injury and conveyancing. After some uncertainty as to their future, the SRA announced in December 2007 that referral fees would continue to be permitted. However, under the Legal Aid, Sentencing and Punishment of Offenders Act 2012 (LASPO), the payment or receipt of referral fees in claims for damages following personal injury or death has been prohibited. LASPO also prohibits payment for other claims for damages arising from the same circumstances. For example, if a personal injury claim resulting from a road traffic accident is referred to a solicitor, together with a claim in relation to uninsured loss recovery resulting from the same accident, the solicitor could not pay a referral fee in relation to either claim.

The SRA has warned solicitors that they should only deal with claims management companies that are appropriately regulated (ie, by the Financial Conduct Authority). It is envisaged, however, that the ban on referral fees for personal injury work will result in a reduction in the claims management company industry and so result in a loss of client leads which firms previously derived from this source.

In the Codes of Conduct, where it appears to the SRA that a solicitor has made or received a 'referral fee', the payment will be treated as such a fee unless the solicitor is able to show otherwise (Code of Conduct for Solicitors, para 5.2 and Code of Conduct for Firms, para 7.1(b)). The term 'referral fee' in this context is defined in the SRA Glossary by reference to the relevant provisions of LASPO and so, as outlined above, refers to prohibited fees in personal injury cases by 'regulated persons', namely solicitors, barristers, claims management companies and insurers.

9.5 EXAMPLES

EXAMPLE 1

Question: Your firm is conducting a marketing drive. Your marketing department has identified a number of former clients who have not used your firm for a number of years. The marketing department suggests that the firm telephones these former clients to try to convince them to use the firm again.

Your marketing department also suggests a campaign of door-to-door visits on a nearby new housing development where a representative of the firm would tell the home owners about the services provided by your firm's private client and property teams and take their contact details for a follow-up email.

Can your firm do this?

Answer: Your firm must comply with the general law concerning advertising and publicity and also with the Codes of Conduct. Whilst a firm must not make unsolicited telephone calls to members of the public, it may do so to current and former clients (Code of Conduct for Solicitors, para 8.9 and Code of Conduct for Firms, para 7.1(c)). Therefore the firm can cold call former clients so long as it complies with the provisions of the data protection legislation and the general law. The firm should have given its clients (and former clients) an opportunity to refuse to receive direct marketing, such as cold calls. If this process has been carried out, the firm must not call those former clients who have withheld their consent.

The proposed campaign of door-to-door visits would amount to unsolicited approaches to members of the public and so would breach the Codes.

EXAMPLE 2

Question: You are contacted by Monks and Co, a well-established local firm of independent financial advisers. Monks and Co proposes entering into an agreement whereby you refer to it all of your clients seeking advice about insurance products. In return, Monks and Co will pay you a small commission for each client referred.

Can you accept this proposition?

Answer You would be able to enter into such an agreement so long as you are satisfied that in referring clients to Monks and Co you are acting with independence (Principle 3), so that, for example, you do not feel that your freedom to refer clients to other providers of financial advice is then restricted. In making the referrals, you must also be acting in the best interests of each client (Principle 7). Clients must be informed of the commission arrangement with Monks and Co (Code of Conduct for Solicitors, para 5.1(a) and (c)). The commission would not be a referral fee of a type prohibited by the SRA (para 5.2). You would also need to account properly to the client for any financial benefit (ie the commission) you receive as a result of that client's instructions (para 4.1) (see **11.3**).

The topic of financial services and solicitors is considered further in **Chapter 17.**

SUMMARY

(1) Solicitors should always be independent when giving advice to a client and ensure that their clients' interests are protected.

(2) Solicitors are free to publicise their practice, provided that they comply with the general law on advertising in force at the time and with the relevant standards of the Codes of Conduct.

(3) A solicitor's promotional material must not be misleading or inaccurate.

(4) Solicitors may enter into a financial arrangement with an introducer, refer clients to third parties and enter into fee-sharing arrangements, provided that they comply with paras 5.1 and 5.2 of the Code of Conduct for Solicitors (which also apply to firms by virtue of para 7.1(c) of the Code of Conduct for Firms).

(5) A solicitor may introduce clients to third parties (such as a financial services provider) or accept referrals from the third party (such as an estate agent) provided they comply with paras 5.1 and 5.3 of the Code of Conduct for Solicitors (which also apply to firms by virtue of para 7.1(c) of the Code of Conduct for Firms).

CHAPTER 10

THE RETAINER

LEARNING OUTCOMES

After reading this chapter you will have learned about:

- accepting and declining instructions
- the duties owed to the client
- ending the relationship.

10.1 INTRODUCTION

The contract between a solicitor and their client is often referred to as a 'retainer'. As with any other contract, the relationship between the solicitor and the client is governed by the general law. However, in addition to considering the general law, a solicitor must also comply with obligations placed upon them by the requirements of professional conduct.

10.2 ACCEPTANCE OF INSTRUCTIONS

10.2.1 Terms of the retainer

As noted above, many of the terms of the retainer will be implied into the contract either by the law, or by the requirements of professional conduct. Some of these terms are considered below. However, the solicitor must ensure that the more basic terms of the retainer are understood by the client. One such critical issue is to ensure that the client understands exactly what work the solicitor has agreed to undertake. Although not required by the Codes, it would be good practice for a solicitor to send a letter to their client at the start of the transaction, confirming to the client exactly what they understand their instructions to be (and also what action, if any, the client must take), along with certain other information to show compliance with the Standards in the Codes of Conduct and the Principles (see **Chapter 11**). This will help to avoid any misunderstandings at a later date, such as where a client makes a complaint against the solicitor for their failure to complete a certain task which the solicitor was unaware they had been instructed to complete.

It is important that a client's expectations are managed at an early stage of the solicitor–client relationship. If the client knows what the solicitor will and will not be doing for them, there will be less scope for problems to arise at a later date.

10.2.2 Identity of the client

A solicitor must identify whom they are acting for in relation to any matter (Code of Conduct for Solicitors, para 8.1, which also applies to firms by virtue of para 7.1(c) of the Code of Conduct for Firms). For example, a solicitor may be instructed by a director of a company concerning the debts of that company. The solicitor will be obliged to clarify whether they are being instructed by the director in her personal capacity, or by the director on behalf of the company (ie, the company will be the client, not the director personally). As noted below, a solicitor owes many duties to their client, and they can ensure that these duties are met only if they know the identity of their client.

A solicitor is also under a separate duty to obtain 'satisfactory evidence' of the identity of their clients (ie, are they who they say they are?). This obligation is imposed by the Money Laundering, Terrorist Financing and Transfer of Funds (Information on the Payer) Regulations 2017 (SI 2017/692) and is considered further at **15.2.3**.

10.2.3 Third party instructions

A solicitor may receive instructions from a third party on behalf of a client. For example, a client's daughter may seek to instruct a solicitor on behalf of her elderly mother, as the mother may have mobility problems in attending the solicitor's office.

Alternatively, a solicitor may receive instructions from one client purporting to instruct the solicitor on behalf of a number of clients. For example, a solicitor may be instructed by Mr Smith to purchase a property on behalf of Mr Smith and Mr Brown.

The Codes of Conduct provide that a solicitor only act for clients on instructions from the client, or from someone properly authorised to provide instructions on their behalf (Code of Conduct for Solicitors, para 3.1 and Code of Conduct for Firms, para 4.1). Therefore, in the examples given above, the solicitor must satisfy themselves that the daughter has the proper authorisation to provide instructions for her mother and that Mr Smith has authority to provide instructions on a joint basis for himself and Mr Brown.

When considering whether to accept instructions from or on behalf of a number of clients, the solicitor must take into account any actual or potential conflicts of interests (see **Chapter 13**).

10.3 REFUSAL OF INSTRUCTIONS TO ACT

10.3.1 Introduction

Solicitors firms spend thousands of pounds in attempting to attract new clients to their business. They will also try to ensure that they retain their existing clients. However, there will be some clients for whom a solicitor will decline to act. For example, a solicitor may decline to act for a client who is known for not paying their legal fees.

Generally, like any other business, a solicitor is free to decide whether to accept or decline instructions to act for a particular client. However, this discretion is limited by the requirements of professional conduct set out in the Codes of Conduct, and also by the general law. A solicitor must not unfairly discriminate by allowing their views to affect their professional relationships and the way in which they provide their services (para 1.1 of both Codes of Conduct), and so they would be in breach of the Code if, by refusing to accept a client's instructions, it could be shown that the solicitor was unfairly discriminating against that client because of, for example, the client's race or gender.

10.3.2 Situations where a solicitor may or has to decline to act

10.3.2.1 Duress or undue influence and vulnerable clients

If a solicitor has reason to suspect that the instructions received from a client, or someone authorised on their behalf, do not represent the client's wishes, they must not act unless they have satisfied themselves that they do (Code of Conduct for Solicitors, para 3.1 and Code of Conduct for Firms, para 4.1). There may be situations, therefore, where a solicitor has reasonable grounds for believing that the instructions are affected by duress or undue influence. The elderly, those with language or learning difficulties or those with mental health issues are particularly susceptible to undue pressure from others. In circumstances in which a solicitor suspects a client's instructions are tainted by duress or undue influence, it would be necessary for them to take appropriate steps to satisfy themselves that the instructions represent the client's genuine wishes, eg by arranging to interview the client alone, away from any third party such as a relative. If, having taken such steps, they are not satisfied, they should decline to act for that client. Alternatively, in circumstances in which the solicitor has concerns that the client is under duress, the solicitor may seek assistance from the High Court to provide its protection under its inherent jurisdiction.

In circumstances where the solicitor has legal authority to act for a client notwithstanding that it is not possible to obtain or ascertain the instructions of their client, then they are subject to the overriding obligation to protect their client's best interests (Code of Conduct for Solicitors, para 3.1 and Code of Conduct for Firms, para 4.1). This would include, for example, where a solicitor has been authorised by the Court of Protection to act for a client who lacks mental capacity under the Mental Capacity Act 2005.

10.3.2.2 Where a solicitor cannot act in the client's best interests

A solicitor must act in the best interests of each client (Principle 7), and so a solicitor should not act where there is an own interest conflict or a client conflict (see **Chapter 13**), or where the solicitor holds 'material' confidential information for an existing or former client which would be relevant to a new instruction (see **Chapter 12**), except when the Codes permit.

A solicitor must ensure that the service provided to clients is competent and delivered in a timely manner and must consider and take account of the client's attributes, needs and circumstances (Code of Conduct for Solicitors, paras 3.2 and 3.4). The same obligations are placed on firms under para 4.2 of the Code of Conduct for Firms. Accordingly, the solicitor must consider the level and quality of service they will be able to provide to the client. Every solicitors' firm will have a maximum capacity of work with which the firm can deal effectively at any one time. If the solicitor or firm does not have the time or resources to deal with the client's matter then it would not be in that client's best interests to accept the instruction.

Equally, if a solicitor is approached by a prospective client about an area of law about which the solicitor knows very little, it would be in the client's best interests to be referred to another solicitor or firm which possesses the requisite knowledge.

10.3.2.3 Gifts from a client

There may be situations where a client proposes to make a gift of a significant amount or leave a legacy in a will to a solicitor, a member of the solicitor's family or to a member of the solicitor's firm or that person's family. This can give rise to an own interest conflict or a significant risk of one arising under para 6.1 of the Codes of Conduct (see **13.5**). The question arises, therefore, as to when it would be appropriate to take such instructions and when it would be appropriate to decline instructions or cease to act if you have already taken instructions or advise the client to take independent legal advice.

In terms of a client wishing to leave a legacy in a will to the solicitor (or someone associated with them), the SRA Guidance on the Drafting and Preparation of Wills provides that, in such circumstances, a solicitor should satisfy themselves that the client has first taken independent legal advice when asked to draft a will where the client wishes to make a gift of 'significant value'. This includes situations in which the intended gift 'is of significant value in relation to the size of the client's overall estate, but also where the gift is of significant value in itself'. If the client does not agree to take legal advice, the SRA advises that the solicitor will usually need to cease acting.

The Law Society has issued a practice note which offers further guidance as to what is likely to be considered a gift of 'significant value'. It advises that a solicitor should carefully consider any gift to determine whether it may be considered significant in the particular circumstances, and that it can be assumed that it would be significant if:

(a) it is worth more than 1% of the client's current estimated net estate;
(b) it might become valuable at some point, especially after the death of the client;
(c) it provides a benefit to an individual which is more valuable than their relationship to the deceased reasonably justifies.

The note advises solicitors, before preparing a will in such circumstances, to consult the firm's compliance officer for legal practice (COLP) or a senior practice member, who will then consider the potential conflict of interests (see **Chapter 13)** and the best interests of the client, and to place a written summary of the decision with the file. The SRA Guidance on the Drafting and Preparation of Wills provides an example of a situation where it may be still appropriate to draft the will even if the client has not received independent legal advice. This is where the solicitor is drafting wills for their own parents and the survivor of them wishes to leave the residuary estate to the solicitor and the solicitor's siblings in equal shares.

10.3.2.4 Compliance with the law and the Codes

In deciding whether to act (or terminate their instructions), a solicitor must act in a way that upholds the constitutional principle of the rule of law, and the proper administration of justice (Principle 1). For example, a solicitor instructed on the sale of a property might be instructed to tamper with a surveyor's report and send it to the buyer in order to hide some defects in the structure of the property. If the solicitor agreed, they would be participating in a fraud against the buyer. Clearly instructions must be refused here.

Where a solicitor becomes aware that their client is involved in criminal conduct, the solicitor must consider very carefully the obligations placed on them by the Proceeds of Crime Act 2002 (see **Chapter 15**). The Civil Liability Act 2018 bans solicitors from inviting a person to offer, offering, making or accepting a payment in settlement of road traffic accident-related whiplash claims without a medical report, regardless of the claim value. Failure to comply with the ban will be treated by the SRA as potential misconduct.

Examples of instructions which would not comply with the Codes are where:

(a) there is, or is likely to be, a conflict of interest between the solicitor and their client, or between two or more clients (see **Chapter 13**);
(b) the solicitor holds material confidential information for an existing or former client which would be relevant to a new instruction (see **Chapter 12**);
(c) the client instructs the solicitor to mislead or deceive the court (see **16.1.1**).

A solicitor must also be able to justify their decisions and actions in order to demonstrate compliance with their obligations under the SRA's regulatory arrangements (Code of Conduct for Solicitors, para 7.2), which includes under the Codes of Conduct.

10.4 DUTIES TO THE CLIENT DURING THE RETAINER

10.4.1 Introduction

A solicitor will owe the client a number of duties throughout the retainer. These duties are prescribed by the common law and the requirements of professional conduct. Some of these duties (such as the duty of confidentiality) will continue even after the retainer has been terminated. The following are examples of some of the duties that solicitors owe to their clients.

10.4.2 Duty of reasonable care and skill

In addition to the solicitor's duty of care in common law, s 13 of the Supply of Goods and Services Act 1982 provides that a supplier of services will carry out those services with reasonable care and skill. This term is implied into the retainer between a solicitor and their client, and therefore the solicitor may be sued for a breach of contract if the term is breached. However, this implied term does not apply to advocacy services provided before a court, tribunal, inquiry or arbitrator (Supply of Services (Exclusion of Implied Terms) Order 1982 (SI 1982/1771), art 2).

Nevertheless, the solicitor may be sued for negligence in both contentious and non-contentious proceedings. The House of Lords removed an advocate's protection from negligence claims in *Arthur JS Hall & Co v Simons* [2002] 1 AC 615. Accordingly, a solicitor who acts as an advocate may be sued in the tort of negligence if they breach their duty of care to their client within court proceedings.

In certain circumstances, a solicitor may owe a duty of care to third parties, such as beneficiaries of an estate (see **16.5.6**).

10.4.3 Duty to act in the best interests of the client

As has been noted throughout this Part, a solicitor must act in the best interests of their client. This duty is taken from the Principles, and also from common law.

The solicitor–client relationship is said to be a 'fiduciary relationship'. Under the common law, a fiduciary relationship is one where one party must act in the best interests of the other party. This means that the solicitor must put the interests of their client before their own. Another example of a fiduciary relationship is the doctor–patient relationship. Directors of a company also owe a fiduciary duty to the company itself.

Where such a relationship exists, one party may not make a secret profit at the expense of the other party. For example, a solicitor may be paid commission, say £50, when referring a client to a third party such as an accountant (see **Chapter 9**). As the solicitor owes a fiduciary duty to their client, this £50 must be accounted for to the client. This duty to account is also mirrored by the Codes (see **11.14**). A solicitor is also under a more general obligation to safeguard money and assets entrusted to them by clients (and others) (Code of Conduct for Solicitors, para 4.2, and mirrored in para 5.2 of the Code of Conduct for Firms).

Equally, there is a presumption of undue influence where a fiduciary duty exists. This means that in any dealings between a solicitor and their client, there will be a rebuttable presumption that the solicitor has exercised undue influence in persuading the client to enter into that dealing. In order to rebut this presumption, the solicitor would need to show that such influence had not been exercised, for example by making a full disclosure of all relevant facts, ensuring that the client took independent legal advice and understood the transaction, and ensuring that all dealings were fair and at arm's length.

10.4.4 Taking advantage of the client

As a result of the fiduciary relationship between the solicitor and client, the solicitor must not take advantage of the client. This is reflected in Principle 5, which provides that a solicitor must act with integrity, and in para 1.2 of both Codes of Conduct: 'You [must] not abuse your position by taking unfair advantage of clients or others.'

10.4.5 Confidentiality

A solicitor and their firm have a duty to keep the affairs of their client confidential. This duty continues even after the retainer has been terminated. This topic is considered in detail in **Chapter 12**.

10.4.6 Disclosure

A solicitor owes the client a duty to disclose all relevant information to the client, regardless of the source of this information. This topic is considered in detail in **Chapter 12**.

10.4.7 Client care and costs

A solicitor is obliged to provide information on costs – at the time of engagement and, when appropriate, as the client's matter progresses – and other information to enable the client to make informed decisions. A solicitor must also deal with the client's matter in a competent and timely manner and taking account of the client's attributes, needs and circumstances (see **Chapter 11**).

10.5 THE CLIENT'S AUTHORITY

A solicitor may derive authority from the retainer to bind the client in certain circumstances. This authority can be limited expressly by the client in the terms of the retainer. However, the solicitor should never seek to rely on this implied authority to bind the client. Express instructions should always be taken from the client prior to the solicitor taking any step in the proceedings or matter.

10.6 TERMINATION OF THE RETAINER

10.6.1 Introduction

As with any contractual relationship, the retainer may be terminated by either party, or by the general law.

10.6.2 Termination by the client

A client may terminate the retainer at any time for any reason. However, the client is likely to be liable to pay the solicitor's fees for work done up until the point of termination. A solicitor may require their costs to be paid prior to forwarding the file to the client (see **10.7**).

10.6.3 Termination by the solicitor

In contrast to the right of a client to terminate the retainer at will, a solicitor must consider whether they will be able justify a decision to terminate the retainer having regard to their obligations under the SRA's regulatory arrangements (including the Principles and the Codes of Conduct) (see Code of Conduct for Solicitors, para 7.2). Although there are no express references to this particular issue in the Codes, the following examples were provided by the SRA in a former version of the Code of Conduct and may still provide useful guidance as to what is likely to be considered a good reason for terminating the retainer:

(a) the solicitor has to terminate the retainer because the instructions would involve the solicitor in a breach of the law or the requirements of professional conduct;

(b) the solicitor cannot obtain proper instructions from the client;

(c) there has been a breakdown in confidence within the relationship between the solicitor and client (eg, the client is not willing to accept the advice of the solicitor).

Good practice dictates that a client be provided with reasonable notice of termination. As to what would amount to reasonable notice will depend on the circumstances. However, previous guidance from the SRA stated that it would rarely be acceptable to stop acting for the client immediately before a court hearing, where it would be impossible for the client to find someone else to represent them at the hearing.

10.6.4 Termination by law

The retainer will be terminated automatically by law in certain circumstances. These include where the solicitor is declared bankrupt or either party loses mental capacity after the retainer has commenced.

Where the solicitor does not practise as a sole practitioner, their being declared bankrupt or losing mental capacity will have little practical effect, as one of their partners or other colleagues will take over the client's matter.

Where the client loses mental capacity, the solicitor should have regard to the Mental Capacity Act 2005 and its accompanying Code.

10.6.5 Responsibilities on termination

As a matter of good practice, a solicitor should confirm to the client in writing that the retainer has been terminated, explain, where appropriate, the client's possible options for pursuing the matter, and take steps to deal with any property of the client which may be held by the solicitor. For example, the solicitor may be holding client monies which, subject to the position on costs, should be returned to the client as soon as possible, together with any interest. The solicitor will also have to deal with the client's paperwork. Where the client's matter is ongoing and the client has instructed another firm of solicitors, it may be advisable to retain a copy of the file. The solicitor should also consider the client's rights and the solicitor's obligations under the Data Protection Act 2018. The Act requires that any personal data in those files are retained only for the purpose for which they were collected, although this will not prevent the solicitor from retaining a copy of the file in order to defend themselves from any future claims of negligence. Firms need to comply with the data protection regime set out in the UK GDPR.

10.7 LIENS

A lien is a legal right that allows a creditor to retain a debtor's property until payment. Accordingly, a solicitor may hold on to property already in their possession, such as a client's papers, until their proper fees are paid. The SRA's guidance in a former Code of Conduct suggested that, where possible, an undertaking to pay the costs should be accepted instead of the solicitor retaining the client's papers under a lien.

The court has the power under s 68 of the Solicitors Act 1974 to order the solicitor to deliver up any papers to the client. The SRA also has a similar power where it has intervened in a solicitor's practice (see **7.8.1**).

Alternatively, a solicitor may apply to court under s 73 of the Solicitors Act 1974 for a charging order over any personal property of the client recovered or preserved by the solicitor within litigation proceedings. The charging order may cover the solicitor's taxed costs for those proceedings.

10.8 EXAMPLES

EXAMPLE 1

Question You are instructed by Mr Evans on behalf of his elderly mother. He instructs you to transfer his mother's house into his name. He gives you a letter purportedly from his mother confirming these instructions. He explains that her age means that she is unable to visit your office to speak with you in person.

Should you accept these instructions?

Answer There are two issues here. First, as you have received these instructions from a third party, you should satisfy yourself that Mr Evans has the proper authority to give those instructions.

Secondly, the circumstances (Mrs Evans' age, the facts that she is gifting away a valuable asset and her absence from your office) should give reasonable grounds to suspect duress or undue influence. You should therefore not act for Mrs Evans without satisfying yourself that the instructions represent her wishes (Code of Conduct for Solicitors, para 3.1). To do so, you would need to interview Mrs Evans away from her son and assess whether you believe she genuinely wishes to transfer her house to her son.

Where there is no actual evidence of undue influence but the client wants to act against his or her best interests, it would be advisable to explain the consequences of the instructions and ask the client whether he or she wishes to proceed, and for this advice and consent to be documented.

EXAMPLE 2

Question — You have acted for Ms Caldicott for a number of years, and consider her to be a good client. You are currently dealing with the sale of one of her businesses. She contacts you to express her disappointment that your firm has recently been acting in defence of a large corporation accused of polluting a local river. On this basis she demands that you transfer her files to Jones & Co Solicitors. You do not consider that you have done anything wrong and wish to dispute Ms Caldicott's right to transfer solicitors. Can you do this?

Answer — No. A client can terminate at any time and for any reason. Whilst you have a right to claim a lien over Ms Caldicott's files until any outstanding bills are paid, previous SRA guidance suggests that you should accept an undertaking from Jones & Co to pay your costs rather than exercising this right.

SUMMARY

Acceptance of instructions

(1) The solicitor must ensure that the client understands the extent of the retainer between the solicitor and client.

(2) The solicitor must only act for clients on the instructions from the client, or someone properly authorised to provide instructions on their behalf. If the solicitor has reason to suspect that the instructions do not represent their client's wishes, they should take steps to satisfy themselves that they do.

Refusal of instructions

(1) A solicitor's ability to accept or decline instructions is limited by the general law and the requirements of professional conduct.

(2) A solicitor must not unfairly discriminate when refusing instructions to act for a client.

Duty to the client during the retainer

(1) The solicitor has a duty to act with reasonable skill and care when providing services (such as legal advice).

(2) The solicitor has a fiduciary duty to act in the best interests of the client. Accordingly, a solicitor must not take advantage of their client.

(3) A solicitor owes various duties to the client throughout the retainer, including a duty of confidentiality and a duty of disclosure.

(4) A solicitor should not seek to rely on any implied authority to bind their client.

Termination of the retainer

(1) The retainer may be terminated by either party, or by law.

(2)	The solicitor's right to terminate the retainer is restricted by the law and the requirements of professional conduct.
(3)	As a matter of good practice, a solicitor should deal promptly with the papers and property of the client within their possession. In certain circumstances a solicitor may exercise a lien over this property until their fees are paid.

CHAPTER 11

CLIENT CARE AND COSTS

LEARNING OUTCOMES

After reading this chapter you will be able to understand:

- the obligation to give the client information
- the controls which exist over the charges solicitors may make to their clients
- how a client may challenge the charges made by a solicitor
- the need to account to clients for commissions received.

11.1 INTRODUCTION

The marketplace for legal services is a very competitive area. From high street firms to large city firms, the competition to work for the best clients in a particular matter is often fierce.

Firms often spend large amounts of money on marketing budgets to attract clients. It is therefore in a firm's best interests to try to keep its clients from instructing other firms by providing a high level of service.

Where a client becomes dissatisfied with their solicitor, it is often due to a lack of information concerning issues such as costs or how the matter is progressing. Accordingly, the Code of Conduct for Solicitors and the Code of Conduct for Firms set out the minimum standards of service and competence that a client can expect to receive. This links to Principle 7: a solicitor must act in the best interests of each client. This includes providing a proper standard of service to their clients. More generally, the Codes of Conduct provide that a solicitor must not abuse their position by taking advantage of clients (para 1.2 of both Codes) or mislead or attempt to mislead them either by their own acts or omissions or allowing or being complicit in the acts or omissions of others (para 1.4).

The Codes are not prescriptive on how a firm should comply with the obligations relating to a standard of service, as different types of legal services providers will have in place differing client care systems. Also, the introduction to the Code of Conduct for Solicitors makes clear that a solicitor must exercise their judgement in applying the standards bearing in mind their areas of practice and the nature of their clients. So, for example, a client providing instructions on a conveyancing matter is unlikely to need the same information as a sophisticated commercial client who instructs the firm on a regular basis.

11.2 CLIENT CARE

11.2.1 Clients able to make informed decisions

A solicitor must give clients information in a way they can understand and ensure that clients are in a position to make informed decisions about the services they need, how their matter will be handled and the options available to them (Code of Conduct for Solicitors, para 8.6, which also applies to firms by virtue of para 7.1(c) of the Code of Conduct for Firms).

As part of this process, therefore, it may be appropriate for the solicitor, for example, to discuss whether the potential outcomes of the client's matter are likely to justify the expense or risk involved, including any risk of having to pay someone else's legal fees. A common complaint from clients is that they were unaware that it would cost so much to achieve so little.

11.2.2 Level of service

The service provided by a solicitor must be competent and delivered in a timely manner (Code of Conduct for Solicitors, para 3.2 and Code of Conduct for Firms, para 4.2).

In seeking to achieve a competent level of service, the solicitor must consider and take account of their client's attributes, needs and circumstances (Code of Conduct for Solicitors, para 3.4 and Code of Conduct for Firms, para 4.2). For example, in terms of the type and frequency of communications with a client during the matter, some clients may want to be updated in writing on a regular basis, whilst some may want to hear nothing from a solicitor until a certain stage of a transaction has been reached.

11.2.3 Responsibilities

Both the solicitor and client will have their own responsibilities during a matter, and so it is good practice to ensure that these responsibilities are explained and agreed with the client at the outset of the matter and prudent to have a written record of this. For example, one of the responsibilities of the solicitor could be to keep the client informed of progress and seek the client's instructions where required. The solicitor will also expect the client to keep them updated as the matter progresses and inform them of anything that occurs which may materially affect the matter or change the basis of the client's instructions.

Where a client has been referred to the solicitor by a third party and/or because of the way the client's matter is funded, there may be conditions placed on how the solicitor may act for the client. For example, a client may be referred to a solicitor by the client's insurer. Under the terms of acting, the solicitor may not be able to issue proceedings without the authority of the insurer (who will be funding any such action). Accordingly, it is important that the solicitor explains at the outset and throughout the matter any limitations or conditions on what they can do for the client for the avoidance of any misunderstanding or potential source of grievance on the part of the client.

11.2.4 Competence and supervision

In order to provide a proper level of service to clients, it is obvious that a solicitor should have a knowledge of the current law and the skills to enable them to carry out their role effectively. Accordingly, the Code of Conduct for Solicitors provides that a solicitor must maintain their competence to carry out their role and keep their professional knowledge and skills up to date (para 3.3)

It is important not only that the solicitor provides a competent level of service to clients, but also that they ensure that those they supervise or manage do so too. As a result, the Code of Conduct for Solicitors obliges a solicitor to ensure that the individuals they manage are competent to carry out their role and keep their professional knowledge and skills, as well as an understanding of their legal, ethical and regulatory obligations, up to date (para 3.6). The Code also makes it clear that a solicitor, when supervising or managing others providing legal services, remains accountable for the work carried out through them and must effectively supervise work they do for clients (para 3.5).

The Code of Conduct for Firms has a provision which mirrors the requirements set out above (para 4.3) with an additional obligation to have in place an effective system for supervising clients' matters (para 4.4).

11.2.5 Information on regulation

A solicitor must ensure that clients understand whether and how the services being provided are regulated. This includes the solicitor explaining which activities will be carried out by them as an 'authorised person' (defined in the SRA Glossary as a person who is authorised by the SRA or another approved regulator to carry out a legal activity as set out in s 12 of the Legal Services Act 2007), which services being provided are regulated by an approved regulator, and ensuring that they do not represent any business or employer which is not authorised by the SRA as being regulated by the SRA (Code of Conduct for Solicitors, para 8.10). There is also an obligation to ensure that clients understand the regulatory protections available to them (Code of Conduct for Solicitors, para 8.11), for example, entitlement to the protection of the SRA Compensation Fund (see **7.11**) and the firm's indemnity insurance (see **18.5**). For solicitors, the regulator will be the SRA and, in some circumstances, the Financial Conduct Authority (see **Chapter 17**). These obligations also apply to firms (see Code of Conduct for Firms, para 7.1(c)).

11.3 INFORMATION ABOUT COSTS

11.3.1 Introduction

One of the most important issues for a client is the overall cost of legal services. When an individual goes into a shop to buy something, it is easy for that person to work out how much the thing will cost and therefore whether they want to spend that amount of money on buying the product.

The provision of legal services often does not work in the same way. Nevertheless, the client must be given the best possible information as to the overall costs of the matter if the client is to be able to make an informed decision about whether they want to go ahead with it.

11.3.2 Best possible information

A solicitor is obliged to provide clients with the best possible information about how their matter will be priced and, both at the time of engagement and when appropriate as their matter progresses, about the likely overall cost of a matter and any costs incurred (Code of Conduct for Solicitors, para 8.7). This obligation is also placed on firms by virtue of para 7.1(c) of the Code of Conduct for Firms. The term 'costs' in the Codes is defined in the SRA Glossary as meaning the solicitor's fees and disbursements.

As for how a solicitor can show that they have provided the best possible information about costs, there is no specific guidance in the Codes of Conduct as, again, the intention is for solicitors and firms to exercise their own judgement in applying the standards, taking into account their areas of practice and the nature of their clients. As a matter of good practice, however, the solicitor should clearly explain how their fees are calculated and if and when they are likely to change. For example, the client may be charged a fixed fee, or by reference to an hourly charge-out rate. Warning the client about any other payments for which they may be responsible is also advisable. For example, when dealing with a residential conveyancing matter, the solicitor will be obliged to obtain details concerning the property from local authority and Land Registry searches, and so disbursements will be incurred for such searches and be payable in addition to the fees charged for the work being carried out by the solicitor.

It will often be impossible to provide an accurate estimate of the overall cost of a matter at the start. However, just providing the client with details of the solicitor's charge-out rate will rarely be sufficient. For example, if the only information the solicitor provides to a client is that their charge-out rate will be £300 per hour, the client will not know whether they will have to pay £300 for the matter to be finished (if the solicitor puts in one hour's work) or £30,000 (if the solicitor puts in 100 hours' work).

If a precise figure is not possible, the SRA's guidance in a previous Code of Conduct suggested that the solicitor should explain why the precise figure cannot be given and agree either:

(a) a ceiling figure, above which the solicitor's costs cannot go, without the client's permission; or

(b) a review date when the parties will revisit the costs position.

The solicitor must not forget expressly to include VAT in any hourly rate or quote. For example, a solicitor may quote their hourly rate as £300 plus VAT. If the solicitor fails to quote with VAT, the price the client pays will be deemed to include VAT. Accordingly, if a solicitor were to say that their charge-out rate was £300 per hour, that is all that the client would be liable to pay. The solicitor would have to pay the VAT element to the authorities from this £300, and would therefore lose out.

In seeking to provide clients with a competent service as required by the Codes of Conduct, the solicitor should discuss how the client will pay for the legal services, including whether the client may be able to have some or all of their costs covered by someone else, such as a trade union, or by legal expenses insurance. Consideration should also be given, where appropriate, as to whether the client may be eligible for public funding and, if so, how this would operate.

The SRA Transparency Rules impose additional obligations on solicitors and firms in providing costs information. These were considered in **Chapter 9**.

11.3.3 Costs issues in litigation

Providing a competent level of service is likely to include the solicitor discussing with the client whether the potential outcomes of the matter are likely to justify the expense or risk involved. This would include discussing any risk of having to pay someone else's legal fees. For example, in litigation the client may be ordered to pay some of the costs of the winning party. The solicitor should consider whether these costs might be covered by legal expenses insurance.

Regardless of any costs order the court may make in favour of the client concerning litigation, it would be good practice for the client to be advised that they may still be liable to pay their own solicitor's costs. For example, the amount that the losing party in litigation is ordered to pay to the winning party will be assessed by the court, and it is unlikely to cover the entirety of the winning client's legal costs and, under the fixed recoverable costs regime in civil litigation cases, the circumstances in which the client may be responsible for any shortfall between the costs incurred and the costs recovered from the other side. Where the solicitor wishes to charge the client for any such excess, the solicitor must have entered into a written agreement with the client to that effect (see CPR, r 48.8(1A)).

The client will also remain liable to pay their solicitor's costs where the losing party is unable to meet the costs order. Again, it would be good practice for this to be made clear to the client prior to starting any litigious proceedings.

Specific obligations relating to providing costs information in the context of certain court or tribunal proceedings are contained in the SRA Transparency Rules (see **Chapter 9**).

11.4 CLIENT CARE LETTER

Solicitors and firms must give clients information in a way they can understand (Code of Conduct for Solicitors, para 8.6 and Code of Conduct for Firms, para 7.1(c)). Under a previous Code of Conduct , a solicitor was obliged to provide the necessary client care information to a client in writing, and this was routinely done in the form of a letter sent out to the client after the first interview, known as the 'client care letter'. Although only information about the complaints procedure is now required to be in writing by the Codes of Conduct (see **7.4**), it is likely that solicitors will continue to provide the client care information and the terms of the firm's retainer in the form of a letter to the client for the avoidance of doubt, and to help show compliance with the Codes and the Principles. Additional, but in many respects overlapping, obligations on the provision of information to clients are contained in the Provision of Services Regulations 2009 (SI 2009/2999) (for example, stating the firm's VAT number). As with the information specified in the Code, this will usually be provided in the client care letter.

11.5 CONSUMER CONTRACTS REGULATIONS 2013

Solicitors need to ensure that they comply with the Consumer Contracts (Information, Cancellation and Additional Charges) Regulations 2013 (SI 2013/3134). These apply to a wide range of contracts made between solicitors and their clients and would include a contract to carry out legal work for a client. The Regulations distinguish between 'on-premises' and 'off-premises' contracts. Whilst most contracts will be concluded between a solicitor and their client at the solicitor's place of business ('on-premises'), there may be situations which will result in the contract falling within the definition of an 'off-premises' contract, for example where a solicitor visits a client at home and the client offers to engage them to carry out legal work. Even if the offer is accepted by the solicitor telephoning the client from their office the next day, this would be considered an 'off-premises' contract.

The Regulations specify that certain pieces of information must be provided to clients before they enter into the contract. Much of the information that solicitors are required to provide under the Regulations is likely to be included in their client care letter; however, the information required varies depending on what type of contract it is. For example, where a client has agreed to an 'off-premises' contract, they must additionally be informed that they have the right to cancel it without giving any reason or incurring any liability during the cancellation period (which in most cases is 14 days beginning on the date after the contract is entered into). Failure to do so is an offence under the Regulations. For this reason, solicitors need to ensure that if they are likely to enter into contracts in different types of circumstances, their standard letters contain any additional information required under the Regulations. Legal aid contracts do not fall within the Regulations.

11.6 FEES AND COSTS

11.6.1 Introduction

The retainer between the solicitor and client is a contract, and so the fees and charges the solicitor will levy for acting for the client will be agreed between the parties at the start of the retainer. However, restrictions are placed upon the fees a solicitor may charge, and also upon how the solicitor will be remunerated by the SRA and the general law. The rest of this chapter offers a summary of the main provisions; it is not intended to be a comprehensive guide.

These restrictions vary depending upon what type of work the solicitor has agreed to carry out for the client. A distinction is made between 'contentious' business and 'non-contentious' business. This distinction is particularly relevant when considering whether, and how, a client can challenge the bill of a solicitor.

11.6.2 Contentious business

Contentious business is defined as 'business done, whether as a solicitor or an advocate, in or for the purposes of proceedings begun before a court or an arbitrator, not being business which falls within the definition of non-contentious business or common form probate business' (Solicitors Act 1974, s 87). Accordingly, contentious business is work done in relation to proceedings. However, contentious business starts only once proceedings have been issued.

For example, a client may seek the advice of a solicitor with a view to suing the client's previous firm for negligence. The solicitor advises that the client should start proceedings, but suggests that a letter is sent to the previous firm beforehand, giving that firm seven days to offer appropriate compensation. The client is clearly contemplating litigious proceedings, but if the firm makes an acceptable offer before proceedings are issued, the solicitor's work will be classified as non-contentious.

11.6.3 Non-contentious business

Non-contentious business is defined as 'any business done as a solicitor which is not contentious business' (Solicitors Act 1974, s 87). This includes obvious examples such as conveyancing or commercial drafting work. The definition also includes all proceedings before tribunals, except the Lands Tribunal and the Employment Appeals Tribunal.

Non-contentious business is governed by the Solicitors' (Non-Contentious Business) Remuneration Order 2009 (SI 2009/1931).

11.7 OPTIONS AVAILABLE FOR SOLICITOR'S FEES

A solicitor may agree to charge a client for work done on a number of different bases. Some of these options are considered below. Whichever method of charging the client and solicitor agree, the overall amount of the charge will be regulated by statute and so the client may be able to challenge the bill at a later date (see **11.10**). As explained above, solicitors and firms are required by the Codes of Conduct to ensure that clients receive the best possible information about how their matter will be priced.

11.7.1 Hourly rate

Perhaps the most common method of charging clients is by use of an hourly rate, ie the client is charged for the time spent on the file. The client is informed at the start of the matter which fee earner will be working on the client's files, and the fee earner's respective charge-out rates. However, in order to ensure that the client receives the best possible information about the likely overall cost of the matter, as required by the Codes of Conduct, it is unlikely that merely giving an hourly rate will be acceptable (see **11.3.2**).

11.7.2 Fixed fee

Alternatively a solicitor may agree to complete the work for a fixed fee, or a fixed fee plus VAT and disbursements. Fixed fees are often used for conveyancing transactions. If the solicitor agrees to act in return for a fixed fee, this fee cannot be altered at a later date (unless the client agrees) if the work turns out to be more expensive than the solicitor first expected.

11.7.3 Variable fees

A solicitor is permitted, in certain circumstances, to charge a fee which varies according to the outcome of the matter. One such example of a variable fee is a contingency fee. However, a solicitor must bear in mind the obligation under the Codes of Conduct to take account of the client's needs and circumstances when deciding to enter into fee agreements and to ensure that any such agreements are legal.

Agreements which are permitted by law are conditional fee agreements (CFAs) and damages-based agreements (DBAs). An example of a conditional fee agreement is the 'no win, no fee' basis of charging that is popular in areas of work such as personal injury. Under such an agreement, the solicitor may agree to charge nothing if the client loses, but will charge their fees plus an agreed 'uplift' (or 'success fee', for example an extra 20%) in the event of success.

In respect of litigation or advocacy services, a solicitor may enter into (and enforce) a CFA if it complies with s 58 of the Courts and Legal Services Act 1990 (see also the Conditional Fee Agreements Order 2013 (SI 2013/689)). For example, the agreement must be in writing, signed by both the solicitor and the client, and, where a success fee is to be paid, specify the percentage of the success fee. The success fee cannot exceed a percentage specified by the Lord Chancellor (currently 100% uplift in the normal hourly charge rate, with the exception of personal injury cases where the cap is 25% of general damages recovered). The solicitor must carry out a proper risk assessment to calculate the amount of the success fee. A solicitor cannot enter into a CFA for any criminal work or family proceedings.

The CFA must also comply with the additional requirements specified by the Consumer Contracts (Information, Cancellation and Additional Charges) Regulations 2013 (see **11.5**). To aid compliance, The Law Society has published a model CFA for use by the profession.

If a client instructs a solicitor on a CFA (for example, on a 'no win, no fee' basis), this does not mean that the client will not have to pay any legal costs if they lose the case. Although the client may not be liable to pay their solicitor's fees, they will usually have to pay disbursements such as court fees, barristers' fees and VAT. The client may also have to pay their opponent's costs. A solicitor should explore whether the client can obtain insurance to cover these costs in the event of losing the case (known as after-the-event insurance). The solicitor should also ask whether the client has before-the-event insurance which will cover the costs.

Following recommendations made by Lord Justice Jackson, significant changes have been introduced in respect of the costs of civil litigation, including CFAs. These changes have been effective since 1 April 2013, when the relevant provisions of the Legal Aid, Sentencing and Punishment of Offenders Act 2012 came into force. For example, with a few exceptions, the success fee and after-the-event insurance premiums will now be paid by the client, not the other side, if the client is successful.

A DBA (defined by s 58AA(3)(a) of the Courts and Legal Services Act 1990 and covered by the Damages-Based Agreements Regulations 2013 (SI 2013/609)) provides that, if the client recovers damages, the solicitor's fee is an agreed percentage of those damages. The DBA must not provide for a payment above an amount which, including VAT, is equal to 50% of the sums ultimately recovered by the client. Also, personal injury cases are subject to a cap of 25% of the general damages recovered. The points made above in respect of combining a CFA with after-the-event insurance cover (or before-the-event insurance cover) apply equally to a DBA.

The SRA Transparency Rules also require that, in relation to specified services (see **Chapter 9**), costs information required to be published includes the circumstances in which clients may have to make any payments themselves for the services provided by the solicitor (including from any damages) if CFAs or DBAs are used.

A solicitor may enter into a contingency fee arrangement in respect of non-contentious work, but to be enforceable this must be in the form of a non-contentious business agreement (see **11.11**).

11.7.4 Other methods

A solicitor may agree to be remunerated by some other means. One such example would be a solicitor agreeing to accept shares in a new company in return for their work, rather than costs. However, in such circumstances the client should be advised to seek independent advice about such a costs agreement.

11.8 MONEY ON ACCOUNT

It is common for a solicitor to require a client to pay a sum of money to the solicitor at the start of the transaction on account of the costs and disbursements that will be incurred.

In contentious business, a solicitor may require a client to pay a reasonable sum to the solicitor on account of costs. If the client does not pay this money within a reasonable time, the solicitor may terminate the retainer (Solicitors Act 1974, s 65(2)).

There is no such statutory right in non-contentious business. Accordingly, where the solicitor requires money on account before starting a matter, the solicitor should make this a requirement of the retainer.

11.9 SOLICITOR'S BILL

11.9.1 Introduction

For a solicitor to be able to obtain payment from the client, certain formalities need to be complied with in respect of the solicitor's bill. These matters include (but are not limited to) the following:

(a) The bill must contain enough information for the client to be satisfied that the bill is reasonable, and also provide details of the period to which the bill relates.

(b) The bill must be signed by the solicitor or on their behalf by an employee authorised to do so. Alternatively, the solicitor/authorised employee may sign a covering letter which refers to the bill (Solicitors Act 1974, s 69(2A)).

(c) The bill must be delivered by hand to the client, by post to their home, business address or last known address, or by e-mail if the client has agreed to this method and provided an appropriate e-mail address (Solicitors Act 1974, s 69(2C)).

11.9.2 Interim bills

A solicitor may wish to bill their client for work done on the client's file before the matter has completed. This will particularly be the case where the client's matter is likely to go on for some months, such as protracted litigation. A solicitor may wish to issue interim bills throughout the matter.

There are two different types of interim bills. The first type are known as interim 'statute bills' because they comply with the provisions of the Solicitors Act 1974. Although they are interim bills, they are also self-contained final bills in respect of the work covered by them. Consequently, the solicitor may sue the client for non-payment of such bills and the client may apply to have them assessed by the court (see **11.10.1**). However, interim statute bills are rare and may arise during the retainer in only two ways:

(a) there is authority for issuing such bills in a 'natural break' in lengthy proceedings, but there is little authority as to what will actually amount to a natural break, and so this should perhaps be avoided as a basis for statute bills except in the clearest of cases;

(b) by agreement with the client, and The Law Society recommends that this right should be expressly reserved within the retainer. The Law Society's guidance provides that the solicitor must specify the time-limit within which the client must pay the interim bill, and must also expressly reserve the right to terminate the retainer in the event of non-payment.

The second, and more common, type of interim bill is the 'bill on account'. Such bills are effectively requests for payments on account of the final bill which will be delivered at the end of the matter/retainer. An advantage of this type of interim bill is that it does not need to represent the final figure for costs in respect of the work covered by it, so that when preparing their statute bill at the end of the matter the solicitor can assess a fair overall costs figure for all of the work done since the start of the retainer. However, unlike with an interim statute bill, a solicitor is unable to sue the client for non-payment of such a bill, and the client cannot apply to have the bill assessed. If the client does not pay the bill on account within a reasonable time then in contentious business the solicitor may terminate the retainer under s 65(2) of the Solicitors Act 1974 (see **11.8**). In the event that the client regards the amount of the bill as excessive, they can request that the solicitor issues a statute bill which the client may then apply to have assessed by the court.

11.9.3 Interest on bills

In a non-contentious matter a solicitor may charge interest on the whole or the outstanding part of an unpaid bill with effect from one month after delivery of the bill, provided that notice of the client's right to challenge the bill has been given to the client. The rate of interest chargeable must not exceed that which is payable on judgment debts. At the time of writing the rate is currently 8%.

In contentious business, The Law Society's guidance provides that a solicitor may charge interest on an unpaid bill where the solicitor expressly reserves this right in the retainer, or the client later agrees for a 'contractual consideration' to pay interest. Alternatively, where a solicitor sues the client for non-payment of fees, the court has the power to award the solicitor interest on the debt under s 35A of the Senior Courts Act 1981 or s 69 of the County Courts Act 1984.

The rate of interest will be the rate payable for judgment debts unless the solicitor and client expressly agree a different rate.

11.9.4 Enforcement

Subject to certain exceptions, a solicitor may not commence any claim to recover any costs due to the solicitor (such as suing the client) until one month has passed since the solicitor delivered their bill (Solicitors Act 1974, s 69). The bill must also be in the proper form (see **11.9.1**).

However, the High Court has the power under s 69 to allow the solicitor to commence such a claim against the client within this one-month period where the court is satisfied that the client is about to leave the country, be declared bankrupt (or enter into a composition with their creditors), or do anything else which would prevent or delay the solicitor obtaining their fees.

11.10 CLIENT'S RIGHT TO CHALLENGE THE BILL

The client may challenge the amount of a solicitor's bill, provided that the client complies with certain requirements. These requirements depend upon how the client wishes to go about challenging the bill.

11.10.1 Assessment by the court

A client may apply to have their bill assessed by the court in both contentious and non-contentious proceedings. This is sometimes referred to as a bill being 'taxed'.

A client has the right to have a bill assessed if an application is made to the court within one month of delivery of the bill. Where no such application has been made within this month, the court still has the power to order assessment within 12 months of delivery of the bill, or even after this time if the client can show special circumstances. However, assessment is not permitted if more than 12 months have expired since payment of the bill. 'Payment' in this context requires the client's acceptance of and agreement to the amount charged (*Oakwood Solicitors Ltd v Menzies* [2024] UKSC 34).

The costs will be assessed by a judge or district judge sitting as a 'costs officer'. The costs officer has the power to assess the fees and disbursements of the solicitor.

The costs will (with certain exceptions) be assessed on an 'indemnity basis'. The court will allow only costs that have been reasonably incurred by the solicitor and which are reasonable in amount. Any doubt as to what is to be considered reasonable is resolved in the favour of the solicitor. However, the client may be ordered to pay the costs of the solicitor arising from the assessment process.

11.10.1.1 Non-contentious proceedings

Where a court is asked to assess a solicitor's bill in non-contentious proceedings, in deciding what is reasonable, the court must have regard to the following circumstances (Solicitors' (Non-Contentious Business) Remuneration Order 2009):

(a) the complexity of the matter, or the difficulty or novelty of the questions raised;
(b) the skill, labour, specialised knowledge and responsibility involved;
(c) the time spent on the business;
(d) the number and importance of the documents prepared or considered, without regard to length;
(e) the place where and the circumstances in which the business or any part thereof is transacted;
(f) the amount or value of any money or property involved;
(g) whether any land involved is registered;
(h) the importance of the matter to the client; and
(i) the approval (express or implied) of the entitled person, or the express approval of the testator, to:
    (i) the solicitor undertaking all or any part of the work giving rise to the costs, or
    (ii) the amount of the costs.

11.10.1.2 Contentious proceedings

The factors the court must take into account when considering whether costs are reasonable are set out in CPR, r 44.5. These include (but are not limited to):

(a) the conduct of the parties;
(b) the amount or value of any money or property involved;
(c) the importance of the matter to the parties;
(d) the particular complexity of the matter, or the difficulty or novelty of the questions raised;
(e) the skill, effort, specialised knowledge and responsibility involved;
(f) the time spent on the case; and
(g) the place where and the circumstances in which work, or any part of it, was done.

Subject to certain exceptions, a client cannot apply for an assessment of costs where the solicitor and client have entered into a contentious business agreement (see **11.12**).

11.10.2 Using the firm's complaints procedure

Solicitors must ensure that clients are informed in writing at the time of engagement about their right to complain about the service provided by them and their charges (Code of Conduct for Solicitors, para 8.3).

If the client is not satisfied with the firm's response, the solicitor must inform the client in writing of any right they have to complain to the Legal Ombudsman (Code of Conduct for Solicitors, para 8.4). The Legal Ombudsman may then limit the solicitor's fees by, for example, directing the solicitor to refund all or part of any amount paid, or to remit all or part of their fees (see **Chapter 7** generally).

These obligations are also placed on firms by virtue of para 7.1(c) of the Code of Conduct for Firms.

11.11 NON-CONTENTIOUS BUSINESS AGREEMENTS

A solicitor and client may enter into a non-contentious business agreement in respect of the solicitor's remuneration for any non-contentious work. Under this agreement the solicitor may be remunerated by a gross sum, commission, a percentage, a salary, or otherwise.

To be enforceable, the agreement must comply with s 57 of the Solicitors Act 1974. For example, the agreement must:

(a) be in writing;
(b) be signed by the client;
(c) contain all the terms of the agreement (including whether disbursements and VAT are included in the agreed remuneration).

Where the relevant provisions have been complied with, the client will be unable to apply to have their bill assessed by the court. However, the court may set the agreement aside if the amount charged by the solicitor is unfair or unreasonable.

11.12 CONTENTIOUS BUSINESS AGREEMENTS

A solicitor may enter into a contentious business agreement in respect of their remuneration for contentious work completed on behalf of the client (see Solicitors Act 1974, ss 59–63).

The agreement may provide for the solicitor to be remunerated by reference to a gross sum, an hourly rate, a salary or otherwise. However, the solicitor may not be remunerated by a contingency fee.

In order to be enforceable, the agreement must comply with certain requirements, including:

(a) the agreement must state it is a contentious business agreement;
(b) the agreement must be in writing;
(c) the agreement must be signed by the client; and
(d) the agreement must contain all the terms.

Where the contentious business agreement is enforceable, the client will be unable to apply to court for an assessment of costs (except where the agreement provides that the solicitor is to be remunerated by reference to an hourly rate.) However, the court may set aside the agreement if it is unfair or unreasonable.

11.13 OVERCHARGING

A solicitor must act in the best interests of the client and must treat their clients fairly. Therefore a solicitor must not overcharge for work done. Where a costs officer (when assessing a solicitor's bill in a non-contentious matter) reduces the amount of the costs by more than 50%, the costs officer must inform the SRA. Overcharging the client will be considered a breach of professional conduct.

11.14 COMMISSION

The solicitor–client relationship is a fiduciary relationship (see 10.4.3), and so a solicitor must not make a secret profit whilst acting for the client. Paragraph 4.1 of the Code of Conduct for Solicitors obliges a solicitor to properly account to a client for any financial benefit they receive as a result of the client's instructions, except where they have agreed otherwise. The term 'financial benefit' includes any commission, discount or rebate (SRA Glossary). This is mirrored in para 5.1 of the Code of Conduct for Firms.

For example, a client may require specialist tax advice, and so may be referred by the solicitor to a tax consultant. The tax consultant may pay the solicitor commission in return for this referral (see **9.4**).

In showing that they have properly accounted to the client for the financial benefit received, the solicitor could:

(a) pay it to the client; or
(b) offset it against their fees; or
(c) keep it where the client has agreed to this.

This is usually dealt with as part of the client care letter or the terms and conditions otherwise agreed upon in acting for the client.

Where the solicitor is carrying out an exempt regulated activity in respect of financial services (see **Chapter 17**), the solicitor must consider s 327 of the Financial Services and Markets Act 2000. Accordingly, to comply with s 327(3), the solicitor must likewise account to the client for all commission received.

11.15 EXAMPLE

Question	You have just submitted your final bill to Mr Waugh in respect of a partnership dispute. You managed to resolve the matter without having to issue proceedings. The next day you receive a call from Mr Waugh who claims your bill (£7,000 plus VAT) is too high. Assuming that your bill complies with the relevant formalities, what options are available to Mr Waugh to challenge your bill?
Answer	Mr Waugh has two options: (a) Assessment by the court Mr Waugh has the right to have the bill assessed by the court if he applies within one month of delivery of the bill (the court may allow assessment after this time in certain circumstances). Both you and Mr Waugh will be bound by the results. (b) Using the firm's complaints procedure Mr Waugh could make a formal complaint about the bill in accordance with the firm's complaint's procedure. If he is not satisfied with the firm's response he may complain to the Legal Ombudsman. In the event that the Legal Ombudsman makes a determination about the bill (which can include a direction that you remit all or part of your fees) which is accepted by Mr Waugh, it will be binding on both of you.

SUMMARY

Client care

(1) A solicitor must ensure that the service they provide to clients is competent and delivered in a timely manner.

(2) The solicitor must ensure that clients are in a position to make informed decisions about the services they need, how their matter will be handled and the options available to them.

(3) The solicitor must inform clients in writing of their right to complain to the firm about the service they receive and the costs and any right they have to complain to the Legal Ombudsman, both at the time of engagement and at the conclusion of the firm's complaint procedure.

(4) A solicitor must not take unfair advantage of clients or mislead or attempt to mislead them.

Information about costs

(1) A solicitor must give their client the best possible information about how their matter will be priced and as to the likely overall costs of a matter and any costs incurred, both at the outset and when appropriate as the client's matter progresses.

(2) The information must be given in a way that clients can understand.

Fees and costs

(1) A solicitor and client may agree the level of costs the solicitor may charge. However, this agreement is regulated by statute and the common law.

(2) A distinction is made between costs in contentious matters and costs in non-contentious matters.

(3) A solicitor's bill must contain prescribed information in order for the bill to be enforceable.

(4) A client may challenge the costs of a solicitor both in contentious and non-contentious proceedings.

(5) Generally, a solicitor may not sue to recover their costs from the client until one month has elapsed since the bill was delivered.

CHAPTER 12

CONFIDENTIALITY

LEARNING OUTCOMES

After reading this chapter you will be able to understand:

- the nature and extent of the duty of confidentiality
- the duty to disclose relevant information to the client
- legal professional privilege.

12.1 DUTY OF CONFIDENTIALITY

> You [must] keep the affairs of current and former clients confidential unless disclosure is required or permitted by law or the client consents. (Codes of Conduct, para 6.3)

12.1.1 Introduction

Confidentiality is a fundamental principle of the solicitor–client relationship. For example, it is important that a solicitor receives all the relevant information from a client in order to give the best possible advice. A client would be dissuaded from informing their solicitor of all the relevant facts if they thought that this information would be released to the public. However, the obligation of confidentiality extends beyond obviously confidential information given to a solicitor by their client and includes all information about a client or matter, regardless of the source of that information. This means that firms must have in place effective systems to enable risks to client confidentiality to be identified and managed. This is covered in the Code of Conduct for Firms, which obliges firms to have effective governance structures, arrangements, systems and controls in place to ensure that the firm, its managers and employees comply with all the SRA's regulatory arrangements (para 2.1).

This duty will continue after the retainer has been terminated. Accordingly, as made clear in the wording of the Codes, a solicitor will owe a duty of confidentiality to former, as well as existing, clients. The duty also continues after the death of the client, whereupon the right to enforce or waive the duty of confidentiality is passed to the client's (or former client's) personal representatives. All members of a firm, including support staff, owe a duty of confidentiality to clients of the firm.

The duty of confidentiality attaches to all information given by, or behalf of, a client in connection with the retainer in respect of which the solicitor is instructed. The SRA Guidance on Confidentiality of Client Information provides an example of a solicitor attending a client at a police station and, whilst there, the client steals someone's phone. In such circumstances, the solicitor would not be breaching their duty of confidentiality in providing the police with a statement about the theft of the phone as it is unrelated to the matter on which they are acting.

Any breach of the duty of confidentiality will be a breach of professional conduct. The solicitor may be disciplined by the SRA, or by the Solicitors Disciplinary Tribunal (see **Chapter** 7). In addition, the client (or former client) may sue the solicitor for any breach of this duty.

12.1.2 Specific examples

The Codes themselves provide no further guidance on the duty of confidentiality (however, the SRA has published Guidance on Confidentiality of Client Information). The previous Code of Conduct contained specific examples of when the duty would be breached, and these may still provide useful guidance in practice:

(a) disclosing the content of a will on the death of a client (including a former client), unless consent has been provided by the PRs for the content to be released;

(b) disclosing details of bills sent to clients (including former clients) by the firm to third parties, such as debt-factoring companies in relation to the collection of book debts, unless the client has consented.

A solicitor will have to take various practical steps to safeguard the identity of their clients. For example, they will have a file, or files, for particular clients and the client's name (and often address and type of matter, such as divorce) may be written on the file. If a solicitor routinely interviews clients at their desk, steps should be taken to ensure that the covers of these files are not left where they could be read by any other clients.

A number of solicitors' firms use the names of their clients in their marketing and publicity to illustrate the quality of clients that instruct their firm. Where solicitors wish to use the names of their clients in marketing materials, they must obtain the consent of these clients beforehand.

Clients' confidential information may be put at particular risk where two or more firms merge their businesses and where an individual leaves one firm and joins another, and so particular vigilance would be needed to ensure compliance with the Codes and to maintain the duty of confidentiality in such circumstances.

The investigation of third party complaints against firms by the Legal Ombudsman ('LeO') (see **7.5**) can result in a potential conflict between the duty to cooperate with the LeO under the Codes (see **18.9.1**) and the duty of confidentiality owed to clients. The SRA's advice in its Guidance in these circumstances is to notify the client of the LeO's request for information and the basis of its stated authority to request it and inform the client that the information will be provided unless the client objects. If the client does object, the LeO should be notified of this and required to serve a notice under s 147 of the Legal Services Act 2007 which the firm would then comply with. Such a notice, however, would not of itself extend to any material covered by legal professional privilege (see **12.4**).

12.1.3 Where confidential information may be disclosed

Disclosure is permitted with the client's consent. In obtaining such consent, steps should be taken to ensure that the client knows to whom their information is to be made available, when and for what purpose. Even where the client may have given their general consent, it may still be appropriate to obtain the client's consent to a specific piece of information being disclosed as the issue arises.

Although no specific examples are contained in the Codes as to when confidential information may be disclosed in the absence of the client's consent, there are circumstances in which disclosure is permitted by law. By way of example:

(a) pursuant to a statutory requirement, eg to HMRC in certain circumstances and to the LeO under a notice issued under s 147 of the Legal Services Act 2007 (see **12.1.2**);

(b) pursuant to a statutory duty, such as in the Proceeds of Crime Act 2002 and the Money Laundering, Terrorist Financing and Transfer of Funds (Information on the Payer)

Regulations 2017 (SI 2017/692) (see **Chapter 15**), and under the anti-terrorism legislation;

(c) under a court order, or where a police warrant permits the seizure of confidential documentation;

(d) disclosure of certain matters to the court when a solicitor is acting for a client under a power of attorney or a court-appointed deputy where the disclosure falls within the scope of their authority.

If a solicitor is uncertain as to whether to disclose the confidential information, they should consider taking legal advice or contact the SRA's Professional Ethics Guidance Team. The solicitor must also bear in mind legal professional privilege (see **12.4**).

The SRA Guidance on Confidentiality of Client Information sets out examples of circumstances which, although still technically amounting to a breach of the duty of confidentiality, may be taken into account as mitigation in the context of disciplinary action. It should be noted that none of them allows for disclosure after the event. The main examples set out in the guidance are as follows:

(a) *Where a client has indicated their intention to commit suicide or serious self-harm.* The SRA advises that, in the first instance, the solicitor should consider seeking consent from the client to disclose that information to a third party (for example, a ward nurse where the client is in hospital) but, where this is not possible or appropriate, the solicitor may decide to disclose the information to the relevant person or authority without consent in order to protect the client or another person.

(b) *Preventing harm to children or vulnerable adults.* This covers situations where the child or adult indicates that they are suffering sexual or other abuse, or where the client discloses abuse either by themselves or by another adult against a child or vulnerable adult. Whilst there is no requirement in law to disclose this information, the solicitor may consider that the threat to the person's life or health is sufficiently serious to justify a breach of the duty of confidentiality.

(c) *Preventing the commission of a criminal offence.* At common law there is no confidence in information of an iniquitous nature and so, if a solicitor is being used by a client to perpetrate a fraud or any other crime, the duty of confidentiality does not arise. In other circumstances, a breach may be mitigated where disclosure is made to the extent that the solicitor believes it necessary to prevent the client or a third party from committing a criminal act that the solicitor believes, on reasonable grounds, is likely to result in serious bodily harm.

12.2 DUTY OF DISCLOSURE

Where a solicitor is acting for a client on a matter, they must make the client aware of all information material to the matter of which the solicitor has knowledge (Code of Conduct for Solicitors, para 6.4). The wording of this obligation in the Code of Conduct for Firms ('.... all information material to the matter of which the individual has knowledge ...' at para 6.4) makes it clear that this is a personal duty, and so the knowledge of the information in question must be that of the individual themselves, ie rather than the material being known within the firm as a whole or within the knowledge of another individual in the firm.

12.2.1 Limitations

The Codes of Conduct set out specific exceptions to the requirement to disclose all information material to the client's matter of which the solicitor is personally aware (para 6.4 in both Codes):

(a) the disclosure of the information is prohibited by legal restrictions imposed in the interests of national security or the prevention of crime;

(b) the client gives informed consent, given or evidenced in writing, to the information not being disclosed to them;
(c) the solicitor has reason to believe that serious physical or mental injury will be caused to the client or another if the information is disclosed to the client; or
(d) the information is contained in a privileged document that the solicitor has knowledge of only because it has been mistakenly disclosed (see **12.2.2**).

12.2.2 Use of confidential material received by mistake

Due to the volume of information which passes between solicitors on a daily basis, occasionally mistakes may be made and information destined for a third party may be inadvertently disclosed to a solicitor. For example, a solicitor acting for one party in a matter may misaddress correspondence destined for their client to the solicitor acting for the other party. In this case, immediately on becoming aware of the error, the receiving solicitor must return the papers to the originating solicitor without reading them or otherwise making use of the information contained therein (*Ablitt v Mills & Reeve* (1995) *The Times*, 25 October). In the Codes of Conduct, there is an express exception to the duty on the solicitor to disclose to their client details of such material received in such circumstances (see **12.2.1**).

12.3 PLACING CONFIDENTIAL INFORMATION AT RISK

12.3.1 Introduction

In order to protect against any accidental disclosure, the Codes provide that a solicitor or firm must not act in certain circumstances.

A solicitor must act in the best interests of the client (Principle 7) and so must not place themselves in a situation where any relevant information could be disclosed to another client, as any such disclosure would be against the best interests of the client to whom the solicitor owes a duty of confidentiality.

Accordingly, a solicitor or firm must not act for a client in a matter where that client has an interest adverse to the interest of another current or former client for whom confidential information which is material to that matter is held unless either of the exceptions set out in the Codes is met (para 6.5 of both Codes of Conduct).

12.3.2 Is the information material?

For the purposes of para 6.5 of the Codes of Conduct, the confidential information must be 'material'. The SRA's guidance in a previous Code of Conduct defined this as information which is:

(a) relevant to your client's matter; and
(b) of more than inconsequential interest to the client (ie, will the decision affect the client's decision-making?).

The question of whether the information is 'material' relates to the client to whom the duty of disclosure concerning the information is owed.

12.3.3 Do the clients have an 'adverse' interest?

Adversity relates to the relationship between two respective clients, namely the client for whom the solicitor or firm is considering acting and a current or former client for whom the solicitor or firm holds confidential information. The SRA guidance in a previous Code of Conduct provided that this relationship will be said to be adverse where the client to whom the firm owes the duty of confidentiality is, or is likely to become, an opposing party in a matter to the client who is owed the duty of disclosure.

This would include a situation where the clients litigate against each other, are involved in mediation, or even if the clients are on opposing sides of a negotiation. There is a view, however, that the concept of an adverse interest should be interpreted in a wider sense, that is, in relation to a particular matter, whether the one client would want to receive the information because it is potentially of value to them, and whether the other client would want that information to remain confidential.

12.3.4 When it is possible to act

Where the same individual within a firm holds confidential information for one party which is relevant to another client, that particular solicitor will be unable to act for both clients unless the client to whom the duty of confidentiality is owed consents to the information being disclosed or the other client gives informed consent, given or evidenced in writing, to the information not being disclosed to them. This will be regardless of whether the two clients have an interest adverse to each other. This is because that individual owes a personal duty of disclosure to one client (see **12.2**) whilst owing a duty of confidentiality to the other and so a conflict of interests arises (see **Chapter 13**).

However, the Codes provide that it would be possible to act for a client in a matter where that client has an interest adverse to the interest of another current or former client for whom confidential information is held which is material to that matter if either of the following exceptions are met:

- effective measures have been taken which result in there being no real risk of disclosure of the confidential information; or
- the current or former client whose information is held has given informed consent, given or evidenced in writing, to the solicitor or firm acting, including to any measures taken to protect their information. (para 6.5 of both of the Codes).

In practice, it is more likely that these exceptions will apply where the client to whom the duty of confidentiality is owed is a former client.

12.3.4.1 Effective measures to safeguard information

Effective measures would include information barriers, which are practical steps taken to ensure that confidential information cannot pass from one client to another client. On a practical level they aim to prevent confidential information, given by a client to one part of a firm, from being made available to another part of the same firm.

The SRA Guidance on Confidentiality of Client Information contains examples of effective measures which would result in there being no real risk of disclosure:

(a) systems that identify the potential confidentiality issue;
(b) separate teams handling the matters, at all levels including non-fee-earning staff;
(c) separate servers (and printers) so that information cannot be cross accessed;
(d) information being encrypted, and password protected;
(e) individuals in the firm being aware of who else in the organisation is working on the respective matters so that they know who they can and cannot discuss the matter with;
(f) appropriate organisational policies and training for staff.

Given the nature of these measures, information barriers will not be appropriate in every situation, for example where:

(a) the firm is small; or
(b) the physical structure or layout of the firm means that it will be difficult to preserve confidentiality; or
(c) the clients are not sophisticated users of legal services.

Again, however, the introduction to the Codes makes it clear that judgement must be exercised by solicitors or firms in applying the standards, bearing in mind areas of practice and the nature of their clients.

12.3.4.2 Informed consent

In broad terms, the client(s) must consent after having understood and considered the risks and rewards involved in the situation. The SRA's guidance in a previous Code of Conduct indicated that one of the difficulties with seeking such consent is that it is often not possible to disclose sufficient information about the identity and business of the other client without breaching that other client's confidentiality. It would be for the firm to decide in each case whether it would be able to provide sufficient information for the client to be able to give 'informed consent'.

The SRA considered that 'informed consent' would generally be of use only to 'sophisticated clients', such as large companies with in-house legal advisers or other expertise, who would be able to assess the risks of giving their consent based on the information provided, and there is no reason to doubt that this will continue to be the case under the Code.

The exception allowing solicitors to act where they are holding confidential information will rarely be of use to, for example, family clients or personal injury clients.

12.3.5 Professional embarrassment

Even where one of the exceptions set out in para 6.5 applies and so allows a firm to act for two clients, where the firm holds confidential information for one client that was material to the other client's matter, a solicitor might still be obliged to refuse to act on the grounds of professional embarrassment.

A firm should decline to act where the information which it cannot disclose to the client would cause severe embarrassment to the firm if the fact that it had agreed to act in those circumstances ever came out.

The SRA's guidance in a previous Code of Conduct provided a useful example in which a firm agrees to act for a company to draft a contract of employment for a prospective employee, where the firm knows (but is unable to disclose to the client due to confidentiality) that the prospective employee is under investigation for fraud. The embarrassment here would stem from the fact that the firm would know that the client seeking to employ the prospective employee was wasting legal fees on an outcome that (if it knew all the facts) it would not wish to pursue.

The firm should also consider the Principles, such as whether it will be able to act in the best interests of the client in question, and public trust in the legal profession. Acting in the above situation would clearly not be in the best interests of the client, and arguably would also damage the reputation of the profession.

EXAMPLE

Mr Smith instructs a firm to purchase a derelict plot of land from X Ltd in order for him to build a new house. Another one of the firm's clients, Mrs Brown, sold the land to X Ltd two years ago at a knock-down price having revealed to the firm that the land is contaminated. This information would be material to Mr Smith's matter as information concerning the state of the land is relevant to whether Mr Smith will want to buy it. However, the two clients are not instructing the firm in relation to the same matter and so their interests are not adverse to one another; therefore, providing the confidential information could be protected, the Codes would not prevent the firm acting for both parties (subject to any conflict of interest). However, the firm could not inform Mr Smith of the contamination – the firm's duty of confidentiality to Mrs Brown would remain. Nevertheless, the firm should decline instructions on the basis of professional embarrassment.

12.4 CONFIDENTIALITY AND PRIVILEGE

The obligation of confidentiality which a solicitor owes to their client is distinct from the issue of legal professional privilege. While confidentiality prevents a solicitor from disclosing any information relating to a client without that client's consent, legal professional privilege allows a solicitor to withhold specific information which they would otherwise be required to disclose, for example in court proceedings.

Legal professional privilege applies to information which is passed between a solicitor and a client, whether written or oral, directly or indirectly. The rationale behind this right to withhold information, even from the court, is similar to the rationale for the obligation of confidentiality – it exists to enable a client to speak to their solicitor without worrying that the information passed over might be disclosed at a later date.

However, there are limitations in place to prevent legal professional privilege being used as a cloak to hide information which a client does not wish a court to see. One type of legal professional privilege is legal advice privilege. It applies only to information passed between the client and a solicitor *acting in the capacity of a solicitor*. In other words, the communication must relate to the request for, or the provision of, advice to the client by the solicitor. If documents are sent to or from an independent third party, even if they are created for the purpose of obtaining legal advice, they will not be covered by this privilege, and therefore simply 'copying in' a solicitor will not mean the information can be withheld. If the communication is made for the purpose of committing a fraud or a crime, it will not attract privilege (*R v Cox and Railton* (1884) LR 14 QBD 153).

Clients and solicitors may also claim litigation privilege in respect of documents created for the sole or dominant purpose of litigation or other adversarial proceedings which have already commenced or are contemplated. This privilege also extends to communications between a solicitor and third parties. A related issue which also arises in the case of litigation is that anything said by a solicitor whilst speaking in court as an advocate is privileged. Therefore the solicitor cannot be sued for defamation in such circumstances.

A House of Lords case, *Three Rivers DC v Bank of England* [2004] UKHL 48, examines closely the limits of legal professional privilege. It was concerned with advice given in complex matters involving large corporate clients, but left unanswered important questions concerning which representatives of a large corporate client can be regarded as the client for the purpose of claiming privilege. A Court of Appeal case suggests that solicitors will have to take care to identify and restrict those within the client corporation from whom they take instructions and to whom they give advice.

Like the obligation of confidentiality, privilege continues beyond the death of a client (*Bullivant v A-G for Victoria* [1901] AC 196).

The court has power to decide whether or not a particular item is privileged.

The UK General Data Protection Regulation (GDPR) and the Data Protection Act 2018 impose a high level of transparency on firms in the context of informing clients and other individuals if it is processing their personal data and providing a copy of that data if they request it (by a 'subject access request'). The Data Protection Act 2018 contains an exception to these requirements in Sch 2 for information in respect of which a claim to legal professional privilege could be maintained in legal proceedings or in respect of which the duty of confidentiality is owed to a client by a professional legal adviser. As a result, data subjects' rights under the data protection regime do not take precedence over legal professional privilege or client confidentiality when it comes to transparency.

12.5 EXAMPLES

EXAMPLE 1

Question: You acted for Mrs Evans for a number of years and drew up her will. Sadly Mrs Evans dies, and the following week you are contacted by her daughter, who is one of the beneficiaries in the will. She asks whether you can tell her who will receive her mother's house. Can you give her this information?

Answer: You must keep the affairs of all clients confidential (Codes of Conduct, para 6.3) and this duty continues after a client's death. In this case the duty of confidentiality will pass to Mrs Evans' PRs. Accordingly, you cannot disclose the contents of the will to the daughter without the consent of the PRs.

EXAMPLE 2

Question: You are an assistant solicitor acting for both X Co Ltd and Y Co Ltd in a patents dispute. They are both being sued by Z Co Ltd for breach of a patent. X Co Ltd manufactures widgets and Y Co Ltd distributes these products. Due to Y Co Ltd's lack of funds, X Co Ltd is paying your fees in respect of both clients.

You get a call from the managing director of X Co Ltd who tells you that he has concerns about the financial situation of Y Co Ltd. He states that it has fallen behind in paying X Co Ltd's invoices and he is likely to issue a winding-up petition within the next few days.

Can you continue to act for both parties?

Answer: You owe a duty of confidentiality to X Co Ltd under para 6.3 of the Code of Conduct for Solicitors, but you also owe a personal duty to Y Co Ltd to disclose any 'material' information under para 6.4 of the Code. Is this information 'material' to Y Co Ltd, ie relevant to its matter and more than of inconsequential interest to it?

This information is clearly relevant to Y Co Ltd, particularly as X Co Ltd is currently funding the litigation.

Can you continue to act for both parties? Unless X Co Ltd is willing to waive confidentiality to allow you to inform Y Co Ltd of your conversation, or Y Co Ltd gives specific informed consent (given or evidenced in writing) to non-disclosure (para 6.4(b) of the Code), then, no, you cannot continue to act for both parties due to a conflict of interests.

SUMMARY

(1) A solicitor (and their staff) must keep the affairs of their clients confidential.

(2) The duty of confidentiality continues until the client permits disclosure or waives the confidentiality.

(3) The duty of confidentiality may be overridden in exceptional circumstances.

(4) The solicitor also has a personal duty to disclose to the client all information that is relevant to the client's matter.

(5) A firm must not risk breaching confidentiality by acting for a client where that client has an interest adverse to the interest of another current or former client for whom the firm holds confidential information which is material to that matter, unless appropriate safeguards can be put in place to prevent disclosure of the confidential information or the client to whom the duty of confidentiality is owed gives informed consent to the firm acting.

(6) In addition to the duty of confidentiality, a solicitor must also consider legal professional privilege. Where legal professional privilege applies, a solicitor can refuse to disclose communications between themselves and a client.

CHAPTER 13

Conflicts of Interests

LEARNING OUTCOMES

After reading this chapter you will have learned about:

- the principles governing conflicts of interests
- identifying and dealing with such conflicts.

13.1 INTRODUCTION

A solicitor must act in the best interests of their clients (Principle 7). There will be situations where the interests of two clients (or prospective clients) conflict. Where this happens it will be practically impossible for the solicitor to act in the best interests of the two clients simultaneously.

For example, a solicitor is asked to act for Mr Lacey and Mr Roberts, who are suing each other over a boundary dispute (an obvious situation where the interests of the two clients conflict). Both clients will ultimately want to win their case, and so the solicitor will have a duty to act in the best interests of each client and take steps to try to ensure that they are successful in their litigation. However, the solicitor would be placed in an impossible situation, as anything done to help Mr Lacey win his case will be detrimental to Mr Roberts' case (and therefore not in Mr Roberts' best interests).

For this reason, the SRA prohibits solicitors from acting where there is a conflict of interests between two or more clients, except in specified limited circumstances.

13.2 TYPES OF CONFLICTS OF INTERESTS

There are two situations where a conflict of interest may arise:

(a) a conflict between two or more clients (a 'conflict of interest'); or

(b) a conflict between the client's interests and the solicitor's interests (an 'own interest conflict').

A solicitor can never act where there is a conflict between themselves and a current client, but there are limited circumstances in which a solicitor can act where there is a conflict between two or more current clients. Even in these circumstances, the overriding consideration will be the best interests of each of the clients concerned, and in particular whether the solicitor is satisfied that it is reasonable to act for all or both of the clients.

13.3 CONFLICT OF INTEREST BETWEEN CLIENTS

13.3.1 Introduction

For the purposes of the Codes of Conduct, a conflict of interest means 'a situation where the solicitor's or firm's separate duties to act in the best interests of two or more clients conflict' (SRA Glossary).

Paragraph 6.2 of the Code of Conduct for Solicitors and the Code of Conduct for Firms provides that a solicitor or firm must not act in relation to a matter or particular aspect of it if there is a conflict of interest or a significant risk of such a conflict in relation to that matter or aspect of it, unless:

(a) the clients have a substantially common interest in relation to the matter or the aspect of it, as appropriate; or

(b) the clients are competing for the same objective (see **13.3.5**).

13.3.2 Former clients – confidential information.

A conflict of interest may arise only between two current clients of the firm. Where a client's retainer has been terminated the firm no longer owes a duty to act in that client's best interests, and so a conflict of interest cannot arise concerning the affairs of a former client.

However, even in the absence of a conflict of interest, a firm may be prevented from acting for a client where it holds confidential information for the former client which would be material to the work done for the new client. See **Chapter 12** for further details.

13.3.3 The same matter or particular aspect of it

It is easy to see how a conflict of interest might arise when advising two clients about the same matter. The first example in this chapter (at **13.1**) concerned two clients involved in the same matter – a court case. Acting for clients whose interests are in direct conflict, for example claimant and defendant in litigation, will inevitably result in a conflict of interest and so it would not be possible to act for both parties in those circumstances. Likewise, acting for two or more clients where the solicitor may need to negotiate on matters of substance on their behalf, for example negotiating on price between a buyer and a seller of property, is also likely to result in a conflict of interest as separate duties will be owed to each client to act in their best interests and those duties conflict or there is a significant risk that they will do so. Care should be taken in situations where there is an inequality of bargaining power between the clients as, again, a conflict of interest is likely to arise.

A conflict of interest can also arise concerning a particular aspect of a matter rather than the matter as a whole. For example, you could not act to sell a new house for one client whilst also acting for another client who is alleging that a part of the house has been built on their land. However, there would need to be some reasonable degree of relationship (such as in the above example) for a conflict to arise.

Where the only conflict between the parties is their wider business interests then this will not create any conflict of interest issues. For example, imagine that Isla Cola and Samet Cola are the two main cola distributors in England and Wales. A firm of solicitors could represent Isla Cola on a purchase of a new IT system for their factory, whilst also representing Samet Cola in the purchase of a fleet of cars for their management. Although the interests of Isla Cola and Samet Cola will conflict (as they will both want to sell more cola than the other firm), a solicitors' firm may act for both at the same time without breaching the Codes as the purchases of the IT system and the cars are not the same matter.

13.3.4 Significant risk of a conflict of interest

An actual conflict of interest is not required. A significant risk that a solicitor's duties to act in the best interests of each client may conflict will be enough to bring it within para 6.2 of the Codes.

For example, if Mr and Mrs Rowntree sought to instruct the same solicitor to act for them in dealing with the division of their financial assets following their divorce from one another, the solicitor could not act for both of them. This would remain the case even if they explained that their divorce was an amicable one, and they had agreed the division of their assets. Even if there was no actual conflict between their interests (an unlikely event), the solicitor could not act, as there would be a significant risk that the duty to act in their best interests might conflict. For instance, Mrs Rowntree might want more of the matrimonial assets once the solicitor has advised her about her legal rights, and Mr Rowntree might not agree to this.

There is also a significant risk of a conflict arising where there is inequality of bargaining power between the clients.

13.3.5 Exceptions

13.3.5.1 Introduction

Where a conflict of interest exists, or where there is a significant risk that a conflict may exist, a firm of solicitors may still act for both parties in defined circumstances and with the informed consent of both parties.

The following exceptions were originally introduced by The Law Society and contained in the previous Codes of Conduct following a period of lobbying by parts of the profession to liberalise the conflict of interest rules, which prohibited a firm acting where there was a conflict, or where the firm held confidential information for one client which was relevant to another client. The exceptions are now contained within para 6.2 of both Codes.

The substantially common interest exception (para 6.2(a))

Where there is a conflict of interest or a significant risk of one, a solicitor or firm can still act where the clients have a substantially common interest in relation to the matter or the aspect of it, as appropriate.

The SRA Glossary defines 'a substantially common interest' as a situation where there is a clear common purpose between the clients and a strong consensus as to how it is to be achieved.

An example of when this exception might be used is where a solicitor is instructed by a group of people who want to set up a company. Whilst those providing instructions may not necessarily agree on every aspect involved in setting up a new business venture, so long as they have agreed upon the key, fundamental matters (such as funding, shareholdings, management structure and roles etc), it is likely that a clear common purpose and a strong consensus as to how this will be achieved can be said to exist and so enable the solicitor to act for the group in setting up the company. However, if differences were to arise within the group during the course of the matter which could be seen as undermining the common purpose and strong consensus, the solicitor is likely to come to the conclusion that the exception no longer applies and so would have to cease to act for the group as a conflict of interest has arisen.

The competing for the same objective (or 'commercial') exception (para 6.2(b))

The SRA Glossary sets out the meaning of some of the terminology used in this exception to aid in its interpretation. Clients will be 'competing for the same objective' in a situation in which two or more clients are competing for an 'objective' which, if attained by one client, will make that 'objective' unattainable to the other client or clients. The term 'objective' is further defined as

> an asset, contract or business opportunity which two or more clients are seeking to acquire or recover through liquidation (or some other form of insolvency process) or by means of an auction or tender process or a bid or offer, but not a public takeover.

This exception is likely, therefore, to continue to be used for corporate clients only. For example, it would enable one firm to act for two companies bidding to take over a third company, despite the fact that the obligations to act in the best interests of the clients would conflict (both want to be successful in their bid to acquire the company, and any step taken by the firm to try to make this happen for one client would be detrimental to the interests of the other client).

13.3.5.2 Conditions for acting under either of the exceptions

A set of conditions must be met where a solicitor or firm is looking to act for two or more clients under either of the exceptions in para 6.2 of the Codes and are set out in that paragraph:

(a) all the clients have given informed consent, given or evidenced in writing, to the solicitor or firm acting:

(b) where appropriate, effective safeguards are put in place to protect the clients' confidential information; and

(c) the solicitor or firm is satisfied it is reasonable for them or it to act for all the clients.

13.3.5.3 Informed consent

A client simply agreeing to the solicitor acting will not be enough. The consent must be 'informed', meaning that the client must appreciate the issues and risks involved (having had these explained to them by the solicitor, where appropriate) and make a decision based on those risks. Informed consent may be easier to obtain from sophisticated users of legal services, such as large companies with in-house legal departments to advise them on the risks involved of being represented under one of the exceptions.

13.3.5.4 Confidential information

Where a firm does decide to act by taking advantage of one of the above exceptions, the firm may well put itself in a position where it holds confidential information for one client which is material to the other client(s). Where this is the case, the firm will need to put in place effective safeguards to protect the confidential information. See **Chapter 12** for more details.

13.3.5.5 Is it reasonable to act?

When considering whether to use one of the above exceptions it also must be reasonable for the solicitor or firm to act for all the clients.

The solicitor should consider – both at the outset and throughout the duration of the retainer – whether one client is at risk of prejudice if they are not represented separately (ie by another firm) from the other client(s). This will particularly be the case where one client is vulnerable, the clients cannot be represented even-handedly or where the parties do not have equal bargaining power.

13.4 CONFLICT OF INTEREST BETWEEN TWO EXISTING CLIENTS

A solicitor may have agreed to act for two clients where, at the beginning of the transaction, there was no actual conflict or any significant risk of a conflict. However, a conflict may arise during the retainer.

Where such a conflict does arise between two existing clients, a solicitor must have regard not only to the conflict of interest, but also to the issues surrounding confidential information. The solicitor may continue to act for one of the clients but must ensure that their duty of confidentiality is not put at risk (see **Chapter 12** for more details).

13.5 OWN INTEREST CONFLICT

Paragraph 6.1 of both Codes of Conduct provides that a solicitor or firm must not act where there is an 'own interest' conflict, or a significant risk of an 'own interest' conflict. This refers to any situation where a solicitor's or firm's duty to act in the best interests of any client in relation to a matter conflicts, or there is a significant risk that it may conflict, with their or its own interests in relation to that or a related matter (SRA Glossary). In such a situation, the solicitor or firm must consider whether to decline to accept the retainer, cease to act where instructions have already been accepted or advise the client to seek independent legal advice on that aspect of the matter.

For example, a solicitor could not act for a client suing a company where the solicitor was a major shareholder in that company. The solicitor would be obliged to act in the best interests of the client and take steps to try to ensure that the client was successful in suing the company. In taking those steps the solicitor would be acting to the detriment of the company. If the client was successful, the company would have to pay the client damages and so its share price might drop. This would be detrimental to the company's shareholders – including the solicitor.

Further examples of situations in which a solicitor's interest might conflict with that of their client are contained in a Law Society Practice Note on conflict of interest:

(a) a client wants to make a gift of a significant amount to a solicitor, or to leave them a legacy in their will (see **10.3.2.3**);
(b) a solicitor lends money to, or borrows from, a client;
(c) a solicitor sells to, or buys from, their client;
(d) a solicitor has an interest in a business which they then recommend as an investment to a client;
(e) there is a personal relationship with the client which impacts on the solicitor's ability to advise them independently, impartially, and as to what is in their best interests;
(f) there has been a negligent act or omission on a matter in which the solicitor or someone else within their firm is acting.

A solicitor must act in the best interests of their client (Principle 7). Thus a solicitor must not make a secret profit whilst acting for the client. Paragraph 4.1 of the Code of Conduct for Solicitors (mirrored in para 5.1 of the Code of Conduct for Firms) obliges a solicitor to account properly to clients for any financial benefit they receive as a result of their instructions (see **11.14**).

13.6 SYSTEMS AND CONTROLS FOR IDENTIFYING CONFLICTS

The Code of Conduct for Firms provides that firms must have effect systems and controls in place to ensure that they comply with all of the SRA's regulatory requirements (para 2.1(a)). Given that the proper handling of conflicts of interests is important for public protection and for being able to act in the best interests of each client, it is important, therefore, that firms have in place appropriate and effective systems and controls to identify and assess potential conflicts of interests. The form that such systems take and the detail regarding what such systems and controls need to assess will differ, however, depending on the size and complexity of the firm, the nature of the clients and work undertaken, and whether they relate to an 'own interest' conflict or a client conflict of interests.

In terms of identifying 'own interest' conflicts, the following factors used as guidance in the previous Code of Conduct may continue to be helpful considerations. The firm should assess all the relevant circumstances, including whether the solicitor's ability as an individual, or that of anyone within the firm, to act in the best interests of the client(s) is impaired by:

(a) any financial interest;
(b) a personal relationship;
(c) the appointment of the solicitor, or a member of their family, to public office;
(d) commercial relationships; or
(e) their employment.

Many firms maintain a register of personal interests held by its managers and employees which aid in identifying potential 'own interest' conflicts.

Likewise, the following may be helpful in identifying conflicts of interests between clients. The firm should assess all relevant circumstances, including whether:

(a) the clients' interests are different;
(b) the ability to give independent advice to the clients may be fettered;
(c) there is a need to negotiate between the clients;
(d) there is an imbalance in bargaining power between the clients; or
(e) any client is vulnerable.

A conflict of interest check should be carried out before accepting instructions to act on any new matter, using details such as the names and addresses of the client and other relevant parties (and their relevant business interests, where appropriate).

13.7 PROFESSIONAL EMBARRASSMENT

Even where there is no conflict of interest, nor any significant risk of a conflict, a solicitor may still decline to act for a client due to professional embarrassment. (See also **12.3.5** above.)

A solicitor should consider whether accepting instructions to act for a client would breach one of the Principles. One example might be acting against a former client. There would be no conflict of interest, as a conflict cannot arise between a current client and a former client. However, the solicitor must consider whether they would feel restricted in doing their best for the current client on the basis that they were acting against a former client (with whom the solicitor may have built up a good relationship). If so, the solicitor would not be acting in the best interests of the current client in accepting the instructions.

A solicitor may also take into account their own commercial considerations when deciding whether to accept instructions from a new client. For example, if your firm's major client is Isla Cola and you are asked to act for its major rival on a completely unrelated matter, you might decline to do so if you thought that Isla Cola would instruct another firm as a result.

13.8 LIMITED RETAINER

Where a conflict arises between two clients, either at the beginning of or during a transaction, an alternative to relying on one of the exceptions set out above (at **13.3.5**) may be to accept a limited retainer. The solicitor could be retained to act only in relation to those areas where no conflict exists, with each client seeking independent advice on the conflicting areas. It is necessary to make clear the terms of the retainer, and that there are defined areas where the solicitor cannot advise.

13.9 CONVEYANCING

The area of conveyancing is subject to additional requirements regarding acting for more than one party within a transaction. These are considered in more detail in ***Property Law & Practice***.

13.10 EXAMPLES

EXAMPLE 1

Question You are approached by Mr Smith and Mr Jones. They are the sole partners of Smith, Jones & Co, a firm of solicitors. Mr Jones explains that he wishes to leave the partnership and that Mr Smith has agreed to buy his interest in the partnership. They suggest to you that they both have the same aim and do not wish to go to the expense of instructing different solicitors to act from them.

Can you or your firm act for both of them in agreeing the sale of Mr Jones' interest in the partnership?

Answer Is there a conflict of interests here? Yes. You would owe separate duties to act in the best interests of both clients in relation to the same matter. Do these interests conflict? Yes. Mr Jones will wish to receive as high a price as possible for his share in the partnership, whereas Mr Smith will want to pay as little as possible. Other issues of conflict will also arise in relation to liability for debts, etc.

Can the 'substantially common interest' exception be used here? Although it may appear initially that the two clients have a common interest – one wishes to sell and the other wishes to buy – their interest conflicts for the reasons stated above.

You must send at least one client to another firm of solicitors.

EXAMPLE 2

Question X Co Ltd is put up for sale as a result of continuing financial difficulties. A number of parties enter negotiations to buy the company as a going concern. Can your firm act for two of these parties (Party A and Party B)?

Answer Is there a conflict of interest here? Yes – clearly the interests of Party A and Party B conflict on the same matter as they both wish to buy X Co Ltd.

Therefore your firm would usually be prevented from acting for both parties. However, does an exception apply? It is possible that the 'competing for the same objective' exception under para 6.2(a) of the Codes of Conduct could allow the firm to act for both parties on the basis that the clients are competing for the same objective (ie, to buy X Co Ltd as a going concern) which, if attained by one client, will make that objective unattainable to the other, and as long as the following conditions are met:

(a) both clients have given informed consent, given or evidenced in writing, to your firm acting;

(b) the firm puts in place effective safeguards (including information barriers) to protect each client's confidential information as the information obtained from either client would be 'material' to the other client, and both clients have an interest adverse to one another by virtue of competing for the same objective (see **12.3**); and

(c) you are satisfied it is reasonable for the firm to act for both clients.

SUMMARY

(1) A solicitor must not act where there is a conflict, or significant risk of a conflict, between the interests of two or more clients, or between the interests of the client and the solicitor.

(2) Where there is a conflict between two or more clients, a solicitor may act if they can satisfy the requirements of the substantially common interest exception or the competing for the same objective exception.

(3) Regardless of the requirements concerning conflicts of interests, the solicitor must also consider their duty of confidentiality.

(4) A solicitor may decline to act if they are professionally embarrassed, or for commercial considerations.

CHAPTER 14

UNDERTAKINGS

LEARNING OUTCOMES

After reading this chapter you will be able to understand:

- what an undertaking is
- the operation and effect of giving an undertaking
- 'policing' and risk management of undertakings.

14.1 INTRODUCTION

In the SRA Glossary, an undertaking is defined as 'a statement given orally or in writing, whether or not it includes the word "undertake" or "undertaking" to someone who reasonably places reliance on it, that you or a third party will do something or cause something to be done, or refrain from doing something'. In other words, an undertaking could be said to be an enforceable promise. Any statement made by a solicitor to do or not do something, whether given to a client or to a third party (such as another solicitor), may be an undertaking. Indeed, even if such a promise is made on a solicitor's behalf by a member of their staff, it may constitute an undertaking.

A solicitor must perform all undertakings given by them and do so within an agreed timescale or, if no timescale has been agreed, then within a reasonable amount of time (para 1.3 of the Code of Conduct for Solicitors and the Code of Conduct for Firms).

As the definition makes clear, it is not necessary to use the word 'undertake' for the undertaking to be binding. Even a promise to give an undertaking will usually be interpreted as an undertaking, and therefore will be binding on the solicitor concerned.

Once the undertaking has been relied upon by the recipient, it can be withdrawn only by agreement.

A solicitor is not obliged to give or accept an undertaking. Given the consequences of breaching an undertaking (see **14.3** below), indeed a solicitor should think carefully when considering whether to give an undertaking.

14.2 WHY UNDERTAKINGS ARE NECESSARY

Undertakings are often given by solicitors in order to smooth the path of a transaction. They are a convenient method by which some otherwise problematic areas of practice can be avoided.

> **EXAMPLE**
>
> Imagine a solicitor is acting for Mr Taylor concerning the sale of his business. Mr Taylor has agreed that he will pay the legal costs of the purchaser if the purchaser buys the business. However, the purchaser of the business wants Mr Taylor to pay this money (an agreed £10,000) up front before the deal takes place, in order to fund the necessary due diligence process (eg, to examine the contracts and leases of the business to establish whether the business is worth the asking price).
>
> The solicitor could give an undertaking to the purchaser's solicitors to pay £10,000 towards the purchaser's costs from the proceeds of sale of the business (assuming that the proceeds of sale would cover the £10,000). If accepted, the purchaser's solicitors might well be happy to complete the due diligence work without any money on account from their client. In the absence of such an undertaking the client would have to fund paying the £10,000 before receiving the proceeds of sale from the business.

14.3 BREACH OF AN UNDERTAKING

Where a solicitor gives an undertaking, the terms of that undertaking will be personally binding on the individual solicitor concerned.

For example, a solicitor is acting for a client who is in arrears with their mortgage payments. The client is taken to court by their mortgage company to repossess their house. To prevent the house being repossessed the client offers to pay the arrears (£10,000) within seven days. The mortgage company agrees to withdraw the repossession proceedings, but only on the basis that the solicitor gives an undertaking to pay the mortgage company £10,000 within seven days. If the solicitor agreed to give the undertaking in those terms and the client didn't come up with the money, the solicitor would be personally liable to pay the £10,000.

If a solicitor fails to comply with such an undertaking, the solicitor may be sued personally by the recipient. The solicitor will also breach the Code of Conduct and may be disciplined by the SRA or the Solicitors Disciplinary Tribunal (see **14.8**). The solicitor's firm may also be disciplined for a lack of supervision. As there is an obligation on firms to maintain records to demonstrate compliance with their obligations under the SRA's regulatory arrangements (Code of Conduct for Firms, para 2.2) and on solicitors to be able to justify their decisions and actions in order to comply with their obligations under those arrangements (Code of Conduct for Solicitors, para 7.2), it will be necessary for firms and solicitors to maintain an effective system that records when undertakings have been given and when they have been discharged.

14.4 ORAL AND WRITTEN UNDERTAKINGS

An undertaking will be binding regardless of whether it is given orally or in writing (SRA Glossary), but it is advisable to give undertakings in writing, so that there can be no dispute as to the terms of the undertaking. If, however, it is necessary in the circumstances to give an oral undertaking, the solicitor should ensure that an attendance note recording the undertaking is placed on the client's file and that it is confirmed in writing as soon as possible.

14.5 TERMS OF THE UNDERTAKING

14.5.1 Introduction

An undertaking is not a contract. For example, there is no obligation for consideration (whether in monetary or other forms) to be present for an undertaking to be enforceable against a solicitor. However, given the binding effect of undertakings, and the consequences for breach, a solicitor should take just as much care in drafting undertakings as they would do when drafting a contract for a client.

14.5.2 Wording of an undertaking

The SRA's guidance in a previous Code of Conduct provided that any ambiguity in the wording of the undertaking would be interpreted in favour of its recipient. As this is still likely to be the case, great care should be taken by the solicitor when drafting undertakings.

14.5.3 Acts outside the solicitor's control

From time to time, a solicitor may be called upon to undertake to perform an action which is outside of their control, such as to forward documents which are not in their possession. The simple fact that the solicitor is unable to perform the undertaking without the cooperation of their client or another third party does not discharge the solicitor's obligation to perform, and the undertaking remains enforceable.

Providing an undertaking which is wholly reliant on the action/inaction of a third party should be avoided given the binding nature of such an undertaking. In other appropriate circumstances, a solicitor may seek to give an undertaking that, in respect of our example above, they will use their 'reasonable endeavours' to obtain and provide the documents requested. This will impose a lesser obligation upon the solicitor, just as such a 'reasonable endeavours' obligation in contract imposes a lesser obligation on the contracting party. However, it may not give the party who might seek to rely on it the same comfort as an absolute undertaking, and that party may therefore choose not to accept it, which may cause delay to the transaction.

Further, it would not be appropriate to give a 'reasonable endeavours' undertaking in circumstances in which a solicitor would be unable or unwilling to take any steps themselves in order to achieve the objective, or where there is likely to be scope for dispute as to whether reasonable endeavours have been used.

14.5.4 Undertakings 'on behalf' of a client

Whilst an undertaking is almost always made for the benefit of the solicitor's client (in order to smooth the transaction as explained above), it is made in the solicitor's name. However, an undertaking may be drafted as being made 'on behalf of' the solicitor's client. This will not prevent the undertaking from being enforceable as against the solicitor, who will remain personally liable.

It is possible for a solicitor to give an undertaking 'on behalf' of a client and exclude personal liability, but in order to do so the SRA's guidance in a previous Code of Conduct provided that the solicitor must clearly and expressly disclaim personal liability, or make it clear that they are simply informing the other side of their client's intentions. This is likely to remain the case under the current Codes of Conduct.

Therefore an undertaking that seeks to exclude personal liability on behalf of the solicitor is legally possible. However, it is unlikely to be accepted by the proposed recipient, as their ability to enforce it (and therefore rely on it) will be greatly reduced.

14.5.5 Timescale

Paragraph 1.3 of the Codes expressly provides that undertakings must be performed 'within an agreed timescale', and therefore it is important that any such timescale is expressed when the undertaking is given. Where no timescale has been agreed, however, para 1.3 provides that the undertaking must be performed within a 'reasonable amount of time'. What is 'reasonable' will depend upon the facts of each case, and so this element of uncertainty should be a consideration when preparing to give or receive such undertakings.

14.5.6 Costs

Where an undertaking is given in respect of the payment of costs of another party, the term 'costs' will be implied to mean proper costs unless a specific amount is agreed. Therefore, a solicitor is able to request an assessment of the costs by the court if costs are not agreed.

14.6 CLIENT'S AUTHORITY

As has been made very clear in this chapter, an undertaking is a personal obligation on the solicitor who gave it, and therefore the solicitor will be held liable for it, even if performance would put the solicitor in breach of their duty to their client. A solicitor should therefore ensure that they have clear and express authority from their client before giving any undertakings. When such authority has been received, it may be withdrawn by the client at any time until the solicitor has acted upon it, even if it is expressed to be irrevocable.

14.7 CHANGE OF CIRCUMSTANCES

An undertaking will remain binding upon the solicitor if the circumstances change so that it is impossible to fulfil it, either wholly or partially. However, the recipient may agree to its variation or discharge. Where an undertaking is given which is dependent upon the happening of a future event and it becomes apparent that the future event in question will not occur, good practice will be to notify the recipient of this.

14.8 ENFORCEMENT

14.8.1 The courts

The court is able to enforce an undertaking against a solicitor as an officer of the court and likewise against an unincorporated law partnership. Accordingly, where an undertaking has been breached, an aggrieved party may seek compensation for any loss (for example, see *Udall v Capri Lighting Ltd* [1987] 3 All ER 262). Firms are obliged to carry indemnity insurance to cover such claims. However, the value of such claims may well fall within the excess of those policies, leading to personal liability for the solicitor concerned.

As outlined below, a breach of an undertaking is likely to be a breach of professional conduct. However, given the court's jurisdiction over solicitors concerning undertakings, the SRA's previous guidance provided that the SRA would not investigate a breach of an undertaking given to the court itself, unless the court reported the matter to the SRA, and this is likely to remain the case.

In *Harcus Sinclair v Your Lawyers* [2021] UKSC 32, the Supreme Court confirmed that an undertaking given by an incorporated law practice, ie a limited company or LLP, is not capable of being enforced against that practice under the court's supervisory jurisdiction over solicitors as officers of the court. This is because such a practice has a separate legal existence which is not a solicitor. Upon breach of an undertaking by an incorporated practice, therefore, the form of redress would be a claim under contract, negligence or breach of trust, depending on the facts. The practice can still face action for professional misconduct. The Law Society has produced a Practice Note on Professional Undertakings which includes considerations concerning the impact of different types of business structure on the enforcement of undertakings.

14.8.2 The SRA and the Solicitors Disciplinary Tribunal

If a solicitor fails to comply with the terms of an undertaking they have given, this will be a breach of professional conduct. The Legal Ombudsman, the SRA and the Solicitors Disciplinary Tribunal have no power to enforce the performance of an undertaking. Neither can these organisations direct that a solicitor pay compensation to an aggrieved third party. However, they may investigate the solicitor's conduct and impose disciplinary sanctions (up to and including, in the case of the Solicitors Disciplinary Tribunal, striking the solicitor off the roll of solicitors).

However, the SRA's previous guidance provided that where an undertaking has been obtained by fraud or deceit, it is unlikely that any action will be taken against the solicitor who has breached the undertaking.

14.9 LIABILITY OF OTHERS

The obligation in para 1.3 of the Code of Conduct for Firms covers undertakings given by solicitors, non-admitted staff, and also undertakings given by anyone held out by the firm as representing the firm. For example, if an undertaking given by an assistant solicitor is not honoured, there will be a breach of professional conduct by the solicitor and also the partners of the firm. Accordingly, many firms have strict procedures in respect of recording undertakings given, and who within the firm is authorised to give undertakings.

14.10 STANDARD FORMS OF UNDERTAKING

Any written undertaking given by a solicitor should be tailored carefully to the circumstances. However, standard forms of wording exist for common undertakings, for example in conveyancing transactions.

14.11 EXAMPLES

EXAMPLE 1

A solicitor is instructed by a landlord regarding the renewal of a lease of a domestic property. The solicitor is told that the landlord is very keen to retain the existing tenant, rather than going to the expense of advertising the property and having it stand empty for possibly weeks whilst a new tenant is found.

The solicitor is told that the tenant will attend the solicitor's office tomorrow (the day the lease is due to expire), to 'tie up a few loose ends' and sign a new tenancy agreement.

The following day the tenant duly arrives at the solicitor's office. However, it soon becomes clear that there are problems to be resolved before the tenant will agree to the new tenancy. The tenant explains that the house is in a shabby state, and the only way that the tenant would be willing to agree to a new tenancy is if the landlord agrees to redecorate the entire house and fit new carpets.

The solicitor tries to negotiate with the tenant that the landlord will look at the matter after the new lease is signed. However, the tenant states that unless the issues are dealt with today, he will terminate the existing lease and rent some other property. The solicitor is unable to contact the landlord and so reluctantly gives an undertaking on behalf of the landlord that the property will be redecorated and the carpets replaced within one month. The tenant happily renews the lease.

The solicitor informs her client of the undertaking the next day. The landlord is outraged, and refuses to carry out the work.

The undertaking was given on behalf of a client, but as the solicitor did not expressly disclaim personal liability, the solicitor will be bound to comply with the undertaking (Code of Conduct for Solicitors, para 1.3). The tenant can enforce the undertaking by suing the solicitor. If the client maintains his stance and refuses to comply, the solicitor will personally have to pay for the redecoration and carpets and ensure that this is done within the timescale stated. In addition to being sued by the tenant, the solicitor could also be reported to the SRA and the Legal Ombudsman in the form of a complaint about the services provided by her.

The solicitor should not have given the undertaking without obtaining her client's authority and consent.

EXAMPLE 2

A solicitor is acting for a client concerning a large debt. The client owes Berkin Finance £100,000 and is being pressed to pay the debt. The client agrees to sell his holiday cottage by auction in order to pay the debt. The cottage is valued at £120,000 and the client is hopeful that he will receive at least this price at the auction.

Berkin Finance writes to the client stating that unless the debt is paid in full within seven days, it will commence court proceedings. As the auction is to be held in 10 days' time, the solicitor (acting on the instructions of the client) undertakes to Berkin Finance to pay £100,000 from the proceeds of sale of the cottage.

The cottage is sold at auction for £90,000. Berkin Finance demands the full £100,000 from the solicitor. The solicitor must perform the undertaking given by her (Code of Conduct for Solicitors, para 1.3). Unfortunately for the solicitor, the SRA's previous guidance provided that where an undertaking is given to make a payment from the proceeds of sale of an asset, the solicitor must pay the full amount (ie, £100,000), regardless of whether the proceeds of sale are sufficient, and this is still likely to be the case under the current Codes of Conduct.

The solicitor should have drafted the undertaking to state clearly that her liability would be limited to the money she received from the sale, or to make it clear that she was disclaiming all personal liability.

SUMMARY

(1) An undertaking is any statement, whether or not it includes the word 'undertake' or 'undertaking', made by or on behalf of a solicitor or their firm to someone who reasonably places reliance upon it, that the giver of the statement or a third party will do something or cause something to be done, or refrain from doing something.

(2) A solicitor will be personally bound to honour an undertaking, regardless of whether the undertaking was given orally or in writing.

(3) Any ambiguity in the wording of an undertaking is likely to be construed against the party that gave it.

(4) A solicitor should obtain their client's express authority before giving an undertaking.

(5) An undertaking by a solicitor and an unincorporated law partnership may be enforced by the court.

(6) The SRA/Legal Ombudsman/Solicitors Disciplinary Tribunal do not have the power to enforce an undertaking. However, any breach of an undertaking may be considered a breach of professional conduct, or result in a complaint about services provided by a solicitor which may lead to sanctions against the solicitor concerned.

CHAPTER 15

Money Laundering and the Proceeds of Crime Act 2002

LEARNING OUTCOMES

After reading this chapter you will be able to understand:

- solicitors' obligations under the Money Laundering Regulations 2017
- solicitors' obligations concerning money laundering under the Proceeds of Crime Act 2002.

15.1 INTRODUCTION

'Money laundering' is the process by which criminals seek to alter or 'launder' their proceeds of crime so that it appears that these funds come from a legitimate source.

Suppose a thief has stolen £1 million. The thief then instructs a number of intermediaries each to invest a relatively small proportion of the money. The investments can later be sold, and the thief then appears to be in possession of the proceeds of a legitimate transaction.

In this particular example the 'audit trail' by which investigators follow the proceeds of crime is not too difficult, but it does not take a great deal of imagination to see how a series of deals using different intermediaries and types of investment could throw the investigators off track.

Solicitors are targets for criminals in their efforts to launder their proceeds of crime. The purpose of regulation in this area is to disrupt serious crime (including terrorism) by inhibiting criminals' ability to reinvest or benefit from the proceeds of crime. The Government has also introduced an economic crime levy on anti-money laundering regulated businesses, including law firms, to fund the fight against this type of crime. The levy is in the form of a fixed fee based on the size of the firm as determined by its UK revenue (with smaller firms being exempt).

The purpose of this chapter is to introduce some of the issues relating to the Government's anti-money laundering legislation. Further guidance can be sought from The Law Society, which produces detailed advice on this subject.

15.2 MONEY LAUNDERING REGULATIONS 2017

15.2.1 Introduction

The Money Laundering, Terrorist Financing and Transfer of Funds (Information on the Payer) Regulations 2017 (SI 2017/692) ('the Regulations') came into force on 26 June 2017 and repealed and replaced the Money Laundering Regulations 2007. The 2017 Regulations have since been amended by the Money Laundering and Terrorist Financing (Amendment) Regulations 2019 and the Money Laundering and Terrorist Financing (Amendment) (EU Exit) Regulations 2020.

The Regulations apply to persons acting in the course of businesses carried out in the UK. This includes 'independent legal professionals' (reg 8), defined in reg 12 as:

> a firm or sole practitioner who by way of business provides legal or notarial services to other persons, when participating in financial or real property transactions ....

The definition of a 'tax adviser' has been expanded in reg 11 to include providing material aid, or assistance or advice, on tax affairs of other persons including where provided through a third party. Therefore, the vast majority of solicitors' firms will be subject to the Regulations. Failure to comply with the Regulations is a criminal offence.

There is a requirement for the 'beneficial owners, officers or managers' of the firm and sole practitioners to apply to the SRA for approval under the Regulations, and such approval must be granted unless they have been convicted of a 'relevant offence' (a long list of offences which fall within this definition is set out in Sch 3 and includes offences under previous money laundering legislation, the Terrorism Act 2006 and any offence which has deception or dishonesty as one of its components). Acting without such approval after 26 June 2018 is a criminal offence and may result in imprisonment, a fine or both (reg 26).

A firm is required to take appropriate steps to identify and assess the risk of money laundering and terrorist financing to which the business is subject (reg 18). This will entail a firm-wide risk assessment to include risk factors relating to, for example, its clients, the countries in which it operates and its transactions, as well as information made available by The Law Society and the SRA. The Legal Sector Affinity Group also provide guidance from time to time. The National Risk Assessment published by HM Treasury in 2017 specifies the following services provided by law firms as most likely to be targeted by money launders: trust and company formation, conveyancing and client account services – and so firms need to ensure that their risk assessment addresses the risks in these specialist areas. A firm is required to keep an up-to-date written record of all of the steps it has taken in terms of the risk assessment.

Firms which are subject to the Regulations must comply with, for example, the matters discussed in **15.2.2** to **15.2.5** below. What follows is simply an overview of the often complex requirements imposed upon solicitors. More guidance can be obtained via www.lawsociety.org.uk.

15.2.2 Nominated officers and reporting procedures

A firm is required to establish and maintain written policies, controls and procedures (proportionate to its size and nature and approved by its senior management) to mitigate and manage effectively the money laundering and terrorist financing risks identified in its risk assessment (reg 21). This will include risk management practices, how the firm conducts client due diligence, the firm's reporting and record keeping systems, policies put in place when new technology products or business practices are adopted and in relation to complex or unusually large transactions, or unusual patterns of transactions which have no apparent economic or legal purpose.

A firm must have a 'nominated officer' (MLRO) to receive reports from within the firm concerning any instances of suspected money laundering and to liaise, if necessary, with the National Crime Agency (NCA) (reg 21(3)). In addition, a firm must appoint an individual at the level of senior management to be responsible for compliance with the Regulations (reg 21(1)(a)). This can be the same individual as the MLRO or the 'compliance officer' (COLP) provided that they are of sufficient seniority.

In addition to the above, a firm is required to adopt two further internal controls:

(a) The screening of relevant employees prior to and during the course of their employment to assess their skills, knowledge, conduct and integrity. This relates to employees whose work in the firm is relevant to compliance with the Regulations or who otherwise contribute towards the identification, prevention and detection of money laundering and terrorist financing (reg 21(1)(b)).

(b) Establishing an independent audit function to examine, evaluate, make recommendations and monitor the firm's policies, controls and procedures adopted to comply with the Regulations (reg 21(1)(c)).

A firm must also establish and maintain controls which enable it to 'respond fully and rapidly' to enquiries from law enforcement as to whether it maintains, or has maintained during the past five years, a business relationship with any person and the nature of that relationship (reg 21(8)).

15.2.3 Client due diligence (client identification)

15.2.3.1 Introduction

Subject to limited exceptions, firms carrying out relevant business are obliged to obtain verification of the identity of each of their clients (referred to as 'customer due diligence' in the Regulations). The need to verify the client's identity includes the following circumstances (reg 27):

(a) if the client and solicitor agree to form a business relationship;

(b) carrying out an occasional transaction (ie one not carried out as part of a business relationship) that amounts to a 'transfer of funds' (essentially any transaction at least partially carried out by electronic means on behalf of a payer through a payment service provider, for example, a credit transfer) exceeding €1,000 euros;

(c) carrying out an occasional transaction that amounts to €15,000 euros or more, whether the transaction is executed in a single operation or in several operations which appear to be linked;

(d) where the solicitor suspects money laundering or terrorist financing;

(e) where the solicitor doubts the veracity or adequacy of documents or information supplied to verify the client's identity.

The verification (as set out in reg 28) must take place before a business relationship is established or the carrying out of the transaction (reg 30). Proof of registration or an excerpt from the relevant register must be collected before establishing a business relationship with a company (registered or unregistered) or a limited liability partnership. Any discrepancies encountered between this information and the information subsequently gathered during the business relationship is to be reported to Companies House as soon as reasonably possible. However, a solicitor may verify otherwise the identity of the client during the establishment of a business relationship if:

(a) there is little risk of any money laundering or terrorist financing occurring;

(b) it is necessary not to interrupt the normal conduct of business; and

(c) the identity is verified as soon as practicable after contact is first established.

However, if the solicitor is unable to complete the client due diligence in time, they cannot:

(a) carry out a transaction with or for the client through a bank account; or

(b) establish a business relationship or carry out a transaction otherwise than through a bank account,

and in such circumstances they must also terminate any existing business relationship and consider making a disclosure to the NCA (reg 31).

How the solicitor must verify the identity of the client varies according to the type of client involved and the risk of money laundering.

15.2.3.2 Simplified due diligence

Simplified due diligence is permitted where a firm determines that the business relationship or transaction presents a low risk of money laundering or terrorist financing, taking into account the risk assessment discussed above. The factors to be taken into account in determining whether a client or transaction poses a lower risk include whether the client is a company listed on a regulated market and the location of the regulated market and where a client is established and does business (reg 37(3)). However, the Regulations make it clear that the presence of one or more of the factors set out does not necessarily indicate that there is a lower risk in a particular situation.

The solicitor must obtain evidence that the transaction and the client are eligible for simplified due diligence. The exact verification required depends on the identity of the client, and the solicitor will not necessarily need to obtain information on the beneficial owners (see **15.2.3.3**). For example, for a well-known plc listed in the UK, the solicitor must obtain confirmation of the company's listing on the Stock Exchange.

15.2.3.3 Standard due diligence

Standard due diligence will apply to most clients. The solicitor is obliged to verify the identity of the client on the basis of 'documents or information in either case obtained from a reliable source which is independent of the person whose identity is being verified' and take reasonable measures to understand the ownership and control structure of non-natural persons such as trusts and companies (reg 28).

For natural persons, evidence of identity may be based on documents such as passports and photocard driving licences. The Law Society considers it good practice to have either:

(a) one government document which verifies name, address and date of birth; or

(b) a government document which verifies the client's full name and supporting documents which verify their address and date of birth.

For non-limited liability partnerships, it will be necessary to obtain information on the constituent individuals who make up the partnership. However, where partnerships are well-known, reputable organisations with long histories in their industries and with substantial public information about them, The Law Society's guidance advises that it should be sufficient to obtain their name, registered or trading address and nature of business.

For companies, it is necessary to verify the existence of the company. The standard identifiers are:

(a) its name;

(b) its company number or other registration; and

(c) the registered office address and principal place of business (if different).

Unless it is a company listed on a regulated market, reasonable measures are to be taken to obtain and verify the law to which it is subject, its constitution or other governing documents and the names of the board of directors or other senior persons responsible for its operations (reg 28). The firm must also collect proof of registration (eg, via the client) or an excerpt from the relevant register before establishing a business relationship with a UK company or a UK limited liability partnership or Scottish Partnership.

Firms should be assisted in this regard by the obligation placed on a 'UK body corporate' (which includes listed and unlisted companies and limited liability partnerships) to provide certain information on request when it forms a business relationship with a firm (and other persons to whom the Regulations apply), which includes the information listed above (reg 43). The Law Society's guidance advises that it may also be appropriate to consider whether the person providing the instructions on behalf of the company has the authority to do so. In addition, where simplified due diligence does not apply (see **15.2.3.2**) it will be necessary to consider the identity of beneficial owners.

Beneficial owners

A solicitor must verify the identity of any 'beneficial owner' where the beneficial owner is not the client. The definition of a beneficial owner varies depending on the nature of the client.

In the case of companies, reg 5(1) defines a beneficial owner as:

(a) any individual who exercises ultimate control over the management of the body corporate;
(b) any individual who ultimately owns or controls (in each case whether directly or indirectly), including through bearer share holdings or by other means, more than 25% of the shares or voting rights in the body corporate; or
(c) an individual who controls the body corporate.

This regulation does not apply to a company listed on a regulated market. It does apply to UK limited liability partnerships.

EXAMPLE

A Co Ltd instructs a firm of solicitors. The solicitors will have to obtain documentary confirmation of the name, number, registered address and the other information set out in reg 28. This can be obtained by carrying out a company search at Companies House. However, the solicitors also need to identify any 'beneficial owner' of the company.

If Mr Smith owns 50% of the shares, Mr Jones owns 30% of the shares and Mr McConnell owns the remaining 20%, Smith and Jones will be the beneficial owners.

However, what happens if A Co Ltd is owned by B Co Ltd? The Law Society's guidance states that a risk-based decision should be taken as to whether to make further enquiries. However, it is common for law firms to seek to identify the beneficial owners of any parent company up to and including the ultimate parent entity.

Therefore, if A Co Ltd is owned by B Co Ltd, the solicitor is likely to make enquiries to identify the beneficial owners of B Co Ltd and so on.

In the case of a partnership (other than a limited liability partnership), reg 5(3) defines a beneficial owner as any individual who:

(a) ultimately is entitled to or controls (whether the entitlement or control is direct or indirect) more than a 25% share of the capital or profits of the partnership, or more than 25% of the voting rights in the partnership; or
(b) otherwise exercises control over the management of the partnership (ie the ability to manage the use of funds or transactions outside of the normal management structure and control mechanisms).

In the case of a trust, beneficial owner means each of the following (reg 6(1)):

(a) the settlor;
(b) the trustees;
(c) the beneficiaries;
(d) where the individuals (or some of the individuals) benefiting from the trust have not been determined, the class of persons in whose main interest the trust is set up, or operates;
(e) any individual who has control over the trust, ie one who has power (whether exercisable alone, jointly with another person or with the consent of another person)

under the trust instrument or by law, for example, to add or remove a person as beneficiary, or to appoint or remove trustees.

As a trust does not have legal personality, the trust itself will not be the client, and so where a solicitor advises any individual client in relation to a trust, they will be required to understand who the other beneficial owners of the trust are, as defined above.

Whilst generally the beneficiaries of a trust will be individuals, they may at times be a company. If this is the case, it is necessary to apply reg 6(4) to determine the beneficial owners of the company in question.

In the case of other arrangements or entities, for example unincorporated associations and foundations, beneficial owner means those individuals who hold equivalent or similar positions to those set out above in reg 6(1).

15.2.3.4 Enhanced due diligence

The Regulations set out a list of circumstances in which enhanced due diligence must be carried out (reg 33). These include where:

(a) the case has been identified as one where there is a high risk of money laundering or terrorist financing in the firm's risk assessment or in the information made available by the SRA and The Law Society;

(b) either the client or other party to the transaction is established in a high-risk third country (as listed on the Financial Action Task Force website);

(c) the client has provided false or stolen identification documentation or information and the solicitor has decided to continue dealing with the client;

(d) the client is a politically exposed person (PEP), or a family member or known close associate of a PEP (see below);

(e) a transaction is complex or unusually large, or where there is an unusual pattern of transactions, or the transactions have no apparent economic or legal purpose;

(f) in any other situation where there is a higher risk of money laundering or terrorist financing. In determining this, there is a wide range of factors for a firm to take into account, for example, whether the business relationship is conducted in unusual circumstances (such as where a solicitor has not met the client face to face), or payments will be received from unknown or associated third parties.

In these situations, a solicitor must take measures, as far as reasonably possible, to examine the background and purpose of the transaction and consider whether it is appropriate, for example, to obtain further independent verification of the client's or beneficial owner's identity or more detail on the ownership, control structure and financial situation of the client. It will also be necessary to conduct enhanced ongoing monitoring of the business relationship.

A PEP is an individual who is entrusted with prominent public functions, other than as a middle-ranking or more junior official (reg 35(12)). PEPs have been a focus for the Financial Action Task Force, EU members and other countries due to growing concerns about PEPs using their political positions to corruptly enrich themselves. Individuals with prominent public functions include the following:

(a) Heads of State, heads of government, ministers and deputy or assistant ministers;

(b) members of parliament;

(c) members of supreme courts, of constitutional courts or of other high-level judicial bodies whose decisions are not generally subject to further appeal, except in exceptional circumstances;

(d) members of courts of auditors or of the boards of central banks;

(e) ambassadors, chargés d'affaires and high-ranking officers in the armed forces;

(f) members of the administrative, management or supervisory bodies of State-owned enterprises.

Family members include a spouse, civil partner, children, their spouses or civil partners and parents. Known close associates include those with whom there are close business relationships.

Changes to the Regulations now mean that domestic PEPs (defined as individuals entrusted with prominent public functions by the UK), whilst still needing to be subject to enhanced due diligence, must be treated as lower risk than overseas PEPs. The exception to this would be if there were enhanced risk factors present with the individual concerned, ie risk factors other than their position as a domestic PEP.

Where the solicitor is dealing with the PEP (and this includes where a PEP, family member or close associate is a beneficial owner of a client), additional obligations are placed on the solicitor, namely having approval of senior management (for example, the managing partner) to act for the client, taking adequate measures to establish the source of wealth and source of funds involved in the business relationship or proposed transactions, and conducting enhanced ongoing monitoring of the business relationship (reg 35(5)).

15.2.3.5 Ongoing monitoring

A solicitor is obliged to undertake ongoing monitoring of business relationships, to ensure that the transactions are consistent with the solicitor's knowledge of the client (reg 28(11)).

15.2.4 Training

Firms are obliged to provide (and maintain a record of) training to their employees and any agents used for the purpose of its business in respect of money laundering (reg 24). Employees should be made aware of the law relating to money laundering, terrorist financing and to the requirements of data protection relating to them. The Regulations also specify that employees should be given regular training on how to recognise (and then deal with) transactions that potentially involve money laundering or terrorist financing.

The Regulations do not specify how the training should take place. However, guidance provided by The Law Society suggests that appropriate methods of delivery may include face-to-face learning or e-learning. The Law Society's guidance also recommends the use of a staff manual on money laundering issues.

Where no such training is given, this may provide the employee with a defence to some of the offences under the Proceeds of Crime Act 2002 (see **15.3.3.7**).

15.2.5 Record keeping

A firm must keep various records in respect of money laundering. The records are a copy of any documents and information obtained by the solicitor to satisfy the due diligence requirements and sufficient supporting records (consisting of the original documents or copies) in respect of a transaction which is the subject of due diligence measures or ongoing monitoring to enable the transaction to be reconstructed (reg 40). These records must be kept for at least five years from when the business relationship ends or the end of the occasional transaction.

15.3 PROCEEDS OF CRIME ACT 2002

15.3.1 Introduction

The Proceeds of Crime Act 2002 makes it an offence to become involved in money laundering. For example, under s 327, it is an offence to conceal, disguise, convert or transfer criminal property, or remove criminal property from England and Wales, Scotland or Northern Ireland.

This chapter will focus on the three offences which most concern solicitors in their day-to-day practice.

15.3.2 Arrangements

15.3.2.1 Introduction

> A person commits an offence if he enters into or becomes concerned in an arrangement which he knows or suspects facilitates (by whatever means) the acquisition, retention, use or control of criminal property by or on behalf of another person. (Proceeds of Crime Act 2002, s 328(1))

15.3.2.2 Definitions

Section 328 is drafted very widely. For example, if a solicitor transferred a house to a relative of a client, where the solicitor knew or suspected that the house was purchased with the proceeds of crime, then the solicitor would '[become] concerned in an arrangement' and so would breach s 328(1).

There is no requirement that the funds pass through the hands of the person concerned with the arrangement, ie the solicitor.

'Criminal property' is defined by s 340 of the Act as a person's direct or indirect benefit from criminal conduct (if the offender knows or suspects that the property constitutes or represents such a benefit).

'Criminal conduct' is defined very widely, and includes any offence committed within the United Kingdom. This would include offences ranging from armed robbery to fraudulent receipt of welfare benefits. The definition also includes an international element. For example, if the offence occurred outside of the United Kingdom, it would still constitute criminal conduct if it would be classed as an offence if it had occurred within the United Kingdom. For example, a criminal robs a bank in France. This would still constitute 'criminal conduct' under the Act as robbery is an offence within the United Kingdom. It is irrelevant whether robbery is an offence in France. (However, there are exceptions to this international element – see **15.3.2.6**.)

15.3.2.3 Authorised disclosure

Disclosure prior to the act taking place

A solicitor does not commit an offence under s 328 if they make an authorised disclosure to the firm's nominated officer as soon as is practically possible prior to the transaction taking place, and the authorisation of the nominated officer or the NCA is obtained to complete the transaction.

However, once the nominated officer has made a suspicious activity report to the NCA, the nominated officer is unable to give consent for the transaction to proceed until one of the following conditions is met:

(a) the nominated officer, having made a disclosure to the NCA, receives the consent of the NCA;

(b) the nominated officer, having made a disclosure to the NCA, hears nothing for seven working days (starting with the first working day after the disclosure is made);

(c) where consent is refused by the NCA, the nominated officer may not give consent for the transaction to proceed unless consent is subsequently granted within 31 days starting on the day refusal is given, or a period of 31 days has expired from the date of refusal. This 31-day period gives the authorities time to take action to seize assets or take other action with respect to the money laundering.

Disclosure during the prohibited act

A solicitor may seek to make an authorised disclosure whilst the prohibited act is ongoing. However, if the solicitor is to avoid breaching s 328 by making the disclosure, they must satisfy the provisions of s 338(2A):

(a) the disclosure is made whilst the prohibited act is ongoing; and

(b) when the alleged offender began to do the act, they did not know or suspect that the property constituted or represented a person's benefit from criminal conduct; and

(c) the disclosure is made as soon as is practicable after the alleged offender first knows or suspects that the property constitutes or represents a person's benefit from criminal conduct, and the disclosure is made on the alleged offender's own initiative.

Take the example of a solicitor conducting a conveyancing transaction on behalf of a client. Until the client exchanges contracts to sell the property, the solicitor has no knowledge or suspicion that the house was bought with the proceeds of crime. Accordingly, there is no breach of s 328, as the solicitor does not possess the requisite knowledge or suspicion. After contracts have been exchanged, the solicitor correctly begins to suspect that the house was bought with the proceeds of crime. Accordingly, they are now concerned in an arrangement which facilitates the acquisition, retention, use or control of criminal property and therefore is in breach of s 328.

In order to seek the protection of making an authorised disclosure, the solicitor must disclose their suspicions to their nominated officer on their own initiative, and must do so as soon as is practicable after their first suspicions arise.

Disclosure after the prohibited act

A solicitor may also seek to make an authorised disclosure after the prohibited act has been completed. However, the solicitor must have a good reason for their failure to disclose prior to their completing the act (s 338(3)). The disclosure must be made as soon as is practicable, and again the solicitor must make the disclosure on their own initiative.

15.3.2.4 Reasonable excuse for non-disclosure

A solicitor may have a defence to breaching s 328 where they intended to make an authorised disclosure but has a reasonable excuse for failing to do so. The Law Society's guidance states that a 'reasonable excuse' has not been defined by the courts. However, the guidance advises solicitors to document their reasons for non-disclosure.

15.3.2.5 Litigation proceedings

In *Bowman v Fels* [2005] EWCA Civ 226, the Court of Appeal considered whether taking steps in litigation could be construed as 'arranging' under s 328. The Court concluded that taking steps in litigation (including pre-action steps) and the resolution of issues in a litigious context were excluded from the scope of s 328. Therefore a solicitor would not be obliged to make an authorised disclosure.

EXAMPLE

A solicitor is acting for Mr Smith in divorce proceedings. Financial relief proceedings are issued by Mrs Smith, as she wishes to have the matrimonial home transferred into her sole name. The solicitor becomes aware that the house was purchased by Mr Smith with the proceeds of crime. The solicitor will not breach s 328 by merely conducting the litigation on behalf of Mr Smith.

It was originally thought that transferring the house from Mr Smith to Mrs Smith after the court proceedings would have fallen into the definition of an arrangement. However, the current Law Society guidance provides that dividing assets in accordance with a court judgment would not fall within this definition, therefore no consent would be required. However, the guidance goes on to state that careful consideration should be made of whether the client would be committing an offence by receiving stolen property.

The solicitor would not be able to take advantage of this exclusion if the litigation was a sham created for the purposes of money laundering. The SRA issued guidance in January 2025 drawing attention to the potential threat posed by sham litigation and outlining the steps that lawyers could take to protect themselves and their firms.

15.3.2.6 'Overseas' defence

Despite the wide definition of 'criminal conduct' (see **15.3.2.2** above), a solicitor will not commit an offence under s 328 where the criminal conduct occurred outside of the United Kingdom and was not unlawful in the country where it happened. However, this defence is not available (subject to certain exceptions) where the offence would carry a sentence of imprisonment for 12 months or more were it to be carried out within the United Kingdom (see the Proceeds of Crime Act 2002 (Money Laundering: Exceptions to Overseas Conduct Defence) Order 2006 (SI 2006/1070)).

15.3.2.7 Penalties

An individual convicted under s 328 may receive a maximum sentence of 14 years' imprisonment.

15.3.3 Acquisition, use or possession

15.3.3.1 Introduction

A person commits an offence under s 329 of the Proceeds of Crime Act 2002 if they acquire, use or have possession of criminal property.

15.3.3.2 Adequate consideration defence

An issue may arise in connection with s 329 where, for example, a solicitor receives money for their costs for work carried out for a client charged with a criminal offence and there is a possibility that the money in question is criminal property.

The adequate consideration defence applies if there was adequate consideration for acquiring, using and possessing the criminal property, unless the individual knew or suspected that those goods or services might help to carry out criminal conduct. The Crown Prosecution Service guidance for prosecutors says that this defence applies where professional advisers, such as solicitors, receive money for or on account of costs, including disbursements. However, the fees charged must be reasonable and the defence is not available if the value of the work is significantly less than the money received.

It must be borne in mind that returning the balance of money in an account to a client may be an offence under s 328 if the solicitor knows or suspects that the money is criminal property. In that case, an authorised disclosure must be made to avoid such an offence being committed (see **15.3.2.3**).

15.3.4 Failure to disclose

15.3.4.1 Introduction

A person commits an offence under s 330 of the Proceeds of Crime Act 2002 if:

(a) they know or suspect, or have reasonable grounds to know or suspect, that a person is engaged in money laundering; and

(b) the information comes to them in the course of a business in the regulated sector; and

(c) the information may assist in identifying the money launderer or the location of any laundered property; and

(d) they do not make an authorised disclosure as soon as is practicable.

15.3.4.2 Objective test

A solicitor will commit this offence even where they genuinely did not know or suspect that a person was engaged in money laundering. The court will consider, based on the information available to the solicitor at the time, whether they *should* have known (or at least suspected) that money laundering was occurring. Accordingly, turning a blind eye to a transaction will not provide the solicitor with a defence.

15.3.4.3 Regulated sector

Firms will be within the 'regulated sector' if they undertake relevant business (see the Proceeds of Crime Act 2002, Sch 9). Most solicitors firms will fall within the regulated sector for at least some of the work with which they deal. The definition of 'regulated sector' is closely aligned to the definition given in the Money Laundering Regulations 2017 (see **15.2.1**).

15.3.4.4 The information

The information obtained by the solicitor must be of some use to the authorities. Accordingly, the solicitor must be able to identify, or believe the information may assist in identifying:

(a) the money launderer; or
(b) the location of the laundered property.

If the solicitor is genuinely unable to provide this information, the solicitor will not breach s 330.

The solicitor cannot blindly assume that the information will be of no use to the authorities. When considering whether the solicitor has breached s 330, the court will consider whether it would have been reasonable to expect the solicitor to believe that the information would assist in identifying the offender, or locating the laundered property.

15.3.4.5 Authorised disclosure

A solicitor will be provided with a defence to s 330 if they make an authorised disclosure to the firm's nominated officer as soon as practically possible. The disclosure on its own will be enough to grant an effective defence under s 330. However, the nominated officer will still consider whether the information should be forwarded to the NCA.

15.3.4.6 Reasonable excuse for non-disclosure

Once again, a solicitor will not commit this offence where they intended to make a disclosure and have a reasonable excuse for not doing so (see **15.3.2.4**).

15.3.4.7 Training

A further defence under s 330 concerns the training provided to an individual. Firms undertaking 'relevant business' are obliged to provide anti-money laundering training to their employees. If an employee does not know or suspect that a client is engaged in money laundering due to a lack of training then the employee may not commit the offence (see **15.2.2**).

15.3.4.8 Confidentiality and privilege

The position concerning a solicitor's duty of confidentiality in the Codes of Conduct is considered below at **15.4**.

A solicitor is also under a duty at common law to keep confidential certain information given to them by a client. This is referred to as legal professional privilege (LPP). Communications will be protected from disclosure if they fall within 'advice privilege' or 'litigation privilege' (see **12.4**). However, LPP cannot be relied upon where the communication takes place with the purpose of carrying out an offence.

The Proceeds of Crime Act 2002 mirrors the common law position, in that a solicitor is not obliged under s 330 to disclose any information that comes to them as a professional legal adviser in privileged circumstances, eg in connection with giving or seeking legal advice, or in relation to legal proceedings, whether contemplated or actual. However, this exemption does not apply where the information is communicated with the intention of furthering a criminal purpose (eg, money laundering).

15.3.4.9 'Overseas' defence

A solicitor will not breach s 330 for failing to disclose where they believe that the money laundering is taking place outside of the United Kingdom, and money laundering is not unlawful in that country. The Secretary of State has the power to limit this defence, but at the time of writing has not taken any steps to do so.

15.3.4.10 Penalties

A person convicted of an offence under s 330 may receive a maximum sentence of five years' imprisonment.

15.3.5 Tipping off

15.3.5.1 The offences

There are two aspects of tipping off that must be avoided under s 333A.

Disclosing a suspicious activity report (s 333A(1))

It is an offence to disclose to any person that a suspicious activity report (on money laundering) has been made if that disclosure is likely to prejudice any investigation that follows such a report. For example, this offence would apply where a solicitor informs their client that an authorised disclosure has been made, with the intention of the client taking steps to frustrate any action taken by the law enforcement authorities. This would apply where a disclosure of suspicion is made to a MLRO, the NCA, the Police, or to HMRC.

EXAMPLE

Mr Wilkinson instructs his solicitor to sell his house. The solicitor suspects that the house was purchased with the proceeds of tax evasion and so makes an authorised disclosure under s 328. The transaction cannot be completed until the solicitor obtains the consent of his MLRO or the NCA (see **15.3.2.3**). Mr Wilkinson demands to know why his house sale has not been completed. The solicitor's trainee receives Mr Wilkinson's call and, having checked the file, informs Mr Wilkinson that an authorised disclosure has been made to the NCA. In these circumstances the trainee may breach s 333A unless he can rely on one of the defences (see **15.3.4.2**).

Disclosing an investigation (s 333A(3))

This is a more general offence, and applies regardless of whether or not a suspicious activity report has been made. The offence is committed where a disclosure is made to any person that an investigation into money laundering is being carried out, or is being contemplated, and that disclosure is likely to prejudice the money laundering investigation. In November 2023 the Serious Fraud Office secured its first ever conviction against a solicitor for tipping off a client. The solicitor had informed his client about an SFO money laundering investigation into a loan taken out by the client to fund a property purchase. The solicitor was sentenced to nine months imprisonment suspended for 18 months.

The idea behind both offences is to ensure that information is not leaked to the money launderer or another third party before the authorities have had the opportunity to investigate the matter and consider whether any enforcement action is necessary.

15.3.5.2 Defences

There are a number of defences to tipping off. These include that the person who made the disclosure did not know or suspect that the disclosure would prejudice an investigation into money laundering (s 333D (3) and (4)). Another defence is that the disclosure is made to the client for the purposes of dissuading the client from engaging in the alleged money laundering (s 333D(2)), although this exception should be treated with caution.

15.3.5.3 Penalties

Both the offences set out in **15.3.5.1** above carry a maximum penalty of an unlimited fine, and/or a maximum prison sentence of two years.

15.3.5.4 'Regulated sector'

These sections (ss 333A to 333D) only apply to the regulated sector. However, similar provisions apply to work completed outside of the regulated sector by virtue of s 342.

15.4 CONFIDENTIALITY

A solicitor is under a duty under para 6.3 of the Codes of Conduct to keep confidential the affairs of clients (including former clients) unless disclosure is required or permitted by law or the client consents (see **Chapter 12**). When making a disclosure under s 328 or s 330, the legislation expressly provides that such a disclosure will not breach this duty and so is permitted by law. Nevertheless, the SRA's previous guidance advised that a solicitor should be mindful of the importance of the duty of confidentiality, and seek advice when uncertain as to whether to report confidential information.

15.5 ECONOMIC CRIME AND THE UK FINANCIAL SANCTIONS REGIME

With effect from 30 September 2017, the Criminal Finances Act 2017 introduced the corporate offence of failure to prevent the criminal facilitation of tax evasion, and it applies to law firms as 'relevant bodies'.

The offence makes a firm liable for failing to prevent tax evasion offences by its employees or other 'associated persons'. Such offences include the fraudulent evasion of VAT, income tax, national insurance contributions and the common law offence of cheating the public revenue. There is strict liability for the offence in that no knowledge or intention is required on the part of the firm or its senior management. The only defence available is that the firm had in place reasonable prevention procedures or is able to show that it was reasonable not to have had such procedures in place. The penalty for breach is unlimited fines, and confiscation of assets may be ordered.

Firms should already have policies and procedures in place to comply with their obligations under the Bribery Act 2010 and the money laundering legislation (see **15.2**). However, the 2017 Act is likely to involve firms in having to review and add to such policies and procedures in order to comply with it. For example, due diligence procedures will need to take into account specifically the risk of criminal facilitation of tax evasion posed by its partners and employees as well as by other 'associated persons' (ie agents of the firm or those who perform services for or on behalf of it, such as barristers, surveyors and foreign law firms) and be adapted or introduced accordingly. A firm-wide risk assessment, internal procedures, staff training and ongoing monitoring will also be required.

Under the legislation which makes up the UK financial sanctions regime, serious and extensive restrictions are imposed on those, including law firms, dealing with people or entities who are on the 'sanctions list' as a result of the UK government having imposed sanctions unilaterally or implemented sanctions imposed by the United Nations or European Union (termed 'designated persons'). The regime covers all firms, regardless of whether or not they are subject to the Money Laundering Regulations regime, and imposes duties in addition to this. There is a requirement to inform the Office of Financial Sanctions Implementation (OFSI) if it is known or reasonably suspected that a person is a 'designated person' or has committed offences under financial sanctions and asset freezing regimes. If a firm decides that it still wishes to act for such a person, it will need to apply for a licence from OFSI to receive reasonable fees for the provision of legal advice unless covered by a general licence issued by OFSI, eg, the Legal Services General Licence for Russia and Belarus issued in October 2022. As the 'sanctions list' is public information, it will not amount to a tipping off offence under the Proceeds of Crime Act 2002 where a person's sanctioned status is discussed with them. Under the provisions of the Economic Crime (Transparency and Enforcement) Act 2022, firms can now face liability for fines even where they have no knowledge or reasonable cause to suspect that a transaction to which they are a party is in breach of the sanctions regime. The Economic Crime and Corporate Transparency Act 2023 (ECCTA 2023) introduced an objective into the Legal Services Act 2007 to prevent economic crime and promote its detection. The SRA can issue unlimited fines in relation to solicitors and firms who commit economic crimes under the Act.

On 1 September 2025, s 199 of the ECCTA 2023 is due to come into force. This creates the new offence of 'failure to prevent fraud', which will apply to corporate bodies and partnerships that meet the criteria to be a 'large organisation'. A large organisation is such if it meets at least two of the following criteria in the financial year that precedes the fraud offence:

- turnover greater than £36 million
- more than £18 million in total assets
- more than 250 employees.

The offence will be punishable by an unlimited fine (ECCTA 2023, s 199(12)).

More guidance on all of the above can be obtained from the practice notes produced by The Law Society.

15.6 EXAMPLES

EXAMPLE 1

Question	You are acting on a corporate transaction. Your client is buying X Co Ltd. During the course of your due diligence you discover that a number of X Co Ltd's lucrative contracts were obtained by paying bribes. What obligations are you now under? Can you complete the transaction?
Answer	You need to consider whether anything of a criminal nature has occurred. Obtaining property using bribes is a criminal offence. These contracts will have generated cash which will be owned by X Co Ltd. Therefore when your client buys the company, it will be acquiring the proceeds of crime, which is an offence under s 329 of the Proceeds of Crime Act 2002. Simply by completing the transaction you will be concerned in an arrangement which facilitates the acquisition, retention, use or control of criminal property, which is an offence under s 328 of the Proceeds of Crime Act 2002. Therefore you need to report the matter to your Money Laundering Reporting Officer as soon as possible. He will then need to seek the consent of the NCA for the transaction to proceed.

EXAMPLE 2

Question This is a continuation of the above question. The above information comes to you on the morning of the day for completion of the deal. You are unable to obtain the consent of the NCA in time to complete the deal. Therefore you must postpone completion of the deal to allow you to obtain this consent. Can you explain your reasons for the delay to the solicitors representing X Co Ltd?

Answer No. This would constitute 'tipping off' – an offence under ss 333A–333D of the Proceeds of Crime Act 2002. This will place you in a very difficult position. Therefore it is vital that you disclose any suspicion to the Money Laundering Reporting Officer as soon as possible to attempt to avoid this situation.

SUMMARY

(1) Money laundering is the process whereby the proceeds of crime are changed so that they appear to come from a legitimate source.

(2) The Government has introduced legislation to disrupt this process.

(3) Solicitors who undertake relevant business must comply with the Money Laundering, Terrorist Financing and Transfer of Funds (Information on the Payer) Regulations 2017 (SI 2017/692).

(4) Under the 2017 Regulations, firms must appoint a nominated officer, who will receive internal reports concerning money laundering and must consider whether to report the matter to the NCA.

(5) A person commits an offence under s 328 of the Proceeds of Crime Act 2002 where they become concerned in an arrangement involving money laundering.

(6) Section 328 does not apply to steps taken in litigation.

(7) A person commits an offence under s 329 of the Proceeds of Crime Act 2002 if they acquire, use or have possession of criminal property.

(8) A solicitor within the regulated sector is obliged to disclose any suspected money laundering activity to their nominated officer under s 330 of the Proceeds of Crime Act 2002.

(9) It is an offence to disclose to any person that a disclosure has been made where this may prejudice an investigation.

CHAPTER 16

Duties Owed to the Court and Third Parties

LEARNING OUTCOMES

After reading this chapter you will be able to understand the duties owed by solicitors to:

- the court
- third parties generally
- other solicitors
- barristers.

16.1 INTRODUCTION

16.1.1 Duty to the court

The Code of Conduct for Solicitors sets out obligations in the context of dispute resolution and proceedings before courts, tribunals and inquiries (paras 2.1 to 2.7). These obligations apply also to firms by virtue of para 7.1(a) of the Code of Conduct for Firms. The SRA Glossary defines 'court' as any court, tribunal or inquiry of England and Wales, or a British court martial, or any court of another jurisdiction.

A solicitor is an officer of the court and as such owes a duty to the court. Although a solicitor has a duty to act in the best interests of each client (Principle 7), their overriding duty is to act in a way that upholds the constitutional principle of the rule of law and the proper administration of justice (Principle 1), and the potential for conflict between these duties can present itself particularly in the context of conducting litigation. The introduction to the SRA Principles makes it clear that, should the Principles come into conflict, those which safeguard the wider public interest take precedence over an individual client's interests and that a solicitor should, where relevant, inform their client of the circumstances in which their duty to the court and other professional obligations outweigh their duty to the client.

A basic and self-explanatory duty is found in para 1.4 of the Code of Conduct for Solicitors, which provides that a solicitor must not mislead or attempt to mislead the court (or others), either by their own acts or omissions or allowing or being complicit in the acts or omissions of others (including their client). This duty is replicated in para 1.4 of the Code of Conduct for Firms. Further, a solicitor must not misuse or tamper with evidence or attempt to do so (Code of Conduct for Solicitors, para 2.1) and must only make assertions or put forward statements, representations or submissions to the court or others which are properly arguable (para 2.4). Examples of breaches of these duties are wide-ranging and include:

(a) calling a witness whose evidence the solicitor knows is untrue;
(b) continuing to act for a client if the solicitor becomes aware that the client has committed perjury or misled (or attempted to mislead) the court. In such circumstances, the solicitor should obtain the client's agreement to disclose the truth to the court and cease to continue to act where the client declines to provide this. However, the SRA's guidance in a previous Code of Conduct stated that a solicitor is not obliged to stop acting where the client gives inconsistent evidence – there must be an intention on behalf of the client to submit false evidence, and this is likely to remain the case under the current Codes;
(c) constructing facts to support a client's case or drafting documents relating to proceedings containing statements or contentions which the solicitor does not consider to be properly arguable before a court.

A solicitor must not place themselves in contempt of court and must comply with court orders which place obligations on them and must not waste the court's time (Code of Conduct for Solicitors, paras 2.5 and 2.6 respectively).

A report produced by the SRA entitled 'Balancing duties in litigation' outlines various instances of misconduct in the conduct of litigation following an increase in reports to it of solicitors misleading the courts. SRA Guidance on Conduct in Disputes was subsequently published. Examples of the conduct encountered include:

(a) 'predatory litigation', which is when solicitors bring a large number of claims against third parties with only a limited amount of prior investigation into the facts and/or the legal basis of the claim. This may result in the third parties seeking to settle the claims in the amount requested (often without seeking their own legal advice) on the basis that this may be less costly than if the matter proceeded to court. A particular spotlight was turned on claims brought against hotels on behalf of clients alleging gastric illnesses suffered on holiday. The SRA had received reports of such claims being dismissed by the court as being dishonest and the solicitors either not having investigated the evidence properly or, in some instances, having actively encouraged their clients to destroy evidence which may have harmed their case;
(b) unnecessary or improper litigation, which is when the courts or general court process is used for purposes not directly connected to resolving a dispute, for example to incur unmanageable costs for a commercial rival of a client, silencing criticism or stalling another process. A particular concern in relation to litigation misconduct that has emerged in recent years are so-called Strategic Lawsuits against Public Participation (SLAPPs). In essence, a SLAPP involves the bringing or threatening of proceedings as a means of intimidation or harassment. The aim is to stop the 'target' publishing information relating to a matter of public interest, such as whistle-blowing or the results of investigative journalism. SLAPPs can take a variety of forms, but typically involve bringing/threatening proceedings for defamation or misuse of information (for more detail see the SRA Warning Notice, 30 May 2024);
(c) solicitors accepting instructions for weak or unwinnable cases without first explaining the potential costs or risks to the client, encouraging clients to proceed with litigation where there is little or no legal merit, or 'touting' for claimants for government-backed compensation schemes that do not actually require the claimant to have legal advice or representation.

Lastly, solicitors appearing before the court should exercise considerable caution when communicating with judges outside of the courtroom. It is advised by the SRA that advocates should communicate with judges in this fashion only when invited to do so and in the presence of the legal representative of the other client.

16.1.2 Witnesses

A solicitor must not seek to influence the substance of evidence, including generating false evidence or persuading witnesses to change their evidence (Code of Conduct for Solicitors, para 2.2). In the report produced by the SRA, 'Balancing duties in litigation', mentioned at **16.1.1**, examples of such behaviour reported to it include where solicitors have knowingly helped criminal clients to create a false alibi and, where they have known that their client has obtained information to help their case by illegal means, helped them provide a false explanation as to where it came from. Should a solicitor wish, or require, in the best interests of their client, to take statements from a witness or potential witness, they may do so at any point in the proceedings. This remains the case whether or not that individual has already been interviewed by another party or has been called as a witness by another party. However, a solicitor must not provide or offer to provide any benefit to witnesses dependent upon the nature of their evidence or the outcome of the case (Code of Conduct for Solicitors, para 2.3). The SRA's previous guidance suggested that the witness be interviewed in the presence of their legal representative.

16.1.3 Duty to disclose law and facts

A solicitor who appears before the court for the defence in a criminal case, or for either party in a civil case, has no duty to inform the court of any evidence or witnesses which would prejudice the solicitor's own client.

However, there is a duty on the part of a solicitor to draw the court's attention to relevant cases and statutory provisions or procedural irregularities of which they are aware and which are likely to have a material effect on the outcome of the proceedings (Code of Conduct for Solicitors, para 2.7). Whilst no express mention is made in the Code of a situation in which to do this would not be in the interests of the solicitor's own client, the introduction to the SRA Principles states that, should the Principles come into conflict, those which safeguard the wider public interest take precedence over an individual client's interests. As a result, it is likely that, in such a situation, Principle 1 (upholding the rule of law and the proper administration of justice) will take precedence over Principle 7 (acting in the best interests of the client).

Different considerations apply to a solicitor who appears before the court for the prosecution in a criminal case. The requirement placed on the prosecution to present evidence in a dispassionate manner means that in addition to complying with the duty under para 2.7, the solicitor must, for example, put all relevant facts before the court and notify the defence of evidence which may assist the defendant.

16.2 REFUSING INSTRUCTIONS TO ACT

There are no longer any specific references in the Code to situations in which a solicitor must not refuse to act as an advocate. A solicitor is generally free to decide whether or not to accept instructions in any matter, provided that they do not discriminate unlawfully (see also **10.3.2**).

If it is clear to a solicitor appearing as an advocate, or acting in litigation, that they or anyone else in their firm will be called as a witness in the matter, they should decline to appear/act unless they are satisfied that this will not prejudice their independence as an advocate or a litigator (Principle 3), the interests of their clients (Principle 7) or the interests of justice (Principle 1).

16.3 INSTRUCTING COUNSEL

A solicitor is obliged to act in the best interests of their client, to include ensuring that the service provided is competent and delivered in a timely manner (Code of Conduct for Solicitors, para 3.2 and Code of Conduct for Firms, para 4.2). Accordingly, where the client requires advocacy services, the solicitor must consider, based on the complexity of the case and the solicitor's own experience, whether it would be in the best interests of that client to instruct another solicitor within the firm or counsel to act as the advocate in the proceedings.

16.3.1 Duty to counsel

If it is in the client's best interests to instruct counsel, it remains the solicitor's duty to ensure that adequate instructions are provided to the chosen barrister. As an extension of the solicitor's duty to their client, they should ensure that these instructions, including any relevant supporting statements, information or documents, are provided in good time to allow adequate preparation of the case.

In order to provide such information, it may be necessary, if practicable, to arrange a conference with counsel, either with or without the client, to enable the barrister to discuss directly the nature of the case, obtain instructions or further information, and provide advice in a direct manner. It is a matter for the solicitor to ascertain whether such a conference would be appropriate and in the client's best interests, and if so, to arrange it.

16.3.2 Duty to the client when instructing an advocate

Notwithstanding the appointment of counsel and the duties the chosen barrister may owe to a solicitor's client, all the solicitor's duties to their client remain in full force and effect. Instructing counsel does not relieve the solicitor of those duties, particularly the overriding duty to act in the best interests of the client.

The solicitor must therefore exercise care in choosing the appropriate barrister for the case, taking into consideration the experience and seniority of counsel available. The solicitor should also ensure they are happy with the quality of the advice given, to ensure that there are no obvious errors or inconsistencies. If such errors are apparent, clarification should be requested or a second opinion obtained (see, for example, *Regent Leisuretime v Skerrett* [2005] EWHC 2255 (QB)).

16.3.3 Counsel's fees

A solicitor is responsible for appointing counsel and (subject to limited exceptions) is therefore responsible personally for the payment of counsel's fees. This applies regardless of whether the solicitor's client has provided the requisite monies. Many solicitors therefore request that their clients provide money on account to cover prospective barristers' fees.

16.3.4 Discrimination – choice of advocate

As noted at **16.3.2** above, a solicitor should select an advocate of sufficient seniority and experience to represent their client adequately in court. A solicitor may consult with their client when choosing a barrister. However, a solicitor must not unlawfully discriminate by allowing their personal views to affect their professional relationships and the way in which they provide their services (para 1.1 of both of the Codes of Conduct), and they must act in a way that encourages equality, diversity and inclusion (Principle 6). Consequently, a solicitor must not discriminate when instructing a barrister on the grounds of, for example, age, race, sex or disability. If the client's request appears to be based on discriminatory grounds (eg, a male client defending himself in an Employment Tribunal against an allegation of sex discrimination may request to be represented by a female advocate), the solicitor should discuss the issue with the client and, if necessary, ask the client to change their instructions. Where the client refuses, it will usually be appropriate for the solicitor to cease to act.

16.4 IMMUNITY FOR ADVOCACY WORK

In previous years, immunity was granted to advocates against claims of negligence or breach of contract in respect of advocacy work undertaken. However, this was abolished by the House of Lords in *Arthur JS Hall & Co (A Firm) v Simons* [2000] 3 All ER 673.

16.5 DUTY TO THIRD PARTIES

16.5.1 Not taking an unfair advantage

Dispute resolution and conducting proceedings before the court will often involve the solicitor communicating with third parties (ie in addition to witnesses). A solicitor must not abuse their position by taking unfair advantage of not only their client but others (para 1.2 of both of the Codes of Conduct). For this reason, it must be borne in mind that third parties may well have a lack of legal knowledge or proper understanding of legal procedures, and a solicitor must not seek to take unfair advantage of this in pursuing a case for a client. Particular care must be taken in situations where the opponent is unrepresented or is vulnerable, for example due to age or mental capacity. The SRA in its report 'Balancing duties in litigation' conceded that there can be a 'fine line between proper defence of the client's interest and taking unfair advantage of others, usually highlighted by any form of deceit or misinformation'. Specific examples of conduct reported to the SRA in this context include overbearing threats of claims or poor outcomes, legalistic letters to minors or others who might be vulnerable and threats of litigation where no legal claims arises. The SRA has issued a warning notice on the use of non-disclosure agreements (NDAs) following their use, for example, in relation to allegations of harassment.

The SRA views the protection of the vulnerable as an important part of its role. The Enforcement Strategy makes clear that the SRA will consider an allegation to be 'particularly serious' where the vulnerability of the client or third party is relevant to the solicitor's behaviour.

The SRA's guidance in a previous Code of Conduct suggested that the solicitor should advise unrepresented individuals to seek independent legal advice.

In the event that a solicitor provides some form of help to an unrepresented third party, care should be taken that a retainer does not arise between the solicitor and the third party.

16.5.2 Public office and personal interests

Solicitors may sometimes be appointed to a public office, such as being a member of a planning committee or a district judge. The public office may provide the solicitor with confidential information or inside knowledge of, for example, policy, which may affect the solicitor's advice to the client or their approach to the matter.

The 'inside information' might also be available to the solicitor if another individual at the solicitor's practice (whether partner, member or employee) held such an office, or indeed if it was held by a member of the solicitor's family.

If a solicitor takes unfair advantage of a public office held by them, a member of their family or their firm, it is unlikely that they will be acting in a way that upholds public trust and confidence in the solicitors' profession or with integrity, and so they will breach Principles 2 and 5.

16.5.3 Giving references

Under the general law of negligence, a solicitor will owe a duty of care to the subject of any reference given by that solicitor (see *Spring v Guardian Assurance plc* [1994] 3 All ER 129, HL). Accordingly, great care must be taken when giving any such reference to avoid incurring liability. Many firms have in place policies with regard to the giving of references, covering who may give them and the nature of the content.

Furthermore, giving a false reference would almost certainly breach the Codes of Conduct, eg for damaging the public trust and confidence in the solicitors' profession (Principle 2).

16.5.4 Offensive communications

A solicitor is under a duty to act with integrity (Principle 5) and in a way that upholds public trust and confidence in the profession (Principle 2). Accordingly, a solicitor must not communicate with any third party in a manner that could be considered to be offensive. The SRA issued a Warning Notice on offensive communications (including emails, texts and the use of social media networks) on 24 August 2017 (updated in 2019) to which it will have regard when exercising its regulatory functions. Such communications may be sent or posted in a work context (within a firm, or externally to clients or third parties), but the SRA may also take action if the sender is identifiable as someone regulated by the SRA (even if acting in a personal capacity) and the communication would tend to damage public confidence in the profession.

16.5.5 Beneficiaries

Where a solicitor is instructed to administer the estate of someone who has died, the solicitor's client will be the personal representatives of the deceased's estate. However, in certain circumstances a solicitor will also owe a duty of care to the beneficiaries of that estate.

For example, in *Ross v Caunters* [1980] 1 Ch 297 a solicitor failed to warn a testator that the will should not be witnessed by a beneficiary. Accordingly, the beneficiary who witnessed the will was unable to claim her share of the estate. The solicitor was held liable in negligence to the beneficiary. See also *White v Jones* [1995] 1 All ER 891, where a solicitor was instructed to draw up a will. The client died approximately a month later, before the will had been drafted. The solicitor was successfully sued in negligence by the beneficiaries who missed out on their share of the estate as a result of the solicitor's failure to draft the will.

16.5.6 Contacting a represented third party

Where a client instructs a solicitor, it is often because the client lacks legal knowledge and skills and therefore seeks the assistance of a legal expert. Care must be taken, therefore, in the context of a solicitor communicating with another party when they are aware that the other party has retained a lawyer in a matter. There is nothing specific in the Codes of Conduct dealing with this situation, but it is suggested that guidance contained in the previous Code of Conduct provides best practice, namely that such communication should be avoided except:

(a) to request the name and address of the other party's lawyer; or

(b) where the other party's lawyer consents to the solicitor communicating with the client; or

(c) where there are exceptional circumstances.

16.5.7 Dealing with unrepresented parties

The SRA's previous guidance provided that where a solicitor is dealing with an unrepresented third party, care should be taken that an implied retainer does not arise from the solicitor's dealings with that third party (see **16.5.1**).

Particular care should be taken when a solicitor discovers they are dealing with an unqualified person (see **18.2.1**) who is carrying out work reserved for solicitors, such as preparing papers for a grant of probate. The solicitor is advised to inform the SRA and seek immediate advice from the Professional Ethics Guidance Team.

16.5.8 Agents' costs

As with counsel's fees, a solicitor is personally responsible for meeting the fees of agents or others they appoint on behalf of their client. This extends only to costs properly incurred. Again, this applies whether or not the solicitor has been put in funds, and therefore the solicitor may ask for monies on account prior to incurring such expenditure. Alternatively, the solicitor and agent may agree that the agent's fee will become payable on receipt by the solicitor of the client's payment.

16.6 RELATIONS WITH OTHER SOLICITORS

A solicitor must act with integrity (Principle 5). Therefore a solicitor must treat other solicitors with due respect in all their communications, whether written or oral.

16.6.1 Agency

As noted at **16.5.9** above, solicitors are personally liable to pay the fees of any agent they instruct on behalf of their clients. This applies even when that agent is another solicitor. Solicitors frequently appoint other solicitors to attend court on their behalf, for example where it is not cost-efficient for the solicitor to travel some distance to attend court. The instructing solicitor therefore remains liable for meeting such costs, regardless of whether their client has put them in funds, unless they agree otherwise with the solicitor-agent.

16.7 EXAMPLES

EXAMPLE 1

Question You are representing your client in an employment tribunal. Your client is suing for unfair dismissal. He was sacked for allegedly stealing a laptop. During cross-examination he denies that he ever had the laptop in his possession. Later that day he confides in you that he took the laptop and sold it to a friend to fund a holiday. What should you do here?

Answer You must not mislead or attempt to mislead the court, or be complicit in another person doing so (including your client), which includes the tribunal (Code of Conduct for Solicitors, para 1.4). Following your conversation, you are aware that your client has committed perjury within the proceedings, and so you should refuse to continue to act for the client unless the client agrees to disclose the truth to the tribunal. You cannot inform the tribunal of the truth (or your reasons for withdrawal) without the consent of the client as to do so would be a breach of confidentiality (para 6.3).

EXAMPLE 2

Question A solicitor instructs counsel on behalf of a client to provide advice on a particular piece of law. Counsel's fee is £1,000 plus VAT. Before the solicitor can bill the client, the client is declared bankrupt. Who is responsible for the counsel's fee?

Answer The solicitor. This is why many solicitors request that their clients provide them with money on account before instructing counsel.

SUMMARY

The solicitor and the court

(1) A solicitor must not mislead or attempt to mislead the court or allow or be complicit in others doing so (including their client). A solicitor must also not place themselves in contempt of court and must comply with any order of the court which places obligations on them.

(2) A solicitor must not offer to provide any benefits to witnesses dependent upon their evidence or the outcome of the case.

(3) A solicitor must not misuse or tamper with evidence or influence the substance of evidence, including generating false evidence or persuading witnesses to change their evidence.

(4) There is a duty on a solicitor to draw the court's attention to relevant cases and statutory provisions or procedural irregularities of which they are aware and which are likely to have a material effect on the outcome of the proceedings.

(5) A solicitor still owes their client a duty to act in the client's best interests even when the solicitor has instructed counsel to act for that client.

Duty to third parties

(1) A solicitor must not take an unfair advantage of clients or others.

(2) A solicitor will be breaching the Principles if they take unfair advantage of a public office held by them.

(3) In certain circumstances a solicitor owes a duty of care to third parties, such as beneficiaries.

(4) A solicitor must act with integrity when dealing with other solicitors.

CHAPTER 17

FINANCIAL SERVICES

LEARNING OUTCOMES

After reading this chapter you will be able to understand:

- the structure of financial services regulation
- how solicitors are regulated in carrying out financial services work.

17.1 INTRODUCTION

From time to time, solicitors engage in financial services work. To do this, they must be sufficiently competent in that area of practice, and in some cases will need to comply with certain regulations imposed by the Financial Conduct Authority (FCA) and/or the Solicitors Regulation Authority (SRA).

Such work could arise:

(a) in conveyancing, if a client needs help in finding a mortgage and a supporting package, which could include a life insurance policy;

(b) in probate, when the executors sell off the deceased's assets;

(c) in litigation, if helping a successful client to invest damages just won;

(d) in company work, in making arrangements for a client to buy or sell shares in a company, and also in arranging corporate finance;

(e) in family work, if arrangements have to be made on a divorce in respect of endowment life policies and/or a family business;

(f) in tax planning or portfolio management, for a private client including trustees.

Under Principle 7, a solicitor would be in breach of their duty to act in the client's best interests if they did not have sufficient expertise in the area concerned. Therefore, a trainee solicitor should not give investment advice to a client unless the trainee is an expert in that field.

However, many activities in connection with investments are subject to regulation under the Financial Services and Markets Act 2000 (FSMA 2000) and, for example, to give advice on these, or even to make arrangements for clients to acquire or dispose of them, may require the solicitor to be authorised to carry out that activity. To do this without authority could involve the commission of a criminal offence. Thus you will, when handling a matter in which investments are involved, even if only peripherally, need to be doubly careful before advising and assisting such clients. You will need to ask yourself two questions:

(a) Have I got the necessary skill and knowledge?
(b) What am I 'permitted' to do under the financial services regulations?

17.2 SOURCE MATERIAL

The FSMA 2000 gained Royal Assent on 14 June 2000. It contains 433 sections and 22 Schedules. The regulatory regime for financial services came into force at midnight on 30 November 2001. The Financial Services Act 2012, which received Royal Assent of 19 December 2012, extensively amends the FSMA 2000. The provisions of that Act will come into force, or in some cases have already come into force, on such dates as the Treasury specifies in commencement orders. The Financial Services and Markets Act 2023 (FSMA 2023) also makes some extensive amendments to the FSMA 2000. The substance of the provisions of the FSMA 2000 discussed below, however, has remained unchanged.

The FSMA 2000 provides only a general framework, and the detail is in secondary legislation (eg, Orders in Council made by the Treasury). In order to understand the whole of the regulation, it is necessary to study the FSMA 2000 and the various Orders made by the Treasury, for example:

(a) Financial Services and Markets Act 2000 (Regulated Activities) Order 2001, SI 2001/544 (RAO 2001);
(b) Financial Services and Markets Act 2000 (Professions) (Non-Exempt Activities) Order 2001, SI 2001/1227;
(c) Financial Services and Markets Act 2000 (Financial Promotion) Order 2005, SI 2005/1529 (FPO 2005);
(d) Financial Services and Markets Act 2000 (PRA-regulated Activities) Order 2013, SI 2013/556.

The regulation of financial services is a complex and detailed area. This chapter will serve only as an introduction to the regulatory framework. Further guidance may be sought from The Law Society.

Materials on financial services work include:

(a) the SRA Financial Services (Scope) Rules (Scope Rules);
(b) the SRA Financial Services (Conduct of Business) Rules (COB Rules).

These may be found on the SRA's website at <www.sra.org.uk> and form part of the SRA Standards and Regulations.

17.3 FINANCIAL SERVICES REGULATORY STRUCTURE

The FSMA 2000 in effect established the Financial Services Authority (FSA) whose authority was vast and included the regulation of financial services. Following the financial crisis of 2007/08 and criticisms of the regulatory system at the time, the Government announced major reforms in the regulatory structure, including the abolition of the FSA in its current form. Three new regulatory bodies were established under the Financial Services Act 2012: the Financial Conduct Authority (FCA), the Prudential Regulation Authority (PRA) and the Financial Policy Committee (FPC). The FCA and PRA have taken over the majority of the FSA's functions, whilst the FPC (a committee of the Bank of England) is responsible for monitoring the stability of the whole UK financial system and so will not of itself directly supervise firms. The new regulatory structure came into effect on 1 April 2013.

17.3.1 The Financial Conduct Authority (FCA)

The FCA inherited most of the FSA's market regulatory functions, including responsibility for the conduct of business regulation of all firms (such as solicitors' firms), including dual-regulated firms (see **17.3.2**), and for the prudential regulation of firms (ie their safety and soundness) not regulated by the PRA (known as FCA-authorised or FCA-only firms).

The FCA is set the following objectives in the FSMA 2000 (as amended):

(a) securing an appropriate degree of protection for consumers (the consumer protection objective);

(b) protecting and enhancing the integrity of the UK financial system (the integrity objective);

(c) promoting effective competition in the interests of consumers in the market, including for regulated financial services (the competition objective).

It also shares a set of 'regulatory principles' with the PRA and these are set out in s 3B of the FSMA 2000.

The FCA has been given powers not previously granted to the FSA, including being able to require firms to withdraw or amend misleading financial promotions (see **17.11**) with immediate effect and to block the launch of, or stop, a service or product. On 1 April 2014 the FCA took over responsibility for the regulation of consumer credit and second charge mortgages secured over property, both formerly regulated by the Office of Fair Trading (see **17.9**).

17.3.2 The Prudential Regulation Authority (PRA)

The PRA is a subsidiary of the Bank of England and is responsible for the authorisation, prudential regulation and general supervision of those firms which manage significant financial risks, namely banks, building societies, insurers, credit unions, certain investment firms and Lloyd's of London. These firms are known as PRA-authorised firms or dual-regulated firms, as they will also be regulated by the FCA for conduct purposes (see **17.3.1**).

The Financial Services and Markets Act 2000 (PRA-regulated Activities) Order 2013 sets out which regulated activities in the RAO 2001 (see **17.6**) are PRA-regulated activities, and any firm with permission to carry out such activities will be designated a PRA-authorised firm. The activities include accepting deposits and effecting a contract of insurance and dealing with investments as principal.

17.4 THE GENERAL FRAMEWORK

Businesses carrying on certain activities, known as 'regulated activities', will need to be authorised by the appropriate regulator, which in the case of a solicitors' firm will be the FCA. The FSMA 2000 contains a special provision for professional firms which do not carry out 'mainstream' investment business but may carry out a regulated activity in the course of carrying out their professional work, such as corporate work. If certain conditions are satisfied, such a firm will be exempt from having to obtain authority from the FCA, provided it is regulated and supervised by a professional body designated by the Treasury (a designated professional body or 'DPB'). The SRA is a DPB for these purposes.

17.5 THE NEED FOR AUTHORITY

There are two main restrictions of most relevance to solicitors:

(a) carrying out a regulated activity;

(b) making a financial promotion.

Section 19 of the FSMA 2000 provides that: 'No person may carry on a regulated activity in the UK unless authorised or exempt' (the 'General Prohibition'). Authorised persons are persons with permission granted by the appropriate regulator (the FCA) under the FSMA 2000. A further offence is that of making an unauthorised financial promotion under s 21. Breach of either of these provisions could result in the commission of a criminal offence. Breach of s 19 could also render unenforceable any resulting agreement which has as a party to it the person who contravened s 19, or made with an authorised person carrying on a regulated activity.

17.6 REGULATED ACTIVITY

17.6.1 The four tests

The definition of a 'regulated activity' is set out in s 22 of the FSMA 2000 and has been substantially amended by the Financial Services Act 2012.

In order to determine if an activity is regulated there are four tests:

(a) Are you in business?

(b) Is there a specified activity (see **17.6.3** below)?

(c) Is there a specified investment (see **17.6.2** below), or does the specified activity relate to information about a person's financial standing or administering a benchmark?

(d) Is there an exclusion?

The particular activities and investments are specified by the Treasury in the RAO 2001 (as amended) under the FSMA 2000, s 22. Information about a person's financial standing includes providing, or advising upon, credit reference and credit information services (FSMA 2000, Sch 2). Benchmarks are used in markets to help set prices, measure performance or work out the amounts payable under financial contracts or the value of financial instruments. The term 'benchmark' is defined in s 22(6A) of the FSMA 2000. The FCA has been given enhanced powers in relation to the authorisation and registration of UK benchmark administrators and the supervising of administrators, contributors and users of them. This was against a background of widespread concerns about one such benchmark, the London Interbank Offered Rate (LIBOR), including attempts by some to manipulate it.

17.6.2 Specified investments

These include:

(a) company stocks and shares (but not shares in the share capital of open-ended investment companies or building societies incorporated in the UK);

(b) debentures, loan stock and bonds;

(c) government securities, such as gilts;

(d) unit trusts and open-ended investment companies (OEICs), which are similar to unit trusts, but use the structure of a company rather than a trust;

(e) insurance contracts (including life policies and annuities) (see **17.10**);

(f) certain types of mortgage contracts termed 'regulated mortgage contracts'. Broadly, these are mortgages to individuals secured over land at least 40% of which is or is intended to be used in connection with a dwelling. This would therefore cover residential mortgages to individual borrowers. Commercial mortgages and some other types of mortgages do not fall within this definition, the detail of which is outside the scope of this book;

(g) home reversion/home purchase plans (the former enables a homeowner to sell the whole or a proportion of their property to a finance provider in order to raise funds, and they then become a tenant of the property, whilst the latter serves the same purpose as a mortgage but is structured in a way that is compliant with Islamic law);

(h) deposits. (These would include cash ISAs and sums of money held in bank or building society accounts. However, the only specified activity relating to these investments is 'accepting deposits', which is mainly carried out by banks and building societies. The main specified investment activities set out in **17.6.3** do not apply to deposits. Sums received by solicitors acting in the course of their business are exempt under the RAO 2001.)

Investments that will not be relevant include:

(a) interests in land;
(b) certain National Savings products.

17.6.3 Specified investment activities

In relation to specified investments, these include (but are not limited to):

(a) dealing as agent;
(b) arranging;
(c) managing;
(d) safeguarding;
(e) advising;
(f) lending money on/administering a regulated mortgage contract.

There are also specified activities that are very particular in their scope, such as establishing, operating or winding up a collective investment scheme or personal pension scheme.

17.6.3.1 Dealing as agent

This involves buying, selling, subscribing for or underwriting the investments where you deal on behalf of a client (ie, rather than on your own account) and commit that client to transactions. For example, selling shares on behalf of a client pursuant to a financial order made on divorce.

17.6.3.2 Arranging

Solicitors will have many clients whose transactions involve investments (eg, endowment policies in conveyancing, unit trusts and shares in probate, etc). The solicitor will very often be involved as the contact between the client and the life company, or the client and the stockbroker. It is in this context that the solicitor may be 'arranging'. Arrangements are excluded where the solicitor merely introduces clients to a person authorised by the FCA (an authorised third person – ATP) and the introduction is made with a view to the provision of independent advice to the client. However, this exclusion does not apply where the transaction relates to an insurance contract. If you do something more than just introduce the client in respect of the investment (eg, you help the client to complete an application form), you will be 'arranging'.

17.6.3.3 Managing

Managing requires active participation beyond the mere holding of investments and applies only to 'discretionary management' (ie, involving the exercise of discretion). This investment activity will be most common in firms that undertake probate and trust work, where the solicitor is acting as trustee or personal representative.

17.6.3.4 Safeguarding

This involves safeguarding and administering investments belonging to a client. This is also particularly relevant for firms which undertake probate and trust work.

17.6.3.5 Advising

This involves giving advice to a person in their capacity as an investor on the merits of their buying, selling, subscribing for, or underwriting an investment. Advice must be about a specific investment; generic advice is outside the scope of the FSMA 2000. Thus you can, if you have the knowledge, advise a client to invest in shares rather than gilts, but if you advise the client to buy shares in a particular company, say Tesco, this will be a regulated activity.

If you do not have the requisite knowledge to provide generic advice, or if the client requires advice on a specified investment, you could refer them to a person authorised by the FCA (an ATP) with a view to the ATP providing that advice. Thus if a client wants advice on what shares to buy, you could refer them to an authorised stockbroker. It will be the stockbroker who 'advises' the client under the FSMA 2000. The referral to the ATP would not amount to a specified activity.

17.6.3.6 Example

EXAMPLE

You have recently managed to secure a large settlement in respect of your client's recent litigation matter. The client tells you that he wishes to invest this money in buying shares in a local company, and asks you which company he should invest in.

Referring to the four-stage test described at **17.6.1**, the client is seeking your advice in your capacity as a solicitor, so you are 'in business'. Shares are a specified investment, and you have been asked to advise on the purchase of these shares – advising is a specified investment activity. Therefore if you are to give this advice you need to take advantage of an exclusion or exemption (see below). If you provide this advice without relying on an exclusion or exemption, you will breach the 'general prohibition' under s 19 of the FSMA 2000, which is a criminal offence.

17.6.4 Exclusions

There are various exclusions set out in the RAO 2001. If an exclusion applies to a particular activity you are carrying out, you do not need to be authorised for that particular transaction. Those exclusions likely to be relevant to solicitors include:

(a) introducing (see **17.6.3.2**);
(b) using an ATP;
(c) acting for an execution-only client;
(d) acting as trustee or personal representative;
(e) the 'professional/necessary' exclusion;
(f) the 'takeover' exclusion.

17.6.4.1 Authorised third persons – the ATP exclusion

If you do something more than merely 'introduce' the client to an ATP (see **17.6.3.5**), you could be 'arranging' or even ' dealing as the client's agent'. However, these will be excluded under RAO 2001, arts 22 and 29 if the transaction is entered into with or through an ATP on the advice given to the client by the ATP.

You cannot rely on this exclusion if you receive from any person other than the client any pecuniary reward (eg, commission) or other advantage, for which you do not account to your client, arising out of the client entering into the transaction.

This exclusion will not apply if the transaction relates to an insurance contract.

17.6.4.2 The execution-only client exclusion

There is an exclusion similar to the ATP exclusion where the client, in their capacity as an investor, is not seeking and has not sought advice from the solicitor as to the merits of the client's entering into the transaction (or, if the client has sought such advice, the solicitor has declined to give it but has recommended that the client seek such advice from an authorised person). There is the same restriction in respect of commissions and contracts of insurance.

17.6.4.3 Trustees or personal representatives

The exclusion applies to arranging, managing, safeguarding and advising fellow trustees and/or beneficiaries. It also applies to lending money on, or administering a regulated mortgage contract.

This exclusion has limitations. It is available to a solicitor acting *as* a trustee or PR, and not to a solicitor acting *for* a trustee or PR. However, the exclusion does apply if a member of the firm is a trustee or PR but the activity is actually carried out by other members of the firm. Note that the exclusion does not apply if the solicitor is remunerated for what they do 'in addition to any remuneration they receive as trustee or personal representative, and for these purposes a person is not to be regarded as receiving additional remuneration merely because their remuneration is calculated by reference to time spent'. For managing and safeguarding, the exclusion is also not available if the solicitor holds themselves out as providing a service comprising managing or safeguarding.

The Law Society's guidance provides that this exclusion will not apply to contracts of insurance. It also does not apply to taking up or pursuing insurance distribution (see **17.10**).

17.6.4.4 Activities carried on in the course of a profession or non-investment business – the 'professional/necessary' exclusion

This applies to advising, arranging, safeguarding and dealing as agent. There is an exclusion if the activity is performed in the course of carrying on any profession or business and may reasonably be regarded as a necessary part of other services provided in the course of that profession or business, ie where it is not possible for the other services to be provided unless the regulated activity is also provided. Examples of where this exclusion may apply include: in acting on the acquisition of a company, giving advice on the merits of buying it and arranging for the acquisition of its shares; or, in probate work, arranging for the sale of all of the assets to pay IHT.

However, the exclusion does not apply if the activity is remunerated separately from the other services. Further, as a result of the Insurance Distribution Directive (2016/97/EC), if the activity consists of taking up or pursuing insurance distribution (see **17.10**), this exclusion is not available.

17.6.4.5 Activities carried on in connection with the sale of a body corporate – the takeover exclusion

This exclusion applies to arranging, advising and dealing as agent. It will apply to a transaction to acquire or dispose of shares in a body corporate (other than an OEIC), or for a transaction entered into for the purposes of such an acquisition or disposal, if:

(a) the shares consist of or include 50% or more of the voting shares in the body corporate; and

(b) the acquisition or disposal is between parties each of whom is a body corporate, a partnership, a single individual or a group of connected individuals.

It is possible to add the number of shares being acquired by a person to those already held by them in order to determine whether the 50% limit has been achieved.

Even if the above criteria are not met, eg the number of shares acquired is less than 50%, but the object of the transaction may nevertheless reasonably be regarded as being the acquisition of day-to-day control of the affairs of the body corporate, the exclusion still applies.

This is an extremely valuable exclusion for the corporate department where a client is seeking to take over, or sell its interest in, a company, whether public or private.

This exclusion does not apply to advising on, arranging, or dealing as an agent in respect of buying or selling contracts of insurance.

17.6.4.6 Summary table

The table below summarises the specified investment activities to which the exclusions apply.

Specified activity	Applicable exclusions
Dealing as agent	• ATP • Execution-only • Professional/necessary • Takeover
Arranging	• Introducing • ATP • Execution-only • Professional/necessary • Acting as trustee/PR • Takeover
Advising	• Professional/necessary • Acting as trustee/PR • Takeover
Managing	• Acting as trustee/PR
Safeguarding	• Professional/necessary • Acting as trustee/PR

17.6.4.7 Example

EXAMPLE

You are approached by Mrs Patel, who owns 100% of the share capital in X Co Ltd. Mrs Patel wishes to sell 75% of these shares to her son.

Referring to the four tests described at **17.6.1**, the client is seeking your advice and assistance in your capacity as a solicitor, so you are 'in business'. Shares are a specified investment, and in dealing with the matter you will be carrying out specified investment activities (eg advising and arranging). Therefore you need to rely on an exclusion or exemption to avoid breaching s 19 of the FSMA 2000 and committing a criminal offence.

Here you are transferring more than 50% of X Co Ltd, and so can rely on the takeover exclusion described above. Therefore you may complete this work without breaching the general prohibition.

17.7 EXEMPTION FOR PROFESSIONAL FIRMS – s 327 EXEMPTION

17.7.1 Introduction

Under s 326 of the FSMA 2000, the Treasury can designate a professional body (a DPB), and has so designated The Law Society (this role will now be undertaken by the SRA).

Under s 327, the general prohibition in s 19 of the FSMA 2000 will not apply to a regulated activity carried on by a firm of solicitors if the following conditions are met:

(a) the firm must not receive from a person other than its client any pecuniary or other advantage arising out of the activity for which it does not account to its client;

(b) the manner of providing 'any service in the course of carrying on the activities must be incidental to the provision' by the firm of professional services, ie services regulated by the SRA.

(c) the firm must carry out only regulated activities permitted by the DPB, ie the SRA.

(d) the activities must not be prohibited by an order made by the Treasury, or any direction made by the FCA under s 328 or s 329;

(e) the firm must not carry on any other regulated activities.

Each of these criteria is discussed further below.

17.7.2 The firm must not receive from a person other than its client any pecuniary or other advantage

If the firm wishes to take advantage of the s 327 exemption then it must account for any such pecuniary advantage to its client. This is mirrored by para 4.1 of the Code of Conduct for Solicitors and para 5.1 of the Code of Conduct for Firms.

17.7.3 Incidental

There are two 'incidental' tests: a specific test and a general test.

The 'specific' test relates to the particular client concerned. Under the Scope Rules, the relevant regulated activity must arise out of, or be complementary to, the provision of a particular professional service to a particular client. The firm could not, therefore, carry out a regulated activity in isolation for a client; the relevant regulated activity must 'arise out of' or be 'complementary to' some other service being provided by it. This other service must not be a regulated activity but must be a 'professional', ie legal, service (eg, in corporate work, giving legal advice, drafting documents or dealing with a regulatory matter; or in probate work, winding up the estate or giving tax advice). It follows that the professional service being provided to the client should be the primary service, and the regulated activity should be 'incidental' or 'subordinate' to the provision of the professional service. Note also that both the professional service and the regulated activity must be supplied to the same person. Thus, in a probate matter, where the probate client is the executor, advice to a beneficiary under the will would not satisfy this test.

To satisfy the 'general' test of being incidental, the activities carried out by the firm which would otherwise be regulated cannot be a major part of the firm's activities. For example, a firm will be ineligible if its income from investment business is half or more of its total income. Further factors are:

(a) the scale of regulated activity in proportion to other professional services provided;

(b) whether and to what extent the exempt regulated activities are held out as separate services; and

(c) the impression given of how the firm provides those activities, for example through advertising its services.

17.7.4 The firm must carry out only regulated activities permitted by the DPB

The role of setting out rules concerning the s 327 exemption, once occupied by The Law Society, now falls to the SRA. Accordingly, the SRA has published the SRA Financial Services (Scope) Rules (see below) and the SRA Conduct of Business (COB) Rules for this purpose (see **17.8**). Firms must comply with the requirements prescribed by these rules at all times when seeking to use this exemption.

For example, under the SRA Financial Services (Scope) Rules:

(a) A solicitor or firm must not carry on any activity that is specified in an order made by the Treasury under s 327(6) of the FSMA 2000. Examples of such activities include recommending to a client to dispose of any rights they have under a personal pension scheme and advising a client to become a member of a particular Lloyd's syndicate. Further prohibited activities are set out in the Scope Rules themselves, such as creating or underwriting a contract of insurance.

(b) If a firm wishes to undertake insurance distribution activities (see **17.10**), it must notify the SRA, be registered in the Financial Services Register and have appointed an insurance distribution officer who will be responsible for such activities.

(c) There are further restrictions in the context of corporate finance and credit-related regulated financial services activities.

For more detail on the above, please consult the Scope Rules, which may be found on the SRA's website at <www.sra.org.uk> and in the SRA *Handbook*.

17.7.5 The activities must not be prohibited by Treasury order or the FCA

The Treasury has set out, in the FSMA 2000 (Professions) (Non-Exempt Activities) Order 2001, a list of activities that cannot be provided by professional firms under the s 327 exemption. The activities that are most relevant to solicitors are incorporated into the SRA Financial Services (Scope) Rules (see **17.7.4(a)**).

The FCA also has power, under s 328, to issue directions (in writing) limiting the application of the exemption in respect of different classes of persons or different descriptions of regulated activities.

17.7.6 The firm must not carry on any other regulated activities

The s 327 exemption cannot be used by firms which are authorised by the FCA. For example, a firm could be authorised by the FCA concerning defined regulated activities. Such a firm could not use s 327 for any other 'non-mainstream' regulated activities.

17.8 THE SRA FINANCIAL SERVICES (CONDUCT OF BUSINESS) RULES

17.8.1 When do the Rules apply?

The SRA Financial Services (Conduct of Business) Rules (COB Rules) apply only when the firm is carrying out an exempt regulated activity; they do not apply if the firm is not carrying out a regulated activity at all.

17.8.2 Status disclosure (COB Rules, r 2.1 and 2.2)

A firm must provide clients with certain information concerning the status of the firm. For example, the firm must confirm to the client that it is not authorised by the FCA, and explain that complaints and redress mechanisms are provided through the SRA and the Legal Ombudsman. Any information that is provided under these rules must be given in a manner that is clear, fair and not misleading.

17.8.3 Best execution (COB Rules, r 3.1)

A solicitor must act in the best interests of their clients (Principle 7). Therefore, the firm must carry out transactions for clients as soon as possible unless it reasonably believes that it is in the client's best interest not to.

17.8.4 Transactions (COB Rules, r 4.1 and 4.2)

The firm must keep records of:

(a) instructions from clients to carry out transactions; and

(b) instructions to third parties to carry them out.

17.8.5 Commissions (COB Rules, r 5.1)

Under the COB Rules, r 5.1, the firm must keep records of commissions received in respect of regulated activities and how those commissions were dealt with.

17.8.6 Execution-only clients (COB Rules, r 7.1)

Where a firm acts for an execution-only client (see **17.6.4.2**) and the investment concerned is a retail investment product (eg life policies, unit trusts, stakeholder and personal pension schemes), it must send a letter to the client confirming that the client is not relying on the advice of the solicitor, and the firm must keep a copy of this letter.

This rule would apply, for example, when the packaged retail investment product is a contract of insurance. Here the 'execution only' exclusion would not apply, and therefore the solicitor would have to rely on the exemption for professional firms (see **17.7**) (and thus comply with the COB Rules).

17.8.7 Insurance distribution activities (COB Rules, Part 3)

There are stringent requirements which must be met when any insurance distribution activities are carried out. For example, all information about insurance distribution must be communicated to clients in a way that is clear, fair and not misleading, and information on the nature of the remuneration received in relation to a contract of insurance must be provided to the client before the conclusion of the initial contract.

17.9 CONSUMER CREDIT ACTIVITY

With effect from 1 April 2014, consumer credit activity (for example, credit brokerage, debt collecting under a consumer credit or hire agreement, debt advice and debt management or administration) became a regulated activity for the purposes of s 22 of the FSMA 2000, following the transfer of responsibility for the regulation of such activities from the Office of Fair Trading to the FCA. The activities (known as credit-related regulated financial services activities) are set out in Pt 2 and Pt 3A of the RAO 2001. Accordingly, solicitors carrying out such activities will need to be authorised by the FCA to carry out this business, or ensure that the activities fall within the s 327 exemption (see **17.7**). Representing a client in a litigation matter which has arisen from a consumer credit or hire agreement is not a credit-related activity for these purposes.

A solicitor could be carrying out a credit-related activity by virtue of the way in which they accept the payment of their fees, including allowing a client time to pay. However, such an arrangement will be regarded as an exempt agreement under the RAO 2001 if all of the following conditions apply:

(a) the number of repayments does not exceed 12;

(b) the payment term does not exceed 12 months; and

(c) the credit is provided without interest or other charges.

In most other cases, such arrangements are likely to be covered by the s 327 exemption (in which case Part 4 of the COB Rules will apply).

17.10 INSURANCE DISTRIBUTION

The Government decided to extend regulation to all general insurance selling and administration in order to comply first with the Insurance Mediation Directive (2002/92/EC) approved by the European Parliament on 30 September 2003 and subsequently the Insurance Distribution Directive (2016/97/EC), which came into effect on 1 October 2018. This Directive was later repealed by the FSMA 2023 following the United Kingdom's departure from the EU; however, its effect on the RAO 2001 was retained.

The definition of 'insurance distribution' in the RAO 2001, as amended by the Insurance Distribution (Regulated Activities and Miscellaneous Amendments) Regulations 2024, means:

> Any regulated activity of the kind specified by article 21, 25(1) or (2), 39A, 53, or, so far as relevant to any of those articles, article 64, which is carried on in relation to a contract of insurance.

This would include the activities of advising on, arranging, dealing as agent or assisting in the administration and performance of a contract of insurance.

'Contracts of insurance' are defined widely, and include life policies (eg endowment policies), car insurance, buildings and contents insurance, defective title insurance, after-the-event legal insurance, and annuities.

Rights under contracts of insurance are specified investments (see **17.6.1**), and in addition to the specified investment activities discussed in **17.6.3** there are other specified activities set out in the RAO 2001 which specifically cover insurance contracts, such as assisting in the administration and performance of a contract of insurance. Law firms carrying out probate, property and personal injury work are most likely to be involved in such activities. Whatever the type of contract of insurance involved, if a solicitor assists a client in obtaining one, even if all they do is to introduce the client to an insurance broker, the solicitor will be carrying out a specified activity. Similarly, if a solicitor is involved in an insurance claim against an insurance company, this will also be caught. All of these activities involve insurance distribution. There is a detailed definition of 'insurance distribution activity' in the SRA Glossary.

Given that the main exclusions will almost certainly not apply to insurance distribution, the firm will have to rely on the s 327 exemption (see **17.7**), seek authorisation from the FCA, or rely on the limited exceptions available for insurance distribution activities (which are beyond the scope of this book).

EXAMPLE

You are acting for Mr George on purchasing a commercial property. Your client needs to obtain defective title insurance. You offer to arrange this for your client.

Using the four tests described at **17.6.1**, you are providing this service to your client and so are 'in business'. Contracts of insurance are a specified investment and arranging is a specified investment activity. Therefore you need to rely on an exclusion or exemption to avoid breaching s 19 of the FSMA 2000 and committing a criminal offence.

However, none of the exclusions will apply here. Therefore, in order to arrange the insurance, you must use the s 327 exemption. Here, arranging the insurance is incidental to your dealing with the property transaction. If your firm can comply with the other conditions outlined above (eg the COB and Scope Rules) then you will be able to arrange the defective title insurance without breaching the general prohibition.

17.11 FINANCIAL PROMOTIONS

17.11.1 Financial Services and Markets Act 2000, s 21

As a result of the FSMA 2000, s 21, a solicitor who is not authorised by the FCA will be unable to make a financial promotion (ie, 'communicate an invitation or inducement to engage in investment activity') unless its contents are approved by an authorised person with approval from the FCA. The structure of the definitions is similar to that for regulated activities, with the Treasury having power by order to specify which investments and activities are 'controlled'. Broadly, the definitions are much the same, although not quite identical.

The result is that you can use almost the same tests as for regulated activities, namely:

(a) Are you in business?

(b) Are you making an invitation or inducement?

(c) In connection with an investment?

(d) In connection with an investment activity?

Notice, however, that the 'exclusion' test is not applicable. Thus, although you may be carrying out an activity which is not regulated, it may be 'controlled' and subject to the restrictions on financial promotions. The result is that almost anything you may say or write in connection with many transactions could be construed as a financial promotion. Thus if a solicitor advises PRs to sell the deceased's assets, this could be an invitation to deal in investments if, for example, the estate included shares or gilts.

All communications are caught, both real-time and non-real-time. A real-time communication is any communication made in the course of a personal visit, telephone conversation or other interactive dialogue. A non-real-time communication is any other communication, eg, letters e-mails, or brochures. Therefore communications to the other side (eg, letters) and communications to advisers (eg, a fax to a broker) are included just as much as communications to clients.

A real-time communication is 'solicited' where it is made in the course of a personal visit, telephone call or other interactive dialogue, if that call, visit or dialogue:

(a) was initiated by the recipient (eg, the client) of the communication; or
(b) takes place in response to an express request from the recipient of the communication (see FPO 2005, art 8).

17.11.2 Exemptions

There are then some exemptions set out in the FPO 2005. Many of these are in terms similar to the exclusions for regulated activities. These include:

(a) trustees, PRs (FPO 2005, arts 53/54);
(b) takeover of body corporate (FPO 2005, art 62).

17.11.3 Exemption for exempt professional firms

There are two exemptions designed specifically for firms claiming the special exemption under the FSMA 2000 for exempt regulated activities (see **17.7**). These deal with real-time and non-real-time promotions.

17.11.3.1 Real-time promotions (FPO 2005, art 55)

A solicitor who carries on exempt regulated activities may make a real-time promotion, for example during a meeting or a telephone conversation:

(a) if made to a client who has, prior to the communication being made, engaged the solicitor to provide professional services; and
(b) where the controlled activity to which the communication relates is exempt because of the exemption for professional firms, or is excluded from being a regulated activity by the 'necessary' exclusion; and
(c) where the controlled activity to which the communication relates would be undertaken for the purposes of, and be incidental to, the provision of professional services to or at the request of the client.

The effect is that if the activity is excluded from being a regulated activity by an exclusion other than the 'necessary' exclusion, art 55 does not apply.

17.11.3.2 Non-real time promotions (FPO 2005, art 55A)

This applies to letters, e-mails, brochures, websites, etc, where the solicitor carries on exempt regulated activities, provided the promotion contains certain specific statements.

17.11.4 One-off promotions (FPO 2005, arts 28/28A)

One-off, non-real-time communications and solicited real-time communications are exempt under the FPO 2005, art 28 if certain conditions are satisfied. Basically the communication must be one that is personal to the client.

One-off, unsolicited real-time communications are exempt under art 28A, provided the solicitor believes on reasonable grounds:

(a) that the client understands the risks associated with engaging in the investment activity to which the financial promotion relates; and

(b) that, at the time of the communication, the client would expect to be contacted by the solicitor in relation to that investment activity.

17.11.5 Introducers (FPO 2005, art 15)

You may make any real-time communication in order to introduce a client to an ATP, provided:

(a) you are not connected to (eg, a close relative of) the ATP;

(b) you do not receive other than from the client any pecuniary reward or other advantage arising out of making the introduction; and

(c) the client is not seeking and has not sought advice from you as to the merits of the client engaging in investment activity (or, if the client has sought such advice, you have declined to give it, but have recommended that the client seeks such advice from an authorised person).

17.12 EXAMPLES

EXAMPLE 1

Question You are approached Mr McParlane and Mr Ferguson. Between them and Mr Smith they own 100% of the share capital in Y Co Ltd, the company they founded. Mr McParlane owns 40% of the share capital, Mr Ferguson owns 40% and Mr Smith owns the remaining 20%. The shares carry equal voting rights.

They inform you that Mr McParlane wishes to retire from the business, and Mr Ferguson wishes to buy out his interest in the company. They want you to act for both of them in negotiating and arranging this transfer.

You decline to act for both of them due to the conflict of interest between them (see Chapter 13), but agree to act for Mr McParlane in the sale of his shares to Mr Ferguson. Your firm is not authorised by the FCA. Can you act for Mr McParlane without breaching s 19 of FSMA 2000?

Answer You are advising Mr McParlane as a solicitor, so you are 'in business'. Shares are a specified investment, and in dealing with the sale you would be taking part in a specified investment activity (arranging or advising). Therefore you need to take advantage of an exclusion or exemption.

Can you use the takeover exclusion? This applies to a transaction to acquire or dispose of shares in a body corporate. Although the transfer of shares does not include 50% or more of the voting shares in the company, the transfer will give Mr Ferguson more than 50% of the voting shares; therefore the exclusion will apply. You can act for Mr McParlane without breaching the general prohibition and committing a criminal offence.

EXAMPLE 2

Question: Review the example given at **17.10**. Would it have made any difference if the client was dealing with the property purchase himself, and just came to you to arrange the defective title insurance?

Answer: Yes.

You are still in business, and carrying out a specified investment activity (arranging) in relation to a specified investment (a contract of insurance). None of the exclusions will apply.

However, here the s 327 exemption is not available as the work you have been instructed to do is not incidental to your provision of legal work.

SUMMARY

Regulated activity

In order to determine if an activity is regulated there are four tests:

(1) Are you in business?

(2) Is there a specified investment?

(3) Is there a specified investment activity (or an activity related to information about a person's financial standing or administering a benchmark)?

(4) Is there an exclusion?

Specified investments

(1) These include:

  (a) shares (but not shares in the share capital of an open-ended investment company or building society incorporated in the UK);

  (b) debentures;

  (c) gilts;

  (d) unit trusts and OEICs;

  (e) contract of insurance;

  (f) regulated mortgage contracts;

  (g) home reversion/home purchase plans;

  (h) deposits.

(2) Investments that will not be relevant include:

  (a) interests in land;

  (b) National Savings products.

Specified investment activities

These include:

(1) dealing as agent;

(2) arranging;

(3) managing;

(4) safeguarding;

(5) advising.

Exclusions

These include:

(1) introducing;

(2) ATP;

(3) execution-only;

(4) trustee/PR;
(5) professional/necessary;
(6) takeover.

Exempt regulated activities

(1) A firm not authorised by the FCA should pay attention to:
  (a) FSMA 2000;
  (b) RAO 2001;
  (c) any rules made by the FCA;
  (d) SRA Scope Rules.
(2) Conditions set out in the FSMA 2000, the RAO 2001 and the Scope Rules overlap.
(3) The main conditions for claiming the s 327 exemption are:
  (a) the activity must arise out of, or be complementary to, the provision of a particular professional service to a particular client;
  (b) the manner of provision by the firm of any service in the course of carrying out the activities is incidental to the provision by the firm of professional services;
  (c) the firm must account to the client for any reward or other advantage which the firm receives from a third party;
  (d) the Scope Rules do not prohibit the firm using the exemption.
(4) Most credit-related regulated financial services activities and insurance distribution carried out by firms are likely to be carried out under the s 327 exemption.

Conduct of Business Rules

(1) The SRA COB Rules apply only when the firm is carrying out an exempt regulated activity; they do not apply if the firm is not carrying out a regulated activity at all.
(2) The SRA COB Rules cover:
  (a) best execution;
  (b) records of transactions;
  (c) records of commissions;
  (d) letters to execution-only clients
  (e) insurance distribution activities;
  (f) credit-related regulated financial services activities.

Financial promotions

(1) There are four questions:
  (a) Are you in business?
  (b) Do you make an invitation or inducement?
  (c) Is there a specified investment?
  (d) Is there a specified investment activity?
(2) There are two special exemptions for professional firms:
  (a) real-time promotions;
  (b) non-real-time promotions.
(3) Other exemptions include:
  (a) one-off promotions;
  (b) introducers;
  (c) trustees, PRs;
  (d) takeover of body corporate.

CHAPTER 18

REQUIREMENTS OF PRACTICE

LEARNING OUTCOMES

After reading this chapter you will be able to understand:

- the need to satisfy the SRA Assessment of Character and Suitability Rules
- the need to hold a practising certificate and comply with other practising requirements
- the need to submit accountants' reports
- the requirement for indemnity insurance
- the need for effective supervision.

18.1 THE SRA ASSESSMENT OF CHARACTER AND SUITABILITY RULES

18.1.1 Applicability and assessment

The Rules apply to:

(a) all individuals applying for admission to the roll of solicitors (including those applying to the SRA for an early assessment of their character and suitability, eg, whilst a student or trainee solicitor);

(b) qualified lawyers from other jurisdictions applying for or renewing their registration to be a Registered European Lawyer (REL) or a Registered Foreign Lawyer (RFL) (see **6.5.5**);

(c) those applying to become an authorised role holder, eg, a Compliance Officer for Finance and Administration (COFA) or a Compliance Officer for Legal Practice (COLP) (or their equivalents for a licensable body) (see **6.5**); and

(e) former solicitors seeking restoration to the roll of solicitors.

According to Part 1 of the Rules, when considering an individual's character and suitability under the Rules, the SRA will take into account the overriding need to protect the public and the public interest and maintain public trust and confidence in the solicitors' profession and in legal services provided by 'authorised persons' (as defined in the SRA Glossary). In doing so, it will take into account the nature of the applicant's role and their individual circumstances on a case-by-case basis. In the case of a compliance officer, the SRA will consider whether the applicant is of sufficient seniority and in a position of sufficient responsibility to fulfil the requirements of the role.

18.1.2 Conduct and behaviour

Part 2 of the Rules sets out the conduct and other behaviour that the SRA will consider when assessing an individual's character and suitability, which fall into two main heads: criminal conduct and other conduct or behaviour. There is a non-exhaustive list in Part 3 of the Rules which sets out the types of aggravating and mitigating factors that the SRA will take into account under either of these heads.

18.1.2.1 Criminal conduct

If an applicant has been involved in criminal conduct, the action taken by the SRA will depend upon the type of conduct involved. These are dealt with in the following categories:

(a) *Most serious.* A finding in this category is likely to result in the application being refused. These include where an applicant has been convicted by a court of a criminal offence resulting in a custodial or suspended sentence, involving dishonesty, perjury, fraud and/or bribery, of a violent or sexual nature, associated with obstructing the course of justice, associated with terrorism or which demonstrated behaviour showing signs of discrimination towards others. Also included are cases where a caution has been accepted from the police for an offence involving dishonesty, violence or discrimination or a sexual offence or the applicant has been included on the Violent and Sex Offender register.

(b) *Serious.* A finding in this category may result in the application being refused. These include where a caution has been accepted for, or the individual has been convicted of, a criminal offence not falling within the 'most serious' category and where an individual is subject to a conditional discharge or bind over by a court.

18.1.2.2 Other conduct and behaviour

The Rules set out a non-exhaustive list of examples of the other types of conduct and behaviour that the SRA will take into account. These include where:

(a) the applicant has behaved in a way which is dishonest, violent, threatening or harassing or where there is evidence of discrimination towards others;

(b) the applicant has committed and/or has been adjudged by an education establishment to have committed a deliberate assessment offence, which amounts to plagiarism or cheating, in order to gain an advantage for themselves or others;

(c) there is evidence that the applicant has deliberately sought to avoid responsibility for their debts, dishonestly managed their finances, been declared bankrupt or cannot satisfactorily manage their finances;

(d) the applicant has been made the subject of serious disciplinary or regulatory findings or sanctions.

18.1.3 Disclosure

On making an application for admission or restoration to the roll of solicitors (or for an early assessment), an individual must disclose all matters, wherever they have taken place (including overseas), which are relevant to the assessment of character and suitability and provide any further information requested by the SRA by the date specified. Failing to disclose any material information relating to the application will be taken into account by the SRA when making its determination. It is important to note that there is an ongoing obligation on those covered by the Rules to tell the SRA promptly about anything that raises a question about their character and suitability, or any change to information previously disclosed to the SRA. This includes following an individual's admittance as a solicitor (see **18.2.4**).

18.2 PRACTISING CERTIFICATES

18.2.1 Requirement to hold a certificate

Section 1 of the Solicitors Act 1974 states:

> No person shall be qualified to act as a solicitor unless—
>
> (a) he has been admitted as a solicitor, and
>
> (b) his name is on the roll, and
>
> (c) he has in force a certificate issued by the Society ... authorising him to practise as a solicitor (in this Act referred to as a 'practising certificate').

Any person who does not comply with this section will fall within the definition of an 'unqualified person' (Solicitors Act 1974, s 87) and so cannot practise as a solicitor.

Any person who practises as a solicitor without having a practising certificate will commit a criminal offence.

18.2.2 Eligibility requirements

An admitted solicitor is eligible to apply to the SRA for a practising certificate if their name is on the roll (see **18.2.3**), they have sufficient knowledge of written and spoken English or Welsh and they are not suspended from practice as a solicitor. Subject to limited exceptions, the certificate then entitles a solicitor to carry on all 'reserved legal activities' (except notarial activities) which include the right of audience before a court, the conduct of litigation and probate activities. The carrying out of immigration work, claims management services and financial services activities (see **Chapter 17**) are subject to further qualifications set out in the SRA Authorisation of Individuals Regulations.

18.2.3 The roll and registers

The SRA keeps a list of all solicitors, called 'the roll', containing details such as their date of admission as a solicitor, main practising address and the name of all organisations through which they practise in the case of a practising solicitor. In addition, it will provide details of any conditions on, or suspension of, their practising certificate and any disciplinary decisions. A solicitor does not have to hold a practising certificate to remain on the roll of solicitors. Under the SRA Roll, Registers and Publication Regulations, the SRA is required to keep in electronic form the following:

(a) the roll;

(b) a register of all solicitors who hold practising certificates;

(c) a register of European lawyers;

(d) a register of foreign lawyers; and

(e) a register of authorised bodies.

The SRA is obliged to publish the entries on the roll and registers, and so this information is available for inspection by the public.

18.2.4 Issue of certificates

Those who are required to hold a practising certificate must apply to the SRA each year to have their certificates renewed. All practising certificates become due for renewal on 31 October each year. A fee is payable on renewal of the certificate. A new fee policy was put in place in 2010 which splits the fee between the individual solicitor (flat fee) and the firm (a fee based on its turnover), although in reality the firm may be willing to pay the fee in its entirety.

Solicitors and firms also have to make a fixed yearly contribution to the SRA's Compensation Fund (see **7.11**).

A solicitor is obliged to inform the SRA promptly of any material changes to relevant information about themselves or their practice, including any change to information recorded on the roll or register (see **18.2.3**), if they are subject to any criminal charge, conviction or caution, or if a relevant insolvency event occurs in relation to them (for example, bankruptcy) (Code of Conduct for Solicitors, para 7.6).

18.2.5 Refusal of certificates and imposition of conditions

As the issuer of practising certificates, the SRA, pursuant to the SRA Authorisation of Individuals Regulations, has a certain level of discretion regarding their issue. If the SRA considers it to be in the public interest to do so, it must refuse an application for a practising certificate or, at any time, it may impose conditions on an existing certificate as it thinks fit in accordance with the regulations. The SRA may impose such conditions if it is satisfied that the solicitor:

(a) is unsuitable to undertake certain activities or engage in certain business or practising arrangements;
(b) is putting, or is likely to put, at risk the interest of clients, third parties or the public;
(c) will not comply with, or requires monitoring of compliance with, the SRA's regulatory arrangements; or
(d) should take specified steps conducive to the regulatory objectives.

The conditions imposed may specify certain requirements to be met or steps to be taken, restrict the carrying on of certain activities, the holding of certain roles or prohibit the taking of specified steps without the SRA's approval.

A decision by the SRA to refuse an application for a practising certificate or to impose conditions on one can be made the subject of an application for a review by the SRA or appealed to the High Court.

18.2.6 Post-admission training requirements

In place of solicitors undertaking a set number of hours of training each year, the SRA's approach to ensure that solicitors remain competent post admission involves:

(a) reflection on the quality of their practice by reference to a Competence Statement (consisting of a statement of solicitor competence, the threshold standard and a statement of legal knowledge) and addressing learning and development needs; and
(b) making an annual declaration that they have considered their training needs and taken measures to maintain their competence.

This links to para 3.3 of the SRA Code of Conduct for Solicitors which requires solicitors to maintain their competence to carry out their role and keep their professional knowledge and skills up to date.

18.3 ADDITIONAL PRACTISING REQUIREMENTS

18.3.1 Higher rights of audience

Solicitors are granted rights of audience in all courts upon qualification, but cannot exercise those rights in the higher courts, namely the Crown Court, High Court, Court of Appeal and Supreme Court, until they have successfully completed, as appropriate, the Higher Courts (Civil Advocacy) Qualification or the Higher Courts (Criminal Advocacy) Qualification, which entitle the solicitor to exercise rights of audience in all civil or criminal proceedings in the higher courts (including judicial review proceedings in any court) respectively.

18.4 ACCOUNTANTS' REPORTS

Under s 34 of the Solicitors Act 1974 and the SRA Accounts Rules, unless exempt, solicitors who have held or received client money must obtain an accountant's report within six months of their accounting period.

The purpose of the report is to certify compliance with the SRA Accounts Rules. Any breach of the Rules should be identified by the accountant, and, if the accountant finds it necessary to qualify the report such that money belonging to clients or third parties is, or has been, or is likely to be placed, at risk, such a report must be delivered to the SRA within six months of the end of the accounting period. The report must be prepared and signed by an accountant who is a member of one of the chartered accountancy bodies and who is, or works for, a registered auditor. The SRA may require the delivery of an accountant's report to it on reasonable notice in any other circumstances where it considers that it is in the public interest to do so.

18.5 INDEMNITY INSURANCE

18.5.1 Requirement for insurance

Firms are required to assess and purchase the level of professional indemnity insurance that is appropriate for their current and past practice. The insurance must meet certain minimum requirements set out in the SRA Indemnity Insurance Rules.

The requirement does not apply to assistant solicitors, trainees, or other individuals employed by a solicitors' practice, who will be covered by any insurance taken out by the firm or their principal. However, a solicitor practising in a non-commercial body (for example, a law centre) and providing reserved legal activities for the public must ensure that the body takes out and maintains appropriate indemnity insurance for the services they provide (Code of Conduct for Solicitors, para 5.6). Freelance solicitors and solicitors working for unregulated entities are also obliged to take out and maintain indemnity insurance (see **6.5.3**).

This insurance protects the solicitor against civil claims made against them in the course of their practice; it also protects an injured client by ensuring that solicitors in practice have sufficient monies in place to meet claims made against them.

In previous years, The Law Society ran its own insurance scheme and firms were obliged to obtain their insurance through this scheme. However, firms must now take out insurance with one or more participating insurers in accordance with the SRA Indemnity Insurance Rules and ensure that they have qualifying insurance in place at all times. The participating insurer has to comply with certain minimum terms and conditions (for example, see **18.5.2**). In the unlikely event that a claim is identified beyond the usual six-year term of firms' indemnity insurance cover, clients can claim compensation from the Solicitors Indemnity Fund (now under the direct control of the SRA).

Claims against uninsured firms are dealt with by way of grants from the SRA Compensation Fund (see **7.11**).

18.5.2 Amount of cover

The sum insured for any one claim (exclusive of defence costs) must be at least £3,000,000 for recognised and licensed bodies, and at least £2,000,000 in all other cases. However, this may not be the minimum level of cover they need in order to provide adequate insurance protection for their practice. Firms may therefore take out 'top-up' cover to increase the amount covered under their insurance.

Under the Provision of Services Regulations 2009 (SI 2009/2999), it is necessary to make available to clients information about the firm's compulsory layer of professional indemnity insurance, including details of the insurer and the territorial coverage of its insurance.

18.6 RESPONSIBILITY OF MANAGERS IN SRA AUTHORISED BODIES

Managers of SRA authorised bodies must ensure that their practice complies with the Code of Conduct for Firms. This responsibility is joint and several where management is shared (para 8.1). There are separate duties for compliance officers, but the details of these are outside of the scope of this book.

18.7 MANAGEMENT, CONTROL AND SUPERVISION

18.7.1 Requirements

Under the SRA Authorisation of Firms Rules, a body authorised by the SRA must ensure that the SRA has approved any manager or owner. In general terms, this means that the individual is fit and proper to undertake the role, in accordance with the SRA Assessment of Character and Suitability Rules (see **18.1**). The body must also have at least one manager or employee who:

(a) is a lawyer (ie, a solicitor or a barrister) of England and Wales and has practised as such for a minimum of three years; and

(b) supervises the work undertaken by that body.

18.7.2 Compliance and business systems

Both solicitors and firms are required to keep up to date with and follow the law and regulation governing the way they work (Code of Conduct for Solicitors, para 7.1 and Code of Conduct for Firms, para 3.1). An information report must be provided to the SRA by firms on an annual basis (or such other period specified by it) in a prescribed form (Code of Conduct for Firms, para 3.7).

It is necessary for bodies authorised by the SRA to have effective governance structures, arrangements, systems and controls in place to comply with the SRA's regulatory requirements. These are set out in paras 2.1 to 2.5 of the Code of Conduct for Firms and include the following:

(a) keeping and maintaining records to demonstrate compliance;

(b) actively monitoring its financial stability and business viability. Once it becomes aware that it will cease to operate, it must effect the orderly wind-down of its activities; and

(c) identifying, monitoring and managing all material risks to the business.

There are further requirements to notify the SRA promptly in specific circumstances (for example, if there are indicators of the firm being in serious financial difficulty) and if the firm becomes aware of any material changes to information previously provided to the SRA about itself, its managers, owners or compliance officers (Code of Conduct for Firms, paras 3.6 and 3.8 respectively).

The body is required to ensure that its managers and employees comply with the SRA's regulatory arrangements. It remains accountable for compliance with those regulatory arrangements where its work is carried out through others, including its managers and those it employs or contracts with (Code of Conduct for Firms, para 2.3). The Code does not go on to specify the precise arrangements that should be put in place to meet these obligations, as these will differ depending on the size and complexity of the firm, the number, experience and qualifications of the employees, the number of offices and the nature of work undertaken.

18.7.3 Treating colleagues fairly and with respect

Individual solicitors are required to treat colleagues fairly and with respect and not bully or harass them or discriminate unfairly against them. Managers are under a further duty to challenge behaviour that does not meet this standard (Code of Conduct for Solicitors, para 1.5). Guidance published by the SRA on the workplace environment explains that the term 'colleagues' for these purposes covers not only individuals employed by firms, but also those with whom solicitors and firms work closely, eg, contractors, consultants, barristers and experts instructed by the firm. The guidance further makes clear that the requirement on firms to have effective systems and controls in place to comply with the SRA's regulatory requirements (see **18.7.2**) covers systems to supervise work and monitor concerns which may affect the wellbeing and competence of individuals working in the firm.

18.8 SEPARATE BUSINESSES

A separate business essentially means a business which is owned by or connected with a body authorised by the SRA, or which owns the authorised body or in which the authorised body directly participates in the provision of its services and which is not itself authorised by the SRA or another approved regulator or an overseas practice (see the SRA Glossary). The SRA considers it important that the public is not confused or misled by a solicitor or firm incorporating non-regulated services into their practice, not least because the protection (if any) they obtain in using such services can be different from that for mainstream legal services regulated by the SRA.

Solicitors and firms should ensure that they do not represent any separate business as being regulated by the SRA (Code of Conduct for Solicitors, para 8.10(c), which applies to firms by virtue of para 7.1(c) of the Code of Conduct for Firms). Historically, examples of the kinds of services that a separate business offered are alternative dispute resolution, financial services and an estate agency. However, the SRA Authorisation of Firms Rules permit recognised bodies and sole practices to offer a wider range of services than before, including the kind of services mentioned above (see annex 2 of the Rules), and so a separate business would no longer be required in order to offer these.

A solicitor can only refer, recommend or introduce a client to the separate business or divide, or allow to be divided, a client's matter between their regulated business and the separate business where the client has given informed consent (Code of Conduct for Solicitors, para 5.3, which applies to firms by virtue of para 7.1(b) of the Code of Conduct for Firms).

18.9 DUTY TO THE SOLICITORS REGULATION AUTHORITY

18.9.1 Duty to cooperate

A solicitor must cooperate with the SRA as well as other regulators, ombudsmen, and those bodies with a role overseeing and supervising the delivery of, or investigating concerns in relation to, legal services (Code of Conduct for Solicitors, para 7.3 and Code of Conduct for Firms, para 3.2). A solicitor must also respond promptly to the SRA and provide full and accurate explanations, information and documents in response to any request or requirement and ensure that relevant information is available for inspection by the SRA (Code of Conduct for Solicitors, para 7.4 and Code of Conduct for Firms, para 3.3). Such information may be required where the SRA is investigating whether the solicitor or firm is complying with the requirements of professional conduct (see **7.6**). Any remedial action requested by the SRA must be acted upon promptly (Code of Conduct for Solicitors, para 7.10 and Code of Conduct for Firms, para 3.4). Lastly, a solicitor or firm must not attempt to prevent anyone from providing information to the SRA or any other body exercising regulatory, supervisory, investigatory or prosecutory functions in the public interest (Code of Conduct for Solicitors, para 7.5 and Code of Conduct for Firms, para 3.11). In its warning notice on the use of non-disclosure agreements, the SRA makes it clear that such agreements should not be entered into to prevent a person from reporting such information.

18.9.2 Investigating claims for redress

The Codes of Conduct require that solicitors and firms are 'honest and open' with clients if things go wrong and, if a client suffers loss or harm as a result, put matters right (if possible) and explain fully and promptly to the client what has happened and the likely impact. If required to do so by the SRA, the solicitor or firm must investigate whether anyone may have a claim against them, provide the SRA with a report on the outcome of the investigation and notify relevant persons that they may have such a claim accordingly (Code of Conduct for Solicitors, para 7.11 and Code of Conduct for Firms, para 3.5).

18.9.2.1 Reporting serious misconduct

A solicitor is obliged to ensure that a prompt report is made to the SRA of any serious breach of its regulatory arrangements by any person regulated by it (including themselves) of which they are aware (Code of Conduct for Solicitors, para 7.7 and Code of Conduct for Firms, para 3.9). If requested to do so by the SRA, a firm is under an obligation to investigate whether there have been any serious breaches that should be reported to the SRA (Code of Conduct for Firms, para 3.9). Notwithstanding this, the SRA must be informed promptly of any facts or matters which the solicitor or firm reasonably believes should be brought to its attention in order that it may investigate whether a serious breach has occurred or otherwise exercise its regulatory powers (Code of Conduct for Solicitors, para 7.8 and Code of Conduct for Firms, para 3.10). Further, a solicitor or firm must not subject any person to detrimental treatment for making or proposing to make a report or providing information based on a reasonably held belief to the SRA or other regulator, irrespective of whether any investigation or action subsequently takes place (Code of Conduct for Solicitors, para 7.9 and Code of Conduct for Firms, para 3.12). In its published guidance on Reporting and Notification Obligations, the SRA indicates that it will take reports of such adverse treatment of individuals in this context extremely seriously.

18.10 EXAMPLES

EXAMPLE 1

Question You are a manager in an SRA authorised body. You learn that one of your clients has complained to the Legal Ombudsman that one of the assistant solicitors under your supervision has been acting on a matter where his interests conflict with those of the client. Who may be disciplined by the SRA in these circumstances?

Answer The SRA may discipline the solicitor concerned. However, instead of or in addition to this action, the SRA will look at whether this solicitor was adequately supervised. Therefore the SRA could pursue you as the manager responsible and/or the authorised body in this regard.

EXAMPLE 2

Question You are a manager in an SRA authorised body. Whilst completing a file review of an assistant solicitor, you discover that he has persuaded an elderly client to transfer his house (worth £300,000) to him for £50,000. It appears that the assistant solicitor convinced the client that the house was worth only £40,000. What are you obliged to do?

Answer You are obliged to report any serious breaches of the Codes of Conduct by a solicitor to the SRA (Code of Conduct for Firms, para 3.9). Whether the breach can be considered 'serious' will depend on the circumstances, but conduct involving deception, dishonesty or a serious criminal offence will amount to a serious breach. Given the circumstances, the solicitor's conduct is clearly a serious breach. You must report the matter to the SRA promptly.

SUMMARY

SRA Assessment of Character and Suitability Rules

(1) Those applying for admission or restoration to the roll of solicitors and those seeking to become authorised role holders within authorised bodies must satisfy the SRA Assessment of Character and Suitability Rules.

(2) Certain behaviour, including the committing of certain criminal or assessment offences, is likely to, or may, result in the application to become a solicitor/authorised role holder being refused by the SRA.

Practising certificates and related matters

(1) The Solicitors Act 1974, s 1 states:

> No person shall be qualified to act as a solicitor unless—
> (a) he has been admitted as a solicitor, and
> (b) his name is on the roll, and
> (c) he has in force a certificate issued by the Society ... authorising him to practise as a solicitor (in this Act referred to as a 'practising certificate').

(2) Practising certificates are issued annually by the SRA.

(3) The SRA may grant or refuse an application for a certificate. The SRA may also grant a certificate subject to specified conditions.

(4) Solicitors wishing to exercise higher rights of audience must complete the appropriate higher courts advocacy qualification.

(5) Solicitors' firms are obliged to obtain an annual accountant's report.

Indemnity insurance

(1) The SRA Indemnity Insurance Rules require solicitors to take out compulsory insurance cover against the risks of professional negligence or other civil liability claims.

(2) Firms can insure with any approved commercial insurer.

(3) Recognised and licensed bodies must obtain cover to a minimum £3 million per individual claim (a minimum of £2 million in all other cases). Voluntary top-up cover may be required.

Supervision

(1) At least one manager or employee of an authorised body must be a lawyer of England and Wales who has practised for a minimum of three years and who supervises the work of that body.

(2) Authorised bodies must have effective governance structures, arrangements, systems and controls in place to ensure that it and its managers and employees comply with the SRA's regulatory arrangements.

APPENDIX TO PART II

SRA CODES OF CONDUCT

Please check www.sra.org.uk for updates.

SRA PRINCIPLES

Introduction

The SRA Principles comprise the fundamental tenets of ethical behaviour that we expect all those that we regulate to uphold. This includes all individuals we authorise to provide legal services (solicitors, RELs and RFLs), as well as authorised firms and their managers and employees. For licensed bodies, these apply to those individuals, and the part of the body (where applicable), involved in delivering the services we regulate in accordance with the terms of your licence.

Should the Principles come into conflict, those which safeguard the wider public interest (such as the rule of law, and public confidence in a trustworthy solicitors' profession and a safe and effective market for regulated legal services) take precedence over an individual client's interests. You should, where relevant, inform your client of the circumstances in which your duty to the Court and other professional obligations will outweigh your duty to them.

The Principles and Codes are underpinned by our Enforcement Strategy, which explains in more detail our approach to taking regulatory action in the public interest.

This introduction does not form part of the SRA Principles.

Principles

The principles are as follows:

You act:

1. in a way that upholds the constitutional principle of the rule of law, and the proper administration of justice.
2. in a way that upholds public trust and confidence in the ***solicitors'*** profession and in legal services provided by ***authorised persons.***
3. with independence.
4. with honesty.
5. with integrity.
6. in a way that encourages equality, diversity and inclusion.
7. in the best interests of each ***client***.

Please check www.sra.org.uk for updates.

SRA CODE OF CONDUCT FOR SOLICITORS, RELS AND RFLS (EXTRACTS)

Introduction

The Code of Conduct describes the standards of professionalism that we, the SRA, and the public expect of individuals (solicitors, registered European lawyers and registered foreign lawyers) authorised by us to provide legal services.

They apply to conduct and behaviour relating to your practice, and comprise a framework for ethical and competent practice which applies irrespective of your role or the environment or organisation in which you work (subject to the Overseas Rules which apply to your practice overseas); although paragraphs 8.1 to 8.11 apply only when you are providing your services to the public or a section of the public.

Conduct does not need to take place in a workplace in order to relate to your practice – these requirements capture conduct which touches realistically upon your practice of the profession, in a way that is demonstrably relevant.

You must exercise your judgement in applying these standards to the situations you are in and deciding on a course of action, bearing in mind your role and responsibilities, areas of practice, and the nature of your clients (which in an in house context will generally include your employer and may include other persons or groups within or outside your employer organisation).

You are personally accountable for compliance with this Code - and our other regulatory requirements that apply to you - and must always be prepared to justify your decisions and actions.

A serious failure to meet our standards or a serious breach of our regulatory requirements may result in our taking regulatory action against you. A failure or breach may be serious either in isolation or because it comprises a persistent or concerning pattern of behaviour. In addition to the regulatory requirements set by us in our Codes, Principles and our rules and regulations, we directly monitor and enforce the requirements relating to referral fees set out in section 56 of the Legal Aid, Sentencing and Punishment of Offenders Act 2012, and provisions relating to anti money laundering and counter terrorist financing, as set out in regulations made by the Treasury as in force from time to time.

All these requirements are underpinned by our Enforcement Strategy. That strategy explains in more detail our views about the issues we consider to be serious, and our approach to taking regulatory action in the public interest.

This introduction does not form part of the SRA Code of Conduct for Solicitors, RELs and RFLs.

Maintaining trust and acting fairly

1.1 You do not unfairly discriminate by allowing your personal views to affect your professional relationships and the way in which you provide your services.

1.2 You do not abuse your position by taking unfair advantage of **clients** or others.

1.3 You perform all ***undertakings*** given by you, and do so within an agreed timescale or if no timescale has been agreed then within a reasonable amount of time.

1.4 You do not mislead or attempt to mislead your **clients**, the **court** or others, either by your own acts or omissions or allowing or being complicit in the acts or omissions of others (including your **client**).

1.5 You treat colleagues fairly and with respect. You do not bully or harass them or discriminate unfairly against them. If you are a ***manager*** you challenge behaviour that does not meet this standard.

Service and competence

3.1 You only act for **clients** on instructions from the **client**, or from someone properly authorised to provide instructions on their behalf. If you have reason to suspect that the instructions do not represent your **client's** wishes, you do not act unless you have satisfied yourself that they do. However, in circumstances where you have legal authority to act notwithstanding that it is not possible to obtain or ascertain the instructions of your **client**, then you are subject to the overriding obligation to protect your **client's** best interests.

3.2 You ensure that the service you provide to **clients** is competent and delivered in a timely manner.

3.3 You maintain your competence to carry out your role and keep your professional knowledge and skills up to date.

3.4 You consider and take account of your **client's** attributes, needs and circumstances.

3.5 Where you supervise or manage others providing legal services:

(a) you remain accountable for the work carried out through them; and

(b) you effectively supervise work being done for **clients**.

3.6 You ensure that the individuals you manage are competent to carry out their role, and keep their professional knowledge and skills, as well as understanding of their legal, ethical and regulatory obligations, up to date.

Conflict, confidentiality and disclosure

Conflict of interests

6.1 You do not act if there is an ***own interest conflict*** or a significant risk of such a conflict.

6.2 You do not act in relation to a matter or particular aspect of it if you have a ***conflict of interest*** or a significant risk of such a conflict in relation to that matter or aspect of it, unless:

(a) the **clients** have a ***substantially common interest*** in relation to the matter or the aspect of it, as appropriate; or

(b) the **clients** are ***competing for the same objective***,

and the conditions below are met, namely that:

(i) all the **clients** have given informed consent, given or evidenced in writing, to you acting;

(ii) where appropriate, you put in place effective safeguards to protect your **clients**' confidential information; and

(iii) you are satisfied it is reasonable for you to act for all the clients.

Confidentiality and disclosure

6.3 You keep the affairs of current and former **clients** confidential unless disclosure is required or permitted by law or the **client** consents.

6.4 Where you are acting for a **client** on a matter, you make the **client** aware of all information material to the matter of which you have knowledge, except when:

(a) the disclosure of the information is prohibited by legal restrictions imposed in the interests of national security or the prevention of crime;

(b) your **client** gives informed consent, given or evidenced in writing, to the information not being disclosed to them;

(c) you have reason to believe that serious physical or mental injury will be caused to your **client** or another if the information is disclosed; or

(d) the information is contained in a privileged document that you have knowledge of only because it has been mistakenly disclosed.

6.5 You do not act for a **client** in a matter where that **client** has an interest adverse to the interest of another current or former **client** of you or your business or employer, for whom you or your business or employer holds confidential information which is material to that matter, unless:

(a) effective measures have been taken which result in there being no real risk of disclosure of the confidential information; or

(b) the current or former **client** whose information you or your business or employer holds has given informed consent, given or evidenced in writing, to you acting, including to any measures taken to protect their information.

When you are providing services to the public or a section of the public

Client identification

8.1 You identify who you are acting for in relation to any matter.

Complaints handling

8.2 You ensure that, as appropriate in the circumstances, you either establish and maintain, or participate in, a procedure for handling complaints in relation to the legal services you provide.

8.3 You ensure that **clients** are informed in writing at the time of engagement about:

(a) their right to complain to you about your services and your charges;

(b) how a complaint can be made and to whom; and

(c) any right they have to make a complaint to the ***Legal Ombudsman*** and when they can make any such complaint.

8.4 You ensure that when **clients** have made a complaint to you, if this has not been resolved to the **client's** satisfaction within 8 weeks following the making of a complaint they are informed, in writing:

(a) of any right they have to complain to the **Legal Ombudsman**, the time frame for doing so and full details of how to contact the **Legal Ombudsman**; and

(b) if a complaint has been brought and your complaints procedure has been exhausted:

(i) that you cannot settle the complaint;

(ii) of the name and website address of an alternative dispute resolution (ADR) approved body which would be competent to deal with the complaint; and

(iii) whether you agree to use the scheme operated by that body.

8.5 You ensure that complaints are dealt with promptly, fairly, and free of charge.

Client information and publicity

8.6 You give **clients** information in a way they can understand. You ensure they are in a position to make informed decisions about the services they need, how their matter will be handled and the options available to them.

8.7 You ensure that **clients** receive the best possible information about how their matter will be priced and, both at the time of engagement and when appropriate as their matter progresses, about the likely overall cost of the matter and any **costs** incurred.

8.8 You ensure that any **publicity** in relation to your practice is accurate and not misleading, including that relating to your charges and the circumstances in which **interest** is payable by or to **clients**.

8.9 You do not make unsolicited approaches to members of the public, with the exception of current or former **clients**, in order to advertise legal services provided by you, or your business or employer.

8.10 You ensure that **clients** understand whether and how the services you provide are regulated. This includes:

(a) explaining which activities will be carried out by you, as an ***authorised person***;

(b) explaining which services provided by you, your business or employer, and any ***separate business*** are regulated by an ***approved regulator***; and

(c) ensuring that you do not represent any business or employer which is not authorised by the **SRA**, including any ***separate business***, as being regulated by the **SRA**.

8.11 You ensure that **clients** understand the regulatory protections available to them.

Please check www.sra.org.uk for updates.

SRA CODE OF CONDUCT FOR FIRMS (EXTRACTS)

Introduction

This Code of Conduct describes the standards and business controls that we, the SRA, and the public expect of firms (including sole practices) authorised by us to provide legal services.

These aim to create and maintain the right culture and environment for the delivery of competent and ethical legal services to clients. These apply in the context of your practice: the way you run your business and all your professional activities (subject, if you are a licensed body, to any terms of your licence).

Conduct does not need to take place in a workplace in order to relate to your practice – these requirements capture conduct which touches realistically upon your practice of the profession, in a way that is demonstrably relevant.

Paragraphs 8.1 and 9.1 to 9.2 set out the requirements of managers and compliance officers in those firms, respectively.

A serious failure to meet our standards or a serious breach of our regulatory requirements may lead to our taking regulatory action against the firm itself as an entity, or its managers or compliance officers, who each have responsibilities for ensuring that the standards and requirements are met. We may also take action against employees working within the firm for any breaches for which they are responsible. A failure or breach may be serious either in isolation or because it comprises a persistent or concerning pattern of behaviour.

In addition to the regulatory requirements set by us in our Codes, Principles and our rules and regulations, we directly monitor and enforce the requirements relating to referral fees set out in section 56 of the Legal Aid, Sentencing and Punishment of Offenders Act 2012, and provisions relating to anti money laundering and counter terrorist financing, as set out in regulations made by the Treasury as in force from time to time.

All of these requirements are underpinned by our Enforcement Strategy, which explains in more detail our views about the issues we consider to be serious, and our approach to taking regulatory action in the public interest.

This introduction does not form part of the SRA Code of Conduct for Firms.

Compliance and business systems

2.1 You have effective governance structures, arrangements, systems and controls in place that ensure:

(a) you comply with all the ***SRA's regulatory arrangements***, as well as with other regulatory and legislative requirements, which apply to you;

(b) your ***managers*** and employees comply with the ***SRA's regulatory arrangements*** which apply to them;

(c) your ***managers*** and ***interest holders*** and those you employ or contract with do not cause or substantially contribute to a breach of the ***SRA's regulatory arrangements*** by you or your ***managers*** or employees;

(d) your ***compliance officers*** are able to discharge their duties under paragraphs 9.1 and 9.2 below.

2.2 You keep and maintain records to demonstrate compliance with your obligations under the ***SRA's regulatory arrangements***.

2.3 You remain accountable for compliance with the ***SRA's regulatory arrangements*** where your work is carried out through others, including your ***managers*** and those you employ or contract with.

2.4 You actively monitor your financial stability and business viability. Once you are aware that you will cease to operate, you effect the orderly wind-down of your activities.

2.5 You identify, monitor and manage all material risks to your business, including those which may arise from your ***connected practices***.

Cooperation and accountability

3.1 You keep up to date with and follow the law and regulation governing the way you work.

3.2 You cooperate with the **SRA**, other regulators, ombudsmen and those bodies with a role overseeing and supervising the delivery of, or investigating concerns in relation to, legal services.

3.3 You respond promptly to the **SRA** and:

(a) provide full and accurate explanations, information and documentation in response to any requests or requirements;

(b) ensure that relevant information which is held by you, or by third parties carrying out functions on your behalf which are critical to the delivery of your legal services, is available for inspection by the **SRA**.

3.4 You act promptly to take any remedial action requested by the **SRA**.

3.5 You are honest and open with **clients** if things go wrong, and if a **client** suffers loss or harm as a result you put matters right (if possible) and explain fully and promptly what has happened and the likely impact. If requested to do so by the **SRA** you investigate whether anyone may have a claim against you, provide the **SRA** with a report on the outcome of your investigation, and notify relevant persons that they may have such a claim, accordingly.

3.6 You notify the **SRA** promptly:

(a) of any indicators of serious financial difficulty relating to you;
(b) if a ***relevant insolvency event*** occurs in relation to you;
(c) if you intend to, or become aware that you will, cease operating as a legal business;
(d) of any change to information recorded in the ***register***.

3.7 You provide to the **SRA** an information report on an annual basis or such other period as specified by the **SRA** in the **prescribed** form and by the **prescribed** date.

3.8 You notify the **SRA** promptly if you become aware:

(a) of any material changes to information previously provided to the **SRA**, by you or on your behalf, about you or your ***managers***, ***owners*** or ***compliance officers***; and
(b) that information provided to the **SRA**, by you or on your behalf, about you or your ***managers***, ***owners*** or ***compliance officers*** is or may be false, misleading, incomplete or inaccurate.

3.9 You report promptly to the **SRA**, or another ***approved regulator***, as appropriate, any facts or matters that you reasonably believe are capable of amounting to a serious breach of their ***regulatory arrangements*** by any **person** regulated by them (including you) of which you are aware. If requested to do so by the **SRA**, you investigate whether there have been any serious breaches that should be reported to the **SRA**.

3.10 Notwithstanding paragraph 3.9, you inform the **SRA** promptly of any facts or matters that you reasonably believe should be brought to its attention in order that it may investigate whether a serious breach of its ***regulatory arrangements*** has occurred or otherwise exercise its regulatory powers.

3.11 You do not attempt to prevent anyone from providing information to the **SRA** or any other body exercising regulatory, supervisory, investigatory or prosecutory functions in the public interest.

3.12 You do not subject any **person** to detrimental treatment for making or proposing to make a report or providing, or proposing to provide, information based on a reasonably held belief under paragraph 3.9 or 3.10 above or 9.1(d) or (e) or 9.2(b) or (c) below, or under paragraph 7.7 or 7.8 of the SRA Code of Conduct for Solicitors, RELs and RFLs, irrespective of whether the **SRA** or another approved regulator subsequently investigates or takes any action in relation to the facts or matters in question.

Service and competence

4.1 You only act for **clients** on instructions from the **client**, or from someone properly authorised to provide instructions on their behalf. If you have reason to suspect that the instructions do not represent your **client's** wishes, you do not act unless you have satisfied yourself that they do. However, in circumstances where you have legal authority to act notwithstanding that it is not possible to obtain or ascertain the instructions of your **client**, then you are subject to the overriding obligation to protect your **client's** best interests.

4.2 You ensure that the service you provide to **clients** is competent and delivered in a timely manner, and takes account of your **client's** attributes, needs and circumstances.

4.3 You ensure that your ***managers*** and employees are competent to carry out their role, and keep their professional knowledge and skills, as well as understanding of their legal, ethical and regulatory obligations, up to date.

4.4 You have an effective system for supervising **clients'** matters.

Client money and assets

5.1 You properly account to **clients** for any ***financial benefit*** you receive as a result of their instructions, except where they have agreed otherwise.

5.2 You safeguard money and **assets** entrusted to you by **clients** and others.

SRA Glossary (extracts)

asset	includes money, documents, wills, deeds, instruments and other property
authorised body	means: (a) a body that has been authorised by the SRA to practise as a licensed body or a recognised body; or (b) a sole practitioner's practice that has been authorised by the SRA as a recognised sole practice
client	means the person for whom you act and, where the context permits, includes prospective and former clients. In the SRA Financial Services (Scope) Rules, in relation to any regulated financial services activities carried on by an authorised body for a trust or the estate of a deceased person (including a controlled trust), means the trustees or personal representatives in their capacity as such and not any person who is a beneficiary under the trust or interested in the estate
client money	has the meaning given in rule 2.1 of the SRA Accounts Rules
competing for the same objective	means any situation in which two or more clients are competing for an "objective" which, if attained by one client, will make that "objective" unattainable to the other client or clients, and "objective" means an asset, contract or business opportunity which two or more clients are seeking to acquire or recover through a liquidation (or some other form of insolvency process) or by means of an auction or tender process or a bid or offer, but not a public takeover
conflict of interest	means a situation where your separate duties to act in the best interests of two or more clients conflict
costs	means your fees and disbursements
court	means any court, tribunal or inquiry of England and Wales, or a British court martial, or any court of another jurisdiction
financial benefit	includes any commission, discount or rebate, but does not include your fees or interest earned on any client account
introducer	means any person, business or organisation who or that introduces or refers clients to your business, or recommends your business to clients or otherwise puts you and clients in touch with each other
own interest conflict	means any situation where your duty to act the best interests or any client in relation to a matter conflicts, or there is a significant risk that it may conflict, with your own interests in relation to that or a related matter
person	includes a body or persons (corporate or incorporate)
publicity	includes all promotional material and activity, including the name or description of your firm, stationery, advertisements, brochures, websites, directory entries, media appearances, promotional press releases, and direct approaches to potential clients and other persons, whether conducted in person, in writing, or in electronic form, but does not include press releases prepared on behalf of a client
referral fee	means a referral fee as defined within section 57(7) of the Legal Aid, Sentencing and Punishment of Offenders Act 2012

separate business	means, where you own, manage, or are employed by an authorised body, a separate business: (a) which you own; (b) which you are owned by; (c) where you actively participate in the provision of its services, including where you have any direct control over the business or any indirect control over the business through another person, or (d) which you are connected with, and which is not an authorised body, an authorised non-SRA firm, or an overseas practice
substantially common interest	means a situation where there is a clear common purpose between the clients and a strong consensus on how it is to be achieved
undertaking	means a statement, given orally or in writing, whether or not it includes the word "undertake" or "undertaking", to someone who reasonably places reliance on it, that you or a third party will do something or cause something to be done, or refrain from doing something

PROCEEDS OF CRIME ACT 2002

PART 7
MONEY LAUNDERING

OFFENCES

327. Concealing etc

(1) A person commits an offence if he—
  (a) conceals criminal property;
  (b) disguises criminal property;
  (c) converts criminal property;
  (d) transfers criminal property;
  (e) removes criminal property from England and Wales or from Scotland or from Northern Ireland.

(2) But a person does not commit such an offence if—
  (a) he makes an authorised disclosure under section 338 and (if the disclosure is made before he does the act mentioned in subsection (1)) he has the appropriate consent;
  (b) he intended to make such a disclosure but had a reasonable excuse for not doing so;
  (c) the act he does is done in carrying out a function he has relating to the enforcement of any provision of this Act or of any other enactment relating to criminal conduct or benefit from criminal conduct.

(2A) Nor does a person commit an offence under subsection (1) if—
  (a) he knows, or believes on reasonable grounds, that the relevant criminal conduct occurred in a particular country or territory outside the United Kingdom, and
  (b) the relevant criminal conduct—
    (i) was not, at the time it occurred, unlawful under the criminal law then applying in that country or territory, and
    (ii) is not of a description prescribed by an order made by the Secretary of State.

(2B) In subsection (2A) 'the relevant criminal conduct' is the criminal conduct by reference to which the property concerned is criminal property.

(2C) A deposit-taking body, electronic money institution or payment institution that does an act mentioned in paragraph (c) or (d) of subsection (1) does not commit an offence under that subsection if—
  (a) it does the act in operating an account maintained with it; and
  (b) the value of the criminal property concerned is less than the threshold amount determined under section 339A for the act.

(2D) A person ('P') who does an act mentioned in paragraph (c) or (d) of subsection (1) does not commit an offence under that subsection if—
  (a) P is carrying on business in the regulated sector that is not excluded business,
  (b) P does the act, in the course of that business—
    (i) in transferring or handing over to a customer or client money or other property of, or owing to, the customer or client, and
    (ii) for the purposes of the termination of P's business relationship with the customer or client,
  (c) the total value of the criminal property so transferred or handed over to the customer or client by P for those purposes is less than the threshold amount determined under section 339A for the act, and
  (d) before the act is done, P has complied with the customer due diligence duties.

(2E) For the purposes of subsection (2D)—
  (a) business is 'excluded' if it is of a description specified in regulations made by the Secretary of State for the purposes of this paragraph;

(b) a reference to property being transferred or handed over to the customer or client includes a reference to property being transferred or handed over to another person at the direction of the customer or client;

(c) 'customer due diligence duties' means all duties imposed on P in relation to the customer or client by regulation 28(2), (3), (3A), (4), (8) or (10) of the Money Laundering, Terrorist Financing and Transfer of Funds (Information on the Payer) Regulations 2017 (S.I. 2017/692) (customer due diligence measures).

(2F) A person ('P') who does an act mentioned in paragraph (c), (d) or (e) of subsection (1) does not commit an offence under that subsection if—

(a) P is carrying on business in the regulated sector,

(b) P does the act in the course of that business, on behalf of a customer or client, in operating an account or accounts maintained with P or in connection with holding any property for the customer or client,

(c) at the time of the act, P knows or suspects that part but not all of the funds in the account or accounts, or of the property so held, is criminal property ("the relevant criminal property"),

(d) it is not possible, at the time the act takes place, to identify the part of the funds or property that is the relevant criminal property, and

(e) the value of the funds in the account or accounts, or of the property so held, is not, as a direct or indirect result of the act, less than the value of the relevant criminal property at the time of the act.

(2G) Where subsection (2F) applies—

(a) if P does the act in operating an account or accounts, the funds in the account or accounts immediately after the act are assumed to include the relevant criminal property, and

(b) if P does the act in connection with holding any property for the customer or client, such of that property as is held by P immediately after the act is assumed to include the relevant criminal property.

(3) Concealing or disguising criminal property includes concealing or disguising its nature, source, location, disposition, movement or ownership or any rights with respect to it.

328. Arrangements

(1) A person commits an offence if he enters into or becomes concerned in an arrangement which he knows or suspects facilitates (by whatever means) the acquisition, retention, use or control of criminal property by or on behalf of another person.

(2) But a person does not commit such an offence if:

(a) he makes an authorised disclosure under section 338 and (if the disclosure is made before he does the act mentioned in subsection (1)) he has the appropriate consent;

(b) he intended to make such a disclosure but had a reasonable excuse for not doing so;

(c) the act he does is done in carrying out a function he has relating to the enforcement of any provision of this Act or of any other enactment relating to criminal conduct or benefit from criminal conduct.

(3) Nor does a person commit an offence under subsection (1) if—

(a) he knows, or believes on reasonable grounds, that the relevant criminal conduct occurred in a particular country or territory outside the United Kingdom, and

(b) the relevant criminal conduct—

(i) was not, at the time it occurred, unlawful under the criminal law then applying in that country or territory, and

(ii) is not of a description prescribed by an order made by the Secretary of State.

(4) In subsection (3) 'the relevant criminal conduct' is the criminal conduct by reference to which the property concerned is criminal property.

(5) A deposit-taking body, electronic money institution or payment institution that does an act mentioned in subsection (1) does not commit an offence under that subsection if—

(a) it does the act in operating an account maintained with it; and

(b) the arrangement facilitates the acquisition, retention, use or control of criminal property of a value that is less than the threshold amount determined under section 339A for the act.

(6) A person ('P') who does an act mentioned in subsection (1) does not commit an offence under that subsection if—

(a) P is carrying on business in the regulated sector that is not excluded business,

(b) P does the act, in the course of that business—
(i) in transferring or handing over to a customer or client money or other property of, or owing to, the customer or client, and
(ii) for the purposes of the termination of P's business relationship with the customer or client,
(c) the total value of the criminal property so transferred or handed over to the customer or client by P for those purposes is less than the threshold amount determined under section 339A for the act, and
(d) before the act is done, P has complied with the customer due diligence duties.

(7) For the purposes of subsection (6)—
(a) business is 'excluded' if it is of a description specified in regulations made by the Secretary of State for the purposes of this subsection;
(b) a reference to property being transferred or handed over to the customer or client includes a reference to property being transferred or handed over to another person at the direction of the customer or client;
(c) 'customer due diligence duties' means all duties imposed on P in relation to the customer or client by regulation 28(2), (3), (3A), (4), (8) or (10) of the Money Laundering, Terrorist Financing and Transfer of Funds (Information on the Payer) Regulations 2017 (S.I. 2017/692) (customer due diligence measures).

(8) A person ('P') who does an act mentioned in subsection (1) does not commit an offence under that subsection if—
(a) P is carrying on business in the regulated sector,
(b) P does the act in the course of that business, on behalf of a customer or client, in operating an account or accounts maintained with P or in connection with holding any property for the customer or client,
(c) at the time of the act, P knows or suspects that part but not all of the funds in the account or accounts, or of the property so held, is criminal property ('the relevant criminal property'),
(d) it is not possible, at the time the act takes place, to identify the part of the funds or property that is the relevant criminal property, and
(e) the value of the funds in the account or accounts, or of the property so held, is not, as a direct or indirect result of the act, less than the value of the relevant criminal property at the time of the act.

(9) Where subsection (8) applies—
(a) if P does the act in operating an account or accounts, the funds in the account or accounts immediately after the act are assumed to include the relevant criminal property, and
(b) if P does the act in connection with holding any property for the customer or client, such of that property as is held by P immediately after the act is assumed to include the relevant criminal property.

329. Acquisition, use and possession

(1) A person commits an offence if he—
(a) acquires criminal property;
(b) uses criminal property;
(c) has possession of criminal property.

(2) But a person does not commit such an offence if:
(a) he makes an authorised disclosure under section 338 and (if the disclosure is made before he does the act mentioned in subsection (1)) he has the appropriate consent;
(b) he intended to make such a disclosure but had a reasonable excuse for not doing so;
(c) he acquired or used or had possession of the property for adequate consideration;
(d) the act he does is done in carrying out a function he has relating to the enforcement of any provision of this Act or of any other enactment relating to criminal conduct or benefit from criminal conduct.

(2A) Nor does a person commit an offence under subsection (1) if—
(a) he knows, or believes on reasonable grounds, that the relevant criminal conduct occurred in a particular country or territory outside the United Kingdom, and
(b) the relevant criminal conduct—

(i) was not, at the time it occurred, unlawful under the criminal law then applying in that country or territory, and

(ii) is not of a description prescribed by an order made by the Secretary of State.

(2B) In subsection (2A) 'the relevant criminal conduct' is the criminal conduct by reference to which the property concerned is criminal property.

(2C) A deposit-taking body, electronic money institution or payment institution that does an act mentioned in subsection (1) does not commit an offence under that subsection if—

(a) it does the act in operating an account maintained with it; and

(b) the value of the criminal property concerned is less than the threshold amount determined under section 339A for the act.

(2D) A person ('P') who does an act mentioned in subsection (1) does not commit an offence under that subsection if—

(a) P is carrying on business in the regulated sector that is not excluded business,

(b) P does the act, in the course of that business—

(i) in transferring or handing over to the customer or client property of, or owing to, a customer or client, and

(ii) for the purposes of the termination of P's business relationship with the customer or client,

(c) the total value of the criminal property so transferred or handed over to the customer or client by P for those purposes is less than the threshold amount determined under section 339A for the act, and

(d) before the act is done, P has complied with the customer due diligence duties.

(2E) For the purposes of subsection (2D)—

(a) business is 'excluded' if it is of a description specified in regulations made by the Secretary of State for the purposes of this subsection;

(b) a reference to property being transferred or handed over to the customer or client includes a reference to property being transferred or handed over to another person at the direction of the customer or client;

(c) 'customer due diligence duties' means all duties imposed on P in relation to the customer or client by regulation 28(2), (3), (3A), (4), (8) or (10) of the Money Laundering, Terrorist Financing and Transfer of Funds (Information on the Payer) Regulations 2017 (S.I. 2017/692) (customer due diligence measures)."

(2F) A person ('P') who does an act mentioned in subsection (1) does not commit an offence under that subsection if—

(a) P is carrying on business in the regulated sector,

(b) P does the act in the course of that business, on behalf of a customer or client, in operating an account or accounts maintained with P or in connection with holding any property for the customer or client,

(c) at the time of the act, P knows or suspects that part but not all of the funds in the account or accounts, or of the property so held, is criminal property ('the relevant criminal property'),

(d) it is not possible, at the time the act takes place, to identify the part of the funds or property that is the relevant criminal property, and

(e) the value of the funds in the account or accounts, or of the property so held, is not, as a direct or indirect result of the act, less than the value of the relevant criminal property at the time of the act.

(2G) Where subsection (2F) applies—

(a) if P does the act in operating an account or accounts, the funds in the account or accounts immediately after the act are assumed to include the relevant criminal property, and

(b) if P does the act in connection with holding any property for the customer or client, such of that property as is held by P immediately after the act is assumed to include the relevant criminal property.

(3) For the purposes of this section—

(a) a person acquires property for inadequate consideration if the value of the consideration is significantly less than the value of the property;

(b) a person uses or has possession of property for inadequate consideration if the value of the consideration is significantly less than the value of the use or possession;

(c) the provision by a person of goods or services which he knows or suspects may help another to carry out criminal conduct is not consideration.

330. Failure to disclose: regulated sector

(1) A person commits an offence if the conditions in subsections (2) to (4) are satisfied:

(2) The first condition is that he—

(a) knows or suspects; or

(b) has reasonable grounds for knowing or suspecting,

that another person is engaged in money laundering.

(3) The second condition is that the information or other matter—

(a) on which his knowledge or suspicion is based; or

(b) which gives reasonable grounds for such knowledge or suspicion,

came to him in the course of a business in the regulated sector.

(3A) The third condition is—

(a) that he can identify the other person mentioned in subsection (2) or the whereabouts of any of the laundered property; or

(b) that he believes, or it is reasonable to expect him to believe, that the information or other matter mentioned in subsection (3) will or may assist in identifying the other person or the whereabouts of any of the laundered property.

(4) The fourth condition is that he does not make the required disclosure to—

(a) a nominated officer; or

(b) a person authorised for the purposes of this Part by the Director General of the National Crime Agency,

as soon as is practicable after the information or other matter mentioned in subsection (3) comes to him.

(5) The required disclosure is a disclosure of—

(a) the identity of the other person mentioned in subsection (2), if he knows it;

(b) the whereabouts of the laundered property, so far as he knows it; and

(c) the information or other matter mentioned in subsection (3).

(5A) The laundered property is the property forming the subject-matter of the money laundering that he knows or suspects, or has reasonable grounds for knowing or suspecting, that other person to be engaged in.

(6) But he does not commit an offence under this section if—

(a) he has a reasonable excuse for not making the required disclosure;

(b) he is a professional legal adviser or ... relevant professional adviser, and

(i) if he knows either of the things mentioned in subsection (5)(a) and (b), he knows the thing because of information or other matter that came to him in privileged circumstances, or

(ii) the information or other matter mentioned in subsection (3) came to him in privileged circumstances, or

(c) subsection (7) or (7B) applies to him.

(7) This subsection applies to a person if:

(a) he does not know or suspect that another person is engaged in money laundering; and

(b) he has not been provided by his employer with such training as is specified by the Secretary of State by order for the purposes of this section.

(7B) This subsection applies to a person if—

(a) he is employed by, or is in partnership with, a professional legal adviser or a relevant professional adviser to provide the adviser with assistance or support,

(b) the information or other matter mentioned in subsection (3) comes to the person in connection with the provision of such assistance or support, and

(c) the information or other matter came to the adviser in privileged circumstances.

(7C) Nor does a person commit an offence under this section if—

(a) he knows, or believes on reasonable grounds, that the money laundering is occurring in a particular country or territory outside the United Kingdom, and

(b) the money laundering—

(i) is not unlawful under the criminal law applying in that country or territory, and

(ii) is not of a description prescribed in an order made by the Secretary of State.

(7D) Nor does a person commit an offence under this section if—

(a) the information or other matter mentioned in subsection (3) consists of or includes information that was obtained only in consequence of the carrying out of a status check under

section 40 of the Immigration Act 2014 or an immigration check under section 40A of that Act or both, and
(b) but for the information so obtained the person would not have reasonable grounds for knowing or suspecting that another person is engaged in money laundering.

(8) In deciding whether a person committed an offence under this section the court must consider whether he followed any relevant guidance which was at the time concerned:
(a) issued by a supervisory authority or an appropriate body;
(b) approved by the Treasury; and
(c) published in a manner it approved as appropriate in its opinion to bring the guidance to the attention of persons likely to be affected by it.

(9) Disclosure to a nominated officer is a disclosure which—
(a) is made to a person nominated by the alleged offender's employer to receive disclosures under this section; and
(b) is made in the course of the alleged offender's employment.

(9A) But a disclosure which satisfies paragraphs (a) and (b) of subsection (9) is not to be taken as a disclosure to a nominated officer if the person making the disclosure—
(a) is a professional legal adviser or ... relevant professional adviser,
(b) makes it for the purpose of obtaining advice about making a disclosure under this section, and
(c) does not intend it to be a disclosure under this section.

(10) Information or other matter comes to a professional legal adviser or ... relevant professional adviser in privileged circumstances if it is communicated or given to him:
(a) by (or by a representative of) a client of his in connection with the giving by the adviser of legal advice to the client;
(b) by (or by a representative of) a person seeking legal advice from the adviser; or
(c) by a person in connection with legal proceedings or contemplated legal proceedings.

(11) But subsection (10) does not apply to information or other matter which is communicated or given with the intention of furthering a criminal purpose.

(12) Schedule 9 has effect for the purpose of determining what is—
(a) a business in the regulated sector;
(b) a supervisory authority.

(13) An appropriate body is any body which regulates or is representative of any trade, profession, business or employment carried on by the alleged offender.

(14) A relevant professional adviser is an accountant, auditor or tax adviser who is a member of a professional body which is established for accountants, auditors or tax advisers (as the case may be) and which makes provision for—
(a) testing the competence of those seeking admission to membership of such a body as a condition for such admission; and
(b) imposing and maintaining professional and ethical standards for its members, as well as imposing sanctions for non-compliance with those standards

331. Failure to disclose: nominated officers in the regulated sector

(1) A person nominated to receive disclosures under section 330 commits an offence if the conditions in subsections (2) to (4) are satisfied—

(2) The first condition is that he—
(a) knows or suspects; or
(b) has reasonable grounds for knowing or suspecting,

that another person is engaged in money laundering.

(3) The second condition is that the information or other matter—
(a) on which his knowledge or suspicion is based; or
(b) which gives reasonable grounds for such knowledge or suspicion,

came to him in consequence of a disclosure made under section 330.

(3A) The third condition is—
(a) that he knows the identity of the other person mentioned in subsection (2), or the whereabouts of any of the laundered property, in consequence of a disclosure made under section 330,
(b) that that other person, or the whereabouts of any of the laundered property, can be identified from the information or other matter mentioned in subsection (3), or

(c) that he believes, or it is reasonable to expect him to believe, that the information or other matter will or may assist in identifying that other person or the whereabouts of any of the laundered property.

(4) The fourth condition is that he does not make the required disclosure to a person authorised for the purposes of this Part by the Director General of the National Crime Agency as soon as is practicable after the information or other matter mentioned in subsection (3) comes to him.

(5) The required disclosure is a disclosure of—

(a) the identity of the other person mentioned in subsection (2), if disclosed to him under section 330,

(b) the whereabouts of the laundered property, so far as disclosed to him under section 330, and

(c) the information or other matter mentioned in subsection (3).

(5A) The laundered property is the property forming the subject-matter of the money laundering that he knows or suspects, or has reasonable grounds for knowing or suspecting, that other person to be engaged in.

(6) But he does not commit an offence under this section if he has a reasonable excuse for not making the required disclosure.

(6A) Nor does a person commit an offence under this section if—

(a) he knows, or believes on reasonable grounds, that the money laundering is occurring in a particular country or territory outside the United Kingdom, and

(b) the money laundering—

(i) is not unlawful under the criminal law applying in that country or territory, and

(ii) is not of a description prescribed in an order made by the Secretary of State.

(6B) Nor does a person commit an offence under this section if—

(a) the information or other matter disclosed to the person under section 330 consists of or includes information that was obtained only in consequence of the carrying out of a status check under section 40 of the Immigration Act 2014 or an immigration check under section 40A of that Act or both, and

(b) but for the information so obtained the person would not have reasonable grounds for knowing or suspecting that another person is engaged in money laundering.

(7) In deciding whether a person committed an offence under this section the court must consider whether he followed any relevant guidance which was at the time concerned:

(a) issued by a supervisory authority or any other appropriate body;

(b) approved by the Treasury; and

(c) published in a manner it approved as appropriate in its opinion to bring the guidance to the attention of the persons likely to be affected by it.

(8) Schedule 9 has effect for the purpose of determining what is a supervisory authority.

(9) An appropriate body is a body which regulates or is representative of a trade, profession, business or employment.

332. Failure to disclose: other nominated officers

(1) A person nominated to receive disclosures under section 337 or 338 commits an offence if the conditions in subsections (2) to (4) are satisfied.

(2) The first condition is that he knows or suspects that another person is engaged in money laundering.

(3) The second condition is that the information or other matter on which his knowledge or suspicion is based came to him in consequence of a disclosure made under the applicable section.

(3A) The third condition is—

(a) that he knows the identity of the other person mentioned in subsection (2), or the whereabouts of any of the laundered property, in consequence of a disclosure made under the applicable section,

(b) that that other person, or the whereabouts of any of the laundered property, can be identified from the information or other matter mentioned in subsection (3), or

(c) that he believes, or it is reasonable to expect him to believe, that the information or other matter will or may assist in identifying that other person or the whereabouts of any of the laundered property.

(4) The fourth condition is that he does not make the required disclosure to a person authorised for the purposes of this Part by the Director General of the National Crime Agency as soon as is practicable after the information or other mater mentioned in subsection (3) comes to him.

(5) The required disclosure is a disclosure of—
   (a) the identity of the other person mentioned in subsection (2), if disclosed to him under the applicable section;
   (b) the whereabouts of the laundered property, so far as disclosed to him under the applicable section; and
   (c) the information or other matter mentioned in subsection (3).

(5A) The laundered property is the property forming the subject-matter of the money laundering that he knows or suspects that other person to be engaged in.

(5B) The applicable section in section 337 or, as the case may be, section 338.

(6) But he does not commit an offence under this section if he has a reasonable excuse for not making the required disclosure.

(7) Nor does a person commit an offence under this section if—
   (a) he knows, or believes on reasonable grounds, that the money laundering is occurring in a particular country or territory outside the United Kingdom, and
   (b) the money laundering—
      (i) is not unlawful under the criminal law applying in that country or territory, and
      (ii) is not of a description prescribed in an order made by the Secretary of State.

333A. Tipping off: regulated sector

(1) A person commits an offence if—
   (a) the person discloses any matter within subsection (2);
   (b) the disclosure is likely to prejudice any investigation that might be conducted following the disclosure referred to in that subsection; and
   (c) the information on which the disclosure is based came to the person in the course of a business in the regulated sector.

(2) The matters are that the person or another person has made a disclosure under this Part—
   (a) to a constable,
   (b) to an officer of Revenue and Customs,
   (c) to a nominated officer, or
   (d) to a National Crime Agency officer authorised for the purposes of this Part by the Director General of that Agency,

   of information that came to that person in the course of a business in the regulated sector.

(3) A person commits an offence if—
   (a) the person discloses that an investigation into allegations that an offence under this Part has been committed is being contemplated or is being carried out;
   (b) the disclosure is likely to prejudice that investigation; and
   (c) the information on which the disclosure is based came to the person in the course of a business in the regulated sector.

(4) A person guilty of an offence under this section is liable—
   (a) on summary conviction to imprisonment for a term not exceeding three months, or to a fine not exceeding level 5 on the standard scale, or to both;
   (b) on conviction on indictment to imprisonment for a term not exceeding two years, or to a fine, or to both.

(5) This section is subject to—
   (a) section 333B (disclosures within an undertaking or group etc),
   (b) section 333C (other permitted disclosures between institutions etc), and
   (c) section 333D (other permitted disclosures etc).

333B. Disclosures within an undertaking or group etc

(1) An employee, officer or partner of an undertaking does not commit an offence under section 333A if the disclosure is to an employee, officer or partner of the same undertaking.

(2) A person does not commit an offence under section 333A in respect of a disclosure by a credit institution or a financial institution if—
   (a) the disclosure is to a credit institution or a financial institution,
   (b) the institution to whom the disclosure is made is situated in the United Kingdom or an EEA State or in a country or territory imposing equivalent money laundering requirements, and

(c) both the institution making the disclosure and the institution to whom it is made belong to the same group.

(3) In subsection (2) 'group' has the same meaning as in Directive 2002/87/EC of the European Parliament and of the Council of 16th December 2002 on the supplementary supervision of credit institutions, insurance undertakings and investment firms in a financial conglomerate.

(4) A professional legal adviser or a relevant professional adviser does not commit an offence under section 333A if—

(a) the disclosure is to professional legal adviser or a relevant professional adviser,

(b) both the person making the disclosure and the person to whom it is made carry on business in the United Kingdom or an EEA State or in a country or territory imposing equivalent money laundering requirements, and

(c) those persons perform their professional activities within different undertakings that share common ownership, management or control.

333C. Other permitted disclosures between institutions etc

(1) This section applies to a disclosure—

(a) by a credit institution to another credit institution,

(b) by a financial institution to another financial institution,

(c) by a professional legal adviser to another professional legal adviser, or

(d) by a relevant professional adviser of a particular kind to another relevant professional adviser of the same kind.

(2) A person does not commit an offence under section 333A in respect of a disclosure to which this section applies if—

(a) the disclosure relates to—

(i) a client or former client of the institution or adviser making the disclosure and the institution or adviser to whom it is made,

(ii) a transaction involving them both, or

(iii) the provision of a service involving them both;

(b) the disclosure is for the purpose only of preventing an offence under this Part of this Act;

(c) the institution or adviser to whom the disclosure is made is situated in the United Kingdom or an EEA State or in a country or territory imposing equivalent money laundering requirements; and

(d) the institution or adviser making the disclosure and the institution or adviser to whom it is made are subject to equivalent duties of professional confidentiality and the protection of personal data (within the meaning of Parts 5 to 7 of the Data Protection Act 2018 (see section 3(2) and (14) of that Act)).

333D. Other permitted disclosures etc

(1) A person does not commit an offence under section 333A if the disclosure is—

(a) to the authority that is the supervisory authority for that person by virtue of the Money Laundering, Terrorist Financing and Transfer of Funds (Information on the Payer) Regulations 2017;

(aa) for the purposes of proceedings under section 336A (power of court to extend moratorium period);

(ab) made in good faith by virtue of section 339ZB (disclosures within the regulated sector); or

(b) for the purpose of—

(i) the detection, investigation or prosecution of a criminal offence (whether in the United Kingdom or elsewhere),

(ii) an investigation under this Act, or

(iii) the enforcement of any order of a court under this Act.

(1A) Where an application is made to extend a moratorium period under section 336A, a person does not commit an offence under section 333A if—

(a) the disclosure is made to a customer or client of the person,

(b) the customer or client appears to the person making the disclosure to have an interest in the relevant property, and

(c) the disclosure contains only such information as is necessary for the purposes of notifying the customer or client that the application under section 336A has been made.

'Moratorium period' and 'relevant property' have the meanings given in section 336D.

(2) A professional legal adviser or a relevant professional adviser does not commit an offence under section 333A if the disclosure—
 (a) is to the adviser's client, and
 (b) is made for the purpose of dissuading the client from engaging in conduct amounting to an offence.

(3) A person does not commit an offence under section 333A(1) if the person does not know or suspect that the disclosure is likely to have the effect mentioned in section 333A(1)(b).

(4) A person does not commit an offence under section 333A(3) if the person does not know or suspect that the disclosure is likely to have the effect mentioned in section 333A(3)(b).

333E. Interpretation of sections 333A to 333D

(1) For the purposes of sections 333A to 333D, Schedule 9 has effect for determining—
 (a) what is a business in the regulated sector, and
 (b) what is a supervisory authority.

(2) In those sections—
'credit institution' has the same meaning as in Schedule 9;
'financial institution' means an undertaking that carries on a business in the regulated sector by virtue of any of paragraphs (b) to (i) of paragraph 1(1) of that Schedule.

(3) References in those sections to a disclosure by or to a credit institution or a financial institution include disclosure by or to an employee, officer or partner of the institution acting on its behalf.

(4) For the purposes of those sections a country or territory imposes 'equivalent money laundering requirements' if it imposes requirements equivalent to those laid down in Directive 2015/849/EU of the Council of 20th May 2015 on the prevention of the use of the financial system for the purpose of money laundering and terrorist financing, as amended by Directive 2018/843 of the European Parliament and of the Council of 30th May 2018.

(5) In those sections 'relevant professional adviser' means an accountant, auditor or tax adviser who is a member of a professional body which is established for accountants, auditors or tax advisers (as the case may be) and which makes provision for—
 (a) testing the competence of those seeking admission to membership of such a body as a condition for such admission; and
 (b) imposing and maintaining professional and ethical standards for its members, as well as imposing sanctions for non-compliance with those standards.

334. Penalties

(1) A person guilty of an offence under section 327, 328 or 329 is liable—
 (a) on summary conviction, to imprisonment for a term not exceeding six months or to a fine not exceeding the statutory maximum or to both; or
 (b) on conviction on indictment, to imprisonment for a term not exceeding 14 years or to a fine or to both.

(2) A person guilty of an offence under section 330, 331 or 332 is liable:
 (a) on summary conviction, to imprisonment for a term not exceeding six months or to a fine not exceeding the statutory maximum or to both; or
 (b) on conviction on indictment, to imprisonment for a term not exceeding five years or to a fine or to both.

(3) A person guilty of an offence under section 339(1A) is liable on summary conviction to a fine not exceeding level 5 on the standard scale.

CONSENT

335. Appropriate consent

(1) The appropriate consent is—
 (a) the consent of a nominated officer to do a prohibited act if an authorised disclosure is made to the nominated officer;
 (b) the consent of a constable to do a prohibited act if an authorised disclosure is made to a constable;

(c) the consent of a customs officer to do a prohibited act if an authorised disclosure is made to a customs officer.

(2) A person must be treated as having the appropriate consent if—

(a) he makes an authorised disclosure to a constable or a customs officer, and

(b) the condition in subsection (3) or the condition in subsection (4) is satisfied.

(3) The condition is that before the end of the notice period he does not receive notice from a constable or customs officer that consent to the doing of the act is refused.

(4) The condition is that—

(a) before the end of the notice period he receives notice from a constable or customs officer that consent to the doing of the act is refused; and

(b) the moratorium period has expired.

(5) The notice period is the period of seven working days starting with the first working day after the person makes the disclosure.

(6) The moratorium period is the period of 31 days starting with the day on which the person receives notice that consent to the doing of the act is refused.

(6A) Subsection (6) is subject to—

(a) section 336A, which enables the moratorium period to be extended by court order in accordance with that section, and

(b) section 336C, which provides for an automatic extension of the moratorium period in certain cases (period extended if it would otherwise end before determination of application or appeal proceedings etc).

(7) A working day is a day other than a Saturday, a Sunday, Christmas Day, Good Friday or a day which is a bank holiday under the Banking and Financial Dealings Act 1971 in the part of the United Kingdom in which the person is when he makes the disclosure.

(8) References to a prohibited act are to an act mentioned in section 327(1), 328(1) or 329(1) (as the case may be).

(8A) Subsection (8) is subject to—

(a) section 336A, which enables the moratorium period to be extended by court order in accordance with that section, and

(b) section 336C, which provides for an automatic extension of the moratorium period in certain cases (period extended if it would otherwise end before determination of application or appeal proceedings etc).

(9) A nominated officer is a person nominated to receive disclosures under section 338.

(10) Subsections (1) to (4) apply for the purposes of this Part.

336. Nominated officer: consent

(1) A nominated officer must not give the appropriate consent to the doing of a prohibited act unless the condition in subsection (2), the condition in subsection (3) or the condition in subsection (4) is satisfied.

(2) The condition is that—

(a) he makes a disclosure that property is criminal property to a person authorised for the purposes of this Part by the Director General of the National Crime Agency, and

(b) such a person gives consent to the doing of the act.

(3) The condition is that—

(a) he makes a disclosure that property is criminal property to a person authorised for the purposes of this Part by the Director General of the National Crime Agency, and

(b) before the end of the notice period he does not receive notice from such a person that consent to the doing of the act is refused.

(4) The condition is that—

(a) he makes a disclosure that property is criminal property to a person authorised for the purposes of this Part by the Director General of the National Crime Agency,

(b) before the end of the notice period he receives notice from such a person that consent to the doing of the act is refused, and

(c) the moratorium period has expired.

(5) A person who is a nominated officer commits an offence if—

(a) he gives consent to a prohibited act in circumstances where none of the conditions in subsections (2), (3) and (4) is satisfied, and

(b) he knows or suspects that the act is a prohibited act.

(6) A person guilty of such an offence is liable—
(a) on summary conviction, to imprisonment for a term not exceeding six months or to a fine not exceeding the statutory maximum or to both, or
(b) on conviction on indictment, to imprisonment for a term not exceeding five years or to a fine or to both.
(7) The notice period is the period of seven working days starting with the first working day after the nominated officer makes the disclosure.
(8) The moratorium period is the period of 31 days starting with the day on which the nominated officer is given notice that consent to the doing of the act is refused.
(9) A working day is a day other than a Saturday, a Sunday, Christmas Day, Good Friday or a day which is a bank holiday under the Banking and Financial Dealings Act 1971 in the part of the United Kingdom in which the nominated officer is when he gives the appropriate consent.
(10) References to a prohibited act are to an act mentioned in section 327(1), 328(1) or 329(1) (as the case may be).
(11) A nominated officer is a person nominated to receive disclosures under section 338.

...

DISCLOSURES

337. Protected disclosures

(1) A disclosure which satisfies the following three conditions is not to be taken to breach any restriction on the disclosure of information (however imposed).
(2) The first condition is that the information or other matter disclosed came to the person making the disclosure (the discloser) in the course of his trade, profession, business or employment.
(3) The second condition is that the information or other matter—
(a) causes the discloser to know or suspect, or
(b) gives him reasonable grounds for knowing or suspecting,
that another person is engaged in money laundering.
(4) The third condition is that the disclosure is made to a constable, a customs officer or a nominated officer as soon as is practicable after the information or other matter comes to the discloser.
(4A) Where a disclosure consists of a disclosure protected under subsection (1) and a disclosure of either or both of—
(a) the identity of the other person mentioned in subsection (3), and
(b) the whereabouts of property forming the subject-matter of the money laundering that the discloser knows or suspects, or has reasonable grounds for knowing or suspecting, that other person to be engaged in,
the disclosure of the thing mentioned in paragraph (a) or (b) (as well as the disclosure protected under subsection (1)) is not to be taken to breach any restriction on the disclosure of information (however imposed).
(5) A disclosure to a nominated officer is a disclosure which—
(a) is made to a person nominated by the discloser's employer to receive disclosures under section 330 or this section, and
(b) is made in the course of the discloser's employment.

338. Authorised disclosures

(1) For the purposes of this Part a disclosure is authorised if—
(a) it is a disclosure to a constable, a customs officer or a nominated officer by the alleged offender that property is criminal property, . . . and
(c) the first, second or third condition set out below is satisfied.
(2) The first condition is that the disclosure is made before the alleged offender does the prohibited act.
(2A) The second condition is that—
(a) the disclosure is made while the alleged offender is doing the prohibited act,
(b) he began to do the act at a time when, because he did not then know or suspect that the property constituted or represented a person's benefit from criminal conduct, the act was not a prohibited act, and
(c) the disclosure is made on his own initiative and as soon as is practicable after he first knows or suspects that the property constitutes or represents a person's benefit from criminal conduct.

(3) The third condition is that—
  (a) the disclosure is made after the alleged offender does the prohibited act,
  (b) he has a reasonable excuse for his failure to make the disclosure before he did the act, and
  (c) the disclosure is made on his own initiative and as soon as it is practicable for him to make it.

(4) An authorised disclosure is not to be taken to breach any restriction on the disclosure of information (however imposed).

(4A) Where an authorised disclosure is made in good faith, no civil liability arises in respect of the disclosure on the part of the person by or on whose behalf it is made.

(5) A disclosure to a nominated officer is a disclosure which—
  (a) is made to a person nominated by the alleged offender's employer to receive authorised disclosures, and
  (b) is made in the course of the alleged offender's employment.

(6) References to the prohibited act are to an act mentioned in section 327(1), 328(1) or 329(1) (as the case may be).

339. Form and manner of disclosures

(1) The Secretary of State may by order prescribe the form and manner in which a disclosure under section 330, 331, 332 or 338 must be made.

(1A) A person commits an offence if he makes a disclosure under section 330, 331, 332 or 338 otherwise that in the form prescribed under subsection (1) or otherwise than in the manner so prescribed.

(1B) But a person does not commit an offence under subsection (1A) if he has a reasonable excuse for making the disclosure otherwise than in the form prescribed under subsection (1) or (as the case may be) otherwise than in the manner so prescribed.

(2) The power under subsection (1) to prescribe the form in which a disclosure must be made includes power to provide for the form to include a request to a person making a disclosure that the person provide information specified or described in the form if he has not provided it in making the disclosure.

(3) Where under subsection (2) a request is included in a form prescribed under subsection (1), the form must—
  (a) state that there is no obligation to comply with the request, and
  (b) explain the protection conferred by subsection (4) on a person who complies with the request.

(4) A disclosure made in pursuance of a request under subsection (2) is not to be taken to breach any restriction on the disclosure of information (however imposed).

(5) . . .

(6) . . .

(7) Subsection (2) does not apply to a disclosure made to a nominated officer.

339ZA. Disclosures to the NCA

Where a disclosure is made under this Part to a constable or an officer of Revenue and Customs, the constable or officer of Revenue and Customs must disclose it in full to a person authorised for the purposes of this Part by the Director General of the National Crime Agency a soon as practicable after it has been made.

...

THRESHOLD AMOUNTS

339A. Threshold amounts

(1) In this section—
  (a) subsections (2) to (6) apply for the purposes of sections 327(2C), 328(5) and 329(2C), and
  (b) subsection (6A) applies for the purposes of sections 327(2D), 328(6) and 329(2D).

(2) The threshold amount for acts done by a deposit-taking body, electronic money institution or payment institution in operating an account is £1,000 unless a higher amount is specified under the following provisions of this section (in which event it is that higher amount).

(3) An officer of Revenue and Customs, or a constable, may specify the threshold amount for acts done by a deposit-taking body, electronic money institution or payment institution in operating an account—

(a) when he gives consent, or gives notice refusing consent, to the body's or institution's doing of an act mentioned in section 327(1), 328(1) or 329(1) in opening, or operating, the account or a related account; or

(b) on a request from the body or institution.

(4) Where the threshold amount for acts done in operating an account is specified under subsection (3) or this subsection, an officer of Revenue and Customs, or a constable, may vary the amount (whether on a request from the deposit-taking body, electronic money institution or payment institution or otherwise) by specifying a different amount.

(5) Different threshold amounts may be specified under subsections (3) and (4) for different acts done in operating the same account.

(6) The amount specified under subsection (3) and (4) as the threshold amount for acts done in operating an account must, when specified, not be less than the amount specified in subsection (2).

(6A) The threshold amount for acts done by a person carrying on business in the regulated sector, for the purposes of the termination of a business relationship with a customer or client, is £1000.

(7) The Secretary of State may by order vary the amount for the time being specified in subsection (2) or (6A).

(8) For the purposes of this section, an account is related to another if each is maintained with the same deposit-taking body, electronic money institution or payment institution and there is a person who, in relation to each account, is the person or one of the persons entitled to instruct the body or institution as respects the operation of the account.

INTERPRETATION

340. Interpretation

(1) This section applies for the purposes of this Part.

(2) Criminal conduct is conduct which—

(a) constitutes an offence in any part of the United Kingdom, or

(b) would constitute an offence in any part of the United Kingdom if it occurred there.

(3) Property is criminal property if—

(a) it constitutes a person's benefit from criminal conduct or it represents such a benefit (in whole or part and whether directly or indirectly), and

(b) the alleged offender knows or suspects that it constitutes or represents such a benefit.

(4) It is immaterial—

(a) who carried out the conduct;

(b) who benefited from it;

(c) whether the conduct occurred before or after the passing of this Act.

(5) A person benefits from conduct if he obtains property as a result of or in connection with the conduct.

(6) If a person obtains a pecuniary advantage as a result of or in connection with conduct, he is to be taken to obtain as a result of or in connection with the conduct a sum of money equal to the value of the pecuniary advantage.

(7) References to property or a pecuniary advantage obtained in connection with conduct include references to property or a pecuniary advantage obtained in both that connection and some other.

(8) If a person benefits from conduct his benefit is the property obtained as a result of or in connection with the conduct.

(9) Property is all property wherever situated and includes—

(a) money;

(b) all forms of property, real or personal, heritable or moveable;

(c) things in action and other intangible or incorporeal property.

(10) The following rules apply in relation to property—

(a) property is obtained by a person if he obtains an interest in it;

(b) references to an interest, in relation to land in England and Wales or Northern Ireland, are to any legal estate or equitable interest or power;

(c) references to an interest, in relation to land in Scotland, are to any estate, interest, servitude or other heritable right in or over land, including a heritable security;

(d) references to an interest, in relation to property other than land, include references to a right (including a right to possession).

(11) Money laundering is an act which—

(a) constitutes an offence under section 327, 328 or 329,
(b) constitutes an attempt, conspiracy or incitement to commit an offence specified in paragraph (a),
(c) constitutes aiding, abetting, counselling or procuring the commission of an offence specified in paragraph (a), or
(d) would constitute an offence specified in paragraph (a), (b) or (c) if done in the United Kingdom.

(12) For the purposes of a disclosure to a nominated officer—
(a) references to a person's employer include any body, association or organisation (including a voluntary organisation) in connection with whose activities the person exercises a function (whether or not for gain or reward), and
(b) references to employment must be construed accordingly.

(13) References to a constable include references to a person authorised for the purposes of this Part by the Director General of the National Crime Agency.

(14) 'Deposit-taking body' means—
(a) a business which engages in the activity of accepting deposits,...
(b) the National Savings Bank, or
(c) a person specified, or of a description specified, in regulations made by the Treasury or the Secretary of State.

(14A) In subsection (14)(a)—
(a) the reference to the activity of accepting deposits is a reference to that activity so far as it is, for the time being, a regulated activity for the purposes of the Financial Services and Markets Act 2000 by virtue of an order under section 22 of that Act, but
(b) the reference to a business which engages in that activity does not include a person specified, or of a description specified, in regulations made by the Treasury or the Secretary of State.

(14B) Before making regulations under subsection (14A)(b), the Treasury or the Secretary of State (as appropriate) must consult such persons likely to be affected by the regulations, or such representatives of such persons, as they consider appropriate.

(14C) 'Electronic money institution' has the same meaning as in the Electronic Money Regulations 2011 (SI 2011/99) (see regulation 2 of those Regulations).

(15) 'Information order' means an order made under section 339ZH.

(16) 'Payment institution' means an authorised payment institution or a small payment institution (each as defined in regulation 2 of the Payment Services Regulations 2017 (SI 2017/752)).

(17) 'Business relationship' means a business, professional or commercial relationship between a person carrying on business in the regulated sector and a customer or client, where the relationship—
(a) arises out of the business of that person, and
(b) is expected by that person, at the time when contact is established, to have an element of duration.

PART II SUMMARIES

PROFESSIONAL CONDUCT

Chapter 6: The Legal Profession

Topic	*Summary*
Professional conduct	Professional conduct is the term that is used to describe the rules, regulations and requirements with which a solicitor must comply. Solicitors are in a position of trust, and so a higher standard of behaviour is expected of them than of members of the public.
Solicitors Regulation Authority (SRA)	The SRA regulates solicitors, law firms and those owning, managing and working for other bodies authorised by the SRA to provide legal services in England and Wales. It also controls such matters as training and entry into the profession.
The Law Society	The Law Society is the representative body for solicitors in England and Wales. Membership is voluntary, but all solicitors (and those who are employed by them) are bound by the requirements of professional conduct whether or not they are members of The Law Society.
Different aspects of practice	The legal profession is made up of a number of different types of organisation. Within these organisations, there are a number of roles that a solicitor may fill. However, most solicitors in private practice are employed by recognised bodies.

Chapter 7: Regulating the Profession

Topic	*Summary*
Solicitors Regulation Authority (SRA)	The SRA publishes and enforces standards, rules and requirements concerning how solicitors, authorised bodies and their owners, managers and employees behave and conduct their business. The subject matter of this Part are the SRA Codes of Conduct and accompanying rules and regulations.
Complaints against solicitors	Every solicitor and firm must have a complaints handling procedure, and must ensure that complaints are dealt with promptly, fairly, openly and free of charge. If a complaint cannot be resolved by the solicitor or firm, the client must be given details of the Legal Ombudsman.

Topic	Summary
Legal Ombudsman	The Legal Ombudsman is the sole point of receipt for complaints concerning services provided by solicitors and other types of individuals providing legal services, and refers any allegations of breaches of the requirements of professional conduct concerning solicitors to the SRA.
Powers of the Legal Ombudsman	Where the Legal Ombudsman makes a determination following a complaint, it has the power to order the firm of solicitors to limit its fees, or to direct that the firm must compensate the client up to the sum of £50,000 (plus interest) amongst other sanctions. The Legal Ombudsman cannot pay compensation to a client itself.
Powers of the SRA – professional misconduct	Where a finding of professional misconduct is made, the SRA may discipline the firm or regulated individual by imposing disciplinary sanctions, or referring the matter to the Solicitors Disciplinary Tribunal. The SRA may also revoke or suspend authorisation of the firm.
Solicitors Disciplinary Tribunal	The Solicitors Disciplinary Tribunal hears and determines applications relating to allegations of professional misconduct. It is independent of the SRA and The Law Society. It has the power to suspend a solicitor, to fine a solicitor an unlimited amount and, in the most extreme cases, to strike a solicitor off the roll – which will effectively end their career.
Negligence	In addition to or instead of the actions that the SRA may take against a solicitor, a solicitor may be sued by their client in the tort of negligence. A solicitor owes their client a duty of care. Where this duty is breached, and the client suffers a foreseeable loss as a result of that breach, the solicitor may be sued for negligence. Firms must carry compulsory indemnity insurance against such actions. Certain categories of solicitor must also ensure that their services are covered by indemnity insurance.
The SRA Compensation Fund	The SRA Compensation Fund is maintained by the SRA. Payment may be made from the Fund when a client has suffered loss as a result of a defaulting practitioner's act or omission.

Chapter 8: The Principles

Topic	Summary
The SRA Codes of Conduct	The profession is regulated by the Government and by standards of conduct set out by the SRA.
The Principles	The Principles are contained within the SRA *Handbook*. They underpin all of the *Handbook* requirements, including the Codes of Conduct. They define the fundamental ethical and professional standards expected of all firms and individuals when providing legal services.

Topic	Summary
Conflict between Principles	Where two or more of the Principles come into conflict, those which safeguard the wider public interest (Principles 1 and 2) take precedence over the individual interests of a client.
Breach of the Principles	Where a solicitor breaches the Principles, they may well be guilty of professional misconduct. In serious cases, this could also lead to them being 'struck off' the roll of solicitors, which would effectively end their career.

Chapter 9: Obtaining Instructions

Topic	Summary
General principles	A solicitors' firm must take steps to try to maintain and increase its market share in order to prosper. However, a solicitor must at all times comply with the general law and the Codes of Conduct. In particular, no matter what financial pressure they are under, a solicitor should always be independent and impartial when giving advice to a client.
Advertising	Solicitors and firms are free to publicise their practices, provided that they comply with the general law on advertising and publicity in force at the time and with paras 8.6 to 8.11 of the Code of Conduct for Solicitors.
Publicity	All publicity issued by, or on behalf of, firms and solicitors must not be misleading or inaccurate, including that relating to charges. The SRA Transparency Rules also set out requirements concerning the publication of costs for certain services.
Cold calling	A solicitor and firm may not cold call the general public. However, this restriction does not apply to contacting clients or former clients.
Referrals and introductions of business	A solicitor or firm may enter into an arrangement with a third party to refer clients to that third party or to have clients introduced to him/it by a third party. However, such arrangements must comply with paras 5.1 and 5.2 of the Code of Conduct for Solicitors.
Separate businesses	A solicitor or firm may refer, recommend or introduce a client to a separate business (as defined in the SRA Glossary) but only where the client has given informed consent.
Payments for referrals or introductions	A solicitor or firm may make payments to or receive payments from a third party for introductions and referrals, but must comply with para 5.1 of the Code of Conduct for Solicitors. Making or receiving a referral fee in relation to claims for damages arising from death or personal injury is prohibited by legislation and the Codes of Conduct.

Topic	Summary
Fee sharing	Clients must be informed of any fee-sharing arrangement with a third party that is relevant to their matter, and the agreement must be in writing.

Chapter 10: The Retainer

Topic	Summary
The retainer	The contract between a solicitor and their client is often referred to as a retainer. The contract is governed by the general law, and also the requirements of professional conduct.
Acceptance and refusal of instructions	A solicitor and firm must identify whom they are acting for in relation to any matter. They must also not unfairly discriminate and this includes when accepting or refusing instructions.
Acceptance of third party instructions	A solicitor or firm can only act for clients on instructions from the client or from someone properly authorised to provide instructions on the client's behalf. If there is reason to suspect that instructions do not represent a client's wishes, the solicitor or firm must not act unless they satisfy themselves that they do.
Duty to the client during the retainer	A solicitor owes the client a number of duties throughout the retainer. For example, s 13 of the Supply of Goods and Services Act 1982 provides that a supplier of services (such as a solicitor) will carry out those services with reasonable care and skill. Other duties are set out in the Codes of Conduct.
Termination of the retainer	A client may terminate the retainer at any time and for any reason. Ceasing to act for a client without good reason and without providing reasonable notice is unlikely to be acting in the best interests of that client and so not in compliance with the Principles and the Codes of Conduct.
Responsibilities on termination	It is good practice for a solicitor to confirm to the client in writing that the retainer has been terminated, and to take steps to deal with any property of the client that may be held by the solicitor. In certain circumstances a solicitor may exercise a lien over the property until their fees are paid.

Chapter 11: Client Care and Costs

Topic	Summary
Client care	A solicitor and firm must achieve the standards set out in the Codes of Conduct on service and competence, including that the service provided is competent and delivered in a timely manner.

Topic	*Summary*
Client's ability to make informed decisions	A solicitor and firm must ensure that clients are given information in a way that they can understand and that clients are in a position to make informed decisions about the services they need, how their matter will be handled and the options available to them.
Level of service	A solicitor must maintain their competence to carry out their role and keep their professional knowledge and skills up to date. In addition to ensuring that the service being provided to clients is competent and delivered in a timely manner, a solicitor and firm must consider and take account of the attributes, needs and circumstances of the individual client.
Costs information	A solicitor and firm are obliged to provide clients with the best possible information as to how their matter will be priced and the likely overall costs of a matter, both at the time of engagement and when appropriate as the matter progresses.
Solicitor's fees	A solicitor and client may agree the level of costs that the solicitor may charge. However, this agreement is regulated by statute and the common law. A distinction is made between costs in contentious matters and costs in non-contentious matters.
Solicitor's bill	A solicitor's bill must contain prescribed information in order for the bill to be enforceable.
Client's right to challenge the bill	A client may challenge the costs of a solicitor in both contentious and non-contentious matters. Generally speaking, in both types of matters the client may apply to have the costs assessed by the court. The client may also complain to the firm about the level of charges under the firm's complaints procedure, and subsequently to the Legal Ombudsman.
Suing on a bill	Generally, a solicitor may not sue to recover their costs from the client until one month has elapsed since the bill was delivered.
Overcharging	A solicitor must act in the best interests of the client and must not take unfair advantage of his client. Therefore a solicitor must not overcharge for work done. Overcharging may well be considered by the SRA as a breach of professional conduct.

Chapter 12: Confidentiality

Topic	*Summary*
Duty of confidentiality	A solicitor, firm and their staff must keep the affairs of current clients and former clients confidential except where disclosure is required or permitted by law or the client consents.

Duty of disclosure	The solicitor also has a duty to disclose to the client all information that is material to the client's matter of which they have personal knowledge except in the circumstances set out in the Codes of Conduct.
Placing confidential information at risk	Where a solicitors' firm holds confidential information for a current or former client, it must not risk breaching confidentiality by acting for (or continuing to act for) another client on a matter where the information is material, and where the clients have an adverse interest to one another, unless effective measures have been taken to avoid the risk of disclosure of the confidential material, or the client for whom confidential information is held has given informed consent (in writing) to it acting, including to any measures taken to protect that information.
Professional embarrassment	Even when a solicitor and firm would be permitted to act for two or more clients on a matter pursuant to the Codes, they may still have to refuse instructions on the basis of professional embarrassment.
Privilege	In addition to the duty of confidentiality, a solicitor must also consider legal professional privilege. Where legal professional privilege applies, a solicitor can refuse to disclose communications between themselves and a client.

Chapter 13: Conflicts of Interests

Topic	*Summary*
General principles	A solicitor and firm must not act where there is an own interest conflict or a significant risk of such a conflict. There are no exceptions to this. A solicitor and firm must also not act where there is a conflict, or a significant risk of a conflict, between the interests of two or more clients unless either of the exceptions in para 6.2 of the Codes applies and specified conditions are met.
Same matter or a particular aspect of it	The conflict of interest between clients must arise in relation to the same matter, or a particular aspect of it, eg if it concerns the same asset or liability. However, there would need to be some reasonable degree of relationship for a conflict to arise.
Former clients	Due to the definition of a conflict of interest, a conflict cannot arise with a former client. However, the solicitor may still be prevented from acting if they hold confidential information concerning the former client.
Exceptions	Where there is a conflict between two clients, a solicitor may act if they can satisfy the requirements of the substantially common interest exception or the competing for the same objective exception and the conditions set out in para 6.2 of the Codes of Conduct are met.

Topic	Summary
Systems and controls for identifying conflicts	Firms must have in place effective systems and controls in place to ensure that they and their employees comply with the SRA's regulatory arrangements which apply to them. This will include having in place controls to enable the firm to identify and assess potential conflicts of interests.

Chapter 14: Undertakings

Topic	Summary
Definition	An undertaking is a statement, given orally or in writing, whether or not it includes the word 'undertake' or 'undertaking', to someone who reasonably places reliance on it, that the solicitor, their firm or a third party will do something or cause something to be done, or refrain from doing something (SRA Glossary). Essentially an undertaking is an enforceable promise.
Effect and time for performance	An undertaking is personally binding on the giver of the undertaking. All undertakings must be performed within an agreed timescale or, if no timescale has been agreed, within a reasonable amount of time.
Ambiguity	Any ambiguity in the wording of the undertaking is likely to be construed against the party that gave the undertaking.
Undertakings 'on behalf of a client'	It is possible for a solicitor to give an undertaking on behalf of a client and exclude personal liability. However, the solicitor must clearly and expressly disclaim personal liability or make it clear that they are simply informing the other side of their client's intentions.
Change of circumstances	An undertaking will remain binding upon a solicitor even if the circumstances change so that it is impossible to fulfil the undertaking. Accordingly, in circumstances where an undertaking is given which is dependent upon the happening of a future event and it becomes apparent that the future event will not occur, the solicitor should notify the recipient of this.
Effective systems to record undertakings	Firms must have in place effective systems and controls in place to ensure that they and their employees comply with the SRA's regulatory arrangements which apply to them. This will include having an effective system for the recording of undertakings given and discharged.
Breach	Breach of an undertaking is prima facie professional misconduct. The SRA/Legal Ombudsman/Solicitors Disciplinary Tribunal do not have the power to enforce an undertaking. However, any breach may lead to sanctions against the solicitor concerned.

Topic	Summary
The courts	The court is able to enforce an undertaking against a solicitor as an officer of the court and likewise a law firm partnership (but not an incorporated practice). Accordingly, where an undertaking has been breached, the aggrieved party may sue the solicitor or firm for compensation for any loss.

Chapter 15: Money Laundering and the Proceeds of Crime Act 2002

Topic	Summary
Money laundering	'Money laundering' is the process by which criminals seek to alter or 'launder' their proceeds of crime so that it appears that these funds come from a legitimate source. Solicitors are often targets for criminals in their efforts to launder the proceeds of their crimes. The Government has introduced legislation to disrupt this process.
Money Laundering Regulations 2017	Solicitors who undertake 'relevant business' must comply with the Money Laundering, Terrorist Financing and Transfer of Funds (Information on the Payer) Regulations 2017 (SI 2017/692). 'Relevant business' includes the provision of legal services which involves participation in a 'financial or real property transaction', and so the vast majority of solicitors' firms will be subject to the Regulations.
Nominated officer	Under the 2017 Regulations, firms must appoint a nominated officer, who will receive internal reports concerning money laundering and must consider whether to report the matter to the National Crime Agency.
Arrangements	A person commits an offence under s 328 of the Proceeds of Crime Act 2002 where he becomes concerned with an arrangement involving money laundering. However, s 328 does not apply to steps taken in litigation. An individual convicted under s 328 may receive a maximum sentence of 14 years' imprisonment.
Acquisition, use or possession	A person commits an offence under s 329 of the Proceeds of Crime Act 2002 if he acquires, uses or has possession of criminal property. The adequate consideration defence may be available to a solicitor in relation to money received for or on account of costs from a client.
Failure to disclose	A solicitor within the regulated sector is obliged to disclose any suspected money laundering activity to their nominated officer (s 330). Failure to do so may result in a maximum sentence of five years' imprisonment.

Topic	Summary
Tipping off	It is an offence to disclose to any person that a disclosure has been made to a nominated officer or the National Crime Agency where this disclosure may prejudice an investigation (ss 333A–333D), or that an investigation into money laundering is being carried out or contemplated. An individual convicted under ss 333A–333D may receive a maximum penalty of two years' imprisonment.

Chapter 16: Duties Owed to the Court and Third Parties

Topic	Summary
Misleading or deceiving the court and contempt	A solicitor and firm are under a duty never to mislead the court or be complicit in the acts or omissions of others (including a client) to do so. A solicitor and firm must also comply with any orders of the court, and must not become in contempt of court.
Witnesses	A solicitor and firm must not provide (or offer to provide) any benefit to witnesses dependent upon the nature of the evidence given, or on the outcome of the case. They must also not seek to influence the substance of evidence, including generating false evidence or persuading witnesses to change their evidence.
Duty to the court	Where relevant, clients must be informed of the circumstances in which a solicitor's duties to the court outweigh their obligations to the client. A solicitor must comply with their duties to the court, including not wasting the court's time and only making assertions or putting forward statements, representations or submissions which are properly arguable.
Instructing counsel	A solicitor and firm must act in the best interests of their clients. Accordingly, if it is in the client's best interests to instruct counsel, the solicitor must ensure that adequate instructions are provided to the chosen barrister. Instructing counsel does not relieve the solicitor of their duties towards their client, particularly the duty to act in the client's best interests.
Duty to third parties	A solicitor and firm must not take an unfair advantage of clients or any other person. Particular care should be taken when dealing with unrepresented third parties.
Represented third parties	Subject to limited exceptions, a solicitor and firm should avoid communicating directly with third parties where it is known that the third party has instructed a legal representative.

Topic	Summary
Beneficiaries	In certain circumstances, a solicitor owes a duty of care to third parties, such as beneficiaries. If this duty is breached, the solicitor may be sued by the third party.
Dealings with other solicitors	A solicitor must act with integrity. Therefore a solicitor must treat other solicitors with due respect in all their communications.

Chapter 17: Financial Services

Topic	Summary
General prohibition	Section 19 of the Financial Services and Markets Act (FSMA) 2000 provides that 'no person may carry on a regulated activity in the UK unless authorised or exempt'.
Regulated activity	A person carries out a regulated activity when, while in business, he carries out a specified investment activity in relation to a specified investment or a specified activity related to information about a person's financial standing or administering a benchmark, and cannot take advantage of an exclusion.
Specified investment	Specified investments include company stocks and shares, debentures, unit trusts, insurance contracts and regulated mortgage contracts.
Specified investment activities	Specified investment activities include advising, arranging, dealing as agent, managing and safeguarding.
Exclusions	Numerous exclusions exist, such as the authorised third party exclusion. Each exclusion has different conditions and restrictions. If a solicitor can take advantage of an exclusion, they will not be carrying out a regulated activity.
Exempt regulated activities	As an alternative to using an exclusion, a firm may seek to use the s 327 exemption to avoid breaching the general prohibition. Once again, a number of conditions must be satisfied. These include that the activity the firm carries out must be incidental to the provision of legal services by the firm. The firm must also comply with the Scope and COB Rules.
Financial promotions	A solicitor who is not authorised by the Financial Conduct Authority is unable to make a financial promotion unless its contents are approved by an authorised or exempt person (FSMA 2000, s 21). Once again, this prohibition is subject to exclusions.

Chapter 18: Requirements of Practice

Topic	*Summary*
SRA Assessment of Character and Suitability Rules	Those intending to become solicitors, those seeking registration as an REL or RFL, authorised role holders and former solicitors seeking restoration to the roll of solicitors must satisfy the SRA Assessment of Character and Suitability Rules. Certain behaviour can result in an application being refused by the SRA.
Requirement to hold a practising certificate	No person may act as a solicitor unless they have been admitted as a solicitor, their name is on the roll of solicitors, and they hold a current practising certificate.
Practising certificates	Practising certificates are issued annually by the SRA, which has a certain level of discretion as to whether to issue a certificate to a particular person. In certain circumstances the SRA may decline to issue a certificate or may impose conditions on the certificate.
Additional practising requirements	Solicitors who wish to exercise higher rights of audience in the civil or criminal courts must have completed the appropriate additional qualification.
Accountants' reports	All solicitors who hold a practising certificate and also hold client monies must obtain an independent accountant's report each year. The purpose of the report is to certify compliance with the SRA Accounts Rules. One report may be obtained for a firm as a whole.
Indemnity insurance	The Solicitors Indemnity Insurance Rules require solicitors to take out compulsory insurance cover against the risks of professional negligence or other civil liability claims. Firms can insure with any approved commercial insurer. Recognised and licensed bodies must obtain cover to a minimum of £3 million per individual claim (a minimum of £2 million in all other cases). Voluntary top-up cover may be required.
Responsibility of managers	Managers must ensure that their firm complies with the requirements of professional conduct. In certain cases, managers will be held liable for any breach.
Supervision	At least one manager or employee of an SRA authorised body must be a lawyer of England and Wales, who has practised for a minimum of three years and who supervises the work of that body.
Duty to the SRA and other regulators	A solicitor is under a duty to cooperate with the SRA and other legal service regulators and ombudsmen.
Reporting serious regulatory breaches	A solicitor and firm are obliged to report promptly to the SRA any serious breach of its regulatory arrangements by any person regulated by the SRA of which they are or it is aware.

PART III

EU LAW

CHAPTER 19

Sources of EU Law

LEARNING OUTCOMES

After reading this chapter you will be able to understand:

- what types of EU legislation there are
- the various treaties which have developed EU law
- the status of the decisions of the Court of Justice
- the key elements of the latest EU Treaty.

19.1 INTRODUCTION

The UK has now left the EU, as of 31 January 2020, with transitional arrangements ending at the end of 2020. This means that EU Treaties, EU free movement rights and the general principles of EU law now no longer apply in the UK.

EU law will in any event continue to be important for many UK lawyers, as their clients will often be multinational and/or operate within Europe. Even if advising clients which operate solely within the UK, lawyers will often deal with UK laws which have been influenced by EU principles in their drafting. It is important therefore that you gain a sound understanding of principles of EU law despite the UK's departure from the EU.

As the UK has now left the EU, references to the UK in **Chapters 19–26** are historical, based primarily on their involvement in EU case law. The legal principles from these cases remain valid in the EU, but are not valid in UK courts save to the extent that they are reflected in UK law.

19.2 BACKGROUND

The Treaty on European Union (the 'Maastricht Treaty') took Europe into a new stage of development, with more ambitious objectives, in order, in the words of the preamble to the Treaty, 'to continue the process of creating an ever closer union among the peoples of Europe'. This drive towards a closer union continued with the Treaty of Amsterdam, the Treaty of Nice and the Treaty of Lisbon, all of which made amendments to (rather than replaced) the original EC Treaty (the Treaty of Rome 1957) and the Treaty on European Union. The Treaty on European Union retains its original name, but the EC Treaty, post-Lisbon, is now called the

Treaty on the Functioning of the European Union (TFEU). It should be noted that Articles of the EC Treaty which survived Lisbon are numbered differently in the TFEU – see **19.10**.

Post-Lisbon, the European Court of Justice was renamed the Court of Justice, and the court below it (the Court of First Instance) was renamed the General Court. Perhaps confusingly, the two courts together form an institution called the Court of Justice of the European Union (CJEU). Most decisions that you will look at as a lawyer will be of the (higher) Court of Justice, although commentators are likely to continue calling it the European Court of Justice (or ECJ) for some time.

The sources of EU law are:

(a) the Treaties;
(b) Regulations;
(c) Directives;
(d) the jurisprudence of the CJEU (and its predecessors).

Regulations and Directives are secondary legislation made under Article 288 TFEU. How these sources of law become part of English law will be discussed in **Chapter 21**.

Article 288 TFEU also provides for the making of Decisions, Recommendations and Opinions. Of these, only Decisions are legally binding, and they bind only the person (Member State, company or individual) to whom they are addressed.

The Court of Justice has been highly influential in developing both substantive areas of EU law (eg, the free movement of goods) and general principles of EU law, such as proportionality.

19.3 THE TREATIES

19.3.1 The Treaty of Rome 1957

The primary aim of the Treaty of Rome ('the EEC Treaty') was to create a European Economic Community, a common market, for the original six signatories: France, West Germany, Italy, The Netherlands, Belgium and Luxembourg. This common market required not only the abolition of customs duties and quotas for goods passing between the six, but also a recognition on the part of the Member States that their populations had a right to share directly in the benefits of the new system. In particular, the Member States had to recognise the right of workers to move freely throughout the Community, and the right of individuals and companies to set up in business or to provide services throughout the Community.

From its very beginning, it was apparent that the Community was more than a mere free trade zone. One of the stated objectives in the preamble to the Treaty was 'to lay the foundations of an ever closer union among the peoples of Europe'. It is also central to an understanding of the Treaty to remember that it created supra-national institutions, not least the Court of Justice (see **Chapter 20**). The result was, in the words of the Court itself in *Van Gend en Loos v Nederlandse Belastingadministratie* [1963] ECR 1, a 'new legal order of international law for the benefit of which the States have limited their sovereign rights, albeit within limited fields, and the subjects of which comprise not only Member States but also their nationals' (see **Chapter 21**).

The most important provisions, as far as the achievement of a common market is concerned, are those dealing with free movement, in particular of goods, persons and services, and competition law. These will be considered at **Chapters 23–26**.

19.3.2 The Merger Treaty 1965

Since the Treaty of Paris 1951, there had existed a European Coal and Steel Community (ECSC), created by the original six signatories of the Treaty of Rome. That Treaty had also established supra-national institutions, including a High Authority, the equivalent of the EC Commission.

In 1957, at the same time as the European Economic Community was established, the same signatories created the European Atomic Energy Community (EurAtom). The European Economic Community and EurAtom shared with the ECSC only the Court and the Assembly set up under the Treaty of Paris. In 1965, the institutions of the three Communities were merged. The Merger Treaty is therefore concerned with their integration within a single organisational structure.

19.3.3 The Accession Treaties

In 1973, the UK, the Republic of Ireland and Denmark joined the Community, followed in 1981 by Greece and in 1986 by Spain and Portugal. Sweden, Finland and Austria joined on 1 January 1995. The European Union welcomed 10 new countries in 2004: Cyprus, the Czech Republic, Estonia, Hungary, Latvia, Lithuania, Malta, Poland, Slovakia and Slovenia. Bulgaria and Romania joined on 1 January 2007, and Croatia joined on 1 July 2013. The UK left on 31 January 2020, bringing the total number of Member States to 27. Current candidate countries at the time of writing are: Albania, Iceland, Montenegro, Serbia, the former Yugoslav Republic of Macedonia and Turkey; and potential candidates are Bosnia and Herzegovina, and Kosovo. No date has yet been set for their accession.

19.3.4 The Single European Act 1986

The Single European Act 1986 saw further significant developments in the Community. It formalised as an objective the completion of the single European market envisaged in the EC Treaty, and set a date for its achievement: 31 December 1992. This required enormous legislative activity by the Community in an attempt to overcome remaining barriers to trade, not least the problem of varying trading standards. In order to make this a manageable task, the Single European Act introduced a streamlined legislative process. When single market measures came to the Council for approval, unanimity was not to be required. Instead, only a qualified majority would be needed (see **Chapter 20**). The Single European Act also extended the areas which would be expressly within the Community's competence, including areas such as the environment and the health and safety of workers.

19.3.5 The European Economic Area Treaty 1992

The effect of the European Economic Area Treaty was to create a 'European Economic Area' (EEA) consisting of the Member States of the EC and the European Free Trade Agreement (EFTA) countries (Sweden, Norway, Finland, Austria and Iceland, but not Switzerland which decided in referendum not to ratify the Treaty). Within this area, EC law relating to free movement and to competition law applies, together with all the related Regulations and Directives. The EEA came into effect on 1 January 1994. However, on 1 January 1995, Sweden, Finland and Austria all joined the European Union, leaving just Norway, Iceland and Liechtenstein as members of the EEA but not of the EU. Switzerland remains in EFTA.

19.3.6 The Treaty on European Union 1992 ('the Maastricht Treaty')

The Treaty on European Union (TEU), signed at Maastricht, came into force on 1 November 1993. It officially renamed the 'EEC' the 'EC' and founded, on the base of the European Community, a European Union. It also renamed the Treaty of Rome the EC Treaty. It made a number of important amendments to the Treaty, in particular:

(a) the EC undertook to act in any given area only if Community action was a better means of achieving the desired end than action by the individual Member States (the principle of subsidiarity);

(b) every EC national became a citizen of the European Union;

(c) the EC specifically assumed responsibility for developing policies in areas such as public health, consumer protection and education. These had previously been dealt with primarily as issues affecting free movement;

(d) the European Parliament was given greater powers (co-decision));

(e) the Council was to take decisions on a qualified majority basis on a wider range of matters, such as consumer protection, using the co-decision procedure.

The Maastricht Treaty did not just amend the Treaty of Rome. It also set out Union objectives, the most important being the promotion of economic and social progress to be achieved by economic and monetary union. The Union also agreed to develop a common foreign and security policy, and to cooperate in the fields of justice and home affairs. Importantly, the Union also undertook expressly to respect fundamental rights, as guaranteed by the European Convention for the Protection of Human Rights and Fundamental Freedoms 1950. Previous European Court case law had already shown, however, that Member States must respect human rights law when acting on a Community matter.

19.3.7 The Amsterdam Treaty

The Amsterdam Treaty entered into force at the beginning of May 1999. The Treaty paved the way for EU enlargement. It also provided for greater cooperation in employment matters and for incentive measures to help boost employment. It incorporated into the EC the TEU Social Chapter, which means that all Member States are bound by its provisions. The Treaty also established a new section on freedom, security and justice, which brings some areas into the framework of the EC Treaty from the 'third pillar' (Justice and Home Affairs) of the Maastricht Treaty. It also strengthened provisions relating to environmental protection. There was a strengthening of public health and consumer protection, and the principle of subsidiarity was clarified. Lastly, there was an increase in the number of matters to be decided under qualified majority rules and a substantial increase in the use of the co-decision procedure (see **20.4.2**). In the TEU, there is a revised section on common foreign and security policy.

19.3.8 The Treaty of Nice

The Treaty of Nice came into force on 1 February 2003 and made changes to the Institutions of the Community with a view to accommodating enlargement. In particular it reduced the number of decisions where a power of veto may be used in the Council. This was felt necessary due to its being less likely that unanimous agreement might be reached with an increased number of countries. In addition, a change was made in the weighting of the votes which each country has in Council meetings. The Treaty also made numerical changes to the Parliament and the Commission, with each Member State having only one Commissioner each.

19.3.9 The Treaty of Lisbon

The Treaty of Lisbon brought to an end several years of negotiation about institutional issues. Its main highlights include:

(a) the European Council (a body composed of the leaders of the Member States) became a formal EU institution, with an independent President;

(b) the European Parliament became an equal co-legislator with the Council of Ministers in the vast majority of cases;

(c) national vetoes were removed in a number of areas, including fighting climate change, energy security and emergency aid;

(d) EU competencies widened to cover areas which were previously the realm of Member States, eg international trade, energy policies, judicial and police cooperation;

(e) the European Union became a single organisation; there is no longer a European Community. This means that it is no longer correct to speak of EC law; rather, it should be referred to as EU law;

(f) qualified majority voting was adjusted to be based on a 'double majority' of 55% of Member States' votes, accounting for 65% of the EU's population.

19.4 REGULATIONS

Article 288 TFEU envisages that secondary legislation is needed to put its broad objectives into effect. It provides that the Council and the Commission 'shall, in accordance with the provisions of this Treaty make Regulations ... '. It goes on to state that a Regulation shall have general application (ie, it will apply throughout the EU in exactly the terms in which it is made). Further, Article 288 TFEU states that a Regulation shall be directly applicable in all Member States, ie no Member State need pass any implementing measure to make the contents of the Regulation form part of its own national law, except in the unusual situation when the Regulation itself expressly requires the Member State to do so. In fact, according to the European Court in *Variola sPA v Amministrazione Italiana della Finanze* [1973] ECR 981, it would ordinarily be wrong for a Member State to disguise the EU origin of the measure by introducing national legislation to enact it.

Many important EU legal measures have taken the form of Regulations, for example, Regulation 1612/68, which sought to make a reality of the free movement of workers provisions in the Treaty, and the Merger Regulation, Regulation 4064/89, under which big multi-national mergers are vetted by the Commission for their effect on competition.

Upon Brexit occurring (at the end of 2020), the UK preserved most EU Regulations in the UK via s 3 of the European Union (Withdrawal) Act 2018 (as amended in the run up to the departure date). This was done to prevent the wholesale loss of rights and obligations which would have left a large hole in UK laws at the beginning of 2021. They were renamed as Direct EU legislation and they remained supreme over conflicting pre-Brexit UK legislation. Following the passing of the Retained EU Law (Revocation and Reform) Act 2023, however, they were renamed Direct Assimilated legislation and the priorities were reversed. So although most EU Regulations remain in the UK legal system as this new category of law, they are subordinate to any pre-existing or new UK laws.

19.5 DIRECTIVES

Article 288 TFEU also gives the Council and the Commission power to issue Directives. It is clear from that Article, however, that their legal effect is quite different from that of Regulations. A Directive is stated to be 'binding, as to the result to be achieved, upon each Member State to which it is addressed, but shall leave to the national authorities the choice of form and methods'. Unlike Regulations, Directives therefore do need a response from each Member State. Unless the national law of the Member State already achieves the objective of the Directive, the Member State must implement it within the specified time-limit. The form of implementing measure may vary from State to State, as may the precise words used to give effect to the Directive. This means that, unlike Regulations, Directives are not of general application throughout the EU in the terms in which they are drafted.

Directives have been issued across a wide range of areas, for example, Directive 2006/54, known as the Equal Treatment Directive, the several Company Law Directives, the Environmental Protection Directive (85/337) and the Product Liability Directive (85/374). In order to bring the Single Market into being, the Commission drafted over 200 separate Directives.

As with Regulations, the UK could not realistically leave the EU upon Brexit without at least initially preserving rights and obligations contained in implemented Directives. Since 1972 (the date the UK joined the EU) it had created UK legislation covering the content of EU Directives, and it was important that these were not removed in entirety by the European Union (Withdrawal) Act 2018 until a thorough review of them could be carried out. The Act therefore preserved them as EU-derived domestic legislation. Subsequently the Retained EU Law (Revocation and Reform) Act 2023 has removed around 600, and has removed the supremacy of the rest. They therefore have no special status above any other UK law and can be repealed or amended as Parliament wishes.

19.6 THE JURISPRUDENCE OF THE COURT OF JUSTICE

The fundamental principles of EU law found in the TFEU and earlier versions of it are set out in outline only, so the Court has inevitably played a leading role in developing EU law. The Court has not been reluctant to assume this role and has made a major contribution to the evolution of the EU. By interpreting the Treaty and secondary legislation according to the overall purposes of the EU, the Court has often pushed governments further than they might have initially intended to go.

Judgments of the Court are now vital to an understanding of the freedoms upon which the EU is based and to the principles of competition law (another major field of EU activity). In addition, the Court has developed certain general principles of EU law, of which the most important are proportionality (see **Chapter 25**), legal certainty and respect for fundamental rights (see **Chapter 27**). As far as the last of these is concerned, the Court's approach can be seen in *Nold (J) KG v EC Commission* [1974] ECR 491, where it stated that fundamental rights, derived from the constitutional traditions common to the Member States and from the international treaties to which they are signatories (in particular, the European Convention on Human Rights), form an integral part of the general principles of EU law.

In applying 'legal certainty' the Court has sometimes ruled that its more surprising interpretations of the Treaty should be non-retrospective, for example in *Defrenne (Gabrielle) v SABENA* [1976] ECR 455 and *Barber v Guardian Royal Exchange Assurance Group* [1991] 1 QB 344 (see **21.3.1**) where direct claims for equal pay and equal pensions were allowed under what is now Article 157 TFEU. To have held otherwise would have had serious financial consequences in the Member States. Ordinarily, Court judgments are retrospective, ie they go back to the date of the original legislation that the Court is interpreting.

Following Brexit, the ECJ no longer has jurisdiction over the UK. This does not mean that it does not continue to have influence, however, at least in terms of its previous decisions. First, it should be noted that no court in the UK will be bound by future ECJ decisions. Secondly, previous decisions of the ECJ remain good case law in the UK unless and until their principles are affected by a later judgment of a UK appellate court, such as the Court of Appeal or Supreme Court. As with Regulations and Directives, therefore, we may see a slow departure from the existing jurisprudence of the ECJ.

19.7 OTHER EU MEASURES

Apart from the measures already indicated, there exist two other EU measures which have only limited legal effect under Article 288 TFEU.

Decisions are binding only on the parties to whom the Decisions are addressed (Article 288 TFEU). The best examples are Commission Decisions under the competition rules in Articles 101 and 102 TFEU. Their Decisions that an agreement or conduct infringes Article 101 or 102 TFEU, that an exemption should be given under Article 101(3) TFEU, or that fines be imposed are all subject to review by the General Court. Subject to this, they bind the parties and must be given effect by national courts. Thus, a Decision that an agreement is exempt will (subject to review) validate the agreement before a national court.

The least effective measure of all is a Council Recommendation. This is certainly not legally binding and cannot create any Community rights, but is still worth referring to as 'persuasive opinion' on a particular issue. A good example is the Code of Practice on Sexual Harassment set out at [1992] OJ L49/1. This can be referred to for guidance to determine whether employers who have allowed such conduct are guilty of sex discrimination under the Sex Discrimination Act 1975 (see *Wadman v Carpenter Farrer Partnership* [1993] 3 CMLR 93 (EAT)).

19.8 CONCLUSION

If a client has a problem which has an EU dimension, this could be because it clearly raises questions of substantive EU law, perhaps in relation to one of the freedoms such as free movement of goods or workers. In this case, a solicitor must, of course, pay careful attention to the TFEU itself. It will often be necessary to look at the secondary legislation which supplements that particular area of the Treaty, as well as at decided cases on the subject.

On the other hand, a client's problem may have an EU aspect because of the ever-increasing pervasiveness of EU law: for example, a business client may be concerned about the significance of the recent Directives on workplace safety. In this case, a detailed consideration of the relevant legislation will be vital, including an appreciation of how it can interact with relevant domestic law (see further **Chapter 21**).

For information as to how to research a problem of EU law and how to use the possible sources, see Chapter 7 of ***Skills for Lawyers***.

19.9 OVERVIEW OF THE TREATY ON THE FUNCTIONING OF THE EUROPEAN UNION

(1) To create the internal market, the TFEU guarantees four freedoms:
   (a) free movement of goods (Articles 34–36 TFEU);
   (b) free movement of services (Article 56 TFEU);
   (c) free movement of persons, ie workers (Article 45 TFEU) and firms (Article 49 TFEU right of establishment);
   (d) free movement of capital (Articles 63–66 TFEU).

(2) To create the customs union, it imposes a common external tariff and prohibits internal custom duties (Article 30 TFEU).

(3) To prevent distortion in the market, it:
   (a) prohibits anti-competitive practices by undertakings (Articles 101, 102 TFEU);
   (b) prohibits discrimination against EU nationals, both generally (Article 18 TFEU) and under particular Articles (eg, on free movement), or through indirect taxes (Article 110 TFEU);
   (c) guarantees equal pay between men and women (Article 157 TFEU).

19.10 CONVERSION TABLE – NOTABLE ARTICLE NUMBERS

Pre-Amsterdam	Post-Amsterdam	Post-Lisbon
Article 5 (State obligations)	Article 10	Article 4(3) TEU
Article 30 (goods)	Article 28	Article 34 TFEU
Article 36 (goods – excl)	Article 30	Article 36 TFEU
Article 48 (workers)	Article 39	Article 45 TFEU
Article 52 (establishment)	Article 43	Article 49 TFEU
Article 59 (services)	Article 49	Article 56 TFEU
Article 85 (competition)	Article 81	Article 101 TFEU
Article 86 (competition)	Article 82	Article 102 TFEU
Article 119 (sex discrimination)	Article 141	Article 157 TFEU
Article 177 (references)	Article 234	Article 267 TFEU

CHAPTER 20

THE INSTITUTIONS

LEARNING OUTCOMES

After reading this chapter you will be able to understand:

- the identity of the various institutions which make up the EU
- their composition
- their roles
- how they work together to create EU legislation.

20.1 INTRODUCTION

The Treaty of Rome established the following institutions of the Community (now 'Union'):

(a) the Council;

(b) the Commission;

(c) the Parliament;

(d) the Court.

The Single European Act created the Court of First Instance. This was renamed 'the General Court' by the Treaty of Lisbon. The Treaty on European Union made the already existing Court of Auditors into a fifth institution. Although they do not have the status of institutions, mention will be made below of the Committee of Permanent Representatives (COREPER), the Economic and Social Council and the Committee of the Regions (see **20.9–20.11**). There will also be a brief explanation of how EU law is made.

The Treaty of Lisbon made the European Council a formal institution for the first time.

20.2 THE COUNCIL

20.2.1 What is its membership?

The Council consists of one government representative from each Member State. The representative need not be the same person at every Council meeting: it depends on the matters on the agenda at that particular meeting. If, for example, the Council were discussing the environment, the representatives would be the ministers responsible for the environment. The Heads of State meet as a separate body – the European Council.

Each Member State takes it in turn to be the President of the Council; the Presidency rotates every six months.

20.2.2 What is its role?

The Treaty of Rome gave the Council responsibility for ensuring that the Treaty's objectives were attained. The Council ensures the coordination of policies and, above all, takes decisions within the Union. This means that it is the Council, acting with the Parliament, rather than the Commission which is responsible for the final decision as to whether a Regulation should be made or a Directive should be issued, although the Commission does have some decision-making powers (see **20.4**).

20.2.3 How does it take decisions?

After the Treaty of Lisbon, almost all policy areas are decided by qualified majority vote. A qualified majority is obtained when at least 55% of Member States, comprising at least 65% of EU citizens, vote in favour of a proposal. This does not apply, however, when the Council votes on a matter not proposed by the Commission, where 72% of Member States must vote in favour (while the population requirement remains the same).

Clearly, the population threshold has an element of weighted voting in it, with the larger nations being able to contribute bigger populations to the calculation. For example, Germany has 16.5% of the EU's population within her borders (a pre-Brexit figure), giving Germany a greater say under this new system.

20.3 THE EUROPEAN COUNCIL

20.3.1 What is its membership?

The European Council consists of the Heads of State or Government of the Member States, together with its President and the President of the Commission.

20.3.2 What is its role?

The European Council defines the general political direction and priorities of the European Union. However, it does not exercise legislative functions. It meets twice every six months and, except where the Treaties provide otherwise, its decisions are by consensus. In some cases, however, the Treaties provide for the European Council to adopt decisions by unanimity or by qualified majority.

Article 15 TEU requires the President of the European Council to:

(a) chair it and drive forward its work;
(b) ensure the preparation and continuity of its work;
(c) endeavour to facilitate cohesion and consensus within it; and
(d) present a report to the European Parliament after every European Council meeting.

20.4 THE EUROPEAN COMMISSION

20.4.1 What is its membership?

There are 27 EU Commissioners, one from each Member State, each of whom is responsible for a particular area of Union competence. The Commission is divided into 23 Directorates-General which are responsible for such matters as the environment (Directorate-General XI) and competition law (Directorate-General IV). The Commissioners are appointed by the Council (ie effectively by the Member States), but once appointed they must be independent of national loyalties. They cannot be recalled by their appointing State. They hold office for a fixed term of five years, although this is subject to renewal. Each Commissioner's appointment must be approved by all Member States and, since Amsterdam, by the President and by the European Parliament. The President of the Commission is appointed by the Council and the European Parliament. The appointment is for a fixed term of two years, although this also is renewable. The Commission is based in Brussels.

20.4.2 What is its role?

The Treaty of Rome required the Commission to pursue infringements of EU law. It can, for example, take action before the European Court against Member States who breach EU law. It is also responsible for enforcing EU competition policy and has the power to exact fines for any breach. Above all, however, the Commission is responsible for initiating EU policy and legislation. It has some delegated powers of law making, particularly in the field of competition law, where (under the authority of an enabling Council Regulation 19/65) it has issued Block Exemption Regulations (see **Chapter 26**).

20.4.3 How does it reach its decisions?

Within the Commission, decisions are taken on a simple majority basis.

20.5 THE PARLIAMENT

20.5.1 What is its membership?

There are 678 members of the European Parliament (MEPs) (677 plus a President) post-Brexit. All MEPs are directly elected, although the voting systems throughout the Union are not uniform. The number of MEPs which each State has is set by the Council and the Parliament itself. A draft decision fixing the numbers was annexed to the TFEU. Numbers per State are roughly in line with the size of the State, eg Germany was allocated 96 seats, France 74 and so on, down to Malta with 6 seats.

The MEPs sit in the Parliament according to their political sympathies (political groups) rather than according to national origin. MEPs are elected for a five-year term. The Parliament holds plenary sessions in Strasbourg for one week per month. Much of its work is, however, done in committees (and plenary sessions) in Brussels. It is organised by an Executive (including a President, ie Speaker) based in Luxembourg.

20.5.2 What is its role?

The Parliament's role was traditionally a consultative one. In a number of areas, the Treaty of Rome provided that once the Commission had initiated a proposal for legislation and the Council had given its preliminary approval to it, the Parliament had to be given an opportunity to comment. It had to respond to the proposal within a reasonable time and the Council had to take its responses into account, although it was not bound by them.

The Single European Act developed the role of the Parliament by introducing a co-operation procedure in certain areas, for example single market legislation. This meant that if the Council did not wish to accept the Parliament's comments, the Parliament had to be given a second opportunity to respond. If it continued to object to the Council's version of the measure, the Council could adopt it in its original form only if it did so unanimously within three months. The Single European Act also increased the number of matters on which the Parliament had to be consulted so as to include most matters relating to the single market.

The Treaty on European Union further increased the role of the Parliament. In certain limited areas it introduced a 'co-decision' procedure which involved the Parliament further in the legislative process. If the Parliament proposed amendments to draft legislation and these amendments were not accepted by the Council, the Parliament could veto the legislation. This procedure applied to measures intended to develop the single market.

The Amsterdam and Nice Treaties greatly extended the areas in which the co-decision procedure was used. They also streamlined this procedure.

The Treaty of Lisbon made further changes, so that virtually all decisions are now made under the co-decision procedure. It also renamed this procedure the 'ordinary legislative procedure'.

Consequently, the Parliament's role has increased greatly over the years, from a simple consultative role to being a major part of the decision-making process. Today, almost all Regulations and Directive require Parliament's approval or they do not become law.

The Parliament has the right to ask questions of the Commission and, in the last resort, it has the power to remove the whole Commission, though not individual Commissioners. (This almost happened at the beginning of 1999. The Commission actually resigned around four weeks after the threat of censure.) The Council, too, must report to the Parliament.

20.6 THE COURT OF JUSTICE

20.6.1 What is its membership?

There are currently 27 judges of the Court of Justice (one from each Member State), each of whom must be eligible for appointment to the highest judicial office in the country from which they come. Each judge is appointed for six years at a time. Their appointments are staggered, so they do not all retire at once. There is no retirement age for a judge, nor can one be recalled by the Member State which made the appointment. A judge can be removed only by the unanimous resolution of the other judges and Advocates-General. The judges elect one of their number to be President of the Court for a three-year term.

In addition to the judges, there are also nine Advocates-General. Their task is to assist the judges in reaching their decisions. One Advocate-General will be assigned to each case, and will hear the evidence and read the papers available to the Court. They will then prepare a reasoned opinion indicating the conclusion to which they would come in that case. The Court is not bound to follow that opinion. When the case is reported, the Advocate-General's opinion is reported, together with the decision of the Court. The Court sits in Luxembourg.

20.6.2 What is its role?

The Treaty of Rome required the Court to ensure that EC law (now EU law) is observed throughout the EU. The three usual ways in which a case may come before it are:

(a) as a result of a reference by a national court under the Article 267 TFEU preliminary rulings procedure (see **21.7**);

(b) as a result of an action brought by the Commission against a Member State pursuant to its powers under Article 258 TFEU;

(c) as a result of an action brought by one Member State against another under Article 259 TFEU.

If a Member State fails to comply with a judgment of the Court of Justice, the Treaty on European Union allows the Court to impose a fine on that Member State.

20.6.3 How are such cases heard?

The Court of Justice usually sits in chambers and consists of three, five or seven judges. In particularly important cases, 13 judges will hear the case. In very rare situations, they can sit as a full court. The procedure is largely by means of written submissions, following a typical civil law (as distinct from common law) pattern. There is very limited scope for oral argument. Barristers and solicitors have a right of audience before the Court, although if a solicitor wishes to appear in the Court following an Article 267 TFEU reference (see **21.7**) they may do so only if they had a right of audience before the court or tribunal which made the reference.

The working language of the court during deliberations is French, although, at hearings, the parties present their arguments in their own language (with simultaneous translation). Each case will have its own official language. One judge (*le juge rapporteur*) puts together a draft judgment synthesising judicial opinions on which the judges then vote.

When the Court has reached a decision, it delivers a single, succinct judgment. No dissenting judgments are delivered.

20.6.4 The nature of EU legal reasoning

The Treaty of Rome was drafted by States which shared a civil law heritage. The original judges of the Court of Justice had been trained in civil law systems which, although they might diverge significantly in their substantive provisions, shared a similar approach to legal reasoning. In particular, such judges were familiar with legislation which provided a framework of principles and which was not intended to be interpreted in an exclusively literal way. They were therefore accustomed to drawing inspiration from the spirit behind legislation. This approach was particularly necessary when interpreting the Treaty of Rome, which is very much a framework treaty. In addition, the early judges of the Court were conscious of the role entrusted to them by the Treaty and the accompanying responsibility to ensure that EC law (now EU law) was a uniform body of legal principles which took effect in the same way throughout the entire Community.

Thus, from a very early stage, it is possible to recognise the purposive (or 'teleological') approach adopted by the Court of Justice. This entailed the Court interpreting the Treaty of Rome, and later subordinate legislation, in accordance with the ethos of the Treaty of Rome. In doing so it had to bear in mind the fundamental freedoms upon which the Community was expressly stated to be based and, in particular, Article 12 EC (now Article 18 TFEU), which prohibits discrimination on the grounds of nationality.

20.6.5 Precedent

In accordance with the civil law tradition, there is no use of precedent as such in the Court of Justice. However, although the Court is not bound by its own previous decisions, it has tended to develop a body of consistent case law. The Court may cite earlier cases in its judgment, and the Advocate-General is likely to discuss earlier decisions in their opinion.

Decisions of the Court are reported in an official set of reports, the *European Court Reports* (ECR). There is also a commercial series of reports called the *Common Market Law Reports* (CMLR).

20.7 THE GENERAL COURT

The Court of First Instance (CFI) was established by the Single European Act because of the heavy work-load faced by the Court of Justice. Many of the cases before the Court of Justice concerned disputes between Community institutions and their employees. These staff cases were assigned to the CFI, as were competition law cases (ie, appeals from Commission decisions banning agreements, imposing fines, etc). As a result of provisions in the Treaty on European Union, the Council transferred to the CFI all of the Court of Justice's jurisdiction apart from most preliminary references and cases involving infringement proceedings against Member States. Appeals on points of law lay to the Court of Justice itself. The Treaty of Nice contained provisions for the CFI to share more of the Court of Justice's workload.

The Treaty of Lisbon renamed the CFI 'the General Court', but otherwise made few changes to its role and the way it operates.

20.8 THE COURT OF AUDITORS

The Court of Auditors is responsible for auditing the accounts of the EU and its institutions. It has 27 members appointed by the Council.

20.9 THE COMMITTEE OF PERMANENT REPRESENTATIVES (COREPER)

The Committee of Permanent Representatives (COREPER) was created by the Merger Treaty. It comprises ambassadors of the Member States. They undertake much of the detailed analysis of Commission proposals on behalf of the Council. If COREPER can agree a response to such a proposal, that response will be automatically approved by the Council. Only if there is disagreement at COREPER level will a matter be actively discussed in the Council.

20.10 THE ECONOMIC AND SOCIAL COMMITTEE (ESC)

The Economic and Social Committee (ESC) is a body which comprises representatives of different sectional interests throughout the EU. There are 353 representatives, for example, of business, of the trade unions and of consumers. The ESC's role is purely consultative.

20.11 THE COMMITTEE OF THE REGIONS

The role of this Committee is purely advisory. It consists of 353 members appointed by the Council.

SUMMARY

The four main institutions have the following primary responsibilities:

(1) the Commission develops policy and proposes legislation;

(2) the Council and the Parliament are the decision-making bodies;

(3) the Court ensures that the law which emerges from these three institutions is interpreted correctly and consistently.

CHAPTER 21

The Relationship Between EU Law and National Law

LEARNING OUTCOMES

After reading this chapter you will be able to understand:

- what it means to be an EU citizen
- how EU laws can be applied directly in court
- how national courts can take EU law into account in making decisions
- which law has priority where there is a conflict between EU law and national law
- how courts resolve doubts about the meaning of EU law.

21.1 INTRODUCTION

The primary source of EU law is the Treaty on the Functioning of the European Union (TFEU). Each Member State has incorporated it in its national constitution in whichever way is necessary for it to have legal effect. The Court of Justice has developed two key concepts to allow it to be enforced:

(a) that EU law can, in certain circumstances, be relied on directly in national proceedings; and

(b) that, when it is utilised, it takes priority over any conflicting national law.

Taken together, these two concepts can give a client a right of action and a remedy which otherwise might not be available under national law.

21.2 EU LAW AND THE EU CITIZEN

European Union law may have two possible effects on the citizen. First, it may have 'direct effect' (see **21.3**), ie it can create rights which may be relied on in national courts directly against the State or another legal person. Secondly, EU law (in particular, Directives) may have 'indirect effect' (see **21.5**) in that courts should comply with EU law when interpreting national legislation.

21.3 THE CONCEPT OF DIRECT EFFECT

In *Van Gend en Loos v Nederlandse Belastingadministratie* [1963] ECR 1 (see **22.2.1**), the Court of Justice recognised the existence of the Community as a 'new legal order'. In that case, an importer of goods from Germany into The Netherlands argued that Article 12 of the EC Treaty (now Article 30 TFEU), which prohibited any increase in customs tariffs for goods passing from one Member State to another, meant that a reclassification of his products into a higher tariff was unlawful. Consequently, he sought to rely on Article 12 of the EC Treaty to claim back from the Dutch customs authorities, which had extracted the increased tariff, the money he had paid. The question for the Court was whether the Treaty could be used in that way by an individual citizen rather than a Member State or the Commission. The Court of Justice held that it could if the provision in question met certain conditions: it would have to be clear, precise and unconditional; and it would have to leave the Member State with no discretion as to how it should be implemented. In other words, if the provision in question is sufficiently clear, precise and unconditional to create an 'enforceable right' for the client, as did Article 12 of the EC Treaty, that right can be enforced through the national courts in preference to national law. In *Van Gend en Loos* itself, the Court found that an individual could rely on Article 12 of the EC Treaty directly to recover the extra tax from the government.

21.3.1 Direct effect and the provisions of the Treaty

It has now been established that, applying the criteria set out in *Van Gend en Loos*, all the fundamental Treaty provisions have direct effect, in particular:

(a) Article 34 TFEU (ex Article 30 EC) on free movement of goods (*Ianelli and Volpi sPA v Meroni* [1977] ECR 557);

(b) Article 45 TFEU (ex Article 48 EC) on free movement of workers (*Van Duyn v Home Office* [1974] ECR 1337);

(c) Article 49 TFEU (ex Article 52 EC) on freedom of establishment (*Reyners v The Belgian State* [1974] ECR 631);

(d) Article 56 TFEU (ex Article 59 EC) on freedom to provide services (*Van Binsbergen (JHM) v Bestuur van de Bedrijfsvereniging voor de Metaalnijverheid* [1974] ECR 1299);

(e) Article 101 TFEU (ex Article 85 EC) on anti-competitive agreements (*Belgische Radio en Televisie v SV SABAM* [1974] ECR 313);

(f) Article 102 TFEU (ex Article 86 EC) on abuse of a dominant position (*Garden Cottage Foods v Milk Marketing Board* [1984] AC 130); and

(g) Article 157 TFEU (ex Article 119 EC) on equal pay (*Defrenne (Gabrielle) v SABENA* [1976] ECR 455).

In addition, Article 18 TFEU (ex Article 6 EC) (discrimination), Articles 63–66 TFEU (ex Articles 73b–73g EC) (capital), Article 107 TFEU (ex Article 92 EC) (State aids) and Article 111 TFEU (ex Article 95 EC) (discriminatory indirect taxes on goods) are considered to have direct effect.

21.3.2 Direct effect and Regulations

Regulations are said by Article 288 TFEU to be 'directly applicable', ie they are part of national law and do not need implementing legislation. They are binding in the form in which they are made. However, they still have to be sufficiently 'clear, precise and unconditional' to create directly effective rights.

21.3.3 Direct effect and Directives

Directives are not of general application throughout the Community but require implementing measures, which are likely to vary from one Member State to another. Despite this, the Court of Justice has held, for example in *Van Duyn v Home Office* (see **21.3.1**), that in appropriate circumstances even Directives may be directly effective. The reason for this is that

Article 288 TFEU expressly states that a Directive is to be legally binding on the State to which it is addressed; this would be meaningless unless there was some possibility that Directives themselves could be relied on where the Member State failed to implement them. However, in the case of Directives, any rights they contain can have direct effect only after the time-limit for implementing the Directive has elapsed (see, eg, *Pubblico Ministero v Ratti* [1979] ECR 1629). Thereafter, again provided that the rights in the Directive are sufficiently clear, precise and unconditional, they can be relied on *against the State*, even though not implemented in national law.

21.3.4 'Horizontal' direct effect

In the early cases on direct effect, the defending party was always the State or some State agency, such as the customs authorities in *Van Gend en Loos* ('vertical' direct effect). Subsequent cases have shown that a party may rely on a Treaty provision, or even a Regulation (but not a Directive), where the other party is not a State body ('horizontal' direct effect). So, for example, in *Defrenne v SABENA* (see **21.4.1**) the plaintiff relied on Article 119 of the EC Treaty (now Article 157 TFEU) against a private employer.

Again, Directives are different. A Directive can be used only against a Member State or an 'emanation of the State'. This is clear from *Marshall v Southampton and South West Hampshire Area Health Authority (Teaching)* [1986] ECR 723. The rationale here is that allowing the use of a Directive against a Member State that is in delay encourages it to implement that Directive. A non-State body, on the other hand, has no power to influence the implementation of a Directive. If it is clear that the defendant is the State or a State body, it is also apparent from *Marshall* that it makes no difference whether or not the State is fulfilling a public function in the circumstances which gave rise to the case. In *Marshall*, the defendant health authority had dismissed the female plaintiff because she had reached the age of 62, although a male employee would not have been dismissed until the age of 65. The plaintiff argued that this breached the Equal Treatment Directive. The defendant conceded that it was a State body but argued that, as it was acting purely as an employer of the plaintiff, the Directive could not be relied upon against it. This argument failed before the Court of Justice.

From cases following *Marshall*, it appears that other emanations of the State for this purpose include a police force (*Johnston v Chief Constable of the RUC* [1986] ECR 1651) and a local authority (*Re London Boroughs* [1990] 3 CMLR 495 and *East Riding of Yorkshire County Council v Gibson* [2000] 3 CMLR 329).

The Court of Justice has subsequently given guidance on the meaning of the term 'emanation of the State'. According to *Foster v British Gas* [1990] ECR I-3133, it must be some body (whatever its legal form) which is carrying out a public service under the control of the State, or which has for that purpose special powers. In *Foster*, the English court applied that definition to find that British Gas prior to privatisation was an emanation of the State. On the other hand, it has since been held by the Court of Appeal in *Doughty v Rolls Royce plc* [1992] IRLR 126 that Rolls Royce was not an emanation of the State when it was in public ownership because it was not providing a public service. By contrast, the High Court has ruled that even the privatised water boards are sufficiently controlled by State regulators to satisfy the criteria in *Foster* (see *Griffin v South West Water Services Ltd* [1995] IRLR 15). Clearly even the privatised British Gas or British Telecom could be regarded as State bodies if this case is correct.

This distinction between public and non-public bodies inevitably means that some individuals will be protected by the provisions of a Directive while others will not. This is especially evident in the employment field, where employees of the State or State bodies will have an advantage over employees of a private employer. The Court of Justice in *Marshall* pointed out that such unfairness is easily countered by the Member State: it can implement the Directive.

Lastly, it should be remembered that even though enforceable only against the State, a Directive may still have indirect consequences for private persons. In *R v Durham, ex p Huddleston* [2000] 1 WLR 1484, a developer obtained from a planning authority permission to develop a site. An objector argued that the development had not been subjected to an environmental impact assessment as required by Directive 85/337. This had direct effect against the local planning authority (an emanation of the State) which was compelled to reconsider the permission. The effect was financially disastrous for the developer.

21.4 THE SUPREMACY OF EU LAW

The Court of Justice, in the seminal case of *Amministrazione delle Finanze dello Stato v Simmenthal* [1978] ECR 629, held that it was fundamental to EU law that EU law should be supreme over the domestic law of the Member States. In this way, EU law would apply uniformly throughout the EU. According to *Simmenthal*, 'every national court must ... accordingly set aside any provision of national law which may conflict with' EU law. The Court of Justice has reinforced that message on numerous occasions.

The courts of individual Member States have, from time to time, found the concept of supremacy difficult to accept. After the European Communities Act 1972, the English courts tended to rely upon interpreting English law to comply with EU law as far as possible. In recent years, however, the courts have been increasingly prepared to give effect to the *Simmenthal* doctrine. This can be seen in the case of *R v Secretary of State for Transport, ex p Factortame (No 2)* [1990] 3 WLR 818, in which some Spanish fishermen challenged the Merchant Shipping Act 1988 as being incompatible with EU law. The House of Lords referred the matter to the Court of Justice under the procedure in Article 177 of the EC Treaty (now Article 267 TFEU) (see **21.7**). In the meantime, the fishermen sought interim relief to suspend the operation of the Act until the Court of Justice replied to the reference. They argued that if the Act continued to operate, their livelihoods would be so seriously affected that the ruling of the Court of Justice might prove to be academic. The House of Lords refused relief, partly because it had no power to suspend the effect of an Act of Parliament, and partly because under English law an interim injunction could not be granted against the Crown. The House of Lords did, however, refer to the Court of Justice a second question: Was it right to refuse relief? The Court responded that where an individual seeks to rely on EU law, a rule of national procedure cannot be invoked in the national courts which would effectively deny the individual that right. The English court then granted the interim relief (see further **22.4**).

21.5 THE CONCEPT OF INDIRECT EFFECT

It would therefore seem clear that when a national court is confronted by national legislation and directly-effective EU legislation which conflict, the court should, under the principle of the supremacy of EU law, apply EU law to the dispute. However, there may be situations in which EU legislation does not have direct effect and a staightforward preference for it cannot be made. This might be the case where a Directive lacks the qualities necessary to give direct effect, as where it is being used against a non-State body.

In such cases, it may be possible to argue that the Directive has indirect effect. The national court is not asked to apply the Directive instead of the national legislation, but is asked to *interpret* the national legislation in the light of the EU Directive.

Accordingly, in *Litster v Forth Dry Dock & Engineering Co Ltd* [1990] 1 AC 546, the House of Lords interpreted the Transfer of Undertakings (Protection of Employment) Regulations 1981 (SI 1981/1794) in the light of Directive 77/187, which the Regulations purported to implement, even though that interpretation was contrary to the meaning on the face of the Regulations. In *Marleasing SA v La Comercial Internacional de Alimentacion SA* [1990] ECR I-4135, the Court of Justice took the concept of 'indirect effect' a stage further by ruling that national law should be interpreted, as far as possible, to give effect to an EU Directive, whether or not the Directive pre-dates the national law. The Court of Justice expressly based the latter decision on Article 5 of the EC Treaty (now Article 4(3) TEU), which requires Member States to take all necessary steps to ensure the fulfilment of their obligations. Contrary to its earlier ruling in *Duke v GEC Reliance Ltd (formerly Reliance Systems)* [1988] AC 618, the House of Lords later conceded that, in interpreting the Sex Discrimination Act 1975, it must take account of the Equal Treatment Directive 76/207 and Court rulings on its interpretation. See *Webb v EMO Air Cargo (UK)* [1994] IRLR 482, where the House of Lords accepted that (from 1978 onwards) it was obliged to interpret the Act in line with the later Directive, even though, in their Lordships' view, the result was not what Parliament had intended when passing the Act.

21.6 ACTION AGAINST A STATE FOR FAILURE TO IMPLEMENT A DIRECTIVE

The European Commission has the responsibility of monitoring the implementation rates of Member States, and it has the power to bring a State in default before the Court of Justice. An individual cannot take this action. However, following *Francovich* and *Bonifacti v Italy* [1992] IRLR 84, an individual may, in appropriate circumstances, sue a State for damages for failure to implement a particular Directive. In that case, Italy had failed to implement Directive 80/987 which would have established a fund available to employees dismissed by insolvent businesses which could not pay them their arrears of salary. Although the Directive was sufficiently precise in the rights it set out to create, these rights were conditional on there being a relevant fund. They were thus not directly effective. However, the Court of Justice gave a right of action against the State itself for non-implementation, relying on Article 5 of the EC Treaty (now Article 4(3) TEU), which requires Member States to take all appropriate measures to ensure the fulfilment of their obligations. The Court of Justice said that a right of action arises where three conditions are met:

(a) the Directive confers rights on individuals;
(b) the content of the rights is identifiable from the Directive;
(c) there is a causal link between the failure to implement and the damage.

This is clearly what we would call in English law a claim in tort.

The action itself would be brought before the relevant national court in accordance with the appropriate national procedure (in England, this would be a High Court action against the Attorney-General). That procedure would have to ensure an effective remedy for the plaintiff.

In *R v Secretary of State for Transport, ex p Factortame (No 4)* [1996] 2 WLR 506, the Court ruled on whether the Spanish fishermen could recover damages for breach of Article 52 of the EC Treaty (now Article 49 TFEU) for being denied the right to form UK fishing companies (see **22.4–22.5**). The Court introduced a further condition for State liability in this type of case, ie damages are recoverable only where the breach of the Treaty is sufficiently serious, that is where the State manifestly and gravely disregards the limits on its own powers. This extra condition has also been applied in a case of an incorrectly implemented Directive. In *R v HM Treasury, ex p British Telecommunications plc* [1996] All ER (EC) 411, it was held that no damages are recoverable against the State if it has made a reasonable mistake in interpreting the Directive when drafting its implementing legislation. This is a very important case for governments, because the broad principles of EU law do provide plenty of scope for innocent, non-negligent interpretation. This will not, however, excuse governments which rely on negligent advice from their lawyers, as happened in the *Factortame* case. The British Government was eventually required to pay damages; the House of Lords accepting that the law on establishment and discrimination being clear, there was a sufficiently serious breach (*R v Secretary of State for Transport, ex p Factortame (No 5)* [1999] 4 All ER 906, HL).

However, note that the non-implementation of a Directive will still be assessed under the original *Francovich* test, since non-implementation is a sufficiently serious breach in itself (see *Dillenkofer and Others v Germany* [1996] 3 CMLR 469).

21.7 ARTICLE 267 TFEU REFERENCE PROCEDURE

21.7.1 What is the purpose of this procedure?

The Article 267 TFEU reference procedure enables the Court of Justice to give a preliminary ruling to a national court principally on the interpretation of the Treaty, although it can also rule on the validity of acts of Union institutions. This means that the Court of Justice will not, as such, rule on the compatibility of national law with EU law, or on the application of EU law to particular facts. This is the national court's responsibility. Thus, in *Foster v British Gas* [1990] ECR I-3133 (see **21.3.4**) the Court of Justice explained how an emanation of the State could be recognised, and the English court then applied the definition to British Gas. It may be, however, that in stating the principle, the Court of Justice, in effect, indicates how it must apply to the facts before the national court. The advantage of Article 267 TFEU is that it provides a mechanism which enables the Court of Justice to ensure that EU law develops along parallel lines throughout the Union.

21.7.2 How does the procedure work?

Article 267 TFEU distinguishes two situations.

21.7.2.1 Where the case is being heard before a court from which there is no judicial remedy

In this case, the national court must make a reference if it believes that a clarification of the EU point is necessary in order to decide the case. It may not be necessary where the point of EU law is irrelevant to the case, where there is an existing Court of Justice judgment on the matter, or where the court believes the correct interpretation to be obvious (see *CILFIT Srl v Ministro della Sanitro* [1982] ECR 3415).

A particularly striking example of this is the case involving part-timers (*Equal Opportunities Commission v Secretary of State for Employment* [1994] 1 All ER 910 (HL)). This is another illustration of the point that discrimination, here in relation to pay between men and women (Article 157 TFEU), always includes unjustifiable indirect discrimination. In this context, paying part-timers less than full-timers means indirectly paying women less than men because most part-timers are women. Thus, the House of Lords ruled that legislation requiring part-timers to work for five years before qualifying for redundancy payments/unfair dismissal compensation (whereas full-timers qualified after two years) was unlawful because it was a breach of equal pay under Article 157 TFEU. There was no objective reason for the discrimination. The House emphatically rejected Government arguments that it would create new jobs by reducing the burdens on business, saying that there was no evidence that this was the case. No reference was made to the Court of Justice because the position in EU law was clear. The provisions of the Employment Protection (Consolidation) Act 1978, which had stood for 13 years, were declared unlawful without the need for a reference. The Act has since been amended. In the light of subsequent cases (notably *R v Secretary of State for Employment, ex p Seymour-Smith* [1999] 3 WLR 460), it is suggested that the House of Lords should have made a reference.

21.7.2.2 Where the case is being heard before any other court or a tribunal that is exercising a judicial function

In this case, the court or tribunal has a discretion whether to make a reference. Again, the Court of Justice's opinion must be necessary in order for a decision to be reached. Throughout the Union, a wide range of lower courts and tribunals have made references under Article 267 TFEU (or its predecessors, Article 177 and Article 234 EC), including UK magistrates' courts and social security appeal tribunals.

In either case, the question whether a reference should be made is one for the court rather than the parties to the case. Once the court has decided that a reference should be made, it should then draft the questions to which it requires a reply. In certain cases, the Court of

Justice has reformulated these questions so that they more accurately reflect the issue that needs to be addressed. Although the Court has no discretion, as such, as to whether it replies to a reference, it has refused to respond where there is no genuine dispute between the parties and where the reference was made in order to raise wider political issues (*Foglia v Novello* [1980] ECR 745).

21.8 BREXIT

The UK ceased to be part of the EU legal system at the end of the transition period on 31 December 2020, and so it is no longer required to adhere to the TFEU and Regulations and to implement Directives, and it is not subject to decisions of the ECJ or General Court. It should be remembered, however, that activities that take place within the EU will be subject to EU rules and jurisdiction, so for example a UK business wishing to export to the EU will have to adhere to EU product restrictions, and a UK business operating within Europe could be fined for breach of EU competition law by the EU Commission.

It should also be remembered that large portions of UK domestic laws have been created to comply with previous EU Directives. The UK will have the ability to change these UK laws over time after departure and so, coupled with the fact that new Directives will not be implemented, there may be a slow departure from alignment with the laws of EU Member States. In the short term, however, it is likely that most EU-derived UK laws will remain unchanged.

Departure removes the ECJ and General Court from the UK's court hierarchy, and this means that the UK's courts can depart from ECJ and General Court guidance and decisions.

SUMMARY

If a client seeks advice on a problem where there could be an EU dimension, remember:

(1) EU law can also be used in its own right if it meets the criteria for direct effect (see **21.3**);

(2) if there is EU legislation which has direct effect, an English court or tribunal must prefer it to conflicting domestic law (see **21.4**);

(3) EU legislation can affect the interpretation of domestic law (see *Marleasing SA v La Comercial Internacional de Alimentacion SA* [1990] ECR I-4135 at **21.5**);

(4) in case of doubt as to the meaning of EU law, consider a reference to the Court of Justice under Article 267 TFEU (see **21.7**).

CHAPTER 22

SEEKING A REMEDY IN NATIONAL COURTS

LEARNING OUTCOMES

After reading this chapter you will be able to understand:

- how to use EU law to defend yourself in a legal action
- how to use EU law offensively in court and what remedies you may be entitled to
- the limits on the use of EU law, both in terms of the amount of compensation and the time limits for use.

22.1 INTRODUCTION

This chapter is an attempt to consolidate the rules and think more practically about how they can be applied in Member States' national courts when acting for a client. Lawyers must be clear on which laws apply to a client's situation. Post-Brexit, in a truly UK-only situation, only UK law will apply, but for lawyers with multinational clients, it could well be that EU law also applies to activities that take place within Europe, as well as any relevant national laws of some Member States.

This chapter analyses the use of EU law in the domestic courts of Member States. Post-Brexit it will not be possible to use EU law in the UK courts in the way described.

22.2 EU LAW AS A DEFENCE

As EU law overrides conflicting national law, directly-effective EU law can always be used as a defence to any civil claim, prosecution or tax claim that is based on that national law. Thus, for example, since Article 101 TFEU makes restrictive agreements void, a defendant can plead Article 101 TFEU when sued in a civil claim for breach of the agreement. Likewise, if Articles 34, 45, 49 and 56 TFEU make measures restricting free movement of goods, services and working persons unlawful, a client prosecuted under such national measures can plead the Articles of the Treaty as a defence. In tax claims, a client can plead the VAT Directive (77/388) or the Treaty provisions on non-discrimination (Article 110 TFEU). Thus, where an exemption from VAT exists in the Directive but not in the local tax legislation, a taxpayer can plead the Directive as defence to a demand for tax; VAT is very much an EU tax and cannot be collected in circumstances not allowed for under the Directive.

22.3 EFFECTIVE REMEDIES

In relation to more active remedies, the Court of Justice has made it plain in cases like *R v Secretary of State for Transport, ex p Factortame (No 2)* [1990] 3 WLR 818, that national courts must provide a sufficient remedy to protect EU rights. In general, this would be the nearest equivalent national remedy. Where no adequate remedy is available under national law, the court must provide one to protect the EU right in question (as it did in *Factortame*). Thus, a client may be better protected by asserting an EU right than under national law (examples being *Marshall v Southampton Area Health Authority (No 2)* [1993] 3 CMLR 293, discussed below at **22.9**, and *R v Secretary of State for Transport, ex p Factortame (No 4)* [1996] 2 WLR 506).

It should also be noted that administrative decisions affecting EU law must be reasoned, 'proportional' and subject to review by a higher tribunal. Neither the duty to give reasons nor 'proportionality' are well established under English administrative law, so that once again the client asserting an EU right may be better protected when dealing with administrative institutions.

22.4 INJUNCTIONS/INTERIM INJUNCTIONS

If one thinks of actual remedies available to protect EU rights, probably the first thing one would think of would be an injunction. This is usually available to be used against a private person to restrain a breach of Articles 101 or 102 TFEU (see *Garden Cottage Foods v Milk Marketing Board* [1984] AC 130), depending on the Member State's legal system. Thus, a client who feels they are being excluded from a particular market because of a restrictive agreement breaching Article 101 TFEU, or an abuse of a dominant position breaching Article 102 TFEU, can get an injunction to restrain such unlawful behaviour, and get back into the market.

However, the remedy of injunction or interim injunction is also usually available against a Member State government to restrain a breach of EU rules. In *Factortame*, some Spanish fishermen had set up a UK company to operate UK trawlers with the intention of exploiting the UK fishing quota in the North Sea. The Merchant Shipping Act 1988 provided that, in order to qualify as a UK company for this purpose, the company must itself be owned at least 75% by UK nationals who were UK residents. Not surprisingly, the Spanish fishermen who found themselves excluded by this rule complained that the Act was contrary to the Treaty in that it denied their right of establishment as a UK company (Article 52 of the EC Treaty (now Article 49 TFEU)) and discriminated against them as EC (now EU) nationals (Article 6 of the EC Treaty (now Article 18 TFEU)). Faced with this issue, the House of Lords felt obliged to make a reference to the Court of Justice, but the question then arose as to whether the House of Lords would be bound to grant interim relief protecting the fishermen's rights until the Court could rule on the main issue. This issue, too, was referred to the Court of Justice, which replied, somewhat more promptly than normal, that the national court must grant an interim injunction to suspend the Act of Parliament where this was necessary to protect the EC (now EU) rights pending the ruling from the Court. Eventually, the ruling came back (*R v Secretary of State for Transport, ex p Factortame (No 3)* [1991] 3 All ER 769) that the 1988 Act did contravene the Treaty and therefore, in relation to EC (now EU) nationals, the provisions concerned had to be suspended indefinitely.

It should be noted that *Factortame* involved an urgent case where the fishermen's livelihood was being threatened in circumstances where damages (at the time uncertain) would not have been an adequate remedy. The ruling does not mean that in EU cases the court need not follow the normal balance of convenience test when deciding when to grant an interim injunction, nor that the court need not take into account other factors, for example public policy, when exercising its discretion. In two other cases, a reference was made but an interim injunction was refused in the meantime. These cases are *R v HM Treasury, ex p British Telecommunications plc* [1994] 1 CMLR 621 and *R v Heritage Secretary, ex p Continental TV (Red Hot TV)* [1993] 2 CMLR 333. Both cases rested on the 'balance of convenience', with the adequacy of damages being a particular fact in the first case and public policy (protecting sensitive viewers from pornographic television) being a factor in the second.

22.5 DAMAGES FOR BREACH OF EU RIGHTS

Damages are usually available against private persons for breach of their statutory duty, for example for anti-competitive behaviour under Articles 101 or 102 TFEU. This will depend on the legal system of each Member State, but the award of damages is usual as the ECJ has ruled that remedies for breach of EU law must be adequate.

See also **21.6**.

22.6 REPAYMENT OF DISCRIMINATORY TAX/VAT

Again, if the tax has been unlawfully collected in breach of Article 110 TFEU or in breach of the VAT Directives, the requirement that an adequate remedy be given means that this tax must be repaid in full with interest (see the Court's ruling in *Amministrazione delle Finanze dello Stato v Spa San Giorgio* [1983] ECR 359). For reasons which will be explained at **22.8**, it may be that the normal time-limit for reclaiming tax under national tax law cannot run to protect the Government until such time as the Government brings its own tax law into line with EU law. This case does recognise a principle of 'unjust enrichment'. Thus, tax should not be repaid where it has been passed on to a customer who cannot themselves be traced.

22.7 STATUTORY REMEDIES

Initially when asserting an EU right, one starts by looking at the nearest equivalent national remedy. Thus, the client who asserts EU rights in the context of employment law, for example equal pay under Article 157 TFEU, or sex discrimination under the Equal Treatment Directive (2006/54), is effectively asserting statutory employment rights and therefore must take their claim to the relevant national court where the remedies and procedures they will be seeking must be adequate to address the wrong. In two respects, however, time-limits and limits on compensation, the remedies provided for breach of these EU rights may be better than those for the equivalent rights under national law.

22.8 TIME-LIMITS

Although initially the national time-limits will apply to the claim, the Court of Justice has made it clear that these cannot be used to protect a government where the claim is based on a Directive which that government has failed to implement. In other words, the claimant cannot be deprived of a right by the government delaying implementation for so long that the claimant is out of time. In such circumstances the government is estopped from relying on its own wrong, and therefore the time-limit begins to run only when it has righted that wrong by introducing national legislation that complies with the Directive (see *Emmott v Minister for Social Welfare and Attorney-General* [1991] IRLR 387). The Court seems to have reduced the effectiveness of this ruling in *Johnson v Chief Adjudication Officer (No 2)* [1995] IRLR 187, where it indicates that a time-limit which limits back-payments of social security may be enforceable even where the government is in breach of a Directive. The same rule applies to tax (see now *Edilizia Industriale v Ministero delle Finanze* [1999] 2 CMLR 995. The normal national time-limits will of course be available to protect a private person, for example an employer faced with a claim for equal pay under Article 157 TFEU. But even these may not start to run until the employee is aware of their rights under Article 157 TFEU (see *Cannon v Barnsley Metropolitan Borough Council* [1992] IRLR 474). The Court has made it clear in the case of *Fischer* [1994] IRLR 662, that the time-limit must not make it impossible to exercise the EU rights which national courts and governments are obliged to protect. There are thus two basic rules that national time-limits must satisfy (see *Comet BV v Produktschap voor Siergewassen* [1997] ECR 2043). First, they must still leave the applicant with an effective remedy and not make recovery virtually impossible. Secondly, they must be equivalent to time-limits in similar national claims. This second principle of non-discrimination is well-illustrated by the case of *Levez v TH Jennings (Harlow Pools) Ltd* [1999] IRLR 764, where the two-year time-limit on back pay in equal pay cases was held to be unlawful as in other similar claims for race and disability discrimination there was no such limit.

22.9 LIMITS ON COMPENSATION

As indicated above, EU rules like those protecting against sex discrimination under the Equal Treatment Directive do require an adequate remedy. Thus, the Court of Justice has ruled that national limits on compensation cannot be used to protect a State employer in a claim based on an EU Directive. This is the now famous case of *Marshall v Southampton Area Health Authority (No 2)* [1993] 3 CMLR 293. Mrs Marshall, who established her right to compensation for breach of the EU Directive in *Marshall v Southampton and West Hampshire Area Health Authority (Teaching)*, then went back to an industrial tribunal where her compensation was assessed at over £20,000. This figure included an assessment of interest. However, both the EAT and the Court of Appeal ruled that the compensation had to be restricted to the limit set by the Sex Discrimination Act 1975, which not only restricted compensation (at the time to £6,000) but also denied the award of interest. On a reference from the House of Lords, the Court ruled that compensation must be awarded without limit and that in assessing compensation the tribunal must, to give an adequate remedy, award interest. The Government reacted promptly and commendably to this ruling by removing both the upper limit and the restriction on interest for all discrimination and equal pay claims with effect from November 1993 (see Sex Discrimination and Equal Pay (Remedies) Regulations 1993, SI 1993/2798).

CHAPTER 23

FREE MOVEMENT OF WORKERS

LEARNING OUTCOMES

After reading this chapter you will be able to understand:

- what EU nationality means
- what EU nationality grants in terms of rights for the workforce
- the extent to which a worker can take their family to another Member State whilst working there
- the circumstances in which a worker and/or their family can be denied entry into a Member State.

23.1 INTRODUCTION

The EC Treaty gave (and the TFEU now gives) the right of free movement within the Union to people who wished to take up offers of employment made from outside their home State. This fundamental Treaty right has been buttressed by a considerable amount of secondary legislation. Further, EU law has developed to the stage where the rights of individuals to move within the EU are not necessarily dependent on the desire to take up employment. Indeed, as a consequence of the Single European Act, from 1 January 1993, internal barriers to movement within the EU should have been removed. Further, Article 20 TFEU now states that every EU national shall be a citizen of the European Union. Under Article 21 TFEU, the Union citizen has the right to move and reside freely within the territory of the Member States, subject to the limitations and conditions in the Treaty and in other legislation.

23.2 WHAT DOES THE TREATY PROVIDE?

Free movement of workers is guaranteed by Article 45 TFEU, which gives the EU worker the right of entry and residence for the purpose of taking up employment. According to Article 45(2) TFEU, Member States must abolish

> any discrimination based on nationality between workers of the Member States as regards employment, remuneration and other conditions of work and employment.

'Work and employment' has been interpreted very widely to include sportspeople. Hence, in *Union Royale Belge des Sociétés de Football Association ASBL v Bosman* [1996] All ER (EC) 97, the Court of Justice made it plain that restrictions on the number of EU nationals in football teams imposed by UEFA and requirements for large transfer fees in cross-border transfers were both illegal.

23.2.1 How is nationality interpreted?

Nationality is entirely a matter for the domestic law of each Member State, which means that, inevitably, rules vary. In particular, not all Member States permit their nationals to hold dual nationality. One result of this was seen in *Micheletti v Delegacion del Gobierno en Cantabria* [1992] ECR I-4238. The case concerned a dual national of Argentina and Italy who sought entry into Spain. Entry was refused because under Spanish law only the nationality of the State in which the person had last been habitually resident was recognised, and in this case that was Argentina. The Court of Justice found, however, that, as he was an Italian national under Italian law, he was an EC (now EU) migrant worker protected by Article 48 of the EC Treaty (now Article 45 TFEU), so that entry into Spain could not be denied.

23.2.2 What rights of residence does the EU national obtain under Article 45 TFEU?

The EU national has an absolute right of residence so long as they remain in work. If the worker becomes involuntarily unemployed, Directive 2004/38 will continue to guarantee them a right to reside in the host State. However, if they become voluntarily unemployed their position is changed as (in accordance with most social security systems) they would be disqualified from social security benefits. Under Directive 2004/38, the worker has a right of residence simply by being a citizen of another Member State as long as they have sufficient resources not to be a burden on the host State. If a worker becomes permanently disabled or reaches retirement age, their right of permanent residence continues under this Directive as well.

An individual can claim the rights of a worker as long as they are genuinely employed, even if their work is part time and obtained so that EU rights can be asserted, and even if the salary paid is below a minimum wage limit (*Levin v Secretary of State for Justice* [1982] 1 ECR 1035).

A period of five years' residence gives the worker and/or their family (see **23.4**) a right of permanent residence.

23.2.3 What terms of employment is an EU national entitled to expect?

An EU national can claim the same terms as those offered to a national of the host State. Article 45(2) TFEU expressly refers to the right not to be discriminated against as regards conditions of work. So, in the case of *Allué (Pilar) and Coonan (Mary Carmel) v Università degli Studi di Venezia* [1991] 1 CMLR 283, an Italian law which provided that non-Italians who accepted jobs in Italy to teach a language could only enter into fixed-term contracts for one year was contrary to Article 48(2) of the EC Treaty (now Article 45(2) TFEU). In addition, Regulation 492/2011, Article 7, and Directive 2004/38, Article 24 prohibit discrimination in relation to conditions of employment, dismissal, social and tax advantages, training and union membership.

23.2.4 What about their social security rights?

Social security rights are governed by Regulation 1408/71, which basically guarantees to EU nationals the social security benefits of the host State. However, where the benefits are dependent on contributions, a worker's entitlement will take into account contributions to the equivalent benefit in their home State or other Member States in which they have worked. The Regulation does not provide for harmonisation of benefits or of levels of benefits throughout the Union.

23.2.5 Does an EU national have a right of entry to look for work?

Article 45 TFEU (or its predecessors) has been interpreted to mean that an EU national has a right of entry to look for work and a reasonable period of residence to find it. This is confirmed in Directive 2004/38, which grants a three-month right of residence without qualifying as a worker. In the UK, the immigration rules used to allow such a person to be deported if they did not succeed in finding work after six months. The Court of Justice held this rule to be consistent with EU law in *R v Immigration Appeals Tribunal, ex p Antonissen* [1991] 2 CMLR 373, although it stressed that the job seeker might still have a right of residence if they had reasonable prospects of finding work. An EU national has a right to remain in the host

State as an ordinary citizen if their resources are adequate and they are covered by health insurance by virtue of Directive 2004/38 on the right to residence for EU citizens.

23.3 WHEN DOES THE TREATY ALLOW MEMBER STATES TO DENY ENTRY?

Article 45(3) TFEU permits derogations on grounds of public policy, public security and public health. Because these are derogations from one of the fundamental freedoms of the EU, the Court of Justice has interpreted them strictly. Further, Directive 2004/38 has made it clear that only personal conduct can be taken into account. Even prior criminal convictions will not necessarily entitle the Member State to deny entry. They will do so only where they indicate that the individual represents a current threat to public security. For example, in *Astrid Proll v Entry Clearance Officer* [1988] 2 CMLR 387, the former Baader Meinhoff terrorist was allowed entry into the UK because she did not represent a present threat.

Article 45(4) TFEU provides that the rights granted earlier in the Article do not apply to employment in the public service. This has been interpreted strictly by the Court of Justice in *Commission of European Communities v Belgium; Re Public Employees (No 1)* [1980] ECR 3881 to mean only 'posts involving the exercise of official authority and functions related to safeguarding the general interests of the State'.

23.4 CAN THE WORKER BRING THEIR FAMILY WITH THEM?

Because a worker might be deterred from moving to another Member State if they could not take their family with them, Directive 2004/38 enables the worker to do so. It does, however, limit the family members who are entitled to entry to the spouse, registered partner, children under 21 and dependent relatives of the worker or spouse/partner. Member States do, however, have an obligation to 'facilitate entry and residence' of any other family members who are dependants or members of the household. It is not necessary for family members to be EU nationals. The host State can refuse entry to family members only in those circumstances which allow it to refuse entry to the worker (see **23.3** above). The rights of a spouse are not dependent on their residing with the worker, and thus can terminate only if the worker leaves the host State permanently (*Diatta v Land Berlin* [1985] ECR 567). Prior to Directive 2004/38 there was no clear European authority as to whether deportation could follow divorce, but in *Baumbast v Secretary of State for the Home Department* [2002] ECR I-7091 the mother of children was entitled to remain having been awarded custody. Directive 2004/38 provides for the spouse (or unmarried cohabitee) to remain in the country if they have resided for three years, or if they have been awarded custody or access to children, or alternatively if the court feels that allowing them to remain is warranted in the circumstances.

Directive 2004/38 lays down formal requirements for entry (including visa) and for obtaining residence documents. Thereafter, the family have the same rights as the worker to jobs, social security and education.

SUMMARY

If an EU national or a family member is refused entry or residence rights by a Member State's immigration authorities, they will be allowed to invoke their EU rights before the appropriate immigration authority or court, or as a defence in criminal proceedings where deportation is being considered.

If an EU national believes that they have been discriminated against in relation to employment, they should, as usual, follow the appropriate national procedure in the host State to obtain a suitable remedy. It is important to remember that, to comply with EU law, such national procedure must not discriminate, even indirectly, against the EU national and must give an effective remedy for breach of EU law (see **22.9**).

CHAPTER 24

FREEDOM OF ESTABLISHMENT AND PROVISION OF SERVICES

LEARNING OUTCOMES

After reading this chapter you will be able to understand:

- the rights which a self-employed individual or business has to ply their trade in another Member State temporarily
- the rights which a self-employed individual or business has to establish themselves permanently in another Member State
- the possibility of persons relying on the above rights to bring their family with them
- what exceptions exist which may stop someone relying on their rights
- the right of the recipient of services to travel to another Member State to receive services.

24.1 INTRODUCTION

The freedom of establishment is the right to base one's business in another Member State permanently. This right is guaranteed by the TFEU, with the important qualification that it cannot give the establishing business greater rights than those enjoyed by businesses operated by nationals of the host Member State. Thus a French business wishing to establish itself in England would have to comply with laws affecting an English business relating, for example, to employment, health and safety, and taxes and social security (except to the extent that these might discriminate directly or indirectly against the foreign firm). The governing Article in the TFEU is Article 49.

The freedom to provide services guarantees that a business can provide a service across an EU frontier even if that business does not want to be permanently based outside its home State. As with the right of establishment, the right to provide services is granted on the basis that the services will be provided subject to the same conditions as apply to nationals of the State in which the service is supplied (again subject to these rules constituting indirect discrimination). The governing Article in the TFEU is Article 56.

Although under both Articles the firm concerned must comply with the same conditions which apply to local nationals, those conditions are likely to be tighter for establishment. In

Gebhard v Consiglio dell'Ordine degli Avvocati e Procuratori di Milano [1996] All ER (EC) 139, it was held that a German lawyer giving advice on German law in Italy was prima facie 'established' there by virtue of his permanent office and his adoption of the title Avvocato. Had he merely been providing services, he could have relied on his home title as a German lawyer and the earlier Directive on free movement of legal services. However, by establishing himself in Italy, he had to requalify as an Italian lawyer.

In the cases taken to the Court of Justice under Articles 49 and 56 TFEU, emphasis has often successfully been placed on Article 18 TFEU which prohibits discrimination on the ground of nationality, wherever the matter is covered by the Treaty.

Article 18 TFEU has direct effect, so that provisions of national statutes can be disapplied by national courts in so far as they directly or indirectly discriminate against other EU nationals. Residence requirements are a good example of indirect discrimination.

24.2 THE RIGHT OF ESTABLISHMENT: ARTICLE 49 TFEU

Article 49 TFEU provides that restrictions on the freedom of establishment by nationals of a Member State in the territory of another Member State must be abolished. This freedom is stated to include the right to take up and pursue activities as self-employed persons and to set up and manage undertakings, in particular companies or firms, under the conditions laid down for its own nationals by the law of the country where the establishment is effected.

24.2.1 What is the implication of this Article?

Article 49 TFEU means that no Member State can, through its legislation or administrative practices, impose a nationality barrier to businesses which wish to be based permanently in another Member State. In *R v Secretary of State for Transport, ex p Factortame (No 3)* [1991] 3 All ER 769, Article 52 of the EC Treaty (now Article 49 TFEU) was invoked by Spanish fishermen who operated British-registered fishing boats but who were prevented from fishing the British quota because the Merchant Shipping Act 1988 laid down nationality and residence requirements for the owners of shares in companies operating such boats. The Court of Justice held that such legislation was contrary to Article 52 of the EC Treaty (see **22.4**).

24.2.2 Are there any limitations on the kind of undertaking which can benefit from Article 49 TFEU?

Article 49 TFEU refers in particular to companies and firms. This phrase is defined in Article 54 TFEU to mean 'companies or firms constituted under civil or commercial law including co-operative societies'. The meaning of company or firm is really a matter for the law of the home State. A French company wishing to set up a branch or subsidiary in England can do so provided it meets the requirements under French law for being a company. It must not hold itself out as having been incorporated under English law. The only qualification here is that EU law requires that an undertaking wishing to rely on Article 49 TFEU must be a profit-making body.

It is particularly important to realise, however, that an entrepreneur wishing to set up a company can choose the State with the least regulatory company regime and then establish a branch back in the State they wish to trade in. In *Centros Ltd v Erhvervsog Selskabsstyrelsen* [1999] 2 CMLR 551, the Court of Justice recognised that it was legitimate to set up a company in the UK and trade through a branch in Denmark, even though the purpose was to avoid the Danish requirements for a minimum paid-up share capital.

24.3 THE RIGHT TO PROVIDE SERVICES: ARTICLE 56 TFEU

According to Article 56 TFEU, restrictions on the freedom to provide services within the EU must be abolished in respect of nationals of Member States who are established in a State of the Community other than that of the person for whom the services are intended. Services for this purpose, according to Article 57 TFEU, are services normally provided for remuneration. In *Commission of European Communities v France* [1991] ECR I-659, for example, it was held that a French law which required tourist guides to hold a licence dependent on the passing of an examination in France was contrary to Article 59 of the EC Treaty (now Article 56 TFEU) as being unnecessary and discriminatory. There are many similar cases. This Article also means that a business providing services in another Member State had the right to bring its own employees into the host State to enable it to perform those services, even where they would not have been entitled to claim rights under Article 48 of the EC Treaty (now Article 45 TFEU) (eg, because of transitional rules for nationals of new EU Member States or because the workforce includes immigrants from outside the EU) (*Rush Portuguesa v Office National d'Immigration* [1990] ECR I-1417, *Van der Elst* [1994] ECR I-3803). The workers would, of course, need to be lawfully employed in the State where the employer is established and might need visas to enter the host country; they would not need fresh work permits. The Court of Justice, however, stresses that the host State can impose its own mandatory rules for workers' protection. Since statutory protection for workers in some countries is less than in other countries (eg, Germany), this might enable British firms to provide services to Germany using their British workforce at cheaper rates than German firms which have to pay their employees a higher minimum wage.

24.4 SECONDARY LEGISLATION

In 2006 the EU passed Directive 2006/123, the 'Services Directive', which was designed to help service providers and recipients benefit from freedom of establishment and freedom to provide services across borders by simplifying administrative procedures and removing obstacles for service activities.

The Directive also applies to freedom of establishment, and so is relevant to Articles 49 and 56 TFEU.

The provisions of the Directive are complex, and beyond the scope of this book; however, the key highlights are:

- Industries are included within it unless expressly excluded (but there is a long list of excluded industries within the Directive).
- The Directive includes an obligation on Member States to set up single points of contact for those wishing to establish or provide services, to make it easier to obtain information.
- Making applications and following procedures must be straightforward, including the possibility of procedures to be completed at a distance and/or by electronic means.
- The Directive sets out restrictions on 'authorisation schemes', ie schemes by which applicants must seek permission from the State before carrying out certain activities. The aim is again to simplify, and to prevent unfair denial of business opportunities.

24.5 CONSTRAINTS UNDER ARTICLES 49 AND 56 TFEU

The in-coming business is subject to the laws that would apply to a business operated by nationals of that State. This can create barriers to the business wishing to operate across a frontier. The host State may require, perhaps, that all such businesses obtain the authority of the State before they can start to operate. Professional people may be required to conform to rules of professional conduct, professional qualifications or to the rules of a professional body within the host State.

Article 57 of the EC Treaty (now Article 53 TFEU) envisaged that a series of Directives would be issued dealing with mutual recognition and harmonisation of professional regulations. In the light of this, the European Commission, recognising the public interest in maintaining standards while wishing to minimise unnecessary barriers to cross-border enterprise, tried to develop uniform codes in certain sectors which would apply throughout the Community. These 'sectoral' Directives apply to medical professions such as doctors, nurses, dentists and vets, but the development of harmonised professional training and qualifications in all professions would have taken many years. So after the Court of Justice held that Articles 52 and 59 of the EC Treaty (now Articles 49 and 56 TFEU) were directly effective (see *Reyners v The Belgian State* [1974] ECR 631 and *Van Binsbergen (JHM) v Bestuur van de Bedrijfsvereniging voor de Metaalnijverheid* [1974] ECR 1299 at **21.3.1**), the Commission changed its approach to one of encouraging mutual recognition of standards. Thus a professional qualified in one State must, in principle, be recognised in another State to the extent that their qualification is equivalent.

A particularly important Directive in this respect is Directive 89/48 on recognition of higher education qualifications. The effect of the Directive is that where entry into a particular profession depends upon the candidate having obtained a 'diploma' which proves that they have completed at least three years' professional education and training, a non-national cannot be denied entry to that profession if they hold the equivalent 'diploma' which would entitle them to enter the profession in their home State. However, if there are substantial differences in the content of the course leading to the diploma in the home State, the Directive allows the host State to require the candidate to follow an adaptation period of no more than three years. As an alternative, the candidate could choose to take an aptitude test. The Directive makes special provision regarding entry to the legal profession. It allows a State to specify whether a candidate must take an aptitude test or follow a period of adaptation. The more recent establishment Directive of 1998 (98/5) provides for automatic requalification after a period of practise as a foreign lawyer.

The principle behind Directive 89/48 has been extended to cover diplomas awarded after one year's post-secondary education by Directive 92/51.

In *Van Binsbergen (JHM) v Bestuur van de Bedrijfsvereniging voor de Metaalnijverheid* [1974] ECR 1299, the Court of Justice held that professional rules of conduct regulating the legal profession would not be in breach of Community (now EU) law provided they did not discriminate against the non-national, they were objectively justifiable and they were not disproportionate to the aim to be achieved. Hence, a lawyer established in France had the right to provide services by representing clients before Belgian tribunals. He could not be forced to establish himself in Belgium. Simply having an address for service in Belgium would be proportional to any need for supervision of his activities. (A Directive has now adopted the *Van Binsbergen* line and allows qualified EU lawyers to represent their clients before foreign tribunals within the EU (see Directive 77/249).) A similar approach can be seen in the case of *Commission of European Communities v Germany* [1988] ECR 5427, which was concerned with the regulation of the German insurance sector. In that case, the Court held that restrictions on the right of an insurance company to provide services in Germany would be acceptable only if they were objectively justified, in the general public good and if they applied to all undertakings so far as they were not regulated in their home State.

Lastly, it would seem that if there is only a tenuous link between the services being provided and a particular restrictive provision, the latter will not be in breach of EU law (see *Society for the Protection of the Unborn Child (Ireland) v Grogan (Stephen)* [1991] 3 CMLR 849). That case concerned Irish legislation prohibiting the supply of information on abortion facilities provided outside Ireland. The Court of Justice acknowledged that the overseas clinics provided services within the meaning of Article 59 of the EC Treaty (now Article 56 TFEU), but went on to hold that since the information in question was being made available by student unions rather than by the clinics themselves, there was an insufficient link between the restriction and the provision of the services. Had the clinics been advertising directly themselves (or through an advertising agency), the position would have been different. (The ban on these leaflets may raise questions of freedom of speech under Article 10 of the European Convention on Human Rights – see **Chapter 27**.)

24.6 CAN THE SELF-EMPLOYED PERSON BRING THEIR FAMILY WITH THEM TO THE HOST STATE?

Directive 2004/38 (as mentioned in **Chapter 23**) applies to freedom of establishment as it does to workers (see **23.4**).

24.7 DEROGATIONS FROM ARTICLES 49 AND 56 TFEU

It is possible to derogate from Articles 49 and 56 TFEU on grounds of public health, public security and public policy (Articles 52 and 62 TFEU). The interpretation of these terms is the same as that under Article 45(3) TFEU and Directive 2004/38 (see **23.3**). Moreover, the right of establishment does not apply to activities involving, even occasionally, 'the exercise of official authority' (Article 51 TFEU). Thus a number of 'legal professions', for example judges, magistrates, court registrars and notaries (but not lawyers), can be reserved to home nationals.

24.8 RIGHTS OF POTENTIAL RECIPIENTS OF SERVICES UNDER EU LAW

In *Luisi and Carbone v Ministero del Tesoro* [1984] ECR 377, the Court of Justice interpreted Article 59 of the EC Treaty (now Article 56 TFEU) to mean that potential recipients of services had the right to go to another Member State to receive those services and that tourists qualified as potential recipients of services. This approach was further developed in *Cowan v Le Trésor Public (The Treasury)* [1989] ECR 195, which concerned a British tourist who was the victim of a criminal assault while in France. His claim for compensation from the French Criminal Injuries Compensation Board was denied because he was not a French national. On an Article 267 TFEU reference, the Court of Justice held that compensation could not be denied to a recipient of compensation services on grounds of nationality.

In a number of cases, the Court of Justice has considered whether this approach entitles a national of a Member State to take advantage of education services elsewhere in the EU. Strictly speaking, State education cannot constitute 'services' because, under Article 57 TFEU, services must normally be paid for. In cases such as *Gravier v City of Liège* [1985] ECR 593, however, it was held that students cannot be asked to pay an additional fee for educational courses because they are non-nationals, provided the course represents vocational training, ie it facilitates access to a particular trade or profession. Even if the courses are normally free (ie not 'services') they still relate to a Treaty matter (training), and therefore any discrimination is unlawful under Article 18 TFEU (see **24.1**).

24.9 SUMMARY AND CONCLUSION

24.9.1 Distinguish between establishment and services

Establishment (Article 49 TFEU) implies permanence; services (Article 56 TFEU) are more temporary. Hence, the presence of a permanent office implies establishment under Article 49 TFEU (see *Gebhard v Consiglio dell'Ordine degli Avvocati e Procuratori di Milano* [1996] All ER (EC) 139 at **24.1**).

24.9.2 Restriction on free movement

Where services are involved, for Article 56 TFEU to apply there must be a restriction on free movement. However, services may move in four different ways.

(a) The provider of services moves to another Member State to provide services on a temporary basis (the normal case).

(b) The recipient of services moves to receive services (eg, as a tourist – see *Cowan v Le Trésor Public* [1989] ECR 195 at **24.8**).

(c) The provider moves to another Member State to provide services to nationals of their own State.

(d) Neither provider nor recipient moves, but services are provided by post, fax, telephone, broadcast, etc.

This last situation arose in the instructive case of *Alpine Investments BV v Minister Van Financien* [1995] All ER (EC) 543, which concerned Dutch financial services laws banning the cold-calling of customers at home or abroad. The Dutch company prosecuted in this case argued that the law banning the cold-calling of foreign clients infringed Article 59 of the EC Treaty (now Article 56 TFEU). Clearly, the law in question did not discriminate against foreign service providers, but it still restricted the export of services because it directly affected access to the market in other States. Nevertheless, the restriction could be objectively justified in the general interest on grounds of consumer protection or the good reputation of the industry. Moreover, the restriction was proportional (the fact that other countries had no (or less strict) controls on cold-calling was considered irrelevant). It should be noted that, as in the *Cassis de Dijon* case (see **25.2.2**), restrictions like this, which apply without distinction to all service providers, could be justified on a wider range of grounds than those which appear in Article 52 TFEU (public policy, public security and public health).

24.9.3 Need to satisfy local conditions

Whether seeking establishment or providing services, the foreign national who tries to work abroad must satisfy local conditions for pursuit of the activity in question. However (according to *Gebhard*; see **24.9.1**), these conditions:

(a) must be non-discriminatory;

(b) must be justified by imperative requirements in the general interest;

(c) must be suitable for securing the attainment of the objective which they pursue; and

(d) must not go beyond what is necessary to achieve it.

24.9.4 General approach to free movement under EU law

The approach of the Court of Justice in *Gebhard* is very similar to that already established by the Court in relation to goods (see the key case of *Cassis de Dijon* at **25.2.2**). It has been stressed that the approach is common to all cases of free movement. It thus applies in relation to workers under Article 45 TFEU (see *Bosman* at **23.2**), to establishment under Article 49 TFEU (*Gebhard*), and to services under Article 56 TFEU (*Alpine Investments* at **24.9.2**).

CHAPTER 25

FREE MOVEMENT OF GOODS

LEARNING OUTCOMES

After reading this chapter you will be able to understand:

- what rights a producer of goods has to take their goods to another Member State in order to sell them
- what rights a Member State's government has to ban or restrict the importation of undesirable goods
- the extent to which a producer is allowed to advertise their goods in another Member State, and the extent to which the government can restrict this
- what a producer can do if they believe their rights to import, advertise and sell their goods are illegally restricted.

25.1 INTRODUCTION

The free movement of goods is one of the fundamental freedoms on which the EU is based. One of the most important aims of the original Treaty of Rome was to create a single market in goods throughout all the Member States of the Community. Following amendments to the Treaty by the Single European Act 1986, this aim was intended to be achieved by 31 December 1992. Because of the importance of this freedom, the Court of Justice has consistently interpreted the relevant Treaty provisions in such a way as to give maximum effect to this basic objective.

25.2 WHAT DOES THE TREATY PROVIDE?

The principal Treaty provision is Article 34 TFEU, which states that:

> Quantitative restrictions on imports and all measures having equivalent effect shall be prohibited between Member States.

Article 35 TFEU makes similar provision in relation to exports, ie the requirement for or refusal of an export licence.

25.2.1 What is meant by 'quantitative restrictions'?

Quantitative restrictions are limitations on the import of goods fixed by reference to quantitative criteria, ie amount or value ('quotas'). A complete ban on the import of a particular type of goods is also such a restriction (see *Commission of European Communities v Italy* [1961] ECR 317).

25.2.2 What is meant by a 'measure having equivalent effect to a quantitative restriction'?

The phrase 'a measure having equivalent effect to a quantitative restriction' (MEQR) is not defined in the Treaty itself but was defined by the Court of Justice in *Dassonville* [1974] ECR 837. In that case, the phrase was said to extend to 'all trading rules enacted by Member States that are capable of hindering, directly or indirectly, actually or potentially, intra-Community trade'.

It is important to note the following about this definition.

(a) A measure having equivalent effect does not have to have an immediate or substantial effect on intra-Community (now Union) trade. In particular, it is clear from *Re Prantl (Karl)* [1984] ECR 1299 that the Court of Justice will not apply a de minimis principle here. This means that any legislation which is capable of affecting trade between Member States, even indirectly, because it is not the primary aim of the legislation, can infringe Article 34 TFEU. However, the case of *Criminal Proceedings Against Keck and Mithouard* [1995] 1 CMLR 101 shows that for 'selling arrangements' the measure must have the effect of putting the imported goods at a disadvantage before it can be said to restrict imports. Contrary to the view expressed earlier in cases involving Sunday trading laws (*Torfaen Borough Council v B&Q plc* [1989] ECR 765), a restriction on volume of imports (ie, the argument that with shops shut there will be fewer sales and therefore fewer imports) is not enough if domestic goods are at the same disadvantage.

(b) A measure having equivalent effect must be taken by an 'organ of the State'. Actions by private individuals, companies or other undertakings cannot fall within this definition. However, this requirement will be satisfied even if the Member State acts through another undertaking. In *Commission of European Communities v Ireland; Re 'Buy Irish' Campaign* [1982] ECR 4005, the Irish Government initiated a campaign to encourage Irish consumers to buy home-produced goods. The campaign was launched by an Irish Government Minister and was funded by the Government, but was actually managed by a guarantee company set up for the purpose. The fact that it was not the Irish Government which was directly running the campaign did not prevent it being a measure having effect equivalent to a quantitative restriction. Likewise, other State bodies, for example local authorities, licensing authorities or courts, may see their 'measures' (eg, injunctions) controlled in the same way.

(c) A measure having equivalent effect need not affect imported products alone, that is, be 'distinctly applicable' to imports. It could be a measure applying to all goods, domestic and imported, without distinction ('indistinctly applicable'), for example national technical standards. The difference is that whereas the latter can be justified under the 'rule of reason' and so do not infringe Article 34 TFEU at all (see *Cassis de Dijon* below), the former are justifiable only under Article 36 TFEU. The following cases involved distinctly applicable measures. In *International Fruit Co NV v Produktschap voor Groenten en Fruit (No 3)* [1971] ECR 1107, a requirement that a licence be obtained before apples could be imported into France was struck down by the Court of Justice as an infringement of Article 30 of the EC Treaty (now Article 34 TFEU). Similarly, in *Rewe-Zentralfinanz e GmbH v Landwirtschaftskammer* [1975] ECR 843, a requirement that apples had to be inspected before they could be imported into Germany was also held to breach Article 30 of the EC Treaty. Although these types of measure do not completely prevent the marketing of the product, they do result in delay and inconvenience for the importer, which may lead to fewer such products being imported. In both these cases, the measures could not be justified under Article 36 of the EC Treaty (now Article 36 TFEU) which is restrictively interpreted.

Increasingly, the Court of Justice has found measures to be within the *Dassonville* definition, and therefore caught by Article 34 TFEU, where the domestic product is also affected by the measure in question. The leading case is *Rewe Zentral v Bundesmonopolverwaltung fur Branntwein (Cassis de Dijon)* [1979] ECR 649. A German law required that spirits such as Cassis de Dijon should be of a stipulated alcoholic strength. Cassis was significantly less strong and therefore could not be sold on the German market. The Court held that the German law fell within the *Dassonville* definition and was in breach of Article 30 of the EC Treaty (now Article 34 TFEU). The case is considered vital to the development of a single market in that it shows that imported products do not have to be changed to meet national technical standards unless the need to do so is justified. The case is considered further in **25.3.1**.

25.3 ARE THERE CIRCUMSTANCES IN WHICH ARTICLE 34 TFEU WILL NOT APPLY?

25.3.1 The 'rule of reason'

Although it is no answer to an Article 34 TFEU complaint to say that the measure in question affects the equivalent domestic product as well as the imported one, it is important to know whether or not this is the case. This is because only such a measure can benefit from the 'rule of reason' approach of the Court of Justice in *Cassis de Dijon* referred to above. The Court recognised in that case that if goods were lawfully manufactured in a particular way in a given Member State, they should ordinarily be entitled to move throughout the rest of the Union. However, where the EU itself had not imposed Union-wide standards, disparities between Member States' legislation could be acceptable. In the words of the Court:

> [O]bstacles to movement within the Community [now Union] resulting from disparities between the national laws relating to the marketing of products must be accepted in so far as those provisions are necessary in order to satisfy mandatory requirements relating in particular to the effectiveness of fiscal supervision, the protection of public health, the fairness of commercial transactions and the defence of the consumer.

The list of mandatory requirements is not closed. The Court has since added to them the protection of the environment (see *Commission of European Communities v Denmark; sub nom Re Disposable Beer Cans* [1989] 1 CMLR 619), the protection of culture (eg, the cinema from the threat of video cassettes in *Cinethèque v Fédération Nationale des Cinemas Français* [1986] 1 CMLR B65) and employment in the Sunday trading cases. The list inevitably includes (but is much wider than) the list of justifications in Article 36 TFEU.

In order for a measure to be 'necessary' to satisfy a mandatory requirement, the aim of the measure in question must be justifiable in EU law and the measure taken must be *proportionate* to that aim. Therefore, if the aim could be achieved by a measure which was less restrictive of the free movement of goods, the measure taken will be held to be disproportionate. In *Cassis de Dijon*, the German Government successfully argued that the law in question was for the defence of the consumer, but the Court found that it was nevertheless disproportionate to its objective: the same aim could have been achieved by a law requiring that such spirits should be clearly labelled with their alcoholic strength.

25.3.2 The Treaty on the Functioning of the European Union

Where a government measure is distinctly applicable (ie, provides different conditions for imported goods), it can only be justified under the terms of the Treaty, ie Article 36 TFEU.

Article 36 TFEU provides a number of important exceptions to Article 34 TFEU. It states that:

> The provisions of Articles 34 to 35 shall not preclude prohibitions or restrictions on imports, exports or goods in transit justified on grounds of public morality, public policy or public security; the protection of health and life of humans, animals or plants; the protection of national treasures possessing artistic, historical or archaeological value; or the protection of industrial or commercial property. Such prohibitions or restrictions shall not, however, constitute a means of arbitrary discrimination or a disguised restriction on trade between Member States.

As this Article derogates from a fundamental principle of the EU, the Court construes it strictly; in particular, no further justifiable restrictions can be read into the list given above.

Further, the burden of establishing that a measure does come within Article 36 TFEU will fall on the relevant Member State.

The following points should be borne in mind when considering the exceptions in Article 36 TFEU.

25.3.2.1 Public morality

The Court of Justice will not seek to impose its own standards of morality; what is required in this area will be a matter for each Member State (see *DPP v Darby; DPP v Henn* [1979] ECR 3795). It is important to appreciate the significance of the final sentence of Article 36 TFEU, ie the measure taken by the Member State must not amount to arbitrary discrimination against the imported product, or to a disguised restriction on trade. In *Darby and Henn*, the seizure of imported pornography by UK customs was not in breach of Article 30 of the EC Treaty (now Article 34 TFEU) as that type of pornography could not be lawfully sold in the UK. On the other hand, in *Conegate v Customs and Excise Commissioners* [1986] ECR 1007, the import of rubber dolls into the UK could not be prevented because if they had been produced in this country they could lawfully have been sold here.

25.3.2.2 Public policy

A Member State cannot invoke public policy whenever it is convenient to do so to avoid falling foul of Article 34 TFEU. The Court of Justice has made it clear that this exception can be used only where there is a serious threat to a fundamental interest of society. See, for example, *R v Thompson (Brian Ernest)* [1978] ECR 2247, where it was applied to the right to mint coinage. Economic reasons, for example protection of industry from competition, are never, however, acceptable.

25.3.2.3 Public security

Similarly, public security cannot be readily called upon in defence of a breach of Article 34 TFEU. It seems clear only that it extends to the need to safeguard essential public services. Note *Campus Oil Ltd v The Minister for Industry and Energy* [1984] ECR 2727, where the Irish Government required importers of petrol to buy a percentage of their needs from an Irish refinery to ensure that the refinery remained viable. It seems that it can relate to the State's internal as well as external security (*Minister of Finance v Richardt* [1992] 1 CMLR 61).

25.3.2.4 Public health

In the absence of EU standards, Member States are entitled to decide what is appropriate for their own citizens in the field of public health. In the case of *Aragonesa de Publicidad v Departmamento de Sanidad y Seguridad Social de la Generalitat de Cataluna* [1991] OJ C220/8, the Court of Justice upheld on public health grounds Spanish legislation which prohibited roadside advertisements for strong spirits. Despite the later case of *Keck and Mithouard* (see **25.4.1**), this case may still involve a measure equivalent to quantitative restriction (MEQR) as it may be indirectly discriminatory against imported spirits not known to the Spanish public. It is, however, clearly justified.

Again, it is essential to pay close attention to the last sentence of Article 36 TFEU. For example, in *Commission of European Communities v United Kingdom; sub nom Re Imports of Poultry Meat* [1982] ECR 2793, where the UK Government prohibited the import of French poultry into the UK, ostensibly in order to avoid the spread of Newcastle Disease, the evidence indicated that the prohibition was unnecessarily restrictive and in reality was intended to protect the English poultry industry. It should be noted that in most areas there are now Directives laying down the minimum requirements for health or animal welfare. For example, EU Directives lay down minimum rules for the carriage of live animals and their stunning before slaughter. It is not a sufficient justification for the refusal of an export licence for live animals that these rules may be ignored in the importing State (see *R v Ministry of Agriculture, Fisheries and Food, ex p Hedley Lomas (Ireland) Ltd* [1996] All ER (EC) 493). The refusal will breach Article 35 TFEU.

25.3.2.5 The protection of national treasures and intellectual property rights

The exception for the protection of national treasures, although not yet used, is likely to be of value where a Member State wishes to impose an export ban on items representing part of its national heritage, ie in breach of Article 35 TFEU.

Intellectual property rights have posed difficulties for the Court of Justice. In the absence of Union-wide regimes, such rights are granted by individual Member States and relate only to the territory of the State in question. This offers enterprises an opportunity to divide up the market on national lines. This is clearly contrary to the spirit of the Union. Because of this the Court of Justice has been careful not to over-extend the protection given to intellectual property rights in Article 36 TFEU. Accordingly, the Court has distinguished between the existence and the exercise of intellectual property rights. Thus, measures (eg, court injunctions keeping out imports of goods infringing a patent) are not caught by Article 34 TFEU even if their effect is to restrict imports (because of Article 36 TFEU).

In order to protect the existence of intellectual property rights, however, the Court has had to decide what the existence of each right amounts to. It has done this by developing the concept of the 'specific subject matter' of a right. Thus, for example, the specific subject matter of a patent is the exclusive right to use an invention for the manufacture of products and to be the first to market them (*Centrafarm BV and De Peijper v Sterling Drug Inc* [1974] ECR 1147). This means that once a company has marketed (or consented to the marketing of) a drug in, say, France, it cannot thereafter purport to use its patent rights in, say, the UK to prevent the import of the patented product. The products marketed in France could therefore be re-imported into the UK and the patent holder or UK court could not interfere with their free movement. The company's rights over that particular product were 'exhausted' when it consented to its marketing in France. The Court of Justice has adopted a similar approach to trade mark rights and copyright. This protection of 'parallel imports' through exhaustion of rights applies only where the goods are marketed within the EU. The Court has ruled in *Silhouette International Schmied GmbH & Co KG v Hartlauer Handelsgesellschaft mbH* [1998] 3 WLR 1218 that following the harmonisation of trade mark rights through the 1989 Directive, Member States' laws can no longer recognise a wider principle of world-wide exhaustion (ie, through marketing outside the EU). Thus manufacturers can use their national trade marks to keep out goods which they authorised for sale only in countries outside the EU.

25.4 SUMMARY OF THE POSITION REGARDING TRADING MEASURES

The problem may be tackled by asking a series of questions.

25.4.1 Is the measure an MEQR (*Dassonville* test)?

To be an MEQR, the rule in question must affect the product itself, ie require some change, before it can be sold in the territory. In general, rules about *selling arrangements* (ie, the arrangements for selling the product once it is imported), for example Sunday trading, licensing hours, and prohibitions on selling at a loss (*Keck and Mithouard*), do not come within the *Dassonville* formula and thus (in the absence of discrimination) need no justification. Although they may restrict the volume of imports (if you sell less, you import less), these measures do not put imports at a disadvantage and thus cannot count as MEQRs.

Advertising restrictions, for example bans on leaflets (*GB-INNO-BM v Confédération du Commerce Luxembourgeoise Asbl* [1991] 2 CMLR 801) or comparative advertising (*Unwesen in den Wirtschaft eV v Yves Rocher GmbH* (1994) *Financial Times*, 9 June), may well put the imported product at a disadvantage because advertising is the most effective way for new imported products to penetrate a market. The rival domestic products may well be better known. It would, however, seem that restrictions on retailers advertising their sales (eg, *Hünermund v Landespothekerkammer*

Baden-Württemberg [1993] ECR I-6787, where German pharmacists were prohibited from advertising off the premises, or *Leclerc v TFI Publicité* [1995] ECR I-179, where French retailers could not advertise at all on French television and thus were restricted in advertising their cheap foreign fuel) are to be treated as selling arrangements under *Keck and Mithouard*. By contrast, a blanket ban on advertising a particular product, for example alcoholic products or toys, would be seen, it is felt, as either a restriction to be justified under the 'rule of reason' in *Cassis de Dijon* or a case of indirect discrimination against imports which would have to be justified on similar objective criteria (see *Konsumentombudsmannen (KO) v De Agostini (Svenska) Forlag AB; Konsumentom-budsmannen (KO) v TV-Shop I Sverige AB (De Agostini)* [1997] All ER (EC) 687).

25.4.2 If it is an MEQR, does it apply only to imports (ie distinctly applicable measures) or directly discriminate (as selling arrangements)?

The best example of this is the French ban on British beef. This could only be justified under Article 30 EC (now Article 36 TFEU) (eg, protection of public health) but the French failed to prove a sufficient health risk. It therefore was a distinctly applicable breach which the French had failed to justify.

Likewise, an injunction prohibiting the imports of goods said to infringe a national patent could only be justified under Article 36 TFEU (protection of intellectual property rights).

25.4.3 Does the measure apply to all products (ie indistinctly applicable measures) or (if a selling arrangement) indirectly discriminate?

Measures which apply to all goods (domestic and imported) without distinction will be caught by Article 34 TFEU only if they put the imported goods at a disadvantage compared with domestic goods. Thus, where the imported product has to be adapted before it can be sold on the domestic market it is prima facie at a disadvantage compared with domestic products which are made to domestic specifications. Here, because we are dealing with indirect discrimination, the measure infringes Article 34 TFEU unless it can be shown to be justified by a public interest objective (eg, consumer protection, health, environment, etc – the list given in *Cassis de Dijon* is not exhaustive) which is proportional and takes precedence over the free movement of goods. If so justified, there is no Article 34 TFEU infringement. Measures falling into this category would be German measures on purity of spirits (*Cassis de Dijon*), sausages, beer, etc; packaging rules (eg, Danish or German rules on recyclable bottles or containers – these may be justified on environmental protection grounds (see *Commission of European Communities v Kingdom of Denmark; sub nom Re Disposable Beer Cans* [1989] 1 CMLR 619)), rules on labelling, weight, trade marks, etc. In *Verband Sozialer Wettbewerb eV v Clinique Laboratories SNC and Estée Lauder Cosmetics* (Case C-315/92) [1994] ECR I-317, the cosmetic 'Clinique' could not be marketed under that mark in Germany because it was considered to suggest therapeutic properties which it did not have. Since the cosmetic had to be repackaged for sale in Germany, there was clearly an indirect restriction on imports which could not be justified on the basis of protecting consumers from confusion.

Since the effect of *Cassis de Dijon* is that Member States must mutually recognise different product standards which give equivalent protective effect, modern product standard Directives under the '1992' campaign (and after) have merely set a minimum level of protection ('the essential requirements') which different national products can satisfy. The obligatory Euro standard is a thing of the past, except for hazardous products like drugs and motor cars where full harmonisation of the specification requirements may be needed. In other areas, Euro standards are considered optional.

25.5 HOW TO USE ARTICLE 34 TFEU

Article 34 TFEU is directly effective; this means it can be relied upon before national courts and tribunals. It can therefore be used defensively, for example in response to a criminal prosecution for breach of trading standards in another Member State, or offensively, for example to challenge a 'buy national' campaign. In the latter case, the challenger must follow the most appropriate national procedure and claim the most effective national remedy. The Court of Justice has made it clear that a Member State is under an obligation to provide an effective remedy for infringement of EU rights. Thus (using a pre-Brexit UK example), a challenge to a Government-sponsored 'buy national' campaign would be made by judicial review proceedings for a declaration that the Government was acting ultra vires, accompanied by a claim for an injunction (see *R v Secretary of State for Transport, ex p Factortame (No 2)* (Case C-213/89) [1990] 3 WLR 818) or possibly damages (see *R v Secretary of State for Transport, ex p Factortame (No 4)* [1996] 2 WLR 506). The case of *Brasserie du Pêcheur*, decided with *Factortame (No 4)*, concerned a damages claim under Article 30 of the EC Treaty (now Article 34 TFEU) by beer importers who fell foul of Germany's purity laws. Since the particular restrictions (relating to a ban on additives) were not manifestly unlawful at the time, no damages were payable.

It should be noted that all new national rules on product standards have to be notified to Brussels under Directive 83/189. The failure to do so will invalidate the national law because Directive 83/189 has direct effect. (See *CIA Security International SA v Signalson SA* [1996] 2 CMLR 781.) This, too, may be used as a defence.

CHAPTER 26

COMPETITION LAW

LEARNING OUTCOMES

After reading this chapter you will be able to understand:

- what restrictions there may be on a business's ability to make arrangements with other businesses which relate to how they ply their trade
- what restrictions there may on a business's ability to make decisions which impact on other businesses
- what consequences there may be for breach of legislation is this area
- what exceptions may be relied upon to escape liability.

26.1 INTRODUCTION

The regulation of competition between businesses is as important to the Union as the attainment of the freedoms discussed in the previous chapters. It is of little use to provide that goods can move freely throughout the Union unless at the same time businesses are able to trade across frontiers without facing improper competition. Improper competition, particularly where it has the effect of dividing up markets along national lines, must be controlled. Thus, Article 3(1)(b) TFEU states that one of the activities of the Union is the institution of a system ensuring that competition in the internal market is not distorted. This system is principally established in two Articles of the Treaty: Articles 101 and 102 TFEU. Article 101 TFEU controls anti-competitive agreements, while Article 102 TFEU regulates an abuse of a dominant position. It should be remembered that the object of any competition law is greater customer choice, either of manufacturers (different brands) or of dealers supplying the same brand. More competition equals more choice; this in turn compels competing manufacturers (or dealers) to cut costs and improve quality of goods or services.

26.2 ANTI-COMPETITIVE AGREEMENTS: ARTICLE 101 TFEU

26.2.1 What does Article 101 TFEU provide?

Article 101 TFEU provides that:

> The following shall be prohibited as incompatible with the internal market: all agreements between undertakings, decisions by associations of undertakings and concerted practices which may affect trade between Member States and which have as their object or effect the prevention, restriction or distortion of competition within the internal market ...

It then gives examples of the types of conduct which would be caught by this definition, such as fixing prices, controlling production and sharing markets. To discover what other practices may be within Article 101 TFEU, it is necessary to look at the Article in detail.

26.2.1.1 Agreements between undertakings

The term 'undertaking' is not defined in the Treaty but is taken to include any business enterprise, whatever legal form it may take. In particular, under English law it will include a company or a partnership, a sole trader or a trade association. A parent and a subsidiary company are usually taken to amount to a single undertaking for this purpose. Likewise, agreements between a company and its employees or agents are unlikely to be agreements 'between undertakings' as they lack the necessary independence.

Not only written agreements between two or more such undertakings but also less formal arrangements, such as a mere understanding or 'gentlemen's agreement', may breach Article 101 TFEU (see the *Quinine Cartel* case, *Boehringer Mannheim GmbH v Commission of the European Communities* [1970] ECR 661). It was originally thought that Article 85 of the EC Treaty (now Article 101 TFEU) applied only to agreements between potential competitors, ie 'horizontal agreements' between undertakings at the same level of the production process, for example the traditional cartel where manufacturers meet in secret to carve up markets or fix prices. The agreement may, however, be a 'vertical' one, that is between undertakings involved at different stages of the manufacturing or trading process, for example an agreement between a wholesaler and a retailer. Even if the manufacturer is not involved in distribution itself, restrictions, eg on prices or exports, can affect competition between distributors (see, for example, *Consten SA and Grundig-Verkaufs-GmbH (Etablissements) v EEC Commission* [1996] CMLR 418).

26.2.1.2 Decisions by associations of undertakings

The phrase 'decisions by associations of undertakings' would include, for example, decisions taken by a trade association, whether or not they were legally binding.

26.2.1.3 Concerted practices

An enterprise may breach Article 101 TFEU if it deliberately co-ordinates its behaviour with another business in the same market, for example if they agree to raise prices at the same time and by the same amount. It is not necessary to be able to prove an agreement that they should do so; the fact of synchronised activity may be enough, so that, in the words of the European Court in *Dyestuffs* [1972] ECR 619, 'the parties have substituted practical co-operation for the risks of competition'. It is important to appreciate that a business is entitled to respond to market conditions, including the behaviour of its competitors. This may well mean that enterprises operating within the same market do show similar behaviour without there being a 'concerted practice'.

26.2.1.4 How much of an effect does there have to be on trade between Member States?

Article 101 TFEU states that it is necessary that the agreement, etc 'may' have an effect on trade. According to the Court of Justice in *STM v Maschinenbau Ulm* [1966] ECR 235:

> it must be possible to foresee with a sufficient degree of probability on the basis of a set of objective factors of law or fact that the agreement in question may have an influence, direct or indirect, actual or potential, on the pattern of trade between Member States.

Such an effect may result even where the parties to the agreement or concerted practice are based within one Member State if the effect is to distort competition elsewhere in the EU, for example because a company based in another Member State is unable to break into that market (see *Vereeniging van Cementhandelaren v Commission of the European Communities (No 2)* (Case 8/72) [1972] ECR 977 (the *Dutch Cement* case)).

It can even occur where the parties are based outside the EU, provided the agreement or practice is implemented within it (*Re Wood Pulp Cartel* [1988] ECR 5193).

It has been held by the Court of Justice that Article 101 TFEU can apply to exclusive distribution agreements in countries outside the EU (here Russia, the Ukraine and Slovenia), which contain restrictions on exporting into the EU. Here, the distribution agreements for Yves St Laurent Perfumes were subject to French law and jurisdiction. The French courts therefore would be entitled to rule that the agreements were invalid under Article 81(2) EC (now Article 101(2) TFEU) (see *Javico v Yves St Laurent* (1998) *Financial Times*, 13 May).

This part of Article 101 TFEU therefore determines the jurisdiction of the EU competition authorities. But it also sets out clearly the policy of EU competition law, which is partly to create a single market. Agreements which have the effect of partitioning the single market (eg, exclusive territories for dealers) are prima facie likely to infringe Article 101 TFEU.

26.2.1.5 '. . . which have as their object or effect'

If, objectively, the parties intend the agreement or the practice to prevent, restrict or distort competition, there is no need to consider further what the effect of the agreement might be. On the other hand, if that is not the object, but it would be its effect, then Article 101 TFEU will still be breached.

26.2.1.6 'the prevention, restriction or distortion of competition'

The words 'the prevention, restriction or distortion of competition' are given their ordinary meaning. However, if the effect is likely to be minimal, Article 101(1) TFEU will not be breached (*Volk v Verwaecke* [1969] ECR 295). See further the Commission's Notice on Agreements of Minor Importance in **26.2.4**.

It should be remembered that even if the agreement has no effect on competition between the parties, it may still be prohibited by Article 101 TFEU if its effect is to restrict competition with third parties. This is the case with vertical agreements such as the exclusive distribution agreement which may restrict intra-brand competition between the different dealers.

26.2.2 Can an undertaking apply for clearance that its arrangements are outside Article 101 TFEU?

This possibility was removed as from 1 May 2004, except that the Commission does have the power 'to adopt a decision of a declaratory nature finding that the prohibition in Article [101] or Article [102] of the Treaty does not apply'. Indications are that this power will be used sparingly. Parties must generally now 'self-assess', ie decide for themselves whether their arrangement is permitted by Article 101(3) TFEU. Their decision may be challenged by national competition authorities, the Commission, or by national courts, should it be relevant in court proceedings.

26.2.3 What is the result if there is a breach of Article 101 TFEU?

According to Article 101(2) TFEU, any agreement or decision prohibited by Article 101(1) TFEU is automatically void. This means that any agreement is unenforcable. It may be possible to sever offending clauses from the agreement and leave the rest of it standing. Whether this is possible depends on the domestic law to which the agreement is subject. Thus, under English law, such clauses can be severed if the remaining agreement still reflects accurately the agreement reached by the parties (*Chemidus Wavin v Société pour la Transformation et l'Exploitation des Resines Industrielles SA* [1978] 3 CMLR 514). Because Article 101(1) TFEU has been held to be directly effective, it seems that a party whose business interests are being or have been harmed by the anti-competitive agreement may seek an injunction to restrain operation of the agreement and may be able to claim damages (*Garden Cottage Foods v Milk Marketing Board* [1983] 3 WLR 143). In addition, the Commission and national competition authorities have the power to levy fines upon the parties to an anti-competitive agreement, the size of the fine (up to a maximum of 10% of turnover) being dependent on the degree of fault. A recent fine for Microsoft was in the sum of £335 million.

26.2.4 Are there any ways out for a business which seems to be at risk of breaching this Article?

There are primarily three ways in which a business may avoid breaching Article 101 TFEU.

26.2.4.1 The Notice on Agreements of Minor Importance

The Commission, which is responsible for implementing the EU's competition policy, has issued a Notice on Agreements of Minor Importance. According to this Notice, only agreements which have an appreciable effect on trade between Member States should be taken as breaching Article 101 TFEU. The questions parties must ask themselves to decide whether they fit within the Notice are:

- Does the parties' combined market share exceed 10% in the case of a *horizontal* arrangement (ie between those at the same level of the supply chain, such as competitors) or 15% in the case of a *vertical* arrangement (such as between supplier and distributor, or distributor and wholesaler)? If it does, the Notice does not apply.
- Is competition in the market restricted by the cumulative effect of similar agreements entered into by a number of suppliers or distributors? If so, the Notice will not apply if the parties' market share is not less than 5%.
- If the arrangement is horizontal, does it have provisions which have as their object the prevention, restriction or distortion of competition, such as those fixing prices, limiting exports or sales, or allocating markets or customers? If so, the Notice will not apply.
- If the arrangement is vertical, does it contain any 'hardcore' restrictions prohibited by the vertical restraints block exemption (see **26.2.5**)? If not, the Notice will not apply.

If the parties meet the requisite criteria, the Notice will apply and the arrangement will be assumed not to have an appreciable effect on trade and so will be taken as not breaching Article 101.

The Notice does not give complete legal protection because the market may be a very specialised one where even small companies (especially with patent protection) may have more than the relevant percentage.

26.2.4.2 Article 101(3) TFEU

It may be possible to avoid the effects of Article 101(2) TFEU for a particular agreement because of the operation of Article 101(3) TFEU. This provides for exemption for any agreement which:

(a) contributes to improving the production or distribution of goods, or to promoting technical or economic progress; and

(b) allows consumers a fair share of the resulting benefit; and

(c) does not impose on the undertakings concerned restrictions which are not indispensable to the attainment of these objectives; and

(d) does not afford such undertakings the possibility of eliminating competition in respect of a substantial part of the products in question.

Thus, to satisfy Article 101(3) TFEU, the agreement must bring with it certain benefits while at the same time not including excessive restriction of competition.

As mentioned at **26.2.2** above, parties must decide for themselves whether they fit within Article 101(3) TFEU.

26.2.4.3 Using a block exemption

The Commission in the early years of the Community was inundated with individual notifications, and it was not unusual for years to go by without a reply being received from the

Commission. To try to deal with this volume of agreements, the Commission began to introduce block exemptions (as Article 101(3) TFEU and its predecessors allow them) for particular categories of agreement which fulfil the conditions for an exemption.

Note that since the Commission alone can give an exemption, severance by national courts is not possible as the parties must stick to the terms of the block exemption before it can apply (see *Delimitis v Henninger Braü* [1991] ECR 1-935). Thus, firms which wish to have the certainty of a valid agreement must take particular care to draft their agreements to fit the relevant block exemption. If they include restrictions which are not allowed by the block exemption, the block exemption cannot apply and the national court generally cannot sever restrictions before applying the block exemption.

26.2.5 Using a typical block exemption: vertical restraints

In June 2022, a block exemption was passed which covers all types of vertical arrangements, such as exclusive distribution, exclusive purchasing (eg, beer ties) and franchising. This is Regulation 2022/720. Regulation 2022/720 exempts in Article 2(1) all vertical agreements (ie, between two or more parties at different levels of the production or distribution chain). There are basically four things to check.

26.2.5.1 Is it vertical?

Under the exemption in Article 2(1), the parties to the agreement must be at different levels, but this would take in a number of different agreements involving goods or services, such as exclusive distribution, selective distribution, franchises and exclusive purchasing. Exemptions would also cover exclusive supply agreements (eg, where a large retailer persuades a supplier of parts to supply only the retailer). Unlike previous block exemptions, it is no longer necessary to identify which type of vertical agreement one is dealing with.

The exemption can apply to multi-party agreements provided they are still vertical. Thus Article 2(2) specifically refers to agreements between a supplier and a trade association of small retailers. There is no reason why a British manufacturer wishing to distribute its product in France should not agree to supply the various retailers in such a trade association and achieve national retail coverage that way rather than supply an individual distributor.

It can also apply even though the chosen distributor is another manufacturer and thus a potential competitor. There is a danger here of the arrangements operating as a horizontal cartel, but provided the arrangements are not reciprocal the exemption can still apply (Article 2(4)).

The exemption does not apply to agreements which are primarily concerned with licensing intellectual property (IP) rights, for example patent, trade mark, copyright or software licences (Article 2(3)). Licensing of 'technology' (patents, software copyright, know-how) is covered by a Technology Transfer Block Exemption (Regulation 316/2014).

26.2.5.2 Prohibited list

Assuming that the agreement is vertical then the exemption under Article 2(1) applies to all vertical restraints otherwise prohibited by Article 101 TFEU, unless the agreement contains prohibited clauses. So, the second stage is to check the prohibited list in Article 4. Some of the prohibited clauses are directed to particular types of agreement, so it may be helpful to see how this applies to exclusive distribution and selective distribution.

If it is *exclusive or selective distribution* the clauses to avoid are as follows:

(a) Article 4(a) – price fixing. This includes minimum prices (which effectively prevent discounts) as well as fixed prices. It does not include maximum or recommended prices unless the price has become in practice fixed through pressure from the supplier. It may be worth considering why prices would be recommended – this may be more justified in selective distribution or franchising than in exclusive distribution.

(b) Article 4(b) – Restrictions on the buyer's resales to customers or into other territories. It should be noticed that only restrictions on the buyer (the distributor) are prohibited; the block exemption would certainly cover restrictions on the supplier selling into the buyer's territory (the essence, of course, of exclusive distribution).

The restrictions on buyer resales under Article 4(b) are split into three categories: restrictions where there is an exclusive distribution system, restrictions where there is a selective distribution system (where distributors are appointed according to specified criteria), and restrictions where there are neither. There are minor differences between the restrictions between these categories, and those details are beyond the scope of this chapter, which aims to summarise the main highlights rather than deal with every nuance in the block exemption. Generally, however, restrictions which are permitted by Article 4(b) are:

- active sales restrictions (ie approaching customers) in territories or customer groups reserved for the supplier or a maximum of five other distributors;
- active or passive sales restrictions (passive being where the customer approaches the distributor) into a territory where the supplier operates a selective distribution system (a system where distributors are selected using certain criteria);
- restrictions on the distributor's place of establishment;
- active or passive sales restrictions placed on a wholesaler selling to end users;
- active or passive sales of components to customers who would use them to manufacture the same type of goods as those produced by the supplier.

Article 4 makes special mention of internet sales. It prohibits restrictions which prevent the effective use of the internet by the distributor to sell the goods, subject to the supplier's ability to restrict online advertising that does not have the object of preventing the use of an 'entire online advertising channel'.

26.2.5.3 Market share

Once it is clear there are no prohibited clauses, the agreement (and all its restrictions) is covered by the exemption, but it is still necessary to check whether either party has more than 30% of the relevant market. If either has, the block exemption cannot apply (Article 3). The rationale for this is that the Commission needs to be satisfied that the agreement does not substantially eliminate competition. Equally, the bigger the market share, the closer the firm comes to being dominant on that market, at which point many of the restrictions permitted under the block exemption would be seen as abuses under Article 102 TFEU. Thirty per cent has always been taken as the bottom line for dominance. So, even though most cases would be well over 40%, the Commission would still want to vet these agreements individually to be sure.

26.2.5.4 Severable restrictions

This leaves one final step, which is to check through Article 5 to see whether there are any severable restrictions in the agreement. These restrictions, which all concern non-compete obligations, do not destroy the exemption given to other vertical restraints. The national court is permitted to sever them from the agreement (assuming this is possible under its own national rules). The restrictions are:

(a) *Non-compete obligations (including exclusive purchase)*. These must be for a fixed term under five years, although, for beer ties with tenanted pubs, the duration could be the length of the lease. Any indefinite exclusive purchase obligation will thus be void but severable. Article 1(b) defines such clauses to include those where the buyer has to take more than 80% of their purchases from the supplier. Thus, in beer ties, the pub may well be taking a guest beer. If guest beers make up less than 20% of the beer supply, the supplier needs to be wary of Article 5.

(b) *Post-term restrictive covenants.* These are void if unjustified. But, under Article 5(b), they benefit from the exemption only if they are confined to the same premises, the same goods and a maximum duration of one year. Moreover, and most importantly, they can be justified only if they are there to protect trade secrets ('know-how'). It is unlikely that such covenants could ever be justified in exclusive distribution. There will, however, be trade secrets to protect in franchises, and possibly in selective distribution.

(c) Selective distribution dealers can never be prevented from selling competing goods, but such clauses are severable.

(d) Any obligation on a buyer of online intermediation services (a service normally provided for remuneration, at a distance, by electronic means and at the individual request of a recipient of services) not to sell to end users under more favourable conditions via competing online intermediation services. Any such restriction would be severable.

26.2.6 Agency agreements

The Commission has stated in its Guidelines on Vertical Restraints that such agreements will be outside Article 101 TFEU provided the agent accepts no financial risks and the principal is responsible for setting prices and terms. The point here is that such an agent is integrated into the principal's business and thus is not an independent undertaking. The Commission has now put the Notice in its new guidelines on vertical agreements.

26.2.7 Mergers

In principle, when two companies merge (eg, one takes over the other) they cease to be independent undertakings and thus the agreement between them cannot be caught by Article 101 TFEU.

26.3 ABUSE OF A DOMINANT POSITION: ARTICLE 102 TFEU

26.3.1 What is the general effect of Article 102 TFEU?

Article 102 TFEU renders unlawful any behaviour which amounts to an abuse of its position by an undertaking which is dominant in its particular market. It will therefore be crucially important, when faced with a potential breach of Article 102 TFEU, to identify the relevant market; it will be seen that undertakings with quite small shares of one market can be dominant in a section of that market and so be at risk from Article 102 TFEU. It will also be seen that a distinction has to be drawn between an undertaking legitimately taking advantage of what may be a hard-won dominant position and an undertaking which illegitimately abuses that position.

26.3.2 What does Article 102 TFEU provide?

According to Article 102 TFEU:

> Any abuse by one or more undertakings of a dominant position within the internal market or in a substantial part of it shall be prohibited as incompatible with the internal market in so far as it may affect trade between Member States.

The Article then goes on to give a non-exclusive list of the types of behaviour which might amount to such an abuse, for example an undertaking imposing unfair trading conditions, such as unfair prices.

26.3.2.1 What is a dominant position within the internal market?

It is by no means essential for an undertaking to be in a monopoly position throughout the EU. The guiding principle here is that an undertaking is likely to be dominant where its economic strength allows it to behave independently of other operators within the market (*United Brands Co (New Jersey, USA) and United Brands Continentaal B (Rotterdam, The Netherlands) v EC Commission* [1978] ECR 207). An example of the principle is where a manufacturing company can set prices or conditions of supply to retailers of its product without regard to the prices or conditions imposed by its competitors. This is more likely to be the case where the undertaking has a larger market share. (In *Hilti v Commission of the European Communities* [1992] 4 CMLR 16, for example, an undertaking was held to be dominant with a 70–80% share of its market.) However, a relatively low market share does not necessarily mean that the undertaking is not dominant. In *United Brands*, dominance was established although the company had a market share of only 40–45%. A particularly important factor to take into account here is whether there are barriers to entry for other undertakings who might wish to enter the market. Does the allegedly dominant undertaking, for example, possess intellectual property rights which would create such a barrier? Whether or not an undertaking is dominant can be considered only in relation to a particular market. In order to identify the relevant market it is important to look at two things: the product market and the geographic market.

How is the product market recognised?

The key question in recognising the product market is 'what other product, if any, can be substituted for the product in question, given the nature of it, its price and its intended use?'. If a number of products are interchangeable, from the point of view of the user, it is arguable that they are all part of one market. On the other hand, if there is no acceptable alternative to the product in question then it can form a market on its own. In *United Brands*, the Court of Justice found that bananas represented a single market because, in certain respects, bananas could not easily be replaced by another fruit. In particular, children and the elderly or the infirm might find it easier to digest bananas than any other fruit.

Similarly, in *Hugin Kassareregister AB and Hugin Cash Registers v EC Commission* [1979] ECR 1869, the Court of Justice found that spare parts for Hugin cash registers represented a separate market in their own right because, once a customer had bought a Hugin machine, no other spare parts could be used. Clearly, if the product market is drawn so narrowly, an undertaking may find itself dominant even if its share of, say, the fruit market or the market for spare parts for cash registers generally is very small.

How is the geographic market recognised?

It is important to look at the geographic area within which the undertaking markets the product where the conditions of competition are the same. Here, too, the definition of the geographical scope of the market is based on substitutability; how far will customers look for their substitute product if the firm's product is unobtainable or too pricey. In many cases, this will be the whole of the single market, but factors such as cultural preferences, the personal nature of services contracts and the costs of transporting heavier goods may restrict the market to a particular region or country.

Article 102 TFEU applies where an undertaking is dominant in the common market or a substantial part of it. Dominance within a single Member State is likely to be within a substantial part of the common market.

26.3.2.2 What amounts to an abuse of a dominant position?

There are broadly two types of abusive behaviour: one affects competitors or potential competitors in the field; the other affects consumers. Abuse affecting competitors would include pricing the undertaking's products so low that those competitors are forced out of the market, or requiring purchasers of one type of product to buy other products produced by the same undertaking in order to tie them in to a single supplier. Examples of abuses affecting consumers would be setting prices extortionately high, or requiring the product to be sold in certain outlets only.

26.3.3 Are there any exceptions to Article 102 TFEU?

There is no equivalent in Article 102 TFEU of Article 101(3) TFEU (see **26.2.4.2**); the Commission cannot grant an individual exemption from Article 102 TFEU, nor are there block exemptions. Even if an undertaking is entitled to claim the benefit of a block exemption under Article 101(3) TFEU for its activities, that does not necessarily mean that such activities do not amount to an abuse of a dominant position (*Tetra Pak Rausing SA v Commission of the European Communities* [1991] FSR 654). The Commission will, in theory, give guidance letters on whether an action represents a breach, but it is thought that such guidance letters will be few and far between.

26.3.4 What are the sanctions for breach of Article 102 TFEU?

The Commission and national competition authorities have the power to fine undertakings for breaches of Article 102 TFEU. As there is no possibility of exemption, there is no equivalent of Article 101(3) TFEU. Behaviour in breach of Article 102 TFEU may also give rise to civil liability. It seems that under English law, an injunction can be granted to restrain breaches of Article 102 TFEU, and it is arguable that damages could also be sought (see *Garden Cottage Foods* at **26.2.3**).

26.4 CHAPTER SUMMARY

Article 102 TFEU cases are likely to be rare for most solicitors. Article 101 TFEU, however, is likely to be of much greater relevance.

In drafting commercial agreements, such as licensing agreements for intellectual property rights, distribution agreements, joint ventures (or other arrangements with potential competitors), franchise agreements and exclusive purchasing arrangements (eg, beer ties with public houses or solus agreements for petrol stations), the practitioner has to take Article 101 TFEU into account. They should consider in turn:

(1) whether the restrictive agreement might affect trade between Member States;

(2) whether it is covered by the Notice on Agreements of Minor Importance (but this is only limited security as market share may change). The determination of the relevant market is as critical here as under Article 102 TFEU;

(3) for full certainty that the agreement is valid; however, the parties must draft their agreement to fit the relevant block exemption Regulation (eg Regulation 2022/720);

(4) if the parties wish to include clauses which are not permitted by a block exemption, the agreement is likely to be void under Article 101(2) TFEU and thus (subject to severance) unenforceable in the national courts, unless the parties show that the agreement fits within the exemption contained in Article 101(3) TFEU.

The following is an illustration of how Article 101 TFEU might apply to an exclusive distribution agreement (based on *Consten SA and Grundig-Verkaufs-GmbH v EEC Commission* [1996] CMLR 418).

EXAMPLE

Widgets Ltd, a UK manufacturer with 15% of the EU widgets market, has a network of exclusive distributors at the wholesale level in France, Italy and Germany (see diagram below). It sells to its distributors at €5 per widget and they then mark the price up when selling on to retailers. The Italian distributor (a wholly-owned subsidiary) charges €10, whereas the German distributor charges only €6. To protect its position in Italy, therefore, Widgets Ltd imposes clauses on the German wholesaler which prevent it selling to customers outside its territory (export bans) and from selling to dealers in Germany who could resell outside (ie sales to parallel importers). It is hoped that it would thus have absolute territorial protection from competition on prices with its other EU distributors.

Such protection is, however, contrary to Article 101 TFEU and will attract fines, potential tort claims and void agreements. The block exemption on vertical agreements (Regulation 2022/720) allows territorial exclusivity and a ban on active sales (advertising, etc) outside the territory, but not a ban on passive sales (ie to unsolicited customers who place orders on their own initiative), nor a ban on sales to parallel exporters (see Article 4(b), first indent). Retailers across the EU are perfectly entitled to buy from the cheapest wholesaler in the network.

A DISTRIBUTION SYSTEM

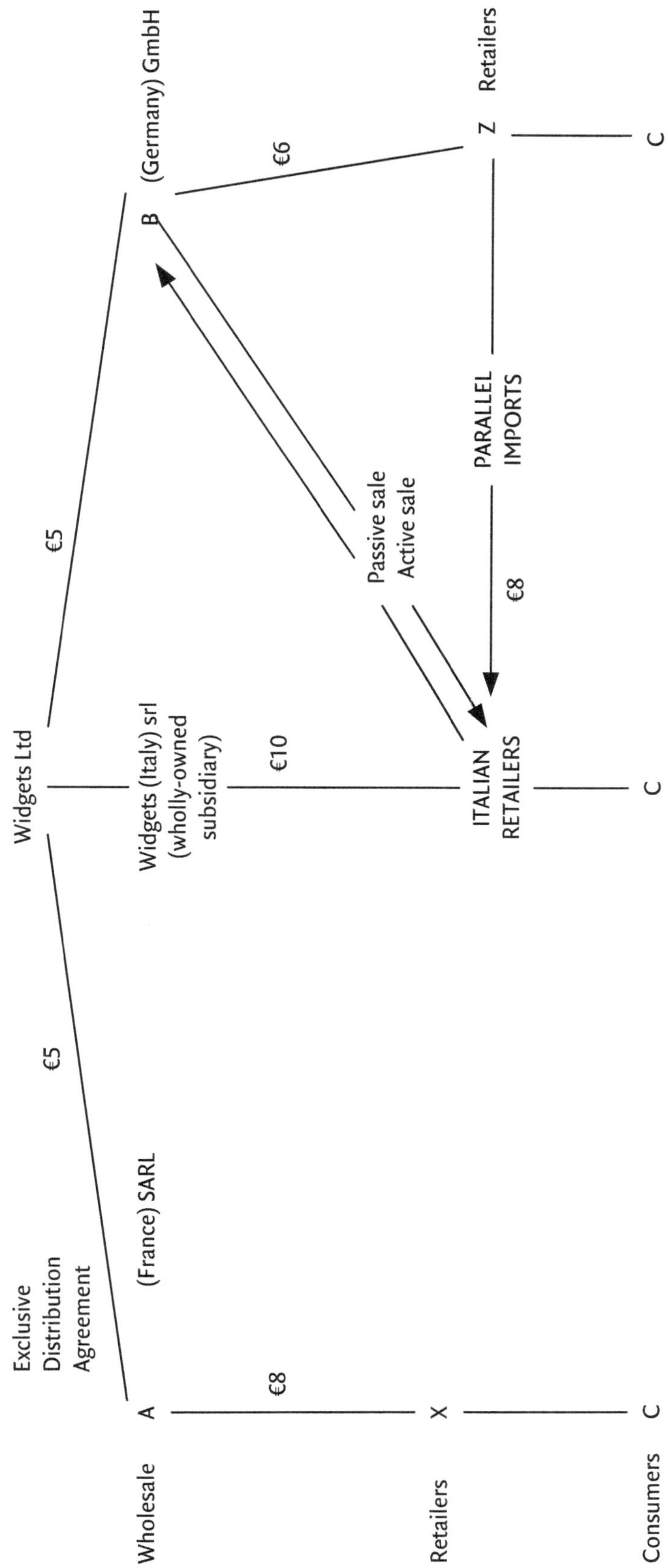

PART IV

HUMAN RIGHTS

CHAPTER 27

The European Convention on Human Rights

LEARNING OUTCOMES

After reading this chapter you will be able to understand:

- the background to the Convention
- how the Convention relates to English and EU law
- how to interpret the Convention
- the main rights that are protected by the Convention
- when a right has been interfered with
- how to petition the European Court of Human Rights.

27.1 INTRODUCTION TO HUMAN RIGHTS

Since the Human Rights Act 1998 (HRA 1998) came into force, the subject of human rights has been treated as a pervasive topic on the Legal Practice Course. Perhaps more than any other pervasive topic, its reach is long, and it has begun to make its presence felt in almost every area of law and practice. A copy of the HRA 1998 may be found at **Appendix 1 to Part IV**.

Before starting a Legal Practice Course students are expected to have a 'basic knowledge and understanding of the relevant human rights conventions and legislation' (see Appendix to the Solicitors Regulation Authority, Legal Practice Course Outcomes, 2019). This part of this book is intended to act as a reminder of the key points and put them in a practical context. This chapter re-introduces you to the European Convention on Human Rights and some of the most important Convention rights. **Chapter 28** deals with the mechanism by which the HRA 1998 makes those rights enforceable in the UK.

27.2 INTRODUCTION TO THE CONVENTION

The UK was instrumental in drafting the European Convention for the Protection of Human Rights and Fundamental Freedoms 1950 (European Convention on Human Rights) (ECHR). The Convention was drafted by members of the Council of Europe (a body unrelated to the European Union) in the aftermath of the Second World War and the human rights abuses which took place during it. The UK was one of the original signatories on 4 November 1950. The Convention came into force on 3 September 1953. However, unlike many of the other signatories, the UK did not incorporate the Convention into its own legal system. The

Government believed that incorporation was unnecessary because the rights contained in the Convention already existed in British common law.

The original ECHR contained the civil and political rights to be found in classical liberal thought, such as freedom of expression, freedom of religion and freedom from interference with privacy. A series of protocols, some of which have been ratified by the UK, deal with certain other matters including the right to education and the right to peaceful enjoyment of private property (First Protocol) and the prohibition of the death penalty (Sixth Protocol).

The most imaginative feature of the ECHR was that it imposed an international judicial system for the protection of human rights on Europe. It is the most developed of regional systems for the protection of human rights.

27.3 THE RELATIONSHIP BETWEEN THE ECHR AND ENGLISH LAW

The HRA 1998 (which came into force in October 2000) has bridged the gap between domestic and international law so far as the Convention is concerned but not unincorporated treaties such as the United Nations Convention on the Rights of the Child (see R *(on the application of SC) v Secretary of State for Work and Pensions* [2021] UKSC 26). Domestic English courts are now empowered to enforce Convention rights, and exactly how they may do so will be discussed in **Chapter 28**.

27.4 THE RELATIONSHIP BETWEEN THE ECHR AND THE EU

While there is a close relationship between the EU and the ECHR, the two are distinct and should not be confused. In particular, bear in mind the following differences.

(a) Far more countries are signatories to the ECHR than are members of the EU.

(b) The EU's concern with human rights has traditionally been limited. Some rights are protected. Article 157 TFEU, for example, deals with sex discrimination.

(c) The ECHR confers rights on everyone within the jurisdiction of a State which is party to the Convention, and not just those who are nationals of the State in question. This is important for asylum seekers, for example: EU law is usually concerned only with the rights of nationals of Member States.

(d) The ECHR has its own institutions and procedures, in particular the European Court of Human Rights (ECtHR) which sits in Strasbourg, not Luxembourg or Brussels.

There have been suggestions since 1977 that the EU might become a party to the ECHR. So far this has not happened, and indeed the Court of Justice ruled that the Council has no power to accede to the ECHR under the Treaty as currently drafted (see *Opinion No 2/94* [1996] ECR I-1759, 28 March 1996). But the Court of Justice has said that EU law will draw upon the jurisprudence of the ECHR because it represents the common traditions of the EU Member States in the field of human rights. Note that the Maastricht Treaty makes an express reference to human rights and in particular to the ECHR: see the Recitals and TEU, Article 6.

27.5 THE SUBSTANTIVE LAW OF THE ECHR

27.5.1 The Convention rights

These are the main rights protected by the Convention:

(a) right to life (Article 2);

(b) prohibition of torture (Article 3);

(c) prohibition of slavery and forced labour (Article 4);

(d) right to liberty and security (Article 5);

(e) right to a fair trial (Article 6);

(f) no punishment without lawful authority (Article 7);

(g) right to respect for family and private life (Article 8);
(h) right to freedom of thought, conscience and religion (Article 9);
(i) right to freedom of expression (Article 10);
(j) right to freedom of assembly and association (Article 11);
(k) right to marry (Article 12);
(l) prohibition of discrimination (Article 14);
(m) right to peaceful enjoyment of possessions (First Protocol, Article 1);
(n) right to education and right of parents to educate children in accordance with religious and philosophical convictions (First Protocol, Article 2).

The most important of these rights are described below (**27.5.3–27.5.9**).

27.5.2 Some general considerations when dealing with Convention rights

27.5.2.1 Drafting

The Convention is drafted in quite a different way from a United Kingdom statute. In the UK, legislative drafting tends to be very tight and exhaustive. The rights in the Convention are deliberately left open-ended, and the Strasbourg organs do not interpret the Convention in the same way as English judges interpret domestic legislation. Lawyers in the UK must appreciate this different way of working.

27.5.2.2 Absolute and limited rights

Some of the Convention rights are absolute. For example, the right to freedom from torture: the Convention allows no circumstances in which torture could be legitimate. But most of the rights are subject to limitations and qualifications. For example, the right to freedom of expression may be interfered with where the matters being expressed are defamatory or harmful to national security. Much of the argument in Convention cases turns not on whether there has been an interference with Convention rights, but on whether that interference is justifiable. In considering the interference, the ECtHR has invented a number of tools with which UK lawyers need to be familiar.

27.5.2.3 Judicial method

Once it has been established that a Convention right has been interfered with, the court must consider whether the interference is justified (unless the right is one which is absolute, in which case no interference is allowed).

There are four key concepts which the ECtHR uses.

The rule of law

No matter how desirable the end to be achieved, any interference with a Convention right must be based on some ascertainable law, and not on an arbitrary executive decision. Without detailed authorisation by law, any interference, however justified, will violate the Convention. For example, telephone tapping by the police in the 1970s was regulated by nothing more than an internal police guidance note which was not available to the public. The interference with the right to respect for correspondence (Article 8) was not therefore justified by law and was contrary to the Convention (*Malone v United Kingdom* (1984) 7 EHRR 14).

Legitimate aims

The defendant must say why the right is being interfered with, and the reason must be a legitimate one. Many of the Articles (eg, Articles 8, 9, 10 and 11) set out what sorts of aims are legitimate, for example the interests of public safety, national security or the protection of the rights and freedoms of others. For example, if a prisoner's correspondence is being read by the prison authorities then the prevention of disorder or crime within the prison would be a legitimate reason for the interference with Article 8 if there was a genuine belief that there was a risk. But the routine reading of mail would not be legitimate (*Campbell v United Kingdom* (1992) 15 EHRR 137).

Proportionality

The cliché usually used to describe the doctrine of proportionality is that the State cannot use a sledgehammer to crack a nut. In the more formal language of the court, any restriction on a right must be 'necessary in a democratic society' or based on some 'pressing social need'. For example, in the domestic UK case of *Lindsay v Customs & Excise Commissioners* [2002] EWCA Civ 267, [2002] STC 588, the defendant had been caught by customs officers driving his Ford Focus car into the UK containing 18,400 cigarettes, 10 kilos of handrolling tobacco, 31 litres of beer and 3 litres of spirits. The goods were for members of his family, for which he had received payment. This was unlawful. As well as seizing the goods, the customs officers seized his car and refused to return it to him. The Court of Appeal held that the interference with the defendant's right to peaceful enjoyment of his possessions by the forfeiture of his car, although within the legal powers of the customs officers, was disproportionate for small-scale smuggling of this nature.

Note that the principle of proportionality in EU law is neither expressed nor applied in the same way as the principle of proportionality under the ECHR. Although there is some common ground, the so-called four-stage analysis of proportionality which was explained in *Bank Mellat v Her Majesty's Treasury (No 2)* [2014] AC 700 at [20] and [72]–[76], in relation to the justification under domestic law (in particular, under the Human Rights Act 1998) of interferences with fundamental rights, is not applicable to proportionality in EU law (see *R (on the application of Lumsdon) v Legal Services Board* [2015] UKSC 41 at [26]).

The application of the proportionality test is more straightforward when only one Convention right is in play: the question then is whether the private right claimed offers sufficient justification for the degree of interference with the fundamental right. It is much less straightforward when two Convention rights are in play, and the proportionality of interfering with one has to be balanced against the proportionality of restricting the other. As each is a fundamental right, there is evidently a 'pressing social need' to protect it. The basic approach (see *In re S* [2003] 3 WLR 1425 and *Duchess of Sussex v Associated Newspapers Ltd* [2021] EWCA Civ 1810) involves the court looking first at the comparative importance of the actual rights being claimed in the individual case; then at the justifications for interfering with or restricting each of those rights; and applying the proportionality test to each.

Margin of appreciation

This is the Strasbourg equivalent of what in Brussels is called subsidiarity. It means that the States which are party to the Convention are allowed a degree of leeway out of sensitivity to their own political and cultural traditions. For example, the case of *Handyside v United Kingdom* (1976) 1 EHRR 737 concerned the publication in England in 1971 of *The Little Red School Book*, a children's book including a section on sex. The publisher had been convicted under the Obscene Publications Act 1959. The ECtHR had to consider the UK Government's argument that the interference with the publisher's right to freedom of expression was necessary for the purpose of the 'protection of morals'. The Court accepted that such a matter was within the competence of national authorities and a standard could not be imposed by an international body:

> By reason of their direct and continuous contact with the vital forces of their countries, state authorities are in principle in a better position than the international judge to give an opinion. (para 48)

The concept of a margin of appreciation is not directly relevant when domestic courts apply the HRA 1998. This is because it is a concept of international law and not domestic law, governing the relationship between an international court and Contracting States. Nevertheless, it is well established that there is an analogous concept which does apply in domestic law under the HRA 1998, which has been variously described as a 'discretionary area of judgement', a 'margin of discretion', a 'margin of judgement', or in other ways, for example to refer to the appropriate weight which is to be given to the judgement of the executive or legislature depending upon the context.

> The margin of judgement which is to be afforded to Parliament in the present context rests upon two foundations. First, there is the relative institutional competence of the courts as compared to Parliament. The court necessarily operates on the basis of relatively limited evidence, which is adduced by the parties in the context of particular litigation. Its focus is narrow and the argument is necessarily sectional. In contrast, Parliament has the means and opportunities to obtain wider information, from much wider sources. It has access to expert bodies, such as the Law Commission, which can advise it on reform of the law. It is able to act upon draft legislation, which is usually produced by the Government and often follows a public consultation exercise, in which many differing views can be advanced by members of the public. Both Government and Members of Parliament can be lobbied by anyone with an interest in the subject in hand. The political process allows legislators to acquire information to inform policy decisions from the widest possible range of opinions. (*R (on the application of McConnell) v Registrar General for England and Wales* [2020] EWCA Civ 559 at [81])

27.5.3 Article 5: The right to liberty and security

> 1. Everyone has the right to liberty and security of person. No one shall be deprived of his liberty save in the following cases and in accordance with a procedure prescribed by law:
>   (a) the lawful detention of a person after conviction by a competent court;
>   (b) the lawful arrest or detention of a person for non-compliance with the lawful order of a court or in order to secure the fulfilment of any obligation prescribed by law;
>   (c) the lawful arrest or detention of a person effected for the purpose of bringing him before the competent legal authority on reasonable suspicion of having committed an offence or when it is reasonably considered necessary to prevent his committing an offence or fleeing after having done so;
>   (d) the detention of a minor by lawful order for the purpose of educational supervision or his lawful detention for the purpose of bringing him before the competent legal authority;
>   (e) the lawful detention of persons for the prevention of the spreading of infectious diseases, of persons of unsound mind, alcoholics or drug addicts or vagrants;
>   (f) the lawful arrest or detention of a person to prevent his effecting an unauthorised entry into the country or of a person against whom action is being taken with a view to deportation or extradition.
> 2. Everyone who is arrested shall be informed promptly, in a language which he understands, of the reasons for his arrest and of any charge against him.
> 3. Everyone arrested or detained in accordance with the provisions of paragraph 1(c) of this Article shall be brought promptly before a judge or other officer authorised by law to exercise judicial power and shall be entitled to trial within a reasonable time or to release pending trial. Release may be conditioned by guarantees to appear for trial.
> 4. Everyone who is deprived of his liberty by arrest or detention shall be entitled to take proceedings by which the lawfulness of his detention shall be decided speedily by a court and his release ordered if the detention is not lawful.
> 5. Everyone who has been the victim of arrest or detention in contravention of the provisions of this Article shall have an enforceable right to compensation.

Article 5 is the lengthiest of the Convention rights. To determine whether there is a deprivation of liberty within the meaning of and engaging the protection of Article 5(1), three conditions must be satisfied:

(a) an objective element of 'a person's confinement to a certain limited place for a not negligible length of time';

(b) a subjective element, namely that the person has not 'validly consented to the confinement in question'; and

(c) the deprivation of liberty must be one for which the State is responsible. See generally *A Local Authority v A, B, C, D and E* [2010] EWHC 978 (Fam), *P (by his litigation friend The Official Solicitor) v Cheshire West & Chester Council* [2014] UKSC 19 and *Secretary of State for Justice v Staffordshire County Council* [2016] EWCA Civ 1317.

As a general principle, detention is arbitrary where there has been an element of bad faith or deception or where there is no genuine conformity with the purpose of the restrictions permitted by Article 5(1). Otherwise, as long as the detention follows and has a sufficient causal connection with a lawful conviction, the decision to impose a sentence of detention and the length of that sentence are matters for the national authorities (*Saadi v United Kingdom* (2008) 47 EHRR 427 and *Knights v Secretary of State for Justice* [2017] EWCA Civ 1053).

The following general principles were recorded by Jackson LJ in *LL v Lord Chancellor (Liability)* [2017] EWCA Civ 237 at [88]:

> (1) A period of detention is lawful if, and only if it complies with the applicable sub-paragraph of Article 5(1).
>
> (2) In the case of detention under Article 5(1)(b):
>
> (i) The underlying court order or legal obligation must be one with which it was feasible for X to comply. And
>
> (ii) The period of detention must be proportionate to that which X was required to do, but failed to do.
>
> (3) Detention under Article 5(1)(a) or (b) will not be lawful if:
>
> (i) The court acted without jurisdiction. Or
>
> (ii) There was a gross and obvious irregularity in the court's procedure. Or
>
> (iii) The court made an order that had no proper foundation in law, because of a failure to observe a statutory condition precedent. Or
>
> (iv) X's detention was arbitrary. In other words the stated grounds for that detention did not comply with the general principle of legal certainty. Or
>
> (v) There were one or more breaches of Article 6 during the proceedings which were so serious as to amount to a flagrant denial of justice.
>
> (4) In considering whether the court's errors amounted to 'gross and obvious irregularity' or 'flagrant denial of justice', where appropriate their cumulative effect can be considered.

Is the continued detention of an arrested adult or juvenile for their own protection, where there exists a reasonable suspicion of their having committed an offence, contrary to Article 5? No, held the Court of Appeal in *Archer v Commissioner of Police of the Metropolis* [2021] EWCA Civ 1662. The Court, however, observed that the pre-trial detention of juveniles should be the exception and not the rule.

Can a control order amount to a deprivation of liberty? In *AH v Secretary of State for the Home Department* [2011] EWCA Civ 787, the control order included the following obligations: a 14-hour curfew between 6pm and 8am in a flat in Norwich; a prohibition on communications equipment other than a landline telephone; and a geographical boundary comprising the centre and inner suburbs of Norwich. At first instance the judge concluded that a curfew of 14 hours was not, by itself, tantamount to a deprivation of liberty. He then addressed 10 individual features of the control order relied upon by the appellant in order to see whether their cumulative effect, when taken with the length of the curfew, was such as to amount to a deprivation of liberty. He concluded that this was not a case of deprivation of liberty but that it 'falls just on the restriction on liberty side of the line and so does not engage Article 5'. The decision was upheld on appeal. Also see *AP v Secretary of State for the Home Department* [2010] 3 WLR 51, where Lord Brown said at (para 4): 'I nevertheless remain of the view that for a control order with a 16-hour curfew to be struck down as involving a deprivation of liberty, the other conditions imposed would have to be unusually destructive of the life the controlee might otherwise have been living.'

Can an adult, in the exercise of parental responsibility, impose, or authorise others to impose, restrictions on the liberty of their child? Yes, but the restrictions so imposed must not in their totality amount to deprivation of liberty that engages the Article 5 rights of the child: see *Neilson v Denmark* (1988) 11 EHRR 175, *Re K* [2002] 2 WLR 1141, *RK (by her litigation friend the Official Solicitor) v BCC* [2011] EWCA Civ 1305 and *Re D (a Child)* [2019] UKSC 42. As to the actions of the police in restraining an autistic, epileptic young man when such restraint was in the circumstances hasty, ill-informed and damaging to him, see *ZH (a protected party by his litigation friend, GH) v Commissioner of Police of the Metropolis* [2013] EWCA Civ 69.

Does the opportunity for a prisoner, who is subject to an indeterminate sentence, to rehabilitate himself and demonstrate that he no longer presents a danger to the public fall within Article 5? Yes, held the ECtHR in *James v UK* (2013) 56 EHRR 12. However, the Supreme Court refused to follow that judgment in *R (on the application of Hanley) v Secretary of State for Justice* [2014] UKSC 66. The Court held that it was only implicit in the scheme of the Article that the State had a duty to provide a reasonable opportunity for a prisoner subject to an indeterminate sentence to rehabilitate himself and demonstrate that he no longer presented a danger to the public. However, that is an ancillary duty, which cannot be brought within the express language of the Article and does not therefore affect the lawfulness of detention.

Article 5 is of particular importance to criminal litigation practitioners, especially in challenging arrests and detentions. Its overall purpose is to ensure that no one is deprived of their liberty in an arbitrary fashion (*Engel v Netherlands* (1979–80) 1 EHRR 647, para 58 and *Austin v Commissioner of Police of the Metropolis* [2009] UKHL 5). Can there be imprisonment at common law without there being a deprivation of liberty under Article 5? Yes, see *R (on the application of Jalloh) v Secretary of State for the Home Department* [2020] UKSC 4.

The Article has two distinct limbs. Paragraph 1 prohibits interference with liberty or security of person except in certain, well-defined circumstances. No distinction tends to be made in Strasbourg jurisprudence between the two concepts of liberty and security of person. Paragraphs 2–5 provide a set of procedural rights for detainees.

27.5.3.1 Lawful detention

Paragraph 1 insists in particular that any detention must be 'lawful' (the word is used in each of sub-paras (a)–(f)). This requires that the domestic law upon which a detention is based must be accessible and precise. The paragraph also requires that the detention be 'in accordance with a procedure prescribed by law'. This calls for a consideration of how the detainer has gone about detaining the individual rather than why. Where there is no procedure prescribed by domestic law, or where the detainer has failed to follow it, Article 5 will have been breached (see *Secretary of State for Justice v RB* [2011] EWCA Civ 1608).

The attempt made in Article 5(1)(a) to (f) to codify the exceptions more precisely makes it unusually inflexible if applied according to its literal meaning in a situation of armed conflict. In some circumstances, some of the six grounds may adventitiously accommodate military detention. But as the Strasbourg Court recognised in *Hassan v UK* (2014) 38 BHRC 358, they are not designed for such a situation and are not well adapted to it. Moreover, *Hassan* does not add a notional seventh ground of permitted military detention in the course of armed conflict.

> Its effect is rather to recognise that sub-paragraphs (a) to (f) cannot necessarily be regarded as exhaustive when the Convention is being applied to such a conflict, because their exhaustive character reflects peacetime conditions. This means that where the armed forces of a Convention state are acting under a mandate from the Security Council to use all necessary measures, article 5(1) cannot be taken to prevent them from detaining persons for imperative reasons of security. (per Lord Sumpton in *Abd Ali Hameed Al-Waheed v Ministry of Defence* [2017] UKSC 2 at para 68)

As a result, in an international armed conflict, a system of judicial control over detention may not always be required.

Is there a breach if the person is detained in the 'wrong' place, for example in prison rather than in a detention centre for deportees? This happened in R *(on the application of Dritan Krasniqi) v Secretary of State for the Home Department* [2011] EWCA Civ 1549. The Court held that a claim cannot be based solely on an irregularity in the selection of the place of detention. It might be different if it was shown that the conditions of detention were unduly harsh, as in *Mayeka v Belgium* [2007] 1 FLR 1726. There, a 5-year-old child was detained for two months, alone among strangers, in an adult detention centre. This caused her such distress and potential psychological damage that it amounted both to inhuman treatment contrary to Article 3 and to a violation under Article 5 of the principle that the place and conditions of detention must be related to the permitted ground of deprivation of liberty. See also R *(on the application of Idira) v Secretary of State for the Home Department* [2015] EWCA Civ 1187. As to the use of the inherent jurisdiction of the High Court to authorise a local authority to deprive a child of their liberty, see *In the matter of T (A Child)* [2021] UKSC 35.

Can Article 5(1)(c) apply in a case of detention for preventive purposes followed by early release, that is, before the person could practicably be brought before a court? Yes – see R *(on the application of Hicks) v Commissioner of Police for the Metropolis* [2017] UKSC 9.

27.5.3.2 Reasons

Paragraph 2 provides a right for those placed under arrest to be given reasons. These do not need to be in writing, and formal notification is not necessary if the reasons are made clear during the arrest (*X v Netherlands* 5 YB 224, at 228).

27.5.3.3 Judicial supervision

Paragraph 3 requires that the person under arrest be brought promptly before a judge (usually a magistrate in the UK). The paragraph also provides for trial within a reasonable time, or for release pending trial (ie bail). There is a presumption that bail will be granted unless there are good reasons not to grant it (for example, because there is a risk that the accused will fail to appear at the trial: *Stögmüller v Austria* (1969) 1 EHRR 155).

27.5.3.4 Challenge and review

Paragraph 4 requires that a speedy procedure must be available by which detention can be challenged. The habeas corpus procedure in the UK fulfils this requirement, so long as it concludes swiftly. The ECtHR has also held that where the circumstances of detention vary over time a regular reviewing procedure must exist.

Many cases turn on the question of whether or not a period of detention is reasonable. In *O'Dowd v UK* [2010] ECHR 1324, the ECtHR stressed that this cannot be assessed in the abstract. Whether it is reasonable for an accused to remain in detention must be considered in each case according to its special features. Continued detention may be justified in a given case only if there are specific indications of a genuine requirement of public interest which, notwithstanding the presumption of innocence, outweighs the rule of respect for individual liberty laid down in Article 5. The persistence of reasonable suspicion that the person arrested has committed an offence is a condition *sine qua non* for the lawfulness of the continued detention, but after a certain lapse of time it no longer suffices. The Court must then establish whether the other grounds given by the judicial authorities continued to justify the deprivation of liberty. Where such grounds were relevant and sufficient, the Court must also be satisfied that the national authorities displayed special diligence in the conduct of the proceedings. In judging whether the special diligence requirement has been met, the Court will have regard to periods of unjustified delay, to the overall complexity of the proceedings and to any steps taken by the authorities to speed up proceedings to ensure that the overall length of detention remains reasonable.

In R *(on the application of Whiston) v Secretary of State for Justice* [2014] UKSC 39, a prisoner was released before he became automatically entitled to release. He was recalled, still within the custodial period of his sentence, because his whereabouts could no longer be monitored in the community. The Secretary of State's recall decision was not subject to judicial control. The issue was whether the recall constituted a fresh deprivation of liberty so as to engage Article 5(4) and provide a right of review, or whether the renewed detention remained justified by the original sentence of imprisonment. The Supreme Court held the latter. In doing so the Court refused to follow its previous decision in R *(on the application of Smith) v Parole Board* [2005] UKHL 1.

27.5.3.5 Compensation

Paragraph 5 provides a right to compensation for any interference with Article 5 rights. In practice, this is unlikely to add anything to the availability of damages (and possibly exemplary damages) in tort for wrongful arrest or unlawful detention.

The enforceable right to compensation is not intended to provide compensation for claimants whose convictions were reached by a lawfully constituted court but which were quashed on appeal: *W v Ministry of Justice* [2015] EWCA Civ 742.

The right to compensation will be important where there is no entitlement to damages at common law, eg the applicant is ordered to remain in custody by a civil court. This happened in *Stellato v Ministry of Defence* [2010] EWCA Civ 1435 where the applicant was unlawfully detained under an order of the Court of Appeal for 14 days until released by the Supreme Court. That he was subsequently unlawfully detained by the defendant for a further 59 days also entitled him to damages at common law.

27.5.4 Article 6: The right to a fair trial

1. In the determination of his civil rights and obligations or of any criminal charge against him, everyone is entitled to a fair and public hearing within a reasonable time by an independent and impartial tribunal established by law. Judgment shall be pronounced publicly but the press and public may be excluded from all or part of the trial in the interest of morals, public order or national security in a democratic society, where the interests of juveniles or the protection of the private life of the parties so require, or to the extent strictly necessary in the opinion of the court in special circumstances where publicity would prejudice the interests of justice.
2. Everyone charged with a criminal offence shall be presumed innocent until proved guilty according to law.
3. Everyone charged with a criminal offence has the following minimum rights:
   (a) to be informed promptly, in a language which he understands and in detail, of the nature and cause of the accusation against him;
   (b) to have adequate time and facilities for the preparation of his defence;
   (c) to defend himself in person or through legal assistance of his own choosing or, if he has not sufficient means to pay for legal assistance, to be given it free when the interests of justice so require;
   (d) to examine or have examined witnesses against him and to obtain the attendance and examination of witnesses on his behalf under the same conditions as witnesses against him;
   (e) to have the free assistance of an interpreter if he cannot understand or speak the language used in court.

Article 6 is arguably the most important, and certainly the most utilised, of all the Convention rights. It provides for a right to fair criminal and civil trials. It lays down certain procedural standards. It is of direct importance to all litigators, and therefore indirectly to all lawyers.

> Article 6 of the Convention guarantees the right of access to justice, with the necessary safeguards to ensure the fairness of the hearing. It is a key human right, not only because access to justice is a pillar of the rule of law, but also because it is the means by which a wide range of other human rights are made enforceable. As the European Court of Human Rights ('the European court') has said, in a

> democratic society the right to a fair administration of justice holds such a prominent place that a restrictive interpretation of article 6(1) would not correspond to the aim and the purpose of that provision: *Delcourt v Belgium* (1970) 1 EHRR 355, para 25. In principle, as the court stated in another judgment, the rule of law implies (among other things) that an interference by the executive authorities with an individual's rights should be subject to an effective control which should normally be assured by the judiciary, at least in the last resort, judicial control offering the best guarantees of independence, impartiality and a proper procedure: *Klass v Germany* (1978) 2 EHRR 214, para 55. (per Lord Reed in *QX v Secretary of State for the Home Department* [2024] UKSC 26 at [60]).

27.5.4.1 Determination of civil rights or a criminal charge

Paragraph 1 lays down the basic 'due process' standards for the determination of civil and criminal matters. The phrase 'in the determination of his civil rights' needs some explanation. It does not simply cover every issue which might be the subject of a trial in civil law as an English lawyer would understand that expression. The Strasbourg case law on this is complex. All proceedings between private individuals and private bodies are included. Not all proceedings involving public authorities are, and here further research may be necessary. Broadly, a distinction is made between those decisions of public bodies which affect private law rights (which are within the scope of the Article) and those affecting public law rights (which are not). For example, disciplinary proceedings that might result in the removal of professional status (*Le Compte v Belgium* [1982] ECC 240) are included. Likewise, planning decisions affect property rights and are included. Actions to sue public authorities for compensation will be included, because private law rights in tort or contract are involved. The fact that a claim depends on a failure to comply with the terms of a government policy, rather than of legislation, is not in itself a reason why it cannot involve the determination of a civil right (R *(on the application of K) v Secretary of State for Defence* [2016] EWCA Civ 1149).

Decisions of public authorities affecting education involve public law, not private law rights, and are not subject to Article 6 requirements (*Simpson v United Kingdom* (1989) 64 DR 188). For the same reason, decisions on the categorisation of prisoners for security purposes are not covered (*Brady v United Kingdom* (1979) 3 EHRR 297), neither are government decisions on asylum (R *(K)(Iran) v Secretary of State for the Home Department* [2010] EWCA Civ 115), or decisions by a local housing authority under s 193(5) of the Housing Act 1996 that it has discharged its duty to secure accommodation available for occupation by a homeless applicant (*Ali v Birmingham CC* [2010] UKSC 8), or decisions of an independent appeal panel as to whether a pupil should be permanently excluded from school (R *(on the application of V) v Independent Appeal Panel for Tom Hood School* [2010] EWCA Civ 142).

What is a criminal charge for the purposes of Article 6? To determine this, three questions must be answered. How is the offence classified in domestic law? What is the nature of the offence? What is the nature and purpose of the penalty; how severe is it? See *Engel v Netherlands* (1979–80) 1 EHRR 647. However, the minor nature of a penalty does not prevent it from being 'criminal' under the Convention and classification under national law is not decisive (*Glantz v Finland* [2014] STC 2263).

Is there a right to legal representation in civil proceedings? The more the proceedings are akin to criminal proceedings, the more positive the answer is yes. For the purposes of Article 6, there is no clear-cut dividing line between civil and criminal proceedings, so the courts approach the issue on the basis of a sliding scale, at the bottom of which are civil wrongs of a relatively trivial nature, and at the top of which are serious crimes meriting substantial punishment. So civil disciplinary proceedings that might lead to a person being barred from practising their profession are likely to attract this right: see R *(on the application of G) v Y City Council* [2010] EWCA Civ 1 and R *(on the application of G) v X School Governors* [2011] UKSC 30.

27.5.4.2 A fair trial

Paragraph 1 sets out the minimum requirements for a fair trial. These are:

(a) a fair and public hearing;
(b) an independent and impartial tribunal;
(c) trial within a reasonable period;
(d) public judgment (with some exceptions); and
(e) a reasoned decision.

As the most litigated Article, a great deal of case law has grown up around these requirements. The approach of the ECtHR in interpreting and applying Article 6(1) is generous to applicants, and the Court reaches its decisions 'bearing in mind the prominent place which the right to a fair trial holds in a democratic society' (*Delcourt v Belgium* (1979–80) 1 EHRR 355). Not only have these decisions built on the requirements expressly contained in the paragraph set out above, but they have also read other rights into the paragraph. These include:

(a) the right of access to a court (eg, *Osman v United Kingdom* (2000) 29 EHRR 245: police immunity a denial of the right of access to a court);
(b) equality of arms (*Dombo Beheer BV v Netherlands* (1994) 18 EHRR 213); and
(c) the right to participate effectively in proceedings (*Stanford v United Kingdom* (Case A/282) (1994) *The Times*, 8 March: poor court room acoustics; *Re L (a child)* (2013) LTL 4 February, CA: refusal to adjourn hearing for legal representation to be obtained; *R v JP* [2014] EWCA Crim 2064: refusal to allow cross-examination of child witness; *Goldtrail Travel Ltd v Onur Air Tasimacilik AS* [2017] UKSC 57: a condition on the grant of permission to appeal which would prevent the appellant from bringing or continuing the appeal). What fairness requires will depend on all the circumstances of the case, eg, as to whether or not a trial should be adjourned due to the illness of a party or a witness (see *Bilta (UK) Ltd (in liquidation) v Tradition Financial Services Ltd* [2021] EWCA Civ 221).

The central question for the Supreme Court in *Griffiths v TUI UK Ltd* [2023] UKSC 48 was whether a party to a civil action is required to challenge by cross-examination the evidence of any witness of the opposing party on a material point which they wish to submit to the court should not be accepted? Yes, held the Court. The rule extends to both witnesses as to fact and expert witnesses. Why? In an adversarial system of justice, the purpose of the rule is to make sure that the trial is fair and that includes fairness to the party who has adduced the evidence of the impugned witness. Maintaining such fairness also includes enabling the judge to make a proper assessment of all the evidence to achieve justice in the cause. The rule is directed to the integrity of the court process itself.

A statutory time limit for lodging an appeal to a court does not impair the essence of the right of access to the court, and it is a proportionate restriction on the exercise of the right of appeal (*Stubbings v United Kingdom*, No 22083/93, [1997] 1 FLR 105). However, the absence of any discretionary power to extend time in exceptional cases is likely to give rise to a breach of Article 6 (*MacCallum v Secretary of State for Education* [2024] EWHC 87 (Admin)).

Can a civil court lawfully stay proceedings for, or order, the parties to engage in a non-court-based dispute resolution process? Yes, provided that the order made: (a) does not impair the very essence of the claimant's right to a fair trial, (b) is made in pursuit of a legitimate aim, and (c) is proportionate to achieving that legitimate aim (*Churchill v Merthyr Tydfil CBC* [2023] EWCA Civ 1416).

Should a fugitive from justice be denied these Convention rights? In *Conde Nast Publications Ltd v UK* (2008) Application No 00029746/05, LTL 29 February, the applicant publishers had been sued successfully for defamation. The claimant had left America and moved to France before being sentenced for an offence in respect of which he had pleaded guilty. The High Court had allowed the claimant to give his evidence by video link from a Paris hotel. The House of Lords had upheld that decision. The applicants argued that the principle of equality of arms was broken and so the proceedings were unfair. The ECtHR held that the UK Government could not be condemned under Article 6 for providing the claimant with facilities that were available to other litigants simply because of his status as a fugitive from justice. Why? Because the deprivation of such facilities would run counter to the Convention guarantee of equal treatment that is inherent in the principle of equality of arms.

Until 2010 there had been a presumption against requiring a child to attend court to give evidence in family proceedings. However, in *Re W (Children)* [2010] UKSC 12, the Supreme Court held that this could not be reconciled with the need to strike a fair balance between the rights protected by Articles 6 and 8 (see **27.5.5**). So a court considering whether to call a child as a witness has to weigh the advantages this will bring to the determination of the truth against the damage it might do to the welfare of that or any other child. Striking that balance in care proceedings might mean that a child is not called in the great majority of cases, but that must be the result of the court's considered judgment and not a presumption.

Furthermore, in civil litigation, paragraph 1 has been held to require a right to legal aid should the circumstances of the case demand it, especially 'by reason of the complexity of the procedure of the case' (*Airey v Ireland* (Case A/32) (1979) 2 EHRR 305; see also *Steel and Morris v United Kingdom* [2005] ECHR 68416/01 (the so-called 'McDonald's libel case'). Article 6(3)(c) expressly requires legal aid in criminal litigation.

When an individual's right to have a fair hearing comes into conflict with the requirements of national security, must their right to a fair hearing prevail? No. As Lord Reed in *R (on the application of Begum) v Special Immigration Appeals Commission* [2021] UKSC 7 explained at [135]:

> If a vital public interest – in this case, the safety of the public – makes it impossible for a case to be fairly heard, then the courts cannot ordinarily hear it. The appropriate response to the problem in the present case is for the appeal to be stayed until Ms Begum is in a position to play an effective part in it without the safety of the public being compromised. That is not a perfect solution, as it is not known how long it may be before that is possible. But there is no perfect solution to a dilemma of the present kind.

Is Article 6 applicable to a review of the Secretary of State's decision to impose a temporary exclusion order under the Counter-Terrorism and Security Act 2015, Pt 1, s 2(2)? Yes, held the Court of Appeal in *QX v Secretary of State for the Home Department* [2022] EWCA Civ 1541.

Does Article 6 confer a right on a party to family proceedings to admit to having committed any criminal offence without the possibility that the admission might be used either (a) as evidence in criminal proceedings, or (b) as a springboard for investigation? No, held the Court of Appeal in *P (Children) (Disclosure)* [2022] EWCA Civ 495.

27.5.4.3 Presumption of innocence

Paragraph 2 provides for the presumption of innocence in criminal trials. 'Reverse onus' provisions, which place the burden of proof upon a defendant to demonstrate their innocence, do not necessarily violate Article 6(2). Despite the bald terms in which the Article is expressed, the right is not unqualified. In *Salabiaku v France* (1988) 13 EHRR 379, which concerned a provision of the French Customs Code whereby any person in possession of smuggled goods was deemed responsible for customs evasion, the ECtHR stated:

> 28 ... Presumptions of fact or of law operate in every legal system. Clearly, the Convention does not prohibit such presumptions in principle. It does, however, require the contracting states to remain within certain limits in this respect as regards criminal law ... Article 6(2) does not therefore regard presumptions of fact or of law provided for in the criminal law with indifference. It requires states to confine them within reasonable limits which take into account the importance of what is at stake and maintain the rights of the defence.

In *Murray v United Kingdom (Right to Silence)* (1996) 22 EHRR 29, the ECtHR ruled that the drawing of adverse inferences from the exercise by the accused of his right to silence did not violate the Article either. However, in *Saunders v United Kingdom* (1996) 23 EHRR 313, the use of statements obtained by compulsion by inspectors exercising statutory powers under the Companies Act 1985 was held to be a violation of Article 6(2).

Since the HRA 1998 came into force the issue of reverse onus provisions has been raised in domestic UK litigation in several motoring cases. For example, in *R v Drummond* [2002] EWCA Crim 527, [2002] 2 Cr App R 25, the defendant was accused of causing death by dangerous driving and driving with excess alcohol. He tried to rely on the 'hip flask' defence, that he had drunk alcohol after the accident and before the arrival of the police to steady his nerves. The legislation placed the burden upon him to prove that this was the case rather than requiring the prosecution to show that he had drunk the alcohol before the accident. The Court of Appeal held that the imposition of this burden on the defendant was justified and he lost his appeal against conviction.

The House of Lords (now the Supreme Court) in *Sheldrake v DPP* [2004] UKHL 43, [2005] 1 AC 264, in a combined appeal, had to consider presumptions against a defendant in two very different contexts: control of a motor vehicle having consumed more than the prescribed limit of alcohol; and membership of a prescribed organisation contrary to the Terrorism Act 2000. Having reviewed the cases, Lord Bingham said at [21]:

> From this body of authority certain principles may be derived. The overriding concern is that a trial should be fair, and the presumption of innocence is a fundamental right directed to that end. The Convention does not outlaw presumptions of fact or law but requires that these should be kept within reasonable limits and should not be arbitrary. It is open to states to define the constituent elements of a criminal offence, excluding the requirement of mens rea. But the substance and effect of any presumption adverse to a defendant must be examined, and must be reasonable. Relevant to any judgment on reasonableness or proportionality will be the opportunity given to the defendant to rebut the presumption, maintenance of the rights of the defence, flexibility in application of the presumption, retention by the court of a power to assess the evidence, the importance of what is at stake and the difficulty which a prosecutor may face in the absence of a presumption. Security concerns do not absolve member states from their duty to observe basic standards of fairness. The justifiability of any infringement of the presumption of innocence cannot be resolved by any rule of thumb, but on examination of all the facts and circumstances of the particular provision as applied in the particular case.

At [31], Lord Bingham concluded:

> The task of the court is never to decide whether a reverse burden should be imposed on a defendant but always to assess whether a burden enacted by Parliament unjustifiably infringes the presumption of innocence.

In *R v Keogh* [2007] EWCA Civ 528, the Court of Appeal held that the reverse burdens of proof contained in s 2(3) and s 3(4) of the Official Secrets Act 1989 were incompatible with Article 6. Why? Because the Act can operate effectively without the imposition of those reverse burdens. The Court held that it was not necessary to impose them and to do so would be disproportionate and unjustifiable.

In *R (on the application of Hallam) v Secretary of State for Justice* [2019] UKSC 2, the Supreme Court had to determine if the Criminal Justice Act 1988, s 133(1ZA) is compatible with Article 6(2). Why? Because it provides that compensation for a miscarriage of justice is only payable if the evidence that had led to the quashing of the conviction demonstrates the applicant's innocence beyond reasonable doubt. By a majority of 4 to 2, the Court held that it is compatible. Subsequently, that has been upheld by the ECtHR in *Nealon and Hallam v United Kingdom* [2024] ECHR 514.

27.5.4.4 Procedural safeguards in criminal trials

Because of the serious nature of criminal litigation, paragraph 3 provides specific procedural rights in this context. These are rights for the defendant:

(a) to be informed promptly of the accusation against them;

(b) to have adequate time and facilities to prepare their defence;

(c) to choose their legal representative and to receive legal aid if necessary;
(d) to call witnesses and to cross-examine witnesses against the defendant; and
(e) to have free access to an interpreter if necessary (see *R v Foronda* [2014] NICA 17).

CASE EXAMPLE

In a criminal trial, if hearsay evidence is admitted against the accused, there is no opportunity to cross-examine that witness. So, is the trial still fair? Yes, provided there is a good reason for the non-attendance of the witness. But what if their statement is the only or decisive evidence against the accused? Then there must be sufficient counterbalancing factors, including strong procedural safeguards, to ensure a fair trial.

The Grand Chamber of the ECtHR applied these tests in *Al-Khawaja and Tahery v UK* (Application Nos 26766/05 and 22228/06) (2011) The Times, 22 December.

Mr Al-Khawaja was a consultant physician. He was charged with indecently assaulting two female patients. Both made statements to the police. However, one complainant committed suicide before the trial. Her statement was admitted as hearsay evidence and read to the jury. The Grand Chamber held that had been necessary as there was no other way the evidence could be given. Moreover, the trial was fair as: (a) the judge directed the jury that her hearsay evidence should carry less weight because she had not been seen, heard or cross-examined; and (b) the jury also heard evidence from the other complainant and two of deceased woman's friends in whom she had confided soon after the incident.

Mr Tahery was charged with stabbing another man in the back during a gang fight. Only one witness claimed to have seen him do this. The witness gave a statement to the police. This was admitted as hearsay evidence and read to the jury because the judge found the witness was afraid of giving evidence. Whilst that may have been a good reason, the Grand Chamber found the trial to have been unfair. The hearsay evidence amounted to an uncorroborated eyewitness statement. The fact that Mr Tahery could challenge the statement himself and the trial judge's clear and forceful warning to the jury in his summing up did not sufficiently counterbalance the difficulties caused to the defence by the admission of the untested evidence.

Is there an interference with an accused person's rights under Article 6(3) in the provision in the Bar of Northern Ireland Code of Conduct, r 20.11 requiring that, in criminal cases where legal aid had been granted for two barristers, one should be a senior counsel? No. Article 6 does not give an accused the right to demand counsel of their choice at public expense independently of the requirements of the interests of justice: see *In the matter of an application by Kevin Maguire for Judicial Review* [2018] UKSC 17.

These rights have caused a great deal of litigation. Reference to the case law or to a specialist work is needed to understand them fully.

27.5.5 Article 8: The right to respect for private and family life

1. Everyone has the right to respect for his private and family life, his home and his correspondence.
2. There shall be no interference by a public authority with the exercise of this right except such as is in accordance with the law and is necessary in a democratic society in the interests of national security, public safety or the economic wellbeing of the country, for the prevention of disorder or crime, for the protection of health or morals, or for the protection of the rights and freedoms of others.

Article 8 has been used creatively by lawyers and judges. Its essential object is to protect the individual against arbitrary action by public authorities (*Kroon v Netherlands* (1994) 19 EHRR 263). It has been used in cases where it might seem quite at home, such as those involving phone tapping or interference with prisoners' mail. But it has also been used in contexts which might come as a surprise to those who drafted it, such as the rights of transsexuals to have official records amended to recognise their status, the right to an environment unpolluted by noise and chemicals, and the right to practise one's sexuality freely.

Paragraph 1 protects four distinct rights.

27.5.5.1 Private life

This encompasses:

(a) noise pollution issues (*Rayner v United Kingdom* (1986) 47 DR 5);

(b) pollution by waste (*López Ostra v Spain* (1994) 20 EHRR 277);

(c) sexual orientation (*Smith and Grady v United Kingdom* (2000) 29 EHRR 548 and *Bull v Hall* [2013] UKSC 73); and gender, including non-binary/non-gendered people (R *(on the application of Elan-Cane) v Secretary of State for the Home Department* [2020] EWCA Civ 363 and R *(on the application of Castellucci) v Gender Recognition Panel* [2024] EWHC 54 (Admin));

(d) the unauthorised disclosure of confidential data to third parties (*MS v Sweden* (1999) 28 EHRR 313) and discharging a reporting restriction order prohibiting the reporting of a defendant's home address in connection with criminal proceedings (R *(on the application of Rai) v Winchester Crown Court* [2021] EWCA Civ 604);

(e) covert police surveillance (*Wood v United Kingdom* [2004] ECHR 23414/02) and covert medical treatment (*A Council v A (By her Litigation Friend, The Official Solicitor)* [2022] EWCOP 44);

(f) the monitoring by an employer of office telephone calls without warning (*Halford v United Kingdom* (1997) 24 EHRR 523);

(g) the opening and censoring of prisoner's confidential correspondence with a court (*Klyakhin v Russia* [2004] ECHR 46082/99);

(h) administration of medication against wishes (*Glass v United Kingdom* [2004] ECHR 61827/00);

(i) a State's obligation to make adequate and effective efforts to assist a person in his attempt to have his child returned to him with a view to exercising his parental rights (*Monory v Romania* [2005] ECHR 71099/01);

(j) unauthorised publication of photographs (*Douglas v Hello!* [2003] 3 All ER 996; *RocknRoll v News Group Newspapers Ltd* [2013] EWHC 24 (Ch) and *Weller v Associated Newspapers Limited* [2015] EWCA Civ 1176);

(k) the retention of fingerprint and DNA data after a person is acquitted of a criminal offence (*Marper v UK* [2007] ECHR 110);

(l) the police's use of automatic recognition technology (whereby digital images of members of the public are captured and processed through a mathematical algorithm to produce a biometric template which is then compared to other biometric templates of people on a watchlist (R *(on the application of Bridges) v Chief Constable of South Wales Police* [2020] EWCA Civ 1058) and the taking and retention of photographs by the police of a member of the public in the street (*Wood v Commissioner of Police of the Metropolis* [2009] EWCA Civ 414);

(m) legal professional privilege relating to the seeking and giving of legal advice by a qualified lawyer but not by an accountant (R *(on the application of Prudential Plc) v Special Commissioner of Income Tax* [2013] UKSC 1);

(n) the reputation of an individual (*In the Matter of Guardian News & Media Ltd v HM Treasury* [2010] UKSC 1 but see *Hurbain v Belgium* [GC], App No 57292/16, 4 July 2023 below) and publication of information about an official criminal investigation into a person's business activities (*Bloomberg LP v ZXC* [2022] UKSC 5);

(o) the prohibition or restriction on the ability to work (*Sidabras v Lithuania* (2006) 42 EHRR 6 and R *(on the application of MA) v National Probation Service* [2011] EWHC 1332 (Admin)) or depriving a person wholly or substantially of the ability to work (*Husson v Secretary of State for the Home Department* [2020] EWCA Civ 329);

(p) the dignity and privacy of prisoners in their cells (*Grant v Ministry of Justice* [2011] EWHC 3379) and their ability to exercise (*Malcolm v Secretary of State for Justice* [2011] EWCA Civ 1538), and the same-sex relationship between two prisoners (*Bright v Secretary of State for Justice* [2014] EWCA Civ 1628);

(q) the administration of a police caution and the requirement to disclose it (R *(on the application of T) v Chief Constable of Greater Manchester* [2014] UKSC 35);

(r) in limited circumstances, the decision to prosecute an individual (*SXH v CPS* [2014] EWCA Civ 90);

(s) the potential humiliation and embarrassment of being searched by a police officer (R *(on the application of Roberts) v Commissioner of Police of the Metropolis* [2014] EWCA Civ 69);

(t) a restraining order imposed as part of a criminal sentence (R *v* R [2019] EWCA Crim 2238 (which also includes the right of the beneficiary of the order to conduct their life free from the risk of violence from the person convicted)) and an exclusion zone imposed by a prison governor as a condition of a prisoner's release on licence (R *(on the application of Bentham) v Governor of Usk & Prescoed Prison* [2014] EWHC 2469 (Admin));

(u) the systematic collection and retention by police authorities of electronic data about individuals (R *(on the application of Catt) v Commissioner of Police of the Metropolis* [2015] UKSC 9, *Re JR38* [2015] UKSC 42 and R *(on the application of Butt) v Secretary of State for the Home Department* [2019] EWCA Civ 256);

(v) the retention and use of gender data by the State (R *(on the application of C) v Secretary of State for Work & Pensions* [2017] UKSC 72 and R *(on the application of McConnell) v Registrar General for England and Wales* [2020] EWCA Civ 559);

(w) the decision of a woman whether or not to have an abortion (*Dulgheriu v London Borough of Ealing* [2019] EWCA Civ 1490) and the denial of a right to a free abortion, thereby putting stress and pressure on women who cannot afford to pay (R *(on the application of A) (A Child By Her Mother and Litigation Friend) v Secretary of State for Health* [2015] EWCA Civ 771);

(x) the denial of citizenship (R *(on the application of Johnson) v Secretary of State for the Home Department* [2016] UKSC 56) and an order to surrender passports and travel documents (*Lakatamia Shipping Co Ltd v Su* [2021] EWCA Civ 1187);

(y) the disclosure of convictions including spent convictions (R *(on the application of T) v Chief Constable of Greater Manchester* [2013] EWCA Civ 25, R *(on the application of P) v Secretary of State for the Home Department* [2017] EWCA Civ 321, *HA v University of Wolverhampton* [2018] EWHC 144 (Admin) and *In the matter of an application by Gallagher for Judicial Review* [2019] UKSC 3);

(z) refusing to comply with a prisoner's food choices (R *(on the application of JJ) v Spectrum Community Health CIC* [2022] EWHC 2440 (Admin)).

The touchstone for Article 8(1)'s engagement in privacy cases is whether the claimant enjoys on the facts a 'reasonable expectation of privacy'. So is it engaged by a teenage boy, involved in an incident of public disorder and rioting, when the police release CCTV still images of some of those involved that include the boy to local newspapers for publication appealing to the public for help in identifying the suspects? The question split the Supreme Court in *In the matter of an application by JR38 For Judicial Review (Northern Ireland)* [2015] UKSC 42. By 3:2 the Court answered the question in the negative.

Does a decision by a public prosecutor to bring criminal proceedings against a person fall potentially within the scope of Article 8 where: (a) the prosecutor has reasonable cause to believe the person to be guilty of the offence with which they are charged; and (b) the law relating to the offence is compatible with Article 8? No, answered the Supreme Court in *SXH v Crown Prosecution Service* [2017] UKSC 30. But, in general, a person does have a reasonable expectation of privacy in a police investigation up to the point of charge. As Simon LJ observed in *ZXC v Bloomberg LP* [2020] EWCA Civ 611 at [83]–[85] (confirmed on appeal, see [2022] UKSC 5):

> I would take the opportunity to make clear that those who have simply come under suspicion by an organ of the state have, in general, a reasonable and objectively founded expectation of privacy in relation to that fact and an expressed basis for that suspicion. The suspicion may ultimately be shown to be well-founded or ill-founded, but until that point the law should recognise the human characteristic to assume the worst (that there is no smoke without fire); and to overlook the fundamental legal principle that those who are accused of an offence are deemed to be innocent until they are proven guilty.
>
> In the present case, the Claimant has not even been arrested.
>
> I would add that the reasonable expectation of privacy is not in general dependant on the type of crime being investigated or the public characteristics of the suspect (for example, engagement in politics or business). The crime need not be sexual: the much maligned Christopher Jefferies (see *Khuja v Times Newspapers Ltd* [2019] AC 161 at [59]) was not suspected of a crime relating to private aspects of his life; and I see no good reason why suspicion relating to a crime concerning business dealings should be an exception to a salutary general approach which is founded on the preliminary stage of a state enforcement agency enquiry into what may or may not lead to a charge. To be suspected of a crime is damaging whatever the nature of the crime: it is sensitive personal information and there can be little justification for a hierarchy of offences giving rise to suspicion; although I would accept that there may be some cases where the reasonable expectation of privacy may be significantly reduced, perhaps even to extinction, due to the public nature of the activity under consideration (rioting, for example).

Removal of an individual from association with others constitutes an interference with the right to respect for private life, such as a prisoner or person in a young offenders' institution who is placed in solitary confinement. That, of course, is subject to justification under Article 8(2): see *R (on the application of AB) v Secretary of State for Justice* [2021] UKSC 28.

After a long-fought litigation battle, the Supreme Court in *R (on the application of Steinfeld and Keidan) v Secretary of State for International Development* [2018] UKSC 32 made a declaration that ss 1 and 3 of the Civil Partnership Act 2004 are incompatible with Article 14 of the ECHR, when taken in conjunction with Article 8, to the extent that they preclude a different sex couple from entering into a civil partnership. The law was subsequently changed by the Civil Partnership (Opposite-sex Couples) Regulations 2019 (SI 2019/1458).

In *R (on the application of Elan-Cane) v Secretary of State for the Home Department* [2021] UKSC 56, the Supreme Court found that identification as non-gendered is an aspect of private life within the meaning of Article 8 but that there is no judgment of the European Court of Human Rights which establishes a positive obligation on a State to recognise a gender category other than male or female, and none which would require the Secretary of State to issue passports without any indication of gender. Likewise, in *R (on the application of Castellucci) v Gender Recognition Panel* [2024] EWHC 54 (Admin), it was held that the inability of a non-binary person to have a certificate issued under the Gender Recognition Act 2004 recording their gender as non-binary is not discrimination contrary to Article 14 of the ECHR.

In *Secretary of State for Justice v Local Authority* [2021] EWCA Civ 1527, the local authority argued that Article 8 obliged the State to allow care workers to make arrangements for those in its care who were over the age of consent to have contact with sex workers where they were unable to make the necessary arrangements themselves. The Court of Appeal held that the European Court of Human Rights had not recognised any right to purchase the services of a sex worker or to be provided with such services by the State, nor had it recognised that Article 8 obliged the State to allow the purchase of sex without fear of criminal sanction.

Does the Abortion Act 1967, by permitting the abortion, without any restriction, of a foetus which is liable to be born seriously handicapped, perpetuate and reinforce negative cultural stereotypes about people with disabilities, essentially to the effect that their lives are less valuable, and thereby both breaches the Article 8 rights of the living disabled and discriminates against them contrary to Article 14? No, held the Court of Appeal in *R (on the application of Crowter) v Secretary of State for Health and Social Care* [2022] EWCA Civ 1559.

What is the scope of the right to respect for an individual's reputation? The ECtHR has held that a person's reputation, even if that person is criticised in the context of a public debate, forms part of their personal identity and psychological integrity and therefore also falls within their private life (*Denisov v Ukraine* [GC], No 76639/11, § 97, 25 September 2018).

However, as in other spheres protected by Article 8, in order for that provision to come into play, an attack on a person's reputation must attain a certain level of seriousness and be made in a manner causing prejudice to personal enjoyment of the right to respect for private life. This requirement pertains to both social and professional reputation. Likewise, Article 8 cannot be relied on in order to complain of a loss of reputation which is the foreseeable consequence of one's own actions, such as the commission of a criminal offence. This rule is not limited to reputational damage but has been expanded to a wider principle according to which any personal, social, psychological and economic suffering that could be foreseeable consequences of the commission of a criminal offence cannot be relied on in order to complain that a criminal conviction in itself amounts to an interference with the right to respect for 'private life'. This extended principle should cover not only criminal offences but also other misconduct entailing a measure of legal responsibility with foreseeable negative effects on 'private life' (*Hurbain v Belgium* [GC], App No 57292/16, 4 July 2023 at [189]).

27.5.5.2 Family life

It is disruption of the family unit which is most likely to offend against this aspect of Article 8. This might include, for example, a situation in which the State wishes to take a child into care or make an adoption order against the wishes of a parent (see *Re Q (a child)* [2011] EWCA Civ 1610). The sentencing of defendants inevitably engages not only their own Article 8 right to family life but also those of their family, and that includes but is not limited to any dependent child or children; and the same will apply in some cases to an adult for whom a defendant is a carer and whether there is a marital or parental link or not (*R v Carla Foster* [2023] EWCA Crim 1196). It is also an extremely important issue for immigration lawyers, as deportation, extradition and immigration controls often result in families being broken up.

In *Schalk and Kopf v Austria* (Application No 30141/04, 24 June 2010) and *Oliari and Others v Italy* (Application Nos 18766/11 and 36030/11, 21 July 2015), the ECtHR recognised that, even absent a legal status, stable and committed same-sex relationships amount to family life. In *Schalk's* case (at para 94) it was held that 'the relationship of the applicants, a co-habiting same-sex couple living in a stable de facto partnership, falls within the notion of "family life", just as the relationship of a different-sex couple in the same situation would'. In *Vallianatos and Others v Greece* (Application Nos 29381/09 and 32684/09, 7 November 2013) (at para 81), the Court stated that civil partnerships 'as an officially recognised alternative to marriage have an intrinsic value for applicants irrespective of the legal effects, however narrow or extensive, that they would produce'. Earlier in its judgment the court found that the measures, in that case making provision for civil partnerships for different-sex couples only, fell squarely within the ambit of Article 8, and stated at para 73 that 'in view of the rapid evolution in a considerable number of member States regarding the granting of legal recognition to same-sex couples, "it [would be] artificial to maintain the view that, in contrast to a different-sex couple, a same-sex couple [could not] enjoy 'family life' for the purposes of Article 8"'.

'Family' clearly includes those with blood and marital links, but has also been extended by the ECtHR to include other emotional ties. In *K v United Kingdom* (1986) 50 DR 199, the ECtHR said 'the question of the existence or non-existence of "family life" is essentially a question of fact depending upon the real existence in practice of close personal ties'. The leading domestic authority on the ambit of family life for the purposes of Article 8 is *Kugathas v Secretary of State for the Home Department* [2003] EWCA Civ 31. The court found that a single man of 38 years who had lived in the UK since 1999 did not enjoy 'family life' with his mother, brother and sister, who were living in Germany as refugees. At [14], Sedley LJ accepted as a proper approach the guidance given by the European Commission for Human Rights in its decision in *S v United Kingdom* (1984) 40 DR 196, at 198:

> Generally, the protection of family life under Article 8 involves cohabiting dependents, such as parents and their dependent, minor children. Whether it extends to other relationships depends on the circumstances of the particular case. Relationships between adults, a mother and her 33-year-old son in the present case, would not necessarily acquire the protection of Article 8 of the Convention without evidence of further elements of dependency, involving more than the normal emotional ties.

Sedley LJ held that there is not an absolute requirement of dependency in an economic sense for 'family life' to exist, but that it is necessary for there to be real, committed or effective support between family members in order to show that 'family life' exists ([17]); 'neither blood ties nor the concern and affection that ordinarily go with them are, by themselves or together', sufficient ([19]); and the natural tie between a parent and an infant is probably a special case in which there is no need to show that there is a demonstrable measure of support ([18]).

Does a private or family life include such interests as an individual's social life; a person's life being centred, or work being dependent on, a particular activity; family involvement in a particular activity; the social and economic impact on a local community of the loss of a particular activity; cultural heritage; loss of job or loss of business? In *R (on the application of the Countryside Alliance and Others) v AG* [2007] UKHL 52, the claimants put forward these interests as part of their case that the ban on hunting wild mammals with dogs under the Hunting Act 2004 engaged Article 8. However, the House of Lords (now the Supreme Court) observed that these arguments stretched the ambit of Article 8 far wider than had ever been recognised in Strasbourg jurisprudence and the House held that Article 8 was not engaged.

> As a matter of everyday experience, no-one could doubt that an individual's wellbeing – their sense of purpose, fulfilment or achievement, their pride and self-esteem, the development of their potential – may be intimately bound up with their working life, their job and their career. The loss of a valued job in any circumstances can hit all of those things hard. When it happens in circumstances of unlawfulness or unfairness, that can of course produce an entirely understandable subjective experience of insult added to injury. At the same time, many people do not have the good fortune of fulfilling work and career prospects. Many jobs may be considered in themselves corrosive of rather than conducive to individual wellbeing, beyond the pure economics. There is no Art.8 protected human right as such to a fulfilling job, a chosen job, or any specific job, to professional development or to career advancement. These are human goods, and their deprivation is a loss, but the addition of a causative unlawful act by a public body does not necessarily make them human rights, nor their deprivation a human rights violation. A Human Rights Act damages claim for lost work requires a claimant to establish not only causative unlawfulness but also a distinctive basis of rights violation deriving, in a case like this, from the impact of the loss on protected private life interests. It is for a claimant to demonstrate that impact, with relevant evidence and to an appropriate level of seriousness. (per Mrs Justice Collins Rice in *Kulumbegov v Home Office* [2023] EWHC 337 (KB) at [67])

Do the values underlying the right of lone parents with children below school age to respect for their family life include those of a home life underpinned by a degree of stability, practical as well as emotional, and thus by financial resources adequate to meet basic needs, in particular for accommodation, warmth, food and clothing? Yes, held the Supreme Court in *R (on the application of DA) v Secretary of State for Work and Pensions* [2019] UKSC 21.

27.5.5.3 Home

Clearly, there is some overlap between private life, family life and home life. This element of Article 8(1) specifically protects the right to occupy one's home without harassment or interference. Noise nuisance can violate this right (*Arrondelle v United Kingdom* (1982) 26 DR 5). So can entry by the police to search or for other purposes. In *McLeod v United Kingdom* (1999) 27

EHRR 493, the police accompanied an estranged husband into the former matrimonial home. As there was little risk of disorder, the ECtHR held that this was a disproportionate interference with the applicant's right to home life.

In the context of housing law, the Article does not extend to the right to have a home (*Buckley v United Kingdom* (1996) 23 EHRR 101). But might it constitute a defence to possession proceedings? Yes, any public sector occupier at risk of losing their home must have the opportunity to have the proportionality of that step considered by the county court, and that consideration can include factors such as their personal circumstances: see *Kay v UK* [2010] ECHR 1322 and *Manchester City Council v Pinnock* [2010] UKSC 45. There is no clear and constant jurisprudence of the ECtHR that the proportionality test implied into Article 8(2) applies where there is a private landlord. In *McDonald (by her litigation friend) v McDonald* [2014] EWCA Civ 1049, a private landlord obtained a possession order of a property held on an assured shorthold tenancy after serving a statutory notice to quit. The Court held that Article 8(2) did not apply. However, the Court noted that the result did not mean that a tenant could not contend that the provisions of the relevant statute did not properly protect the Article 8 rights of the tenant. In *Dean v Mitchell* [2023] EWHC 1479 (KB), it was held that in these circumstances the correct approach can be found in *Moreno Gómez v Spain* (2005) 41 EHRR 40 at [55]:

> Although the object of Art.8 is essentially that of protecting the individual against arbitrary interference by the public authorities, it may involve the authorities' adopting measures designed to secure respect for private life even in the sphere of the relations of individuals between themselves. Whether the case is analysed in terms of a positive duty on the State to take reasonable and appropriate measures to secure the applicants' rights under para.1 of Art.8 or in terms of an interference by a public authority to be justified in accordance with para.2, the applicable principles are broadly similar. In both contexts regard must be had to the fair balance that has to be struck between the competing interests of the individual and of the community as a whole. Furthermore, even in relation to the positive obligations flowing from the first paragraph of Art.8, in striking the required balance the aims mentioned in the second paragraph may be of a certain relevance.

27.5.5.4 Correspondence

It was under this provision that *Malone v United Kingdom* (1984) 7 EHRR 14 was brought, successfully challenging telephone tapping by the police without statutory authority. This resulted in the enactment of the Interception of Communications Act 1985 to grant the police statutory powers. Similar issues were raised in the *Halford* case (see **27.5.5.1**). The Regulation of Investigatory Powers Act 2000 is an important piece of legislation in this area which now, amongst other things, governs interference with communications by employers. As for interference with written correspondence, most of the case law concerns prisoners' rights. Broadly they may correspond freely with their lawyers, but prison authorities may interfere with other correspondence so long as this is justified (*Golder v United Kingdom* (1975) 1 EHRR 524; *Silver v United Kingdom* (1983) 5 EHRR 347).

Following the decision in *Big Brother Watch v United Kingdom* (2022) 74 EHRR 17, s 8(4) of Regulation of Investigatory Powers Act 2000, which conferred a power on the Secretary of State to issue a warrant for 'the interception of external communications in the course of their transmission by means of a telecommunication system', was repealed. Its successor in the Investigatory Powers Act 2016 was held to be compatible with Articles 8 and 10 in *R (on the application of National Council for Civil Liberties) v Secretary of State for the Home Department* [2023] EWCA Civ 926.

At a general level, a person's internet chats fall within the broad ambit of Article 8(1) (*Garamukanwa v United Kingdom* [2019] IRLR 853, ECtHR).

27.5.5.5 Justification for interference

Article 8 is not absolute. Paragraph 2 sets out reasons which may justify interference with para 1 rights. The principle of proportionality requires that the interference must be the minimum necessary to achieve the legitimate aim (see *R (on the application of M) v Chief Constable of Hampshire* [2014] EWCA Civ 1651 and the *McLeod* case at **27.5.5.3** above).

CASE EXAMPLE

In *R (on the application of TT) v Registrar General for England and Wales* [2019] EWHC 2384 (Fam) (confirmed on appeal: [2020] EWCA Civ 559), the claimant had been born female but had transitioned to live as a man. He had obtained a gender recognition certificate confirming his gender as male under the law. However, he suspended testosterone treatment and had intra-uterine insemination with donor sperm whereby he became pregnant and gave birth to a child. He wished to be registered on his child's birth certificate as his child's father or 'parent' but the registrar general concluded that he had to be registered as the child's 'mother'.

The court observed that the requirement for the claimant to be registered as the child's mother interfered with his, and his child's, Article 8 rights. Why? Because the psychological and social reality for them was that the claimant was the child's father. Further, if an occasion arose where the claimant was required to produce the child's full birth certificate, that would cause embarrassment and distress for both parent and child. But a balance had to be struck between the parent's individual right to privacy and the child's right to know about their biological identity, particularly for medical reasons. Moreover, the outcome sought by the claimant would mean that the child would never have a 'mother', which would mark him out from all other children.

The court held that in establishing the scheme of birth registration under the Births and Deaths Registration Act 1953, and in holding by s 12 of the Gender Recognition Act 2004 that the fact that a person's gender had become the acquired gender following the issue of a certificate 'does not affect the status of the person as the father or mother of a child', Parliament had made a social and political judgement as to how the competing interests should be accommodated. In doing so, it had afforded priority to the need for clarity as to parental status. There were child-focused reasons in favour of striking the balance that way. The government was pursuing the legitimate aim of establishing a coherent birth registration system. The requirement that the person who gave birth was registered as the child's mother was fully justified, proportionate and fair. The adverse impact on the claimant was substantially outweighed by the interests of third parties and society at large in the operation of a coherent registration scheme.

27.5.6 Article 10: The right to freedom of expression

1. Everyone has the right to freedom of expression. This right shall include freedom to hold opinions and to receive and impart information and ideas without interference by public authority and regardless of frontiers. This Article shall not prevent States from requiring the licensing of broadcasting, television or cinema enterprises.
2. The exercise of these freedoms, since it carries with it duties and responsibilities, may be subject to such formalities, conditions, restrictions or penalties as are prescribed by law and are necessary in a democratic society, in the interests of national security, territorial integrity or public safety, for the prevention of disorder or crime, for the protection of health or morals, for the protection of the reputation or rights of others, for preventing the disclosure of information received in confidence, or for maintaining the authority and impartiality of the judiciary.

Some forms of self-expression will fall outside the scope of the free speech right, because they amount to no more than vulgar abuse and convey no ideas and no meaningful information, or for other reasons. At the other extreme, information and ideas which aim at the destruction of democracy, or its fundamental freedoms are not protected: see Article 17 of the Convention. But the law does not require courtesy. It is trite law that speech does not lose protection just because the information or ideas that it conveys are offensive, disturbing or even shocking. Communications of that kind are within the scope of the right. (per Lady Carr of Walton-on-the-Hill, LCJ in *R v Casserly* [2024] EWCA Crim 25 at [37])

The ECtHR has described this right as 'one of the essential foundations of a democratic society and one of the conditions of its progress' (*Handyside v United Kingdom* (1976) 1 EHRR 737). It is particularly useful to the press and broadcast media, as well as other publishers and political organisations. Free speech is a fundamental common law right (*R v Shayler* [2002] 1 AC 247). It has been described as 'the primary right' without which 'an effective rule of law is not possible', 'the lifeblood of democracy' and 'a brake on the abuse of power by public officials' (*R v Secretary of State for the Home Department, ex parte Simms* [1999] 2 AC 11 per Lord Steyn at [125G] and [126F]–[126H]). It 'constitutes one of the essential foundations of a democratic society and one of the basic conditions for its progress and for each individual's self-fulfilment': R *(Lord Carlile) v Home Secretary* [2014] UKSC 60 per Lord Sumption at [13].

The right extends to receiving as well as imparting information. However, this does not oblige public authorities to disclose information against their will (*The Gaskin Case* [1990] 1 FLR 167, no right of access to fostering records held by a local authority). It merely prohibits restrictions on the receipt of information, for example information about abortion in Ireland (*Open Door Dublin Well Women v Ireland* (1992) 15 EHRR 244), and internet sites containing legal and educational information in Estonia and Lithunania respectively (*Kalda v Estonia* (2016) (Application No 17429/10) and *Jankovskis v Lithuania* (2017) (Application No 21575/08)). But it can also address the wholesale blocking of websites by governments, for example *YouTube* by Turkey (*Cengiz v Turkey* (2015) (Application Nos 48226/10 and 14027/11)).

There are limits to the important general rule that dissent enjoys a high degree of protection – see *Aldi v General Medical Council* [2023] EWCA Civ 1261 per Popplewell LJ at [50]:

> ... Bean LJ posited a hypothetical example of a doctor who published views that there was no link between cancer and smoking, that smoking was good for health, and that people were encouraged to smoke at least 40 cigarettes a day. In such a case the views would be so far removed from any concept of legitimate medical debate that an appeal to the importance and breadth of the freedom of expression protected by article 10 would be misplaced. All depends upon the facts of each individual case, and Mr Hoar's appeal to some general principle in relation to medical or political debate obscures the need to focus on the particular views expressed by the appellant in this case.

The important policy considerations that underpin free speech show that it is wrong to afford equal protection to all speech.

> That is because the essential contribution that free speech makes to a democratic society depends on a functioning democratic marketplace in free thought and ideas. That marketplace can be distorted by speech itself. In the online world of social media, bots, trolls, cyber troops, false and hacked accounts can be used to drown out genuine free speech and replace it with a dishonest narrative to suit the whim of an autocrat, government or some other powerful body or person. Propaganda, disinformation and misinformation, particularly in time of war, can be corrosive of democracy and national security. (per Mr Justice Johnson in *Phillips v The Secretary of State for Foreign, Commonwealth and Development Affairs* [2024] EWHC 32 (Admin) at [46])

If there is a threat to life within the meaning of Article 2, the court does not have to balance the principle of open justice and the rights of the media under Article 10, as the State through its judicial branch cannot release material into the public domain which would threaten the life of a citizen (*R v Blackman* [2017] EWCA Crim 326).

Justice should be open to public scrutiny, and the media are the conduit through which most members of the public receive information about court proceedings (*R v Cornick* [2014] EWHC 3623 (QB)). So it follows that the principle of open justice is inextricably linked to the freedom of the media to report court proceedings (see *A v BBC* [2014] UKSC 25). It is therefore a general principle that, in the vast majority of cases, a defendant in a criminal case can be expected to be named, unless there is an absolute necessity for anonymity. Similar considerations apply in civil proceedings (*PNM v Times Newspapers Ltd* [2014] EWCA Civ 1132 and *Moss v Information Commissioner* [2020] EWCA Civ 580).

Is an immediate custodial sentence never appropriate for a non-violent crime committed as part of peaceful protest and in breach of Article 10? No, held the Court of Appeal in *R v Roberts* [2018] EWCA Crim 2739.

Why did the College of Policing's 2014 Hate Crime Operational Guidance, which required police to record non-crime hate incidents against individuals, regardless of whether there was evidence of hostility, breach Article 10? The Court of Appeal held that whilst the Guidance pursued the legitimate aims of preventing crime and protecting the rights of others, those aims could have been achieved by less intrusive means. Although the Guidance was revised in 2020, that did not go far enough in addressing the chilling effect of such perception-based recording (*R (on the application of Miller) v College of Policing* [2021] EWCA Civ 1926).

Where there is an interference with Article 10 rights, it will be incompatible with the Convention unless:

(a) it is prescribed by law;
(b) it pursues a legitimate aim (see para 2);
(c) it is necessary in a democratic society; and
(d) it is proportionate.

The appropriate structure for analysing the application of Article 10 rights is the series of questions identified and applied by the Supreme Court in *DPP v Ziegler* [2022] AC 408 at [16] and [58]:

> (1) Is what the defendant did in exercise of one of the rights in Article 10?
> (2) If so, is there an interference by a public authority with that right?
> (3) If there is an interference, is it 'prescribed by law'?
> (4) If so, is the interference in pursuit of a legitimate aim as set out in paragraph 2 of article 10?
> (5) If so, is the interference 'necessary in a democratic society' to achieve that legitimate aim? This question will in turn require consideration of the well-known set of sub-questions which arise in order to assess whether an interference is proportionate:
> (a) Is the aim sufficiently important to justify inference with a fundamental right?
> (b) Is there a rational connection between the means chosen and the aim in view?
> (c) Are there less restrictive alternative means available to achieve that aim?
> (d) Is there a fair balance between the rights of the individual and the general interest of the community, including the rights of others?

EXAMPLES

The Video Recordings Act 2010 requires the British Board of Film Classification (BBFC) to classify all video works, subject to exemptions in respect of educational, sporting or musical works which are not supplied for profit. The purpose of the legislation is to provide information for the public so as to enable choices in viewing material unsuitable for children, or extreme violence or pornography. The classifications of U, PG, 12, 15 and 18 are familiar to all. In *R v Dryzner* [2014] EWCA Crim 2438, the Court held that the classification requirements that the Act imposed are lawful, necessary and proportionate for the protection of public health and morals.

An offence under the Terrorism Act 2000, Part II, s 13(1) of carrying or displaying an article 'in such a way or in such circumstances as to arouse reasonable suspicion' that the accused belonged to or supported a proscribed organisation is an offence of strict liability. However, whilst the offence engages the right to freedom of expression under Article 10, that interference is justified by the legitimate aims of safeguarding national security and ensuring public order and is not disproportionate to those aims (see *Pwr v DPP* [2022] UKSC 2).

For a more contentious case that split the Supreme Court, *see R (on the application of Lord Carlile of Berriew QC) v Secretary of State for the Home Department* [2014] UKSC 60.

27.5.6.1 Defamation

The ECtHR recognises that individuals have a right to have their reputations protected. But defamation claims are an interference with Article 10 rights and so must be justified using the criteria listed above on a case-by-case basis. In *Tolstoy Miloslavsky v United Kingdom; Lord Aldington v Watts* (1995) 20 EHRR 442, for example, the ECtHR found that a damages award of £1.5 million was disproportionate.

The ECtHR has also recognised, however, that criticism of public figures, especially politicians, is more easily justifed under Article 10. In *Lingens v Austria* (1986) 8 EHRR 407 it said:

> The limits of acceptable criticism are ... wider as regards a politician as such than as regards a private individual. Unlike the latter, the former inevitably and knowingly lays himself open to close scrutiny of every word and deed by both journalists and the public at large, and he must consequently display a greater degree of tolerance. (para 42)

What about pressure groups? In *Steel and Morris v United Kingdom* [2005] ECHR 68416/01 (the so-called 'McDonald's libel case') the ECtHR stated that

> [t]he Court considers, however, that in a democratic society even small and informal campaign groups ... must be able to carry on their activities effectively and that there exists a strong public interest in enabling such groups and individuals outside the mainstream to contribute to the public debate by disseminating information and ideas on matters of general public interest such as health and the environment ... If, however, a State decides to provide such a remedy [defamation] to a corporate body, it is essential, in order to safeguard the countervailing interests in free expression and open debate, that a measure of procedural fairness and equality of arms is provided for. ... (paras 89 and 95)

27.5.6.2 Prior restraint

The use of injunctions to prevent publication of material in advance is viewed with suspicion by the ECtHR. In the *Spycatcher* case (*Guardian Newspapers v United Kingdom* (1992) 14 EHRR 153) it said:

> [T]he dangers inherent in prior restraint are such that they call for the most careful scrutiny ... News is a perishable commodity and to delay its publication, even for a short period, may well deprive it of all its value and interest. (para 60)

For example, a journalist was denied an injunction restraining the BBC from broadcasting his image as part of a documentary exposing alleged wrongdoing in investigative journalism, because the evidence had not demonstrated that the risk of harm to him would be materially increased (*Mahmood v BBC* [2014] EWHC 4207 (QB)). However, in *OPO v MLA* [2014] EWCA Civ 1277, an injunction was granted restraining the defendant, a talented performing artist, from publishing a book describing his traumatic upbringing, which included the suffering of sexual abuse. The claimant was the defendant's autistic young son, and the Court held that he had sufficiently favourable prospects of establishing at trial his claim that publication would constitute intentional conduct causing him psychiatric harm.

The concern which the Strasbourg Court has is reflected in s 12 of the HRA 1998 (see the **Appendix to Part IV**).

In *Cream Holdings Ltd and Others v Banerjee and Others* [2004] UKHL 44, the House of Lords stated:

> Section 12(3) makes the likelihood of success at trial an essential element in the court's consideration of whether to make an interim order. ... There can be no single, rigid standard governing all applications for interim restraint orders. Rather, on its proper construction the effect of section 12(3) is that the court is not to make an interim restraint order unless satisfied the applicant's prospects of success at the trial are sufficiently favourable to justify such an order being made in the particular

> circumstances of the case. As to what degree of likelihood makes the prospects of success 'sufficiently favourable', the general approach should be that courts will be exceedingly slow to make interim restraint orders where the applicant has not satisfied the court he will probably ('more likely than not') succeed at the trial. In general, that should be the threshold an applicant must cross before the court embarks on exercising its discretion, duly taking into account the relevant jurisprudence on article 10 and any countervailing Convention rights. But there will be cases where it is necessary for a court to depart from this general approach and a lesser degree of likelihood will suffice as a prerequisite. Circumstances where this may be so include those mentioned above: where the potential adverse consequences of disclosure are particularly grave, or where a short-lived injunction is needed to enable the court to hear and give proper consideration to an application for interim relief pending the trial or any relevant appeal.

See also *Boyd v Ineos Upstream Ltd* [2019] EWCA Civ 515.

The Supreme Court in *PJS v News Group Newspapers Ltd* [2016] UKSC 26 held that: (i) neither Article 8 nor Article 10 has preference over the other; (ii) where their values are in conflict, what is necessary is an intense focus on the comparative importance of the rights being claimed in the individual case; (iii) the justifications for interfering with or restricting each right must be taken into account; and (iv) the proportionality test must be applied. See also *Abbasi v Newcastle upon Tyne Hospitals NHS Foundation Trust* [2023] EWCA Civ 331.

27.5.7 Article 11: The right to freedom of assembly and association

> 1. Everyone has the right to freedom of peaceful assembly and to freedom of association with others, including the right to form and to join trade unions for the protection of his interests.
> 2. No restrictions shall be placed on the exercise of these rights other than such as are prescribed by law and are necessary in a democratic society in the interests of national security or public safety, for the prevention of disorder or crime, for the protection of health or morals or for the protection of the rights and freedoms of others. This Article shall not prevent the imposition of lawful restrictions on the exercise of these rights by members of the armed forces, of the police or of the administration of the State.

This Article contains two distinct rights: freedom of peaceful assembly and freedom of association.

27.5.7.1 Freedom of peaceful assembly

This extends to anyone who intends to organise a peaceful march or static assembly. It does not cover a protest where the organisers or participants engage in violence, have violent intentions, incite violence or otherwise reject the foundations of a democratic society (*Attorney General's Reference (No 1 of 2022)* [2022] EWCA Crim 1259). The possibility of violence arising because of the intentions of counter-demonstrators or extremist infiltrators does not affect the right (*Christians Against Racism and Fascism v United Kingdom* (1980) 21 DR 138). By exercising the right on a public highway, the protesters' activities must not become a nuisance nor unreasonably impede the right of others to pass (see *Secretary of State for the Environment, Food and Rural Affairs v Meier* [2009] UKSC 11). So whilst protesters might assemble peacefully in a public place such as St Paul's Cathedral in London, they are not entitled to establish a substantial encampment of tents on the highway there (see *City of London v Tammy Samede (representative of those persons taking part in a protest camp at St Paul's Churchyard, London EC4)* [2012] EWHC 34).

Deliberately obstructing traffic or seriously disrupting the activities of others is not at the core of the rights guaranteed by Article 11 (*Attorney General's Reference (No 1 of 2022)* [2022] EWCA Crim 1259). Nor do these rights include any ancillary right to trespass, damage private property, or injure others (*Esso Petroleum Co Ltd v Breen* [2023] EWHC 2013 (KB)).

The sorts of restrictions which para 2 envisages include limitations on the location of a demonstration or the route of a march.

Does the right to peaceful assembly under Article 11 mean that the police force has a responsibility to facilitate peaceful protests even if they are technically unlawful? No, held the Supreme Court in *DB v Chief Constable of Police Service of Northern Ireland* [2017] UKSC 7. At para 60 the Court quoted with approval the decision in *Eva Molnar v Hungary* (Application No 10346/05), where the ECtHR considered a complaint that the applicant's rights under Article 11 had been infringed by police dispersing a peaceful demonstration in which she had participated, merely because prior notification of the protest had not been given. At paras 34–38 the ECtHR said this:

> 34. The Court observes that paragraph 2 of article 11 entitles States to impose 'lawful restrictions' on the exercise of the right to freedom of assembly. The Court notes that restrictions on freedom of peaceful assembly in public places may serve the protection of the rights of others with a view to preventing disorder and maintaining the orderly circulation of traffic.
>
> 35. The Court reiterates that a prior notification requirement would not normally encroach upon the essence of that right. It is not contrary to the spirit of article 11 if, for reasons of public order and national security, *a priori*, a High Contracting Party requires that the holding of meetings be subject to authorisation (see *Nurettin Aldemir v Turkey*, nos 32124/02, 32126/02, 32129/02, 32132/02, 32133/02, 32137/02 and 32138/02 (joined) [2007] ECHR 1121, para 42, 18 December 2007).
>
> 36. However, in special circumstances when an immediate response might be justified, for example in relation to a political event, in the form of a spontaneous demonstration, to disperse the ensuing demonstration solely because of the absence of the requisite prior notice, without any illegal conduct by the participants, may amount to a disproportionate restriction on freedom of peaceful assembly (see *Bukta*, cited above, paras 35 and 36). It is important for the public authorities to show a certain degree of tolerance towards peaceful gatherings if the freedom of assembly guaranteed by article 11 of the Convention is not to be deprived of all substance (see *Nurettin Aldemir*, cited above, para 46).
>
> 37. Nevertheless, in the Court's view, the principle established in the case of *Bukta* cannot be extended to the point that the absence of prior notification can never be a legitimate basis for crowd dispersal. Prior notification serves not only the aim of reconciling, on the one hand, the right to assembly and, on the other hand, the rights and lawful interests (including the right of movement) of others, but also the prevention of disorder or crime. In order to balance these conflicting interests, the institution of preliminary administrative procedures is common practice in member states when a public demonstration is to be organised. In the Court's view, such requirements do not, as such, run counter to the principles embodied in article 11 of the Convention, as long as they do not represent a hidden obstacle to the freedom of peaceful assembly protected by the Convention (see *Balcik v Turkey*, no 25/02, para 49, 29 November 2007).
>
> 38. The Court therefore considers that the right to hold spontaneous demonstrations may override the obligation to give prior notification to public assemblies only in special circumstances, namely if an immediate response to a current event is warranted in the form of a demonstration. In particular, such derogation from the general rule may be justified if a delay would have rendered that response obsolete.

27.5.7.2 Freedom of association

This covers the right of individuals to join together, especially in organisations like political parties and trade unions (see, for example, *Independent Workers Union of Great Britain v Central Arbitration Committee* [2021] EWCA Civ 952). So, a finding that a trade union representing the interests of foster carers was not entitled to be listed as a trade union (under the Trade Union and Labour Relations (Consolidation) Act 1992, s 2) breached the Article 11 rights of the union and its members (*National Union of Professional Foster Carers v Certification Officer* [2021] EWCA Civ 548). It also extends to the right not to join such organisations, for example compulsory membership of a union (a 'closed shop') will usually be contrary to the Convention (*Young, James and Webster v United Kingdom* (1982) 4 EHRR 38).

The ECtHR considered the scope of the class of people who have trade union rights under Article 11 in the leading case of *Sindicatul 'Păstorul Cel Bun' v Romania* [2014] IRLR 49 ('The Good Shepherd'). The rights extend to a right to negotiate with employers via collective bargaining (*Demir v Turkey* [2009] IRLR 766) and a right to strike (*Enerji Yapi-Yol Sen v Turkey* [2009] ECHR 2251) but see RMT *v* UK [2014] ECHR 366; as well as a right to claim for unfair dismissal from employment based on political affiliation or opinion (*Redfearn v UK* [2012] ECHR 1878).

Is s 146 of the Trade Union and Labour Relations (Consolidation) Act 1992 compatible with Article 11 in so far as it fails to provide any protection against sanctions, short of dismissal, that are intended to deter or penalise trade union members from taking part in lawful strike action organised by their union? No, held the Supreme Court in *Secretary of State for Business and Trade v Mercer* [2024] UKSC 12.

27.5.8 Article 14: The prohibition on discrimination

> The enjoyment of the rights and freedoms set forth in this Convention shall be secured without discrimination on any ground such as sex, race, colour, language, religion, political or other opinion, national or social origin, association with a national minority, property, birth or other status.

Article 14 draws a distinction between relevant status and difference in treatment, and the former cannot be defined solely by the latter.

> There must be a ground for the difference in treatment in terms of the characteristic which is something more than a mere description of the difference in treatment. [However] there is no requirement that the status should have legal or social significance for other purposes or in contexts other than the difference in treatment of which complaint is made. (per Lord Lloyd-Jones in R *(A) v Criminal Injuries Compensation Authority* [2021] UKSC 27 at [66])

Article 14 is not as important as it may at first appear. It is vital to realise that the right not to be discriminated against cannot be relied upon on its own. It may only be invoked in conjunction with another Convention right.

> As the Court has consistently held, Article 14 of the Convention complements the other substantive provisions of the Convention and the Protocols. It has no independent existence since it has effect solely in relation to 'the enjoyment of the rights and freedoms' safeguarded by those provisions. Although the application of Article 14 does not presuppose a breach of those provisions – and to this extent it is autonomous – there can be no room for its application unless the facts at issue fall within the ambit of one or more of the latter. (*Van Raalte v Netherlands* (1997) 24 EHRR 503 at para 33 and see also R *(SC) v Secretary of State for Work and Pensions* [2021] UKSC 26)

A claimant relying on Article 14 must first establish that a substantive Convention right is in issue. There need not necessarily have been a breach of that right. It must only be shown that the facts fall within the ambit of that provision. What Article 14 prohibits is discrimination. What this means is that if there is a prejudicial difference in treatment of persons in relevantly similar situations on the facts of the particular case, the difference in treatment must have an objective and reasonable justification (see, for example, R *(Chester) v Secretary of State for Justice* [2013] UKSC 63). In deciding whether there has been discrimination in this sense, the position of the claimant must be compared with that of those in 'relevantly similar or analogous' situations (*Larkos v Cyprus* (1990) 30 EHRR 597). If there is a prejudicial difference in treatment, that difference in treatment must pursue a legitimate aim and bear a reasonable relationship to the aim sought to be realised (*Belgian Linguistic Case (No 2)* (1979–80) 1 EHRR 252). There are, therefore, two distinct questions: (i) has there been disadvantageous treatment of persons in relevantly similar situations; and (ii) if so, does it have reasonable and objective justification?

Lieven J in R *(on the application of AM) v Secretary of State for the Home Department* [2022] EWHC 2591 (Admin) at [59] summarised the following relevant propositions:

(1) "The court has established in its case law that only differences in treatment based on an identifiable characteristic, or 'status', are capable of amounting to discrimination within the meaning of article 14."

(2) "Moreover, in order for an issue to arise under article 14 there must be a difference in the treatment of persons in analogous, or relevantly similar, situations."

(3) "Such a difference of treatment is discriminatory if it has no objective and reasonable justification; in other words, if it does not pursue a legitimate aim or if there is not a reasonable relationship of proportionality between the means employed and the aim sought to be realised."

(4) "The contracting state enjoys a margin of appreciation in assessing whether and to what extent differences in otherwise similar situations justify a different treatment. The scope of this margin will vary according to the circumstances, the subject matter and the background."

What about indirect discrimination?

> It has to be shown by the claimant that a neutrally formulated measure affects a disproportionate number of members of a group of persons sharing a characteristic which is alleged to be the ground of discrimination, so as to give rise to a presumption of indirect discrimination. Once a prima facie case of indirect discrimination has been established, the burden shifts to the state to show that the indirect difference in treatment is not discriminatory. The state can discharge that burden by establishing that the difference in the impact of the measure in question is the result of objective factors unrelated to any discrimination on the ground alleged. This requires the state to demonstrate that the measure in question has an objective and reasonable justification: in other words, that it pursues a legitimate aim by proportionate means. (per Lord Reed in *R (SC) v Secretary of State for Work and Pensions* [2021] UKSC 26 at [53])

There has been much debate as to the legal position where the claim is that there has been an infringement of Article 14 in conjunction with Article 8 (see **27.5.5**):

> The claim is capable of falling within Article 14 even though there has been no infringement of Article 8. If the State has brought into existence a positive measure which, even though not required by Article 8, is a modality of the exercise of the rights guaranteed by Article 8, the State will be in breach of Article 14 if the measure has more than a tenuous connection with the core values protected by Article 8 and is discriminatory and not justified. It is not necessary that the measure has any adverse impact on the complainant in a positive modality case other than the fact that the complainant is not entitled to the benefit of the positive measure in question. (per Sir Terence Etherton MR at [55] in *Smith v Lancashire Teaching Hospitals NHS Foundation Trust* [2017] EWCA Civ 1916; see also *Steinfeld v Secretary of State for Education* [2017] EWCA Civ 81)

Where there is an interference with rights falling within Article 8(1) but that is justified under Article 8(2), may that also fall foul of Article 14 if it is discriminatory?

> I do not see why any conduct that interferes with a qualified substantive right such as those in article 8(1) should not fall within the ambit of that substantive right irrespective of whether it is justified; although, of course, in those circumstances the state may be able to show that, as well as its interference with the substantive right, its discriminatory conduct is also justified. (per Hickinbottom LJ at [86] in *R (JCWI) v Secretary of State for the Home Department* [2020] EWCA Civ 542)

CASE EXAMPLES

(1) *Abdulaziz v United Kingdom; Cabales v United Kingdom; Balkandali v United Kingdom* (1985) 7 EHRR 471, an immigration case. The exclusion from the UK of spouses of new entrants in certain circumstances was held not to breach Article 8. However, the admission of the spouses of male entrants but the exclusion of spouses of female entrants breached Article 14.

(2) R *(on the application of Chapti) v Secretary of State for the Home Department* [2011] EWHC 3370, an immigration case. The requirement that a foreign spouse applying to settle in the UK with their partner had to produce a test certificate of knowledge of the English language engaged Article 8. However, the aims of the rule, namely to promote integration and to protect public services, were legitimate aims and did not amount to a disproportionate interference with family life. Was Article 14 breached because nationals of English-speaking countries and those with educational qualifications that were taught in English or obtained from institutions in English-speaking countries were exempt from the requirement? No, held the court, this was rational in the light of the aims of the rule. Further, there was no evidence that the rule indirectly discriminated on the grounds of nationality, ethnic origins or disability.

(3) *Humphreys v Revenue & Customs Commissioners* [2012] UKSC 18, a social security case. The claimant was the father of a child for whom he claimed child tax credits. The refusal of that claim engaged Article 1 of the First Protocol (see **27.5.9**). The refusal was based on the fact that he was the child's minority carer. His mother was awarded the child tax credit as she cared for the child more nights each week. Whilst this was discrimination for the purposes of Article 14, the Supreme Court held that it was justified. See further R *(on the application of SC, CB and 8 children) v Secretary of State for Work and Pensions* [2021] UKSC 26.

You will have noted that Article 14 ends with the words 'other status'. Who might fall within that category? The ECtHR has interpreted this as meaning a personal characteristic (see *Kjeldsen, Busk Madsen and Pedersen v Denmark* (1976) 1 EHRR 711, para 56). It is therefore necessary to examine whether the ground for different treatment in a case amounts to a status in the sense of a personal characteristic (see R *(on the application of S) v Chief Constable of South Yorkshire* [2004] UKHL 39). This led the Court of Appeal, for example, in R *(on the application of RJM) v Secretary of State for Work and Pensions* [2007] EWCA Civ 614, to hold that a person who chooses to be homeless or to sleep rough does not fall within this provision. 'Impecuniosity', at any rate if defined by reference to an inability to pay a particular government fee, is not a relevant status for the purposes of Article 14: R *(on the application of Williams (by his litigation friend)) v Secretary of State for the Home Department* [2017] EWCA Civ 98. However, in R *(on the application of K (a child by her litigation friend MT)) v Secretary of State for the Home Department* [2018] EWHC 1834 (Admin), the court held that being born to a mother married to someone other than one's biological father was an 'other status' for the purposes of Article 14. Likewise, in R *(on the application of Stott) v Secretary of State for Justice* [2018] UKSC 59, [2020] AC 51, the Supreme Court held that the different treatment of prisoners serving extended determinate sentences to consideration of parole when compared to those serving indeterminate or other determinate sentences constituted a ground within the meaning of 'other status' in Article 14. An applicant is entitled to rely on a status provided that it is not defined entirely by the alleged discrimination (*Simawi v Haringey LBC* [2019] EWCA Civ 1770).

Does a status for the purpose of Article 14 have to be permanent? No, held the Supreme Court in R *(on the application of DA) v Secretary of State for Work and Pensions* [2019] UKSC 21.

The historical difference of view between the Supreme Court (when it was formerly the House of Lords) and the ECtHR as to the meaning of the phrase 'other status' in Article 14, which was manifested in the speeches in the House of Lords in R *(Clift) v Secretary of State for the Home Department* [2007] 1 AC 484 and in the judgment of the 4th Section of the ECtHR in *Clift v United Kingdom* (Application No 7205/07, 13 July 2010), was finally resolved in favour of the latter by the Supreme Court in R *(on the application of Stott) v Secretary of State for Justice* (above).

To summarise, in determining whether an individual's Article 14 rights have been breached, the court has to ask whether:

(a) the facts fell within the ambit of one or more of the Convention rights;

(b) there was difference in treatment in respect of that right between the complainant and others put forward for comparison;

(c) those others were in an analogous situation;

(d) the difference in treatment was objectively justifiable, in that it had a legitimate aim and bore a reasonable relationship of proportionality to that aim;

(e) the difference in treatment was based on one or more of the grounds proscribed, whether expressly or by inference, in Article 14 (see further *Wandsworth LBC v Michalak* [2002] EWCA Civ 271, *Ghaidan v Godin-Mendoza* [2004] UKHL 30 and *Gilham v Ministry of Justice* [2017] EWCA Civ 2220).

27.5.9 Protocol 1, Article 1: The right to peaceful enjoyment of possessions

> Every natural or legal person is entitled to the peaceful enjoyment of his possessions.
>
> No one shall be deprived of his possessions except in the public interest and subject to the conditions provided for by law and by the general principles of international law.
>
> The preceding provisions shall not, however, in any way impair the right of a State to enforce such laws as it deems necessary to control the use of property in accordance with the general interest or to secure the payment of taxes or other contributions or penalties.

'Possessions' in this Article has a wide meaning. It includes, amongst other things, land, money, shares and goodwill. Whilst not all contracts are possessions, the starting point must be that a signed and part-performed commercial contract is, prima facie, a possession (*Solaria Energy UK Ltd v Department for Business, Energy and Industrial Strategy* [2020] EWCA Civ 1625). Child maintenance payable under statute but not yet paid does not amount to possessions (R *(on the application of Ingold) v Secretary of State for Work and Pensions* [2023] EWHC 3207 (Admin)).

The Article contains two distinct rights:

(a) the right not to be deprived of possessions, subject to certain conditions; and

(b) the right not to have the State control possessions, subject to certain conditions.

Deprivation covers situations in which title is transferred or extinguished, for example the creation of a presumption of title in land in favour of the State (*Holy Monasteries v Greece* (1994) 20 EHRR 1). Control covers situations falling short of this, for example limiting the amount of rent which a landlord may charge, placing restrictions upon developing property and rules restricting rights of inheritance. Control connotes restraint or regulation: see *King v Environment Agency* [2018] EWHC 65 (QB).

In both cases interference with the right is permissible in the public interest or the general interest (a distinction which is of little importance). The guiding principle is one of fair balance between individual and community interests. In striking this balance regard must always be had to the principle of proportionality (see **27.5.2**) and the split Court of Appeal decision upholding the legislation banning the sale of tobacco from automatic vending machines: R *(on the application of Sinclair Collis Ltd) v Secretary of State for Health* [2011] EWCA Civ 437.

In deprivation cases, proportionality is generally achieved where the compensation paid to the person whose property has been taken is reasonably related to its 'market value', as determined at the time of the expropriation; and a total lack of compensation can be considered justifiable only in 'exceptional circumstances': see, for example, *James and Others v United Kingdom* (Series A, No 98, 21 February 1986) at [54]. In R *(SRM Global Master Finance Ltd) v Commissioners of Her Majesty's Treasury* [2009] EWCA Civ 788, the Court of Appeal noted that there had been only one occasion when the ECtHR had approved a deprivation of property without any compensation: *Jahn v Germany* (2006) 42 EHRR 49, where this result was only justified because of 'the unique context of German reunification'.

In control of use cases, the proportionality test is applied differently: the lack of compensation is a factor to be taken into consideration in determining whether a fair balance has been achieved but is not determinative (*R (on the application of LJ Fairburn & Son Ltd) v Secretary of State for the Environment, Food and Rural Affairs* [2024] EWHC 65 (Admin)).

In *Hammersmith and Fulham LBC v Monk* [1992] 1 AC 478, it was held that at common law a periodic joint residential tenancy is terminated automatically if one joint tenant unilaterally serves a notice to quit on the landlord. Is that incompatible with the other joint tenant's rights under Protocol 1, Article 1? No, held the Supreme Court in *Sims v Dacorum BC* [2014] UKSC 63. A husband had no right to remain in a local authority property as a sole tenant after his wife had left and given notice to the local authority landlord quitting the joint tenancy.

The Social Security (Recovery of Benefits) Act 1997 requires employers' liability insurers to repay certain social security benefits irrespective of any contributory negligence by the person with an injury or disease, or the insured's partial responsibility. Is that incompatible with the insurers' rights under Protocol 1, Article 1? No, held the Court of Appeal in *Aviva Insurance Ltd v Secretary of State for Work and Pensions* [2022] EWCA Civ 15.

27.5.10 Identifying and addressing Convention rights

27.5.10.1 Has there been an interference with a Convention right?

Do the facts complained of disclose an interference with the enjoyment of any particular right or rights?

CASE EXAMPLE 1

Assume that you are a solicitor and a court has made a wasted costs order against you. What rights might be relevant? Is the order a determination of your civil rights such that Article 6 is engaged? Or is it a criminal charge for the purposes of that Article? Otherwise, is it an interference with your possessions for the purposes of the First Protocol, Article 1? In fact, the ECtHR has already answered all these questions in the negative (see, eg, *Tormala v Finland* (2004) Application No 41528/98).

CASE EXAMPLE 2

Assume that you are protesting peacefully against an arms fair being held in London. You are stopped by two police officers and searched. You are handed a copy of Stop/Search Form 5090 which records that you were stopped and searched under s 44 of the Terrorism Act 2000. The search was said to be for 'articles concerned in terrorism'. The whole incident lasts about 20 minutes. What rights might be engaged? Have you been deprived of your liberty under Article 5? Has there been a lack of respect for your private life such that Article 8 is engaged? Have your rights to free expression and free assembly protected by Articles 10 and 11 been infringed? The House of Lords (now the Supreme Court) answered all of these questions in the negative (or otherwise felt that the measures were justified): see *R (on the application of Gillan and Another) v Commissioner of Police for the Metropolis and Another* [2006] UKHL 12. However, for a similar case where the House of Lords held that Articles 10 and 11 were infringed, see *R (on the application of Laporte) v Chief Constable of Gloucestershire* [2006] UKHL 55. Moreover, when the *Gillian* case was heard by the Grand Chamber of the ECtHR, it held that Article 8 was engaged and infringed (see [2010] ECHR 28 (Application No 4158/05)).

CASE EXAMPLE 3

In R *(on the application of Naik) v Secretary of State for the Home Department* [2011] EWCA Civ 1546, the applicant was a leading Muslim writer and public speaker. In 2010, two days before he was due to arrive in the UK on a lecture tour, the Secretary of State excluded him and revoked his existing visa on the basis that he had made a number of statements supporting terrorism. As a foreign national outside the UK, could he rely on Article 10? The Court of Appeal held that Article 10 was engaged in respect of the applicant's supporters in the UK and (without deciding the issue) possibly also in respect of the applicant personally.

How are you going to be able to identify relevant rights in the future? You need to have in mind the structure of the Articles. A breakdown of the key Articles by way of a checklist appears in the **Appendix to Part IV**.

Once any particular qualified right has been identified, the following questions need to be answered. The detail may be found at **27.5.2.3** above:

(a) Is the interference prescribed by law?

(b) Does the interference have a legitimate aim under the relevant Article?

(c) Is the interference proportionate?

(d) Is the interference within any appropriate margin of appreciation?

CASE EXAMPLE

In *Connors v UK* (2004) Application No 66746/01, the applicant, a gypsy, complained that he and his family had been evicted by a local authority from its gypsy caravan site in breach of Article 8.

The parties were agreed that Article 8 was engaged as the eviction of the applicant from the site on which he had lived with his family in his caravan disclosed an interference with his right to respect for his private life, family life and home. The parties were also agreed, in the context of the second paragraph of Article 8, that the interference was in accordance with the law and pursued a legitimate aim, namely, the protection of the rights of other occupiers of the site by the local authority which owned and managed the site. The question for the Court was whether the interference was 'necessary in a democratic society' in pursuit of that aim, ie if there was a 'pressing social need' and, in particular, if it was proportionate to the legitimate aim pursued. As to the scope of the margin of appreciation, the Court indicated that this depends on the context of the case, with particular significance attaching to the extent of the intrusion into the personal sphere of the applicant. The procedural safeguards available to the individual are especially material in determining whether the respondent State has, when fixing the regulatory framework, remained within its margin of appreciation. In particular, the court must examine whether the decision-making process leading to measures of interference was fair and such as to afford due respect to the interests safeguarded to the individual by Article 8.

The Court found that the eviction of the applicant and his family from the local authority site was not attended by the requisite procedural safeguards, namely the requirement to establish proper justification for the serious interference with his rights. Consequently it could not be regarded as justified by a 'pressing social need' or proportionate to the legitimate aim being pursued. There had, accordingly, been a violation of Article 8 of the Convention.

27.5.10.2 Everyday situations in which the HRA 1998 might apply

In June 2009 the Commission for Equality and Human Rights (CEHR – see **28.5**) published a report entitled, *Human Rights Inquiry*. At Chapter 1, section 3, it produced a list of everyday situations in which the HRA 1998 might apply. This is reproduced in the **Appendix to Part IV.**

27.5.10.3 Business and human rights

The publication entitled 'Guiding Principles on Business and Human Rights: Implementing the United Nations "Protect, Respect and Remedy" Framework' recognises the important role that business plays in society and the need for business to respect human rights. In particular, it identifies that business enterprises should:

(a) avoid infringing on the human rights of others and should address adverse human rights impacts with which they are involved;

(b) avoid causing or contributing to adverse human rights impacts through their own activities, and address such impacts when they occur;

(c) prevent or mitigate adverse human rights impacts that are directly linked to their operations, products or services by their business relationships, even if they have not contributed to those impacts;

(d) put in place policies and processes that include a policy commitment to meet their responsibility to respect human rights; a human rights due diligence process to identify, prevent, mitigate and account for how they address their impacts on human rights; and processes to enable the remediation of any adverse human rights impacts they cause or to which they contribute.

A copy of the document is available at <http://www.ohchr.org/Documents/Publications/GuidingPrinciplesBusinessHR_EN.pdf>.

Legislation is starting to push this agenda forward. For example, the Modern Slavery Act 2015 requires certain businesses to prepare and publish a slavery and trafficking statement for each financial year. Further examples of how businesses can impact certain human rights can be found in the 'Reference Annex to the IBA Practical Guide on Business and Human Rights for Business Lawyers'. This is reproduced in the **Appendix to Part IV.** A copy of the entire document is available at <www.ibanet.org/MediaHandler?id=d6306c84-e2f8-4c82-a86f-93940d6736c4>.

See also the Equality and Human Rights Commission's publication, 'Business and human rights: a seven-step guide for managers'. A copy of the document is available at <www.equalityhumanrights.com/sites/default/files/ehrc_business_and_human_rights-_a_seven-step_guide_for_managers_0.pdf>.

27.6 PETITIONING THE COURT IN STRASBOURG

27.6.1 Introduction

Despite the HRA 1998, there will be situations where an individual is denied a remedy under UK law, for example because primary legislation is clearly incompatible with the Convention, or because there is some gap in the legislation which cannot be filled by the common law and in either case the Government will not make amends. In such cases, the individual can petition the ECtHR in Strasbourg. This will be the last resort, however, as the Convention requires the applicant to exhaust domestic remedies (including the HRA 1998) before going to Strasbourg.

27.6.2 Procedural law of the ECHR

A complaint will be addressed to the Secretary of the Court of Human Rights. The initial complaint does not need to be on a special form, although one would have to be completed eventually. Under the rules made under the Eleventh Protocol, a chamber of the court will determine admissibility. Around 90% of complaints are ruled inadmissible, usually because of failure to exhaust domestic remedies, or because they are 'manifestly ill-founded' or because they fail to meet the time-limit of six months from the exhaustion of the final domestic remedy. The initial decision on admissibility will be taken by a committee of three.

Once the committee has judged a complaint admissible, the ECtHR will try to reach a friendly settlement with the government concerned, which must include the reform of any offending rules. Failing a settlement, there will be further submissions, including an oral hearing at which, as well as the parties, relevant organisations like Liberty or Justice may be represented. The ECtHR (usually a chamber of seven, but exceptionally a Grand Chamber of 17) may award compensation as part of its judgment, but the judgment itself does not change the law in the UK. That is a matter for the UK Government. There is also a right of appeal to the Grand Chamber on issues of general importance (subject to the permission of the first chamber). The Rules of Court were published in March 2024 and can be found on the ECtHR website at <www.echr.coe.int/documents/d/echr/Rules_Court_ENG>. A flowchart summarising the procedure follows.

Simplified case-processing flow chart by judicial formation

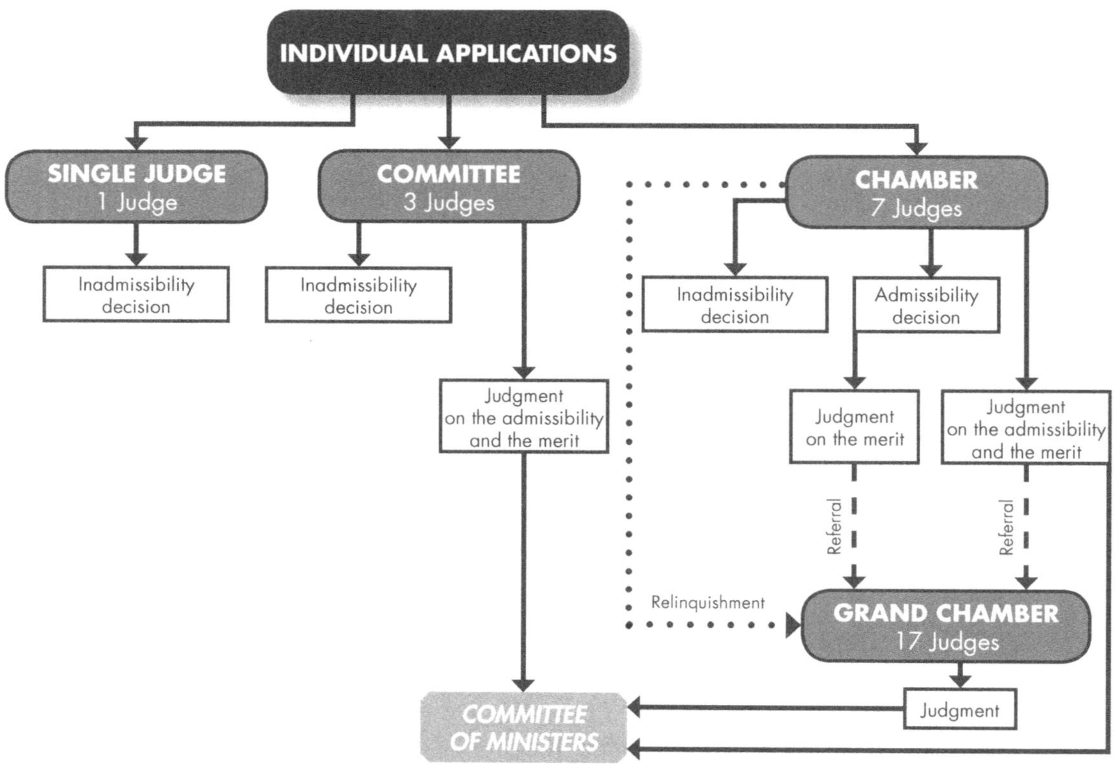

CHAPTER 28

The Human Rights Act 1998

LEARNING OUTCOMES

After reading this chapter you will have learned:

- how the Convention affects statutory interpretation
- when a declaration of incompatibly may be made
- what public authorities fall within the HRA 1998
- what is meant by the doctrine of direct effect
- the procedure for using the HRA 1998
- when damages might be awarded under the HRA 1998
- the role of the Equality and Human Rights Commission.

28.1 INTRODUCTION

> It is clear that the 1998 Act must be given its full import and that long or well entrenched ideas may have to be put aside, sacred cows culled. (per Lord Slynn in *R v Lambert* [2001] UKHL 37 at para 6)

In brief, the effect of the HRA 1998 is to make it possible for litigants in the UK to rely on Convention rights in our own domestic courts without the delay and expense incurred by taking the case to the ECtHR in Strasbourg. The constitutional issues which are raised by this are potentially momentous. Giving the judiciary a yardstick against which they can measure UK legislation and find it to be wanting has obvious impacts on the traditional conception of parliamentary supremacy. The HRA 1998 attempts to defuse this by the device of the declaration of incompatibility (see **28.3.3**). It also shifts power towards the judiciary, giving them greater scope to determine difficult, perhaps emotive and politically charged questions. This raises questions about the accountability of our judges.

28.1.1 Five central planks

There are five central planks of the HRA 1998. First, all legislation, whether primary or subordinate, must, if possible, be interpreted so as to be compatible with the ECHR. Secondly, where it is not possible to interpret primary legislation so as to be compatible with the ECHR, certain courts can make a declaration of incompatibility. Thirdly, where it is not possible to interpret subordinate legislation so as to be compatible with the Convention, the courts have power to disapply it. Fourthly, all public authorities, including courts and tribunals, must, if possible, act in a way that is compatible with the ECHR. Lastly, individuals who believe that their ECHR rights have been infringed by a public authority can rely on the ECHR to take proceedings in English courts rather than having to apply to Strasbourg.

28.1.2 Practice areas

All lawyers in the UK must bear Convention rights in mind. These rights have much more impact in some areas of law than others. For example, criminal law and immigration practitioners need to have regard to the HRA 1998 on a day-to-day basis. However, the HRA 1998 requires that all legislation be read in accordance with Convention rights and that all public authorities make their decisions in accordance with them: any lawyer who makes use of legislation or who has dealings with organs of the State does so against the backdrop of the HRA 1998.

28.2 CONVENTION RIGHTS

The concept of Convention rights is central to the HRA 1998. There are certain rights from the ECHR which are listed in Sch 1 to the 1998 Act. The most important are those discussed in **Chapter 27**.

Section 2 requires that any court or tribunal determining a Convention right must take into account any decision of the Strasbourg institutions, in particular judgments of the ECtHR. Notice that these decisions are not binding in the same way that decisions of higher courts within the UK are, or even decisions of the Court of Justice in the context of EU law. Decisions of the Strasbourg Court need only be taken into account. Clearly, they will be highly persuasive, but should a UK court feel the need to decide the matter differently it is free to do so. See, for example, *R v Horncastle* [2009] UKSC 14.

It has been held that English courts should, in the absence of some special circumstances, follow any clear and constant jurisprudence of the Strasbourg court: *R (Alconbury Developments Ltd) v Secretary of State for the Environment, Transport and the Regions* [2001] UKHL 23 at [26]. As Lord Bingham observed in *R (Ullah) v Special Adjudicator* [2004] 2 AC 323 at [20]:

> This reflects the fact that the Convention is an international instrument, the correct interpretation of which can be authoritatively expounded only by the Strasbourg court. From this it follows that a national court subject to a duty such as that imposed by section 2 should not without strong reason dilute or weaken the effect of the Strasbourg case law. It is indeed unlawful under section 6 of the 1998 Act for a public authority, including a court, to act in a way which is incompatible with a Convention right. It is of course open to member states to provide for rights more generous than those guaranteed by the Convention, but such provision should not be the product of interpretation of the Convention by national courts, since the meaning of the Convention should be uniform throughout the states party to it. The duty of national courts is to keep pace with the Strasbourg jurisprudence as it evolves over time: no more, but certainly no less.

So, what does the principle in the *Ullah* case establish? That an English court should not feel driven on Convention grounds unwillingly to decide a case against a public authority (which could not then seek a corrective judgment in Strasbourg) unless the existing Strasbourg case law clearly compels this. Indeed, the more reluctant the domestic court may be to recognise in the circumstances a violation of the Convention, the readier it should be to reject the complaint unless there exists an authoritative judgment of the Grand Chamber plainly decisive of the point at issue. If, however, the domestic court is content (perhaps even ready and willing) to decide a Convention challenge against a public authority and believes such a conclusion to flow naturally from existing Strasbourg case law (albeit that it could be regarded as carrying the case law a step further), then it should take that further step (see *Rabone v Pennine Care NHS Foundation Trust* [2012] UKSC 2 at [112], as applied in *Fearn v The Board of Trustees of the Tate Gallery* [2020] EWCA Civ 104). For an example where it was a step too far for the Supreme Court, see *Jones v Birmingham City Council* [2023] UKSC 27.

> [I]t is not the function of our domestic courts to establish new principles of Convention law. But that is not to say that they are unable to develop the law in relation to Convention rights beyond the limits of the Strasbourg case law. In situations which have not yet come before the European court, they can and should aim to anticipate, where possible, how the European court might be expected to decide the case, on the basis of the principles established in its case law. Indeed, that is the exercise which the

> High Court and the Court of Appeal undertook in the present case. The application of the Convention by our domestic courts, in such circumstances, will be based on the principles established by the European court, even if some incremental development may be involved. (per Lord Reed in R *(on the application of AB) v Secretary of State for Justice* [2022] AC 487 at [59])
>
> The core concerns advanced before the President were that naming health care professionals might undermine morale, make it more difficult to recruit into the relevant speciality and increase pressure on staff and hospitals. We are aware of no Strasbourg case which has come close to allowing concerns about morale, recruitment or general well-being of health staff to provide a justification for curtailing the right to free expression about individual experiences whilst being cared for, or on matters of general public interest. It would be a strong thing for public debate to be curtailed in these circumstances and, in line with established domestic authority (the Ullah principle), the domestic courts should not run ahead of Strasbourg in finding a principle in the Convention which has not emerged in Strasbourg. (per Lord Burnett of Maldon CJ in *Abbasi v Newcastle upon Tyne Hospitals NHS Foundation Trust* [2023] EWCA Civ 331 at [125])

The courts have stressed in recent years that the Act should not normally be treated as the starting point in any case in which human rights issues arise. Although the importance of the Act is unquestionable, it does not supersede the protection of human rights under the common law or statute, or create a discrete body of law based on the judgments of the ECtHR (*A (A Child) (Withdrawal of Treatment: Legal Representation)* [2022] EWCA Civ 1221).

Decisions on the meaning to be given to Convention rights may involve UK courts and lawyers looking further afield than Strasbourg. The House of Lords (now the Supreme Court) accepted that it is appropriate to look to case law from other jurisdictions in determining such matters (*R v Khan* [1997] AC 558). Most other countries have an established constitutional human rights document with a well-developed jurisprudence, especially those from common law jurisdictions such as New Zealand and Canada.

28.3 THE MECHANISMS OF THE ACT

28.3.1 Introduction

The HRA 1998 seeks to give Convention rights effect in UK law through two pathways. Whenever legislation is relevant, lawyers are able to rely on a rule of statutory interpretation that legislation should be read in line with Convention rights. Even where there is no legislation in issue, all public authorities have an obligation to act in accordance with Convention rights.

28.3.2 The interpretative obligation

Section 3(1) reads:

> So far as it is possible to do so, primary legislation and subordinate legislation must be read and given effect in a way which is compatible with the Convention rights.

This interpretative obligation applies whether the legislation in question was passed before or after the HRA 1998. The obligation under s 3 is imposed not just on the courts, but also on those tasked with interpreting and applying the relevant legislation.

> Nevertheless, the section is not aimed exclusively, or indeed mainly, at the courts. ... section 3 is carefully drafted in the passive voice to avoid specifying, and so limiting, the class of persons who are to read and give effect to the legislation in accordance with it. Parliament thereby indicates that the section is of general application. It applies, of course, to the courts, but it applies also to everyone else who may have to interpret and give effect to legislation. The most obvious examples are public authorities such as organs of central and local government ... (per Lord Rodger of Earlsferry in *Ghaidan v Godin-Mendoza* [2004] 2 AC 557 at [106])

All legislation must be read in such a way as to be compatible with Convention rights, even if it is unambiguous, so long as the wording will bear such an interpretation.

> Looking at section 3, a number of words are important. First, there is the mandatory word 'must' which imposes a duty on the court to read and give effect in a compatible way to legislation. The second words to stress are 'it is possible to do so'. This not an option on the court. The court must act in a way to achieve compatibility with the Convention rights unless it is impossible to do so within the structure of the legislation and the wording of the provision. (per the President of the Family Division in *Re H (Step-Parent Adoption: Human Rights)* [2023] EWHC 3186 (Fam) at [25]).

CASE EXAMPLES

(1) In *Re S* [2002] 2 AC 313, Lord Nicholls described s 3 as 'a powerful tool whose use is obligatory' (para 38). He acknowledged, however, the difficulty of 'identifying the limits of interpretation in a particular case', adding (at para 40): 'For present purposes it is sufficient to say that a meaning which departs substantially from a fundamental feature of an Act of Parliament is likely to have crossed the boundary between interpretation and amendment. This is especially so where the departure has important practical repercussions which the court is not equipped to evaluate ...'. In that case it was held that the proposed re-interpretation (favoured by a majority of the Court of Appeal) would have departed fundamentally from the legislative scheme. Where Parliament had entrusted to local authorities, not the courts, the responsibility for looking after children subject to care orders, the proposed interpretation (involving a so-called 'starring system') would have enabled the court to exercise a 'newly created supervisory function' (para 42).

(2) The case of *R v A (No 2)* [2002] 1 AC 45 concerned the provisions of the Youth Justice and Criminal Evidence Act 1999 that protected complainants in proceedings for sexual offences. Section 41 placed strict limits on the scope for evidence or cross-examination of complainants about their own sexual behaviour. As Lord Steyn said, the practically 'blanket exclusion' of prior sexual history between the complainant and the accused posed 'an acute problem of proportionality' (para 30). Notwithstanding the apparently clear language of the section, it was held that it could be re-interpreted under s 3 to the extent that justice required the admission of such evidence or cross-examination. Lord Steyn said: 'In my view section 3 requires the court to subordinate the niceties of language of section 41(3)(c), and in particular the touchstone of coincidence, to broader considerations of relevance judged by logical and common sense criteria of time and circumstance. After all, it is realistic to proceed on the basis that the legislature would not, if alerted to the problem, have wished to deny the right to an accused to put forward a full and complete defence by advancing truly probative material.' It was held that the section should be read as subject to an implied provision that 'evidence or questioning required to ensure a fair trial under Article 6 of the Convention should not be treated as inadmissible' (para 45).

What about criminal offences? If they are statutory, the interpretative duty imposed by s 3 of the Human Rights Act 1998 may enable the court to construe the relevant provision in a way which renders it compatible with the Convention rights, either by interpreting it in such a way that a conviction will always meet the requirements of proportionality, or by interpreting it so as to allow for an assessment of the proportionality of a conviction in the circumstances of individual cases. For example, a defence of lawful or reasonable excuse may provide a route by which a proportionality assessment can be carried out, where the defence can properly be interpreted, having recourse if need be to s 3 of the Human Rights Act 1998, as including the exercise of Convention rights. But where a criminal offence arises at common law, resort cannot be had to s 3 of the Human Rights Act 1998 since there is no legislation capable of being given a Convention-compliant interpretation. Instead, the question arises whether the court can develop the common law so as to render the offence compatible with Convention rights, either on ordinary principles or by virtue of the duty imposed by s 6(1) of the Act (see **28.3.4**).

28.3.2.1 Nature of opponent irrelevant

This principle applies whether the other party is public or private. So long as a litigant can find a piece of legislation to which the Convention right can be pinned, the nature of their opponent does not matter. For example, *R (on the application of Sacker) v HM Coroner for the County of West Yorkshire* [2004] UKHL 11 involved an inquest into a prisoner's death. The House of Lords (now the Supreme Court) had to rule on the interpretation of the word 'how' in s 11(5) of the Coroners Act 1988, in the context of 'how' the prisoner had died. In order to protect Article 2 rights, the House of Lords held that it was not simply to be interpreted as meaning 'by what means', but rather 'by what means in and in what circumstances'.

28.3.2.2 Ministerial statements

Section 19 gives judges an extra spur to find a construction which is compatible with Convention rights. It provides that all Bills introduced into Parliament must be accompanied by a statement from the sponsoring Minister on the compatibility or otherwise of the Bill with Convention rights. Clearly, Ministers will almost invariably make statements of compatibility because were a Minister to stand up and state that a Bill did not comply with Convention rights, some very good reasons why it should be enacted in spite of this would have to be provided. The doctrine in *Pepper v Hart* [1993] AC 59 allows the courts to look to such ministerial statements in *Hansard* as background evidence of parliamentary intention (see *Wilson v Secretary for Trade and Industry* [2003] UKHL 40). Equipped with such evidence, courts may feel especially justified in straining legislative wording where necessary to give it a meaning compatible with Convention rights. Indeed, in *R v A (No 2)* [2002] 1 AC 45, Lord Hope observed (at para 69):

> These statements may serve a useful purpose in Parliament. They may also be seen as part of the parliamentary history, indicating that it was not Parliament's intention to cut across a Convention right ... No doubt they are based on the best advice that is available. But they are no more than expressions of opinion by the minister. They are not binding on the court, nor do they have any persuasive authority.

28.3.3 Declarations of incompatibility

Section 4 applies to higher courts (the High Court, Crown Courts, the Employment Appeals Tribunal and above). It empowers them to make declarations of incompatibility. This provides a fallback for situations in which a court recognises that legislation does not comply with Convention rights but, because of the clear words used by the legislator, does not feel that it is possible to give it a purposive interpretation. For example, the Divisional Court, the Court of Appeal and the Supreme Court all agreed to make a declaration of incompatibility in respect of s 82 of the Sexual Offences Act 2003 (see *R (on the application of F) v Secretary of State for the Home Department* [2010] UKSC 17). Why? The section imposes on all who are sentenced to 30 months' imprisonment or more for a sexual offence a duty to keep the police notified of where they are living and if they travel abroad. As there is no provision in the Act for any individual review of these requirements, the duty was a disproportionate interference with the Article 8 rights of those individuals.

What approach should the court take? In *R (Chester) v Secretary of State for Justice* [2013] UKSC 63, the Supreme Court strongly urged any court that was considering remedies under the HRA 1998 to adopt the practice of asking in what way the particular claimant's Convention rights had been violated. As Baroness Hales observed at [102]:

> That leaves the possibility of a declaration of incompatibility under section 4(2) of the Human Rights Act 1998. This applies 'in any proceedings in which a court determines whether a provision of primary legislation is compatible with a Convention right': section 4(1). This does appear to leave open the possibility of a declaration in abstracto, irrespective of whether the provision in question is incompatible with the rights of the individual litigant. There may be occasions when that would be

> appropriate. But in my view the court should be extremely slow to make a declaration of incompatibility at the instance of an individual litigant with whose own rights the provision in question is not incompatible. Any other approach is to invite a multitude of unmeritorious claims.

The court is far less likely to grant a declaration of incompatibility where there is a lacuna in the law rather than a specific statutory provision which is incompatible (*Mercer v Alternative Future Group Ltd* [2022] EWCA Civ 379 but successfully appealed in *Secretary of State for Business and Trade v Mercer* [2024] UKSC 12 as the Supreme Court did not find a lacuna in the relevant domestic law).

28.3.3.1 Declaration must be necessary

Any declaration must be 'necessary'. In *R v HM Attorney General, ex p Rusbridger* [2003] UKHL 38, [2003] 3 All ER 784, a newspaper sought a declaration as to the proper construction of s 3 of the Treason Felony Act 1848 (which made it an offence punishable by imprisonment for life or any shorter period to 'compass by publication to deprive or depose the Queen from the Crown'). No prosecution had been brought under the section since 1883. The newspaper wished to publish a series of articles urging abolition of the monarchy and asked the Attorney-General to clarify the legal position under s 3. He refused. The House of Lords (now the Supreme Court) held that it was not appropriate to bring proceedings against the part of s 3 of the 1848 Act that appeared to criminalise the advocacy of republicanism since it was a relic of a bygone age. The idea that it could survive scrutiny under the HRA 1998 was unreal. It was clear that no one who advocated the abolition of the monarchy by peaceful and constitutional means was at any risk of prosecution or conviction. The litigation was therefore unnecessary, and the application was dismissed.

28.3.3.2 Applicant must benefit from declaration

In *Lancashire County Council v Taylor* [2005] EWCA Civ 284, the Court of Appeal had to determine if a litigant can obtain a declaration of incompatibility on a ground from which they cannot benefit. The Court stated that the primary objective of the ECHR is to secure for individuals the rights and freedoms set out in the Convention. The HRA 1998 and the Convention also play an educative role by promoting the observance of human rights and thus the Convention. One way in which this objective is achieved is by requiring a Minister to make a statement of compatibility with regard to any new legislation in accordance with s 9 of the HRA 1998. But it is not the intention of the HRA 1998 or the Convention that members of the public should use these provisions if they are not adversely affected by them to change legislation because they consider that the legislation is incompatible with the Convention.

28.3.3.3 Effect

These declarations are a compromise between the need to provide a remedy in such cases and the attachment of the UK to the doctrine of parliamentary supremacy which prevents courts from striking down Acts of Parliament. They flag up the incompatibility but provide no further redress. They do not affect the continuing operation of the offending legislation (s 4(6)).

Clearing up the aftermath of such a declaration is left to the politically accountable organs of State: the Government and Parliament. Section 10 and Sch 2 allow Ministers to amend an incompatible Act by a 'fast track' procedure rather than having to put amending legislation through the full process in both Houses of Parliament. Broadly speaking, this allows Ministers to lay before Parliament a 'remedial order' amending the offending legislation. The order will take effect after 120 days, so long as no objections are made by either House. In emergencies the remedial order can take effect immediately, but will automatically cease to have effect if not given positive approval by both Houses within 120 days. See, for example, the Terrorism Act 2000 (Remedial) Order 2011 (SI 2011/631) which followed the ECtHR's decision in the case of *Gillian*, detailed in Case Example 2 at **27.5.10.1**.

However, remedial action is optional. The HRA 1998 places no obligation on Ministers to do anything after a declaration of incompatibility is made. Even if they decide to take action, they do not have to do so via the fast track. Remember, though, that the road to Strasbourg is not closed. If a UK court declares legislation to be incompatible with Convention rights and the UK Government does not take adequate steps to put matters right, then a judgment could be sought in the ECtHR. The Government would then have an obligation in international law to act.

28.3.3.4 Subordinate legislation as *ultra vires*

Declarations of incompatibility are reserved in the main for primary legislation, that is Acts of Parliament. Delegated or subordinate legislation (usually made by Ministers under an enabling power in an Act of Parliament) is more easily attacked. Striking out such subordinate legislation does not offend against the principle of parliamentary supremacy. In fact, by ensuring that Ministers only use enabling powers in an appropriate way it reinforces the will of Parliament. Because of this, courts have never shied away from ruling subordinate legislation to be ultra vires and therefore inoperative. They will continue to do so in circumstances in which subordinate legislation is incompatible with Convention rights and it is not possible to place a purposive interpretation upon it in accordance with s 3.

28.3.3.5 Worked example

In *Westminster City Council and The First Secretary of State v Morris; R (on the application of Badu) v London Borough of Lambeth and The First Secretary of State* [2005] EWCA Civ 1184, the Court of Appeal declared s 185 of the Housing Act 1996 incompatible. The Court arrived at its decision by taking the following steps.

(a) The provision made by s 185(4) of the Housing Act 1996 precluding a British parent from establishing a priority need for housing assistance where the claim is based on a resident dependent child who is ineligible for UK citizenship and, therefore, subject to immigration control, was within the ambit of Article 8 of the ECHR.

(b) The effect of s 185(4), when read with Article 8, was plainly discriminatory within the meaning of Article 14 of the Convention because the differential treatment for which it provides turns on national origin, or on a combination of one or more of the following forms or aspects of status: nationality, immigration control, settled residence and social welfare.

(c) Regardless of the precise basis of the differential treatment, it could only be justified, particularly under Article 8, if there were 'very weighty' or 'solid' grounds for it, or if it could be shown that it is a proportionate and reasonable response to a perceived need to discourage 'benefit tourism' by British citizens or the 'overstaying' of any of their dependent children subject to immigration control.

(d) The justification advanced in the proceedings on behalf of the Secretary of State was neither 'very weighty' nor 'solid', nor did it amount to a proportionate and reasonable response by him to his concerns.

(e) It was not apparent that the Executive in proposing, or Parliament in enacting, s 185(4) gave consideration to its potential discriminatory impact in any of the respects proscribed by Article 14 or to the justification, if any, for it; but even if they did, the enactment of such a provision, with such effect, could not have fallen within even the very wide ambit of discretion allowed to the Government and Parliament in such matters.

(f) On the issue of compatibility and whether a court should, in the exercise of its discretion under s 4(2) of the HRA 1998, make a declaration of incompatibility, it is immaterial that there may be other forms of statutory protection, and the Court should grant a declaration.

28.3.3.6 Declarations made

The Ministry of Justice publishes annual reports by the Joint Committee on Human Rights on the Government's response to human rights judgments. The report for 2023–2024 details the 58 declarations that had been made since the HRA 1998 came into force. The details are reproduced in the **Appendix to Part IV.**

28.3.3.7 'Wait and see'

Increasingly, courts appear reluctant to address the issue of formal remedies. In two high profile cases in 2017, the Supreme Court and Court of Appeal side-stepped human rights issues respectively as follows:

> So far as concerns the [Home Office Immigration] instructions, we have indicated those aspects which require revision. However, given the passage of time, including new legislation, it would be wrong for this court to attempt to indicate how those defects should now be corrected. It is preferable to adjourn the question of remedies to allow time for the Secretary of State to consider her position, and to indicate to the appellants and to the court how she proposes to amend the instructions or other guidance to accord with the law as indicated in this judgment. The court will receive written submissions on such proposals, and consider whether a further hearing is necessary. (*R (on the application of MM (Lebanon)) v Secretary of State for the Home Department* [2017] UKSC 10 at para 110)
>
> It is not the role of the court to set a deadline for compliance and the function of the court is certainly not to micro-manage areas of social and economic policy, particularly in sensitive areas such as this where changes will affect society as a whole. It is the court's role to say whether or not the discriminatory measure and the Government's decision to undertake a proper assessment of the optimum way forward in the light of the demand by couples (whether same-sex or different-sex) for civil partnerships as well as marriage is objectively justified now. I therefore do not think it is appropriate to set a deadline for the Government or to give any concrete indication as to when the discriminatory measure will no longer be justified. I do, however, note that as time passes it will become increasingly difficult to persuade the court that there is still a need to 'wait and see' or that an approach to civil partnership primarily based on the demand for that status by same-sex couples alone is justifiable. The Government will have to decide whether to abolish the status of civil partnership or extend it to different-sex couples and it is for the Government and for Parliament to decide how to keep the matter under active review. (per Beatson LJ at para 162 in *Keidan v Secretary of State for Education* [2017] EWCA Civ 81)

28.3.4 Public authorities

Public authorities may find themselves challenged because the statutory framework within which they operate gives rise to the indirect application of Convention rights via the interpretative obligation as described in **28.3.2**. However, in addition, the Convention can be applied directly to their activities: it is not necessary for a litigant first to find a legislative provision to interpret purposively. Section 6(1) provides simply:

> It is unlawful for a public authority to act in a way which is incompatible with a Convention right.

28.3.4.1 What is a public authority?

Section 6 does not fully define public authority but does say that it includes 'any person certain of whose functions are functions of a public nature'. The dividing line between public and private bodies is a difficult one to draw. The question has exercised the minds of judicial review lawyers for some time because only public bodies are susceptible to judicial review (eg, *R v Panel on Takeovers and Mergers, ex p Datafin plc* [1987] QB 815). It has also been an issue for EU lawyers because of the important distinction between the horizontal and vertical effect in EU law (eg, *Foster v British Gas* Case (C-188/89) [1990] ECR I-3133). For the purposes of the HRA 1998 there is no doubt that the departments of central government are public authorities, nor that local government is a public authority. In *R (on the application of Miller) v Prime Minister* [2020] AC 373, the Prime Minister advised the Sovereign to prorogue Parliament. This was the exercise of a public function. But the Conservative Party's election of a new leader, and thereby the Prime Minister in 2023, was not (R *(on the application of Tortoise Media Ltd) v Conservative and Unionist Party* [2023] EWHC 3088 (Admin)).

Large companies which exercise quasi-public regulatory authorities may be regarded as public authorities when exercising their public functions. But there are many grey areas which have been and will in the future be a fertile ground for litigation.

There are two decisions of the House of Lords (now the Supreme Court) which inform the approach courts should take when determining whether a body is a public body within the meaning of the HRA 1998. These are *Aston Cantlow and Wilmcote with Billisley Parochial Church Council v Wallbank* [2003] UKHL 37 and *YL v Birmingham City Council* [2007] UKHL 27. In R *(on the application of Weaver) v London & Quadrant Housing Trust* [2009] EWCA Civ 587, Elias LJ summarised the following principles from these cases:

(1) The purpose of section 6 is to identify those bodies which are carrying out functions which will engage the responsibility of the UK before the ECtHR.

(2) In conformity with that purpose, a public body is one whose nature is, in a broad sense, governmental. However, it does not follow that all bodies exercising such functions are necessarily public bodies; many functions of a kind historically performed by government are also exercised by private bodies, and increasingly so with the growth of privatisation. Moreover, this is only a guide since the phrase used in the Act is public function and not governmental function.

(3) In determining whether a body is a public authority, the courts should adopt what Lord Mance in *YL* described as a 'factor-based approach' (para 91). This requires the court to have regard to all the features or factors which may cast light on whether the particular function under consideration is a public function or not, and weigh them in the round.

(4) In applying this test, a broad or generous application of section 6(3)(b) should be adopted.

(5) In *Aston Cantlow* Lord Nicholls said (para 12) that the factors to be taken into account 'include the extent to which in carrying out the relevant function the body is publicly funded, or is exercising statutory powers, or is taking the place of central government or local authorities, or is providing a public service.'

(6) As to public funding, it was pointed out that it is misleading to say that a body is publicly subsidised merely because it enters into a commercial contract with a public body (Lord Scott, para 27; Lord Neuberger para 141). As Lord Mance observed (para 105): 'Public funding takes various forms. The injection of capital or subsidy into an organisation in return for undertaking a non-commercial role or activity of general public interest may be one thing; payment for services under a contractual arrangement with a company aiming to profit commercially thereby is potentially quite another.'

(7) As to the second matter, the exercise of statutory powers, or the conferment of special powers, may be a factor supporting the conclusion that the body is exercising public functions, but it depends why they have been conferred. If it is for private, religious or purely commercial purposes, it will not support the conclusion that the functions are of a public nature: see Lord Mance in *YL* at paragraph 101. However, Lord Neuberger thought that the 'existence of wide ranging and intrusive set of statutory powers ... is a very powerful factor in favour of the function falling within section 6(3)(b)' and he added that it will often be determinative (para 167).

(8) The third factor, where a body is to some extent taking the place of central government or local authorities, chimes with Lord Nicholls' observation that generally a public function will be governmental in nature. This was a theme running through the *Aston Cantlow* speeches, as Lord Neuberger pointed out in *YL*, para 159. That principle will be easy to apply where their powers are formally delegated to the body concerned.

(9) The fourth factor is whether the body is providing a public service. This should not be confused with performing functions which are in the public interest or for the public benefit. As Lord Mance pointed out in *YL* (para 105), the self-interested endeavour of individuals generally works to the benefit of society, but that is plainly not enough to constitute such activities public functions. Furthermore, as Lord Neuberger observed (para 135), many private bodies, such as private schools, private hospitals, private landlords, and food retailers, provide goods or

services which it is in the public interest to provide. This does not render them public bodies, nor their functions public functions. Usually the public service will be of a governmental nature.

28.3.4.2 Examples

A public broadcaster, such as the BBC, may in certain circumstances be regarded as a public authority under the HRA 1998; for example, when it takes a decision not to broadcast certain matters, it must have regard to Article 10, the right to freedom of expression (*R (on the application of ProLife Alliance) v British Broadcasting Corporation* [2002] EWCA Civ 297, [2002] 2 All ER 756). But, in *R (on the application of Liberal Democrats) v ITV Broadcasting Ltd* [2019] EWHC 3282 (Admin), ITV was not acting as a public body when as a commercial broadcaster it decided to exclude the Liberal Democrats and the Scottish National Party from a leaders' debate prior to the 2019 General Election.

The police, when they exercise their powers at common law to arrest to prevent a breach of the peace, must have regard to Article 5, the right to liberty and security of the person. However, a large and flourishing private-sector provider of residential care homes was not acting as a public authority, and did not have to act in accordance with Convention rights when deciding to close a care home, despite the applicant having lived there for 17 years (*R (on the application of Heather and Others) v Leonard Cheshire Foundation* [2002] EWCA Civ 366). But a private psychiatric hospital exercising its powers of compulsory detention under the Mental Health Act 1983 will be performing functions of a public nature (*Sammut v Next Steps Mental Healthcare Ltd* [2024] EWHC 2265 (KB) and *YL v Birmingham City Council* [2007] UKHL 27).

The members of an inquiry established under the Inquiries Act 2005 are a public authority for the purposes of the HRA 1998. But is an independent inquiry established by the government of a State party to investigate a matter of public concern? Yes, see *Foreign and Commonwealth Office v Warsama* [2020] EWCA Civ 142.

28.3.4.3 Defences

Sometimes a public authority will attempt to argue that it had no choice but to act in the way it did because it was merely obeying obligations imposed by an Act of Parliament. In such cases there are two possibilities. The court may use the interpretative obligation in s 3 to read the offending legislation in such a way that the public authority was not restricted as it thought; in such a case, the public authority will be regarded as having made an error of law and an appropriate remedy will be awarded against it. Alternatively, the court may agree with the public authority's reading of the legislation, which may be so clear that it cannot be purposively interpreted in line with Convention rights. In this case, the public authority will have the defence that as a result of the legislation in question it could not have acted differently (s 6(2)) and the other party will have to content themselves with a declaration of incompatibility against the legislation.

28.3.4.4 Acts of a public authority outside the UK

What is the territorial scope of s 6? Does it apply to a public authority that acts both within and outside the UK? In *R (on the application of Al-Skeini) v Secretary of State for Defence* [2007] UKHL 26, the claimants were relatives of Iraqi citizens who, it was claimed, had been unlawfully killed by members of British armed forces in southern Iraq in 2003. The Secretary of State argued that the 1998 Act did not apply outside the territory of the UK and that the deceased had not been within the jurisdiction of the UK for the purposes of Article 1 of the Convention when they were killed. The House of Lords (now the Supreme Court) rejected these arguments. It held that s 6 should be interpreted as applying not only when a public authority acted within the UK, but also when it acted within the jurisdiction of the UK for the purposes of Article 1 of the Convention but outside the territory of the UK. Why? The House of Lords stated that the purpose of the 1998 Act was to provide remedies in domestic law to those whose human rights had been violated by a UK public authority. Making such remedies available for acts of a

UK authority in the territory of another State is not offensive to the sovereignty of the other State.

> The exception to the territoriality principle acknowledged in *Al-Skeini* in the case of physical power and control over a person depends on the fact of such physical power and control. Its significance is that it enables the contracting state to act to secure certain Convention rights depending on the circumstances and the degree of physical power and control it possesses. (per Lloyd Jones LJ in *Al-Saadoon v Secretary of State for Defence* [2016] EWCA Civ 811 at para 105)

Do British troops operating on foreign soil fall within the jurisdiction of the UK? In *R (on the application of Smith) v Secretary of State for Defence* [2010] UKSC 29, the Supreme Court held that the answer is yes, but only when a soldier is on a British base. Note, however, that when the ECtHR heard the *Al-Skeini* case referred to above (see [2011] ECHR 1093, Application No 55721/07), the Grand Chamber held (at paras 149 and 150):

> It can be seen, therefore, that following the removal from power of the Ba'ath regime and until the accession of the Interim Government, the United Kingdom (together with the United States) assumed in Iraq the exercise of some of the public powers normally to be exercised by a sovereign government. In particular, the United Kingdom assumed authority and responsibility for the maintenance of security in South East Iraq. In these exceptional circumstances, the Court considers that the United Kingdom, through its soldiers engaged in security operations in Basrah during the period in question, exercised authority and control over individuals killed in the course of such security operations, so as to establish a jurisdictional link between the deceased and the United Kingdom for the purposes of Article 1 of the Convention.
>
> Against this background, the Court recalls that the deaths at issue in the present case occurred during the relevant period: the fifth applicant's son died on 8 May 2003; the first and fourth applicants' brothers died in August 2003; the sixth applicant's son died in September 2003; and the spouses of the second and third applicants died in November 2003. It is not disputed that the deaths of the first, second, fourth, fifth and sixth applicants' relatives were caused by the acts of British soldiers during the course of or contiguous to security operations carried out by British forces in various parts of Basrah City. It follows that in all these cases there was a jurisdictional link for the purposes of Article 1 of the Convention between the United Kingdom and the deceased. The third applicant's wife was killed during an exchange of fire between a patrol of British soldiers and unidentified gunmen and it is not known which side fired the fatal bullet. The Court considers that, since the death occurred in the course of a United Kingdom security operation, when British soldiers carried out a patrol in the vicinity of the applicant's home and joined in the fatal exchange of fire, there was a jurisdictional link between the United Kingdom and this deceased also.

28.3.5 Direct effect in cases not involving public authorities

There is a significant gap in the way in which the HRA 1998 allows Convention rights to be enforced. It would appear from s 6 that Convention rights can only be applied directly against public authorities. Experience from the domain of EU law has shown that this can lead to unfairness. For example, employees of public authorities may enjoy more rights than employees of private authorities. Such an interpretation of s 6 would not prevent claimants against private defendants from relying on the interpretative obligation in s 3. But, to take advantage of the interpretative obligation, they would have to be litigating a point which was dealt with by UK legislation which itself was capable of a Convention-compatible interpretation. Claimants against public authorities would have a simpler solution by applying Convention rights directly under s 6.

However, it would seem that a doctrine of direct effect in cases involving private bodies is being developed by the courts. For example, *Venables and Thompson v News Group Newspapers Ltd* [2001] 2 WLR 1038 involved an application to the court by the two boys convicted of murdering Jamie Bulger. After their release from prison, they wanted an injunction preventing the press from revealing their new identities. Their application was based partly on Article 2 because they feared for their lives should their identities become public. It was argued on their behalf that because the court is a public authority (the HRA 1998 says so in s 6(3)), the court has a duty under s 6(1) to ensure that Convention rights are protected even when it decides cases involving private litigants. This was accepted by Dame Elizabeth Butler-Sloss. She said (para 24):

> It is clear that, although operating in the public domain and fulfilling a public service, the defendant newspapers cannot sensibly be said to come within the definition of public authority in s 6(1) of the 1998 Act. Consequently, Convention rights are not directly enforceable against the defendants ... That is not, however, the end of the matter, since the court is a public authority, see s 6(3), and must itself act in a way compatible with the Convention, see s 6(1), and have regard to European jurisprudence ...

The injunction was granted.

28.4 PROCEDURE FOR USING THE ACT

> One principal achievement of the Act is to enable the Convention rights to be directly invoked in the domestic courts. In that respect the Act is important as a procedural measure which has opened a further means of access to justice for the citizen, more immediate and more familiar than a recourse to the Court in Strasbourg. (per Lord Clyde in *R v Lambert* [2001] UKHL 37 at para 135)

The s 3 interpretative obligation (see **28.3.2**) may be raised in any court or tribunal hearing in which the meaning of a legislative provision needs to be construed.

Many HRA points are raised in criminal proceedings by defendants. This may be on the basis that an Act upon which the prosecution seeks to rely does not bear the meaning which the prosecution attributes to it when s 3 is applied. Alternatively, it may be that the defence wish to raise a 'freestanding' HRA point, not linked to any legislation, that the police or the Crown Prosecution Service have acted contrary to Convention rights and therefore have broken s 6.

The other procedure which is commonly used to raise Convention rights against public authorities is judicial review under CPR, Part 54. Under this procedure, the Divisional Court is well accustomed to scrutinising the decisions of public authorities and measuring them against a variety of standards of legality and procedural fairness. The HRA 1998 adds another string to the bow of judicial review lawyers.

28.4.1 *Locus standi* test

The HRA 1998 introduces some special procedural rules for s 6 challenges to public authorities. Section 7(1) introduces a *locus standi* test for such challenges. The claimant must be a 'victim' of the unlawful act 'for the purposes of Article 34 of the Convention if proceedings were brought in the European Court of Human Rights in respect of that act' (see s 7(7)).

> Convention rights are not free-floating entities which are available to and enforceable by anyone who disagrees with a decision of a public authority on the grounds that it breaches, or may breach, somebody's Convention rights. Convention rights have effect in the law of England and Wales to the extent provided for by the 1998 Act. Therefore, the starting point is not article 3, or article 6(1), but that Act. The claimants' case is that the Prime Minister breached section 6(1) of the 1998 Act in deciding not to hold a judicial inquiry, thereby failing to comply with the positive investigative obligation imposed by article 3. The effect of section 7(1) and (7) of the 1998 Act is that a person can bring a claim founded on a Convention right, and only has standing in an application for judicial review, 'if he would be a victim for the purposes of Article 34 of the Convention if proceedings were brought in the [Strasbourg Court] in respect of that act'. The clear purpose of section 7 of the 1998 Act is to permit, and only to permit, a victim to litigate an alleged breach of Convention rights. It is only if the litigant is a victim that the Convention right in question can arguably be a 'civil right' of his for the purposes of article 6(1) . (per Lord Burnett of Maldon CJ in *R (on the application of Reprieve) v Prime Minister* [2021] EWCA Civ 972 at [39])

Strasbourg case law on this expression says that to qualify a person must be actually and directly affected by the act or omission which is the subject of the complaint. Thus, in *Zakharov v Russia* (2016) 63 EHRR 17, it was said at [164]:

> The Court has consistently held in its case-law that the Convention does not provide for the institution of an actio popularis and that its task is not normally to review the relevant law and practice in abstracto, but to determine whether the manner in which they were applied to, or affected, the applicant gave rise to a violation of the Convention. Accordingly, in order to be able to lodge an application in accordance with art.34, an individual must be able to show that he or she was 'directly affected' by the measure complained of. This is indispensable for putting the protection mechanism of the Convention into motion, although this criterion is not to be applied in a rigid, mechanical and inflexible way throughout the proceedings.

So, in R *(on the application of Butt) v Secretary of State for the Home Department* [2019] EWCA Civ 256, where the claimant failed to demonstrate that guidance issued by the Secretary of State had had any concrete impact on him, the claimant was held not to be a victim of the guidance within the meaning of s 7(1). See also *Privacy International v Secretary of State for Foreign and Commonwealth Affairs* [2021] EWCA Civ 330, where the claimants were non-governmental organisations seeking to represent a viewpoint that might be advanced by others who were or would be victims of government secret service policy.

If a victim dies before making a claim, their next-of-kin may be able to do so provided it is related to the death or disappearance of their relative. See further *Milner v Barchester Healthcare Homes Ltd* [2022] EWHC 593 (QB) and the Admissibility Guide published by the Registry of the ECHR (available on the ECtHR's website: <www.echr.coe.int/>).

28.4.2 Limitation

Section 6 challenges are also subject to a one-year limitation period from the date on which the offending act took place (s 7(5)).

> As a matter of ordinary language, the wording of section 7(5)(a) contemplates that an 'act' is a single event which occurred on a single date. No express provision is made for an act which extends over a period of time. There is no difficulty in applying this approach in the paradigm case of a single act which takes place at a clearly identifiable point of time. The act should not be confused with its consequences. If it takes place more than one year before proceedings are brought, the claim is barred by section 7(5)(a) even if its consequences do not appear until later. (per the Master of the Rolls in *O'Connor v Bar Standards Board* [2016] EWCA Civ 775 at para 19)

The period may be extended pursuant to s 7(5)(b) if the court considers it equitable having regard to all the circumstances. As for the approach to the exercise of discretion, see *Williams v London Borough of Hackney* [2017] EWCA Civ 26. At para 85 the Court of Appeal referred to the decision of the Supreme Court in *Rabone v Pennine Care NHS Foundation Trust* [2012] UKSC 2 where Lord Dyson at para 75 identifies the principles that should guide the court in these terms:

> The relevant principles are not in dispute. The court has a wide discretion in determining whether it is equitable to extend time in the particular circumstances of the case. It will often be appropriate to take into account factors of the type listed in section 33(3) of the Limitation Act 1980 as being relevant when deciding whether to extend time for a domestic law action in respect of personal injury or death. These may include the length of and reasons for the delay in issuing the proceedings; the extent to which, having regard to the delay, the evidence in the case is or is likely to be less cogent than it would have been if the proceedings had been issued within the one-year period; and the conduct of the public authority after the right of claim arose, including the extent (if any) to which it responded to requests reasonably made by the claimant for information for the purpose of ascertaining facts which are or might be relevant. However, I agree with what the Court of Appeal said in *Dunn v Parole Board* [2009] 1 WLR 728, paras 31, 43 and 48 that the words of section 7(5)(b) of the HRA mean what they say and the court should not attempt to rewrite them. There can be no question of interpreting section 7(5)(b) as if it contained the language of section 33(3) of the Limitation Act 1980.

What if a claimant is a child when the offending act takes place? Under domestic law, limitation would not begin to run until they had attained 18 years of age. Although that principle is not directly applicable to s 7(5), it is significant factor in the exercise of the court's discretion (*CJ v Chief Constable of Wiltshire* [2022] EWHC 1661 (QB)).

Must any limitation issue be left to be determined at trial? No. It is an important part of the court's case management powers to ensure that hopeless claims (hopeless because they are plainly and obviously statute-barred) do not use up valuable court time and resources by being allowed to proceed to a trial where they are inevitably doomed to fail (see *Solaria Energy UK Ltd v Department for Business, Energy and Industrial Strategy* [2020] EWCA Civ 1625).

The time limit is also subject to any stricter time limit imposed by the particular procedure being used. If judicial review is used, an application must usually be made 'promptly and in any event within three months' (CPR, Part 54).

The s 3 interpretative obligation is not subject to these special provisions for locus standi or limitation period. The usual rules will apply for whatever procedure is chosen.

28.4.3 Remedies

Section 8 provides for remedies in s 6 challenges to public authorities.

> What section 6(1) says is that 'it is unlawful for a public authority to act in a way which is incompatible with a Convention right'. That means that where the remedies provisions of section 8 of the Act refer to an act of a public authority which is 'unlawful', they are referring only to cases where the unlawfulness involves the breach of a claimant's rights under the European Convention on Human Rights. So in bringing a claim in reliance on section 8 of the Act, a claimant has to show how they say their ECHR rights have been breached. (per Mrs Justice Collins Rice in *Kulumbegov v Home Office* [2023] EWHC 337 (KB) at [16])

The court's role is to adjudicate on whether a claim as brought is made out and, if so, what remedy is appropriate. Section 8 empowers a court to award such remedies within its powers as it considers just and appropriate. This will include injunctions to restrain breaches of Convention rights (see, for example, *In the matter of G (Children)* [2019] EWCA Civ 1779) and damages. But it is not for the court to define the legal content of the obligations owed under the Convention (see R *(on the application of Richards) v Environment Agency* [2022] EWCA Civ 26, where the judge sought to prescribe the precise outcomes that the defendant had to achieve and the timescale within which it had to achieve them).

28.4.4 Damages

28.4.4.1 General principles

As provided for under s 8(4)(b), a court asked to consider an award of damages is obliged to take into account principles applied by the ECtHR under Article 41 of the Convention, which states:

> If the Court finds that there has been a violation of the Convention or the Protocols thereto, and if the internal law of the High Contracting Party concerned allows only partial reparation to be made, the Court shall, if necessary, afford just satisfaction to the injured party.

A Practice Direction pertaining to the recovery of damages was issued by the President of the ECtHR on 28 March 2007and subsequently amended on 9 June 2022. It provides that:

> 9. It is for the applicant to show that pecuniary damage has resulted from the violations alleged. A direct causal link must be established between the damage and the violation found. A merely tenuous or speculative connection is not enough.

Rule 60(1) of the ECtHR Rules of Court emphasises the need to find a relevant violation:

> 1. An applicant who wishes to obtain an award of just satisfaction under Article 41 of the Convention in the event of the Court finding a violation of his or her Convention rights must make a specific claim to that effect.

The role of damages in human rights litigation has significant features which distinguish it from the approach to the award of damages in a private law contract or tort action. As Lord Woolf CJ stated in *Anufrijeva v Southwark London Borough Council* [2004] QB 1124:

The following points need to be noted.

(a) The award of damages under the HRA is confined to the class of unlawful acts of public authorities identified by section 6(1): see section 8(1) and (6).

(b) The court has a discretion as to whether to make an award (it must be 'just and appropriate' to do so) by contrast to the position in relation to common law claims where there is a right to damages: section 8(1).

(c) The award must be necessary to achieve 'just satisfaction'; language that is distinct from the approach at common law where the claimant is invariably entitled, so far as money can achieve this, to be restored to the position he would have been in if he had not suffered the injury of which complaint is made. The concept of damages being 'necessary to afford just satisfaction' provides a link with the approach to compensation of the Court of Human Rights under article 41.

(d) The court is required to take into account in determining whether damages are payable and the amount of damages payable the different principles applied by the Court of Human Rights in awarding compensation ... (para 55)

In the following paragraph Lord Woolf said that in considering whether to award compensation and, if so, how much, 'there is a balance to be drawn between the interests of the victim and those of the public as a whole' and that the court has 'a wide discretion in respect of the award of damages for breach of human rights'. He described damages as 'not an automatic entitlement but ... a remedy of last resort'. Later, at para 66, in discussing the principles applied by the Strasbourg Court, he said that the approach is an equitable one and that 'the "equitable basis" has been cited by the Court of Human Rights both as a reason for awarding damages and as a basis upon which to calculate them'.

Lord Woolf's analysis was approved by the House of Lords (now the Supreme Court) in *R (Greenfield) v Secretary of State for the Home Department* [2005] 1 WLR 673 and the Court of Appeal in *Dobson v Thames Water Utilities Ltd* [2009] EWCA Civ 28. To summarise, the Convention serves principally public law aims; the principal objective is to declare any infringement and to put a stop to it. Compensation is ancillary and discretionary. The interests of the individual are part of the equation, but so are those of the wider public.

Note that when the *Dobson* case was tried (see [2011] EWHC 3253), the court held that the defendant was liable to the claimants for its negligent failure to control odour from its sewerage facility. However, the award of damages at common law was made only to the claimants who were property owners, and this was said to constitute just satisfaction for the purposes of s 8(3) of the HRA 1998. As a result, no additional compensation was payable to those claimants who did not have a proprietary interest, such as children living in an affected property. See also *R (on the application of Infinis Plc) v Gas and Electricity Markets Authority* [2011] EWHC 1873 (Admin).

Section 9 of the HRA 1998 prevents damages being awarded in respect of a judicial act done in good faith. In order to show that a judicial act was not done in good faith, a claimant has to show that there was an ulterior purpose (*Webster v Ministry of Justice* [2014] EWHC 3995 (QB)). Is it an abuse of process to make a claim for damages under s 9 against the Lord Chancellor for breaches of the ECHR unless the orders or judicial acts complained of have been appealed against (*Mazhar v Lord Chancellor* [2019] EWCA Civ 1558)? No, see *MTA (a protected party, by his litigation friend, the Official Solicitor) v Commissioner of Police of the Metropolis* [2023] EWHC 117 (KB).

Interest is generally only payable if the damages awarded are not paid on time (*Adegboyega v Secretary of State of the Home Department* (2025) EWHC 155 (KB)).

28.4.4.2 ECtHR principles

The fundamental principle underlying the award of compensation by the ECtHR is that the Court should achieve what it describes as *restitutio in integrum*. The applicant should, insofar as this is possible, be placed in the same position as if their Convention rights had not been infringed.

Where the breach of a Convention right has clearly caused significant pecuniary loss, this will usually be assessed and awarded. For example, awards of compensation were made to homosexuals, discharged from the armed forces, in breach of Article 8, for loss of earnings and pension rights in *Lustig-Prean and Beckett v UK* (2001) 31 EHRR 601 and *Smith and Grady v UK* (2001) 31 EHRR 620. But a problem arises in relation to the consequences of the breach of a Convention right which are not capable of being computed in terms of financial loss.

None of the rights in Part 1 of the Convention are of such a nature that their infringement will automatically give rise to damage that can be quantified in financial terms. Infringements may involve a variety of treatment of an individual which is objectionable in itself. The treatment may give rise to distress, anxiety and, in extreme cases, psychiatric trauma. The primary object of the proceedings will often be to bring the adverse treatment to an end. If this is achieved, it may constitute 'just satisfaction', or it may be necessary to award damages to compensate for the adverse treatment that has occurred.

More particularly, damages may be awarded for anxiety and distress that has been occasioned by the breach. However, an admission of the breach and an apology may be a sufficient remedy where no damage measurable in financial terms has occurred: see *R (on the application of Degainis) v Secretary of State for Justice* [2010] EWHC 137, where the defendant failed promptly to secure a review of the applicant's release from prison, thereby breaching his Article 5(4) rights, but the judge found that that did not cause him to spend longer in custody nor suffer the sort of frustration or anxiety that might otherwise have merited an award of damages under Article 5(5). Contrast that with *R (on the application of Hester) v Secretary of State for Justice* (2011) LTL, 20 December. Here, the breach of Article 5(4) was admitted and the court found that the applicant had been unlawfully detained for 12 weeks. However, the court was not satisfied that the applicant had suffered any distress or medical problems and assessed the appropriate award of damages at £500 per week. That amounted in total to £6,000, but as the Secretary of State had already offered precisely that sum to the applicant, the court ordered that he should pay the defendant's costs from the date of that offer. See also *ZH (a protected party by his litigation friend, GH) v Commissioner of Police of the Metropolis* [2013] EWCA Civ 69 and *Bell v Commissioner of Police of the Metropolis* [2024] EWHC 379 (KB).

CASE EXAMPLES

(1) In *Re Mahmud's Application for Judicial Review* [2021] NIQB 37, the applicant was denied any form of asylum support in breach of his Article 3 rights. This included £31.80 per week in financial support over 167 days. He was awarded damages of £1,750.

(2) In *Goodenough v Chief Constable of Thames Valley* [2020] EWHC 1428 (QB), the court awarded £5,000 each in damages to the mother and sister of a man who had died in police custody. The serious shortcomings in the police investigation had breached their Article 2 rights adding to the considerable distress and anxiety suffered by them.

28.4.4.3 Domestic comparators

Where a court decides that it is appropriate to award damages, the level might be assessed by reference to any existing domestic comparators. These might include guidelines issued by the Judicial College, as well as the levels of awards made by the Criminal Injuries Compensation Board, the Parliamentary Ombudsman and the Local Government Ombudsman. These may all provide some rough guidance where the consequences of the infringement of human rights are similar to that being considered in the comparator selected. For example, in *R (on the application of ZB & DB v London Borough of Croydon* [2023] EWHC 489 (Admin) damages were awarded in line with the payments recommended by the Local Government and Social Care Ombudsman in cases where maladministration has resulted in a child missing out on education.

28.4.4.4 Modest awards

In cases where there is no ready domestic comparator to assist in the assessment of damages (see **28.4.4.3**), the general principle is that the scale of damages should be modest and not aim to be significantly more or less generous than the ECtHR would award (see R *(Greenfield) v Secretary of State for the Home Department* [2005] 1 WLR 673).

See further, for example, *Northamptonshire CC v AS, KS and DS (by his children's guardian)* [2015] EWFC 7 (where the local authority agreed to pay what appear to be modest damages to a child and his mother for breaches of Articles 6 and 8 of the ECHR, arising from its failures in the conduct of care proceedings) and *Re H (a child: breach of Convention rights: damages)* [2014] EWFC 38 (where the amount of damages is discussed at [84] to [91]).

28.4.5 Other claims

Claims which introduce Convention rights indirectly via the interpretative obligation are not subject to s 8. If they are civil claims, they will have available whatever remedies are available for the cause of action being used (eg, tort).

28.5 THE COMMISSION FOR EQUALITY AND HUMAN RIGHTS

The CEHR is a non-departmental public body that is intended to act as a central point of advice and guidance on all equality and human rights issues in Great Britain. Its remit is to promote awareness and understanding of human rights, and to encourage good practice by public authorities in meeting their obligations under the HRA 1998. The CEHR has powers to take human rights cases on behalf of minorities who suffer discrimination (see Equality Act 2006, s 30(3)). The Commission's web address is <www.equalityhumanrights.com>.

Since February 2009 the CEHR has intervened in several cases before the ECtHR involving issues about housing, immigration, family law, employment law, the right to a fair trial and other matters, including whether the concept of family life under the ECHR includes same-sex couples; whether the ban on the use of intercept evidence in court should be lifted; whether persons subject to immigration control who wish to marry outside the Church of England (whether in a civil or religious ceremony) should be subject to requirements that do not apply to those who have a Church of England wedding; and whether the protections of the HRA 1998 extend to the actions of UK troops abroad.

HUMAN RIGHTS ACT 1998

Introduction

1. The Convention Rights

(1) In this Act 'the Convention rights' means the rights and fundamental freedoms set out in—

(a) Articles 2 to 12 and 14 of the Convention,

(b) Articles 1 to 3 of the First Protocol, and

(c) Article 1 of the Thirteenth Protocol,

as read with Articles 16 to 18 of the Convention.

(2) Those Articles are to have effect for the purposes of this Act subject to any designated derogation or reservation (as to which see sections 14 and 15).

(3) The Articles are set out in Schedule 1.

(4) The Secretary of State may by order make such amendments to this Act as he considers appropriate to reflect the effect, in relation to the United Kingdom, of a protocol.

(5) In subsection (4) 'protocol' means a protocol to the Convention—

(a) which the United Kingdom has ratified; or

(b) which the United Kingdom has signed with a view to ratification.

(6) No amendment may be made by an order under subsection (4) so as to come into force before the protocol concerned is in force in relation to the United Kingdom.

2. Interpretation of Convention rights

(1) A court or tribunal determining a question which has arisen in connection with a Convention right must take into account any—

(a) judgment, decision, declaration or advisory opinion of the European Court of Human Rights,

(b) opinion of the Commission given in a report adopted under Article 31 of the Convention,

(c) decision of the Commission in connection with Article 26 or 27(2) of the Convention, or

(d) decision of the Committee of Ministers taken under Article 46 of the Convention,

whenever made or given, so far as, in the opinion of the court or tribunal, it is relevant to the proceedings in which that question has arisen.

(2) Evidence of any judgment, decision, declaration or opinion of which account may have to be taken under this section is to be given in proceedings before any court or tribunal in such manner as may be provided by rules.

(3) In this section 'rules' means rules of court or, in the case of proceedings before a tribunal, rules made for the purposes of this section—

(a) by the Lord Chancellor or the Secretary of State, in relation to any proceedings outside Scotland;

(b) by the Secretary of State, in relation to proceedings in Scotland; or

(c) by a Northern Ireland department, in relation to proceedings before a tribunal in Northern Ireland—

(i) which deals with transferred matters; and

(ii) for which no rules made under paragraph (a) are in force.

Legislation

3. Interpretation of legislation

(1) So far as it is possible to do so, primary legislation and subordinate legislation must be read and given effect in a way which is compatible with the Convention rights.

(2) This section—

(a) applies to primary legislation and subordinate legislation whenever enacted;

(b) does not affect the validity, continuing operation or enforcement of any incompatible primary legislation; and

(c) does not affect the validity, continuing operation or enforcement of any incompatible subordinate legislation if (disregarding any possibility of revocation) primary legislation prevents removal of the incompatibility.

4. Declaration of incompatibility

(1) Subsection (2) applies in any proceedings in which a court determines whether a provision of primary legislation is compatible with a Convention right.

(2) If the court is satisfied that the provision is incompatible with a Convention right, it may make a declaration of that incompatibility.

(3) Subsection (4) applies in any proceedings in which a court determines whether a provision of subordinate legislation, made in the exercise of a power conferred by primary legislation, is compatible with a Convention right.

(4) If the court is satisfied—

(a) that the provision is incompatible with a Convention right, and

(b) that (disregarding any possibility of revocation) the primary legislation concerned prevents removal of the incompatibility,

it may make a declaration of that incompatibility.

(5) In this section 'court' means—

(a) the Supreme Court;

(b) the Judicial Committee of the Privy Council;

(c) the Court Martial Appeal Court;

(d) in Scotland, the High Court of Justiciary sitting otherwise than as a trial court or the Court of Session;

(e) in England and Wales or Northern Ireland, the High Court or the Court of Appeal;

(f) the Court of Protection, in any matter dealt with by the President of the Family Division, the Chancellor of the High Court or a puisne judge of the High Court.

(6) A declaration under this section ('a declaration of incompatibility')—

(a) does not affect the validity, continuing operation or enforcement of the provision in respect of which it is given; and

(b) is not binding on the parties to the proceedings in which it is made.

5. Right of Crown to intervene

(1) Where a court is considering whether to make a declaration of incompatibility, the Crown is entitled to notice in accordance with rules of court.

(2) In any case to which subsection (1) applies—

(a) a Minister of the Crown (or a person nominated by him),

(b) a member of the Scottish Executive,

(c) a Northern Ireland Minister,

(d) a Northern Ireland department,

is entitled, on giving notice in accordance with rules of court, to be joined as a party to the proceedings.

(3) Notice under subsection (2) may be given at any time during the proceedings.

(4) A person who has been made a party to criminal proceedings (other than in Scotland) as the result of a notice under subsection (2) may, with leave, appeal to the Supreme Court against any declaration of incompatibility made in the proceedings.

(5) In subsection (4)—

'criminal proceedings' includes all proceedings before the Court Martial Appeal Court; and

'leave' means leave granted by the court making the declaration of incompatibility or by the Supreme Court.

Public Authorities

6. Acts of public authorities

(1) It is unlawful for a public authority to act in a way which is incompatible with a Convention right.

(2) Subsection (1) does not apply to an act if—

(a) as the result of one or more provisions of primary legislation, the authority could not have acted differently; or

(b) in the case of one or more provisions of, or made under, primary legislation which cannot be read or given effect in a way which is compatible with the Convention rights, the authority was acting so as to give effect to or enforce those provisions.

(3) In this section 'public authority' includes—

(a) a court or tribunal, and

(b) any person certain of whose functions are functions of a public nature,

but does not include either House of Parliament or a person exercising functions in connection with proceedings in Parliament.

(4) . . .

(5) In relation to a particular act, a person is not a public authority by virtue only of subsection (3)(b) if the nature of the act is private.

(6) 'An act' includes a failure to act but does not include a failure to—

(a) introduce in, or lay before, Parliament a proposal for legislation; or

(b) make any primary legislation or remedial order.

7. Proceedings

(1) A person who claims that a public authority has acted (or proposes to act) in a way which is made unlawful by section 6(1) may—

(a) bring proceedings against the authority under this Act in the appropriate court or tribunal, or

(b) rely on the Convention right or rights concerned in any legal proceedings, but only if he is (or would be) a victim of the unlawful act.

(2) In subsection (1)(a) 'appropriate court or tribunal' means such court or tribunal as may be determined in accordance with rules; and proceedings against an authority include a counterclaim or similar proceeding.

(3) If the proceedings are brought on an application for judicial review, the applicant is to be taken to have a sufficient interest in relation to the unlawful act only if he is, or would be, a victim of that act.

(4) If the proceedings are made by way of a petition for judicial review in Scotland, the applicant shall be taken to have title and interest to sue in relation to the unlawful act only if he is, or would be, a victim of that act.

(5) Proceedings under subsection (1)(a) must be brought before the end of—

(a) the period of one year beginning with the date on which the act complained of took place; or

(b) such longer period as the court or tribunal considers equitable having regard to all the circumstances,

but that is subject to any rule imposing a stricter time limit in relation to the procedure in question.

(6) In subsection (1)(b) 'legal proceedings' includes—

(a) proceedings brought by or at the instigation of a public authority; and

(b) an appeal against the decision of a court or tribunal.

(7) For the purposes of this section, a person is a victim of an unlawful act only if he would be a victim for the purposes of Article 34 of the Convention if proceedings were brought in the European Court of Human Rights in respect of that act.

(8) Nothing in this Act creates a criminal offence.

(9) In this section 'rules' means—

(a) in relation to proceedings before a court or tribunal outside Scotland, rules made by the Lord Chancellor or Secretary of State for the purposes of this section or rules of court,

(b) in relation to proceedings before a court or tribunal in Scotland, rules made by the Secretary of State for those purposes,

(c) in relation to proceedings before a tribunal in Northern Ireland—

(i) which deals with transferred matters; and

(ii) for which no rules made under paragraph (a) are in force,

rules made by a Northern Ireland department for those purposes,

and includes provision made by order under section 1 of the Courts and Legal Services Act 1990.

(10) In making rules, regard must be had to section 9.

(11) The Minister who has power to make rules in relation to a particular tribunal may, to the extent he considers it necessary to ensure that the tribunal can provide an appropriate remedy in relation to an act (or proposed act) of a public authority which is (or would be) unlawful as a result of section 6(1), by order add to—

(a) the relief or remedies which the tribunal may grant; or

(b) the grounds on which it may grant any of them.

(12) An order made under subsection (11) may contain such incidental, supplemental, consequential or transitional provision as the Minister making it considers appropriate.

(13) 'The Minister' includes the Northern Ireland department concerned.

7A. Limitation: overseas armed forces proceedings

[omitted]

8. Judicial remedies

(1) In relation to any act (or proposed act) of a public authority which the court finds is (or would be) unlawful, it may grant such relief or remedy, or make such order, within its powers as it considers just and appropriate.

(2) But damages may be awarded only by a court which has power to award damages, or to order the payment of compensation, in civil proceedings.

(3) No award of damages is to be made unless, taking account of all the circumstances of the case, including—

(a) any other relief or remedy granted, or order made, in relation to the act in question (by that or any other court), and

(b) the consequences of any decision (of that or any other court) in respect of that act,

the court is satisfied that the award is necessary to afford just satisfaction to the person in whose favour it is made.

(4) In determining—

(a) whether to award damages, or

(b) the amount of an award,

the court must take into account the principles applied by the European Court of Human Rights in relation to the award of compensation under Article 41 of the Convention.

(5) A public authority against which damages are awarded is to be treated—

(a) in Scotland, for the purposes of section 3 of the Law Reform (Miscellaneous Provisions) (Scotland) Act 1940 as if the award were made in an action of damages in which the authority has been found liable in respect of loss or damage to the person to whom the award is made;

(b) for the purposes of the Civil Liability (Contribution) Act 1978 as liable in respect of damage suffered by the person to whom the award is made.

(6) In this section—

'court' includes a tribunal;

'damages' means damages for an unlawful act of a public authority; and

'unlawful' means unlawful under section 6(1).

9. Judicial acts

(1) Proceedings under section 7(1)(a) in respect of a judicial act may be brought only—

(a) by exercising a right of appeal;

(b) on an application (in Scotland a petition) for judicial review; or

(c) in such other forum as may be prescribed by rules.

(2) That does not affect any rule of law which prevents a court from being the subject of judicial review.

(3) In proceedings under this Act in respect of a judicial act done in good faith, damages may not be awarded otherwise than—

(a) to compensate a person to the extent required by Article 5(5) of the Convention, or

(b) to compensate a person for a judicial act that is incompatible with Article 6 of the Convention in circumstances where the person is detained and, but for the incompatibility, the person would not have been detained or would not have been detained for so long.

(4) An award of damages permitted by subsection (3) is to be made against the Crown; but no award may be made unless the appropriate person, if not a party to the proceedings, is joined.

(5) In this section—

'appropriate person' means the Minister responsible for the court concerned, or a person or government department nominated by him;

'court' includes a tribunal;

'judge' includes a member of a tribunal, a justice of the peace (or, in Northern Ireland, a lay magistrate) and a clerk or other officer entitled to exercise the jurisdiction of a court;

'judicial act' means a judicial act of a court and includes an act done on the instructions, or on behalf, of a judge; and

'rules' has the same meaning as in section 7(9).

Remedial Action

10. Power to take remedial action

(1) This section applies if—

(a) a provision of legislation has been declared under section 4 to be incompatible with a Convention right and, if an appeal lies—

(i) all persons who may appeal have stated in writing that they do not intend to do so;

(ii) the time for bringing an appeal has expired and no appeal has been brought within that time; or

(iii) an appeal brought within that time has been determined or abandoned; or

(b) it appears to a Minister of the Crown or Her Majesty in Council that, having regard to a finding of the European Court of Human Rights made after the coming into force of this section in proceedings against the United Kingdom, a provision of legislation is incompatible with an obligation of the United Kingdom arising from the Convention.

(2) If a Minister of the Crown considers that there are compelling reasons for proceeding under this section, he may by order make such amendments to the legislation as he considers necessary to remove the incompatibility.

(3) If, in the case of subordinate legislation, a Minister of the Crown considers—

(a) that it is necessary to amend the primary legislation under which the subordinate legislation in question was made, in order to enable the incompatibility to be removed, and

(b) that there are compelling reasons for proceeding under this section,

he may by order make such amendments to the primary legislation as he considers necessary.

(4) This section also applies where the provision in question is in subordinate legislation and has been quashed, or declared invalid, by reason of incompatibility with a Convention right and the Minister proposes to proceed under paragraph 2(b) of Schedule 2.

(5) If the legislation is an Order in Council, the power conferred by subsection (2) or (3) is exercisable by Her Majesty in Council.

(6) In this section 'legislation' does not include a Measure of the Church Assembly or of the General Synod of the Church of England.

(7) Schedule 2 makes further provision about remedial orders.

Other Rights and Proceedings

11. Safeguard for existing human rights

A person's reliance on a Convention right does not restrict—

(a) any other right or freedom conferred on him by or under any law having effect in any part of the United Kingdom; or

(b) his right to make any claim or bring any proceedings which he could make or bring apart from sections 7 to 9.

12. Freedom of expression

(1) This section applies if a court is considering whether to grant any relief which, if granted, might affect the exercise of the Convention right to freedom of expression.

(2) If the person against whom the application for relief is made ('the respondent') is neither present nor represented, no such relief is to be granted unless the court is satisfied—

(a) that the applicant has taken all practicable steps to notify the respondent; or

(b) that there are compelling reasons why the respondent should not be notified.

(3) No such relief is to be granted so as to restrain publication before trial unless the court is satisfied that the applicant is likely to establish that publication should not be allowed.

(4) The court must have particular regard to the importance of the Convention right to freedom of expression and, where the proceedings relate to material which the respondent claims, or which appears to the court, to be journalistic, literary or artistic material (or to conduct connected with such material), to—

(a) the extent to which—

(i) the material has, or is about to, become available to the public; or

(ii) it is, or would be, in the public interest for the material to be published;

(b) any relevant privacy code.

(5) In this section—

'court' includes a tribunal; and

'relief' includes any remedy or order (other than in criminal proceedings).

13. Freedom of thought, conscience and religion

(1) If a court's determination of any question arising under this Act might affect the exercise by a religious organisation (itself or its members collectively) of the Convention right to freedom of thought, conscience and religion, it must have particular regard to the importance of that right.

(2) In this section 'court' includes a tribunal.

...

21. Interpretation, etc

(1) In this Act—

'amend' includes repeal and apply (with or without modifications);

'the appropriate Minister' means the Minister of the Crown having charge of the appropriate authorised government department (within the meaning of the Crown Proceedings Act 1947);

'the Commission' means the European Commission of Human Rights;

'the Convention' means the Convention for the Protection of Human Rights and Fundamental Freedoms, agreed by the Council of Europe at Rome on 4th November 1950 as it has effect for the time being in relation to the United Kingdom;

'declaration of incompatibility' means a declaration under section 4;

'Minister of the Crown' has the same meaning as in the Ministers of the Crown Act 1975;

'Northern Ireland Minister' includes the First Minister and the deputy First Minister in Northern Ireland;

'primary legislation' means any—

(a) public general Act;

(b) local and personal Act;

(c) private Act;

(d) Measure of the Church Assembly;

(e) Measure of the General Synod of the Church of England;

(f) Order in Council—

(i) made in exercise of Her Majesty's Royal Prerogative;

(ii) made under section 38(1)(a) of the Northern Ireland Constitution Act 1973 or the corresponding provision of the Northern Ireland Act 1998; or

(iii) amending an Act of a kind mentioned in paragraph (a), (b) or (c);

and includes an order or other instrument made under primary legislation (otherwise than by the Welsh Ministers, the First Minister for Wales, the Counsel General to the Welsh Assembly Government, a member of the Scottish Executive, a Northern Ireland Minister or a Northern Ireland department) to the extent to which it operates to bring one or more provisions of that legislation into force or amends any primary legislation;

'the First Protocol' means the protocol to the Convention agreed at Paris on 20th March 1952;

'the Eleventh Protocol' means the protocol to the Convention (restructuring the control machinery established by the Convention) agreed at Strasbourg on 11th May 1994;

'the Thirteenth Protocol' means the protocol to the Convention (concerning the abolition of the death penalty in all circumstances) agreed at Vilnius on 3rd May 2002;

'remedial order' means an order under section 10;

'subordinate legislation' means any—

(a) Order in Council other than one—

(i) made in exercise of Her Majesty's Royal Prerogative;

(ii) made under section 38(1)(a) of the Northern Ireland Constitution Act 1973 or the corresponding provision of the Northern Ireland Act 1998;

(iii) or amending an Act of a kind mentioned in the definition of primary legislation;

(b) Act of the Scottish Parliament;

(ba) Measure of the National Assembly for Wales;

(bb) Act of the National Assembly for Wales;

(c) Act of the Parliament of Northern Ireland;

(d) Measure of the Assembly established under section 1 of the Northern Ireland Assembly Act 1973;

(e) Act of the Northern Ireland Assembly;

(f) order, rules, regulations, scheme, warrant, byelaw or other instrument made under primary legislation (except to the extent to which it operates to bring one or more provisions of that legislation into force or amends any primary legislation);

(g) order, rules, regulations, scheme, warrant, byelaw or other instrument made under legislation mentioned in paragraph (b), (c), (d) or (e) or made under an Order in Council applying only to Northern Ireland;

(h) order, rules, regulations, scheme, warrant, byelaw or other instrument made by a member of the Scottish Executive, Welsh Ministers, the First Minister for Wales, the Counsel General to the Welsh Assembly Government, a Northern Ireland Minister or a Northern Ireland department in exercise of prerogative or other executive functions of Her Majesty which are exercisable by such a person on behalf of Her Majesty;

'transferred matters' has the same meaning as in the Northern Ireland Act 1998; and

'tribunal' means any tribunal in which legal proceedings may be brought.

(2) The references in paragraphs (b) and (c) of section 2(1) to Articles are to Articles of the Convention as they had effect immediately before the coming into force of the Eleventh Protocol.

(3) The reference in paragraph (d) of section 2(1) to Article 46 includes a reference to Articles 32 and 54 of the Convention as they had effect immediately before the coming into force of the Eleventh Protocol.

(4) The references in section 2(1) to a report or decision of the Commission or a decision of the Committee of Ministers include references to a report or decision made as provided by paragraphs 3, 4 and 6 of Article 5 of the Eleventh Protocol (transitional provisions).

(5) ...

22. Short title, commencement, application and extent

(1) This Act may be cited as the Human Rights Act 1998.

(2) Sections 18, 20 and 21(5) and this section come into force on the passing of this Act.

(3) The other provisions of this Act come into force on such day as the Secretary of State may by order appoint; and different days may be appointed for different purposes.

(4) Paragraph (b) of subsection (1) of section 7 applies to proceedings brought by or at the instigation of a public authority whenever the act in question took place; but otherwise that subsection does not apply to an act taking place before the coming into force of that section.

...

(5) This Act binds the Crown.

(6) This Act extends to Northern Ireland.

(7) ...

SCHEDULE 1

The Convention Rights

Article 2
Right to life

1. Everyone's right to life shall be protected by law. No one shall be deprived of his life intentionally save in the execution of a sentence of a court following his conviction of a crime for which this penalty is provided by law.

2. Deprivation of life shall not be regarded as inflicted in contravention of this Article when it results from the use of force which is no more than absolutely necessary:
   (a) in defence of any person from unlawful violence;
   (b) in order to effect a lawful arrest or to prevent the escape of a person lawfully detained;
   (c) in action lawfully taken for the purpose of quelling a riot or insurrection.

Article 3
Prohibition of Torture

No one shall be subjected to torture or to inhuman or degrading treatment or punishment.

Article 4
Prohibition of Slavery and Forced Labour

1. No one shall be held in slavery or servitude.
2. No one shall be required to perform forced or compulsory labour.
3. For the purpose of this Article the term 'forced or compulsory labour' shall not include:
   (a) any work required to be done in the ordinary course of detention imposed according to the provisions of Article 5 of this Convention or during conditional release from such detention;
   (b) any service of a military character or, in case of conscientious objectors in countries where they are recognised, service exacted instead of compulsory military service;
   (c) any service exacted in case of an emergency or calamity threatening the life or well-being of the community;
   (d) any work or service which forms part of normal civic obligations.

Article 5
Right to Liberty and Security

1. Everyone has the right to liberty and security of person. No one shall be deprived of his liberty save in the following cases and in accordance with a procedure prescribed by law:
   (a) the lawful detention of a person after conviction by a competent court;
   (b) the lawful arrest or detention of a person for non-compliance with the lawful order of a court or in order to secure the fulfilment of any obligation prescribed by law;
   (c) the lawful arrest or detention of a person effected for the purpose of bringing him before the competent legal authority on reasonable suspicion of having committed an offence or when it is reasonably considered necessary to prevent his committing an offence or fleeing after having done so;
   (d) the detention of a minor by lawful order for the purpose of educational supervision or his lawful detention for the purpose of bringing him before the competent legal authority;
   (e) the lawful detention of persons for the prevention of the spreading of infectious diseases, of persons of unsound mind, alcoholics or drug addicts or vagrants;
   (f) the lawful arrest or detention of a person to prevent his effecting an unauthorised entry into the country or of a person against whom action is being taken with a view to deportation or extradition.
2. Everyone who is arrested shall be informed promptly, in a language which he understands, of the reasons for his arrest and of any charge against him.
3. Everyone arrested or detained in accordance with the provisions of paragraph 1(c) of this Article shall be brought promptly before a judge or other officer authorised by law to exercise judicial power and shall be entitled to trial within a reasonable time or to release pending trial. Release may be conditioned by guarantees to appear for trial.
4. Everyone who is deprived of his liberty by arrest or detention shall be entitled to take proceedings by which the lawfulness of his detention shall be decided speedily by a court and his release ordered if the detention is not lawful.
5. Everyone who has been the victim of arrest or detention in contravention of the provisions of this Article shall have an enforceable right to compensation.

Article 6
Right to a Fair Trial

1. In the determination of his civil rights and obligations or of any criminal charge against him, everyone is entitled to a fair and public hearing within a reasonable time by an independent and impartial tribunal established by law. Judgment shall be pronounced publicly but the press and public may be

excluded from all or part of the trial in the interest of morals, public order or national security in a democratic society, where the interests of juveniles or the protection of the private life of the parties so require, or to the extent strictly necessary in the opinion of the court in special circumstances where publicity would prejudice the interests of justice.

2. Everyone charged with a criminal offence shall be presumed innocent until proved guilty according to law.

3. Everyone charged with a criminal offence has the following minimum rights:
   (a) to be informed promptly, in a language which he understands and in detail, of the nature and cause of the accusation against him;
   (b) to have adequate time and facilities for the preparation of his defence;
   (c) to defend himself in person or through legal assistance of his own choosing or, if he has not sufficient means to pay for legal assistance, to be given it free when the interests of justice so require;
   (d) to examine or have examined witnesses against him and to obtain the attendance and examination of witnesses on his behalf under the same conditions as witnesses against him;
   (e) to have the free assistance of an interpreter if he cannot understand or speak the language used in court.

Article 7

No Punishment Without Law

1. No one shall be held guilty of any criminal offence on account of any act or omission which did not constitute a criminal offence under national or international law at the time when it was committed. Nor shall a heavier penalty be imposed than the one that was applicable at the time the criminal offence was committed.

2. This Article shall not prejudice the trial and punishment of any person for any act or omission which, at the time when it was committed, was criminal according to the general principles of law recognised by civilised nations.

Article 8

Right to Respect for Private and Family Life

1. Everyone has the right to respect for his private and family life, his home and his correspondence.

2. There shall be no interference by a public authority with the exercise of this right except such as is in accordance with the law and is necessary in a democratic society in the interests of national security, public safety or the economic well-being of the country, for the prevention of disorder or crime, for the protection of health or morals, or for the protection of the rights and freedoms of others.

Article 9

Freedom of Thought, Conscience and Religion

1. Everyone has the right to freedom of thought, conscience and religion; this right includes freedom to change his religion or belief and freedom, either alone or in community with others and in public or private, to manifest his religion or belief, in worship, teaching, practice and observance.

2. Freedom to manifest one's religion or beliefs shall be subject only to such limitations as are prescribed by law and are necessary in a democratic society in the interests of public safety, for the protection of public order, health or morals, or for the protection of the rights and freedoms of others.

Article 10

Freedom of Expression

1. Everyone has the right to freedom of expression. This right shall include freedom to hold opinions and to receive and impart information and ideas without interference by public authority and regardless of frontiers. This Article shall not prevent States from requiring the licensing of broadcasting, television or cinema enterprises.

2. The exercise of these freedoms, since it carries with it duties and responsibilities, may be subject to such formalities, conditions, restrictions or penalties as are prescribed by law and are necessary in a democratic society, in the interests of national security, territorial integrity or public safety, for the prevention of disorder or crime, for the protection of health or morals, for the protection of the reputation or rights of others, for preventing the disclosure of information received in confidence, or for maintaining the authority and impartiality of the judiciary.

Article 11
Freedom of Assembly and Association

1. Everyone has the right to freedom of peaceful assembly and to freedom of association with others, including the right to form and to join trade unions for the protection of his interests.
2. No restrictions shall be placed on the exercise of these rights other than such as are prescribed by law and are necessary in a democratic society in the interests of national security or public safety, for the prevention of disorder or crime, for the protection of health or morals or for the protection of the rights and freedoms of others. This Article shall not prevent the imposition of lawful restrictions on the exercise of these rights by members of the armed forces, of the police or of the administration of the State.

Article 12
Right to Marry

Men and women of marriageable age have the right to marry and to found a family, according to the national laws governing the exercise of this right.

Article 14
Prohibition of Discrimination

The enjoyment of the rights and freedoms set forth in this Convention shall be secured without discrimination on any ground such as sex, race, colour, language, religion, political or other opinion, national or social origin, association with a national minority, property, birth or other status.

Article 16
Restrictions on Political Activity of Aliens

Nothing in Articles 10, 11 and 14 shall be regarded as preventing the High Contracting Parties from imposing restrictions on the political activity of aliens.

Article 17
Prohibition of Abuse of Rights

Nothing in this Convention may be interpreted as implying for any State, group or person any right to engage in any activity or perform any act aimed at the destruction of any of the rights and freedoms set forth herein or at their limitation to a greater extent than is provided for in the Convention.

Article 18
Limitation on Use of Restrictions on Rights

The restrictions permitted under this Convention to the said rights and freedoms shall not be applied for any purpose other than those for which they have been prescribed.

The First Protocol

Article 1
Protection of Property

Every natural or legal person is entitled to the peaceful enjoyment of his possessions. No one shall be deprived of his possessions except in the public interest and subject to the conditions provided for by law and by the general principles of international law.

The preceding provisions shall not, however, in any way impair the right of a State to enforce such laws as it deems necessary to control the use of property in accordance with the general interest or to secure the payment of taxes or other contributions or penalties.

Article 2
Right to Education

No person shall be denied the right to education. In the exercise of any functions which it assumes in relation to education and to teaching, the State shall respect the right of parents to ensure such education and teaching in conformity with their own religious and philosophical convictions.

Identifying and Addressing Convention Rights: a Checklist

Article 2

- Was there an intentional deprivation of life?
- Was it in execution of a court sentence following conviction of a crime for which the sentence is the death penalty?
- Was it for a ground permitted under para 2?
- Did it comply with the conditions set out in para 2?

Article 3

- Was there torture or inhuman or degrading treatment or punishment?

Article 4

- Was there slavery or servitude (para 1)?
- Was there forced or compulsory labour (para 2) save as excluded by para 3?

Article 5 (para 1)

- Was there a deprivation of liberty?
- Was it in accordance with a procedure prescribed by law?
- Was it for any of the grounds permitted by paras (a) to (f)?

Article 6, civil matters

- Was a civil right or obligation determined?
- Were the rights under para 1 met?

Article 6, criminal matters

- Did the proceedings concern a criminal charge?
- Were the rights under para 1 met?

Article 7

- Did the act or omission constitute a criminal offence at the time it was committed?

Article 8

- Was there an interference with a person's private or family life, home or correspondence?
- Was any interference lawful (para 2)?
- Was any interference necessary pursuant to the reasons set out in para 2?

Article 9

- Was there an interference with a person's freedom of thought or conscience?
- Was there an interference with a person's religion? If so, was it lawful and necessary (para 2)?

Article 10

- Was there an interference with a person's right to freedom of expression?
- Was any interference lawful (para 2)?
- Was any interference necessary pursuant to the reasons set out in para 2?

Article 11

- Was there an interference with a person's freedom of peaceful assembly or association?
- Was any interference lawful (para 2)?
- Was any interference necessary pursuant to the reasons set out in para 2?

Article 12

- Was the person of marriageable age?
- Did the person comply with national laws?

- Was there an interference with a person's right to marry or found a family?

First Protocol, Article 1

- Was there an interference with a person's peaceful enjoyment of their possessions?
- Was any interference lawful?
- Was any interference necessary pursuant to any of the specified grounds?

First Protocol, Article 2

- Was there a denial of the right to education?
- Was there a lack of respect of parents' religious or philosophical views?

Article 14

- Is another ECHR right or freedom in issue?
- Has there been discrimination on any of the specified grounds?

EVERYDAY SITUATIONS IN WHICH THE HRA 1998 MIGHT APPLY

Not being able to eat properly while in hospital or a care home (Articles 2 and 8).

Provision of facilities or food which do not meet religious or cultural needs (Article 9).

Abuse or neglect of older people, those who are learning disabled or other vulnerable people (Articles 2 and 3).

Lack of respect for privacy on a hospital ward (Article 8).

Disproportionate use of stop-and-search powers against young black males and other ethnic minorities (Article 14).

Not respecting gay and lesbian partners as next-of-kin and inheritors of tenancies (Articles 8 and 14).

Excessive surveillance of law-abiding people (Article 8).

Loss of personal data by public officials (Article 8).

Curfews preventing law-abiding young people from going out at night (Article 8).

Failures by the authorities to protect people from being stalked and harassed (Articles 2, 3 and 8).

Not being sufficiently protected from domestic violence (Articles 2, 3 and 8).

Not being allocated suitable housing for special needs that have been identified (Article 8).

Bullying of all kinds in schools (Articles 3 and 8).

Disregard of gay and lesbian couples in adoption policies (Article 14).

Unexplained death in prisons, police stations and psychiatric hospitals (Article 2).

Wearing religious symbols or dress at work or in schools (Article 9 and Protocol 1, Article 2).

Inadequate provision for children with special educational needs (Protocol 1, Article 2 and Article 14).

Refusal to permit the staging or broadcasting of artistic works (Article 10).

Refusal to allow people to attend a demonstration (Articles 10 and 11).

Responding to Human Rights Judgments

Annex A: All declarations of incompatibility

As there is no official database of declarations of incompatibility, this annex lists all the cases in which a declaration has been made.

Since section 4 of the HRA came into force on 2 October 2000 until the end of July 2024, 58 declarations of incompatibility have been made.

Of these, 45 have been fully addressed:

- 12 have been overturned on appeal (and there is no scope for further appeal);
- 5 related to provisions that had already been amended by primary legislation at the time of the declaration;
- 11 have been addressed by Remedial Order;
- 16 have been addressed by primary or secondary legislation (other than by Remedial Order);
- 1 has been addressed by various measures;

and 13 are ongoing:

- 5 are currently open to appeal;
- 5 the Government has proposed to address by Remedial Order;
- 3 are currently under consideration by the Government.

The cases in each category are listed in the table below. They are numbered in chronological order of the initial making of a declaration of incompatibility (rather than any appeals). The 2019 report was the last to give full details of all cases (at that time, cases 1–42). For cases which have been fully addressed since then, the report containing the final update is indicated after the case name in the list below.

Overturned on appeal

1. R (on the application of Alconbury Developments Ltd.) v Secretary of State for the Environment, Transport and the Regions: *Administrative Court; [2001] HRLR 2; 13 December 2000*
3. Wilson v First County Trust Ltd (no.2): *Court of Appeal; [2001] EWCA Civ 633; 2 May 2001*
6. Matthews v Ministry of Defence: *Queen's Bench Division; [2002] EWHC 13 (QB); 22 January 2002*
10. R (on the application of Uttley) v Secretary of State for the Home Department: *Administrative Court; [2003] EWHC 950 (Admin); 8 April 2003*
15. R (on the application of MH) v Secretary of State for Health: *Court of Appeal; [2004] EWCA Civ 1609; 3 December 2004*
20. Re MB: *Administrative Court; [2006] EWHC 1000 (Admin); 12 April 2006*
24. Nasseri v Secretary of State for the Home Department: *Administrative Court; [2007] EWHC 1548 (Admin); 2 July 2007*
25. R (on the application of Wayne Thomas Black) v Secretary of State for Justice: *Court of Appeal; [2008] EWCA Civ 359; 15 April 2008*
31. Northern Ireland Human Rights Commission, Re Judicial Review: *Queen's Bench Division (NI); [2015] NIQB 102; 16 December 2015*
42. R (on the application of the Joint Council for the Welfare of Immigrants) v Secretary of State for the Home Department (2022 report): *Administrative Court; [2019] EWHC 452 (Admin); 1 March 2019*
45. In the matter of an application by JR123 for judicial review (2023 report): *Queen's Bench Division (NI); [2021] NIQB 97; 1 November 2021*
46. R v Marks, Morgan, Lynch and Heaney (2023 report): *Court of Appeal (NI); [2021] NICA 67; 22 December 2021*

Provisions already amended by primary legislation

13. R (on the application of Wilkinson) v Inland Revenue Commissioners: *Court of Appeal; [2003] EWCA Civ 814; 18 June 2003*
14. R (on the application of Hooper and others) v Secretary of State for Work and Pensions: *Court of Appeal; [2003] EWCA Civ 875; 18 June 2003*

21. R (on the application of (1) June Wright; (2) Khemraj Jummun; (3) Mary Quinn; (4) Barbara Gambier) v (1) Secretary of State for Health; (2) Secretary of State for Education & Skills: *Administrative Court; [2006] EWHC 2886 (Admin); 16 November 2006*
22. R (on the application of Clift) v Secretary of State for the Home Department; Secretary of State for the Home Department v Hindawi and another: *House of Lords; [2006] UKHL 54; 13 December 2006*
32. David Miranda v Secretary of State for the Home Department: *Court of Appeal; [2016] EWCA Civ 6; 19 January 2016*

Addressed by Remedial Order

2. R (on the application of H) v Mental Health Review Tribunal for the North and East London Region & The Secretary of State for Health: *Court of Appeal; [2001] EWCA Civ 415; 28 March 2001*
19. R (on the application of Baiai and others) v Secretary of State for the Home Department and another: *Administrative Court; [2006] EWHC 823 (Admin); 10 April 2006*
26. R (on the application of (1) F; (2) Angus Aubrey Thompson) v Secretary of State for the Home Department: *Administrative Court; [2008] EWHC 3170 (Admin); 19 December 2008*
29. R (on the application of Reilly (no.2) and Hewstone) v Secretary of State for Work and Pensions: *Administrative Court; [2014] EWHC 2182; 4 July 2014*
30. Benkharbouche and Janah v Embassy of the Republic of Sudan, and Libya (2023 report): *Court of Appeal; [2015] EWCA Civ 33; 5 February 2015*
35. Z (A Child) (no.2): *Family Court; [2016] EWHC 1191 (Fam); 20 May 2016*
36. R (on the application of Johnson) v Secretary of State for the Home Department: *Supreme Court; [2016] UKSC 56; 19 October 2016*
37. Consent Order in R (on the application of David Fenton Bangs) v Secretary of State for the Home Department: *Administrative Court; 4 July 2017*
38. Smith v (1) Lancashire Teaching Hospitals NHS Foundation Trust; (2) Lancashire Care NHS Foundation Trust; (3) Secretary of State for Justice (2020 report): *Court of Appeal; [2017] EWCA Civ 1916; 28 November 2017*
41. Siobhan McLaughlin, Re Judicial Review (Northern Ireland) (2023 report): *Supreme Court; [2018] UKSC 48; 30 August 2018*
43. Jackson and Simpson v Secretary of State for Work and Pensions (2023 report): *Administrative Court; [2020] EWHC 183 (Admin); 7 February 2020*

Addressed by other primary or secondary legislation

4. McR's Application for Judicial Review: *Queen's Bench Division (NI); [2002] NIQB 58; 15 January 2002*
5. International Transport Roth GmbH v Secretary of State for the Home Department: *Court of Appeal; [2002] EWCA Civ 158; 22 February 2002*
7. R (on the application of Anderson) v Secretary of State for the Home Department: *House of Lords; [2002] UKHL 46; 25 November 2002*
8. R (on the application of D) v Secretary of State for the Home Department: *Administrative Court; [2002] EWHC 2805 (Admin); 19 December 2002*
9. Blood and Tarbuck v Secretary of State for Health: *Unreported; 28 February 2003*
11. Bellinger v Bellinger: *House of Lords; [2003] UKHL 21; 10 April 2003*
12. R (on the application of M) v Secretary of State for Health: *Administrative Court; [2003] EWHC 1094 (Admin);16 April 2003*
16. A and others v Secretary of State for the Home Department: *House of Lords; [2004] UKHL 56; 16 December 2004*
17. R (on the application of Sylviane Pierrette Morris) v Westminster City Council and First Secretary of State (no.3): *Court of Appeal; [2005] EWCA Civ 1184; 14 October 2005*
18. R (on the application of Gabaj) v First Secretary of State: *Administrative Court; unreported; 28 March 2006*
27. R (on the application of Royal College of Nursing and others) v Secretary of State for Home Department: *Administrative Court; [2010] EWHC 2761; 10 November 2010*
28. R (on the application of T, JB and AW) v Chief Constable of Greater Manchester, Secretary of State for the Home Department and Secretary of State for Justice: *Court of Appeal; [2013] EWCA Civ 25; 29 January 2013*
33. R (on the application of P and A) v Secretary of State for the Home Department and Others: *Administrative Court; [2016] EWHC 89 (Admin); 22 January 2016*
34. R (on the application of G) v Constable of Surrey Police & Others (2020 report): *Administrative Court; [2016] EWHC 295 (Admin); 19 February 2016*
39. Steinfeld and another v Secretary of State for International Development (2020 report): *Supreme Court; [2018] UKSC 32; 27 June 2018*
40. K (A Child) v Secretary of State for the Home Department (2022 report): *Administrative Court; [2018] EWHC 1834 (Admin); 18 July 2018*

Addressed by various measures

23. Smith v Scott (2021 report): *Registration Appeal Court (Scotland); [2007] CSIH 9; 24 January 2007*

Open to appeal

48. R (on the application of Jesse Quaye) v Secretary of State for Justice: *King's Bench Division; [2024] EWHC 211 (Admin); 9 January 2024*

55–57. In the matter of an application by the Northern Ireland Human Rights Commission for judicial review, in the matter of an application by JR295 for judicial review and in the matter of the Illegal Migration Act 2023: *King's Bench Division (NI); [2024] NIKB 35; 13 May 2024*

58. R (on the application of Smith) v Secretary of State for the Home Department: *King's Bench Division; [2024] EWHC 1137 (Admin); 14 May 2024*

Proposed to address by Remedial Order

49–53. In the matter of applications by Martina Dillon & Others, Teresa Jordan, Patrick Fitzsimmons & Gemma Gilvary for Judicial Review: King's Bench Division (NI); [2024] NIKB 11; 28 February 2024

44. In the matter of an application by 'JR111' for judicial review (ruling on remedy): *Queen's Bench Division (NI); substantive judgment [2021] NIQB 48 on 13 May 2021; ruling on remedy 21 May 2021*

Under consideration

47. Dean, Haggart and Harding v Mitchell and Secretary of State for Levelling-Up, Housing and Communities: *King's Bench Division*; QB-2022-002460; *29 June 2023*

54. Secretary of State for Business and Trade (Respondent) v Mercer (Appellant): *Supreme Court; [2024] UKSC 12; 17 April 2024*

Examples of How Business Can Impact Certain Human Rights

Relevant human right	**The right explained**	**How business might impact that right**
Right to life	• Right not to be deprived of life arbitrarily or unlawfully; • right to have one's life protected, for example from physical attacks or health and safety risks.	• Lethal use of force by security forces (State or private) to protect company resources, facilities or personnel; • operations that pose life-threatening safety risks to workers or neighbouring communities through accident/exposure to toxic chemicals; • manufacture and sale of products with lethal flaws or dual-use products.
Right to be free from slavery, servitude and forced labour	• Slavery occurs when one human effectively owns another; • freedom from servitude covers other forms of egregious economic exploitation, like trafficking of workers or debt bondage; • rights to freedom from slavery and servitude are absolute rights; • forced or compulsory labour is defined by the ILO as all work or service that is extracted under menace of any penalty and for which the person has not voluntarily offered themselves; • providing wages does not necessarily mean that work is not forced labour if the other aspects of the definition are met.	• Business operations that take place in certain countries or cultural contexts may, knowingly or unknowingly, benefit from forced labour, either directly or through supply chains; • business practices that put workers in a position of debt bondage through company loans, payment of fees or other means; • transportation of people/goods that facilitates the trafficking of forced or bonded labour.

Relevant human right	The right explained	How business might impact that right
Right to privacy	• Individuals have a right to be protected from arbitrary, unlawful or unreasonable interference with their privacy, family, home or correspondence and from attacks on their reputation.	• Failing to protect the confidentiality of personal data on employees, customers or other stakeholders; • providing information to government authorities without the individual's permission, in response to government requests that do not follow required national procedures and/or that are not in line with international human rights law.
Right to health	• Individuals have a right to the highest attainable standard of physical and mental health; • this includes the right to control over one's health and body and freedom from interference.	• Pollution from business operations creates negative health impacts on workers and surrounding communities; • sale of products that are hazardous to the health of end users/ customers; • failure to implement effective OH&S standards.
Rights of protection for the child	• Children are in need of special protection because of their potentially vulnerable status as minors; • a child has the right to a name, to be registered and to acquire a nationality; • children must be protected from sexual and economic exploitation; • ILO standards set minimum employment ages for hazardous work (18 years) and regular work (15 years, unless the country exercises the exception for developing States, which is 14 years), though there are some carefully prescribed exceptions.	• Business activities might be relying on child labour, either directly or through their supply chains; • where child labour is discovered, businesses can impact other rights (such as the right to an adequate standard of living) if they fail to take account of the best interests of the child in determining the appropriate response.
Right of self-determination	• Right of peoples, rather than individuals; • Peoples are entitled to determine their political status, pursue economic, social and cultural development, dispose of their land's natural resources and not be deprived of their own means of subsistence; • The right of indigenous peoples to self-determination has been specifically recognised by the international community.	• Any activity that might have impacts on indigenous peoples or their lands whether through acquisition, construction or operation.

PART V

PROBATE AND ADMINISTRATION

CHAPTER 29

SUCCESSION TO PROPERTY ON DEATH: THE BACKGROUND LAW

LEARNING OUTCOMES

After reading this chapter you will be able to:

- identify what property is capable of passing by will
- identify whether a will is valid
- decide the effect of a will
- explain the intestacy rules and decide who is entitled to property under the rules
- identify the circumstances in which a person can make a claim under the Inheritance (Provision for Family and Dependants) Act 1975 and the factors the court will take into account when considering a claim.

29.1 INTRODUCTION

When a person dies, one of the most important questions is who will inherit that person's property. This chapter explains the matters that are relevant when answering that question.

The first thing people usually ask is whether or not there is a will. However, many valuable assets pass independently of the terms of the will; and even if there is a will, the court may override its terms under the Inheritance (Provision for Family and Dependants) Act 1975 if it concludes that reasonable financial provision was not made for a close relative or dependant.

This chapter therefore looks at all the ways in which property can pass on death and the circumstances in which the court can alter the disposition of property under the Inheritance (Provision for Family and Dependants) Act 1975. It also looks at how to make a valid will and at the way in which wills take effect.

29.2 WHAT PROPERTY CAN PASS UNDER A WILL AND THE INTESTACY RULES?

When an individual dies, they may have provided for the disposition of their property on death by leaving a valid will. A will can operate to dispose of most types of property which an individual may own on death. A gift in a valid will of 'all my estate to my son, John' would include property held in the sole name of the testator at the time of their death in a variety of different forms, such as cash, money in bank and building society accounts, stocks and shares and other investments, land and chattels. It would also pass the testator's share of any property owned as beneficial tenant in common.

If an individual does not dispose of such property by will, it passes on their death according to the intestacy rules.

However, there are some important types of property which pass on death independently of the terms of the will and the intestacy rules. For many people the bulk of their property will pass in this way.

29.3 WHAT PROPERTY PASSES INDEPENDENTLY OF THE WILL AND INTESTACY RULES?

A number of different kinds of property pass independently of the terms of any will or the intestacy rules, some much more significant than others.

29.3.1 Joint property

Where property is held by more than one person as joint tenants in equity, on the death of one joint tenant their interest passes by survivorship to the surviving joint tenant(s).

> **EXAMPLE**
>
> George makes a will leaving all his estate to a charity. He and his brother Harry have a joint bank account and own a house as joint tenants in equity. On George's death his interests in the house and the bank account pass automatically to Harry, not to the charity under the terms of George's will.

The doctrine of survivorship does not apply to land where the beneficial interests are held on a tenancy in common. The share of each tenant in common passes on their death under their will (or under the intestacy rules).

29.3.2 Nominated property

There are statutory provisions allowing individuals to 'nominate' what is to happen to certain types of funds after the nominator's death. The statutory provisions apply to deposits not exceeding £5,000 in certain trustee savings banks, friendly societies, and industrial and provident societies.

A nomination is a direction to the institution to pay the money in the account, on the death of the investor, to a chosen ('nominated') third party.

If an individual has an account to which these provisions apply and has made a nomination, on their death the property passes to the chosen nominee regardless of the terms of the will (if any) or intestacy rules. If no nomination has been made, the money in the account will pass under the will or intestacy in the usual way.

There are very few statutes which allow new nominations to be made, although those already made will continue to be valid unless and until revoked.

29.3.3 Insurance policies

Where a person takes out a simple policy of life assurance, the benefit of that policy belongs to them. On their death, the policy matures and the insurance company will pay the proceeds to their representatives who will distribute the money according to the terms of the person's will or the intestacy rules.

However, a person may take out a life assurance policy expressed to be for the benefit of specified individuals. This is effectively a gift on trust for those individuals. It may be done in two ways:

(a) Under the terms of the Married Women's Property Act 1882, s 11. Under this section, a person taking out a life assurance policy on their own life may express the policy to be for the benefit of their spouse and/or children. This creates a trust in favour of the named beneficiaries.

(b) Alternatively, a policy may be expressly written in trust for or assigned to named beneficiaries.

In either case, once given away, the benefit of the policy does not belong to the policy holder. On the policy holder's death, the policy matures and the insurance company will pay the proceeds to the named beneficiaries (or to trustees for them) regardless of the terms of the deceased's will. The policy holder makes a transfer of value of the policy at the date of the gift. If the gift is made shortly after the policy has been taken out, its surrender value will be low.

29.3.4 Pension benefits

Many pension schemes provide for the payment of benefits if an employee dies 'in service'. Commonly, a lump sum calculated on the basis of employees' salary at the time of their death is paid by the trustees of the pension fund to members of the family or dependants chosen at the trustees' discretion. Such discretionary schemes usually allow employees to leave a letter of wishes for the trustees indicating which people they would like to benefit. The letter of wishes is not binding on the pension fund trustees, but they will normally comply with its terms. Funds remaining undrawn at death in defined benefit pension schemes are treated in the same way.

Such pension benefits do not belong to the employee during their lifetime and pass on death independently of the terms of any will and of the intestacy rules.

A few pension schemes provide that the lump sum must be paid to the employee's personal representatives (PRs). The PRs must then distribute the money according to the terms of the employee's will or the intestacy rules.

PRACTICAL POINT

When trying to decide who is entitled to take assets following a death, always deal with assets in the following order:

(a) property passing independently of the will and intestacy rules;

(b) property passing by will;

(c) property undisposed of by will and therefore passing under the intestacy rules.

29.4 THE REQUIREMENTS FOR A VALID WILL

In order to create a valid will, a testator must have the necessary capacity and intention, and must observe the formalities for execution of wills laid down in the Wills Act 1837. Once the will is made, it may be revoked by subsequent marriage or the formation of a civil partnership, by destruction or by a later will.

29.4.1 Capacity

In order to make a valid will, an individual must be aged 18 or over (with certain limited exceptions) and must have the requisite mental capacity. This testamentary capacity was defined in *Banks v Goodfellow* (1870) LR 5 QB 549 as 'soundness of mind, memory and understanding'. The testator must understand:

(a) the nature of their act and its broad effects;

(b) the extent of their property (although not necessarily recollecting every individual item); and

(c) the moral claims they ought to consider (even if they decide to reject such claims and dispose of their property to other beneficiaries).

In addition, the testator must not be suffering from any insane delusion which affects the disposition of property.

29.4.1.1 Proof and presumptions

At common law, the person who puts forward a will has to prove that all necessary elements, including mental capacity, are present. This is normally not particularly burdensome as, where a person generally showed no sign of mental confusion, it will be presumed that capacity existed at the time the will was made. If, however, there is anything to put the testator's general capacity in doubt, the presumption will not apply and the PRs will have to prove capacity on the basis of the *Banks v Goodfellow* test.

The Mental Capacity Act (MCA) 2005 came into force on 1 April 2007. It introduced a statutory test (contained in s 3) to determine whether a person had capacity to take a decision. Section 1(2) provides that 'for the purposes of this Act a person must be assumed to have capacity unless it is established that he lacks capacity'. There was some uncertainty as to whether the Act applied to capacity to make a will.

In *Scammell v Farmer* [2008] EWHC 1100 (Ch), which was the first case to consider the effect of the Act, the judge concluded that the Act applies only to decisions taken under the Act by the Court of Protection on behalf of another, so it ought not to apply to the assessment of a person's capacity to make their own will. Some later cases doubted this. However, in *Kicks v Leigh* [2014] EWHC 3926 (Ch), Judge Stephen Morris QC reviewed all the cases and said that he preferred the analysis in *Scammell*. In *Walker v Badmin* [2014] All ER (D) 258 (Nov), Judge Nicholas Strauss QC also reviewed the case law and concluded that the *Banks v Goodfellow* test for testamentary capacity applied rather than the MCA 2005 test. The question was considered again in *James v James* [2018] EWHC 43 (Ch) by Paul Matthews J; in *Clitheroe v Bond* [2021] EWHC 1102 (Ch) by Mrs Justice Falk; and in *Baker v Hewston* [2023] EWHC 1145 (Ch) by Tindal J, all of whom came to the same conclusion. Although the Court of Appeal might take a different view, it seems likely that this is the correct answer and the MCA 2005 has not affected either the common law test or the burden of proof of testamentary capacity.

29.4.2 Intention

When the will is signed, the testator must have both general and specific intention. This means that the testator must intend to make a will (as opposed to any other sort of document), and must also intend to make the particular will now being executed (ie the testator must know and approve its contents).

29.4.2.1 Proof and presumptions

The burden of proving the testator's knowledge and approval falls on the person putting forward the will, but there is a presumption which will usually assist.

A testator who has capacity and has then read and executed the will is presumed to have the requisite knowledge and approval. However, this presumption does not apply in the situations listed below.

Testator blind/illiterate/not signing personally

The presumption that the testator knew and approved the contents of their will does not apply if the testator was blind or illiterate, or another person signed the will on the testator's behalf (eg, because the testator had an injured hand).

In these cases, it will be necessary to provide evidence to prove knowledge and approval. It is usual in such cases to include a statement at the end of the will stating that the will was read over to the testator, or read by the testator, who appeared to know and approve the contents.

Suspicious circumstances

Similarly, the presumption of knowledge and approval does not apply if there are suspicious circumstances surrounding the drafting and/or execution of the will (eg, the will has been prepared by someone who is to be a major beneficiary under its terms or who is a close relative of a major beneficiary).

In such cases, because the presumption does not apply, the person putting forward the will must remove the suspicion by proving that the testator did actually know and approve the will's contents.

In *Gill v Woodall* [2010] EWCA Civ 1430, the Court of Appeal found that the presumption did not apply where Mrs Gill, a Yorkshire farmer, who was on excellent terms with her daughter and grandson, left everything to the RSPCA after leading her daughter to believe that she would inherit everything. Mrs Gill had gone with her husband to see a solicitor in order that they would both make wills. She suffered from a severe anxiety disorder and agoraphobia, the result of which was that she would have experienced panic when at the office of the solicitor. There was no evidence that she had read the will or had it explained to her, which meant that the Court of Appeal held that the circumstances of the case were so unusual that the presumption did not apply, and that the RSPCA had not proved that Mrs Gill had known and approved the contents of her will.

Note: Conduct issues for those regulated by the SRA

Those regulated by the SRA are required to act with honesty and integrity and in the best interests of clients (Principles 4, 5 and 7). They must not abuse their position by taking unfair advantage of clients, and they must not act if there is a significant risk that the duty to act in the best interests of the client conflicts with their own interests. There is such a risk where someone prepares a will which benefits themselves or someone close to them.

It is therefore sensible for firms to have a policy of refusing to act where a client proposes to make a gift of significant value to a fee earner or member of their family unless the client takes independent legal advice. The SRA published guidance on 'Drafting and Preparation of Wills' (updated 25 November 2019) which recommended this.

29.4.2.2 Force, fear, fraud, undue influence and mistake

Where a testator with capacity appears to have known and approved the contents of the will, any person who wishes to challenge the will (or any part of it) must prove one or more of the following to prevent some or all of the will from being admitted to probate. (There are no presumptions, so the person claiming invalidity on one of these grounds must prove it.)

Force, fear, fraud or undue influence

A will is invalid if it is shown that the testator made the will (or part of it) as a result of force or fear (through actual or threatened injury), or fraud (eg, after being misled by some pretence) or undue influence (where the testator's freedom of choice was overcome by intolerable pressure, even though their judgement remained unconvinced).

Notice that it is necessary to *prove* undue influence in relation to a will.

This is different from the position in relation to a lifetime gift. If a donor makes a lifetime gift which requires explanation (for example, because it is large in relation to the donor's other assets) to a person who is in a position of trust and confidence, there is a presumption of undue influence. The donee will be able to keep the gift only if they can provide the court with a satisfactory explanation.

There is no such presumption in the case of gifts by will, so the person alleging undue influence must prove it. The need for proof of undue influence in relation to wills makes it very difficult for someone challenging the will to succeed. The testator is dead, so the person alleging undue influence will need to collect evidence from family, friends and carers.

Mistake

All or part of the will may be included by mistake. Any words included without the knowledge and approval of the testator will be omitted from probate. In this respect, it is important to distinguish between actual mistake (ie absence of knowledge and approval) and misunderstanding as to the true legal meaning of words used in the will. In the latter case mistaken words will not be omitted. The court may however interpret the words used in a way which allows it to give effect to the intention of the testator.

29.4.3 Formalities for execution

Section 9 of the Wills Act 1837 (as substituted by Administration of Justice Act 1982, s 17) provides:

> No will shall be valid unless—
>
> (a) it is in writing, and signed by the testator, or by some other person in his presence and by his direction; and
>
> (b) it appears that the testator intended by his signature to give effect to the will; and
>
> (c) the signature is made or acknowledged by the testator in the presence of two or more witnesses present at the same time; and
>
> (d) each witness either—
>
> (i) attests and signs the will; or
>
> (ii) acknowledges his signature,
>
> in the presence of the testator (but not necessarily in the presence of any other witness),
>
> but no form of attestation shall be necessary.

There is one exception to the rule that wills must comply with the requirements of s 9. A will made on actual military service or by a mariner or seaman at sea is valid and may be in any form, including a mere oral statement: Wills Act 1837, s 11. The only requirement is that the 'testator' intends to dispose of their property after their death. It is the circumstances in which the will is made that are important, not the circumstances of death. In *Ayling v Summers* [2010] 1 All ER 410 the testator made an oral statement of wishes in 1990 while he was under orders to join his ship, and died, retired, in 2005; his statement was held to be a valid privileged will.

The requirement that the will must be signed in the presence of two witnesses present at the same time caused concern at the beginning of the Covid-19 pandemic as to how testators would be able to comply with the s 9 requirements. Fortunately, 'presence' has been given a generous interpretation. In the well-known case of *Casson v Dade* (1781) 1 Bro C C 99, the short report says:

> Being asthmatical, and the office very hot, she retired to her carriage to execute the will, the witnesses attending her: after having seen the execution, they returned into the office to attest it, and the carriage was accidentally put back to the window of the office, through which, it was sworn by a person in the carriage, the testatrix might see what passed.

The witnesses then brought out the will, handed it to the testator, telling her that they had attested it. The Lord Chancellor accepted that it was properly attested. The case is generally accepted as authority that what is required for 'presence' is a line of sight.

The existence of a line of sight is not enough; it is also necessary that there is consciousness of what is going on. Justice Gorell Barnes said in *Brown v Skirrow* [1903] P 3:

> You cannot be a witness to an act that you are unconscious of; otherwise the thing might be done in a ball-room 100 feet long and with a number of people in the intervening space. In my view, at the end of the transaction, the witness should be able to say with truth, 'I know that this testator or testatrix has signed this document'. (see p 5)

During the period of social isolation required by the Covid-19 pandemic, most practitioners became adept at ways of procuring 'safe' execution. For example, witnesses can stand outside a window or on the outside of an open door. Some testators have executed wills in parks sitting on adjacent benches, or inside a car with the witnesses signing on a bonnet (for a reported example of such signing see *Baker v Hewston* [2023] EWHC 1145 (Ch), where the court had no difficulty in finding that the will was properly executed).

However, there was argument as to whether or not 'presence' could include virtual presence via a video link. The Law Society of Scotland suggested that it could, but the Law Society of England and Wales said that it could not and most professional bodies agreed. There was pressure for legislation to clarify the position. On 25 July 2020 the Ministry of Justice announced that there would be legislation to allow remote witnessing for a limited period. See **29.4.3.1** below.

29.4.3.1 Remote witnessing

The Wills Act 1837 (Electronic Communications) (Amendment) (Coronavirus) Order 2020 (SI 2020/952) came into force on 28 September 2020. Article 2 amends the Wills Act 1837 as follows.

The existing s 9 becomes s 9(1), and a new s 9(2) provides as follows:

> For the purposes of paragraphs (c) and (d) of subsection (1), in relation to wills made on or after 31 January 2020 and on or before 31 January 2022, 'presence' includes presence by means of videoconference or other visual transmission.

The change was extended to wills made on or before 31 January 2024 by the Wills Act 1837 (Electronic Communications) (Amendment) Order 2022 (SI 2022/18). No further extension has been made so remote witnessing is no longer possible. Wills executed remotely between 28 September 2020 and 31 January 2024 will continue to be valid.

Note that s 9(1)(a) is not amended, so if a will is signed on behalf of a testator, it must be in the actual presence of the testator. Remote presence is not enough.

Article 3 provides that the Order does not allow a remotely witnessed will to be proved if a grant of probate was issued before 28 September 2020. The position in relation to other types of grant is unclear. (As to types of grant, see **Chapter 30**.)

The procedure for remote witnessing is not straightforward. The 'Guidance on making wills using video-conferencing', which the Government published on 25 July 2020 when it announced the temporary change, makes the following points:

- Witnessing pre-recorded videos is not permitted – the witnesses must see the will being signed in real-time.
- The witnesses and testator can all be at different locations, on a three-way link, or two can be physically together with one at a remote location.
- The testator must physically sign the will (or acknowledge an earlier physical signature). Electronic signatures are not permitted. Another person can sign on behalf of the testator if directed to do so, but, as explained above, the person signing must be in the physical presence of the testator. The testator will date the will with the date of signature.
- The will must then be taken or posted to the witnesses.
- The witnesses must physically sign the will in the virtual presence of the testator, and, if possible, in the virtual or physical presence of each other.
- The witnesses will sign with the date on which they are signing, which may be different from the date on which the testator signed and the date on which the other witness signs. The execution process is not complete until everyone has signed.

The will is not valid until both witnesses have signed. If the testator dies before all signatures have been added, the will cannot take effect. The government guidance said: 'The advice remains that where people can make wills in the conventional way they should continue to do so.'

29.4.3.2 Proof and presumptions

If the will includes a clause which recites that the s 9 formalities were observed, a presumption of due execution is raised. The will is valid unless there is proof that the formalities were not observed. Such a clause is called an attestation clause.

An example of an attestation clause is:

> Signed by the testator in our joint presence and then by us in his/hers.

If the will does not contain an attestation clause, the district judge (or registrar) must require an affidavit or witness statement verified by a statement of truth from a witness or any other person who was present during the execution, or, failing that, an affidavit of handwriting evidence to identify the testator's signature, or refer the case to a judge (all of which involve time and expense).

While not essential for validity, in the case of remote witnessing it is desirable that the attestation clause should be amended to recite that remote witnessing took place and that the necessary formalities were complied with. If it is not, the witnesses are likely to have to provide statements as to what occurred. The following is probably the minimum necessary.

> **Testator**
>
> Signed by me in the joint virtual presence of these two witnesses, who are witnessing me doing this remotely via a video-conferencing link
>
> [signature of testator or testatrix]
>
> [Date]
>
> **Witnesses**
>
> Signed by me in the virtual presence of [testator/testatrix] and the [actual] [virtual] presence of [other witness] having watched [testator/testatrix] sign remotely via a video-conferencing link on [date]
>
> [signature of witness]
>
> [Date]

The testator and the two witnesses must enter the date on which they each actually sign. The dates may well differ and, as explained above, the will is not valid until all three have signed.

29.4.3.3 Witnesses

There are no formal requirements relating to the capacity of witnesses, although they must be capable of understanding the significance of being the witness to a signature.

If either of the witnesses is a beneficiary under the will or is the spouse or a civil partner of a beneficiary, the will remains valid but the gift to the witness or to the witness's spouse or civil partner fails (Wills Act 1837, s 15; see **29.5.3**).

It is important for solicitors preparing wills to give clear instructions to their clients explaining how to sign and witness the will, and warning that beneficiaries and those married to or civil partners of beneficiaries should not be witnesses. It is preferable for the clients to execute at the solicitors' office where execution can be supervised.

If the will is returned to the solicitor for storage, the solicitor is under a duty to check the signatures to see whether ss 9 and 15 appear to have been complied with.

Failure to carry out these duties may lead to liability in negligence.

29.4.4 Revocation

Testators can always revoke a will during their lifetime, provided they have testamentary capacity. There are three ways of revoking a will.

29.4.4.1 By a later will or codicil

Under the Wills Act 1837, s 20, a will may be revoked in whole or in part by a later will or codicil. Normally, a will contains an express clause revoking all earlier wills and codicils.

If a will does not contain an express revocation clause, it operates to revoke any earlier will or codicil by implication to the extent that the two are inconsistent.

Exceptionally, the court may decide that a testator's intention to revoke an earlier will by an express revocation clause was conditional upon a particular event (eg, the effectiveness of a gift in the new will). If that condition is not satisfied, the revocation may be held to be invalid so that the earlier will remains effective (this is sometimes called the doctrine of 'dependent relative revocation').

29.4.4.2 By marriage or formation of a civil partnership

If the testator marries or forms a civil partnership after executing a will, the will is automatically revoked (Wills Act 1837, s 18, as substituted by the Administration of Justice Act 1982). The rule does not apply where a testator makes a will prior to a forthcoming marriage or civil partnership if it appears from the will that the testator was expecting to marry or form a civil partnership with a particular person and does not intend the will to be revoked (s 18(3)). Unless the will states that it is conditional on the marriage or civil partnership taking place, it will take effect unless expressly revoked, even if the expected marriage/civil partnership does not happen.

For example, Fred and Frances are engaged. They make wills in expectation of marriage and then have a row and break off the engagement. Fred dies 10 years later without changing his will. Frances will take his estate.

Note that as a result of the Marriage (Same Sex Couples) Act 2013, s 1(1), a marriage may, since 29 March 2014, be between a same sex couple as well as an opposite sex couple.

It is possible for same sex civil partners to convert a civil partnership into a same sex marriage. A new subsection (5) was inserted into s 18 of the Wills Act 1837 to provide that, where a civil partnership is converted to a marriage, the conversion will not revoke an existing will of either party nor affect any dispositions in the wills.

The Civil Partnerships, Marriages and Deaths (Registration etc) Act 2019 came into force on 26 May 2019. Section 2(1) authorised the Secretary of State to make regulations to amend the Civil Partnership Act 2004, so that opposite-sex couples could form civil partnerships in England and Wales (provided that they would be eligible to do so apart from the question of gender).

The Civil Partnership (Opposite-sex Couples) Regulations 2019 came into force on 2 December 2019 under which the formation of new opposite-sex civil partnerships became possible from 31 December 2019 onwards (existing overseas opposite-sex civil partnerships were recognised from 2 December 2019).

Part 8 of the Regulations maintains the current position on conversion rights. Hence, although same sex couples continue to be able to convert a civil partnership into a same sex marriage, opposite sex spouses cannot convert a marriage into an opposite sex civil partnership. Paragraph 91 of *Implementing Opposite-Sex Civil Partnerships: Next Steps* (the government guidance published with the Regulations in July 2019) states:

> This approach avoids making short-term changes ahead of the outcome of the public consultation on the future of conversion rights conducted earlier this year ... Further regulations on conversion rights may follow next year, depending on the outcome of the consultation.

If the testator makes a will and is later divorced, or if the civil partnership is dissolved (or the marriage or civil partnership is annulled or declared void), then under the Wills Act 1837, s 18A (amended by the Law Reform (Succession) Act 1995 with effect from 1 January 1996) the will remains valid but:

(a) provisions of the will appointing the former spouse or civil partner as executor or trustee take effect as if the former spouse or civil partner had died on the date on which the marriage or civil partnership is dissolved or annulled; and

(b) any property, or interest in property, which is devised or bequeathed to the former spouse or civil partner passes as if the former spouse or civil partner had died on that date. See **29.5.3.1** below.

This means that substitutional provisions in the will which are expressed to take effect if the spouse/civil partner predeceases the testator will also take effect if the marriage/civil partnership is dissolved or annulled.

29.4.4.3 By destruction

A will may be revoked by 'burning, tearing or otherwise destroying the same by the testator or by some person in his presence and by his direction with the intention of revoking the same' (Wills Act 1837, s 20). Physical destruction without the intention to revoke is insufficient; a will destroyed accidentally or by mistake is not revoked. If its contents can be reconstructed (eg, from a copy), an order may be obtained allowing its admission to probate as a valid will.

Physical destruction is required: symbolic destruction (eg, simply crossing out wording or writing 'revoked' across the will) is not sufficient, although if a vital part (eg, the signature) is destroyed, this partial destruction may be held to revoke the entire will. If the part destroyed is less substantial or important, then the partial destruction may revoke only that part which was actually destroyed.

Note that the destruction must be in the testator's presence and by their direction. Destruction in another room is ineffective to revoke the will. Where a will is destroyed without the intention to revoke, it is possible to obtain probate of a copy, draft or reconstruction. See **30.5.2.4**. For a recent example, see *Crew v Oakley* [2024] EWHC 2847 (Ch). The testatrix was terminally ill in hospital. She wanted to change her will. In the presence of her solicitor, she tore three-quarters of the way through the will but was too weak to continue. Her solicitor asked if she wanted the solicitor to complete the job and the testatrix nodded. The court held that the partial tearing was not sufficient to revoke but that the testatrix, by nodding, had authorised the solicitor to complete the destruction. The will was, therefore, revoked.

Occasionally, the court may apply the doctrine of dependent relative revocation to save a will, on the basis that the testator's intention to revoke their will by destruction was conditional upon some future event (eg, upon the later execution of a new will). If that event did not in fact take place, the original will may be valid even though it was destroyed. The contents of the original will may be reconstructed from a copy or draft.

29.4.5 Alterations

If a will has been altered, the basic rule is that the alterations are invalid unless it can be proved that they were made before the will was executed, or unless the alterations are executed like a will (the initials of the testator and witnesses in the margin beside the alteration are sufficient for this purpose).

If a will includes invalid alterations, the original wording will stand if the original words are 'apparent', ie can still be read. If the original words have been obliterated in such a way that they can no longer be read, those words have effectively been revoked by destruction. The rest of the will remains valid, and takes effect with the omission of the obliterated words.

Again, the court may decide that the testator's intention to revoke the obliterated words was conditional only. This inference is most likely to be drawn where the testator attempted to replace the obliterated words with a substitution. The implied condition is that the testator intended to revoke the original words only if the substitution was effective. As it is not, the original words remain valid and, if they can be reconstructed (eg, from a copy or draft), they will take effect.

EXAMPLE

Tamal makes a professionally drawn will which leaves '£10,000 to my nephew, Nalin'. After executing the will, Tamal decides he wants to change the legacy to Nalin:

(1) He draws a thin line through '£10,000' and writes above it '£20,000'.

This is an unexecuted alteration and will have no effect. The gift remains a gift of £10,000.

(2) He does exactly the same thing but writes his name next to the alteration and gets two people to witness his signature.

This is an executed alteration and takes effect to alter the gift to £20,000.

(3) He draws a thick line through '£10,000' in such a way that the original wording is wholly unreadable.

This is an obliteration and will be treated as revoking the original gift. The gift is treated as a gift of nothing.

(4) He does exactly the same thing but writes '£20,000' above the obliteration.

This is an obliteration and would be treated as revoking the original gift were it not for the fact that Tamal has substituted words. A court is likely to conclude that Tamal's intention to revoke the original gift was conditional on the substitution being able to take effect. As the substitution is not effective, the original gift will take effect (provided it is possible to discover what the original gift was).

29.5 HOW A WILL TAKES EFFECT

When a testator dies, the people dealing with the estate must decide (usually with the help of a solicitor) the effect of the will in the light of the circumstances at the date of the testator's death. They will need to consider what property the testator owned when the testator died and which of the people named in the will have survived the testator in order to decide the effect of the gifts.

If the will refers to beneficiaries by description, it will be necessary to identify the people fulfilling the description.

The people dealing with the estate will be called executors, if they were appointed by the will, and administrators, if there was no appointment in the will. There are statutory rules as to who is able to act as an administrator (Non-Contentious Probate Rules 1987, r 20). Both executors and administrators may be referred to generically as 'personal representatives' ('PRs').

29.5.1 What property passes under the gifts in the will?

As seen in **29.3** above, certain types of property pass independently of the will either because they have their own rules of succession (eg, joint property), or because the testator did not own them beneficially at death (eg, life assurance policies written in trust).

When the PRs have decided what property is capable of passing under the will, they must apply the terms of the will to the property.

29.5.1.1 Basic rule

The basic rule is stated in the Wills Act 1837, s 24, which provides:

> every will shall be construed, with reference to the real estate and personal estate comprised in it, to speak and take effect as if it had been executed immediately before the death of the testator, unless a contrary intention shall appear by the will.

This means that a gift of 'all my estate' or 'all the rest of my estate' takes effect to dispose of all property the testator owned when they died, whether or not the testator owned it at the time the will was made.

29.5.1.2 Ademption

A specific legacy, ie a gift of a particular item or group of items of property, will fail if the testator no longer owns that property at death. The gift is said to be 'adeemed'. Ademption usually occurs because the property has been sold, given away or destroyed during the testator's lifetime.

EXAMPLE

In her will Ellen gives 'my engraved gold bracelet' to her sister Grace and the rest of her estate to her husband Harry. Ellen no longer owns the bracelet when she dies. Grace receives nothing: her legacy is adeemed. All Ellen's estate passes to Harry under the residuary gift.

Problems may arise where the asset has been retained but has changed its nature since the will was made. For example, where the will includes a specific gift of company shares, the company may have been taken over since the will was made so that the testator's shareholding has been changed into a holding in the new company. In such a case, the question is whether the asset is substantially the same, having changed merely in name or form, or whether it has changed in substance. Only if there has been a change in substance will the gift be adeemed.

Another area of potential difficulty occurs where the testator disposes of the property described in a specific gift but before their death acquires a different item of property which answers the same description; for example a gift of 'my car' or 'my piano' where the original car or piano has been replaced since the will was made. It has been held that the presumption in such a case is that the testator meant only to dispose of the particular asset they owned at the date of the will so that the gift is adeemed. By referring to 'my' car or piano, the testator is taken to have shown a contrary intention as specified in s 24. This construction may vary according to the circumstances, and the respective values of the original and substituted assets may be taken into account.

If the property given is capable of increase or decrease (eg, 'my shares', 'my jewellery'), the testator will normally be taken to have made a gift of any items satisfying the description at death.

EXAMPLE

Thea makes a will leaving 'all my jewellery' to her niece, Nepota. After the date of the will, all her jewellery is stolen. Six months later she receives money from her insurance company and buys new jewellery. Then she dies.

(1) Because Thea has used a phrase which is capable of increase and decrease, she is treated as intending to pass whatever jewellery she has at the date of her death. Nepota will, therefore, take the replacement items.

(2) Had the gift been of 'my pearl necklace', Thea would probably be treated as intending to pass only the necklace she owned at the date of the will. Nepota would not have taken any replacement necklace.

> (3) Had Thea died after receiving the insurance money but before buying replacement assets, Nepota would have taken nothing. She has no right to the insurance money under the terms of the gift.

A testator may wish to add to or change a will in a minor way and so may execute a supplementary codicil. A codicil is a supplement to a will which, to be valid, must be executed in the same way as a will. The significance of a codicil in the context of a gift of property is that it republishes the will as at the date of the codicil. Thus, if the testator makes a will in 1990 leaving 'my gold watch' to a legatee, loses the watch in 2000 and replaces it, the gift of the watch in the will is adeemed. If, however, the testator executes a codicil to the will in 2003, the will is read as if it had been executed in 2003 and so the legatee will take the replacement watch.

29.5.2 Has the beneficiary survived the testator?

29.5.2.1 Basic rule

A gift in a will fails or 'lapses' if the beneficiary dies before the testator. If a legacy lapses, the property falls into residue, unless the testator has provided for the possibility of lapse by including a substitutional gift. If a gift of residue lapses, the property passes under the intestacy rules, unless the testator has included a substitutional gift in the will. Where no conditions to the contrary are imposed in the will, a gift vests on the testator's death. This means that provided the beneficiary survives the testator, for however short a time, the gift takes effect. If the beneficiary dies soon after the testator the property passes into the beneficiary's estate.

It is possible to show a contrary intention, for example by wording a gift to make it clear that the property is to pass to whoever is the holder of a position or office at the date of the testator's death.

There is a presumption that, as regards people, a will is construed at the date it is made. A gift made to 'the eldest son of X' is construed as a gift to the person fulfilling that description at the date the will is made. If that person dies, the gift does not pass to the eldest surviving son. However, if the testator makes a codicil to the will, it republishes the will and the will is treated as made at the date of the republication. Hence, if the eldest son dies between the date of the will and the codicil, the will is construed as referring to the person who is the eldest son at the date of the codicil.

29.5.2.2 Law of Property Act 1925, s 184

The principle outlined above means that if the deaths of the testator and beneficiary occur very close together, it is vital to establish who died first. The law of succession does not accept the possibility that two people might die at the same instant. If the order of their deaths cannot be proved, s 184 provides that the elder of the two is deemed to have died first. If the testator was older than the beneficiary, the gift takes effect and the property passes as part of the beneficiary's estate.

Scarle v Scarle [2019] EWHC 2224 (Ch) is a recent case involving the presumption. There was uncertainty as to the order of deaths of a husband and wife. Mrs Scarle was younger than her husband but there was some forensic evidence that she might have died first.

The order of deaths was crucial as the couple held their house as beneficial joint tenants, together with £18,000 in a joint bank account. The survivor would take the house and bank account by survivorship. It was a second marriage for both and each had one daughter from their previous marriages. The dispute was between the daughters.

Unfortunately for the husband's daughter, the court held that the evidence was not sufficient to establish the order of deaths on the balance of probabilities so the uncertainty remained and the presumption applied. The wife's daughter inherited everything.

29.5.2.3 Survivorship clauses

Commonly, gifts in wills are made conditional upon the survival of the beneficiaries for a specific period of time, such as 28 days. These survivorship provisions prevent a gift from taking effect where the beneficiary survives the testator for only a relatively short time or is deemed to have survived by s 184. As with any other contingent gift, if the beneficiary fails to satisfy the contingency, the gift fails.

29.5.2.4 Lapse of gifts to more than one person

A gift by will to two or more people as joint tenants will not lapse unless all the donees die before the testator. If a gift is made 'to A and B jointly' and A dies before the testator, the whole gift passes to B.

If the gift contains words of severance, for example 'everything to A and B in equal shares', this principle does not apply. If A dies before the testator, A's share lapses and B takes only one share. The lapsed share will pass under the intestacy rules unless, as is often the case, the testator included a substitutional gift to take effect if one of the original beneficiaries predeceased.

If the gift is a class gift (eg, 'to my nephews and nieces, equally if more than one'), there is no lapse unless all the members of the class predecease the testator.

29.5.2.5 Wills Act 1837, s 33: gifts to children and remoter issue

This section applies to all gifts by will to the testator's children or remoter issue (for the meaning of 'issue', see **29.6.2.1**) unless a contrary intention is shown in the will and its effect is to incorporate an implied substitution provision into such gifts. It provides that where a will contains a gift to the testator's child or remoter descendant and that beneficiary dies before the testator, leaving issue of their own who survive the testator, the gift does not lapse but passes instead to the beneficiary's issue. The issue of a deceased beneficiary take the gift their parent would have taken in equal shares.

> **EXAMPLE**
>
> **Tom's will includes a gift of £40,000 to his daughter, Caroline. Caroline and her daughter Sinead both die before Tom, but Caroline's son, Jack, and Sinead's children, Erin and Finola, all survive him. Under s 33, the legacy is saved from lapse. Jack takes half the gift (£20,000). Sinead would have taken the other half but, as she has predeceased Tom, her half passes to her own children equally. Thus, Erin and Finola take £10,000 each.**

Section 33 does not apply if the will shows a contrary intention. This is usually shown by including an express substitution clause.

The Estates of Deceased Persons (Forfeiture Rule and Law of Succession) Act 2011 inserted a new s 33A into the Wills Act 1837, with the result that in certain circumstances for the purposes of the Wills Act 1837 a person may be deemed to have predeceased the testator. See **29.5.3.5** below.

29.5.3 Does the gift fail for any other reason?

29.5.3.1 Divorce or dissolution of a civil partnership

Under the Wills Act 1837, s 18A (as substituted by the Law Reform (Succession) Act 1995), where after the date of the will the testator's marriage or civil partnership is dissolved or annulled or declared void, 'any property which, or an interest in which, is devised or bequeathed to the former spouse or civil partner shall pass as if the former spouse or civil partner had died' on the date of the dissolution or annulment of the marriage or civil partnership.

> **EXAMPLE**
>
> Fauzia makes a will in which she leaves all her estate to her husband, Sabiq, with a substitutional provision that, if Sabiq dies before her, the property should pass to her children equally. Fauzia and Sabiq are later divorced but Fauzia does not change her will. She dies, survived by Sabiq and the children. Under s 18A, the gift to Sabiq fails. Even though Sabiq in fact survived Fauzia, the substitutional gift takes effect and Fauzia's estate passes to the children.

29.5.3.2 Beneficiary witnesses will

Under the Wills Act 1837, s 15, a gift by will fails if the beneficiary, their spouse or civil partner witnesses the will.

29.5.3.3 Disclaimer

Beneficiaries need not accept gifts given to them by will. They can disclaim the gift, which will then fall into residue or, in the case of disclaimer of a gift of residue, pass on intestacy.

However, a beneficiary who has received a benefit from a gift (eg, a payment of income) is taken to have accepted the gift and may no longer disclaim.

29.5.3.4 Forfeiture

The forfeiture rule provides that, as a matter of public policy, a person should not be able to inherit from a person they have been convicted of unlawfully killing. The rule applies in cases both of murder and manslaughter, but not in cases where the killer was insane within the meaning of the *McNaghten* rules. Unlawful killing includes aiding, abetting, counselling or procuring the death of another person, for instance by assisting with their suicide, a crime under s 2 of the Suicide Act 1961. *Amos v Mancini* [2020] EWHC 1063 (Ch) held that the rule applied to causing death by careless driving. This was a sad case where an elderly lady who had been driving for 10 hours drove into the back of a line of cars coming off a motorway, killing her husband who was in the passenger seat. Happily, the court was able to relieve the widow from forfeiture under the Forfeiture Act 1982.

In cases of unlawful killing, other than murder, the killer may apply within three months of conviction for relief from forfeiture under the Forfeiture Act 1982. As mentioned above, this was done successfully in *Amos v Mancini*.

The court has a discretion as to whether or not to grant relief. In *Ninian v Findlay* [2019] EWHC 297 (Ch), Mrs Ninian was held to have assisted her husband to commit suicide by helping with the administrative requirements required by *Dignitas* and organising his trip to *Dignitas* in Zurich. However, the court had no hesitation in granting relief against the forfeiture rule. The couple were described as devoted and the wife had tried to change her husband's mind. She assisted him because he found the effects of his progressive and terminal illness intolerable.

The time limit is strict and the court has no discretion to extend the period. In *Challen v Challen* [2020] EWHC 1330 (Ch) Judge Paul Matthews held that where there is an initial conviction followed by an appeal, and then a subsequent conviction, it is the subsequent conviction which is the relevant one for the purposes of the time limit. It was not strictly necessary for the judge to decide when conviction occurs if the plea is accepted and the defendant is sentenced on different days, as in this particular case the two coincided. However, on the basis that a defendant may with the consent of the judge change their plea at any time up until sentence is passed, the defendant's position is only definitive at the point of sentence and not, if this is earlier, when the court accepts the plea. Judge Matthews concluded that it is only at the point of sentence that there is a conviction within s 2(3) of the 1982 Act, starting the three-month time limit running.

29.5.3.5 The Estates of Deceased Persons (Forfeiture Rule and Law of Succession) Act 2011

This Act came into effect on 1 February 2011. Section 2 inserts a new s 33A into the Wills Act 1837 which provides, subject to contrary intention in the will, that a person who disclaims or forfeits an entitlement under a will is to be treated for the purposes of the Wills Act as having predeceased the testator. This means that if a child of the testator forfeits or disclaims, their issue can be substituted under the Wills Act 1837, s 33.

EXAMPLE

Terry is murdered by his daughter, Denise. His will leaves everything to Denise who has a son, Sean.

Denise forfeits her entitlement under the will but she will be treated as if she had predeceased Terry, with the result that s 33 of the Wills Act 1837 will apply and Terry's property will pass to Sean.

29.5.4 Identifying the beneficiaries

Where the beneficiaries are referred to by name, identification is usually just a matter of locating them.

Where the will refers to a class of beneficiaries, for example 'my children', 'my nieces', there may be some doubt as to who fulfils that description. Unless the will provides otherwise, such a gift will be a gift only to the testator's own children or nieces and not to the children or relatives of the testator's spouse or civil partner (so-called step-children), or to those of a cohabitee.

In *Reading v Reading* [2015] EWHC 946 (Ch) the court found that there was sufficient evidence to demonstrate that the testator had intended his step-children to share a pecuniary legacy with his own children: the will included a substitutional gift of residue to both his own children and his step-children in the event that his second wife predeceased him, the general wording suggested step-children were intended to share in both cases, and the solicitor who prepared the will had recorded in his attendance note that the step-children were to share but had failed to word the will correctly. In *Wales v Dixon* [2020] EWHC 1979 (Ch) the deceased left his estate to the children of 'my' nephews and nieces. The court found that there was sufficient evidence to show that the deceased had intended to include the children of his wife's nephews and nieces.

The normal meaning of issue is direct descendants of any generation so, as well as the testator's children, it will include grandchildren, great-grandchildren and so on.

Adopted children are normally treated as children of the adoptive parents, although the will may provide otherwise. In the case of succession to property under modern wills, it is irrelevant whether or not a child's parents are married to each other.

There are special rules which apply to determine the parentage of children born as a result of assisted reproduction (see Human Fertilisation and Embryology Act 2008). These are beyond the scope of this book.

The Gender Recognition Act 2004 came into force on 4 April 2005. Persons who have obtained a full gender recognition certificate from the Gender Recognition Panel are legally recognised in the acquired gender. Section 15 provides that:

> the fact that a person's gender has become the acquired gender under the Act does not affect the disposal or devolution of property under a will or other instrument made before 4 April 2005.

However, it will do so if the will or other instrument is made after that date.

> **EXAMPLE**
>
> 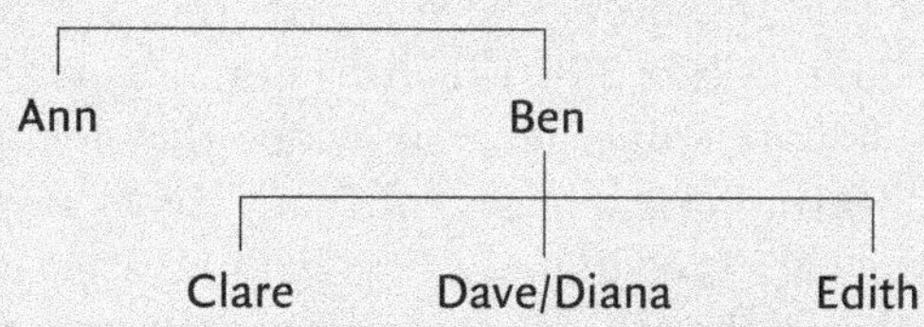
>
>
> Dave obtains a full gender recognition certificate as a woman (Diana) in 2016.
>
> Ann dies in 2022 with a will leaving everything to 'my nieces equally'.
>
> If the will is made before 4 April 2005, Diana cannot share in Ann's estate but she can if the will is made on or after that date.

Section 18 of the Act provides that where the disposition or devolution of any property under a will or other instrument (made on or after the appointed day) is different from what it would be but for the fact that a person's gender has become the acquired gender under the Act, an application may be made to the High Court where expectations have been defeated. Where the court is satisfied that it is just to make an order, it has a wide discretion as to the appropriate order to make. For example, it could order payment of a lump sum, transfer or settlement of property.

Trustees and PRs are protected under s 17 of the Act from: (a) being under any duty to enquire whether a full gender recognition certificate has been issued or revoked before conveying or distributing any property; and (b) being liable to any person by reason of a conveyance or distribution of property made without regard to whether a full gender recognition certificate has been issued to any person or revoked without the trustee or personal representative having been given prior notice. However, the section does not prejudice the right of a person to follow the property, or any property representing it, into the hands of another person who has received it unless that person has purchased it for value in good faith and without notice.

29.6 THE EFFECT OF THE INTESTACY RULES

The intestacy rules contained in the Administration of Estates Act 1925 (AEA 1925) apply to decide who is entitled to an individual's property when they die without disposing of it by will.

This may occur because the deceased has died intestate (ie, without a valid will), or because their will failed to dispose of all their estate (partial intestacy).

The intestacy rules apply only to property which is capable of being left by will (see **29.3**).

> **EXAMPLE**
>
> Laura dies intestate on 1 September 2022, survived by her husband, Michael, and their two children. Laura and Michael owned their house as beneficial joint tenants. Laura had taken out a life assurance policy for £100,000 which is written in trust for the children, and she owned investments worth £150,000. The intestacy rules do not affect Laura's share of the house (which passes to Michael by survivorship) or the life policy (which passes to the children under the terms of the trust). Only the investments pass under the intestacy rules.

Note that the Inheritance and Trustees' Powers Act 2014 made significant changes to the entitlement of surviving spouses and civil partners on intestacy in the case of deaths occurring on or after 1 October 2014. The previous rules made more limited provision for spouses and civil partners. These earlier rules are not considered here.

29.6.1 Statutory trust for payment of debts, etc

The intestacy rules impose a trust over all the property (real and personal) in respect of which a person dies intestate (AEA 1925, s 33). This trust is similar to the usual express trust found in a will and includes a power of sale: it provides that the PRs must pay the funeral, testamentary and administration expenses, and any debts of the deceased. The balance remaining (after setting aside a fund to meet any pecuniary legacies left by the deceased in the will) is the 'residuary estate' to be shared among the family under the rules of distribution set out in s 46 of the AEA 1925. The PRs have power under s 41 to appropriate assets in or towards satisfaction of a beneficiary's share (with the beneficiary's consent).

29.6.2 Spouse or civil partner and issue

29.6.2.1 Definitions

Under the intestacy rules, a spouse is the person to whom the deceased was married at their death, whether or not they were living together. A same sex spouse has exactly the same rights as an opposite sex spouse.

A former spouse is excluded once the decree absolute is obtained. A cohabitee has no rights under the intestacy rules.

Civil partners are treated in the same way as spouses.

The term 'issue' includes all direct descendants of the deceased: ie, children, grandchildren, great grandchildren, etc. Adopted children (and remoter descendants) are included, as are those whose parents were not married at the time of their birth. Descendants of the deceased's spouse or civil partner ('step' children) are not issue of the deceased unless adopted.

29.6.2.2 Entitlements

Where the intestate is survived by both spouse or civil partner and issue, the 'residuary estate' (as defined in **29.6.1**) is distributed as follows:

(a) The spouse or civil partner receives the personal chattels absolutely. 'Personal chattels' are defined in s 55(1)(x) of the AEA 1925 as tangible movable property, other than any such property which—
  (i) consists of money or securities for money, or
  (ii) was used at the death of the intestate solely or mainly for business purposes, or
  (iii) was held at the death of the intestate solely as an investment.

(b) In addition, the spouse or civil partner receives a 'statutory legacy' free of tax and costs plus interest from death until payment. The rate of interest payable is the Bank of England rate that had effect at the end of the day on which the intestate died. The statutory legacy was £250,000 but was increased in line with inflation to £270,000 for deaths on or after 6 February 2020 by the Administration of Estates Act 1925 (Fixed Net Sum) Order 2020 and to £322,000 for deaths after 26 July 2023.

(c) The rest of the residuary estate (if any) is divided in half. One half is held on trust for the spouse or civil partner absolutely. The other half is held for the issue on the statutory trusts.

The intestate's spouse or civil partner must survive the intestate for 28 days in order to inherit. The Law Reform (Succession) Act 1995 provides that, where the intestate's spouse or civil partner dies within 28 days of the intestate, the estate is distributed as if the spouse or civil partner has not survived the intestate.

29.6.2.3 Applying the statutory trusts

The statutory trusts determine membership of the class of beneficiaries, and the terms on which they take, as follows.

(a) The primary beneficiaries are the children of the intestate who are living at the intestate's death. Remoter issue are not included, unless a child has died before the intestate.

(b) The interests of the children are contingent upon attaining the age of 18 or marrying or forming a civil partnership under that age. Any child who fulfils the contingency at the intestate's death takes a vested interest.

(c) If any child of the intestate predeceased the intestate, any children of the deceased child (grandchildren of the deceased) who are living at the intestate's death take their deceased parent's share equally between them, contingently upon attaining 18 or earlier marriage or formation of a civil partnership. Great grandchildren would be included only if their parent had also predeceased the intestate. This form of substitution and division is known as a '*per stirpes*' distribution.

(d) If children or issue survive the intestate but die without attaining a vested interest, their interest normally fails and the estate is distributed as if they had never existed. However, s 3 of the Estates of Deceased Persons (Forfeiture Rule and Law of Succession) Act 2011 amended s 47 of the Administration of Estates Act 1925 so that it now provides that if they die without attaining a vested interest but leaving issue, they will be treated as having predeceased the intestate so that they can be replaced by their own issue (see **29.6.5.1**). To be substituted, the issue must be living at the intestate's death.

EXAMPLE

Joanne dies intestate on 1 October 2022, survived by her husband, Kenneth, and their children, Mark (aged 20, who has a son, Quentin) and Nina (aged 16). Their daughter, Lisa, died last year. Lisa's two children, Oliver and Paul (aged 6 and 4), are living at Joanne's death.

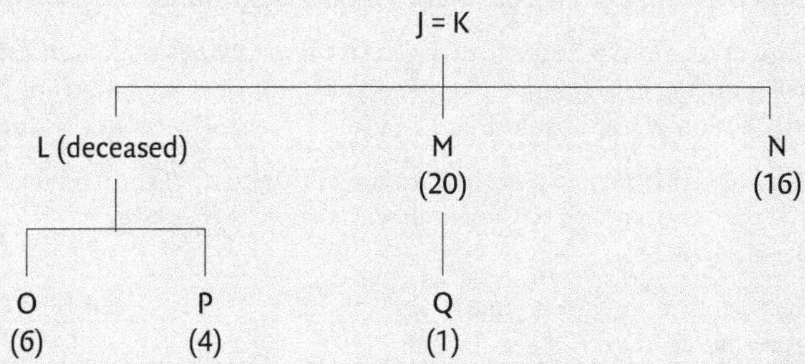

Joanne's estate consists of her share in the house, held as joint tenants with Kenneth, and other property worth £590,000 after payment of debts, funeral and testamentary expenses. This figure includes personal chattels worth £20,000.

DISTRIBUTION

Joanne's share in the house passes to Kenneth by survivorship. The rest of her estate passes on intestacy.

£	
20,000	personal chattels to Kenneth
270,000	statutory legacy to Kenneth

The remaining £300,000 is divided in half.

150,000	for Kenneth absolutely
150,000	for the issue on the statutory trusts
590,000	

The statutory trusts apply to determine the distribution between Joanne's issue as follows.

Mark and Nina, Joanne's children, are living at her death and take one share each. The share Lisa would have taken had she survived is held for her children, Oliver and Paul, in equal shares. The interests of Nina, Oliver and Paul are contingent upon attaining 18 or earlier marriage or formation of a civil partnership.

Thus, Mark has a vested interest in one-third of the issues' half. He is entitled to £50,000 on Joanne's death. If Mark should die shortly after Joanne, his share would form part of his estate on death. Quentin has no entitlement under Joanne's intestacy.

Nina has a contingent interest in one-third of the issues' half, which will vest when she is 18 or if she marries or forms a civil partnership before 18. If Nina should die under the age of 18 and without marrying or forming a civil partnership, her interest would fail. One half of Nina's share would pass to Mark and the other half would be held for Oliver and Paul equally. However, if Nina has a child who is living on Joanne's death, the child would take Nina's place as a result of the changes made by s 3 of the Estates of Deceased Persons (Forfeiture Rule and Law of Succession) Act 2011.

Oliver and Paul each have contingent interests in one-sixth of the issues' half, which will vest at 18 or earlier marriage or formation of a civil partnership. If Oliver should die under the age of 18 and without marrying or forming a civil partnership (or having an illegitimate child), his share would pass to Paul (and vice versa). If both Oliver and Paul were to die under the age of 18 and without marrying or forming a civil partnership (or having an illegitimate child), their shares would be divided equally between Mark and Nina (provided she reaches 18, marries or forms a civil partnership).

29.6.2.4 Right of spouse or civil partner to require appropriation of the matrimonial home

If the matrimonial home forms part of the estate passing on intestacy, the surviving spouse or civil partner can require the PRs to appropriate the matrimonial home in full or partial satisfaction of any absolute interest in the estate (Intestates' Estates Act 1952, s 5).

If the property is worth more than the entitlement of the spouse or civil partner, the spouse or civil partner may still require appropriation provided they pay the difference, 'equality money', to the estate.

The election must be made in writing to the PRs within 12 months of the grant of representation.

29.6.3 Spouse or civil partner and no issue

Where the intestate leaves a surviving spouse or civil partner but no issue, the whole estate, however large, passes to the spouse or civil partner absolutely. Other relatives, such as parents, brothers and sisters, grandparents and cousins, are not entitled.

The spouse or civil partner must survive the intestate for 28 days in order to take. If the spouse or civil partner dies within that period, the estate is distributed as if the spouse or civil partner had not survived the intestate.

29.6.4 Distribution where there is no surviving spouse or civil partner

Where there is no surviving spouse or civil partner (or, for deaths after 1 January 1996, where the spouse or civil partner dies within 28 days of the intestate), the 'residuary estate' is divided between the relatives in the highest category in the list below:

(a) issue on the 'statutory trusts' (see **29.6.2**), but if none,

(b) parents, equally if both alive, but if none,

(c) brothers and sisters of the whole blood on the 'statutory trusts', but if none,
(d) brothers and sisters of the half blood on the 'statutory trusts', but if none,
(e) grandparents, equally if more than one, but if none,
(f) uncles and aunts of the whole blood on the 'statutory trusts', but if none,
(g) uncles and aunts of the half blood on the 'statutory trusts', but if none,
(h) the Crown, Duchy of Lancaster, or Duke of Cornwall (*bona vacantia*).

29.6.4.1 The statutory trusts

Each category other than parents and grandparents takes 'on the statutory trusts'. This means that members of the specified class share the estate equally (children under 18 take their interest contingently upon attaining 18 or marrying earlier), and that issue of a deceased relative may take that relative's share. This means that relatives not mentioned in s 46 (eg, nephews, nieces and cousins) may inherit on intestacy if their parents died before the intestate.

EXAMPLE 1

Tom dies intestate. He was not married to his partner, Penny, although the couple have a son, Simon, aged 13, Tom's only child. Tom's parents predeceased him but he is survived by his only sibling, his brother, Bob, aged 40.

Tom's estate is held on trust for Simon, contingently upon attaining 18 or marrying earlier. If Simon dies before the contingency is fulfilled, Tom's estate passes to Bob absolutely.

EXAMPLE 2

Vera, a widow aged 80, is cared for by her step-daughter, Carol (the child of her deceased husband's first marriage). Her only living blood relatives are cousins, the children of her mother's brothers and sisters. Vera dies intestate. Her estate is divided 'per stirpes' between her cousins (and the children of any cousins who predeceased her). Carol receives nothing from Vera's estate.

Section 3 of the Estates of Deceased Persons (Forfeiture Rule and Law of Succession) Act 2011 provides that a person with an interest on the statutory trusts who dies before reaching the age of 18 or marrying or forming a civil partnership will be treated as having predeceased the intestate. The effect is that if such a person has an illegitimate child living at the intestate's death, the child can take the share their parent would have taken provided the child fulfils the statutory trusts.

29.6.4.2 Adopted and illegitimate children

Adopted children are treated for intestacy purposes as the children of their adoptive parents and not of their natural parents. If a person who was adopted dies intestate without spouse or issue, their estate will be distributed between the closest relatives in the adoptive family. An adopted child may also inherit on the intestacy of any member of their adoptive family.

Similarly, the intestacy rules are applied regardless of whether or not a particular individual's parents were married to each other. However, on the intestacy of an individual whose parents were not married to each other, it is presumed that the individual has not been survived by their father or by any person related to them through their father unless the contrary is shown (Family Law Reform Act 1987, s 18(2)). This presumption avoids any necessity for the PRs to make enquiries where the identity or whereabouts of the father is unknown. The presumption does not apply where the father is named on the intestate child's birth certificate (Family Law Reform Act 1987, s 18(2ZA)).

> **EXAMPLE**
>
> Jawaria, whose parents did not marry, dies intestate. Her only known relative is a half-brother, the child of her mother's later marriage. Nothing is known of Jawaria's father or any other children he may have had. Jawaria's PRs may distribute her estate to her half-brother, relying on the presumption in s 18(2).

The Human Fertilisation and Embryology Act 2008 makes it possible for a child to have a second female parent (where a child is conceived using donated sperm and/or eggs and the mother is in a civil partnership or where the parties have agreed that this is to be the case). The Family Law Reform Act 1987, s 18(2) and s 18(2ZA) apply in the same way to a second female parent as they apply to a father.

If a child with a contingent interest in the estate of an intestate relative is adopted before fulfilling the statutory trusts, the child ceases to be entitled under the intestacy rules to share in the estates of the birth parents. The Inheritance and Trustees' Powers Act 2014 introduced a limited saving. Section 4 provides that any contingent interest (other than a contingent interest in remainder) which the adopted person had immediately before the adoption in the estate of a deceased parent is preserved. The change applies also to gifts in a will of a deceased parent as well as on intestacy, for example '£100,000 to be divided amongst such of my children as reach 18'. The change is limited to parents, so an adopted child will still lose a contingent entitlement to the estate of other relatives.

The Adoption and Children Act 2002 already preserved vested interests of children who are adopted before their interest falls into possession.

There are provisions in the Human Fertilisation and Embryology Act 2008 which apply to children born as a result of surrogacy arrangements and techniques of assisted reproduction. The details are beyond the scope of this book.

29.6.4.3 *Bona vacantia*

Where an estate passes *bona vacantia*, the Crown, Duchy of Lancaster or Duke of Cornwall has a discretion to provide for dependants of the intestate, or for other persons for whom the intestate might reasonably have been expected to make provision.

Genealogists say that it is rare for an estate to be truly *bona vacantia*. They can usually trace some relatives (provided the estate is large enough to meet their fees).

29.7 THE INHERITANCE (PROVISION FOR FAMILY AND DEPENDANTS) ACT 1975

The Inheritance (Provision for Family and Dependants) Act 1975 (I(PFD)A 1975) allows certain categories of people who may be aggrieved because they have been left out of a will, or are not inheriting on an intestacy, to apply for a benefit from the estate following the testator's or intestate's death. The I(PFD)A 1975 may also be used by a person who has received some benefit under the will or intestacy but is dissatisfied with the amount of the inheritance.

Note that the Inheritance and Trustees' Powers Act 2014 made some limited changes to the I(PFD)A 1975 in the case of deaths occurring on or after 1 October 2014. The previous legislation is not considered here.

The I(PFD)A 1975 applies only where the deceased died domiciled in England and Wales. It does not apply where a person originally domiciled in England and Wales has acquired a domicile of choice elsewhere. Note that although domicile has been replaced by long-term residence for tax purposes, this is not the case for other purposes.

Applicants must be living to make a claim. A claim cannot be continued on behalf of the estate of a person who survived the deceased but died before their claim was heard. See *Roberts v Fresco* [2017] EWHC 283 (Ch).

Section numbers below refer to the I(PFD)A 1975 unless otherwise stated.

29.7.1 When should a claim be made?

An application must be brought within six months of the date of issue of the grant of representation to the deceased's estate (s 4). However, the court has a discretion to extend this time-limit. In the case of deaths on or after 1 October 2014 (the date on which the Inheritance and Trustees' Powers Act 2014 came into force) it is possible to make an application before the grant is issued.

29.7.2 Who can make a claim?

The following persons can make a claim (s 1(1)):

(a) the spouse or civil partner of the deceased;

(b) a former spouse or civil partner of the deceased who has not remarried (except where, on the granting of the decree of dissolution or nullity, the court made an order barring the former spouse or civil partner from making a claim);

(c) a child of the deceased (whatever the child's age);

(d) any person treated by the deceased as a child of the family in relation to any marriage or civil partnership of the deceased, or otherwise in relation to any family in which the deceased at any time stood in the role of a parent (eg, a step-child or child of a cohabitee);

(e) any person who, immediately before the death of the deceased, was being maintained by the deceased either wholly or in part. A person is 'maintained' if 'the deceased was making a substantial contribution in money or money's worth towards the reasonable needs of that person, other than a contribution made for full valuable consideration pursuant to an arrangement of a commercial nature' (s 1(3));

(f) any person who, during the whole of the period of two years ending immediately before the date when the deceased died, was living:
   - (i) in the same household as the deceased, and
   - (ii) as the husband or wife of the deceased;

(g) any person who, during the whole of the period of two years ending immediately before the date when the deceased died, was living:
   - (i) in the same household as the deceased, and
   - (ii) as the civil partner of the deceased.

29.7.3 What must the applicant prove?

The only ground for a claim is that 'the disposition of the deceased's estate effected by his will or the law relating to intestacy, or a combination of his will and that law, is not such as to make reasonable financial provision for the applicant'. Section 1(2) sets out two standards for judging 'reasonable financial provision':

(a) 'the surviving spouse standard', which allows a surviving spouse or civil partner such financial provision as is reasonable in all the circumstances 'whether or not that provision is required for his or her maintenance' (s 1(2)(a)); and

(b) 'the ordinary standard', which applies to all other categories of applicant and allows 'such financial provision as it would be reasonable in all the circumstances ... for the applicant to receive for his maintenance' (s 1(2)(b)).

The limitation to maintenance in the ordinary standard means that a person who is able to provide for their own maintenance will not obtain any award.

29.7.4 What factors does the court take into account?

Section 3 contains guidelines to assist the court in determining whether the will and/or intestacy does make reasonable financial provision for the applicant. Some matters should be considered for every claimant (ie, the common guidelines). There are also special guidelines for each category of applicant.

The common guidelines in s 3(1) are:

(a) the financial resources and needs of the applicant, other applicants and beneficiaries of the estate now and in the foreseeable future;
(b) the deceased's moral obligations towards any applicant or beneficiary;
(c) the size and nature of the estate;
(d) the physical or mental disability of any applicant or beneficiary;
(e) anything else which may be relevant, such as the conduct of the applicant.

The special guidelines vary with the category of applicant. For example, where the applicant is the surviving spouse or civil partner, the court takes into account the applicant's age and contribution to the welfare of the family, the duration of the marriage or civil partnership and the likely financial settlement if the marriage or civil partnership had ended in divorce or dissolution rather than death. On an application by a child of the deceased the applicant's education or training requirements are considered.

When considering the common and special guidelines, the court takes into account:

(a) the facts at the date of the hearing (s 3(5)); and
(b) with regard to the financial resources and needs of the applicant:
    (i) their earning capacity; and
    (ii) their financial obligations and responsibilities (s 3(6)).

29.7.5 What orders can the court make?

The court has wide powers to make orders against the 'net estate' of the deceased, including orders for periodical payments, lump sum payments or the transfer of specific property to the applicant.

The 'net estate' against which an order can be made includes not only property which the deceased has, or could have, disposed of by will or nomination, but also the deceased's share of joint property passing by survivorship if the court so orders.

In making an order, the court will declare how the burden of the order is to be borne, ie which beneficiary is to lose part or all of the property they would otherwise have taken.

For inheritance tax (IHT) purposes, the altered disposition of the estate is treated as taking effect from death.

If the order alters the amount passing to the deceased's spouse, the amount of any IHT payable on the estate will be affected.

29.7.6 Protecting the PRs

Personal representatives should be advised not to distribute the estate until six months have elapsed from the issue of the grant. In any event, they must not distribute once they have notice of a possible claim. If PRs do distribute within the six-month period and an applicant subsequently brings a successful claim, the PRs will be personally liable to satisfy the claim if insufficient assets remain in the estate. Where a court permits an application out of time, the PRs will not be liable personally if they have distributed the estate, but the claimant may be able to recover property from the beneficiaries.

SUMMARY

(1) Important types of property pass independently of a will or the intestacy rules.

(2) To be valid a will must:

- (a) be made by a testator with capacity who knows and approves the contents and is not subject to undue influence;
- (b) be properly executed in accordance with Wills Act 1837, s 9;
- (c) remain unrevoked.

(3) Gifts in wills may fail as a result of:

- (a) ademption;
- (b) lapse;
- (c) divorce or dissolution of a civil partnership;
- (d) beneficiary witnesses will;
- (e) disclaimer;
- (f) forfeiture.

(4) The intestacy rules apply to property which is undisposed of by will. The rules are contained in the Administration of Estates Act 1925.

(5) Family members and dependants can ask the court to alter the disposition of the deceased's estate if they feel that reasonable financial provision has not been made for them. The relevant legislation is contained in the Inheritance (Provision for Family and Dependants) Act 1975.

CHAPTER 30

PROBATE PRACTICE AND PROCEDURE

LEARNING OUTCOMES

After reading this chapter you will be able to:

- decide whether a grant of representation is required and, if so, who has the best right to take it
- decide what probate papers are required to obtain the grant
- explain the effect of a grant of representation
- recognise situations in which a limited grant is required
- recognise situations in which the chain of representation is required
- identify situations in which it is appropriate to use caveats and citations.

30.1 INTRODUCTION

When someone dies, it is necessary for assets in their name to be transferred into the names of their beneficiaries. To do this, it is normally necessary to obtain a court document authorising the deceased's personal representatives (PRs) to transfer the deceased's assets. This document is called a grant of representation.

This chapter deals with the process of obtaining a grant of representation by professionals and, in particular, with the various documents that the PRs must produce to the Probate Service and with whether inheritance tax (IHT) is payable.

The final paragraphs look at how to deal with problems that arise where PRs die before completing the administration and at disputes.

The process of applying for a grant is governed by the Non-contentious Probate Rules 1987 (NCPR 1987) (SI 1987/2024) as amended.

30.1.1 Digital probate

The Probate Service is increasingly moving to online applications. Lay applicants can use paper application forms (PA1P and PA1A) but are encouraged to apply online.

The Non-Contentious Probate (Amendment) Rules 2020 (SI 2020/1059) came into force on 2 November 2020. They insert a new Rule 4 into the Non-Contentious Probate Rules 1987 making it obligatory for professionals to apply for grants of probate online unless the application is listed in a new Sch 3 to the 1987 Rules as an exception.

The exceptions include:

- a grant of administration including a grant of administration with will annexed;
- a second grant of probate in respect of the same estate;
- a grant where the person entitled has been convicted of murder or manslaughter of the deceased or has otherwise forfeited the right to apply;
- a grant in respect of a foreign will;
- a grant accompanied by an application to prove a copy of the will;
- a grant, where all those entitled are deceased, to any of their legal personal representatives.

Currently, applications by professionals for letters of administration (with or without a will) do not have to be made online. However, these applications can be made online if certain conditions are fulfilled, for example, where there is only one applicant and they are the only person entitled to the estate.

Where applications are made online, supporting documentation, such as the death certificate, original will and HMRC forms have to be sent separately to HMCTS Probate at Harlow where they are scanned. The scans are then sent to the caseworkers who manage the application process.

30.1.2 Fees

The same fee is payable irrespective of whether the application is made on paper or online. The fee for paper applications is paid by cheque. In the case of online applications made by professionals, the firm must open an 'HMCTS Payment by Account' from which payment is taken automatically when the application is submitted.

The fee paid by professionals used to be lower (£155) than that paid by personal applicants (£215). However, with effect from 26 January 2022, under an amendment to the Non-Contentious Probate Fees Order 2004 (SI 2004/3120) made by the Non-Contentious Probate Fees (Amendment) Order 2021 (SI 2021/1451), application fees in England and Wales increased to £273 for both professional and personal applications where the estate exceeds £5,000. In April 2024 the government announce an inflation linked increase to £300 to be introduced from May 2024. There is no fee if the estate is £5,000 or less. Applicants automatically receive one free copy of the grant. Extra copies can be requested and cost £1.50 each.

30.2 WHO ARE THE PRS?

The PRs will be either the deceased's executors, or intended administrators. 'Personal representative' is a generic term which covers both.

30.2.1 The executors

If the will is valid and contains an effective appointment of executors of whom one or more is willing and able to prove the deceased's will, a grant of probate will be issued to the executor(s) willing to act (see **30.9**).

30.2.2 Administrators with the will annexed

If there is a valid will but there are no persons willing or able to act as executors, then the next persons entitled to act are administrators with the will annexed, who should be appointed in accordance with the NCPR 1987, r 20 (see **30.10**).

30.2.3 Administrators (simple administration)

If a deceased left no will, or no valid will, the estate will be administered in accordance with the law of intestacy by administrators appointed by the application of NCPR 1987, r 22 (see **30.11**).

30.2.4 Number of PRs required

One executor may obtain a grant and act alone. This is so, even if the estate contains land which may be sold during the administration, because a receipt for the proceeds of sale from one executor is sufficient for the purchaser. This is in contrast to the position of trustees where, if a good receipt for the proceeds of sale of land is to be given to a purchaser, it must be given by at least two trustees (or a trust corporation).

In the case of administrators (with or without the will), it is normally sufficient for one to act in the administration of the estate. However, where the will or intestacy creates a life or minority interest, two administrators are normally required.

30.2.5 Authority of PRs before the grant

An executor derives authority to act in the administration of an estate from the will. The grant of probate confirms that authority. Although the executor has full power to act from the time of the deceased's death, the executor will be unable to undertake certain transactions (eg, sale of land) without producing the grant as proof of entitlement to act.

An administrator (with or without the will) has very limited powers before a grant is made. Their authority stems from the grant which is not retrospective to the date of death.

30.3 FIRST STEPS AFTER RECEIVING INSTRUCTIONS

Following a person's death, the PRs and their professional advisers will have to deal with a number of matters quickly.

30.3.1 The deceased's will

Ascertain whether the deceased made a will. If so, ensure all executors named in the will receive copies of it.

30.3.2 Directions as to cremation, etc

Give immediate consideration to the terms of the will to ascertain any special directions by the deceased as to cremation, or the use of their body for medical research or other purposes. It is desirable for testators to make their relatives aware of any such wishes before death.

30.3.3 Details of assets and liabilities

Obtain details of the deceased's property and of any debts outstanding at the date of death, by obtaining building society passbooks, share certificates and details of bank accounts, etc. The deceased may have had a safe deposit bank at a bank containing documents and valuables, but increasingly banks are ceasing to provide this service. Gathering information can be difficult where the deceased dealt with their financial affairs online. However, the income tax return (if one was completed) will show details of income-producing assets. A number of organisations have started to provide assistance with electronic searches for unknown assets and liabilities. From these details, it is possible to begin to evaluate the size of the deceased's estate, and the amount of any liability to IHT.

30.3.4 Details of the beneficiaries

If there is a will, the adviser must establish the identity of the beneficiaries and the nature and extent of their entitlements (eg, whether as legatee or as residuary beneficiary). If specific legacies have been given, it is important to ascertain whether the property given by those specific gifts is part of the estate (if not the gift(s) will have adeemed) (see **29.5.1.2**). If the deceased has died intestate, it is necessary to establish which members of the family have survived so that the basis of distribution of the estate may be established in accordance with the rules discussed at **29.6**.

To comply with the obligations imposed by the UK General Data Protection Regulation, advisers must inform beneficiaries that they are holding personal data on them, the purposes for which the data will be used and the rights of the beneficiaries as data subjects.

30.3.5 Missing and/or unknown creditors and beneficiaries

PRs are responsible for administering the estate correctly. This means that they have to collect in all the assets, pay all the debts and transfer the remaining funds and assets to those entitled under the will or intestacy.

If the PRs fail to pay someone who is entitled either as a creditor or as a beneficiary, they will be personally liable to that person.

PRs may have two problems:

(a) There may be creditors of whom they are unaware or unknown relatives (eg, children born outside marriage whose existence has been kept secret).

(b) They may not know the whereabouts of some beneficiaries who may have lost contact with the deceased's family.

PRs can protect themselves against *unknown* claims by advertising for claimants complying with the requirements of the Trustee Act 1925, s 27. Provided they wait for the time period specified in the section (at least two months), the PRs will be protected from liability if an unknown claimant later appears. However, the claimant will have the right to claim back assets from the beneficiaries who received them.

In relation to unknown claims, the following procedure should be adopted. (Note, however, that if the PRs are aware that a creditor or beneficiary exists but have no contact details, s 27 will not provide any protection. For options in such a case, see **30.3.5.6**.)

30.3.5.1 Early advertisement

In view of the minimum notice period of two months, PRs should advertise as early as possible in the administration. If they are executors, they may advertise at any time after the death; if they are administrators, they have power to advertise at any time after obtaining their grant.

30.3.5.2 Placing the advertisement

The PRs should give notice of the intended distribution of the estate, requiring any person interested to send in particulars of their claim, whether as a creditor or as a beneficiary, by:

(a) advertisement in the *London Gazette*;

(b) advertisement in a newspaper circulating in the district in which land owned by the deceased is situated; and

(c) 'such other like notices, including notices elsewhere than in England and Wales, as would, in any special case, have been directed by a court of competent jurisdiction in an action for administration'.

If the PRs are in any doubt as to what notices should be given, they should apply to the court for directions. Printed forms for the advertisements may be obtained from law stationers.

30.3.5.3 Time for claims

Each notice must require any person interested to send in particulars of their claim within the time specified in the notice, which must not be less than two months from the date of the notice.

30.3.5.4 Searches in case of land

The PRs should also make searches which the prudent purchaser of land would make in the Land Registry, the Land Charges Register and the Local Land Charges Registry, as appropriate. The purpose of these searches is to reveal the existence of any liability in relation to the deceased's ownership of an interest in land, for example a second mortgage.

30.3.5.5 Distribution after notices

When the time-limit in the notice has expired, the PRs may distribute the deceased's estate, taking into account only those claims of which they have actual knowledge, or which they discover as a result of the advertisements. The PRs are not personally liable for any other claim, but a claimant may pursue the claim by following the assets into the hands of the beneficiaries who have received them from the PRs.

The Trustee Act 1925, s 27 will not give any protection to PRs who knows that there is a person with a claim but cannot find them. It protects only against *unknown* claims.

30.3.5.6 Missing known creditors and beneficiaries

Where PRs cannot trace a known beneficiary, they must consider one of the following:

(a) Keeping back assets in case the claimant appears. This is unpopular with the other beneficiaries.

(b) Taking an indemnity from the beneficiaries that they will meet any claims if the claimant reappears. This is dangerous for the PR as the beneficiaries may have no assets when the claimant appears.

(c) Taking out insurance to provide funds. This can be expensive and, as the claimant may be entitled to interest on the amount of their entitlement for the period up to payment, it is difficult to know what sum to insure.

(d) Applying to the court for an order authorising the PRs to distribute the estate on the basis that the claimant is dead. This is referred to as a *Benjamin* order after the case in which it was first ordered (*Re Benjamin* [1902] 1 Ch 723). This protects the PRs from liability, although the claimant retains the right to recover the assets from the beneficiaries. Applying to court is an expensive process, but it is the only solution that offers the PR full protection.

30.4 DECIDING WHETHER A GRANT OF REPRESENTATION IS NECESSARY

A grant enables the PRs to prove their authority to deal with the deceased's assets which passes under the will or the intestacy rules. However, it is not always necessary to obtain a grant of representation to deal with assets. The ability to access assets without a grant is particularly useful where the deceased's family needs funds immediately for paying IHT or other purposes.

A grant may not be required in the three situations which follow.

30.4.1 Assets which may pass to the PRs without a grant

30.4.1.1 Administration of Estates (Small Payments) Act 1965

Orders made under this Act permit payments to be made under various statutes and statutory instruments to persons appearing to be beneficially entitled to the assets without formal proof of title. This facility is restricted, in that it is not available if the value of the asset exceeds £5,000; in addition, as the payments are made at the discretion of the institutions concerned, it is not possible for PRs to insist that payments should be made. If payment is refused, the PRs will have to obtain a grant before the asset can be collected. This can present practical problems where IHT is payable, as the tax normally has to be paid before obtaining the grant and there may be no funds accessible to the PRs. Subject to these points, payments can be made in respect of, for example:

(a) money in the National Savings Bank and Trustee Savings Bank (but not in other bank accounts);
(b) National Savings Certificates and Premium Bonds; and
(c) money in building societies and friendly societies.

30.4.1.2 Chattels

Movable personal property such as furniture, clothing, jewellery and cars can normally be sold without the PRs having to prove formally to the buyer that they are entitled to sell such items.

30.4.1.3 Cash

Normally, the PRs do not require a grant when taking custody of any cash found in the deceased's possession (ie found in the home of the deceased as opposed to deposited in a bank or other account). Although banks and building societies vary, most will release relatively small amounts without requiring a grant.

30.4.2 Assets not passing through the PRs' hands

30.4.2.1 Joint property

On death, any interest in property held by the deceased as beneficial joint tenant with another (whether it is an interest in land or personalty, eg a bank account) passes by survivorship to the surviving joint tenant. As it does not pass via the PRs, any grant is irrelevant. The survivor has access to the property and can prove title to the whole of it merely by producing the deceased's death certificate. Since it is common for married couples and civil partners to own property jointly, there are many occasions where a grant is not required for this reason.

(Conversely, if the property is held by persons as beneficial tenants in common, the share of each tenant in common passes on their death to their PRs for distribution, and a grant will be required.)

30.4.3 Property not forming part of the deceased person's estate

The deceased may have insured their own life, but in such a way that the policy and its proceeds are held in trust for others. This trust may be established by writing the policy under the Married Women's Property Act 1882, s 11 ('a Married Women's Property Act policy') for the spouse or children of the deceased, or by making a separate declaration of trust for those or other beneficiaries. On death, the policy money is payable to the trustees of the policy on production of the death certificate. A grant is not required since the money does not form part of the estate. As the deceased had no beneficial interest in the policy or its proceeds (because of the trust), no IHT will be payable on the proceeds. Such a policy is particularly advantageous, as the proceeds make tax-free provision for dependants of the deceased and can be obtained immediately following the death.

30.4.3.1 Pension benefits

Death in service benefits under a pension scheme and undrawn funds from defined benefit schemes are often payable to persons to be selected at the discretion of the pension fund trustees. Payments are made to the beneficiaries on production of the death certificate. A grant is not required, since the pension benefits do not form part of the deceased's estate. This is currently a method of making tax-free provision for dependants, and such provision can also be obtained immediately following the death. However, from 6 April 2027, pension funds remaining undrawn at the date of death will form part of the deceased's IHT estate even though held in a discretionary trust. The pension fund administrators will be required to pay the IHT attributable to the funds before releasing the balance to the person nominated by the deceased. This will obviously delay payment significantly.

30.5 APPLYING FOR GRANT

A grant of representation is an order of the High Court. Applications used to be dealt with at one of the following:

- the Principal Probate Registry
- a District Probate Registry
- a Sub-Probate Registry.

Sub-Probate Registries have all been closed and District Registries have been reduced to eight in a move towards centralisation and modernisation of the system. Online applications are now dealt with from the Courts and Tribunals Service Centre in Birmingham. Bulk scanning of supporting documents takes place at HMCTS Probate in Harlow. The scanned supporting documents are then transmitted to Birmingham. Paper applications made by professionals are sent to the Newcastle District Probate Registry (or Cardiff in the case of Welsh language applications). Paper applications made by non-professionals are sent to Harlow.

The application is made by lodging such of the following documents as are appropriate to the particular case:

(a) the deceased's will and codicil, if any;

(b) where the application is not being made online, a PA1P if there is a will and a PA1A where there was no will, including, if death was on or after 1 January 2022, statements as to the gross, net and IHT value after deduction of exemptions and reliefs of the estate (see **30.7**);

(c) any supporting evidence which may be required (see **30.5.2**);

(d) probate court fees. This is a flat fee of £300 for estates over £5,000 (see **30.1.2**).

Until 17 January 2024 when applicants were required to submit an IHT400 (as to which see 30.6.1 below), they also had to complete a Form IHT421 showing the amount of IHT due. HMRC would receipt it and send it to HM Courts and Tribunals Service to confirm payment.

HMRC has removed the requirement to complete an IHT421 when submitting an IHT400 as from 17 January 2024. Instead, HMRC's letter to applicants confirming receipt and processing of the IHT400 account includes a unique code and details of the estate values needed to submit a grant application to HM Courts and Tribunals Service.

30.5.1 Admissibility of will to probate

It is important to check the will carefully to make sure that it is valid and admissible to probate. If it is not, application will be made instead for a grant of simple administration. To ensure that the will is admissible, check the following:

(a) the will is the last will of the testator;

(b) that it has not been validly revoked;

(c) that it is executed in accordance with the Wills Act 1837, s 9; and

(d) that it contains an attestation clause which indicates that the will was executed in accordance with the requirements of the Wills Act 1837 and raises a presumption of 'due execution'.

30.5.2 The registrar's additional requirements

If the application is in order, HM Courts and Tribunals Service (HMCTS) will issue the grant. In some cases, before issuing the grant, HMCTS may require further evidence. Evidence used to be required in affidavit form but due to the difficulties caused by social distancing, the President of the Family Division announced that statements of truth could be used instead until 30 July 2020. The period was extended to 30 October 2020. The change was made permanent by the Non-Contentious Probate (Amendment) Rules 2020 (SI 2020/1059).

A new 2A is inserted into the 1987 Rules which says that witness statements must be verified by a statement of truth and that where the existing Rules require an affidavit, the words 'or witness statement' should be added.

30.5.2.1 Evidence of due execution and/or capacity

If there is no attestation clause, or the clause is in some respect defective, or there are circumstances raising doubt about the execution of the will, HMCTS will require evidence in the form of an affidavit or witness statement, preferably from an attesting witness, to establish that the will has been properly executed.

If there is doubt about the mental capacity of the testator to make the will, an affidavit or witness statement from a doctor may be necessary. In such cases, it is helpful if a doctor examined the testator to ascertain whether they had sufficient capacity at the time the will was made.

30.5.2.2 Evidence as to knowledge and approval

There may be doubt as to whether the testator was aware of the contents of the will when they executed it. This may arise through blindness, illiteracy or frailty of the testator, or because of suspicious circumstances, for example where the person who prepared the will for the testator benefits substantially by its terms.

In any of these circumstances, the attestation clause should have been suitably adapted, ideally by indicating that the will was read over to the testator or was independently explained to them. In the absence of this, HMCTS will require to be satisfied that the testator had knowledge and approval of the contents of the will. The evidence is provided by means of an affidavit or witness statement made by someone who can speak as to the facts. Normally, this will be one of the attesting witnesses, but it could be an independent person who explained the provisions of the will to the testator.

30.5.2.3 Evidence as to remote witnessing

Where witnesses were not physically present when the testator signed or acknowledged the will but watched via a video link, questions as to formalities, capacity and knowledge and approval are more likely to arise than in cases of conventional execution. Unless the attestation clause has been amended to give details of such matters, it is likely that evidence in the form of an affidavit or witness statement will be required from the witnesses or anyone else who was present (remotely or physically).

30.5.2.4 Evidence as to plight and condition

If the state of the will suggests that it has been interfered with in some way since execution, the registrar will require further evidence by way of explanation. This may arise:

(a) where the will has been altered since its execution;

(b) where there is some obvious mark on it indicating a document may have been attached to it (eg, the marks of a paper clip, raising a suggestion that some other testamentary document may have been attached); or

(c) where it gives the appearance of attempted revocation.

Generally, the explanation required will take the form of an affidavit or witness statement made by some person having knowledge of the facts, although in the case of an online application the information is included in the application.

30.5.2.5 Lost will

A will which was known to have been in the testator's possession but which cannot be found following the death is presumed to have been destroyed by the testator with the intention of revoking it.

However, if the will has been lost or accidentally destroyed, probate may be obtained of a copy of the will, such as a copy kept in the solicitor's file, or a reconstruction. In such a case, application should be made to the registrar, supported by appropriate evidence in the form of an affidavit or witness statement from the applicant for the grant of probate.

30.6 COMPLETING THE IHT ACCOUNT

30.6.1 Purpose of an IHT account

One of the first steps towards obtaining the grant of representation is the preparation of the appropriate IHT account and the calculation of any IHT payable.

If the estate is not an 'excepted estate' (see **30.7**), for a person domiciled in the UK, the PRs will prepare an IHT400 (IHT401 for a person domiciled elsewhere) and whichever of the supporting schedules are relevant to the estate. For example, if the deceased made lifetime gifts, the PRs must complete schedule 403 which deals with lifetime gifts.

The IHT400 is an inventory of the assets to which the deceased was beneficially entitled and of their liabilities, and is the form for claiming reliefs and exemptions and calculating the IHT payable. It should be delivered within 12 months of the end of the month in which the death occurred. Usually PRs aim to deliver the account within six months to comply with IHT time-limits for the payment of interest. Until the account is submitted no grant of representation can be issued.

Where IHT is payable, it is necessary to apply for a reference number before submitting the IHT400. Application may be made online or by post using schedule IHT422.

IHT is payable on all property to which the deceased was beneficially entitled immediately before their death, whether or not such property vests in their PRs. Certain types of property qualify for tax relief, for example business or agricultural property, or an exemption may apply because of the identity of the beneficiary (ie the surviving spouse or a charity) (see **4.4.3**).

The rate of IHT is 0% on transfers within the nil rate band (£325,000 for tax year 2025/26 and frozen until the end of 2029/30) and 40% on the balance, unless at least 10% of the chargeable estate is passing to charity in which case the reduced rate of 36% is charged.

Where surviving spouses or civil partners die on or after 9 October 2007, they can inherit any unused proportion of the nil rate band of the first spouse or civil partner to die. The PRs of the survivor must make a claim using schedule 402. It does not matter when the first spouse or civil partner died. So long as they had unused nil rate band, it can be transferred.

EXAMPLE

Paul died in January 2008 (when the nil rate band was £300,000). He left £60,000 to his sister and everything else to his civil partner, Leo.

Paul therefore had four-fifths of his nil rate band unused.

> Leo dies in August 2040 when the nil rate band is £500,000, leaving everything to his nephews and nieces. Leo's PRs can claim an additional four-fifths of the 2040/41 nil rate band. As a result the nil rate band available on Leo's death will be £500,000 + ($\frac{4}{5}$ x £500,000) = £900,000.

For deaths on or after 6 April 2017, there is an additional nil rate band (the 'RNRB') available to those who leave a residence or interest in a residence to lineal descendants. The value of the new RNRB was £100,000 in 2017/18, rising by £25,000 a year until 2020/21 when it reached £175,000. It is now frozen until the end of 2027/28.

A surviving spouse or civil partner can inherit unused RNRB from a predeceased spouse or civil partner. The PRs of the survivor make a claim using schedule 436.

> **EXAMPLE**
>
> Jason died in January 2018. He was separated but not divorced from his wife, Minette. He left his half of the residence he owned with his cohabitee (value £175,000) and the rest of his estate (value £200,000) to his cohabitee.
>
> Minette dies in 2022/23 and leaves everything including her residence worth £400,000 to her children. She has £400,000 of other assets.
>
> There is no nil rate band transferred from Jason as the gifts to his cohabitee exhausted it.
>
> His estate did not benefit from the residence nil rate band as his lineal descendants did not inherit his interest in the former matrimonial home. Therefore, Minette's RNRB can be increased by 100% to £350,000.

30.6.1.1 Paying the IHT

IHT on property without the right to pay by instalments (see **4.8.1.2**) must be paid within six months of the end of the month in which the death occurred. Failure to do so causes interest to become payable. For example, if a person dies on 10 January, IHT is due on 31 July, or on delivery of the IHT400 if this is earlier. Until this tax has been paid, no grant can issue to the deceased's estate. It may be possible to obtain a grant on credit where the PRs are unable to raise funds from other sources. HMRC will require the PRs to explain the steps they have taken to obtain funds (for example realising assets that do not require a grant, borrowing from beneficiaries) and to explain when and how they expect to be able to pay the tax due. HMRC's IHT Manual explains the process at IHTM05120–IHTM05137. Where HMRC gives permission, the unique tax code will be qualified to state that some or all of the tax due is outstanding but the PRs will be able to obtain a grant.

Where there is property which qualifies for the right to pay the tax by instalments, none of the tax on that property is due until the expiry of the six-month period. If the option is exercised, only the first instalment of one-tenth must then be paid. In an estate where it is not possible to deliver the IHT400 within that period, all tax on non-instalment option property plus the appropriate number of instalments on property with the option and interest must be paid on delivery of the account. Interest runs on all tax not paid on the due date.

The tax payable on the estate is apportioned between the instalment and non-instalment option property using the method described in **4.7.2**.

30.6.2 Valuations

30.6.2.1 General principles

Assets in the estate are valued at 'the price which the property might reasonably be expected to fetch if sold in the open market' immediately before the death (IHTA 1984, s 160).

30.6.2.2 Jointly-owned assets

There is a special valuation rule where the deceased was the co-owner (as tenant in common or as beneficial joint tenant) of land at their death. The market value of the land at the date of death will normally be discounted to reflect the difficulty of selling a part interest in land. The probate value of the deceased's interest is the discounted market value at the date of death divided proportionately between the co-owners. A discount of 15% is normally considered reasonable for residential property and a discount of 10% for investment property. A share in a residential property is relatively unattractive because of the rights of the other co-owner to occupy the property. Buying a share in an investment property is less unattractive as it is relatively unimportant whether the capital sum spent buys the whole or part of an income stream.

EXAMPLE

Mary and her sister, Nellie, owned a house as joint tenants, in which they live together. The value of the house at Mary's death was £400,000. Apply a 15% discount.

The discount is £400,000 × 15% = £60,000

and her half share £400,000 – £60,000 = £340,000 ÷ 2 = £170,000.

The probate value of Mary's share is £170,000.

The discount is not normally available where the co-ownership is of an asset other than land. For such assets, for example bank and building society accounts, the probate value is the account balance as at the date of death (plus interest) divided proportionately between the joint owners. However, there are other items where there is a reduction in value where the whole is not owned, for example a set of chattels or shares in a company. The question is always 'What is the open market value of the asset?'

Where the co-owners of land are spouses or civil partners, the related property rules (see **4.4.2**) apply. HMRC has always refused to allow any discount in value on the basis of these rules. This normally means that each spouse or civil partner will be treated as owning a proportionate part of the value of the whole. *Arkwright v IRC* [2004] WLTR 181 suggested that if one spouse or civil partner is terminally ill, the value of their share might be reduced. So far there is no reported case in which such a discount has been obtained.

30.6.3 Funding the IHT

Where there is tax to pay on delivery of an IHT400, the PRs must arrange for the appropriate amount of money to be sent to HMRC with the account. When this tax is paid, HMRC sends the applicant a code which must be included in the application for a grant. Funding the tax bill may be problematic as all the deceased's assets vesting in the PRs are 'frozen', and therefore may be untouchable, until the grant issues giving the proof of title to the PRs.

The options which may be available to raise funds to pay the IHT are set out below.

30.6.3.1 Direct payment scheme

HMRC has reached an agreement with the British Banker's Association and the Building Societies Association on a procedure allowing PRs to arrange payment of IHT to HMRC directly from the deceased's accounts.

The scheme is voluntary on the part of the institutions, so PRs must check whether the relevant banks and building societies are part of the scheme.

The procedure is as follows:

(a) The PRs must provide whatever identification the relevant banks and building societies require. They should do this well in advance of applying for a grant so as to avoid any unnecessary delay in the application.

(b) The PRs complete a separate IHT423 for each bank and building society from which money is to be transferred.

(c) The PRs send each IHT423 to the relevant bank or building society at the same time that they send the IHT400 and supporting schedules to HMRC. The IHT423 includes an IHT reference number provided by HMRC to allow HMRC to match up the payment with the correct estate.

(d) The bank or building society will send the money direct to HMRC. Once HMRC has received the money and is satisfied that the amount is correct, it will issue the code indicating that tax has been paid.

The process is not quick, so where there is an urgent need for a grant PRs will want to find an alternative source of funding.

The scheme has been extended to investment providers and form IHT423 has been redesigned. PRs can now use the revised form to ask brokers, investment management firms and pension or life insurance providers to sell shares or assets and release funds from the deceased's investment accounts to pay directly to HMRC. Participation in the scheme is voluntary, and not all investment providers choose to take part.

Solicitors often make private arrangements with banks and building societies under which the bank or building society transfers funds directly to HMRC from the deceased's accounts. This is a relatively quick and easy method of funding.

30.6.3.2 Life assurance

Where the proceeds of a policy of insurance on the deceased's life are payable to the estate, the life assurance company, like a bank, may be willing to release funds to pay the IHT directly to HMRC.

30.6.3.3 Assets realisable without production of the grant

By applying the Administration of Estates (Small Payments) Act 1965 (see **30.4.1**), assets may, in some cases, be realised without production of a grant. The maximum value of any one asset that may be realised is £5,000. The Act gives discretion to the institution to allow assets to be realised in this way. Where an estate is large or complex, this discretion will often not be exercised. In such cases, a grant must first be obtained and produced to release the asset concerned.

30.6.3.4 Loans from beneficiaries

Wealthy beneficiaries may be prepared to fund the tax from their own resources, on condition that they will be repaid from the deceased's estate once the grant issues. Alternatively, beneficiaries may already have received assets as a result of the death which they are prepared to use to pay the tax, such as money from a jointly held bank account, or the proceeds of a life policy vested in them under the Married Women's Property Act 1882. However, many beneficiaries may not be able to afford to make a loan.

30.6.3.5 Bank borrowing

Banks which do not participate in the voluntary scheme will still usually lend against an undertaking to repay the loan given by the PRs. A bank may also require an undertaking from the solicitor to repay the loan from the proceeds of the estate. Whether or not the solicitor is a PR, any undertaking should be limited to 'such proceeds as come into the solicitor's control'. Undertakings to pay money should be carefully worded so as to ensure payment is not due from the solicitor personally.

Bank borrowing is expensive, because the bank will charge an arrangement fee and interest on the amount borrowed. Money borrowed should be repaid at the earliest opportunity so as to honour any undertaking and to stop interest running. Income tax relief is available to the PRs for interest paid on a separate loan account in respect of IHT payable on personalty vesting in them.

30.6.3.6 National Savings and Government stock

Payment of tax may also be made from National Savings Bank accounts or from the proceeds of National Savings Certificates using Form IHT423. British government stock can be used. The PRs write to British Government Stocks (Gilts), Computershare Investor Services plc, The Pavilions, Bristol BS99 6ZW. At the same time, they will send HMRC the IHT 400 and a letter saying how much tax is to be paid out of the stock; HMRC will contact Computershare and ask for the money to be transferred. This could take up to 4 weeks.

30.6.3.7 Heritage property in lieu of tax

Taxpayers can offer HMRC an asset in lieu of tax (IHTA 1984, s 230(1)). The Secretary of State must agree to accept such assets and the standard required of such objects is very high. The item must be 'pre-eminent for its national, scientific, historic or artistic interest'.

30.6.3.8 Obtaining a grant on credit

Where the PRs can demonstrate that they are unable to pay the IHT in advance, HMRC will allow the grant to be obtained on credit. As explained above, PRs must explain to HMRC what steps they have taken to raise IHT and why they are unable to provide the amount due. PRs used to have to provide evidence that they had tried and failed to borrow money commercially, but in the Spring Budget 2024 the Chancellor announced that this would no longer be necessary. However, PRs will be required to provide undertakings as to when and how they will be able to provide the amount due. The process is explained in HMRC's IHT Manual at IHTM05120–IHTM05137.

30.7 EXCEPTED ESTATES

30.7.1 Inheritance Tax (Delivery of Accounts) (Excepted Estates) Regulations 2004

No IHT400 is required if the estate is 'excepted' under the Inheritance Tax (Delivery of Accounts) (Excepted Estates) Regulations 2004 (SI 2004/2543).

For deaths before 1 January 2022, it was necessary to submit an IHT 205 giving limited details of the assets of the estate and their value. However, the Office of Tax Simplification (OTS) in its First Report on Inheritance Tax published on 23 November 2018 criticised HMRC for requiring too much information where no tax was payable. HMRC agreed to simplify the process and finally we have the Inheritance Tax (Delivery of Accounts) (Excepted Estates) (Amendment) Regulations 2021 (SI 2021/1167) which will apply to deaths on and after 1 January 2022.

If the estate is excepted, PRs do not now submit any IHT form to HMRC. Instead, information as to value of the estate is included on the forms submitted to the Probate Service which the Probate Service must pass on to HMRC within one month of the issue of the grant. HMRC has 60 days from the issue of the grant of representation to ask for additional information. If no such request is made, the estate receives automatic clearance. If an estate which initially appears to be excepted is subsequently found not to be so, the PRs must submit the IHT400 within six months of the discovery.

The requirements for qualifying as an excepted estate have been relaxed in response to the criticisms of the OTS, allowing many more estates to qualify. However, the requirements remain extremely complex. You will find it easier to focus on the broad description of the requirements rather than on the detail.

For deaths on or after 1 September 2006, there are three categories of excepted estate, and the requirements for deaths on and after 1 January 2022 are as follows:

- *Category 1 – 'small' estates*

  Broadly, estates falling into this category are those where the gross value of the death estate for IHT purposes, plus the chargeable value of any 'specified transfers' (defined below) in the seven years prior to death, does not exceed the current nil rate threshold.

  The nil rate threshold is increased to take account of any transferred nil rate band. For deaths before 1 January 2022, transferred nil rate band was only taken into account for this purpose if 100% of the nil rate band was transferred from one spouse or civil partner. Where a deceased had more than one previous spouse or civil partner, it was not possible to transfer portions of nil rate band to make up 100%. For deaths on or after 1 January 2022, any percentage of transferred nil rate band is taken into account when calculating the nil rate threshold for this purpose, but it is still only possible to transfer from one predeceased spouse or civil partner.

EXAMPLE

Maria dies in July 2021. She was predeceased by her husband Josef who had 60% of his nil rate band unused. Maria's nil rate band for the purposes of the excepted regulations cannot be increased by the 60% transferred from Josef. Hence her IHT threshold for the purposes of these regulations is £325,000.

However, if Maria dies in July 2022, her nil rate band for the purposes of the excepted regulations can be increased by the 60% transferred from Josef. Hence her enhanced threshold will be £520,000.

If Maria had also been predeceased by a second husband, Xian, who died with 40% of his nil rate band unused, her IHT threshold cannot be increased for the purposes of the excepted estates regulations by two transfers. Her PRs will be limited to claiming one.

(For applications between 6 April and 1 August each year the threshold will be the threshold for the previous tax year.)

In full, the Regulations for this category require the following:

(a) the deceased was a long-term UK resident immediately before their death;

(b) the value of the death estate is attributable wholly to property passing:
  (i) under their will or intestacy,
  (ii) under a nomination of an asset taking effect on death,
  (iii) under a single settlement in which they were entitled to an interest in possession in settled property, or
  (iv) by survivorship in a beneficial joint tenancy or, in Scotland, by survivorship in a special destination;

(c) of that property:
  (i) not more than £250,000 represents property which, immediately before that person's death, was settled property; and
  (ii) not more than £100,000 represents property situated outside the United Kingdom;

(d) the deceased made no chargeable transfers in the seven years before death other than specified transfers (defined below) where the aggregate value transferred (ignoring business or agricultural relief) did not exceed £250,000; and

(e) the aggregate of:
  (i) the gross value of the deceased's death estate, plus
  (ii) the value transferred by any specified transfers (defined below), plus

(iii) the value transferred by any specified exempt transfers (defined below),

did not exceed the nil rate threshold for the deceased, increased by any nil rate band transferred from one deceased spouse or civil partner.

- *Category 2 – 'exempt' estates*

  These are estates where the bulk of the estate attracts the spouse (or civil partner) or charity exemption. The gross value of the death estate for IHT purposes plus specified transfers (defined below) must not exceed £3 million and the net chargeable estate after deduction of liabilities and spouse and/or charity exemption must not exceed the nil rate threshold.

  As with Category 1 estates, transferred nil rate band can increase the nil rate threshold for this purpose. Again, if the death is before 1 January 2022, the threshold is only increased if the whole of the nil rate band is transferred. For deaths on or after 1 January 2022, any transferred nil rate band can be taken into account.

  In full, the Regulations for this category require the following:

  (a) the deceased was a long-term UK resident immediately before their death;

  (b) the value of the death estate is attributable wholly to property passing:

  (i) under their will or intestacy,

  (ii) under a nomination of an asset taking effect on death,

  (iii) under a single settlement in which they were entitled to an interest in possession in settled property, or

  (iv) by survivorship in a beneficial joint tenancy or, in Scotland, by survivorship in a special destination;

  (c) of that property:

  (i) not more than £1 million represents property which, immediately before that person's death, was settled property (but no more than £250,000 of that settled property must pass to anyone other than a UK domiciled spouse or civil partner or charity); and

  (ii) not more than £100,000 represents property situated outside the United Kingdom;

  (d) the deceased made no chargeable transfers during the period of seven years ending with their death other than specified transfers (defined below) where the aggregate value transferred (ignoring business or agricultural relief) did not exceed £250,000;

  (e) the aggregate of:

  (i) the gross value of that person's death estate, plus

  (ii) the value transferred by any specified transfers (defined below) made by that person, plus

  (iii) the value transferred by any specified exempt transfers (defined below),

  did not exceed £3 million;

  (ea) there is property left after deduction of liabilities to pass to spouse or charity; and

  (f) the aggregate of:

  (i) the value of the death estate after deducting allowable liabilities, spouse and charity exemptions, plus

  (ii) specified transfers (defined below), plus

  (iii) specified exempt transfers (defined below),

  did not exceed the nil rate threshold, increased by any percentage of nil rate band transferred from one deceased spouse or civil partner.

'Specified transfers' for Categories 1 and 2

These are chargeable transfers of cash, personal chattels or tangible moveable property, quoted shares or securities, or an interest in or over land (unless the land becomes settled or is subject to a reservation of benefit) made in the seven years before death. This means that if someone makes a gift which does not fall within this category in the seven years before death (for example, a transfer of unquoted shares), the estate cannot be excepted under Categories 1 or 2.

When valuing the specified transfers, business and agricultural property relief is ignored so the unrelieved value has to be taken into account.

'Specified exempt transfers' for Categories 1 and 2

These are transfers of value made during the seven years before death which are exempt under one of the following exemptions:

(a) s 18 (transfers between spouses (or civil partners));
(b) s 23 (gifts to charities);
(c) s 24 (gifts to political parties);
(d) s 24A (gifts to housing associations);
(e) s 27 (maintenance funds for historic buildings, etc); or
(f) s 28 (employee trusts).

Gifts within the annual exemption are not included when calculating the value of specified exempt transfers. In the case of deaths occurring on or after 1 March 2011, gifts which are exempt under the normal expenditure out of income exemption are treated for this purpose as chargeable if they exceed £3,000 in any one tax year.

- *Category 3 – estates where deceased neither domiciled nor long-term resident in UK*

  Before 6 April 2025, liability to inheritance tax was governed by the concept of 'domicile'. It was often difficult to decide where a person was domiciled, so from 6 April 2025 the concept has been replaced with long-term residence. An individual is long-term resident (and in scope for IHT on their non-UK assets) when they are older than 20 and have been resident in the UK for at least 10 out of the 20 tax years before the one in which any transfer takes place. For individuals who are 20 years old or younger, the test will be whether they have been resident in the UK for 50 per cent of the tax years since their birth.

  In full, the Regulations for this category require the following:

  (a) the deceased died on or after 6 April 2004; and
  (b) the deceased:
    (i) was not a long-term UK resident at any time on or after 6 April 2025, and
    (ii) was not domiciled in the UK at any time before that date;
  (bb) the deceased was not beneficially entitled to any UK residential land owned through a close company or partnership;
  (bc) the deceased made no chargeable transfers during the period of seven years ending with their death; and
  (d) the value of the estate situated in the United Kingdom is wholly attributable to cash or quoted shares or securities passing under their will or intestacy or by survivorship in a beneficial joint tenancy or, in Scotland, by survivorship in a special destination, the gross value of which does not exceed £150,000.

EXAMPLE 1

Adam has just died. His will leaves his estate to his wife Brenda and daughter Clare in equal shares. He is UK domiciled and has made no lifetime transfers.

His estate consists of:	£
House owned jointly with Brenda (half share)	80,000
Building society a/c (sole name)	100,000
Personal chattels	2,000
Life interest in a trust fund set up in his father's will (value of capital assets)	30,000
There are debts (funeral bill and credit cards)	(2,000)

This is a Category 1 ('small') excepted estate. This fact will also be noted on the probate application. Adam's estate satisfies the criteria and it has an IHT value of £212,000 gross (note that IHT exemptions and reliefs are ignored when ascertaining the gross IHT estate).

EXAMPLE 2

Davina has just died. Her will leaves £50,000 to her son, Ernst, and the residue to her husband, Ferdinand. She is UK domiciled. Her only specified transfer was made two years ago when she gave £200,000 to Ernst.

Her estate consists of:	£
House owned jointly with Fernando (half share)	1,400,000
Quoted Investments	100,000
Bank and building society accounts	50,000
Personal chattels	15,000
Specified transfer	100,000
There are debts (funeral bill and credit cards)	(5,000)

This is a Category 2 ('exempt') excepted estate. The gross value of the estate, plus the value of specified transfers in the seven years prior to death does not exceed £3 million; the net estate after deduction of liabilities and the spouse exemption does not exceed the current nil rate threshold of £325,000

EXAMPLE 3

Fred has just died leaving everything to his two children. His wife Freda died in 2010 and left half her estate to Fred, half to the children.

Fred's gross death estate is £450,000, and consists of a house and money in the bank. He has made no lifetime gifts.

This is a Category 1 ('small') excepted estate because Fred's nil rate threshold is increased for the purpose of the excepted estates regulations by one half to £487,500 as a result of inheriting an additional 50% of nil rate band.

EXAMPLE 4

Eduardo is an Italian who has never been domiciled in the UK and who was not a long-term UK resident at any time on or after 6 April 2025. He dies with £100,000 in a UK bank account. Under his will, his entire estate passes to his nephew.

The estate is excepted as a 'non-domiciled' estate because it fulfils the requirements:

> - Eduardo was never domiciled in the UK, nor was he long-term resident at any time on or after 6 April 2025.
> - The value of his UK estate is wholly attributable to cash.
> - His whole UK estate passes by will and does not exceed £150,000.

30.7.1.1 Procedure

PRs provide no information directly to HMRC. Instead, they include the following on their applications for a grant:

(a) the deceased's full name and date of death; and

(b) the following details in relation to the deceased's estate:

  (i) the gross value of the 'estate' for IHT;

  (ii) the net value of the 'estate' (after deduction of debts) for IHT;

  (iii) the net non-exempt value of the 'estate';

  (iv) a declaration that the estate is an excepted estate; and

  (v) whether any transferred IHT nil rate band is being claimed.

'Estate' is defined in reg 4(6) of the amended Regulations for this purpose as the total of the death estate plus specified transfers and specified exempt transfers made in the 7 years before death. HM Courts and Tribunals Service will have one month from issue of the grant to pass the information to HMRC.

Personal representatives of non-UK domiciliaries will have to provide rather more information on a Form 207.

HMRC will select a random sample to review within 60 days of the application for a grant. In addition, it 'will use other information sources to identify those estates nearer to the IHT threshold' where it feels that there is a risk that IHT may be payable.

30.7.2 Form IHT400

Form IHT400 must be used whenever the deceased dies domiciled in the UK and the estate is not an 'excepted' estate.

The PRs must complete Form IHT400 and relevant supporting schedules, and sign a declaration that the contents are true. They must calculate the amount of any IHT payable and ensure that any IHT due on delivery of the account is paid.

The schedules required will vary according to the make-up of the estate. So, for example, if the estate includes property eligible for business or agricultural property relief, an IHT412 (unquoted shares), IHT413 (sole trader or partnership) or IHT414 (agricultural property) will be required. If there is foreign property, an IHT417 is required.

Whenever an IHT400 is required, HMRC will issue the applicant with a code and details of the estate values needed to submit a grant application to HM Courts and Tribunals Service. The gross and net value of the estate for probate purposes are often not the same as the IHT values. The probate value is not reduced by IHT exemptions and reliefs but conversely does not include the value of property passing by survivorship or under the terms of a trust.

The application for a grant cannot be made until the code and confirmation of the values are received.

30.8 FORMS PA1P AND PA1A AND ONLINE APPLICATIONS

30.8.1 Background

It used to be necessary for applications for a grant of representation to be supported by an oath sworn or affirmed by the personal representatives before an independent solicitor. The move to online applications made this requirement inappropriate. As a result, the Non-Contentious Probate (Amendment) Rules 2018 (SI 2018/1137), which took effect as from 27 November 2018, enable applications for a grant of representation to be verified by a statement of truth (instead of an oath) and without the will having to be marked with the signature of the applicant.

Before the changes to the Rules, PRs completed different applications for each of the three main grants of representation: probate, administration with will and simple administration.

There are now only two types of paper application:

- Form PA1P where there is a will, irrespective of whether it will lead to a grant of probate or administration with will; and
- Form PA1A where there is no will.

The two PA1 applications are similar but differ in points of detail.

Online applications are made using one form which has different sections depending on whether the application is for a grant of probate, administration with a will or administration on intestacy.

As explained at **30.1.1** above, all applications for probate by professionals have to be made online unless they are one of the excluded applications. The online form is based on the PA1 forms.

When applications are made online by professionals, payment is taken immediately from the firm's 'HMCTS Payment by Account', so it is important for applicants to check that the firm has sufficient funds in the account to allow the fee to be taken.

At the time of writing, the PA1 application forms for lay and professional applicants differ slightly, but there are plans to produce a combined form for use by probate practitioners and personal applicants.

30.8.2 What the application forms do

The purpose of the application forms is to:

(a) establish the basis of the applicants' claim to be entitled to take the grant (for example, in the case of applications by executors it identifies the applicants as the persons named as executors in the will);

(b) confirm that the personal representatives will carry out their statutory duty (contained in Administration of Estates Act 1925, s 25) to:

  (i) collect and get in the real and personal estate of the deceased and administer it according to law;

  (ii) when required to do so by the court, exhibit on oath in the court a full inventory of the estate and when so required render an account of the administration of the estate to the court;

  (iii) when required to do so by the High Court, deliver up the grant of probate or administration to that court;

(c) in the case of applications where there is a will, identify the will and any codicils to it – the date of the will must be included.

Items (b) and (c) are included on the application forms as a legal statement signed by the PR(s) and verified by a statement of truth. Where the application is made online by a professional, the PR(s) can authorise the professional to sign the legal statement on their behalf. The professional must also sign the statement of truth. Typed and handwritten signatures are acceptable.

Paper applications by lay persons are sent to HMCTS Probate at Harlow. Professional applications are sent to Newcastle District Probate Registry.

When applications are made online, supporting documentation is sent to HMCTS Probate at Harlow.

30.9 POINTS COMMON TO BOTH PAPER FORMS

Both forms start with a useful checklist of the documents that may be required. These are:

- IHT Form if required signed by or on behalf of all applicants.
- Any will and codicils to it.
- A copy of any foreign wills or any wills dealing with assets held outside England and Wales (and if not in English, an English translation).
- An official copy (not a photocopy) of the death certificate, or a coroner's interim certificate of the person who has died.
- Any other relevant documents such as supporting affidavits or witness statements.
- Credit/debit card details or a cheque/postal order payable to 'HMCTS' for the application fee, plus a fee for any official copies required. The name of the deceased must be written on the back of the cheque.

30.9.1 Identifying the applicants

The first section of both forms identifies the persons applying for the grant, providing full names, postal and email addresses of all applicants. The names provided must be the same as the applicant's identification documents (for example, a passport or driving licence). A maximum of four people can apply for a grant. Where there is more than one applicant, HMCTS will treat the first applicant as nominated by all applicants to apply on their behalf. All correspondence and the Grant of Representation will be sent to the first applicant or to their legal representative, if named at the end of the section.

Where there is a will, if any applicant's name as written in the will differs from their name as it appears on their identification papers, the name written in the will or codicil must be included on the form.

30.9.2 Identifying the deceased

The form requires the name, address, date of birth and date of death of the deceased, together with their marital status and domicile at the date of death. At the time of writing, the form still refers to domicile. Following the change to long-term residence as from 6 April 2025, this will presumably be altered to refer to long-term residence.

The name of the deceased is normally the name in which the birth was registered or, in the case of a married or divorced woman, the surname of her husband (if she has adopted her husband's name). A person may change their name by:

(a) deed poll; or
(b) habit and repute; however, a name is only regarded as changed by habit and repute if the former name has been completely abandoned over a period of time.

If the deceased was known by any other name, that name must be included if the deceased held assets in that name. It will then be included on the grant. There is no need to include another name if no assets were held in that name.

The deceased's marital status at death must be provided. The form has separate tick boxes for:

- Never married
- Widowed, their lawful spouse or civil partner having died before them
- Married/in a civil partnership – the date is required

- Divorced/civil partnership is dissolved – the date is required
- Judicially separated – the date is required

This section of the form continues with questions about more unusual matters.

If the deceased owned any foreign assets, the total value of their foreign assets (not including houses or land) must be provided.

The form asks whether there was any land vested in the person who has died which was settled previously to their death and which remained settled land not withstanding their death. These settlements are relatively unusual as, since the Trusts of Land and Appointment of Trustees Act 1996, no new Settled Land Act settlement can be created. Old settlements continue and present particular problems in relation to grants of representation. Normally such settled land devolves not on the general personal representatives but on the trustees of the settlement who must take out a special grant of representation limited to the settled land. Therefore normally in such a case, the general personal representatives take out a grant which excludes the settled land. If, however, the settled land devolves on the general personal representatives (for example, where they happen to be the trustees of the settlement), the grant will be made 'including settled land'.

A further question asks whether the deceased had any legally adopted relatives, whether adopted into the family of the deceased or 'adopted out' (became part of someone else's family). This will obviously not be relevant if the estate is fully disposed of to named individuals but may become relevant if gifts fail.

30.9.3 Applications as an attorney

It is quite common for persons to apply for a grant as an attorney on behalf of the person entitled to take out the grant (for example where the person entitled is elderly). Attorneys provide identification information for themselves in the first section of the form and then later identify the person on whose behalf they are applying (Section 5 in the PA1P and Section 4 in the PA1A). They must enclose the signed attorney form with this application. The attorney of one executor and an executor acting in their own right may not jointly apply for a grant of representation.

Where a person lacks capacity to manage their own affairs, medical evidence may be required as will the enduring or lasting power of attorney appointing the applicant to act.

Where no attorney has been appointed and there are no persons entitled in the same degree to take out a grant, a grant will be made to another person for the use and benefit of the incapacitous person.

30.9.4 Foreign domicile or long-term residence

Both forms include a section on foreign domicile. The reference to foreign domicile will presumably be amended to refer to long-term residence outside the UK to reflect the change to long-term residence for tax purposes as from 6 April 2025. The applicant must identify what assets are situate in England and Wales.

In order to obtain a grant for a person domiciled abroad, it is necessary to demonstrate who is entitled to deal with the assets. NCPR 1987, r 30(1) provides that where a person dies domiciled outside England and Wales, a registrar may issue a grant to any of the following:

(a) to the person entrusted with the administration of the estate by the court having jurisdiction at the place where the deceased died domiciled; or

(b) where there is no person so entrusted, to the person beneficially entitled to the estate by the law of the place where the deceased died domiciled or, if there is more than one person so entitled, to such of them as the registrar may direct; or

(c) if in the opinion of the registrar the circumstances so require, to such person as the registrar may direct.

The forms therefore require an applicant to explain the basis of their entitlement to take a grant.

30.9.5 IHT estate and probate estate

The final set of questions relates to the value of the deceased's assets.

The applicant must state whether an IHT400 was completed.

If it was not because the estate was excepted, the following details must be provided:

- gross value of the estate for IHT;
- net value of the estate for IHT;
- net qualifying value of the estate (after deduction of exemptions and reliefs).

As explained at **30.7.1.1** above, 'estate' for this purpose includes specified transfers and specified exempt transfers made in the 7 years before death: see reg 4(6).

30.9.6 Legal statements

Both forms end with a series of declarations and undertakings. The applicants confirm:

(1) That the last will and any codicils referred to in this application is the last will and testament of the person who has died.

As required by Administration of Estates Act 1925, s 25 they will:

(2) collect the whole estate

(3) keep full details (an inventory) of the estate

(4) keep a full account of how the estate has been distributed.

If required, they will:

(5) provide the full details of the estate and how it has been distributed

(6) return the grant of representation to the court.

They understand that:

(7) the application will be rejected if the information is not provided (if asked)

(8) proceedings for contempt of court may be brought against the undersigned if it is found that the evidence provided is deliberately untruthful or dishonest, as well as revocation of the grant.

The applicants confirm that they will administer the deceased's estate in accordance to law, and that the application is truthful.

30.10 FORM PA1P

This form is completed whenever there is a will and irrespective of whether the grant sought is a grant of probate (in the case of executors) or a grant of letters of administration with will (in the case of non-executors). Because one form is being used for differently entitled applicants, not all of the questions asked are relevant but, unless the form says otherwise, all should be answered.

30.10.1 Identification of the will

The original will and any codicils must accompany the application. The date must be entered and details must be provided of any foreign wills in case they revoke the UK will. The form asks whether the deceased married or formed a civil partnership after making the will for the same reason.

If the application is by non-executors, question 3.5 must be answered to ascertain whether there are any minor beneficiaries, in which case two administrators will be required. The form does not deal with the need for two applicants where there is a life interest. Presumably this will be picked up by the Registry, if necessary.

30.10.2 Entitlement of executors to act

Executors have the best right to take a grant which will be a grant of probate. They are appointed by will (which must, of course, be valid). One executor may obtain a grant and act alone.

> **EXAMPLE 1**
>
> Alex by his will appoints Brian and Colin to be his executors and leaves his entire estate to a named charity.
>
> Brian and/or Colin can apply for a grant of probate by lodging a PA1P, and the will, with the Probate Service.

The appointment of executors is not affected by the fact that the will may fail to dispose of some or all of the deceased's estate.

> **EXAMPLE 2**
>
> Diana has just died. Her will appoints Eric as her executor and leaves her entire estate to Freda. Freda died before Diana whose estate will therefore be distributed according to the intestacy rules. Eric is alive and prepared to act as executor. Eric will apply for a grant of probate using a PA1P.

30.10.2.1 Executor lacking capacity to act

Capacity to act as executor is judged at the time of the application for the grant. A person appointed as an executor by the will but who, at the testator's death, lacks capacity to make decisions, cannot apply for the grant. Where one of several executors lacks capacity, the others will take the grant. Where the only executor lacks capacity, NCPR 1987, r 35 provides that a grant can be made for the use and benefit of that person to:

(a) the person authorised by the Court of Protection to apply for a grant or, where there is no such person,

(b) the attorney of the person who lacks capacity appointed under a registered enduring power of attorney or lasting power of attorney, or where there is no attorney or the attorney renounces,

(c) the person entitled to the residuary estate of the deceased.

30.10.2.2 Minors

There is no prohibition on a testator naming a minor as their executor. However, an executor who is still a minor at the testator's death cannot act as an executor nor obtain a grant of probate until attaining majority.

Where one of several executors is a minor, the other(s) being adults, probate can be granted to the adult executor(s) with power reserved to the minor to take a grant at a later date (for an explanation of 'power reserved', see **30.10.2.4**). If the administration of the estate has not been completed by the time the minor attains 18 years, an application for a grant of double probate can be made to enable the former minor to act as executor alongside the other proving executor(s).

EXAMPLE

George dies appointing his wife, Ingrid and his son Harry (aged 16) as his executors.

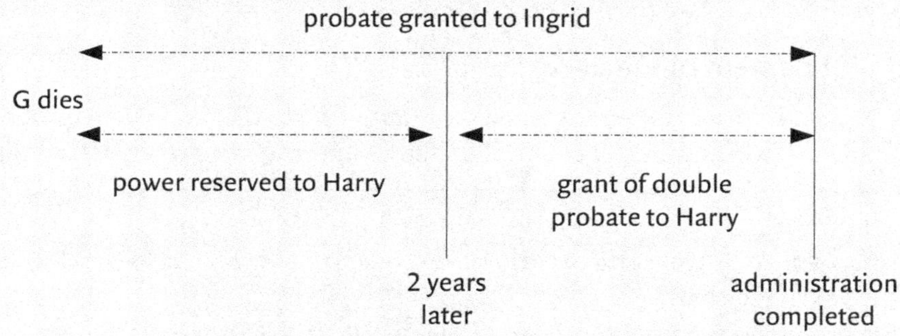

Where the minor is the only executor appointed by the will (or the adult executors are not able or willing to act), someone must take the grant on behalf of the minor as it would be impracticable to leave the testator's estate unadministered until the executor reaches 18 years. A grant of letters of administration with will annexed for the use and benefit of the minor will be made, usually to the parent(s) or guardian(s) of the minor, until the minor attains 18 years. On obtaining majority, the executor may apply for a cessate grant of probate if the administration has not been completed.

30.10.2.3 The former spouse or civil partner

If the testator appointed their spouse or civil partner as their executor and the marriage or civil partnership subsequently ends, that appointment will fail unless the testator has shown a contrary intention in the will (Wills Act 1837, s 18A: see **29.4.4.2**).

If the spouse or civil partner was one of several executors, the others may apply for the grant of probate without the spouse or civil partner. If the spouse was appointed as a sole executor, application should be made for a grant of letters of administration with will annexed. In either case, details should be provided of the fact and date of the divorce.

30.10.2.4 Renunciation

Persons appointed as executors may renounce their right to take the grant, provided that they have not intermeddled in the estate. Intermeddling consists of doing tasks a PR might do, for example notifying the deceased's bank of the death. By intermeddling, executors accept their appointment. Once executors have intermeddled, they must take the grant because they are treated as having accepted office.

Provided there has been no intermeddling, executors who do not wish to act can renounce their rights. Rights as executor then cease and the administration of the estate proceeds as if the executor had never been appointed.

The renunciation must be made using Form PA15, signed by the person renouncing (the signature must be witnessed), and the renunciation must be filed with the Probate Service. This is normally done by the PRs who are applying for a grant when they lodge their application for a grant.

Executors who are also appointed as trustees will remain trustees despite renouncing the executorship. They will have to disclaim the trusteeship as well if they want to act in neither capacity.

30.10.2.5 Power reserved

There is no limit on how many executors can be appointed by the will, but probate will be granted to a maximum of four executors in respect of the same property. Power may be reserved to the other(s) to take out a grant in the future if a vacancy arises.

EXAMPLE 1

Aadit's will appoints B, C, D, E and F to be his executors. All are willing and able to act. C, D, E and F apply for a grant of probate. 'Power is reserved' to B. If F dies before the administration is complete, B can then apply for a grant. B must apply if he wishes to act; there is no automatic substitution.

If there is a dispute between the executors as to which of them should apply for a grant, this may be resolved by summons before a registrar (NCPR 1987, r 27(6)).

There is no need for every executor to act. A person appointed as one of several executors may not wish to act initially but may not want to take the irrevocable step of renouncing the right to a grant of probate.

Details of executors not applying for the grant must be given at 3.6. The options are:

A – They died before the person who has died.

B – They died after the person who has died.

C – They wish to have power reserved to apply at a later date.

D – They have renounced.

E – They have appointed an attorney to take the grant on their behalf.

F – They lack capacity to act as executor.

EXAMPLE 2

Aadit appoints Bala and Chaarvik as his executors. When Aadit dies, Bala is working in Germany but is due to return to England in 12 months' time. Bala does not feel that she should act as executor whilst abroad and is happy to let Chaarvik act alone initially, but she does want to help in the administration if it has not been completed by the time she returns to England.

Chaarvik should apply for the grant 'with power reserved' to Bala to prove at a later stage.

It is possible to obtain a grant limited to part only of the estate (see **30.14** below). This is frequently done where particular expertise is required. For example, an author might appoint literary executors to deal with their books and general executors to deal with everything else. Up to four executors can take the grant limited to the deceased's writings, and up to four can take the grant dealing with the rest of the estate.

One executor is always sufficient. This is not the case for administrators (see below).

30.10.3 Entitlement of administrators to act

If there is a valid will but no executor able and willing to act, and the will does not dispose of all the estate, the appropriate grant is still letters of administration with will annexed. The property undisposed of by the will is distributed according to the intestacy rules (see **29.6**).

30.10.3.1 NCPR 1987, r 20

The order of priority of the person(s) entitled to a grant of letters of administration with will annexed is governed by NCPR 1987, r 20. The rule states as follows:

> Where the deceased died on or after 1 January 1926 the person or persons entitled to a grant in respect of a will shall be determined in accordance with the following order of priority, namely—
>
> (a) the executor ... ;
>
> (b) any residuary legatee or devisee holding in trust for any other person;

(c) any other residuary legatee or devisee (including one for life) or where the residue is not wholly disposed of by the will, any person entitled to share in the undisposed of residue (including the Treasury Solicitor when claiming bona vacantia on behalf of the Crown), provided that—

   (i) unless a registrar otherwise directs, a residuary legatee or devisee whose legacy or devise is vested in interest shall be preferred to one entitled on the happening of a contingency, and

   (ii) where the residue is not in terms wholly disposed of, the registrar may, if he is satisfied that the testator has nevertheless disposed of the whole or substantially the whole of the known estate, allow a grant to be made to any legatee or devisee entitled to, or to share in, the estate so disposed of, without regard to the persons entitled to share in any residue not disposed of by the will;

(d) the personal representative of any residuary legatee or devisee (but not one for life, or one holding in trust for any other person), or of any person entitled to share in any residue not disposed of by the will;

(e) any other legatee or devisee (including one for life or one holding in trust for any other person) or any creditor of the deceased, provided that, unless a registrar otherwise directs, a legatee or devisee whose legacy or devise is vested in interest shall be preferred to one entitled on the happening of a contingency;

(f) the personal representative of any other legatee or devisee (but not one for life or one holding in trust for any other person) or of any creditor of the deceased.

30.10.3.2 Clearing off

Each applicant is listed in priority in r 20. A person in a lower-ranked category may apply only if there is nobody in a higher category willing and able to take the grant. The applicant must explain the basis of their own claim to the grant.

Unless the basis of entitlement is obvious, clearing off information should be provided at question 16 of Section 2.

Details of surviving relatives (which will not always be relevant) have to be provided in Section 4 of the Form.

'(a) the executor ...'

The NCPR 1987, r 20 in fact provides the 'order of priority for grant where deceased left a will'. This covers both grants of probate and letters of administration with the will annexed. An executor who has been appointed in the will and is able and willing to act has first right to a grant.

The remaining categories are relevant where, for whatever reason, no executor is available.

Where executors are named in the will but are not applying, it is necessary to explain at question 3.6 what has happened to them.

'(b) any residuary legatee or devisee holding in trust ...'

> **EXAMPLE**
>
> Abdar has died leaving a will. Although he failed to appoint executors, he left his residue to Buhran and Caliana on trust for Debbie. Buhran and Caliana are the residuary legatees (or devisees, depending on the type of trust property) holding on trust and so they have first right to a grant. Clearly, Abdar was happy for them to deal with his property otherwise he would not have appointed them as trustees.

'(c) any other residuary legatee or devisee ...'

> **EXAMPLE 1**
>
> Amanda has died leaving a will appointing Boris as her executor and giving the residuary estate to Carol, ie Carol is the residuary legatee and devisee.
>
> Carol can apply for a grant only if Boris is unable or unwilling to act. She must explain at 3.6 why Boris is not applying.
>
> The facts are the same as above, but Boris was appointed 'executor and trustee' and the residue was given to Carol for lfe.
>
> Carol must clear off Boris in both capacities by saying, 'the executor and trustee named in the will has [renounced probate] etc ...'.

'... or ... any person entitled to share in the undisposed of residue'

If a partial intestacy arises because the will fails to dispose of all or part of the residuary estate, those people entitled to the residue by virtue of the intestacy rules (see **29.6**) may apply for a grant under NCPR 1987, r 20, but they must show why they are entitled to the grant by explaining what has happened to anyone who would have been in a higher category. Details of the surviving relatives are given in Section 4.

> **EXAMPLE**
>
> Damien's will appoints Errol to be his sole executor and residuary beneficiary. Errol died last month and Damien has just died. Damien's closest living relative is his mother, Florence.
>
> As the sole residuary beneficiary has predeceased the deceased (and the gift is not saved by any substitutional gift), the residue is undisposed of and will be distributed according to the intestacy rules. Damien has left no spouse or civil partner and no issue but is survived by his mother, Florence, who is next entitled to the property.
>
> Florence will apply for a grant of letters of administration with will annexed by clearing off the executor. She must also establish her entitlement to the undisposed of property and, therefore, to the grant. She will explain that the executor and residuary legatee and devisee have predeceased the deceased. She will explain her relationship in Section 4 together with the fact that no spouse, civil partner or issue survive.

'(d) the personal representative of a deceased residuary legatee or devisee ...'

Where there is no proving executor and, for example, the residuary beneficiary survives the testator to take a vested interest in the estate but then dies without having taken the grant, that beneficiary's PR may apply for the grant. This is because the gift under the will forms part of the beneficiary's estate and needs to be collected by their PR.

> **EXAMPLE**
>
> Gazala died last week leaving a will appointing Hafsa as executrix and giving the residuary estate to Imran absolutely. Hafsa has predeceased Gazala; Imran died yesterday. Imran's will appoints Jamila as his sole executrix and beneficiary.
>
> Jamila may apply for a grant of letters of administration with will annexed to Gazala's estate. To do so, Jamila must clear off Hafsa and Imran by saying, 'the sole executrix predeceased the deceased and the sole residuary legatee and devisee named in the said will survived the deceased and has since died without having proved the said will and I am the executrix of the deceased residuary legatee and devisee'.

'(e) any other legatee or devisee ... or any creditor of the deceased ...'

This category covers any other beneficiary under the will, for example, a specific devisee who has been left the deceased's house, or a pecuniary legatee who has been left money by the deceased. It also covers creditors of the deceased.

'(f) the personal representative of any other legatee or devisee ... or of any creditor ...'

This category works on the same principles as category (d) above.

30.10.3.3 Beneficiary with vested interest preferred

Where there is more than one person of equal rank but one has a vested and one a contingent interest in the estate, the court generally prefers an application by the beneficiary with the vested interest.

EXAMPLE

Kalima's will leaves her residuary estate to her two children, Laila and Masoud, contingent on their attaining 25 years of age. There is no executor appointed in the will and at Kalima's death Laila is 30 years old and Masoud 23 years old.

Laila and Masoud can make a joint application, but if they were to apply separately the court would prefer Laila because Masoud's interest is still contingent.

30.10.3.4 Minors

A minor cannot act as administrator with will annexed, nor can they apply for a grant. Their parent(s) or guardian(s) may apply for a grant 'for the minor's use and benefit' on the minor's behalf. The grant is limited until they attain the age of 18.

If there is a person not under a disability who is entitled in the same degree as the minor then that person will be preferred to the guardian of the minor (NCPR 1987, r 27(5)).

30.10.3.5 The number of administrators

Maximum number

If there are several people entitled to act as administrators, then, as with executors, the grant will not issue to more than four of them in relation to the same property (Senior Courts Act 1981, s 114). It is not possible for an administrator to have power reserved to prove at a later stage.

If a person is entitled to act as administrator but does not obtain a grant (eg, because there are four other applicants), this does not affect that person's beneficial entitlement to the estate.

Number in the same category

Subject to the provisions of s 114 of the Senior Courts Act 1981 (see **30.15.1** below), where two or more people are entitled in the same degree, a grant can be made on the application of any one of them without notice to the other or others (NCPR 1987, r 27(4)).

EXAMPLE

Jane dies leaving her residuary estate by will to her two adult brothers, Ken and Larry. Jane's will does not appoint an executor. Larry does not wish to act.

Ken can apply for a grant alone. This does not affect Larry's beneficial entitlement to half the estate.

30.10.3.6 Need for two administrators

Where there is a life interest, or property passes to a minor (whether the interest is vested or contingent), the court normally requires a minimum of two administrators to apply for the grant (Senior Courts Act 1981, s 114). This is made clear at Question 3.5.

EXAMPLE 1

Abhijeet has just died leaving a valid will which:

(a) appoints Balinder his executor;

(b) gives £1,000 to Fraz (aged 6) contingent on reaching 21;

(c) gives the residue of his estate to Pardeep and Parminder.

As executor, Balinder has the best right to take a grant. If Balinder renounces probate, at least two people must apply for a grant of letters of administration because there is a minority interest, ie the legacy to Fraz. Pardeep and Parminder have the best right to take a grant.

EXAMPLE 2

Quentin's will fails to appoint an executor. He leaves his estate to his wife Rose for life, remainder to his adult son, Sam.

Two administrators are required because of Rose's life interest. Rose and Sam should both apply.

EXAMPLE 3

Tahir's will leaves his residuary estate to his friend Una, whom he has also appointed executrix. Una has predeceased Tahir. Tahir is divorced and has three children, Varisha (21), Wahid (19), and Zafir (15).

Tahir therefore dies partially intestate. By virtue of the intestacy rules his children take the residuary estate on the statutory trusts.

Two administrators are required because part of the estate goes to Zafir who is a minor. Varisha and Wahid should both apply.

Section 114(2) of the Senior Courts Act 1981 gives the court power, where it appears to the court to be expedient in all the circumstances, to appoint an individual as sole administrator despite the existence of a minority or life interest.

30.10.3.7 Renunciation

Any person entitled to apply for a grant of letters of administration with will annexed can renounce in the same way as an executor (though using a Form PA16), except that an administrator does not lose the right to renounce by intermeddling. Renunciation does not affect any beneficial entitlement of the administrator or any appointment as a trustee.

30.11 FORM PA1A

This form is completed where the deceased died without a valid will and so is totally intestate.

30.11.1 Entitlement to act

The person or persons entitled to the grant are listed in NCPR 1987, r 22 as set out below. The order is the same as the order or entitlement on intestacy:

(1) Where the deceased died on or after 1 January 1926, wholly intestate, the person or persons having a beneficial interest in the estate shall be entitled to a grant of administration in the following classes in order of priority, namely—

(a) the surviving spouse or civil partner;

(b) the children of the deceased and the issue of any deceased child who died before the deceased;

(c) the father and mother of the deceased;

(d) brothers and sisters of the whole blood and the issue of any deceased brother or sister of the whole blood who died before the deceased;

(e) brothers and sisters of the half blood and the issue of any deceased brother or sister of the half blood who died before the deceased;

(f) grandparents;

(g) uncles and aunts of the whole blood and the issue of any deceased uncle or aunt of the whole blood who died before the deceased;

(h) uncles and aunts of the half blood and the issue of any deceased uncle or aunt of the half blood who died before the deceased.

(2) In default of any person having a beneficial interest in the estate, the Treasury Solicitor shall be entitled to a grant if he claims bona vacantia on behalf of the Crown.

(3) If all persons entitled to a grant under the foregoing provisions of this rule have been cleared off, a grant may be made to a creditor of the deceased or to any person who, notwithstanding that he has no immediate beneficial interest in the estate, may have a beneficial interest in the event of an accretion thereto.

Some of the descriptions of relations require further explanation, as follows.

30.11.1.1 'Children'

On an intestacy, no distinction is drawn between those who have been born legitimate or have been adopted, or those whose parents were not married (subject to the qualification in the Family Law Reform Act 1987, s 18(2) – see **29.6.5.2**).

Equally entitled with the deceased's children are the children or grandchildren of any child who predeceased the deceased. Step-children (ie, children of the deceased's spouse or civil partner) are not children for this purpose unless the deceased adopted them.

30.11.1.2 'Brothers and sisters'

Brothers and sisters of the deceased are also known as 'siblings'. A sibling is of the 'whole blood' where they share both parents in common with the deceased, and of the 'half blood' where they have only one common parent.

EXAMPLE

Susan has been married twice. By Tom she had two children, Una and Victoria, and by Arshad she had a son, Wisan.

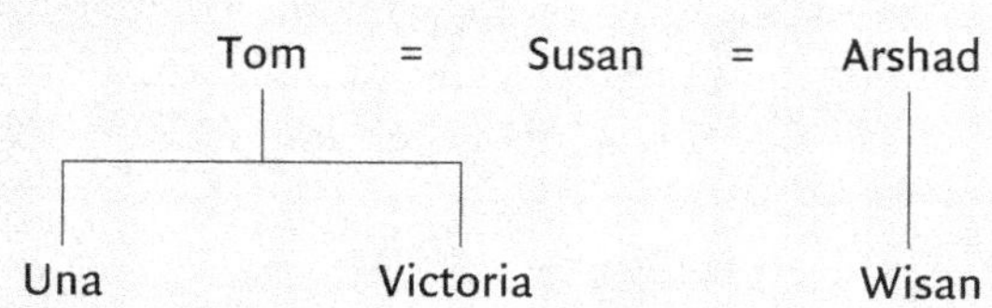

Una and Victoria are sisters of the whole blood.

Wisan is their brother of the half blood.

30.11.1.3 'Uncles and aunts'

Uncles and aunts of 'the whole blood' are the children of both grandparents of the intestate. Aunts and uncles of the 'half blood' are the children of only one of the deceased's grandparents.

> **EXAMPLE**
>
> David has died recently and his closest living relations are his uncles, Ben and Charles. David's mother, Ann, and his uncle, Ben, were children of the same parents; Charles was the son of David's grandfather, Fred, and Fred's mistress, Joan.
>
> 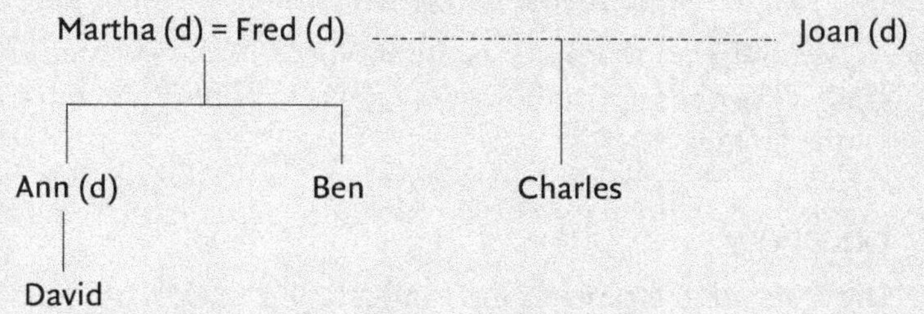
>
>
> Ben is David's uncle of the whole blood.
>
> Charles is David's uncle of the half blood.

30.11.2 Clearing off

Each category is listed in priority in NCPR 1987, r 22. Like the applicant under NCPR 1987, r 20 (see **30.10.2**), an applicant under r 22 must make clear that there is no one in a higher category able to apply for the grant (again, this is called 'clearing off') and describe their own relationship to the deceased.

This is done in Section 3 of the Form. Questions 3.1–3.4 establish what relatives survived the deceased and question 3.5 establishes the relationship of the applicant(s) to the deceased.

> **EXAMPLE 1**
>
> Alice, a widow, has died intestate, survived by her son who will take the grant.
>
> He will state that there was no surviving spouse or civil partner.

> **EXAMPLE 2**
>
> Barraq, who is unmarried, has just died intestate aged 92 years. He is survived by his two brothers who will take the grant.
>
> The brothers will state that there was no surviving spouse or civil partner, no children or issue and no parents.

At 3.5, the applicant(s) will explain their own relationship to the deceased.

30.11.3 The need for a beneficial interest in the estate

Unless the application is made by the Treasury Solicitor or a creditor, the applicant must have a beneficial interest in the estate (or would have such an in interest if there was an accretion to the estate) by virtue of the intestacy rules; hence there is a similarity of entitlement under NCPR 1987, r 22 and under AEA 1925, s 46 (see **29.6**).

EXAMPLE 1

Chandra, who is unmarried, dies intestate survived by her mother and one brother.

Only the mother can apply for the grant because she is solely and absolutely entitled to Chandra's estate under the intestacy rules.

EXAMPLE 2

David dies intestate survived by his wife, Eve, and adult son, Fred. Excluding personal assets, David's estate is valued at £500,000.

As Eve and Fred share the estate by virtue of the intestacy rules, Fred can apply for the grant if Eve does not, although Eve ranks in priority and must be cleared off if Fred applies for the grant.

EXAMPLE 3

The facts are the same as in Example 2 but David's estate is £190,000. Prima facie, Fred would seem to have no interest and would therefore be unable to apply for a grant if Eve failed to do so. But Fred can apply in these circumstances on the basis that if additional assets were found in David's estate, Fred would then share the estate with Eve. It is irrelevant that David's estate never actually increases above £190,000. Again, Eve ranks in priority.

30.11.4 Minors

A minor cannot act as administrator, neither can they apply for a grant. The same procedure as that discussed at **30.10.3** above should be followed.

30.11.5 Renunciation

A person entitled to a grant under NCPR 1987, r 22 can renounce their right to the grant in the same way as an administrator with the will annexed. If they are the only relative of the deceased with a beneficial entitlement, the grant will be made to a creditor of the deceased. Renunciation does not affect any beneficial entitlement of the administrator.

EXAMPLE

Graeme dies intestate survived by one brother, Henry, and an uncle, Jack. Graeme owes Kalya £100.

Henry has the best right to a grant under r 22. As Jack has no beneficial interest in the estate under the intestacy rules, he cannot apply for the grant if Henry fails to do so. In that event Kalya should apply for the grant of letters of administration.

It is common for a creditor to take the grant if the estate is insolvent.

30.11.6 The number of administrators

The rules applying to the number of administrators with will annexed apply equally to administrators of a totally intestate estate.

30.11.6.1 Maximum number

The grant will issue to a maximum of four administrators. If there are more than four people with an equal entitlement, it is not possible to have 'power reserved' to a non-proving administrator.

30.11.6.2 Number in the same category

Where two or more people are entitled in the same degree, a grant can be made on the application of any one of them without notice to the other(s).

30.11.6.3 Need for two administrators

A minimum of two administrators is generally required where the intestacy creates minority interests through property being held for minors on the 'statutory trusts'. The court may dispense with the need for two administrators in special circumstances.

EXAMPLE 1

John dies intestate in March 2019 with a net estate for probate purposes of £300,000, and is survived by his wife, Kala, and children, Laksha (20) and Madesh (16).

Kala and Laksha must take the grant. Two administrators are needed because the intestacy creates a minority interest. Madesh cannot be an administrator because he is a minor.

EXAMPLE 2

Nigel dies intestate, a bachelor without issue. Both his parents are dead.

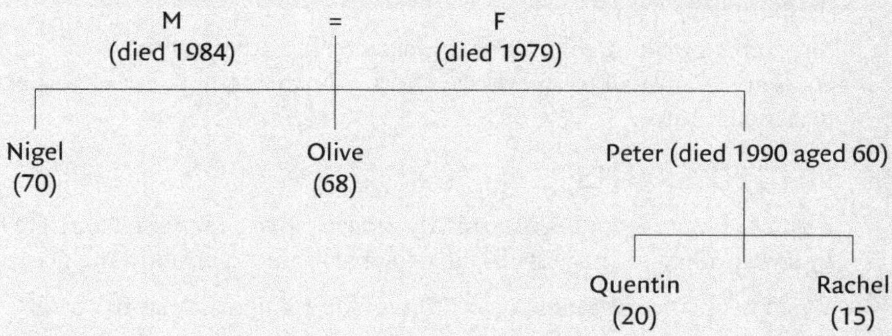

His sister and the issue of his deceased brother are equally entitled to apply for the grant as they share the estate under the intestacy rules. Both Olive and Quentin must apply because Rachel is a minor.

30.12 COMPLETING THE ONLINE APPLICATION

Completing the application online is fairly intuitive, but there is helpful guidance provided by HMCTS at 'Apply for probate with MyHMCTS'. When you start, you will select 'application for grant of representation' from the drop down menu and then indicate which of the three grants you wish to apply for. The questions will then be appropriate for the grant you have selected.

The questions correspond to those on the paper forms.

The legal statement confirming that the information is correct and that the PRs will carry out their duties can be emailed to them, in which case they will add their typed signature, or printed for them to sign in pen.

Alternatively, if the applicants wish to, they can authorise the practitioner to sign on their behalf. The legal statement can be uploaded with the application or sent by post.

Once the application is submitted, a summary appears followed by information about what needs to be done next. This includes a list of the documents that need to be sent. A coversheet can be downloaded which has the list of documents, the case number and where to send them (currently HMCTS Probate at Harlow). Once sent, the documents are scanned. The scanned documents are then made available to the case workers who work on the applications.

There is an optional box where you can give additional details about your application. It is helpful to point out if supporting documentation is double-sided, as this is sometimes missed when documents are scanned. Since case workers work out of the processing centre in Birmingham, they cannot access the physical documents. Hence scanning errors will significantly delay the application.

30.13 EFFECT OF GRANT

30.13.1 Grant of probate

A grant of probate confirms the authority of the executor(s) which stems from the will and arises from the time of the testate's death (see **30.2**).

The grant provides conclusive evidence of the title of the executor(s) and of the validity and contents of the will.

30.13.2 Grant of administration (with or without will)

A grant of administration (with or without will annexed) confers authority on the administrator and vests the deceased's property in the administrator. Until the grant is issued, the administrator has no authority to act and the deceased's property is vested in the President of the Family Division.

The grant provides conclusive evidence of the administrator's title and of the validity and contents of any will (or intestacy). Normally, the grant is not retrospective to the date of the deceased's death.

30.14 LIMITED GRANTS

A grant of representation is normally general, ie it is expressed to relate to 'all the estate which by law devolves to and vests in the personal representatives of the deceased'.

When necessary, a grant may be limited; for example, it may be:

(a) limited as to a specified part of the deceased's property. For example, a novelist might appoint literary executors to administer their literary estate; general executors would be responsible for their general estate;

(b) limited to settled land. Any settled land vested in the deceased is usually excepted from a general grant if the land remains settled after their death. The trustees of the settlement will apply for a grant limited to the settled land;

(c) limited to a special purpose. For example, if the person entitled to apply for a grant is a minor then application should be made by their parent(s) or guardian(s) for a grant for the minor's use and benefits. The practice in making such grants is governed by NCPR 1987, r 2.

30.15 THE CHAIN OF REPRESENTATION AND GRANT DE BONIS NON ADMINISTRATIS

30.15.1 Introduction

If there are several proving PRs administering an estate and one dies after taking the grant but before the administration has been completed, the surviving PRs continue to act. The continuing PRs' powers remain unaffected. Where the death leaves a sole surviving PR, the court may exercise its powers to appoint an additional PR. This might happen, for example, where there is a life or minority interest and the court wishes there to continue to be two PRs (Senior Courts Act 1981, s 114).

If a person entitled to be the PR (either as the executor under a will, or by virtue of NCPR 1987, r 20 or r 22) survives the deceased but then dies themselves without taking out a grant of representation, the AEA 1925, s 5 provides that their rights concerning the grant die with them (unless it is an exceptional case where their PR may apply for a grant under NCPR 1987, r 20).

EXAMPLE 1

Abdul dies, appointing Eman as his executrix and leaving his estate to Rafi. Eman dies a few days after Abdul and without having proved his will. Rafi should apply for a grant of letters of administration with will annexed to Abdul's estate.

The position is more complicated on the death of a sole or sole surviving PR if the administration is incomplete.

EXAMPLE 2

Anthony died six months ago, appointing Edward as his sole executor.

Edward obtained a grant of probate to Anthony's estate and had begun to deal with the assets when he died. The house is on the market but unsold and the final IHT assessment cannot be agreed because tax is being paid on the house by instalments. The administration is therefore incomplete. What happens? That depends on whether or not the chain of representation applies. See **30.15.2**.

30.15.2 Chain of representation

The office of executor is personal to the executor appointed by the testator in their will. Because it is an office of personal trust an executor cannot assign that office (although they can appoint an attorney). However, the AEA 1925, s 7 provides that in one case the office of executor will pass automatically to someone else. This is called the 'chain of representation'. This happens only where an executor who has taken out a grant of probate dies without completing the administration and appoints someone as their own executor. If that person takes out a grant of probate they will automatically become the executor of both estates.

30.15.2.1 Unbroken chain

The chain of representation is applicable only where there is an unbroken sequence of proving executors.

EXAMPLE

Colin died, leaving a will appointing Diane as his executrix.

Diane proved the will and obtained a grant of probate.

Diane died before she had completed the administration of Colin's estate.

Diane's will appointed Eric to be her executor. If Eric applies for probate of Diane's will, he automatically becomes executor of Colin's estate.

It is not possible to accept the office of executor to Diane's estate and refuse to be executor by representation of Colin's estate.

30.15.2.2 AEA 1925, s 7

Section 7 provides that an executor by representation:

(a) has the same rights in respect of the testator's estate as if they were the original executor; and

(b) is, to the extent to which the testator's estate has come into their hands, answerable as if they were the original executor.

30.15.2.3 Broken chain

If for any reason there are no successive executors, the chain of representation will be broken.

> **EXAMPLE 1**
>
> Fiona appointed Graham to be her executor. Graham obtained probate to Fiona's estate. Graham then died intestate. Graham's PR under NCPR 1987, r 22 is Ian, who obtains a grant of letters of administration to Graham's estate. Ian will not become the executor of Fiona's estate.

> **EXAMPLE 2**
>
> Jaan died intestate and Kaleema obtained a grant of letters of administration to his estate. Kaleema died leaving a will appointing Laila to be her executrix. Laila proved Kaleema's will and obtained probate. Laila does not become the executrix of Jaan's estate.

30.15.3 Grant *de bonis non administratis*

In situations where the chain of representation does not apply because there are no successive proving executors, a grant *de bonis non administratis* must be obtained to the original estate (usually known as a 'grant *de bonis non*'). The grant *de bonis non* may be one of administration with the will or one of simple administration, depending on the circumstances.

It is issued in estates where the sole, or sole surviving, PR has died after obtaining the grant but without having completed the administration, and it relates only to the unadministered part of the estate. Two requirements apply:

(a) there must have been a prior grant of probate or letters of administration to a PR who has now died; and

(b) the chain of representation must not apply.

The grant *de bonis non* will issue to the person who would have been entitled had the original PR never taken the grant. The order of priority will depend on NCPR 1987, r 20 or r 22, as appropriate.

30.16 CAVEATS AND CITATIONS

Caveats and citations are available under the NCPR 1987 to assist in the event of a dispute over the right to take out a grant of representation to an estate.

30.16.1 Caveats (NCPR 1987, r 44)

The effect of a caveat is to prevent the issue of a grant of representation. The person lodging or entering a caveat is called a 'caveator'. A caveat might be used, for example, where a beneficiary believes the executor named in the will lacks the mental capacity to act, or where the validity of the will is questioned.

> **EXAMPLE 1**
>
> The will appoints Eric as executor, gives a legacy to Ann and the residue to Ben.
>
> Eric wants to act as executor but Ann challenges his capability. Ann should enter a caveat before a grant of representation is issued so that the court can decide who should act as PR.

> **EXAMPLE 2**
>
> On Dinar's death a homemade will is found appointing Eisaz as executor and sole beneficiary. Fahima would be entitled to Dinar's estate under the intestacy rules and Fahima believes the will is invalid. She should enter a caveat to prevent any grant of representation issuing until the court has decided the validity or otherwise of the will.

An application for a caveat can be made online or using paper form PA8A. The PA8A is posted to HMCTS Probate at Harlow. The fee is £3 to stop an application for six months. The caveat can be renewed but a further application is required.

30.16.2 Citations (NCPR 1987, r 46)

Only executors or persons specified under NCPR 1987, r 20 or r 22 can take a grant of representation. If the person initially entitled to take the grant refuses to do so and also refuses to renounce, the estate would remain unadministered and the beneficiaries would be left waiting indefinitely for their inheritance. In such circumstances, a citation provides a remedy.

There are several types of citation which may be issued by the Probate Service at the request of a beneficiary ('the citor').

30.16.2.1 Citation to take probate

A citation to take probate may be used where an executor has lost their right to renounce probate by intermeddling in the estate (eg, by informing the deceased's bank of their death, see **30.9.3**) but has not applied for a grant of probate and shows no signs of so doing. Once cited, the executor must proceed with an application for a grant of probate. If they do not (without good reason) the citor can apply to the court for an order allowing the executor to be passed over and a grant of letters of administration with will annexed to issue to the person(s) entitled under NCPR 1987, r 20.

30.16.2.2 Citation to accept or refuse a grant

A citation to accept or refuse a grant is the standard method of clearing off a person with a prior right to any type of grant who has not applied, and shows no intention of applying, for a grant. If the person cited does not take steps to take out the grant, a grant may be issued to the citor.

> **EXAMPLE**
>
> Adam's will appoints Bert his executor and Clare the residuary beneficiary. Bert takes no steps towards administering the estate or proving the will. Clare may cite Bert to act and, if Bert does nothing, Clare may apply by virtue of NCPR 1987, r 20 for a grant of letters of administration with will annexed.

30.17 AN ALTERNATIVE TO CITATION

To compel an unwilling person to take a grant is likely to produce more problems than it solves. If a person is unwilling to act as executor in the administration of an estate, it is often preferable to apply to HMCTS under the Senior Courts Act 1981, s 116 for an order passing over that person in favour of someone else. For example, in *Re Biggs* [1966] 1 All ER 358, an executor had intermeddled but then refused to have anything to do with the estate. The applicants obtained an order that he be passed over.

SUMMARY

(1) When a person dies, someone must deal with the administration of the estate. Those who take on this task are referred to generically as 'personal representatives' (PRs). They may be executors or administrators.

(2) Executors are appointed by the will and take a grant of probate.

(3) If there is no executor able and willing to act, those entitled to property take a grant of administration (with the will annexed if there is one). Priority is governed by the Non-Contentious Probate Rules 1987.

(4) Some assets (eg joint property, life policies assigned or written in trust during the deceased's lifetime) do not pass through the hands of the PRs.

(5) The process for obtaining a grant involves completing an IHT400, unless the estate is excepted, and sending it to HMRC with any tax due.

(6) The following should be sent to the Probate Service:

- a Form PA1P or PA1A completed by the PRs explaining their right to take a grant
- any will and codicils
- affidavits or statements of truth explaining any unusual features
- probate fee
- any renunciations of the right to act

If IHT is due, HMRC will send a code confirming that it has been paid which must be included in the application together with the values confirmed by HMRC.

(7) One executor is always sufficient. Two administrators are required if there is a minority or life interest.

CHAPTER 31

ADMINISTRATION OF AN ESTATE

LEARNING OUTCOMES

After reading this chapter you will be able to:

- explain the meaning of the 'administration period'
- explain the duties of a PR during the administration period
- protect the PRs from personal liability
- identify the powers of PRs when dealing with the administration
- identify the steps necessary to administer the estate and complete the administration.

31.1 INTRODUCTION

Once the PRs have obtained the grant, they are able to start the administration of the estate. The work involved in administering an estate is basically the same whether the deceased left a will or died intestate. However, in the latter case, the beneficiaries will be ascertained by application of the law of intestacy rather than from construction of the will.

Broadly speaking, the PRs have to:

- collect the deceased's assets;
- pay the deceased's funeral and testamentary expenses and debts;
- distribute the legacies; and
- complete the administration and distribute the residuary estate.

This chapter looks at the different aspects of the PRs' duties and at how they can protect themselves from personal liability.

31.2 THE ADMINISTRATION PERIOD

The 'administration period' commences at the moment immediately following the death and ends when the PRs are in a position to vest the residue of the estate in the beneficiaries, or the trustees if a trust arises under the will or the intestacy law.

Note, however, that a PR holds office for life. If further assets or liabilities are discovered after the residue has all been transferred, the PRs will still have to deal with them.

31.3 DUTIES OF THE PRS

The Administration of Estates Act 1925 (AEA 1925), s 25 (as substituted by AEA 1971, s 9) states that the PRs of a deceased person shall be under a duty to 'collect and get in the real and personal estate of the deceased and administer it according to law'.

The duties to be undertaken by a PR are onerous. A PR who has accepted liability is personally liable for loss to the estate resulting from any breach of duty they commit as PR (although they are not generally liable for breaches committed by a co-PR). There are several types of breach of duty, including:

(a) failing to protect the value of assets;
(b) failing to pay the people entitled to assets.

The Trustee Act 1925 (TA 1925), s 61 gives the court power at its discretion to relieve a PR from liability for breach of duty if satisfied that the PR 'has acted honestly and reasonably and ought fairly to be excused for the breach'. Alternatively, an executor may be able to rely on a clause in the deceased's will providing protection from liability for mistakes made in good faith.

31.4 PROTECTION AGAINST LIABILITY

As we saw at **30.3.5**, PRs can protect themselves against personal liability to unknown beneficiaries by complying with the requirements of the TA 1925, s 27.

31.4.1 Missing beneficiaries

As we saw at **30.3.5**, the TA 1925, s 27 will not protect PRs against claims from beneficiaries whose existence is known but who cannot be traced. The only way they can fully protect themselves in such a case is to apply to court for a *Benjamin* order.

Before making an order, the court will require evidence that the fullest possible enquiries were made to trace the missing person. If the court considers the advertisements made in addition to the TA 1925, s 27 are insufficient, it will direct that further enquiry be made.

An application to court is expensive so, as an alternative, PRs may take out insurance to cover the risk.

31.4.2 Inheritance (Provision for Family and Dependants) Act 1975

The PRs will be personally liable where an applicant under the I(PFD)A 1975 successfully obtains an order for 'reasonable financial provision' from the estate. They can protect themselves against such liability by waiting more than six months following the date of the grant of representation before distributing the assets. If earlier distribution is required, PRs should ensure they retain sufficient assets to satisfy an order should an applicant be successful within six months of the grant.

31.5 ADMINISTRATIVE POWERS OF PRS

31.5.1 Statutory powers of PRs and trustees

The PRs have a wide range of powers which they may exercise in carrying out the administration of an estate. These powers are largely conferred on them by statute. The AEA 1925 gives some powers specifically to PRs. The TA 1925 and the Trustee Act 2000 (TA 2000) confer powers on trustees for use in administering a trust. Since 'trustee' in the TA 1925 and TA 2000 includes a 'personal representative', PRs (executors and administrators) have these powers as well.

The TA 2000 modifies in various ways powers previously available to PRs and trustees. The main purpose of the Act is to remedy certain deficiencies by bringing the law into line with what has been regarded as good drafting practice for some years.

The TA 2000 deals with powers to invest trust property, appoint agents and nominees, remuneration of trustees (and PRs) and to insure trust property. A duty of care requires trustees (and PRs) when exercising many of their powers under the Act to exercise the skill and care reasonable in the circumstances, having regard to any special knowledge or expertise of the trustee.

31.5.2 Powers granted by a will

31.5.2.1 Modification of statutory powers

Many of the statutory powers may be modified by express provision contained within a will. If there are no executors who prove the will but the will is proved by administrators with the will annexed, they also have these modified powers available to them.

31.5.2.2 Additional powers

In addition to modification of statutory powers, a will often grants powers which are not available at law, for example power to advance capital to a person to whom a life interest has been given, or to lend capital to such a person; in the absence of any such express power, the executors have no implied power to advance or lend capital to a life tenant.

31.5.2.3 Will drafting

It is good drafting practice for a will to set out in full all the powers of the executors so that the position is clear on the face of the will, thus avoiding the possibility of a particular power available at law being overlooked. Whether the following powers are available to the PRs at all, or in modified form, will depend on the terms of the particular will and the circumstances of the estate.

Many professionally drafted wills incorporate the STEP (Society of Trust and Estates Practitioners) Standard Provisions. These represent commonly used administrative provisions. They can be incorporated with or without amendment.

31.5.3 Provisions concerning the administration of the estate

The provisions which follow may be included in the will to simplify the administration of the estate. However, in a homemade will or a very simple professionally-drafted will, the draftsman may decide not to extend the executors' statutory powers.

31.5.3.1 Power to appropriate assets without consent of beneficiary

The statutory provisions

The AEA 1925, s 41 gives PRs the power to appropriate any part of the estate in or towards satisfaction of a pecuniary legacy or share in the residuary estate provided that the appropriation does not prejudice any specific beneficiary. Thus, if the will gives a pecuniary legacy to a beneficiary, the PRs may allow the pecuniary legatee to take chattels or other assets in the estate up to the value of their legacy, provided that these assets have not been specifically bequeathed by the will. The section provides that the beneficiary (or their parent or guardian if they are a minor) must consent to the appropriation.

Specimen clause

> Power to exercise the power of appropriation conferred by section 41 of the Administration of Estates Act 1925 without obtaining any of the consents required by that section.

This provision is commonly included in order to relieve the PRs of the duty to obtain formal consent. Nevertheless, the PRs would informally consult the beneficiaries concerned.

There is no statutory power for trustees to appropriate assets so, if they are to have power to appropriate, an express clause must be included. In the case of a continuing trust, it is sensible to give trustees a power to re-appropriate assets so that if they have appropriated assets to a sub-trust, they can return them to the main trust, substituting other assets if it becomes desirable. A general power to re-appropriate is clearly a useful addition to the power of appropriation because as times change there may be good reasons to make suitable adjustments that are in the interests of the beneficiaries. See *Cotterell v Beaumont* [2020] EWHC 2234 (Ch).

31.5.3.2 Power to insure

The statutory provision

The TA 1925, s 19 (as substituted by TA 2000, s 34) gives PRs and trustees power to insure trust property against any risks, to the full value of the property, and to pay premiums out of either capital or income.

Before the TA 2000, the statutory power of insurance was inadequate, and so it was normal to extend it by including an express power. However, this is no longer necessary.

The TA 2000 only provides trustees with a power to insure trust *property*. If trustees wish to be able to insure the *life* of a beneficiary or of the settlor (eg, where there is a risk of a charge to inheritance tax (IHT) if death occurs within seven years), they will require an express power.

31.5.3.3 Power to accept receipts from or on behalf of minors

The statutory provision

Under the general law, an unmarried minor could not give a good receipt for capital or income. A married minor can give a good receipt for income only (LPA 1925, s 21). Parents and guardians used not to be able to give a good receipt on behalf of minors unless specifically authorised to do so in the will.

The Children Act 1989 provides that parents with parental responsibility have the same rights as guardians appointed under the Act. These rights are set out at s 3 and include the right to receive or recover money for the benefit of the child. Therefore, since the Children Act, parents and guardians have been able to give a good receipt to PRs. See *Re AC (a child)* [2020] EWFC 90 for a discussion of the extent of powers to receive property for a minor.

Extended statutory power

There are often tensions within families, and a client may not be happy for a parent or guardian to give a good receipt for a legacy. In such a case, it may be preferable to leave the legacy to another adult to hold on trust for the minor.

Other alternatives are:

(a) leaving a legacy to trustees to hold for the benefit of the minor rather than to the child directly;

(b) including a clause allowing the PRs to accept the receipt of the child itself if over 16 years old – the provision may be incorporated into the legacy itself, or may be included in a list of powers in the will.

31.5.4 Provisions concerning the administration of a trust

At the end of the administration of an estate, the PRs may be able to distribute the residue to the beneficiaries, thus completing their task. However, in some cases distribution will be delayed and the PRs will hold the residue (or part of it) as trustees. This may happen:

(a) where the beneficiary has a contingent interest, and so cannot be given the property until the interest vests; or

(b) where the interests in the property are divided, for example between income and capital.

In either of these cases, the statutory powers of the trustees may also be extended.

31.5.4.1 Power to invest trust funds

The statutory provision

Under the general law, trustees have a duty to invest trust money. The TA 2000, s 3 gives trustees a 'general power of investment' enabling them to invest as if they were absolutely entitled to the trust property themselves. This wide power excludes investment in land, other than by mortgage, but further powers in relation to land are contained in s 8 (see **31.5.4.2**). In exercising the investment power, trustees are required to take proper advice and to review investments of the trust from time to time. They must have regard to the standard investment criteria, namely the suitability to the trust of any particular investment and to the need for diversification of investments of the trust.

An express investment clause can be included but is no longer necessary.

31.5.4.2 Power to purchase land

The statutory provisions

The TA 2000, s 8 gives trustees power to acquire freehold or leasehold land in the UK for 'investment, for occupation by a beneficiary or for any other reason'. When exercising their power, the trustees are given 'all the powers of an absolute owner in relation to the land'.

The statutory power does not authorise the purchase of land abroad, nor does it allow trustees to purchase an interest in land with someone else (eg, a beneficiary). An express power will be needed if the trustees are to have such powers.

Specimen clause

> My trustees may apply trust money in
> — the purchase of land or an interest in land anywhere in the world, and
> — the improvement of such land.

31.5.4.3 Power to sell personalty

Trustees holding land in their trust have the power to sell it under their powers of an absolute owner. However, there is some doubt whether trustees who do not hold land have an implied power of sale. For this reason, some wills may continue to impose an express trust for sale over residue. The alternative solution is to include power in the will (among the administrative provisions) giving the trustees express power to sell personalty.

Specimen clause

> Power to sell mortgage or charge any asset of my estate as it they were an absolute beneficial owner.

31.5.4.4 Power of maintenance

The statutory powers of maintenance and advancement (see **31.5.4.5**) are extremely important to PRs and trustees.

The statutory provisions

Where trustees are holding a fund for a minor beneficiary, the TA 1925, s 31 gives them power to use income they receive for the minor's maintenance, education or benefit. The section provides that if the trustees continue to hold the trust funds after the beneficiary reaches 18 (for example, where the interest is contingent on reaching 21 or 25), they must pay the income to the beneficiary from 18 onwards.

The TA 1925, s 31 (as amended by the TA 2000 and the Inheritance and Trustees' Powers Act 2014) states (inter alia):

> (1) Where any property is held by trustees in trust for any person for any interest whatsoever, whether vested or contingent, then, subject to any prior interests or charges affecting that property—
>
> (i) during the infancy of any such person, if his interest so long continues, the trustees may, at their sole discretion, pay to his parent or guardian, if any, or otherwise apply for or towards his maintenance, education, or benefit, the whole or such part, if any, of the income of that property as the trustees may think fit, whether or not there is—
>
> (a) any other fund applicable to the same purpose; or
>
> (b) any person bound by law to provide for his maintenance or education; and
>
> (ii) if such person on attaining the age of eighteen years has not a vested interest in such income, the trustees shall thenceforth pay the income of that property and of any accretion thereto under subsection (2) of this section to him, until he either attains a vested interest therein or dies, or until failure of his interest:
>
> (2) During the infancy of any such person, if his interest so long continues, the trustees shall accumulate all the residue of that income by investing it, and any profits from so investing it, from time to time in authorised investments, and shall hold those accumulations as follows:—
>
> (i) If any such person—
>
> (a) attains the age of eighteen or marries under that age or forms a civil partnership under that age, and his interest in such income during his infancy, or until his marriage or his formation of a civil partnership, is a vested interest; or
>
> (b) on attaining the age of eighteen years or on marriage, or formation of a civil partnership, under that age becomes entitled to [the trust capital];
>
> the trustees shall hold the accumulations in trust for such person absolutely ...; and
>
> (ii) In any other case the trustees shall, notwithstanding that such person had a vested interest in such income, hold the accumulations as an accretion to the capital of the property from which such accumulations arose ...;
>
> but the trustees may, at any time during the infancy of such person if his interest so long continues, apply those accumulations, or any part thereof, as if they were income arising in the then current year.
>
> (3) This section applies in the case of a contingent interest only if the limitation or trust carries the intermediate income of the property ...

As originally drafted, s 31 allowed the trustees to apply only so much of the income as was 'reasonable'. This was an objective test and it was common to vary the statutory provision to allow the trustees an unfettered discretion. For trusts *'created or arising'* on or after 1 October 2014, this amendment is no longer required. If a trust is created by will, it is the date of death not execution that is significant.

Application of section 31

EXAMPLE – TRUST 1

The trustees are holding £100,000 on a bare trust for Madhu (16) who has a vested interest in the capital. Under s 31(1), the trustees have the power to pay all or part of the income to Madhu's parent or guardian, or 'otherwise apply' it for Madhu's maintenance, education or benefit. This could include paying bills (eg, school fees) directly.

Section 31(2) directs the trustees to accumulate any income not used for maintenance and invest it. If Madhu dies, the capital and accumulated income is part of his estate.

EXAMPLE – TRUST 2

The trustees are holding £100,000 for Dora (14) who has an interest in the capital contingent on reaching 21. They may pay or apply the income for Dora's maintenance, education or benefit in the same way as the trustees of Trust 1.

The trustees are also holding £100,000 for Charles (19) who has an interest in the capital contingent on reaching 21. Section 31(1)(ii) directs them to pay all the income to Charles until his interest vests (ie until he is 21), when he will receive the capital, or fails (ie if he dies before he is 21). The same will apply to the income from Dora's share from her 18th birthday onwards.

EXAMPLE – TRUST 3

The trustees of a trust created by Debra are holding £200,000 for her husband, Henry (aged 60) for life with remainder to their son, Stephen (10). They have no power to use the income for Stephen's benefit as Henry is entitled to it. If Henry dies while Stephen is still a minor, s 31 will apply to allow the trustees to apply income for Stephen's maintenance, etc during the period from Henry's death until Stephen is 18 (when they will transfer the capital to Stephen).

EXAMPLE – TRUST 4

The trustees are holding £200,000 for Tariq (aged 6) for life with power to appoint capital to him at their discretion. Subject thereto, they are to pay the trust fund to a named charity.

Until Tariq is 18, the trustees may apply income for Tariq's benefit and to the extent that they do not must accumulate it. The accumulations are added to capital, and Tariq will only have a right to receive the accumulated income if he reaches 18 or marries or forms a civil partnership under that age (see s 31(2)(i)(a)).

PRACTICAL POINT

Summary of the effect of the Trustee Act 1925, s 31:

(1) Beneficiaries under 18 with vested or contingent interests. These beneficiaries cannot insist on receiving income as the trustees have a discretion to apply income or accumulate it, ie add it to the capital of the trust fund. (There is an important IHT point here. In order to have an immediate post-death interest, a beneficiary must have a right to receive income. Unless s 31 is varied, a minor given a right to income under a will cannot insist on receiving it until they reach 18 and so will not have an immediate post-death interest.)

(2) *Beneficiaries reaching 18 who become entitled to capital at that age.* These beneficiaries are entitled to receive capital and any accumulated income.

(3) *Beneficiaries reaching 18 who have a right to income but not capital, eg a life tenant.* On reaching 18, these beneficiaries are entitled to receive the available income each year, plus any income from previous years which was accumulated instead of being paid to them.

(4) *Beneficiaries reaching 18 who become entitled to capital at a later age.* From age 18 these beneficiaries have a right to the available income. When they reach the age at which they are entitled to receive the capital, they will get the capital plus any income accumulated before they reached 18. If they fail to attain the required age, the capital together with any unapplied income passes to the beneficiary entitled in default.

Extending section 31 – specimen clause

Section 31 of the Trustee Act 1925 shall apply as if the age of 21 years were substituted for all references to the age of 18 wherever they occur in s 31 (references to 'infancy' being construed accordingly).

The clause removes the right for a contingent beneficiary to receive all the income from the age of 18. The trustees' discretion under s 31 to pay or apply income for maintenance, or to accumulate any surplus will continue until the beneficiary is 21. Thus in Trust 2 the trustees would have a discretion over the payment of income to Charles even though he is over 18.

31.5.4.5 Power to apply capital

The statutory provisions

The TA 1925, s 32 (as amended by the Inheritance and Trustees' Powers Act 2014) allows trustees in certain circumstances to permit a beneficiary with an interest in capital to have capital applied for the beneficiary's benefit before they are entitled to receive it under the basic provisions of the trust.

Section 32 states:

> (1) Trustees may at any time or times pay or apply any capital money subject to a trust, or transfer or apply any other property forming part of the capital of the trust property, for the advancement or benefit, in such manner as they may, in their absolute discretion, think fit, of any person entitled to the capital of the trust property or of any share thereof, whether absolutely or contingently on his attaining any specified age ... and whether in possession or in remainder or reversion ...
>
> Provided that—
>
> (a) property (including any money) so paid, transferred or applied for the advancement or benefit of any person must not, altogether, represent more than the presumptive or vested share or interest of that person in the trust property; and
>
> (b) if that person is or becomes absolutely and indefeasibly entitled to a share in the trust property the money or other property so paid, transferred or applied shall be brought into account as part of such share; and
>
> (c) no such payment transfer or application shall be made so as to prejudice any person entitled to any prior life or other interest, whether vested or contingent, in the money or other property paid, transferred or applied unless such person is in existence and of full age and consents in writing to such payment or application.

As originally drafted, s 32 only allowed the trustees to advance up to one half of a beneficiary's vested or presumptive share. It was common to vary the statutory provision to allow the trustees an unfettered discretion. For trusts *'created or arising'* on or after 1 October 2014, this amendment is no longer required as the statutory provision now allows the trustees to apply amounts up to the level of a beneficiary's vested or presumptive share. If a trust is created by will, it is the date of death not execution that is significant.

Where more than one beneficiary has an interest in a trust fund, any advance made must be brought into account on final distribution (s 32(1)(b)). Advances are brought into account at their cash value at the date of the advance, unless the trustees make the advance on the basis that it is be treated as a proportionate part of the capital (s 32(1A)).

Application of section 32 (these examples relate to the trusts that we looked at in relation to s 31)

EXAMPLE – TRUST 1

Trustees are holding £100,000 on bare trust for Madhu. Section 32 allows the trustees to release some of the capital for Madhu's benefit. 'Benefit' is widely construed: money could be used to pay educational or living expenses. If the trust was created or arose on or after 1 October 2014, the trustees may advance the whole of Madhu's entitlement, ie £100,000. If it was created or arose before that date, they can only advance up to half.

EXAMPLE – TRUST 2

Charles and Dora have contingent interests in capital, their presumptive shares being £100,000 each. If the trust was created or arose on or after 1 October 2014, s 32 applies to allow the trustees to release up to £100,000 for the benefit of either beneficiary. The trustees could transfer money or assets directly to Charles as he is old enough to give a valid receipt. The power applies even though the interests of Charles and Dora are contingent. If either beneficiary dies before the age of 21 there is no right to recover any advance even though that beneficiary's interest in capital has failed. If the trust is created or arose before 1 October 2014, advances are limited to £50,000 to each beneficiary.

If the trustees give £50,000 to Charles now, he will receive £50,000 less than Dora when the fund is finally distributed to them, unless the trustees make the advance on the basis that he is to be treated as having received 25% of the value of the fund, in which case he will receive 25% less.

EXAMPLE – TRUST 3

The trustees are holding £200,000 for Henry for life, remainder to Stephen absolutely. Henry has only an interest in income and s 32 does not permit the release of capital to him. The section does apply to Stephen's vested interest in remainder.

If the trust was created or arose before 1 October 2014, the trustees can apply up to £100,000 (half his interest) for Stephen's benefit. If the trust was created or arose on or after that date, the trustees can apply up to £200,000 for Stephen's benefit.

Such an advance would prejudice Henry since his income would be substantially reduced. Section 32(1)(c) provides that no advance may be made without Henry's written consent.

Extending section 32 – specimen clause 1

> I leave it within the discretion of my trustees whether and to what extent the beneficiary shall bring into account any payments received under this clause.

This clause supersedes s 32(1)(b) and means that if, in Trust 2, £50,000 was advanced to Charles, the trustees could on distribution still divide the remaining fund equally between Charles and Dora.

Extending section 32 – specimen clause 2

> Power to pay or apply capital money from my residuary estate to any extent to or for the benefit of my husband.
>
> Power to advance capital money from my residuary estate to my husband by way of loan to any extent upon such terms and conditions as my trustees may in their absolute discretion think fit.

These provisions would permit the trustees in Trust 3 to give or lend capital from the fund to Henry even though he has only an interest in income, not capital. Such a clause may be included to give more flexibility in case the income proves insufficient for Henry's needs. Henry has no right to capital. He is dependent on the discretion of the trustees.

31.5.4.6 Power to accept receipts from and on behalf of minors

The statutory provisions

Where a trust arises in favour of a beneficiary who is a minor, the trustees have statutory powers of maintenance and advancement under ss 31 and 32 of the TA 1925. Section 31 specifically allows the trustees to pay income to the child's parent or guardian or 'otherwise apply' it for the child's maintenance, education or benefit. Similarly, s 32 empowers the trustees to pay 'or apply' capital for the beneficiary's advancement or benefit. Thus, even before the Children Act 1989, the trustees had no difficulty in obtaining a good receipt when exercising these powers.

31.5.4.7 Control of trustees by beneficiaries

The Trusts of Land and Appointment of Trustees Act 1996 (TLATA 1996), s 19 provides that where beneficiaries are of full age and capacity and together entitled to the whole fund, they may direct the trustees to retire and appoint new trustees of the beneficiaries' choice. This means that in a case where the beneficiaries could by agreement end the trust under the rule in *Saunders v Vautier* (1841) 4 Beav 115, they now have the option of allowing the trust to continue with trustees of their own choice. The provision may be expressly excluded by the testator. If, under the terms of the trust, the position could arise where all the beneficiaries are in existence and aged over 18 but the trust has not ended, the testator may wish to prevent the beneficiaries from choosing their own trustees.

Specimen clause

> The provisions of section 19 of the Trusts of Land and Appointment of Trustees Act 1996 shall not apply to any trust created by this will so that no beneficiary shall have the right to require the appointment or retirement of any trustee or trustees.

31.5.4.8 Trusts of land

The TLATA 1996 gives special powers (see below) to a beneficiary under a trust of land who has an interest in possession. If, under the terms of the will, a trust with an interest in possession could arise the will may amend those powers. The Act does not define 'interest in possession', so it presumably has its usual meaning; a beneficiary has an interest in possession if they are entitled to claim the income of the fund as it arises (normally either because they have a life interest, or because they are over 18 and entitled to claim income under the TA 1925, s 31).

Duty to consult beneficiaries

Trustees exercising any function relating to the land must consult any beneficiary who is of full age and beneficially entitled to an interest in possession in the land and, so far as consistent with the 'general interest of the trust', give effect to the wishes of any such beneficiary (TLATA 1996, s 11). The duty to consult may be excluded by the will and often is.

Specimen clause

> The provisions of section 11 of the Trusts of Land and Appointment of Trustees Act 1996 shall not apply so that it shall not be necessary for my trustees to consult any beneficiaries before carrying out any function relating to land.

Beneficiary's rights of occupation

A beneficiary with a beneficial interest in possession, even if not of full age, has the right to occupy land subject to the trust if the purposes of the trust include making the land available for occupation by them, or if the trustees acquired the land in order to make it so available (TLATA 1996, s 12). There is no power to exclude s 12, but a declaration that the purpose of the trust is not for the occupation of land may be included in the will.

Specimen clause

> The purposes of any trust created by this will do not include making land available for occupation of any beneficiary [although my trustees have power to do so if they wish].

31.5.4.9 Holding the balance between beneficiaries

One of the duties of trustees is to ensure that a fair balance is kept between the interests of the beneficiaries. This is particularly important where different beneficiaries are entitled to income and capital, for example where property is left on trust for X for life with remainder to Y, as in Trust 3 at **31.5.4.5** above. The trustees must ensure that the investments they choose produce a reasonable income for X, the life tenant, and preserve the capital reasonably safely for Y, the remainderman.

The trust instrument may authorise trustees to treat the interests of one beneficiary as of paramount importance and relieve them of the duty to treat beneficiaries impartially. This is particularly common where a trust is created for the benefit of a surviving spouse and others.

Specimen clause

> In exercising the powers conferred by clause [ ] my Trustees shall be entitled to have regard solely to the interests of my surviving spouse and to disregard all other interests or potential interests under my Will.

31.5.4.10 Trusts (Capital and Income) Act 2013

The requirement to preserve a fair balance between income and capital beneficiaries led to the development of various rules, equitable and statutory, requiring apportionment of income and capital.

For example, the Apportionment Act 1870, s 2 provides that income such as rent and dividends is to be treated as accruing from day to day and apportioned accordingly. Thus, where interest is received after death but part relates to the pre-death period, the income would have to be apportioned. The part accruing before death would be capital, while that accruing after death is income.

While designed to achieve fairness between different classes of beneficiaries, the various apportionment rules led to lengthy and expensive calculations, and it was generally accepted that they were more trouble than they were worth. They were routinely excluded in professionally drawn wills.

The Trusts (Capital and Income) Act 2013, s 1 disapplies these apportionment rules for trusts created or arising on or after 1 October 2013, so it is unnecessary to include an express clause in wills prepared after that date.

It will still be necessary to look at earlier trusts to check whether an exclusion is included.

31.5.5 Miscellaneous additional powers

31.5.5.1 Charging clause

Background law

The rule of equity that a trustee may not profit from their trust applies both to trustees and executors. Its effect is that an executor or trustee may claim only out-of-pocket expenses and may not charge for time spent in performing their office unless expressly authorised.

The TA 2000, ss 28–31 have made various changes to the general rule of law governing the remuneration of 'professional' trustees.

Professional trustees are defined as those whose business includes the provision of services in connection with the management or administration of trusts.

A professional trustee charging for services is now entitled to charge for all services, even if they are services which are capable of being provided by a lay person (TA 2000, s 28(2)). Previously, express authority was required.

Where a will or trust instrument does not contain a charging clause, a professional trustee acting in a non-charitable trust can charge reasonable remuneration *if authorised to do so in writing by each of the co-trustees* (s 29(2)). This means that it is still desirable to include a charging clause as a sole trustee will be unable to charge and a co-trustee will be able to do so only with the permission of co-trustees.

A charging clause used to be regarded as a legacy, but this is no longer the case (s 28(4)). This means that a partner in a firm authorised by the will to charge can witness the will without losing the entitlement to charge. If there are insufficient funds to pay the pecuniary legacies in full, the legacies will abate proportionally unless the will provides otherwise. As a charging clause is no longer a legacy, it is not necessary to provide that the charges be paid in priority to other legacies.

Note that, if a person engaged in a profession or business not connected with the administration of trusts is to have power to charge for time spent dealing with the trust, there must be express authority in the trust instrument.

In any case where a professional executor or trustee is appointed such as a bank, a firm of solicitors, an individual solicitor or an accountant, a power to charge should be included in the will. Without a charging clause, an executor cannot make any charge for the work they do unless they obtain the consent of beneficiaries or authorisation from the court. See *Brealey v Shepherd & Co* [2024] EWCA Civ 303. They can, of course, recover out of pocket expenses.

Power to charge – specimen clause

> Any of my trustees being a solicitor or other person engaged in any profession or business may charge and be paid his usual professional charges for work done by him or his firm in the administration of my estate and the trusts arising under my will including acts which a trustee not engaged in any profession or business could have done personally.

A clause in this form would allow a person engaged in a profession or business to charge their usual fees for services of the type they provide in the course of their profession or business but not for time spent. So, an estate agent could charge usual fees if selling a property comprised in the estate, and a valuer could charge usual fees for valuing assets comprised in the estate, but they could not charge for time spent on the general administration of the estate as they do not have 'usual' fees for this type of work. Solicitors do have 'usual' fees for general estate administration and so can charge under such a clause. See *Da Silva v Heselton* [2022] EWCA Civ 880.

Power to appoint a trust corporation – specimen clause

> Power to appoint a trust corporation to be the sole trustee or one of the trustees of my will upon such terms and conditions in all respects as may be acceptable to the corporation so appointed.

Provision of this latter kind is not commonly included in practice. Its purpose is to ensure that, if individual trustees wish to retire and no substitutes can readily be found, a bank (or other trust corporation) may be appointed even though there may be minor beneficiaries who are unable to give the required consent to the bank's usual terms and conditions, particularly in relation to charging.

31.5.5.2 Power to carry on business

Where an estate includes a business which was run by the deceased as a sole (unincorporated) trader, the powers of the PRs to run the business are limited. For example, they may only run the business with a view to selling it as a going concern and may use only those assets employed in the business at the date of death. These powers may be extended by will, although in practice PRs are unlikely to wish to involve themselves in the detailed running of a business. It may be preferable to bequeath the business by specific legacy and to appoint the legatee as a special PR of the business.

31.6 COLLECTING THE DECEASED'S ASSETS

31.6.1 Duty of the PRs

As you saw at **29.2**, some assets pass independently of the will and intestacy rules. The PRs have no obligation, or indeed power, to deal with these assets.

Assets which pass under the will or intestacy rules devolve on the PRs, who are under an obligation to collect and administer it for the benefit of those entitled.

In order to collect the property, the PRs generally produce their grant of representation to whoever is holding the various assets, for example to the deceased's bank or building society. If the bank is holding share certificates or documents of title to land, these also will be handed over to the PRs once the grant has been produced. In most cases, an office copy grant will be accepted as evidence of title.

In some cases, a grant is not required to collect certain assets. As explained at **30.4.1**, it may be possible to realise assets without production of a grant under the Administration of Estates (Small Payments) Act 1965.

31.6.2 Property not devolving on the PRs

The following examples illustrate types of property which do not devolve on the PRs and which therefore will not pass under any will or under the intestacy law.

31.6.2.1 Life interest

EXAMPLE

Terry died some years ago having by his will left property to Henry and Ian on trust for sale 'for Andrew for life, remainder for Ben'. Andrew has recently died. Assuming Ben is of full age and capacity, Henry and Ian will transfer the property to him in accordance with the terms of Terry's will. Andrew's PRs are not required to do anything in relation to the transfer.

31.6.2.2 Joint tenancy

EXAMPLE

Aamir and Barack own property as beneficial joint tenants at law and in equity. On Aamir's death his interest passes by operation of the right of survivorship to Barack the surviving joint tenant.

31.6.2.3 Policy held in trust for others

As explained at **29.2.3**, any proceeds of an insurance policy written in trust for third parties, or written under the Married Women's Property Act 1882, s 11 for the benefit of the deceased's spouse and/or children, will be paid to the trustees of the policy on proof of death, usually by production of the death certificate. The trustees will then distribute the proceeds among the beneficiaries in accordance with the trusts of the policy.

31.6.2.4 Pension schemes

As you saw at **29.3.4** and **30.4.3**, death in service benefits payable under an occupational pension scheme established by the deceased's former employers, where the trustees have a discretion as to whom to pay the benefits, do not devolve on the deceased's PRs and do not form part of the deceased's estate for succession purposes. In exercising their discretion as to payment, the trustees will have regard to any 'letter of wishes' given to them by the deceased person during the deceased's lifetime; however, they are not bound to give effect to these wishes.

31.7 PAYING THE DECEASED'S FUNERAL AND TESTAMENTARY EXPENSES AND DEBTS

31.7.1 Preliminary considerations

31.7.1.1 Immediate sources of money

As soon as monies can be collected from the deceased's bank or building society, or realised through insurance policies etc, the PRs should begin to pay the deceased's outstanding debts and the funeral account. Administration expenses, for example estate agents' and valuers' fees, will arise during the course of administration of the estate and will have to be settled from time to time while the administration is proceeding.

31.7.1.2 Repayment of loan to pay IHT

It may be necessary to raise money to repay a loan from the deceased's bank to pay IHT to obtain the grant. If an undertaking has been given to the bank in connection with the loan, it will probably be a 'first proceeds' undertaking. This means that the PRs must use money first realised by them during the administration to repay the bank. Failure to do so will be a breach of the terms of the undertaking.

31.7.1.3 Which assets to sell?

The PRs must take considerable care when deciding which assets they will sell to raise money for payment of the various outgoings from the deceased's estate. They should consider the following points.

Provisions of the deceased's will

The will may direct from which part of the deceased's estate the debts, funeral account, testamentary and administration expenses should be paid; usually they will be paid from the residue. In the absence of such direction, the PRs must follow the statutory rules for the incidence of liabilities as outlined below. In any event, it will be generally incorrect for PRs to sell property given specifically by will (eg, a gift of the testator's valuable stamp collection to his nephew) unless all other assets in the estate have been exhausted in payment of the debts, etc.

The beneficiaries' wishes

Where possible, the wishes of the beneficiaries of the residuary estate should be respected by the PRs. Although the PRs have power to sell any assets in the residuary estate, it is clearly appropriate that the residuary beneficiaries should be consulted before any sale takes place. Generally, beneficiaries have clear views as to which assets they desire to be retained for transfer to them; other assets may be sold by the PRs to raise the necessary money, possibly following receipt of professional advice as to particular sales.

Tax consequences

Before selling assets, the PRs should consider the amount of any capital gains (or losses) likely to arise as a result of the sale, and the availability of any exemptions, etc. Full use should be made of the annual exemption for CGT. If assets are to be sold at a loss (compared to their value at the date of death) CGT loss relief may be available for the PRs, as may 'loss relief' for IHT purposes. An explanation of these reliefs is contained at **31.9.6**.

31.7.2 Funeral and testamentary expenses and debts

31.7.2.1 Funeral expenses

Reasonable funeral expenses are payable from the deceased's estate. In all cases, it is a question of fact what funeral expenses are reasonable.

31.7.2.2 Testamentary expenses

The phrase 'testamentary and administration expenses' is not defined in the AEA 1925, but it is generally considered to mean expenses incident to the proper performance of the duties of a PR. The phrase will include:

(a) the costs of obtaining the grant;

(b) the costs of collecting in and preserving the deceased's assets;

(c) the costs of administering the deceased's estate, for example solicitors' fees for acting for the PRs, valuers' fees incurred by PRs in valuing the deceased's stocks and shares or other property; and

(d) any IHT payable on death on the deceased's property in the UK which vests in the PRs (IHTA 1984, s 211).

31.7.3 Administration of assets: solvent estate

The rules applying to the payment of funeral and testamentary expenses and debts depend on whether the estate is solvent or insolvent. The insolvent estate is considered at **31.7.4**.

31.7.3.1 The statutory order for payment of debts

Section 34(3) of the AEA 1925 states:

> Where the estate of a deceased person is solvent his real and personal estate shall, subject to rules of court and the provisions hereinafter contained as to charges on property of the deceased, and to the provisions, if any, contained in his will, be applicable towards the discharge of the funeral, testamentary and administration expenses, debts and liabilities payable thereout in the order mentioned in Part II of the First Schedule to this Act.

Part II of the First Schedule lays out an order which the PRs must follow when deciding which part of the deceased's estate should be used for the purposes of payment of the funeral and testamentary expenses and debts. Under the order generally, assets forming part of the residue are to be used before using property given to specific legatees.

'Subject ... to'

However, the effect of the proviso 'subject to' is that the operation of s 34(3) is expressly subject to two important rules or provisions, as follows:

(a) The AEA 1925, s 35, which deals with secured debts, ie debts owing by the deceased which are charged on particular items of property. A common example is a loan secured by legal mortgage on the deceased's house. The effect of this rule is that a beneficiary taking the asset takes it subject to the debt and will be responsible for paying the debt.

(b) The deceased's will can vary the provisions implied by the AEA 1925, ss 34(3) and/or 35. To vary s 35 it is necessary to have an express reference to the mortgage.

A suitable clause would be:

I GIVE my country cottage to my daughter free of mortgage.

A direction to pay 'debts' from residue is not sufficient to vary s 35. It will be construed as a direction to pay from residue debts *other than* those charged on particular assets.

31.7.4 The insolvent estate

31.7.4.1 Meaning of insolvency

An estate is insolvent if the assets are insufficient to discharge in full the funeral, testamentary and administration expenses, debts and liabilities. In such cases, the creditors will not be paid in full (or at all) and the beneficiaries under the will or the intestacy provisions may receive nothing from the estate. In doubtful cases, the PRs should administer the estate as if it is insolvent. Failure to administer an insolvent estate in accordance with the statutory order is a breach of duty by the PRs.

In the case of an insolvent estate which is being administered by the deceased's PRs out of court (this being the most common method of administration), the order of distribution in the Administration of Insolvent Estates of Deceased Persons Order 1986 (SI 1986/1999) should be followed.

Secured creditors, for example those holding a mortgage or charge over the deceased's property, are in a better position than unsecured creditors in that they may (inter alia) realise the security, ie sell the property by exercising a power of sale as mortgagee or chargee.

31.8 PAYING THE LEGACIES

31.8.1 Introduction

Once the funeral, testamentary and administration expenses and debts have been paid, or at least adequately provided for by setting aside sufficient assets for the purpose, the PRs should consider discharging the gifts arising on the death, other than the gifts of the residuary estate. They may also consider making interim distributions to the residuary beneficiaries on account of their entitlement.

31.8.2 Specific legacies

Unless an estate has significant debts, it unusual for property given by specific bequest or devise to be needed for payment of the deceased's funeral and testamentary expenses and debts. Once the PRs are satisfied that the property will not be so required, they should consider transferring it to the beneficiary, or to trustees if a trust arises, for example if the property is given to a beneficiary contingently on attaining a stated age and the beneficiary has not yet reached that age.

The method of transferring the property to the beneficiary or trustee will depend on its particular nature. For example, the legal estate in a house or flat should be vested in a beneficiary by a document known as an assent. If the specific legacy is of company shares, a stock transfer form should be used (unless, as is frequently the case, the shares are held by a nominee in which case the nominee will simply start to hold for the new beneficiary).

In the case of specific gifts only, the vesting of the asset in the beneficiary is retrospective to the date of death, so that any income produced by the property, for example dividends on a specific gift of company shares, belongs to the beneficiary. The beneficiary is not entitled to the income as it arises but must wait until the PRs vest the property in the beneficiary. As the beneficiary is entitled to the income they will be liable to be assessed for any income tax due on that income since the death.

Any costs of transferring the property to a specific legatee, and the cost of any necessary insurance cover taken to safeguard the property are the responsibility of the legatee who should reimburse the PRs for the expenses incurred (subject to any contrary direction in a will indicating that such expenses should be paid from residue). If the deceased's title to the asset is disputed by a third party, the specific legatee will be responsible for the cost of litigation to establish ownership (see *Re Clough-Taylor, Coutts & Co v Banks and Others* [2003] WTLR 15).

31.8.3 Pecuniary legacies – provision by will for payment

Set out below is an example of a clause dealing expressly with the payment of pecuniary legacies:

> I GIVE all my estate both real and personal whatsoever and wheresoever not hereby or by any codicil hereto otherwise specifically disposed of (hereinafter called 'my residuary estate') unto my trustees UPON TRUST to raise and discharge thereout my debts and funeral and testamentary expenses and all legacies given hereby or by any codicil hereto and any and all taxes payable by reason of my death in respect of property given free of tax and subject thereto UPON TRUST to pay and divide the same equally between ...

There is clear intention shown by the testator to pay the pecuniary legacies from the fund of general residue described as 'my residuary estate'. The result would be the same if the clause gave the residuary estate 'subject to' or 'after payment of' the pecuniary legacies. In both cases the legacies should be paid from the fund of residue before the division of the balance between the residuary beneficiaries.

31.8.4 Pecuniary legacies – no provision by will for payment

Where the will makes no provision for the payment of pecuniary legacies, they are paid primarily from residuary personalty.

> **EXAMPLE**
>
> A will leaves a legacy of £5,000 to Dawn. There is no direction as to payment of the legacy. Residue consisting of personalty and realty is given by the will to 'Edward if he shall survive me by 28 days'. He does so survive the testator, and residue is, therefore, fully disposed of. The PRs should pay the legacy from the personalty, with the proceeds of the realty being used afterwards if necessary.

If a partial intestacy arises, for example where part of a gift of residue fails because one of the beneficiaries dies before the testator, it is often unclear as a matter of law which is the appropriate part of the estate for the payment of the pecuniary legacies. It is preferable, therefore, to make express provision for payment of legacies (as in **31.8.3**).

31.8.5 Time for payment of pecuniary legacies

31.8.5.1 The executor's year

The general rule is that a pecuniary legacy is payable at the end of 'the executor's year', ie one year after the testator's death. The AEA 1925, s 44 provides that PRs are not bound to distribute the estate to the beneficiaries before the expiration of one year from the death. It is often difficult to make payment within the year and, if payment is delayed beyond this date, the legatee will be entitled to interest by way of compensation. The rate of interest will either be the rate prescribed by the testator's will, or, in default of such provision, the rate payable on money paid into court and held in the Basic Account. This fluctuates in line with interest rates generally and has been increased to 5.00% from 23 August 2023. If the testator stipulates that the legacy is to be paid 'immediately following my death', or that it is payable at some future date, or on the happening of a particular contingency, then interest is payable from either the day following the date of death, the future date or the date the contingency occurs, as may be appropriate.

31.8.5.2 Interest payable from the date of death

There are four occasions when, as an exception to the normal rule, interest is payable on a pecuniary legacy from the date of the death. These occur when legacies are:

(a) payable in satisfaction of a debt owed by the testator to a creditor;

(b) charged on land owned by the testator;

(c) payable to the testator's minor child (historically this was so that provision was made for maintenance of the child, and interest is not payable under this provision if other funds exist for the child's maintenance); or

(d) payable to any minor (not necessarily the child of the testator) where the intention is to provide for the maintenance of that minor.

31.9 COMPLETING THE ADMINISTRATION AND DISTRIBUTING THE RESIDUARY ESTATE

31.9.1 Introduction

Once the PRs have paid the deceased's funeral, testamentary expenses and debts and any legacies given by the will, they can consider distribution of the residuary estate in accordance with the will or the intestacy rules.

The PRs may have made interim distributions to the residuary beneficiaries on account of their entitlements, at the same time ensuring that they have retained sufficient assets to cover any outstanding liabilities, particularly tax.

Before drawing up the estate accounts and making the final distribution of residue, the PRs must deal with all outstanding matters. Such matters relate mostly to IHT liability, but there will also be income tax and capital gains tax (CGT) to consider.

31.9.2 Adjusting the IHT assessment

Adjustment to the amount of IHT payable on the instalment and non-instalment option property in the estate may arise for a number of reasons, including:

(a) discovery of additional assets or liabilities since the IHT account was submitted;

(b) discovery of lifetime transfers made by the deceased within the seven years before death;

(c) agreement of provisionally estimated values, for example with the shares valuation division of HMRC (in the case of shares in private companies) or the district valuer (in the case of land). The shares valuation division and the district valuer are official agencies established for the formal agreement of valuations on behalf of HMRC with PRs and others. Especially in the case of private company shares, but also in the case of land, valuations may require long negotiations and can often delay reaching a final settlement of IHT liabilities;

(d) agreement between the PRs and HMRC of a tax liability or repayment, in relation to the deceased's income and capital gains before the death;

(e) sales made by the PRs after the deceased's death which have given rise to a claim for IHT 'loss relief'.

31.9.2.1 IHT loss relief

The PRs are often forced to sell assets because they need cash to meet debts, tax liabilities or legacies. The value of quoted shares and land fluctuates depending on market conditions, and PRs may find that they sell these assets for less than their value at the date of death. Loss on sale relief can reduce the IHT liability of the estate in such cases. Where 'qualifying investments' are sold within 12 months of death for less than their market value at the date of death (ie 'probate value') then the sale price may be substituted for the market value at death and the IHT liability adjusted accordingly (IHTA 1984, ss 178–189). 'Qualifying investments' are shares or securities which are quoted on a recognised stock exchange at the date of death and also holdings in authorised unit trusts. The relief must be claimed; it is not automatic. It is normally available only when the PRs make the sale and not where a beneficiary to whom assets have been transferred does so.

If the PRs claim the relief, the value of the qualifying investments at death must be reduced for CGT purposes (s 187). This has the effect of preventing the PRs claiming a loss for CGT purposes where they have claimed IHT loss relief. It would, therefore, be foolish to claim the relief if the estate is passing to a surviving spouse or civil partner as the IHT reduction would be pointless and the estate would no longer be able to claim a CGT loss.

When claiming the relief, PRs must report all sales of qualifying investments made within the 12-month period, including those sold for more than death value, and must substitute the aggregate sale proceeds for the original values.

EXAMPLE

PRs are dealing with an estate which includes holdings in three quoted companies. They sell all the shares in the first 12 months after the death; they make a loss on two of the companies and a gain on the third.

	Value at death	Sale price
	£	£
Shares in XX plc	20,000	10,000
Shares in YY plc	20,000	5,000
Shares in ZZ plc	20,000	40,000
Total value	60,000	55,000

The aggregate sale price is £55,000 so the PRs can reduce the IHT value of the shares from £60,000 to £55,000 saving the IHT on £5,000. Obviously the reduction would have been greater had the PRs not sold the ZZ shares. The CGT acquisition value for the PRs of the XX and YY shares will be reduced to £10,000 and £5,000 respectively.

Loss on sale of shares relief is intended to help those who have to sell investments at a loss to raise money to pay tax, debts, administration expenses or legacies.

To stop PRs selling shares to create a loss and then either buying them back ('bed and breakfasting') or reinvesting the proceeds in other shares, s 180 restricts the relief where the appropriate person buys new qualifying investments within the period starting with death and ending two months after the date of the last sale.

There are similar, though separate, provisions allowing claims for loss relief in relation to the sale of land within four years of a death at a loss (IHTA 1984, ss 190–198).

31.9.3 PRs' continuing IHT liability

31.9.3.1 Payments of IHT by instalments

The PRs may have opted to pay IHT by instalments on the property in the deceased's estate attracting the instalment option. By the time they are ready to transfer the assets to those entitled, probably only one or two instalments will have been paid. The PRs continue to be liable for the remaining instalments. They would be foolish to transfer all the assets to the beneficiaries in reliance on a promise that the beneficiaries will pay the tax. If the beneficiaries become insolvent or disappear, the PRs will be liable for the unpaid tax but will have no assets of the estate to meet the liability. They should consider retaining sufficient assets in the estate. See, for example, *Harris v RCC* [2018] UKFTT 0204 (TC), where the unfortunate administrator distributed all the assets to a beneficiary who immediately returned to his home in Barbados. The administrator is personally liable for unpaid IHT of £341,278.76.

Details of the instalment option facility are discussed at **4.8.1.2**. If any instalment option property is sold, any outstanding IHT on the property sold becomes due immediately.

31.9.3.2 IHT on lifetime transfers

If the deceased dies within seven years of making either a potentially exempt transfer (PET), or a chargeable transfer, IHT (if a PET) or more IHT (if a chargeable transfer) may become payable. Although the general rule is that the donees of lifetime transfers are primarily liable for the tax, the PRs of the donor's estate may become liable if the tax remains unpaid by the donees 12 months after the end of the month in which the donor died. However, the PRs' liability is limited to the extent of the deceased's assets which they have received, or would have received in the administration of the estate, but for their neglect or default.

In addition, if the deceased gave away property during their lifetime but reserved a benefit in that property, such property is treated as part of their estate on death (see **4.3.1.3**). The donee of the gift is primarily liable to pay the tax attributable, but if the tax remains unpaid 12 months after the end of the month of death, the PRs become liable. Again the PRs should consider how they can protect themselves in case this liability materialises.

31.9.4 Corrective account

When all variations in the extent or value of the deceased's assets and liabilities are known, and all reliefs to which the estate is entitled have been quantified, the PRs must report all outstanding matters to HMRC. This report is made by way of a corrective account on Form C4.

31.9.5 IHT clearance

31.9.5.1 Certificate of clearance

PRs will normally want to obtain confirmation from HMRC that there is no further claim to IHT. If HMRC is satisfied that IHT attributable to a chargeable transfer has, or will be, paid, it can, and if the transfer is one made on death must, confirm that this is the case. The effect is to discharge all persons, thus in particular the PRs, from further liability to IHT (unless there is fraud or non-disclosure of material facts). It also extinguishes any charge imposed by HMRC on the deceased's property for the IHT.

HMRC used to send a standard clearance letter when it had finished its checks. In April 2018 it announced that it would no longer do so. Taxpayers who want confirmation must apply for a clearance certificate using form IHT30, 'Application for clearance certificate', once all amendments have been reported to and accepted by HMRC. HMRC provides a certificate of clearance (SL120).

31.9.6 Income tax and CGT

31.9.6.1 The deceased's liability

Immediately following the death, the PRs must make a return to HMRC of the income and capital gains of the deceased for the period starting on 6 April before the death and ending with the date of death. Even though the deceased died part way through the income tax year, the PRs, on the deceased's behalf, may claim the same reliefs and allowances as the deceased could have claimed had they lived throughout the whole year. Any liability to tax is a debt of the deceased which must be paid by the PRs during the administration. The debt will be deductible when calculating the amount of IHT. Alternatively, if a refund of tax is obtained, this will represent an asset, so increasing the size of the estate for IHT purposes.

31.9.6.2 The administration period

For each income tax year (or part) during the administration period, the PRs must calculate their income tax and any CGT liability on assets disposed of for administration purposes, for example raising money to pay debts or pecuniary legacies.

Provided the estate is not classified as a complex estate, at the end of the administration period the PRs can make a one-off informal payment of all the income tax and CGT due without having to provide a tax return.

If the estate is 'complex', they must complete a self-assessment tax return for each tax year of the administration period reporting the estate's income and gains and must pay the tax due each tax year. An estate is considered complex if either: (1) the value of the estate exceeds £2.5 million; or (2) tax due for the whole of the administration period exceeds £10,000; or (3) the value of assets sold in a tax year exceeds £500,000.

These returns for the estate are distinct from the PRs' returns of their own income and capital gains and from the returns for the deceased's income and gains.

Note that since 6 April 2020 there is a special rule for reporting and paying CGT on UK residential land. This has to be paid within a short period of completion of sale irrespective of whether the estate is simple or complex. See **31.9.6.4** below.

31.9.6.3 Income tax

Rate of tax

The rates at which PRs pay income tax depends on the type of income they receive.

PRs do not pay income tax at any higher rate(s) but nor do they benefit from the personal savings and dividend allowances. They do not have a personal allowance.

They will therefore pay tax at the following rates on all income received:

dividends	8.75% (increased from 7.5% from 6 April 2022)
other income	20%

Note, however, that under the Individual Savings Account (Amendment No 3) Regulations 2017 (SI 2017/1089), which took effect on 6 April 2018, investments held in an ISA wrapper will not be liable to income tax (or CGT) during the administration of the deceased's estate, or three years from the death, whichever is the shorter. PRs will, therefore, pay no tax during that period on the deceased's ISA investments.

There is a special rule for low income estates (replacing a more limited informal concession which had existed from 6 April 2016). Where income of the estate in a tax year does not exceed £500, the PRs pay no income tax and neither do the beneficiaries.

Calculation of PRs' liability

In calculating any income tax liability on the income of the administration period, the PRs may be able to claim relief for interest paid on a bank loan to pay IHT. If the PRs use this loan to pay the IHT on the deceased's personal property in the UK which devolves on them in order to obtain the grant, income tax relief is generally available to them.

EXAMPLE

PRs' only income is gross interest of £4,000 for a tax year in the administration period. They pay £1,000 interest to the bank on a loan to pay IHT to obtain their grant.

Gross income	£4,000
Less: interest paid	£1,000
Taxable income	£3,000
Less: tax (20%)	£600
Net income for the beneficiaries	£2,400

Beneficiary's income tax liability

Once the PRs' tax position has been settled, the remaining net income will be paid to the beneficiary. The grossed up amount of this income should be included by the beneficiary in their return of income for the income tax year to which it relates.

EXAMPLE

PRs have completed the administration of an estate and there is bank deposit account interest which, after payment of tax at 20% by the PRs, amounts to £800. That sum is paid by the PRs to the residuary beneficiary.

When the beneficiary makes his return of income he must declare the estate income grossed up at 20%, ie

$£800 \times \frac{100}{80} = £1,000.$

The PRs must supply the beneficiary with a certificate of deduction of tax, on Form R185, which the beneficiary should submit to HMRC as evidence of the payment of the tax by the PRs. Beneficiaries whose income, including the estate income, is not above the level of the personal allowance or the savings or dividend allowances can reclaim the tax paid.

31.9.6.4 Capital gains tax

No disposal on death

On death, there is no disposal for CGT purposes, so that no liability to CGT arises. The PRs acquire all the deceased's assets at their probate value at death. This has the effect of wiping out gains which accrued during the deceased's lifetime so that these gains are not charged to tax. Although there is no disposal, the probate value becomes the PRs' 'base cost' of all the deceased's assets for future CGT purposes.

Calculation of PRs' liability

If the PRs dispose of chargeable assets during the administration of the deceased's estate to raise cash (eg, to pay IHT, or other outgoings or legacies), they are liable to CGT at the higher rates on any chargeable gains that they make (unless the gain arises on the disposal of investments held by the deceased in an ISA wrapper: see **31.9.6.3** above). For gains arising in 2025/26 the rate for PRs is 24%. The rates are flat rates irrespective of the level of income and gains of the estate.

In addition to deducting their acquisition cost (probate value), the PRs may deduct from the disposal consideration the incidental costs of disposal (eg, stockbroker's commission on sale of shares). In addition, they may deduct a proportion of the cost of valuing the deceased's estate for probate purposes. Calculations may be based either on a scale published by HMRC, or on the actual expenditure incurred if this is higher.

The PRs may claim the annual exemption for disposals made in the tax year in which the deceased died and the following two tax years only (if the administration lasts this long). The exemption is the same as for an individual. The annual exemption for individuals was £12,300 for 2022/23 but was reduced to £6,000 for 2023/24 and then to £3,000 for 2024/25. It remains at £3,000 for 2025/26. Maximum advantage will be obtained from this exemption if the PRs plan sales of assets carefully so that gains are realised in stages in each of the three tax years for which it is available.

EXAMPLE

In May 2025 PRs realise they will need to raise £50,000 to pay administration expenses. The investments they are advised to sell will realise a net gain of £6,000. They have no unused losses.

(1) If all sales occur in the same tax year, their CGT position is as follows:

	£	
gain	6,000	
annual exemption	(3,000)	
taxable	3,000	at 24% = £720

(2) If the sales are spread evenly over two tax years, their CGT position for each tax year is as follows:

		£
Year 1	gain	3,000
	annual exemption	(3,000)
	taxable	nil
Year 2	gain	3,000
	annual exemption	(3,000)
	taxable	nil

Sales at a loss

If the PRs sell assets for less than their value at death, an allowable loss for CGT will arise. This loss may be relieved by setting it against gains arising on other sales by the PRs in the same, or any future, tax year in the administration period. Any loss which is unrelieved at the end of the administration period cannot be transferred to the beneficiaries. In view of this limitation, the PRs should plan sales carefully to ensure they can obtain relief for all losses which they realise. If there is a possibility of losses being unused, the PRs should either plan sales of other assets, or consider transferring the assets worth less than their probate value to the beneficiaries (see below).

Accelerated payment of CGT on UK residential land

FA 2019, s 14 and Sch 2 introduced accelerated reporting and payment dates for CGT on UK land disposed of by non-residents starting in tax year 2019/20. The return and payment originally had to be submitted within 30 days of completion of the disposal. However, the short period caused problems, and for disposals that complete on or after 27 October 2021 the period is extended to 60 days from completion. Disposals completed before that date will still need to meet the 30-day requirement.

The change extends to all disposals of UK residential land (ie by UK residents as well as by non-residents) on or after 6 April 2020, but only where tax is due. It applies to disposals made by PRs and trustees as well as to disposals by individuals. The date of disposal is fixed by reference to the date of unconditional exchange of contracts.

EXAMPLE

(1) PRs of Anna exchange contracts for the sale of her residence under an unconditional contract on 31 August 2025 making a chargeable gain of £3,000. Completion takes place on 20 October 2025.

(2) The PRs must make a return to HMRC within 60 days of completion of the sale on 20 October 2025 together with a payment on account within the same 60 days' timescale.

No returns are required for disposals where no tax is due, for example because the gain is:

- within the annual exemption,
- covered by existing losses, or
- to a spouse or civil partner (no gain/no loss disposal).

The calculation of tax is made on the basis of events occurring in the tax year up to the date of payment with an approximation of the level of income expected during the year. The payment made is on account of the tax due at the end of the year, so credit is given at the end of the year for tax already paid. However, it is not necessary to submit a self-assessment tax return at the end of the year if the accelerated tax paid was correct and there is no further need for a return.

Provided the estate is not a complex estate (see **31.9.6.2** above), income tax and CGT are normally paid in one lump sum at the end of the administration period. However, CGT on a disposal of UK residential land will have to be paid within the 30/60 day period even if the estate is a simple one.

Transfer of assets to the legatees

If, instead of selling assets, the PRs vest them in the legatees, ie in the beneficiaries (or trustees if a trust arises), no chargeable gain or allowable loss arises. The beneficiary or trustee is assumed to acquire the asset transferred at its probate value. This 'base cost' of the asset will be relevant to the CGT calculation on a future disposal.

EXAMPLE 1

A testator dies in 2020 and leaves his residuary estate to Parvez. Among the assets forming residue are 1,000 shares in XYZ plc. Probate value of these was £5,000. By the time they were transferred to Parvez the value had risen to £10,000. In 2025/26 Parvez sells them for £17,000.

	£
Disposal consideration	17,000
Less: acquisition (probate) value	(5,000)
Gain	12,000
Less: annual exemption	(3,000)
Chargeable gain	9,000

EXAMPLE 2

If Parvez sells the shares in 2025/26 for £3,000, ie £2,000 less than their probate value, his position would be as follows:

	£
Disposal consideration	3,000
Less: acquisition (probate) value	5,000
Loss	(2,000)

The loss of £2,000 is available to Parvez to set against chargeable gains he may have in the same, or any future, tax year.

PRACTICAL POINTS

Remember the following points on CGT and death:

(1) No CGT is payable on death itself.

(2) If PRs sell assets, they make a disposal. Their acquisition value is the market value at the date of death. They have an annual exemption equal to an individual's in the tax year of death and the two following tax years, so there will often be no tax liability on their disposals.

(3) The rate of tax payable by PRs is 20% except for gains on residential property which are taxed at 28%.

(4) If PRs transfer assets to beneficiaries, they do not make a disposal. The beneficiary acquires the asset at market value at the date of death.

31.9.7 Transferring assets to residuary beneficiaries

31.9.7.1 Interim distributions

Once the outstanding tax, legal costs and other matters have been disposed of, PRs should consider transferring any remaining assets to the residuary beneficiaries. In doing so they must remember that payments may have been made already to the beneficiaries as interim distributions on account of their entitlement. If so, these will be taken into account when determining what and how much more should be transferred to those beneficiaries. These interim distributions will also be shown in the estate accounts.

31.9.7.2 Adult beneficiaries

If the beneficiaries are adults, and have a vested entitlement to property in the residuary estate, their entitlement can be transferred to them. If they have a contingent entitlement, the property cannot be transferred to them but will instead be transferred to trustees to hold on their behalf until the contingency is satisfied.

31.9.7.3 Minor beneficiaries

If any beneficiaries are under 18 years of age, whether the interest enjoyed is vested or contingent, the property will usually be held in trust for them until the age of majority is reached or the contingency is satisfied. If a minor beneficiary has a vested interest the PRs may be able to transfer the minor beneficiary's entitlement to the minor (if expressly authorised in the will), or to parents and guardians on behalf of the minor.

31.9.7.4 Transferring property to the residuary beneficiaries

The manner in which the property is transferred to residuary beneficiaries, or to trustees of their behalf, will depend on the nature of the property remaining in the estate.

Personal property

The PRs indicate that they no longer require property for administration purposes when they pass title to it by means of an assent. Generally, no particular form of assent is required in the case of personalty so that often the property passes by delivery. The beneficiary's title to the property derives from the will; the assent is merely the manner of giving effect to the gift by the PRs. Company shares are transferred by share (stock) transfer form (unless, as is often the case, they are held by a nominee company). The PRs must produce their grant to the company as proof of title to the shares. They, as transferors, transfer the shares 'as PRs of X deceased' to the beneficiary (the transferee), who then applies to be registered as a member of the company in place of the deceased member. No change is required where the shares continue to be held by the nominee.

Freehold or leasehold land

Personal representatives vest the legal estate in land in the person entitled (whether beneficially or as trustee) by means of an assent, which will then become a document of title to the legal estate. If PRs are to continue to hold property in their changed capacity as trustees under trusts declared by the will, or arising under the intestacy law, an assent will again be appropriate. The PRs should formally vest the legal estate in themselves as trustees to hold for the beneficiaries.

By the AEA 1925, s 36(4), an assent must be in writing, it must be signed by the PRs, and it must name the person in whose favour it is made. It then operates to vest the legal estate in the named person. A deed is not necessary to pass the legal estate, but PRs may choose to use a deed, for example if they require the beneficiary to give them the benefit of an indemnity covenant. If the title to the land is registered, the assent must be in the form specified by the Land Registration Rules 2003.

Any person in whose favour the PRs make an assent or conveyance may require notice of it to be endorsed on the original grant of probate or administration. In view of this entitlement, it is good practice that the endorsement should be made by the PRs, or solicitors on their behalf, as a matter of routine at the same time as the assent is given. Indeed, if the PRs have made an assent where the title is unregistered in favour of a beneficiary, endorsement is essential for that beneficiary's protection in view of the provisions of the AEA 1925, s 36(6) benefitting any later purchaser from the PRs.

If the title to the land is registered, two options are open to the PRs:

(a) they can apply to be registered as proprietor in place of the deceased, in which case they must produce the grant of representation when making the application; or

(b) they can transfer the property by assent without being registered as proprietor themselves, in which case the beneficiary must be given a certified copy of the grant of representation so that the beneficiary can present it with their application for registration.

As the register is conclusive as to title, the provisions in the AEA 1925 regarding endorsements on the grant are of no relevance.

31.9.8 Estate accounts

31.9.8.1 Purpose of the accounts

The final task of the PRs is usually to produce estate accounts for the residuary beneficiaries. The purpose of the accounts is to show all the assets of the estate, the payment of the debts, administration expenses and legacies, and the balance remaining for the residuary beneficiaries. The balance will normally be represented by a combination of assets transferred to the beneficiaries in specie, and some cash. The residuary beneficiaries sign the accounts to indicate that they approve them. In the absence of fraud or failure to disclose assets, their signatures will also release the PRs from further liability to account to the beneficiaries.

31.9.8.2 Presentation of the accounts

There is no prescribed form for estate accounts. Any presentation adopted should be clear and concise so that the accounts are easily understood by the residuary beneficiaries. If interim distribution payments were made to the residuary beneficiaries during the administration period, these must be taken into account and shown in the estate accounts.

Vertical presentation

Estate accounts may be presented vertically, disclosing assets less liabilities, etc, and a balance for the beneficiaries, or on a double-sided basis, disclosing receipts opposite the payments. It is customary to use the probate values of the assets for accounting purposes.

Narrative introduction

The accounts generally start with a narrative statement of the date of death, the date of the grant of representation, a summary of the will or succession under the intestacy law, and the value of the deceased's gross and net estate. All this information is provided to make the understanding of the accounts easier for the beneficiaries.

Capital and income accounts

Normally accounts show capital assets, and income produced by those assets during the administration period, in separate capital and income accounts. In small estates this may not be necessary, so that one account showing both capital and income will be sufficient. However, it is always necessary to prepare separate accounts if the will (or the intestacy rules) creates a life or minority interest, since the different interests of the beneficiaries in the capital and income need to be distinguished throughout the period of the trust, and when it ends.

SUMMARY

(1) When PRs administer an estate, they are under a statutory duty to administer it correctly (Administration of Estates Act 1925, s 25 as substituted).

(2) They are personally liable for any errors and so must be careful to protect themselves.

(3) They have various statutory powers contained mainly in the Trustee Acts 1925 and 2000. These powers are sometimes extended by the will. Sections 31 and 32 of the Trustee Act 1925 are particularly important.

(4) As well as paying IHT, PRs may have to pay CGT and income tax:

  (a) The PRs have an individual's CGT annual exemption for the tax year of death and the two following tax years.

(b) Death is not a disposal but the PRs are deemed to acquire the assets at market value at the date of death.

(c) If they sell, they make a disposal. If the disposal is of UK residential land, the accelerated payment rules apply to disposals made on or after 6 April 2020 and any tax due must be paid within 30 days of completion.

(d) If they transfer to beneficiaries, there is no disposal; the beneficiaries acquire at market value at the date of death.

(e) The PRs are liable to income tax on income of the administration period at basic and dividend ordinary rate.

(5) At the end of the administration, PRs prepare estate accounts for approval by the residuary beneficiaries.

PART V SUMMARY

PROBATE AND ADMINISTRATION

Topic	*Summary*	*References*
What happens to property when someone dies?	People usually think that where property goes depends on whether or not there is a will. However, many assets pass independently of a will. For example, property held as beneficial joint tenants passes by survivorship; trust property passes under the terms of the trust. Money due from a pension scheme will be subject to the terms of the scheme which normally give the trustees power to choose who to pay it to. Often, the bulk of a person's wealth passes independently of any will.	See **29.2** and **29.3**.
What are the requirements of a valid will?	A testator must be at least 18 and have testamentary capacity. The testator must know and approve the contents of the will and must not have been subjected to undue influence, force, fear or fraud. The will must be signed and witnessed in accordance with s 9 of the Wills Act 1837.	See **29.4**.
How are wills revoked?	Wills can be revoked by a later will or codicil, by destruction or by a later marriage or the formation of a later civil partnership.	See **29.4.4**.
Failure of legacies	A gift in a will fails if the beneficiary predeceases the testator, witnesses the will or is a spouse or civil partner of a witness. A gift of a specific item will fail if the testator no longer owns the item at death. A gift to a spouse or civil partner fails if the marriage or civil partnership is dissolved.	See **29.5**.
What if there is no valid will?	If there is no valid will or if there is property undisposed of by the will, the undisposed of property passes under the intestacy rules. The deceased's personal representatives hold the property on trust. They pay any debts and inheritance tax due and then pay what is left to the closest members of the deceased's family following the order set out in s 46 of the Administration of Estates Act 1925.	See **29.6**.

Topic	*Summary*	*References*
What if a family member or dependant is inadequately provided for?	Family members and dependants can apply to the court under the Inheritance (Provision for Family and Dependants) Act 1975 for a redistribution of assets if they feel that the deceased did not make reasonable provision for them. The court is limited to providing for the reasonable maintenance of the applicant except in the case of spouses and civil partners who can claim a reasonable share of the deceased's assets.	See **29.7**.
Who deals with the estate of a deceased person?	Someone has to deal with the assets of the deceased. The generic name for people doing this job is 'personal representatives'. There are two types: executors and administrators. Executors are people appointed in the will. If there are no executors able and willing to act then beneficiaries of the estate will act as administrators. The order of entitlement for administrators is set out in rules 19 and 20 of the Non-contentious Probate Rules 1987. Both executors and administrators need proof that they are entitled to act. They need to apply to HMCTS Probate for a grant of representation. Executors get a grant of probate; administrators get a grant of administration. Note that personal representatives deal only with assets capable of passing by will. Other assets such as property held as beneficial joint tenants pass directly to the person entitled.	
Procedure for applying for a grant of representation	This varies depending on what type of grant is involved, but all personal representatives must complete a Form PA1P or PA1A and pay any inheritance tax due.	See **30.5–30.11**.
What do the personal representatives do once they have obtained the grant of representation?	Once the grant is obtained, the personal representatives must pay the debts, finalise the inheritance tax position and distribute the assets to the people entitled. This is a burdensome task as personal representatives are personally liable for errors in payment. They can get limited protection under s 27 of the Administration of Estates Act 1925 by advertising for claimants to the estate. For full protection against later claims, they must apply to the court.	See **Chapter 31**.

Index